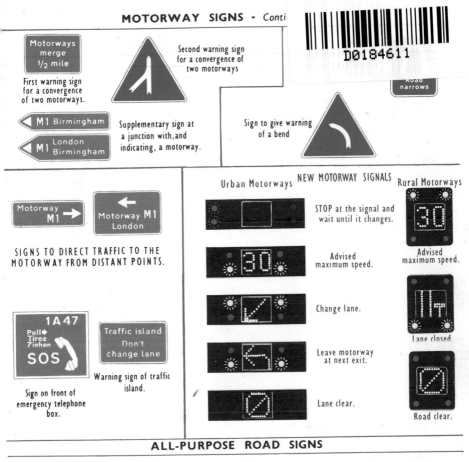

First warning sign for a convergence of two motorways.

Second warning sign for a convergence of two motorways

Road narrows

Supplementary sign at a junction with, and indicating, a motorway.

Sign to give warning of a bend

NEW MOTORWAY SIGNALS

Urban Motorways   Rural Motorways

SIGNS TO DIRECT TRAFFIC TO THE MOTORWAY FROM DISTANT POINTS.

STOP at the signal and wait until it changes.

Advised maximum speed.

Advised maximum speed.

Change lane.

Lane closed.

Leave motorway at next exit.

Warning sign of traffic island.

Sign on front of emergency telephone box.

Lane clear.

Road clear.

ALL-PURPOSE ROAD SIGNS

DIRECTIONAL SIGNS

Advance direction sign for complex junction.

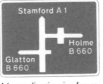

Advance direction sign for use at junction of side turnings with dual-carriageway road.

Advance direction sign for roundabout junction of all-purpose roads with motorway.

SIGNS WHICH MUST BE OBSERVED

Stop and give way.

School Crossing Patrol.

Give way to traffic on major road.

No right turn.

No U turns.

Turn right.

3 miles to 1 inch

ROAD ATLAS
of GREAT BRITAIN

JOHNSTON & BACON PUBLISHERS
Edinburgh & London

Johnston & Bacon a division of
Cassell & Collier Macmillan Publishers Limited, London
35 Red Lion Square, London WC1R 4SG
Tanfield House, Tanfield Lane, Edinburgh EH3 5LL

Sydney, Auckland, Toronto, Johannesburg

An affiliate of Macmillan Inc., New York

First Edition 1940
Reprinted 1941 (thrice), 1942, 1943, 1944, 1945,
          1946, 1947 (twice)

Second Edition 1948
Reprinted 1949, 1950, 1951, 1952, 1953, 1954

Third Edition 1955
Reprinted 1955, 1956

Fourth Edition 1957
Reprinted 1958, 1959, 1960, 1961, 1962

Fifth Edition 1963
Reprinted 1964, 1965, 1966, 1968

Sixth Edition 1970

Revised Edition 1971/1972

Seventh Edition 1973
Reprinted 1974

ISBN 0 7179 3500 0

Printed in Great Britain by
Morrison and Gibb Limited, London and Edinburgh

CONTENTS

Plan of the motorways	4
Town street plans	5–16
Map signs and references	17
Plan of London	18–19
Key to map section	20–27
Map sections	1–324
Index and table of distances	325–372

TOWN STREET PLANS

Bath	8	Leicester	9
Birmingham	6	Lincoln	14
Bristol	8	Liverpool	5
Cambridge	13	London	18–19
Cardiff	11	Manchester	5
Carlisle	15	Newcastle	15
Chester	10	Norwich	14
Derby	10	Nottingham	7
Edinburgh	16	Oxford	13
Exeter	12	Salisbury	12
Glasgow	16	Sheffield	7
Gloucester	11	Wolverhampton	9
Leeds	6		

PLAN OF THE MOTORWAYS

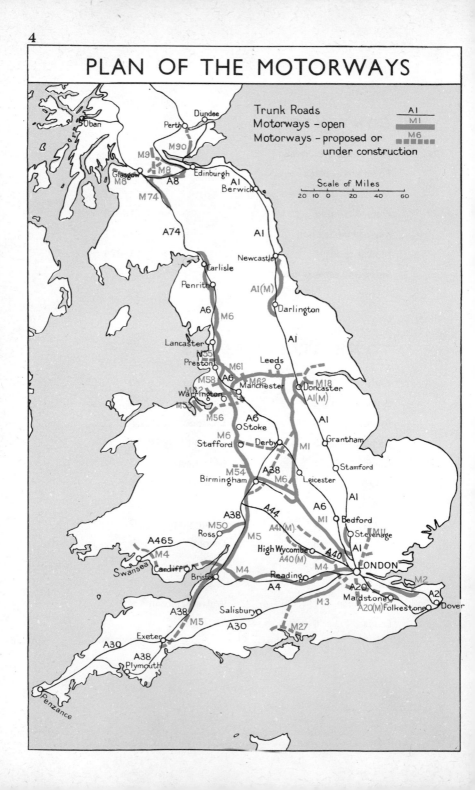

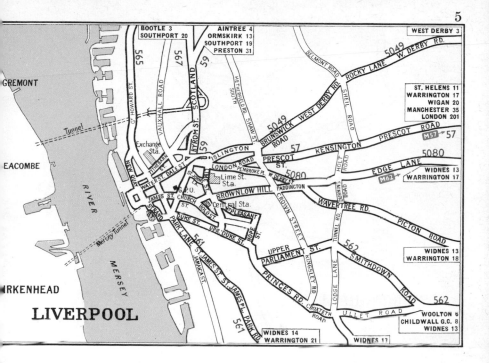

GREMONT

EACOMBE

RKENHEAD

LIVERPOOL

BOOTLE 3
SOUTHPORT 20

AINTREE 4
ORMSKIRK 13
SOUTHPORT 19
PRESTON 31

WEST DERBY 3

ST. HELENS 11
WARRINGTON 17
WIGAN 20
MANCHESTER 35
LONDON 201

M57 57

5080

WIDNES 13
WARRINGTON 17

WIDNES 13
WARRINGTON 18

WOOLTON 6
CHILDWALL G.C. 8
WIDNES 13

WIDNES 14
WARRINGTON 21

WIDNES 12

565   567   59

5049   W. DERBY RD.

BELMONT ROAD   ROCKY LANE

HETHFIELD RD. SOUTH   WEST DERBY RD.   SHEIL ROAD

Tunnel

Exchange Sta.

ISLINGTON

BYROM ST.   59

LONDON ROAD

BRUNSWICK ROAD

PRESCOT ST.

KENSINGTON   PRESCOT ROAD

HOLT ROAD

EDGE LANE   M62

5080

Lime St. Sta.

Pembroke Pl.   W. DERBY

PADDINGTON

BURNING RDS.   TUNNEL RD.

WAVERTREE RD.

PICTON ROAD

BROWNLOW HILL

Central Sta.

Mt. PLEASANT

CROWN STREET

UPPER PARLIAMENT ST.

562

SMITHDOWN ROAD

562

PRINCES RD.

KINGSLEY RD.

CROXTETH ROAD

LODGE LANE

ULLET ROAD

561   Mersey Tunnel

RIVER   MERSEY

G.P.O.

ST. CHURCH

JAMES ST.   561

BOLD ST.

UFR DUKE ST.

DUKE ST.

PARK LANE   561

STRAND

NEW QU

WATER ST.   DALE ST.

VAUXHALL ROAD   G. HOWARD ST.

SCOTLAND   59

SHAW ST.

ST. JAMES PL. PARK RD.

ST. JAMES ST.   JAMAICA ST.

5049

5080

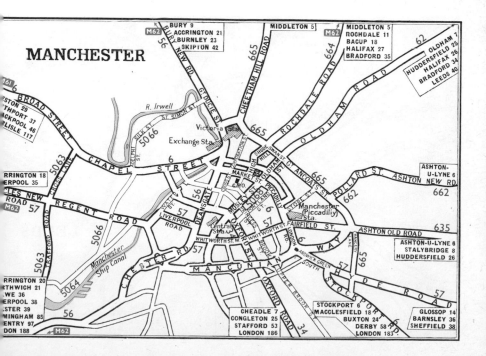

MANCHESTER

BURY 9
ACCRINGTON 21
BURNLEY 23
SKIPTON 42

M62   56   BURY NEW RD.

MIDDLETON 5

MIDDLETON 5
ROCHDALE 11
BACUP 18
HALIFAX 27
BRADFORD 35

M62   62

OLDHAM 7
HUDDERSFIELD 25
HALIFAX 26
BRADFORD 34
LEEDS 40

161   6

BROAD STREET

ESTON 29
THPORT 37
ACKPOOL 46
RLISLE 117

R. Irwell

ST. SIMON ST.

GT. DUCIE ST.

665   CHEETHAM HILL ROAD

664   ROCHDALE ROAD

OLDHAM ROAD

ASHTON-U-LYNE 6
NEW RD.
662

SILK ST.   5066

Victoria

Exchange Sta.

665

ASHTON NEW RD.

ADELPHI ST.   CHAPEL STREET

CROSS LANE   5063   5066

RRINGTON 18
ERPOOL 35

CLES NEW ROAD   M62   57

REGENT ROAD

6

STREET   56

DEANSGATE

MARKET ST.   C.R.O.

PICCADILLY

SWAN ST.   SHUD HILL   STOCKPORT RD.

ANCOATS ST.

POLLARD ST.

662

665

LIVERPOOL ROAD

5066

57

Central Sta.

MOSLEY ST.   OXFORD ST.

WHITWORTH ST.   FAIRFIELD ST.

Manchester (Piccadilly) Sta.

ASHTON OLD ROAD   635

ASHTON-U-LYNE 6
STALYBRIDGE 8
HUDDERSFIELD 26

5063   5064

Manchester Ship Canal

CHESTER RD.   57

WHITWORTH ST. W.

MANCUNIAN   WAY

ARDWICK GREEN SOUTH

HYDE ROAD

665

57

57

RRINGTON 20
RTHWICH 21
WE 36
ERPOOL 38
STER 39
MINGHAM 85
ENTRY 97
DON 188

56   M62

5064

OXFORD ROAD   34

CHEADLE 7
CONGLETON 25
STAFFORD 53
LONDON 186

STOCKPORT 9
MACCLESFIELD 18
BUXTON 24
DERBY 58
LONDON 183

STOCKPORT ROAD

GLOSSOP 14
BARNSLEY 36
SHEFFIELD 38

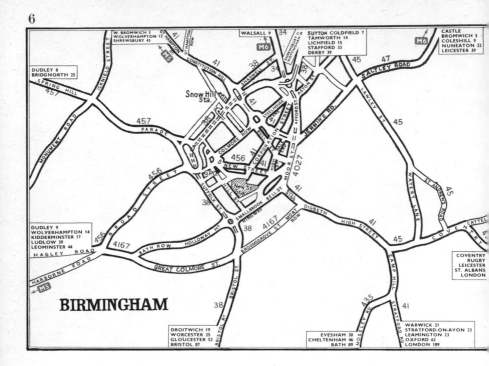

BIRMINGHAM

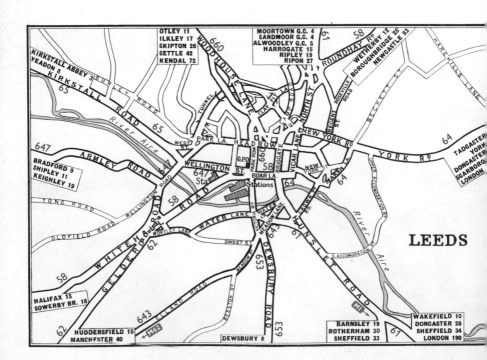

LEEDS

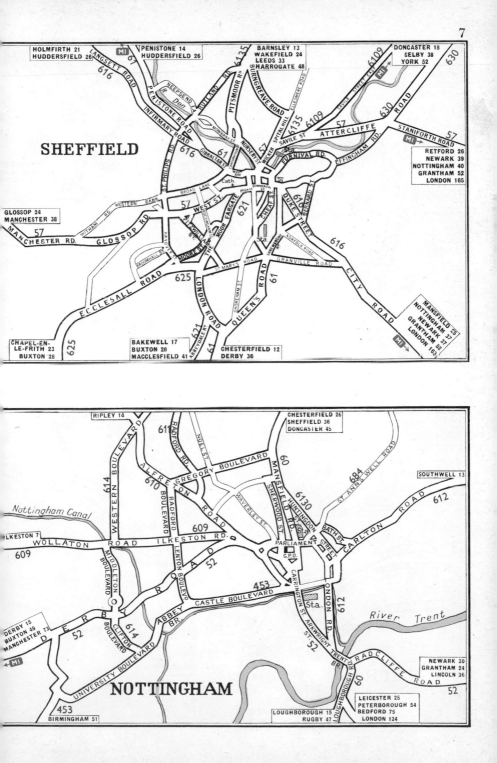

SHEFFIELD

HOLMFIRTH 21
HUDDERSFIELD 26

PENISTONE 14
HUDDERSFIELD 26

BARNSLEY 13
WAKEFIELD 24
LEEDS 33
HARROGATE 48

DONCASTER 18
SELBY 38
YORK 52

RETFORD 26
NEWARK 39
NOTTINGHAM 40
GRANTHAM 52
LONDON 165

GLOSSOP 24
MANCHESTER 38

MANSFIELD 25
NOTTINGHAM 37
NEWARK 52
GRANTHAM 52
LONDON 163

CHAPEL-EN-
LE-FRITH 23
BUXTON 28

BAKEWELL 17
BUXTON 28
MACCLESFIELD 41

CHESTERFIELD 12
DERBY 36

NOTTINGHAM

RIPLEY 14

CHESTERFIELD 26
SHEFFIELD 36
DONCASTER 45

SOUTHWELL 13

Nottingham Canal

ILKESTON 7

DERBY 15
BUXTON 49
MANCHESTER 73

NEWARK 20
GRANTHAM 24
LINCOLN 36

River Trent

LEICESTER 25
PETERBOROUGH 54
BEDFORD 75
LONDON 124

LOUGHBOROUGH 15
RUGBY 47

453
BIRMINGHAM 51

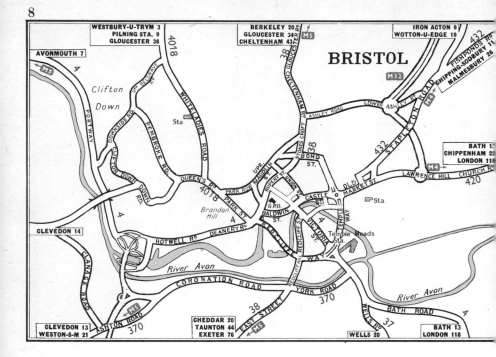

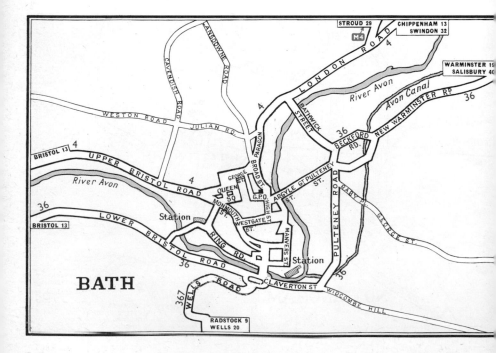

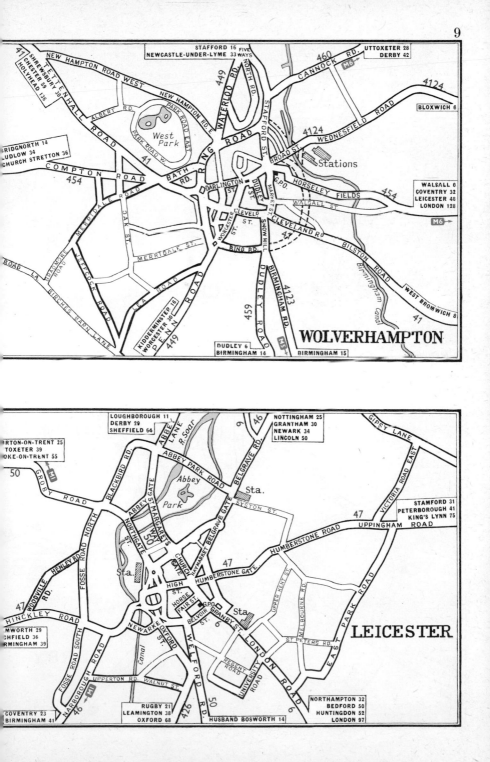

WOLVERHAMPTON

LEICESTER

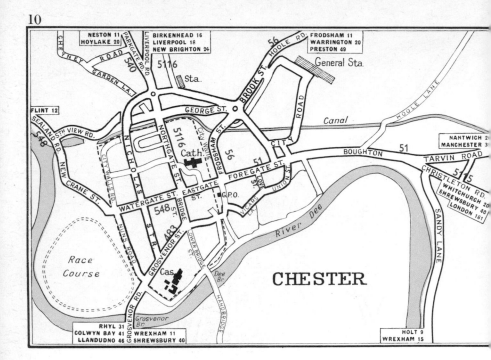

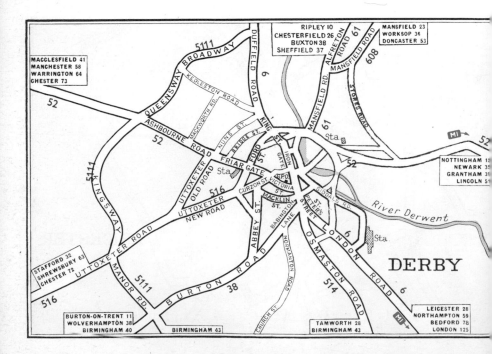

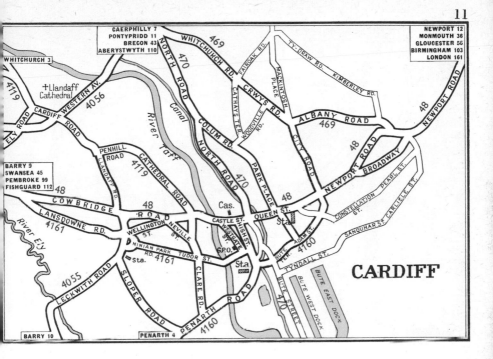

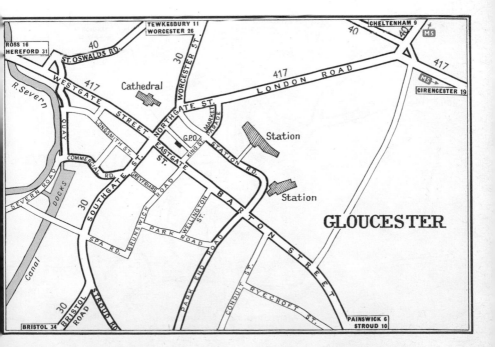

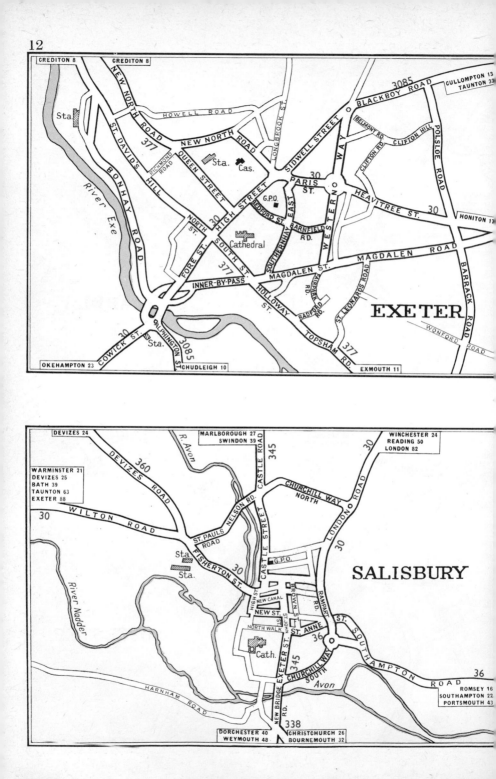

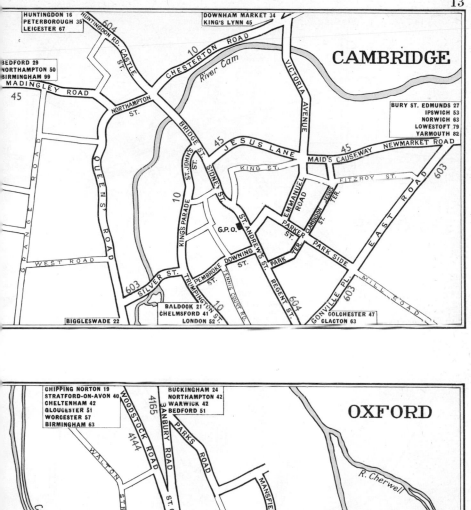

CAMBRIDGE

HUNTINGDON 16
PETERBOROUGH 35
LEICESTER 67

DOWNHAM MARKET 34
KING'S LYNN 45

BEDFORD 29
NORTHAMPTON 50
BIRMINGHAM 99

BURY ST. EDMUNDS 27
IPSWICH 53
NORWICH 63
LOWESTOFT 79
YARMOUTH 82

MADINGLEY ROAD
45
CHESTERTON ROAD
River Cam
VICTORIA AVENUE
10
HUNTINGDON RD.
CASTLE ST.
604
NORTHAMPTON ST.
QUEENS' ROAD
BRIDGE ST.
ST. JOHNS' ST.
SIDNEY ST.
KINGS PARADE
ST. ANDREW'S ST.
JESUS LANE
45
MAID'S CAUSEWAY
NEWMARKET ROAD
45
603
KING ST.
FITZROY ST.
EMMANUEL ROAD
JESUS TER.
CLARENDON ST.
EAST ROAD
GRANGE ROAD
WEST ROAD
10
G.P.O.
PARKER ST.
PARK TER.
PARK SIDE
603
SILVER ST.
603
PEMBROKE ST.
DOWNING ST.
TRUMPINGTON ST.
TENNIS COURT RD.
PARK ST.
REGENT ST.
604
GONVILLE PL.
603
MILL ROAD
10
BALDOCK 21
CHELMSFORD 41
LONDON 52
BIGGLESWADE 22
COLCHESTER 47
CLACTON 63

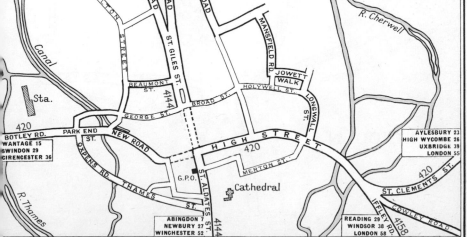

OXFORD

CHIPPING NORTON 19
STRATFORD-ON-AVON 40
CHELTENHAM 42
GLOUCESTER 51
WORCESTER 57
BIRMINGHAM 63

BUCKINGHAM 24
NORTHAMPTON 42
WARWICK 42
BEDFORD 51

R. Cherwell
WOODSTOCK ROAD
4165
BANBURY ROAD
PARKS ROAD
4144
WALTON STREET
ST. GILES ST.
MANSFIELD RD.
JOWETT WALK
Canal
BEAUMONT ST.
4144
HOLYWELL ST.
LONGWALL ST.
Sta.
GEORGE ST.
BROAD ST.
420
BOTLEY RD.
PARK END ST.
NEW ROAD
HIGH STREET
420
AYLESBURY 23
HIGH WYCOMBE 26
UXBRIDGE 39
LONDON 55
WANTAGE 15
SWINDON 29
CIRENCESTER 36
OXPENS RD.
THAMES ST.
G.P.O.
ST. ALDATES ST.
MERTON ST.
Cathedral
4144
ST. CLEMENTS ST.
420
COWLEY ROAD
IFFLEY RD.
4158
R. Thames
ABINGDON 7
NEWBURY 27
WINCHESTER 52
READING 29
WINDSOR 38
LONDON 58

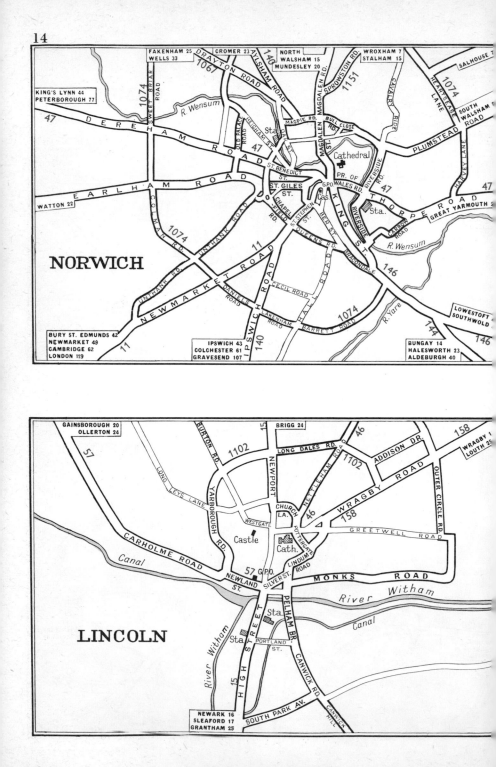

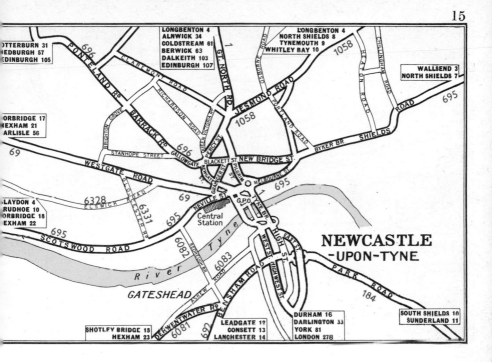

NEWCASTLE
-UPON-TYNE

LONGBENTON 4
ALNWICK 34
COLDSTREAM 61
BERWICK 63
DALKEITH 103
EDINBURGH 107

LONGBENTON 4
NORTH SHIELDS 8
TYNEMOUTH 9
WHITLEY BAY 10

WALLSEND 3
NORTH SHIELDS 7

OTTERBURN 31
EDBURGH 57
EDINBURGH 105

ORBRIDGE 17
HEXHAM 21
CARLISLE 56

LAYDON 4
RUDHOE 10
ORBRIDGE 18
EXHAM 22

SHOTLEY BRIDGE 15
HEXHAM 23

LEADGATE 12
CONSETT 13
LANCHESTER 14

DURHAM 16
DARLINGTON 33
YORK 81
LONDON 278

SOUTH SHIELDS 10
SUNDERLAND 11

PONTELAND RD.
CLAREMONT RD.
RICHARDSON RD.
GT. NORTH RD.
JESMOND ROAD
1058
BARRACK RD.
696
STANHOPE STREET
WESTGATE ROAD
GALLOWGATE
BLACKETT ST.
NEW BRIDGE ST.
BYKER BR.
SHIELDS
695
6328
ELSWICK
6331
695
69
NEVILLE ST.
G.P.O.
TYNE BR.
695
Central Station
6082
River Tyne
6083
SCOTSWOOD ROAD
695
GATESHEAD
DEKWENTWATER RD.
BENSHAM ROAD
6081
690
PARK ROAD
184
HIGH WEST ST.
69
1058

CARLISLE

DUMFRIES 33
EDINBURGH 94
GLASGOW 96

BRAMPTON 9
HEXHAM 39
NEWCASTLE 56

IGTOWN RD
ILLOTH 33
KESWICK 33
WHITEHAVEN 39

PORT ROAD

DALSTON 4

PENRITH 18
LONDON 303

HEXHAM 38
NEWCASTLE 57
DURHAM 70

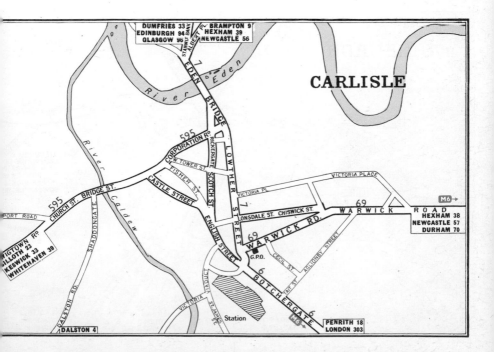

River Eden
EDEN BRIDGE
595
CORPORATION RD.
RICKERGATE
LOWTHER STREET
SCOTCH ST.
FISHER ST.
CASTLE STREET
CHURCH ST.
BRIDGE ST.
595
SHADDONGATE
River Caldew
W. TOWER ST.
ENGLISH STREET
VICTORIA PL.
LONSDALE ST.
CHISWICK ST.
VICTORIA PLACE
WARWICK
ROAD
69
WARWICK RD.
G.P.O.
CECIL ST.
BOTCHERGATE
Station
M6

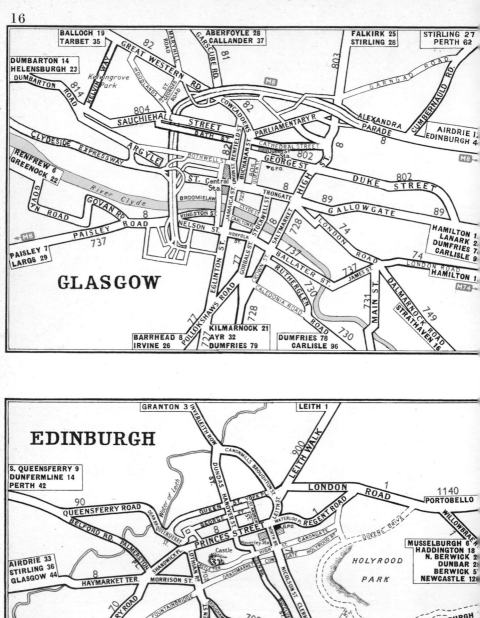

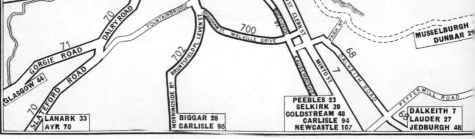

LEGEND

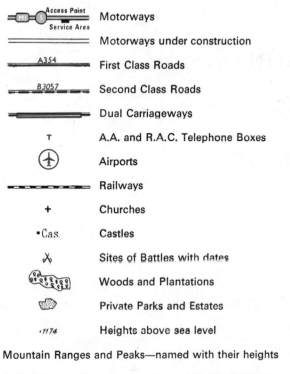

Motorways	
Motorways under construction	
First Class Roads	
Second Class Roads	
Dual Carriageways	
A.A. and R.A.C. Telephone Boxes	
Airports	
Railways	
Churches	
Castles	
Sites of Battles with dates	
Woods and Plantations	
Private Parks and Estates	
Heights above sea level	

Mountain Ranges and Peaks—named with their heights

Antiquities, e.g. Stonehenge—lettered in very thin type

HEIGHTS IN FEET

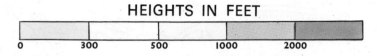

LONDON

Scale of Miles

ST ALBANS 21
FENNY STRATFORD 45
TO MOTORWAY MI

STEVENAGE 32
STAMFORD 91
GRANTHAM III
NEWARK 124

HARROW 2

OXFORD 55
CHELTENHAM 96
GLOUCESTER 103

MAIDENHEAD 25
READING 38
NEWBURY 54
BATH 106
BRISTOL 118

GUILDFORD 28
PORTSMOUTH 73

LEATHERHEAD 19
DORKING 25
HORSHAM 38
WORTHING 57

CROYDON 10
REDHILL 22
BRIGHTON 54

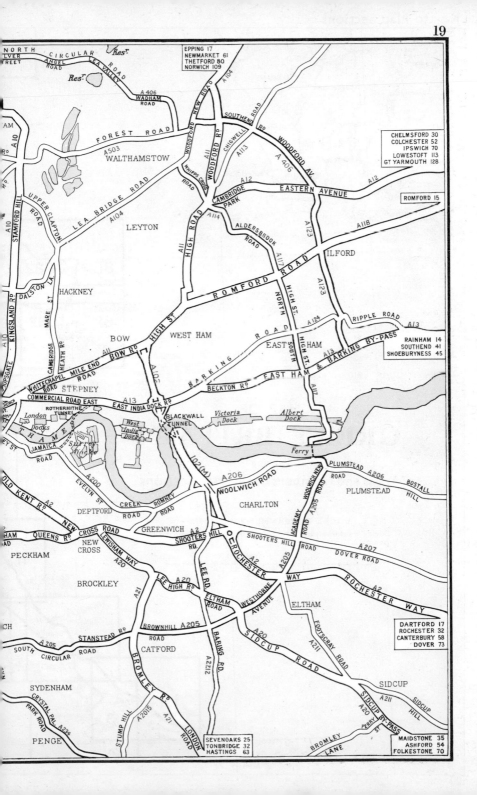

NORTH CIRCULAR ROAD
SILVER
ANGEL
ROAD
Res.
Res.
LEA VALLEY

EPPING 17
NEWMARKET 61
THETFORD 80
NORWICH 109

A406
WARHAM
ROAD

FOREST ROAD
A503
WALTHAMSTOW
WHIPPS CROSS
WOODFORD RD.
WOODFORD NEW RD.
SOUTHEND RD.
CHIGWELL RD.
WOODFORD RD.
A113
A114
A406
WOODFORD AV.
A12
EASTERN AVENUE
A12

CHELMSFORD 30
COLCHESTER 52
IPSWICH 70
LOWESTOFT 113
GT. YARMOUTH 128

ROMFORD 15

STAMFORD HILL
UPPER CLAPTON ROAD
A10
A10
LEA BRIDGE ROAD
A104
LEYTON
HIGH ROAD
A11
CAMBRIDGE PARK
A114
ALDERSBROOK ROAD
A118
A123
ILFORD
A123

KINGSLAND RD.
DALSTON LA.
MARE ST.
HACKNEY
CAMBRIDGE HEATH RD.
BOW
HIGH ST.
A11
BOW RD.
WEST HAM
A102
A11
ROMFORD ROAD
A117
NORTH ROAD
HIGH ST.
EAST HAM
SOUTH HIGH ST.
A124
A13
RIPPLE ROAD
A13
BARKING BY-PASS

RAINHAM 14
SOUTHEND 41
SHOEBURYNESS 45

WHITECHAPEL ROAD
MILE END ROAD
STEPNEY
COMMERCIAL ROAD EAST
A13
EAST INDIA DOCK RD.
BECKTON RD.
EAST HAM
A117
ROTHERHITHE TUNNEL
London Docks
THAMES
JAMAICA ROAD
West India Dock
Surrey Docks
BLACKWALL TUNNEL
Victoria Dock
Albert Dock
Ferry

A200
EVELYN ST.
DEPTFORD
CREEK
ROMNEY ROAD
A2 (M)
A206
WOOLWICH ROAD
CHARLTON
WOOLWICH NEW ROAD
A206
PLUMSTEAD A206
BOSTALL HILL
PLUMSTEAD

OLD KENT RD.
A2
NEW CROSS ROAD
QUEENS RD.
NEW CROSS
LEWISHAM WAY
A20
GREENWICH
A2
SHOOTERS HILL RD.
SHOOTERS HILL
A2
ACADEMY ROAD
A205
A205
DOVER ROAD
A207
ROCHESTER WAY
A2

PECKHAM
BROCKLEY
A21
LEE HIGH RD.
A20
LEE RD.
ELTHAM ROAD
WESTHORNE AVENUE
ELTHAM
ROCHESTER WAY

DARTFORD 17
ROCHESTER 32
CANTERBURY 58
DOVER 73

A205
SOUTH CIRCULAR ROAD
STANSTEAD RD.
BROWNHILL ROAD A205
CATFORD
BROMLEY RD.
BARING RD.
A2212
A20
SIDCUP ROAD
A211
FOOTSCRAY ROAD
SIDCUP
A211
SIDCUP HILL

SYDENHAM
CRYSTAL PAL. A234
PARK ROAD
PENGE
STUMP HILL
A2015
A21
LONDON ROAD
BROMLEY LANE
SIDCUP BY-PASS
A20
PERRY ST.

SEVENOAKS 25
TONBRIDGE 32
HASTINGS 63

MAIDSTONE 35
ASHFORD 54
FOLKESTONE 70

MAP OF
GREAT BRITAIN
Showing
Areas and Numbers of the Map Sections

LOCAL GOVERNMENT ACT, 1972
During transition stage new county boundaries shown on this map only.

Scale of Miles

10 5 0   10   20   30   40   50

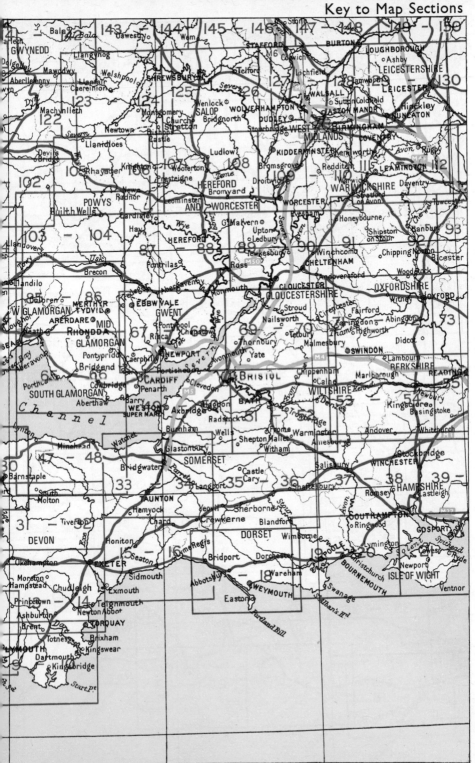

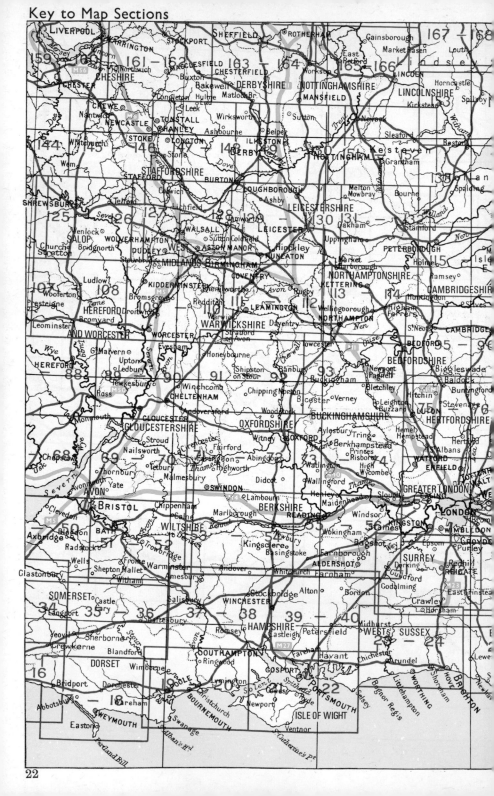

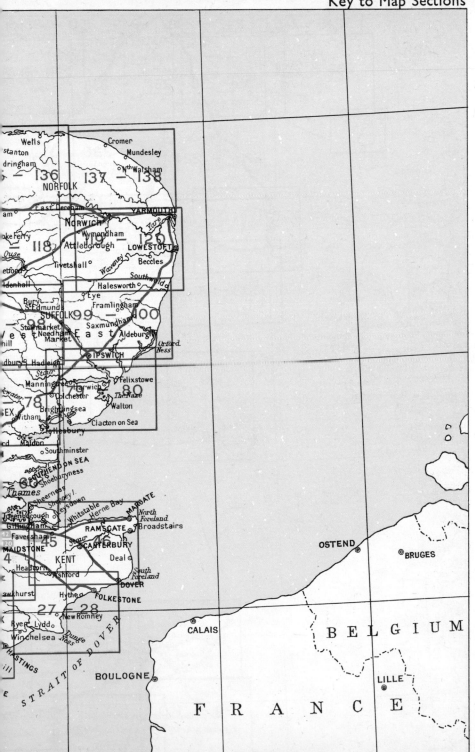

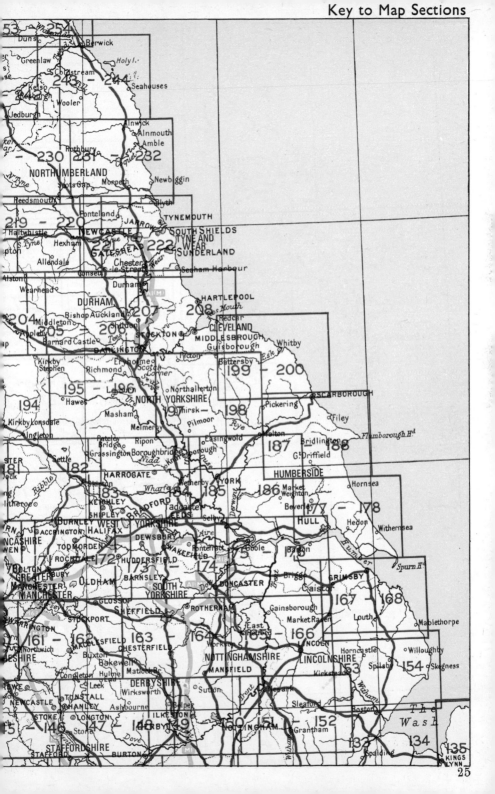

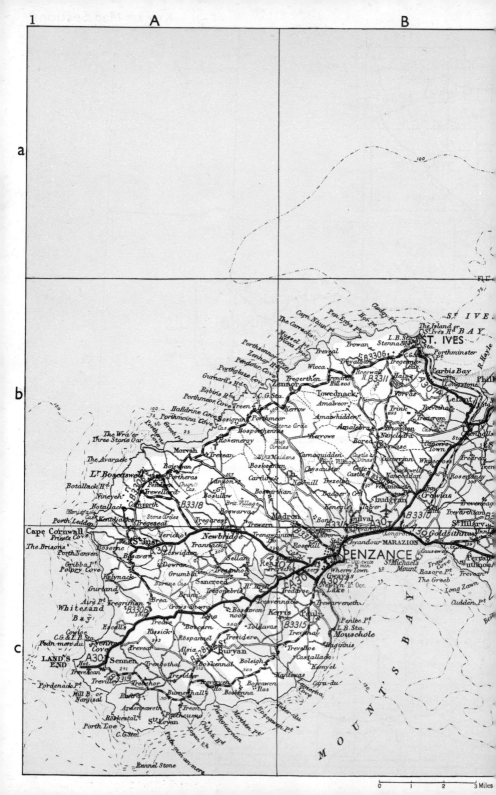

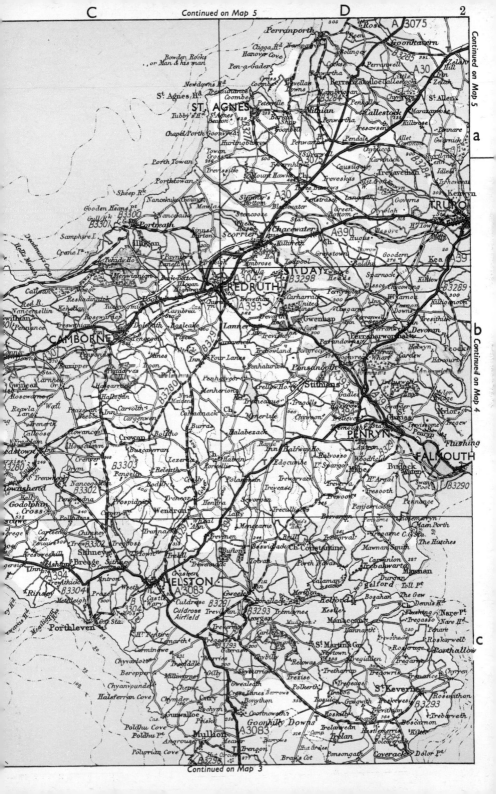

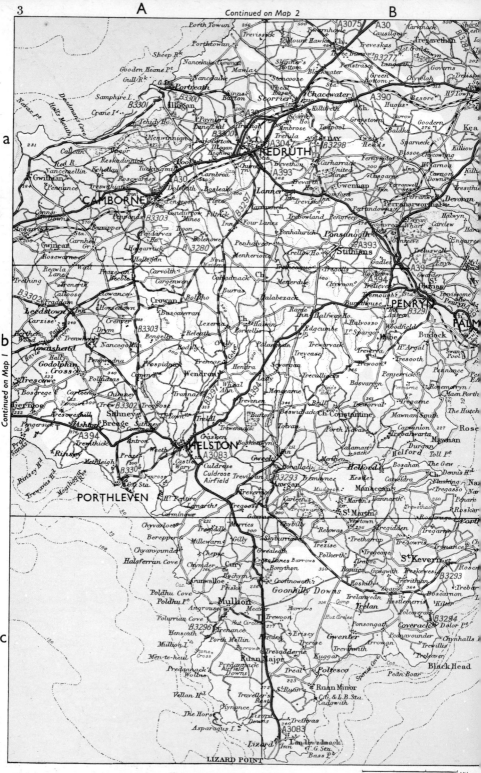

Continued on Map I

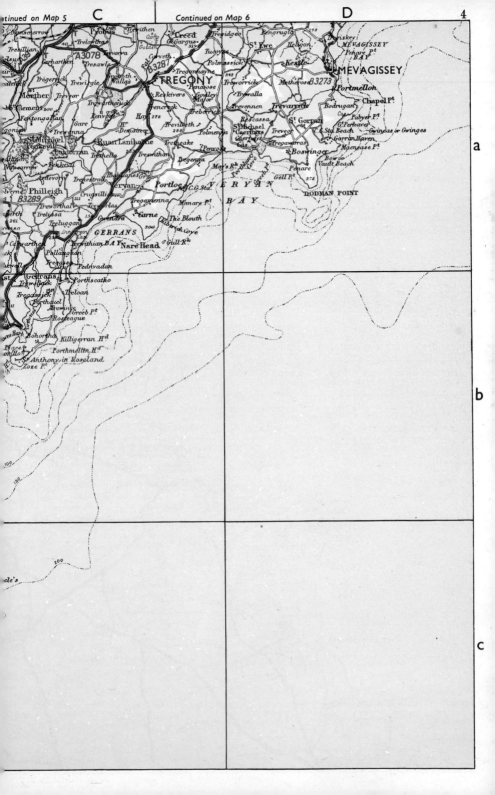

a

b

c

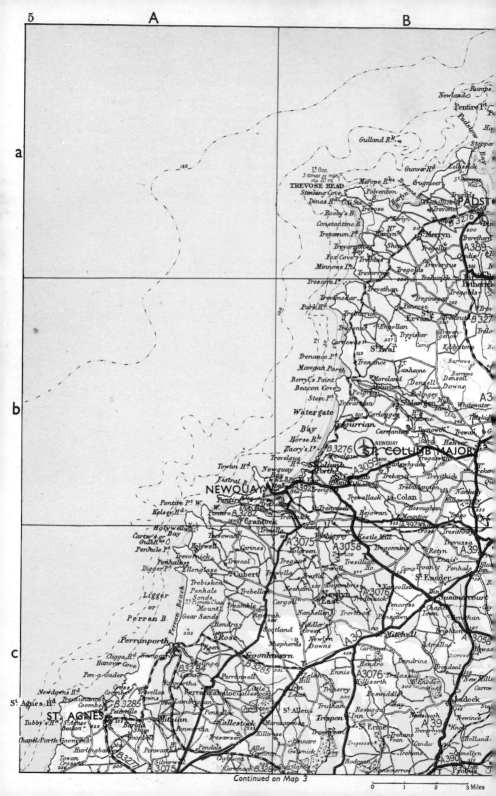

Continued on Map 3

0   1   2   3 Miles

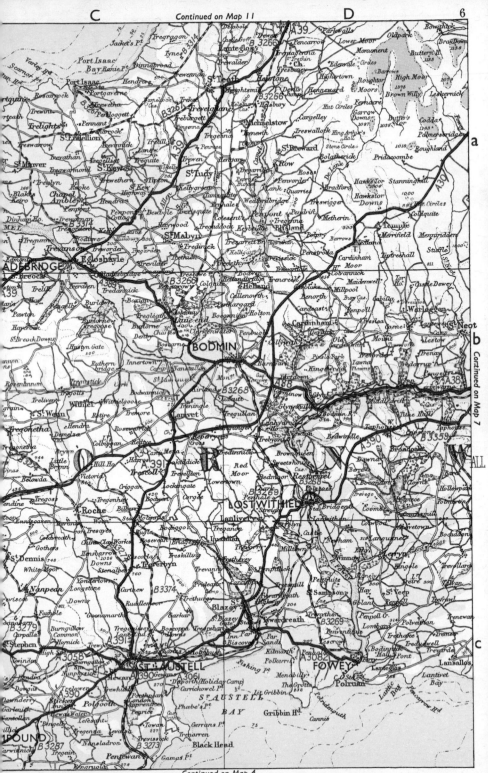

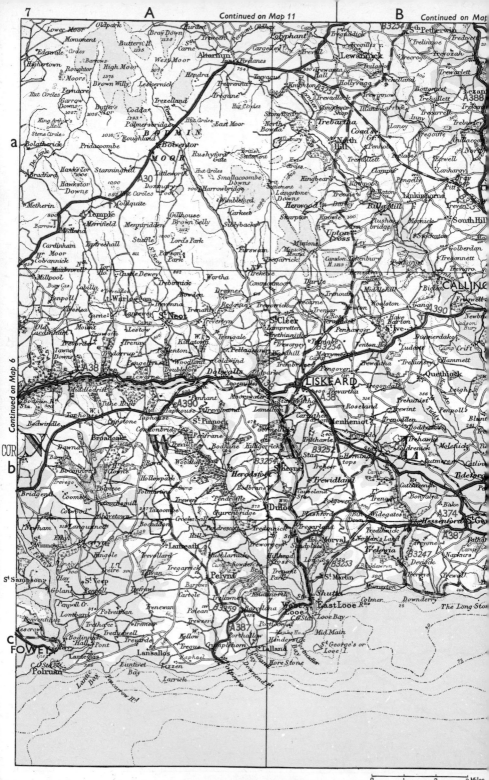

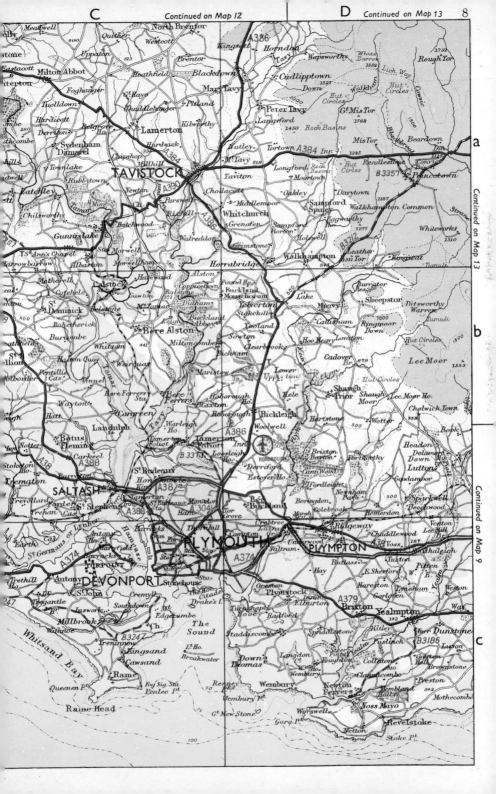

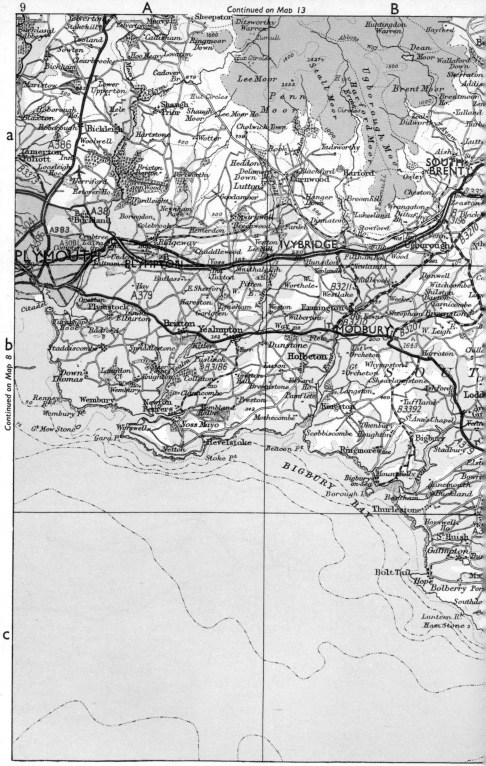

Continued on Map 8

a

b

c

SOUTH BRENT

PLYMOUTH

PLYMPTON

IVYBRIDGE

MODBURY

Yealmpton

Brixton

Holbeton

Kingston

Bigbury

Bigbury-on-Sea

Thurlestone

Bolt Tail

Hope

Bolberry

BIGBURY BAY

Borough I.

0   1   2   3 Miles

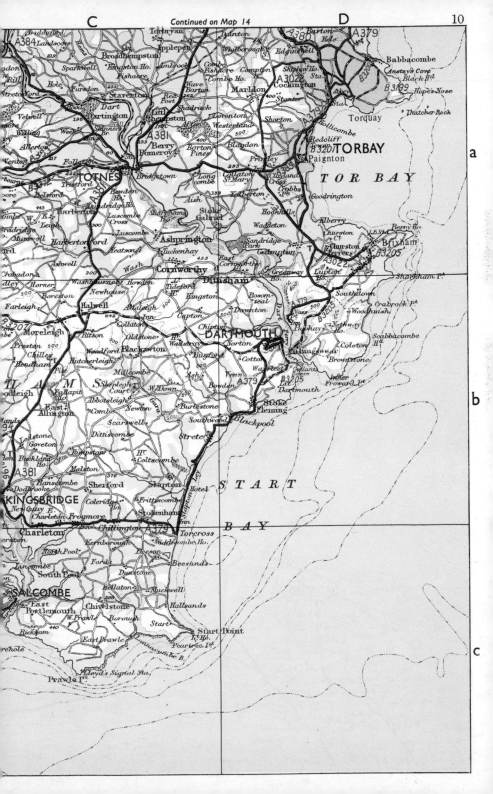

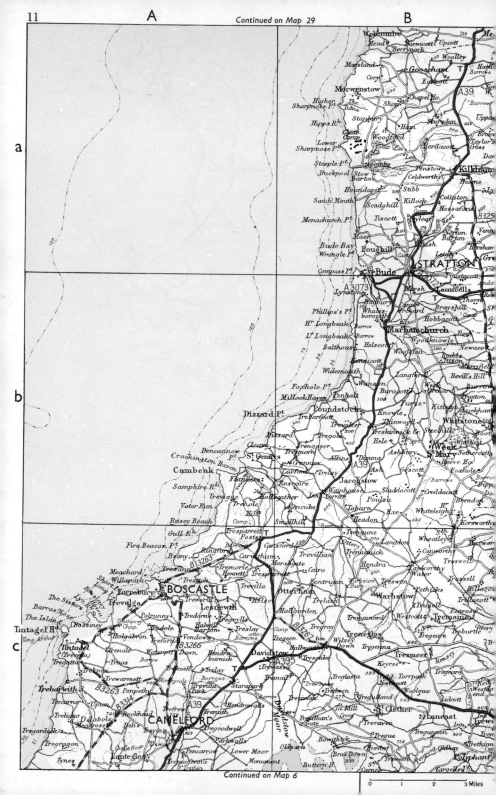

Continued on Map 29

A
B

a

b

c

Welcombe
Mead
Darracott
Berrypark
Upcott
Woolley
Me

Morwenstow
Cory
Gooseham
Eastcott
A39
Hartl
Barrows

Higher
Sharpnose Pt
The Idna
Shop
Chapel Ho.
Shurdon
Uppa

Hippa Rk
Stanbury
Ham
Taylor's
Cross

Lower
Sharpnose Pt
Clean
Camp
Woodford
Berdacott
500
Bro

Steeple Pt
Coombe
Lee
Penstowe
Kilkhampton
Da

Duckpool
Stow
Barton
Coldworthy

Houndapit
Stibb
Killock
Collaton
B325

Sandy Mouth
Scadghill
Tiscott
Hessaford

Menachurch Pt
Tiscott
Norton
Barton

Maer
Bush
Hersham

Bude Bay
Wrangle Pt
Foughill
Camp
Leigh

Compass Pt
Bude
Trustacott

STRATTON

A3073
Marsh
Launcells

Lynstone
Binhamy
Camp
Orchard
Launceston

Phillips's Pt
Whalesborough
Camp
Brayshill
Thorn

Hr Longbeak
Barrow
Hobbacott
St

Lr Longbeak
Barrow
Marhamchurch
Woodknowle

Salthouse
Helscott
Newaco

Widemouth
Wanson
Budds
Dizzard
Marianleigh

Foxhole Pt
Penhalt
Buragott
Langford
West
Orchard
Bevill's Hill
Burro

Millook Haven
Poundstock
Thinwood
Furze
Kitleigh
Buckham

Dizzard Pt
Trebarwith
Trevigo
Knowle
Freskinnick Cr
Steelhill
Whitstone
Boot

Bottreaux
Dizzard
Tresmorn
Trengayor
Hele
Week
St Mary
Nethercott
Wadfast
Boo

Cleave
Trefrouse
Allins
Damma
Ash
Ashbury
Reeve Ho
Foxhole

Crackington Haven
Pencannow
Pt
St Gennys
Grannow
Trelay
Gescott
Barrow
Dipp

Cambeak
Flanders
Roscare
Jacobstow
Wainhouse
Corna
Sladnacott
Geddacott
Brendon

Samphire Rk
Trevigue
Hallagather
Penkuke
Tobarn
Poulza
Whiteleigh
Hr

Voter Run
Trehole
Hill
Smallhill
Exe
Headon

Rusey Beach
Gull Rk
Smallhill
Trevanne
Kersworthy

Tresparrett
Posts
Trenannick
Langdon
Sth.
Wheatley's

Fire Beacon Pt
Carsford
Otter
Canworthy
Marwo

Meachard
Willapark
Bcertram
Ringford
Carthham
Trevillian
Trenannick
Hendra
Tackworthy
Water
Tressell

Short
Long
Trewannet
Tresparret
Cairo
Treswen
Pethicks
Balla

Torpabury
Trevalga
BOSCASTLE
Marshgate
Kentrigan
Burn
Treswen
Treneglos
Penrose

The Sisters
Trewen
Lesnewth
Trevilla
Otterham
Trelash
Tregonnard
Westcott
Tremaine

Barras Nose
Tredarrup
Hilsea
Warbstow

Rossiney
Trevigo
Tregune
Hallgarden
Tregray
Breburtle

Tintagel Hd
Trewarmett
Vendown
Treslay
Camp
Barrows
Tregeen
Wilsey
Down
Inn
Tregeare
Ottery

King Arthur
Tintagel
(Trevena)
Trenale
Truas
Waterpit
Down
Hendra
burnick
Davidstow
Hallworthy
Trygenna
Tresmeer
Kersey

Tregatta
Treknow
Trelabe
Trelay
B395
Trenault
Tregleasta
Torrponk
Wooleux
Tregeare

Trebarwith
B3263
Penpethy
Trevillia
Pask
Staraparok
Trewanna
Tregrenna
Tregunnon
Clether
Lancast

Treberyth
CANELFORD
A39
Tremail
Tregrella
Treneath
Treven
Trefranes
Treragon
Oldhay

Tregardock
Delabole
Meadrose
Heli
Treglasta
Bowithyck
Bray
Down
Butter H.
Treque
Trewen
Polyphant

Continued on Map 6

0   1   2   3 Miles

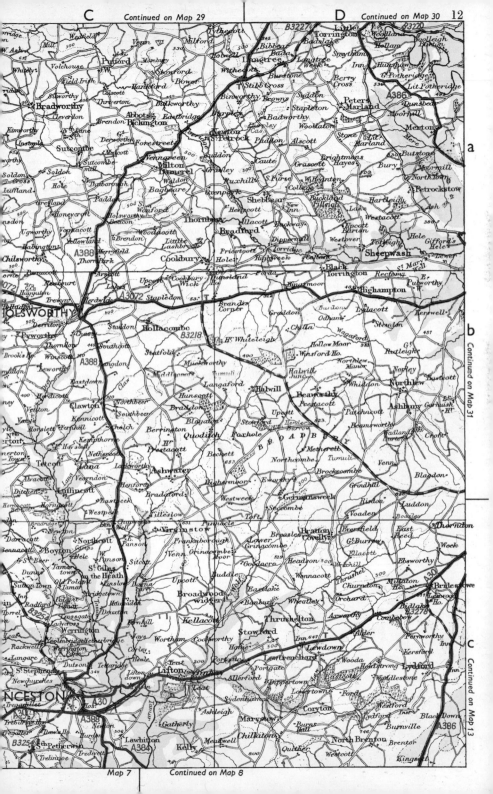

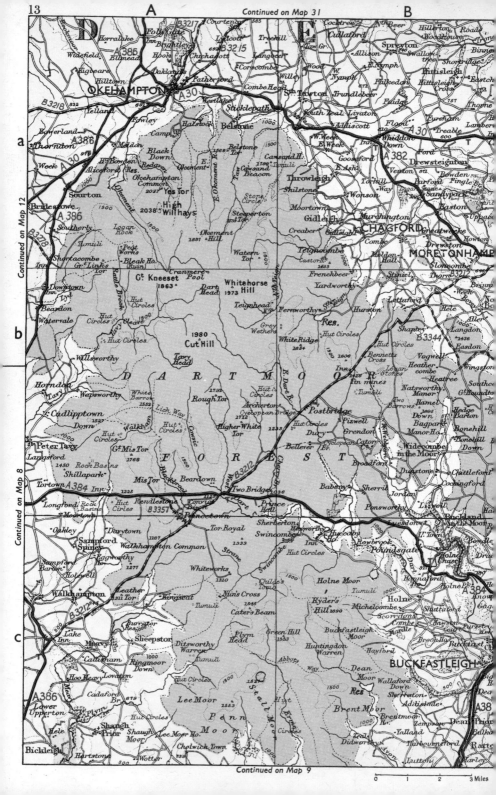

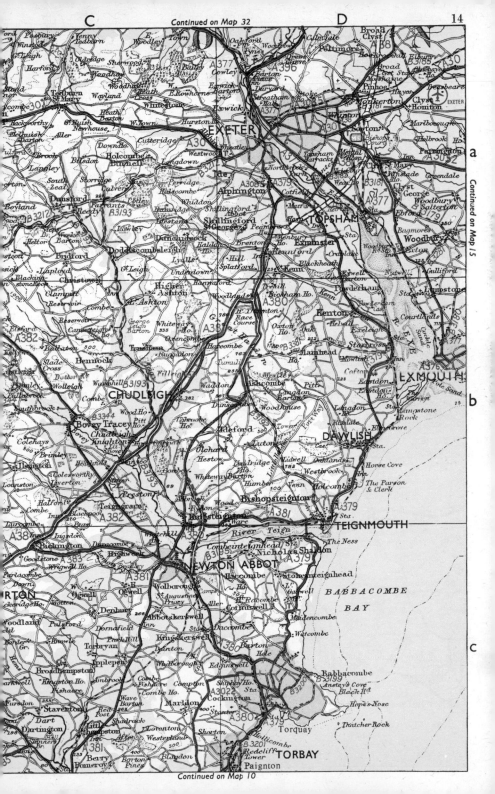

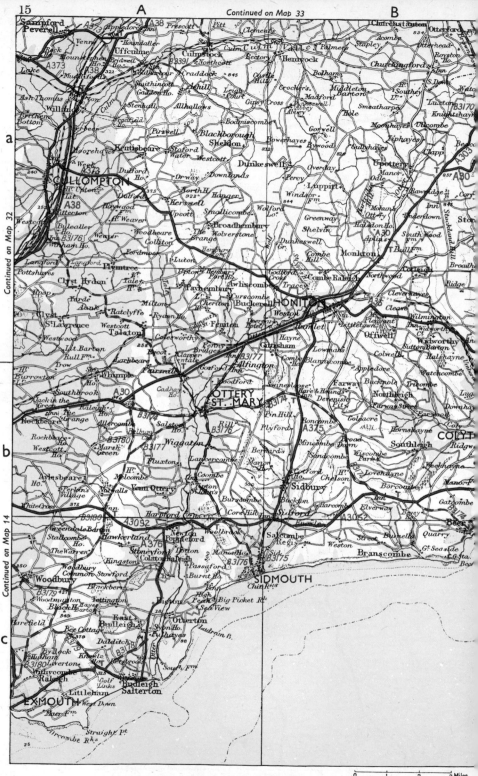

Continued on Map 33
Continued on Map 32
Continued on Map 14

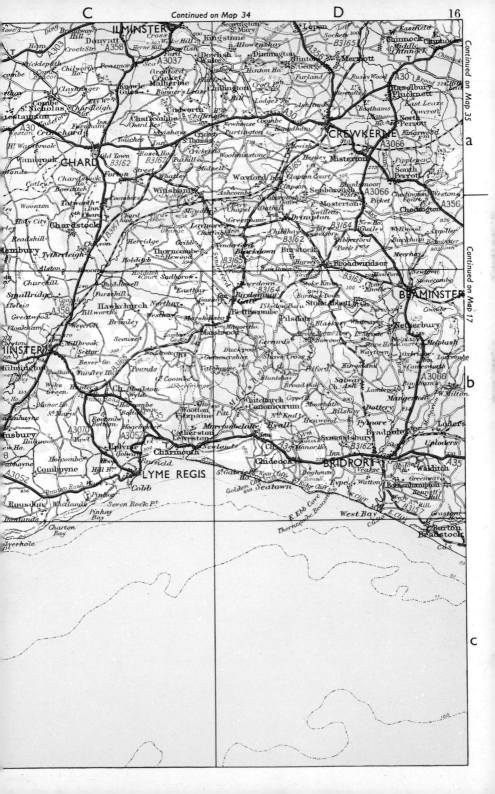

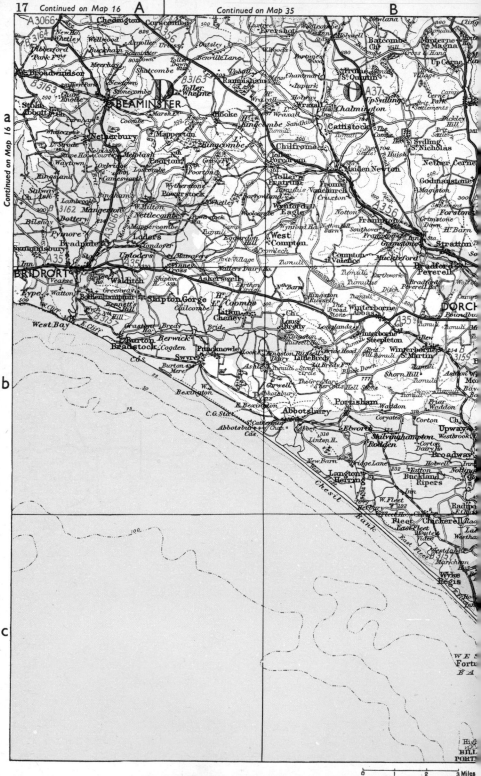

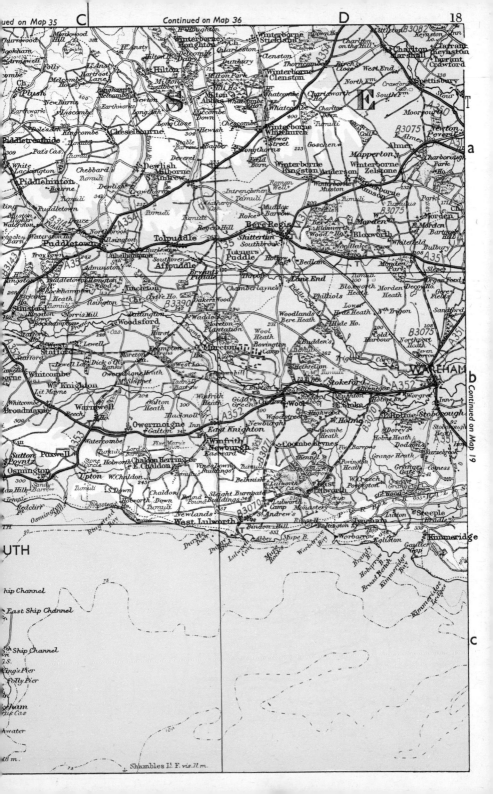

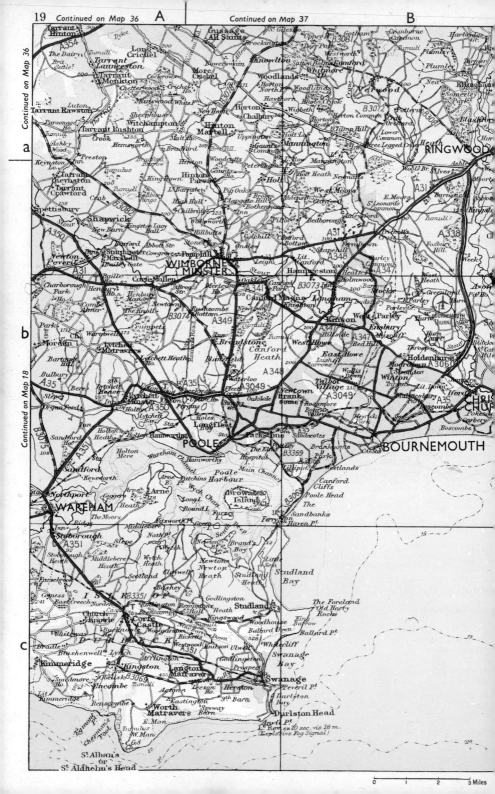

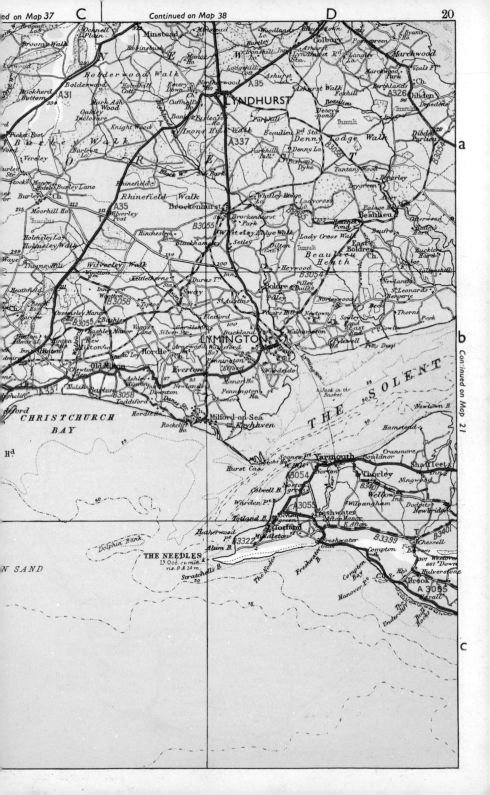

SOUTHAMPTON

Continued on Map 20

a

b

c

SOUTHAMPTON WATER

THE SOLENT

COWES

EAST COWES

SPITH

RYDE

NEWPORT

IS E OF WIGH T

SANDOWN

Sandown Bay

SHANKLIN

VENTNOR

FAREHAM

GOSPOR

0   1   2   3 Mile

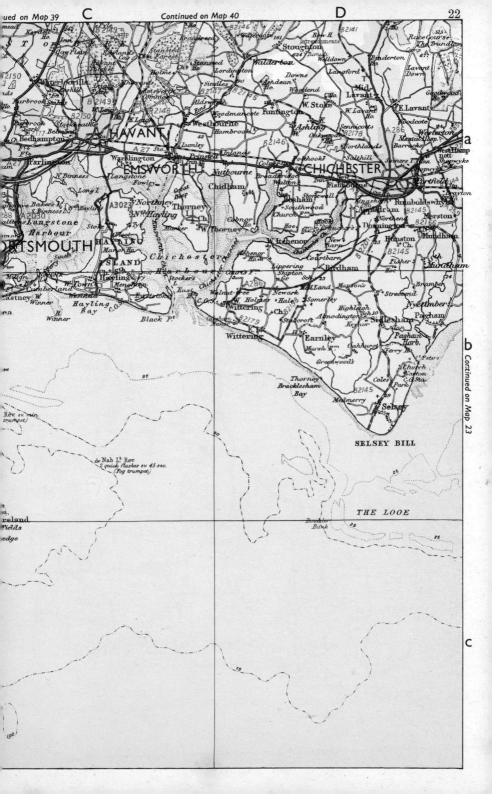

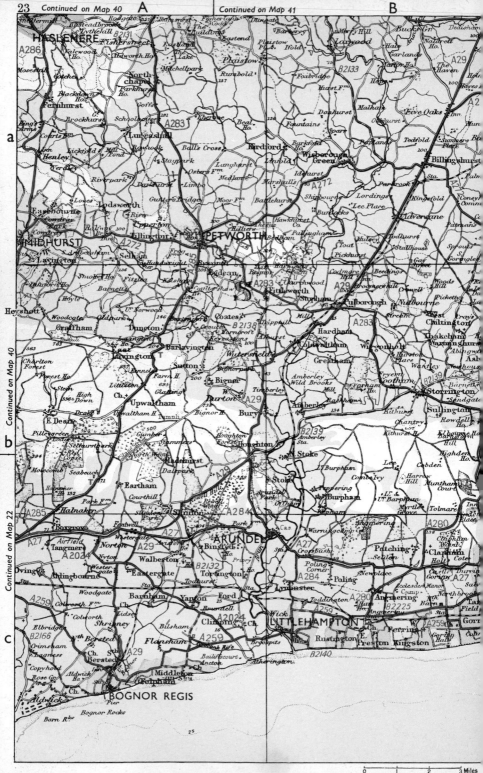

a

b

c

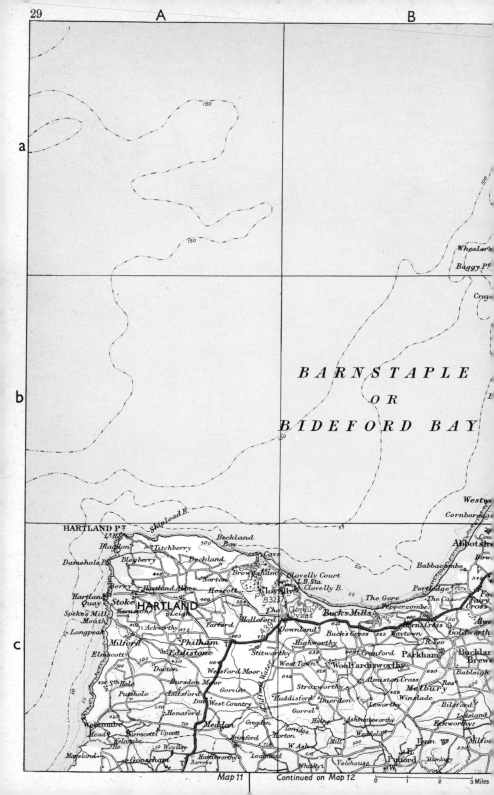

29

A B

a

150

150

Wheeler's

Baggy Pt

Cray

BARNSTAPLE

OR

BIDEFORD BAY

b

50

Westw

Cornborou

HARTLAND PT

L.H.S.

Shipload B.

Beckland

Bay

73

Abbotsh

Cou

Bow

Blagdon

Titchberry

Beckland

Cave

Babbacombe

Damehole Pt

Bleggerry

Browtham

Clovelly Court

L.B.Sta.

Clovelly B.

50

342

Berry

Norton

Hescott

Clovelly

The Gore

Portledge

The Cas

Fo

Hartland Abbey

466

B3237

25

Peppercombe

460

Fairy

Hartland

Quay

Stoke

584

Cha

Clovelly

Dykes

Bucks Mills

Horns Cross

Cross

Alw

Speke's Mill

Mouth

Kernstoke

Leigh

Holloford

Downland

621

Waytown

500

Gold

Longpeak

Ackworthy

477

663

Farford

Bucks Cross

583

R.Yeo

c

Milford

Philham

Stitworthy

Highworthy

658

691

Cranford

Parkham

620

Buckla

Brewe

Elmscott

516

Eddistone

661

West Town

619

Woolfardisworthy

Bableigh

Sth Hole

426

Docton

Welsford Moor

642

Stroxworthy

Almiston Cross

Metbury

500

Pushole

Bursdon Moor

Gorvin

Huddisford

Duerdon

Leworthy

Winslade

Res

Bilsford

423

Lutsford

570

West Country

Gorrel

Hole

Ashmansworthy

Lobeland

Henaford

Iron

718

Greadon

Horridge

Mill

Westfield

Eckworthy

Welcombe

Head

Barracott

Upcott

Welcombe

Ho.

Woolly

Meddon

Brimford

Horton

W.Ash

500

Yeom

Milfo

Yenn

530

Mansland

Gooseham

Hartisworthy

Barrows

Loatmead

Whitty

Volehouse

Putford

Monbury

F.

F.W.

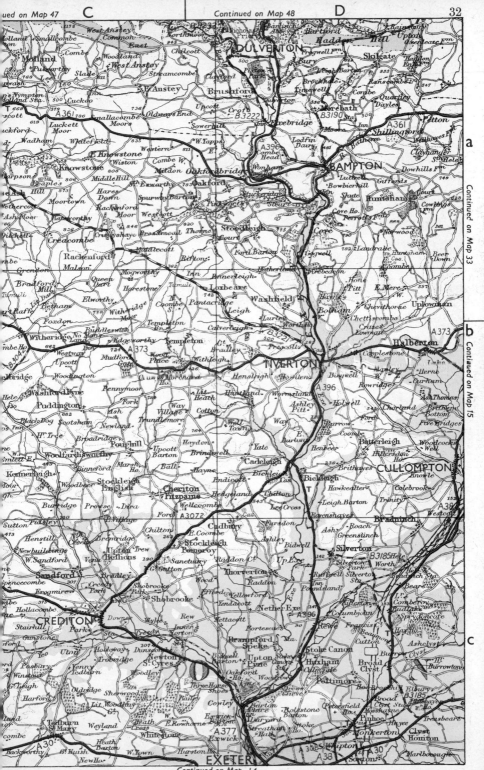

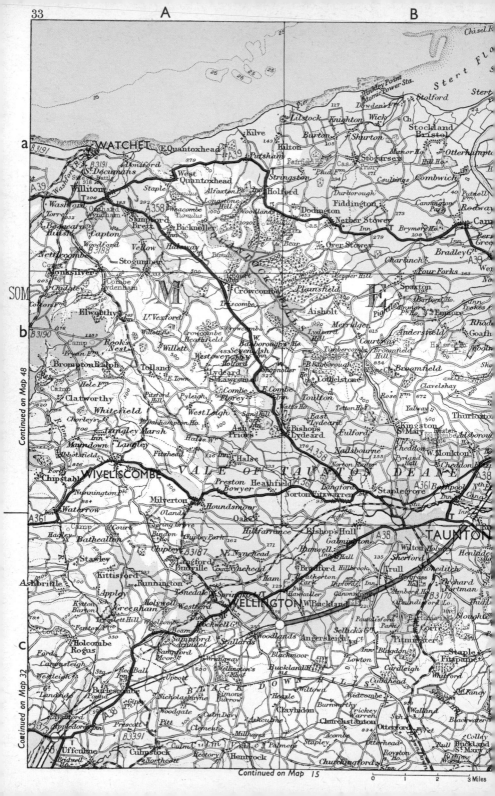

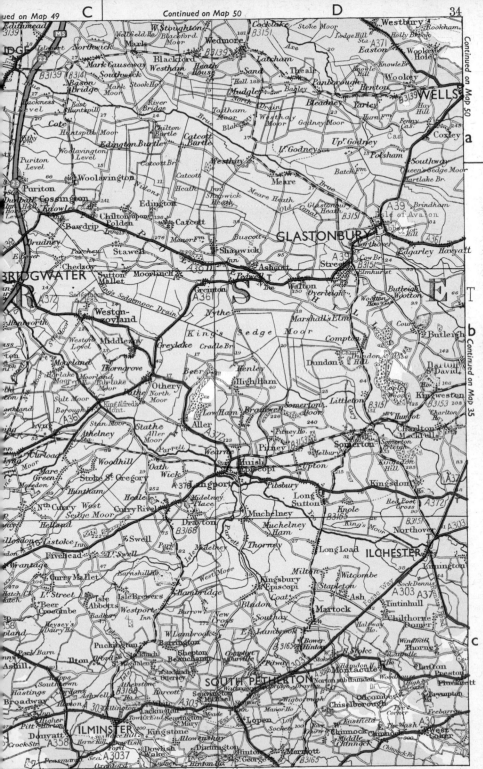

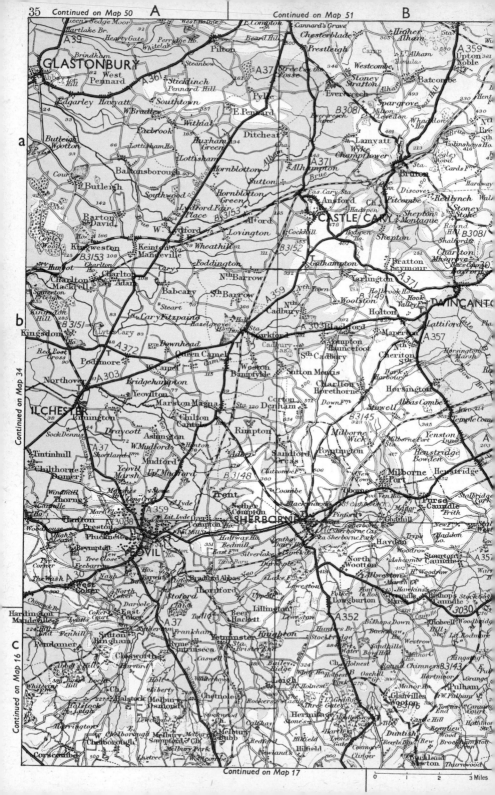

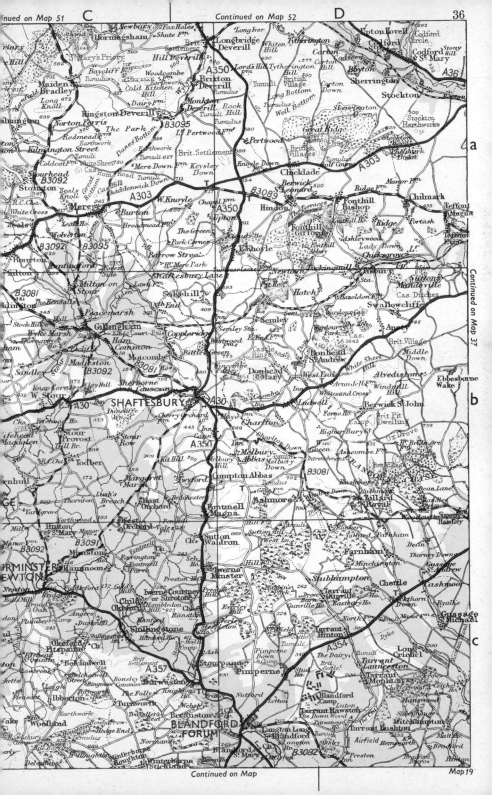

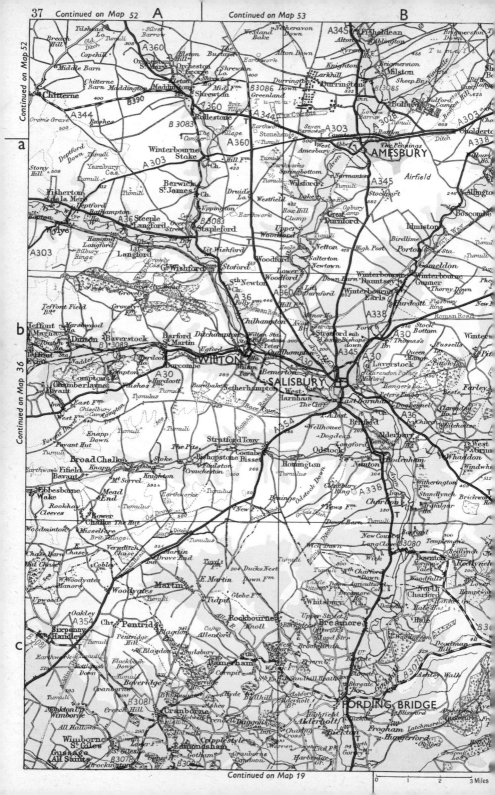

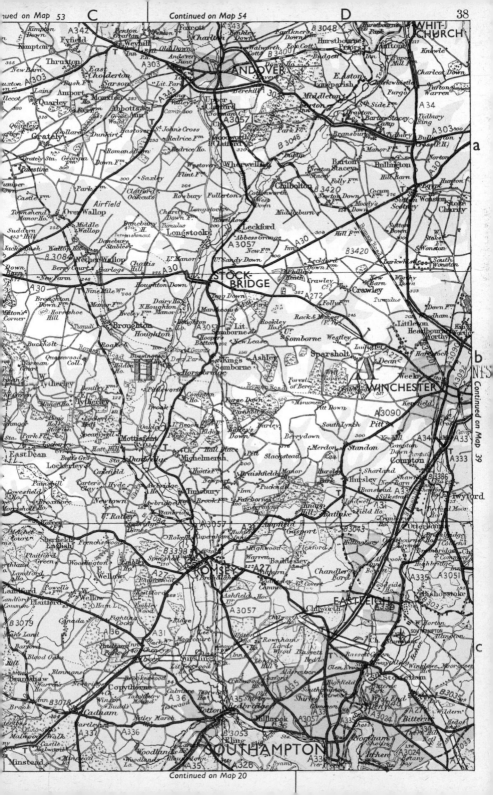

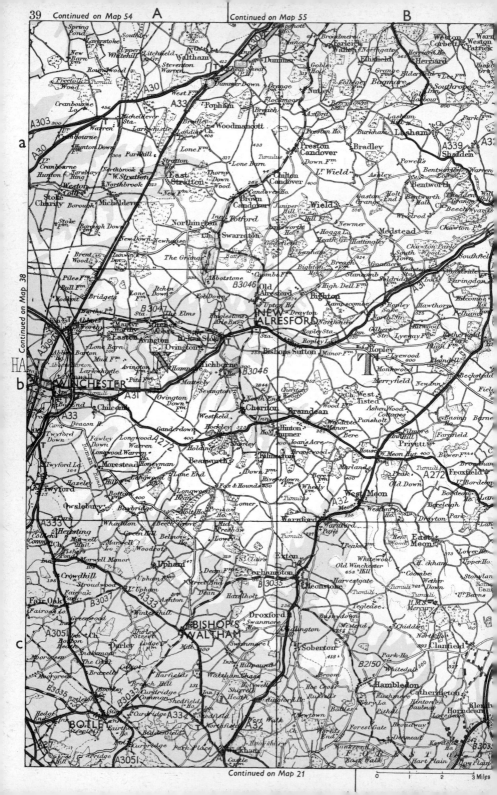

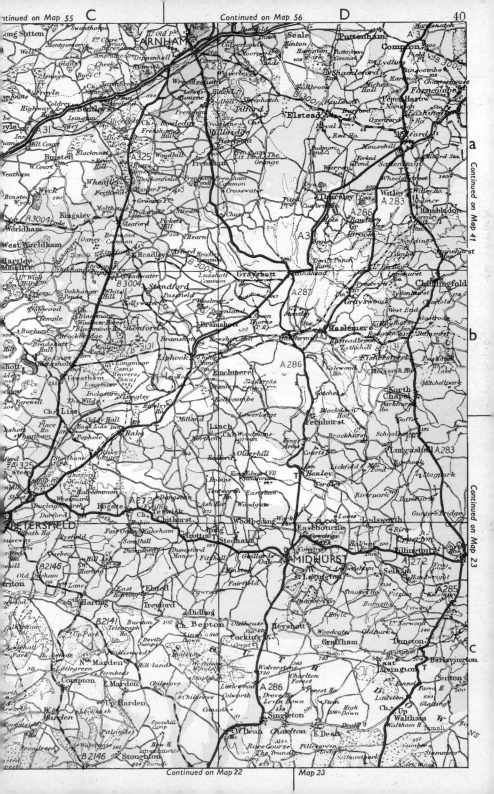

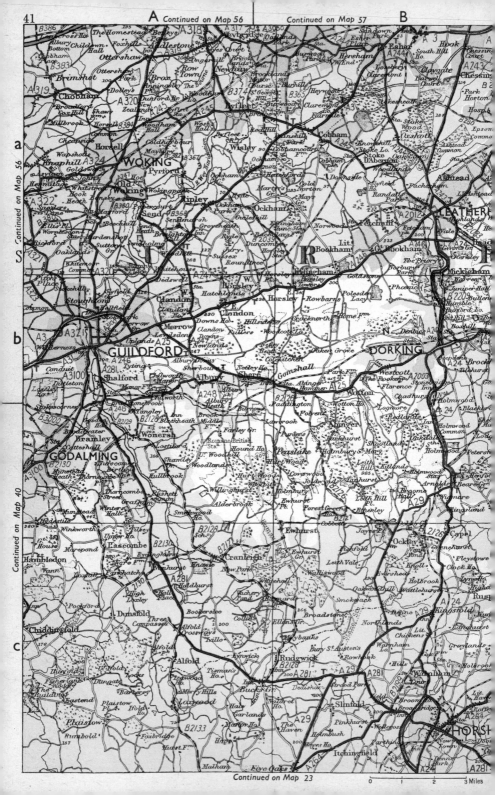

Continued on Map 56
Continued on Map 57
Continued on Map 56
Continued on Map 40
Continued on Map 23

WOKING
GUILDFORD
GODALMING
DORKING
LEATHER
HORSHAM

0   1   2   3 Miles

Continued on Map 43

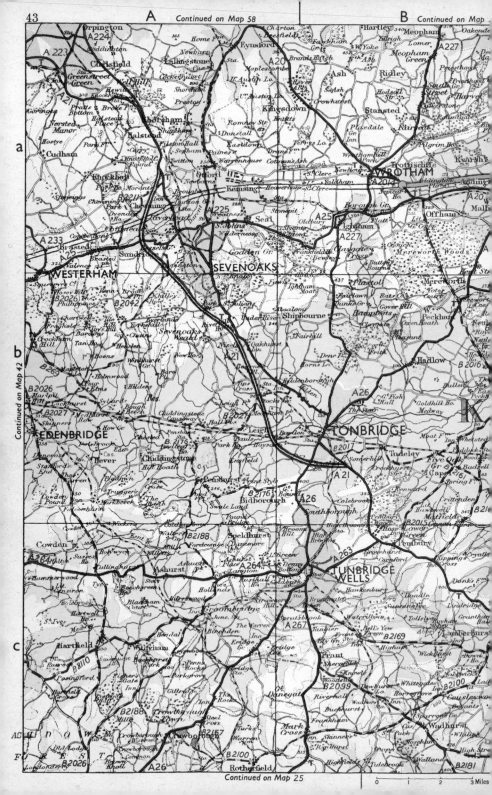

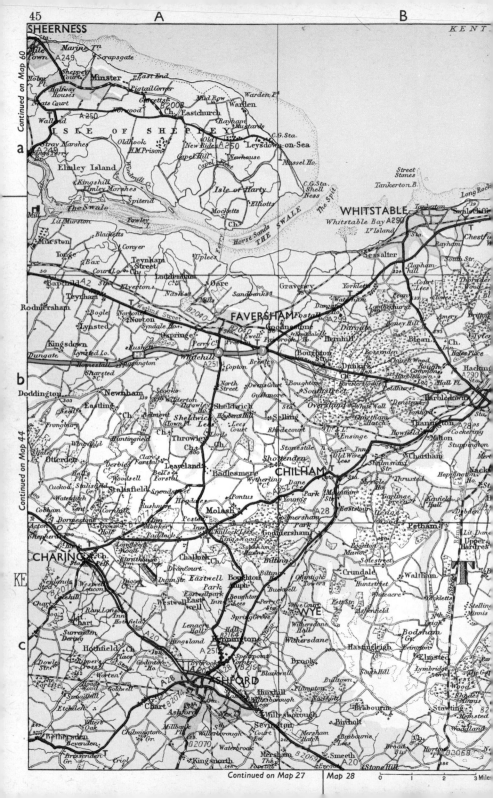

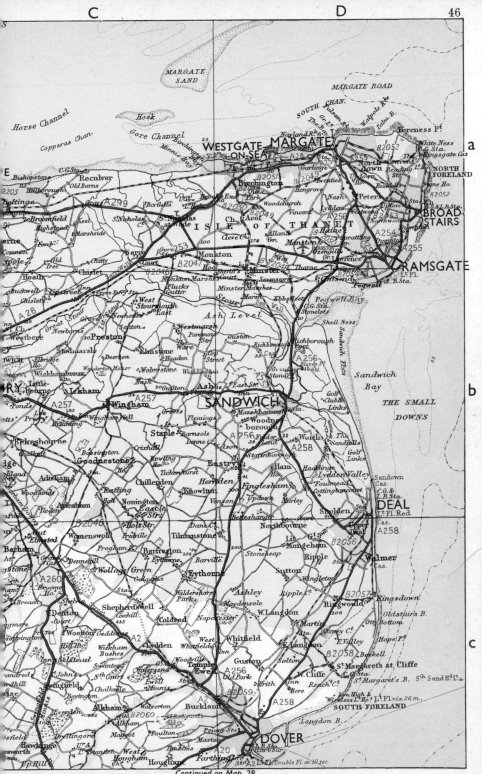

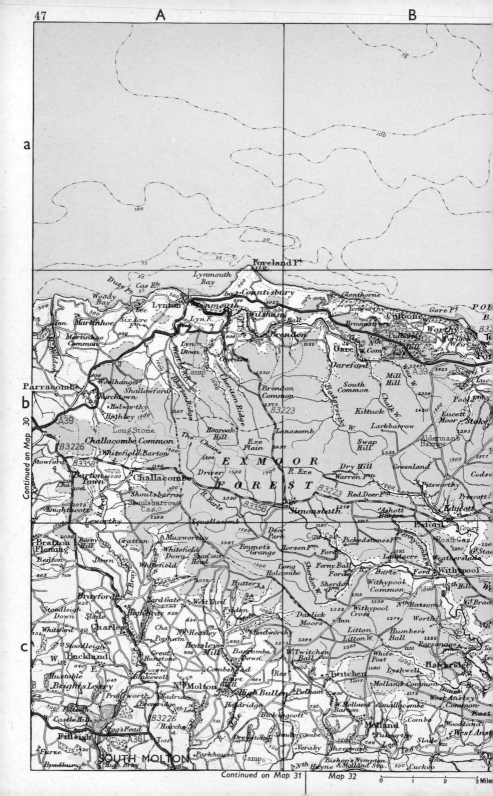

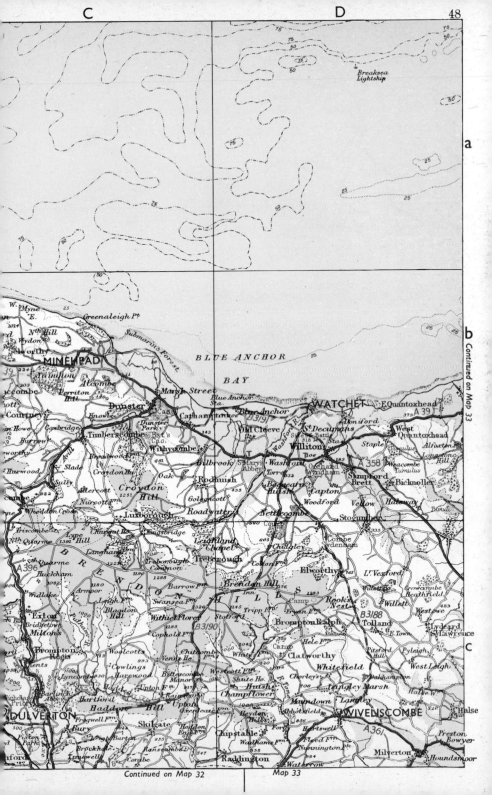

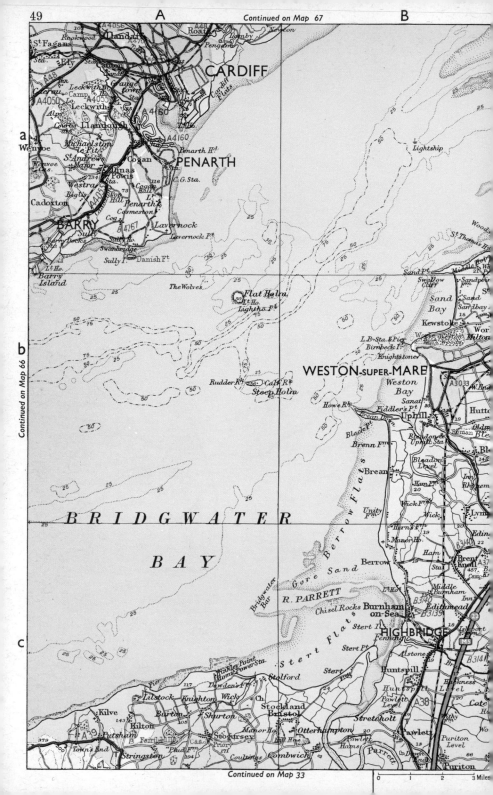

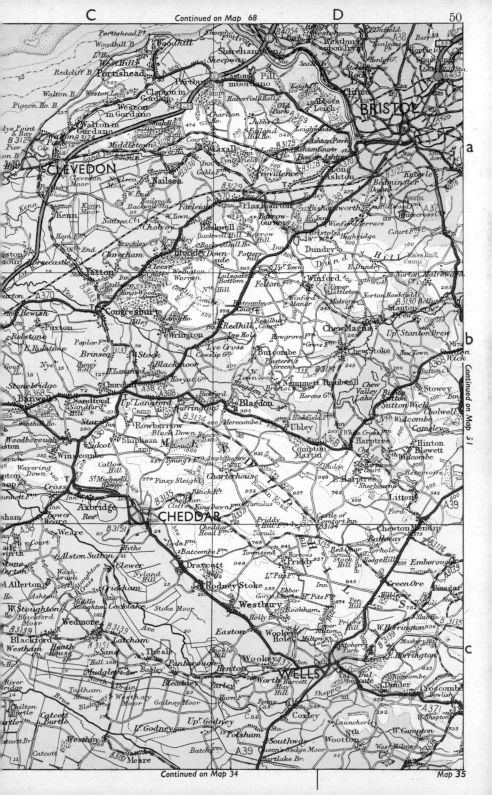

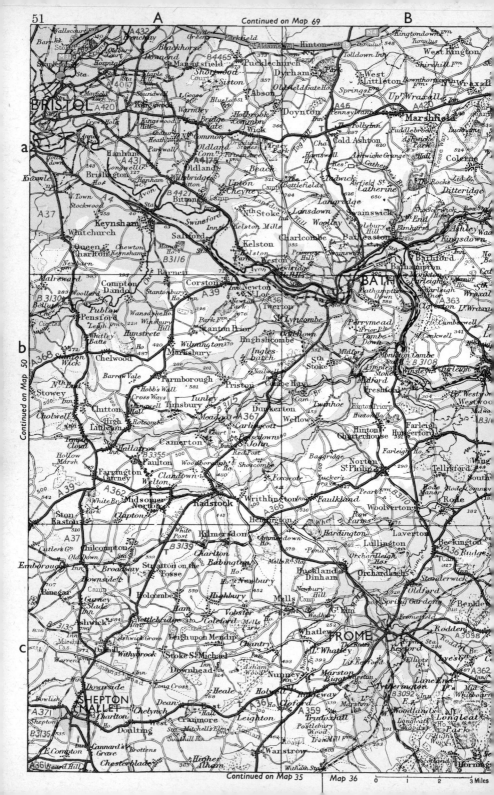

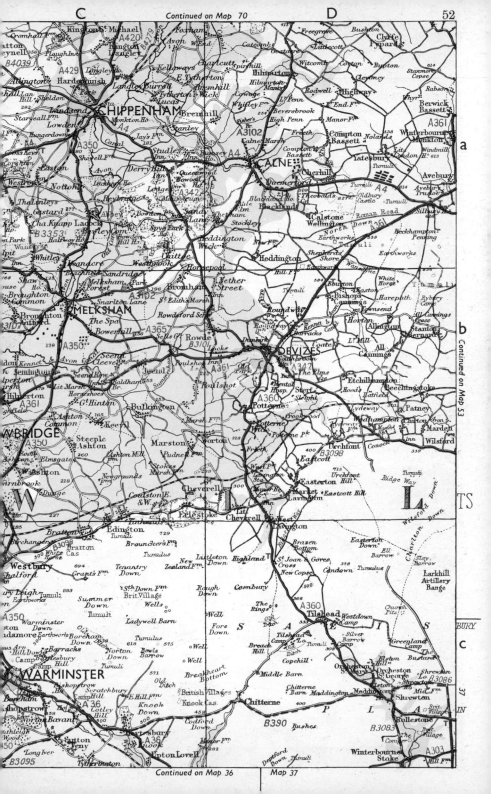

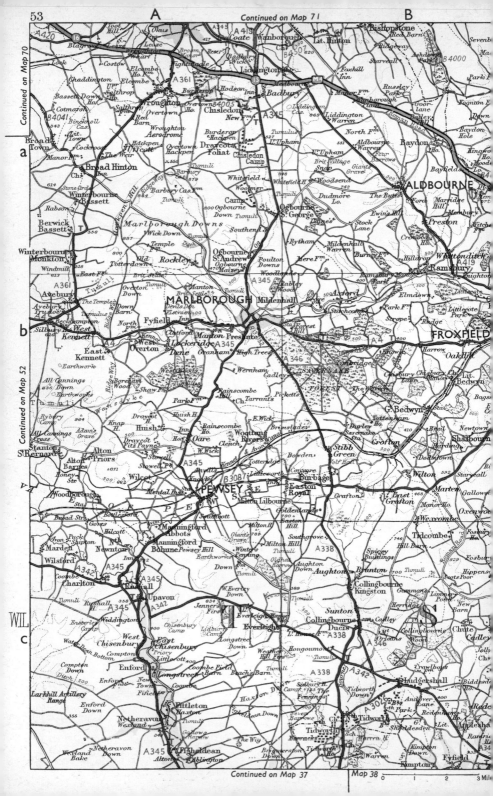

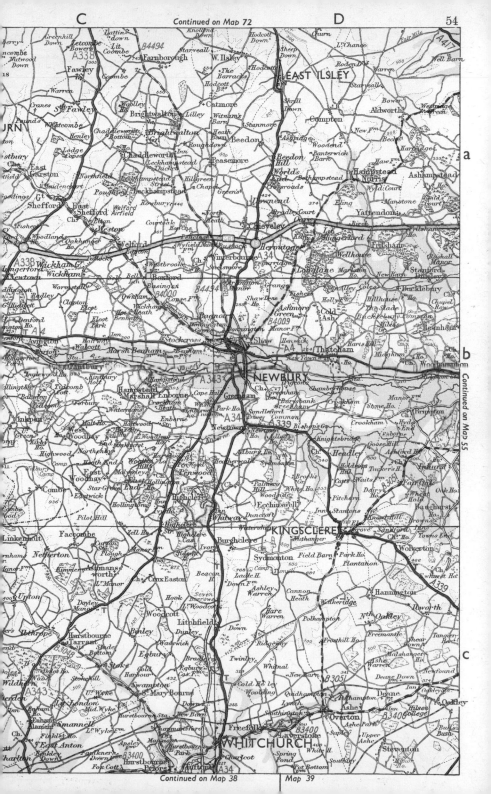

resses
ch

Mr G.F
40 Rec
SW13
Tel :

day noon before

Fee

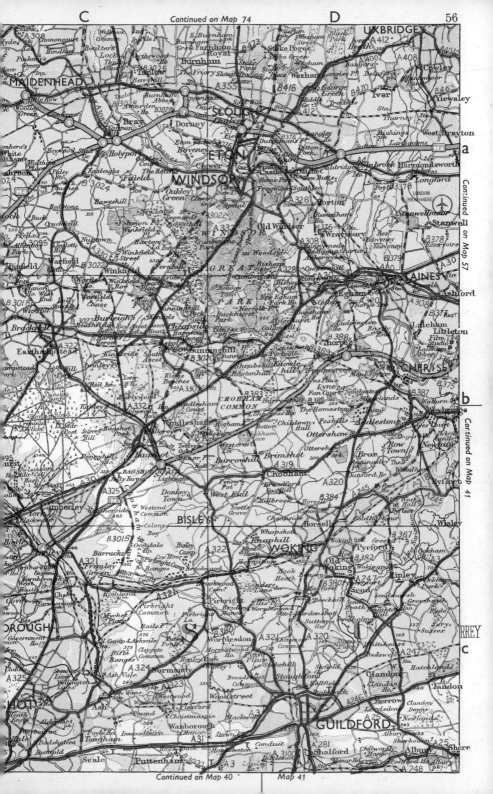

Continued on Map 74

Continued on Map 56

Map 42

Continued on Map 59

Continued on Map 77

A

B

A130

a

Continued on Map 58

b

c

INGATESTONE

BRENTWOOD

BILLERICAY

BASILDON

HAVERING

Ockendon

Orsett

Grays

Thurrock

Tilbury

GRAVESEND

Fobbing

Corringham

Mucking

Chadwell St Mary

East Tilbury

Cliffe

Cooling

Swanscombe

Northfleet

Chalk

Higham

ROCHESTER

CHATHAM

Meopham

Cuxton

Map 43

Continued on Map 44

0   1   2   3 Mile

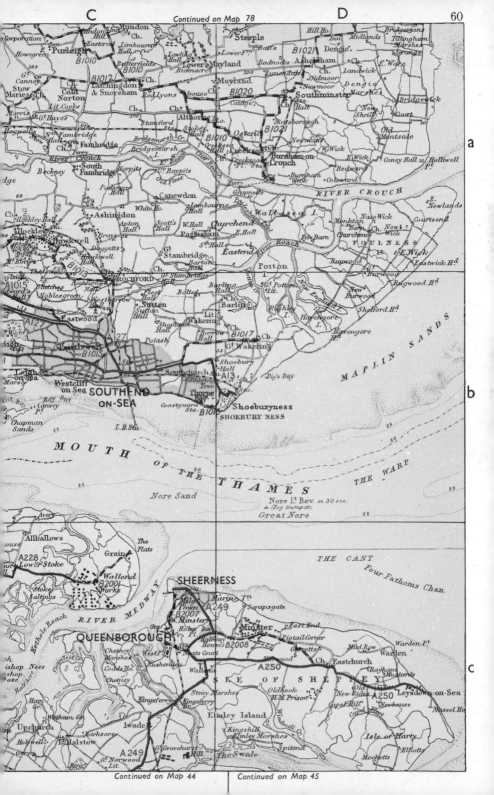

Corporation
Howegreen
Purleigh
B1010
B1012 B1010
Cold Norton
Ch.
Stow Maries
Gt. Canner
Lit. Cooks
Gt. Hayes
Nth Fambridge Hall
Ch.
Fambridge Ferry
South Fambridge
Beckney
Norpits
Pooles Hall
Canewdon
White Ho.
Hockley Hall
Hockley
Ch.
Hawkwell
Hawkwell Hall
Gt. Blixes
Marylands
B1013
Ashingdon
Apton Hall
Scott's Hall
Brays
Daggetts
Hockwell Hall
ROCHFORD
Rochford Hall
Sutton
Sutton Hall
Blatches
Nobles green
Westbarrow Hall
Eastwood
Prittlewell
B1015
Leigh-on-Sea
Westcliff on Sea
SOUTHEND-ON-SEA
I. B. Sta.

Mundon Hill Ch.
Mundon
Eastcroft
Limbourne Hall
Butterfields
Latchingdon & Snoreham
Red Lyons
Inraoo Ch.
Ch.
Ch.
Stamford
Althorne Lo.
Bridgemarsh Ch.
Bridgemarsh I.
Gt. Stambridge Hall
Stambridge
Barton Hall
Gt. Stambridge
Bartons
Ch. Barling
Lit. Barling
Little Wakering
Shopland Hall
Barrow Hall
Potash
Gt. Wakering
B1017
Shoebury Hall
Southchurch Sta.
Cambridge Town
Thorpe Bay
Southchurch
A13
Coastguard Sta.
B101
Shoeburyness
SHOEBURY NESS

Steeple
Lower Fm.
Lawling Hall
Lower Mayland
Mayland
Cadge
B1020
Altar
Creeksea Ch.
Osteud
Creeksea Hall
Creeksea Ferry Sta.
Burnham-on-Crouch
Grapnells
Lambourne Ch.
Churchend
Paglesham
E. Hall
W. Hall
Sth Hall
E. Hall
Eastend
Potton
Gt. Potton Lit.
New England I.
Rushley I.
Havengore I.
Tyle Barn
Batt's
Badnocks
Lunendale
Newmoor
Oldmoor
Asheldham
B1021
Southminster
Ch.
Ratsborough
Newland
Burnham Wick
Coleward
Monkton Barn
Churchend
Courtsend
Nase Wick
New Wick
FOULNESS
Rugwood
Burwood
Gt. Pottom
New Burwood
Shelford Hd.
Rugwood Hd.
Havengore Hd.
Tip's Bay

Hill Ho.
Inn Midlands
Dengie Ch.
Landwick
E. Ware
Dengie Marshes
Bridgwick
Coney Hall
Holliwell Pt.
Old Montsale
E. Newlands
E. Wick
Eastwick Hd.

MAPLIN SANDS

RIVER CROUCH
Wallasea I.
River Roach

MOUTH OF THE THAMES THE WARP
Nore Sand
Chapman Sands
Canvey
Ray Sand Pt.
Nore Lt. Rev. ev. 30 sec.
(Fog trumpet)
Great Nore

THE CANT
Four Fathoms Chan.

Allhallows
The Flats
Grain
Avery
A228
Lower Stoke
Stoke Saltings
Wallend
B2001
Works
SHEERNESS
Mile Town
Marine Tn.
A249
W. Minster
B2007
Hobur Inn
Halfway Houses
QUEENBOROUGH
W. Pt.
Chetney Marshes
Coads Ho.
Chetney
West Pt.
Neats Court
Wallend
Minster
B2008
Garretts
Norwood
A250
ISLE OF SHEPPEY
Scrapsgate
East End
Pigtail Corner
Ch.
Eastchurch
Mud Row
Warden Pt.
Warden
Rayham
Mustards
Newhouse
Isle of Harty
Elliotts
Mockett's
Leysdown-on-Sea
Mussel Ho.
A250
Old New Rides
Capel Hill
Bishop Ness
Ham Gr.
Wetham Gr.
Upchurch
Hollwell Gores.
Barksore
RIVER MEDWAY
Kethole Reach
Kingsferry
Kingsferry
Stray Marshes
Elmley Island
Kingshill
Elmley Marshes
Oldhook
H.M. Prison
Walland
Spitend
Capel Hill
Windmill
Iwade
A249
Grovehurst
Mill
Gt. Norwood Lit.
The Swale

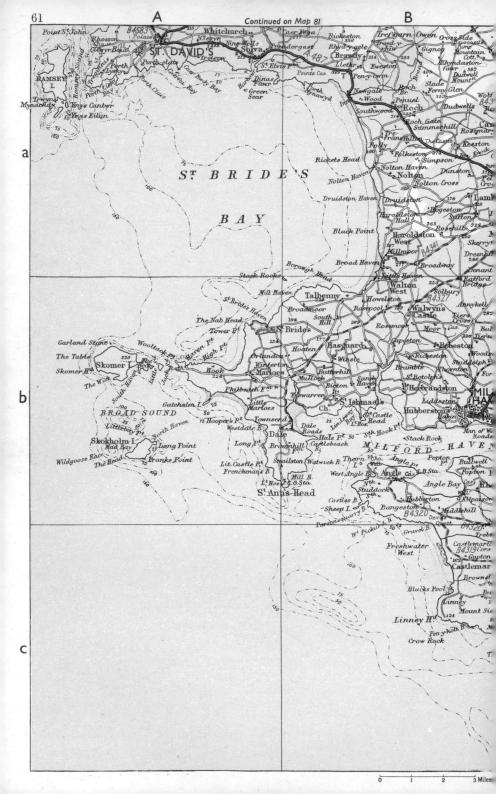

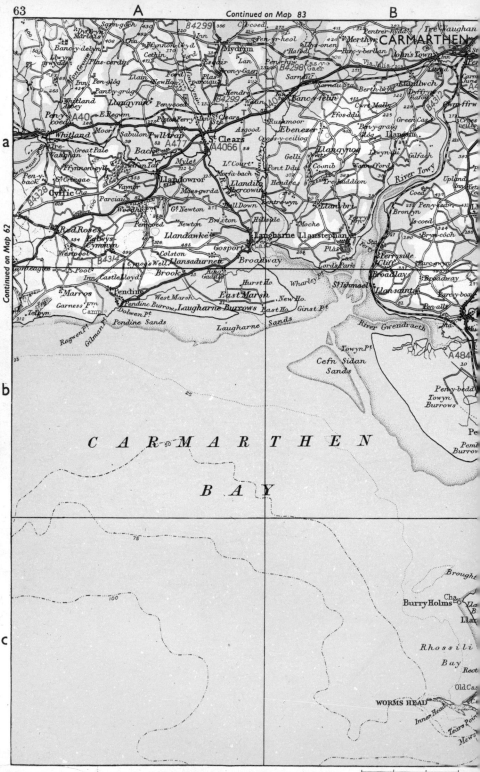

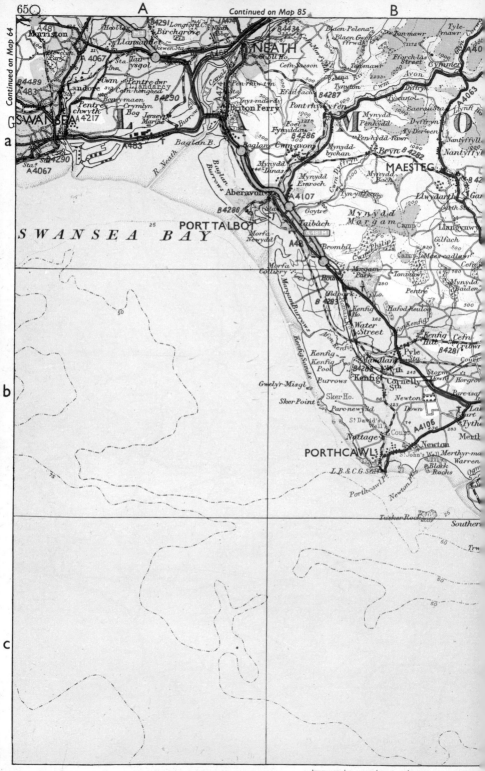

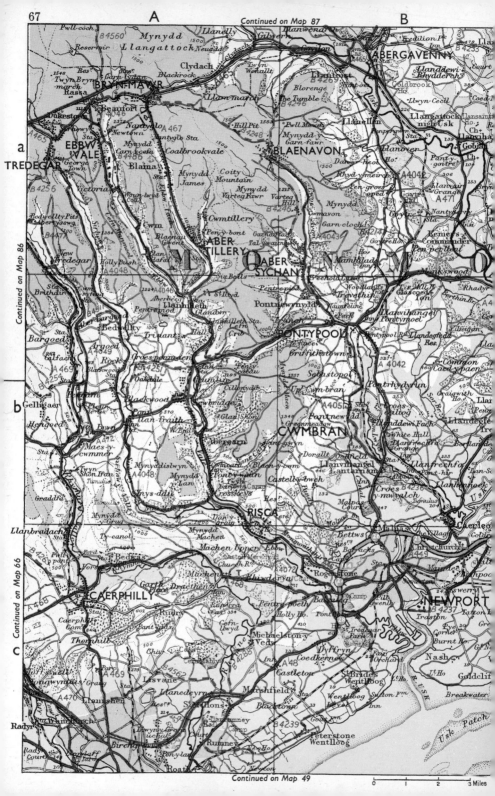

Continued on Map 88

Continued on Map 69

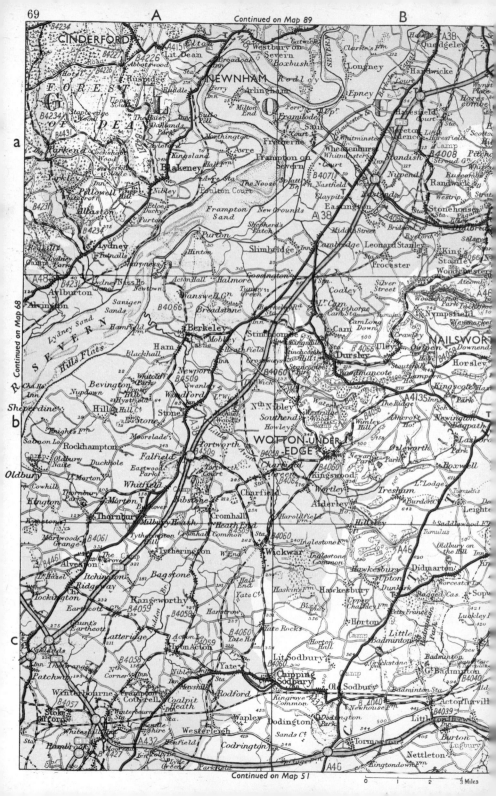

Continued on Map 89

A

B

CINDERFORD

GLOUCESTER

NEWNHAM

FOREST
OF DEAN

a

Blakeney

Lydney

NAILSWORTH

Berkeley

Dursley

Uley

Horsley

b

R. Continued on Map 68

Sheperdine

Rockhampton

Falfield

WOTTON-UNDER-EDGE

Kingswood

Boxwell

Thornbury

Cromhall

Charfield

Alderley

Hillsley

Tytherington

Wickwar

Hawkesbury

Didmarton

Rangeworthy

Horton

Bagstone

C

Iron Acton

Yate

Lit. Sodbury

Gt. Badminton

Winterbourne

Chipping
Sodbury

Old Sodbury

Acton Turvill

Stoke
Gifford

Dodington

Tormarton

Nettleton

Continued on Map 51

0   1   2   3 Miles

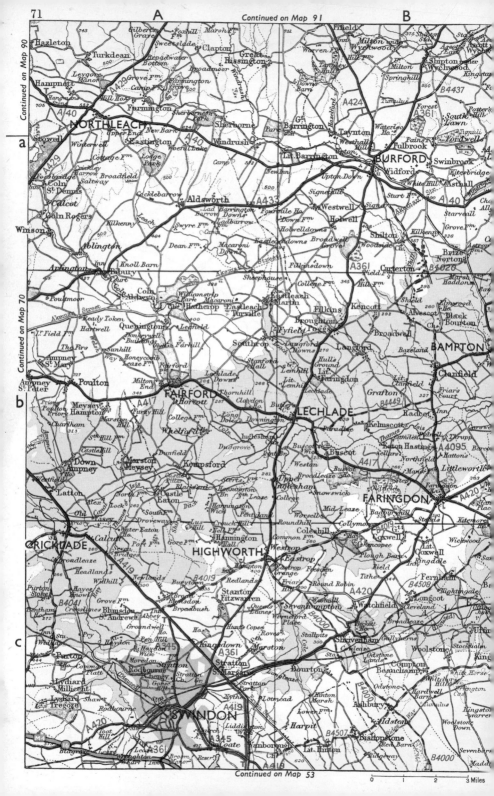

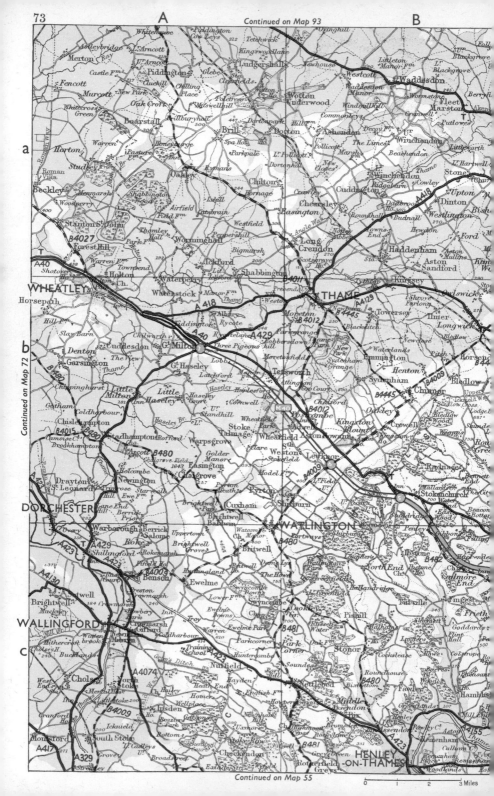

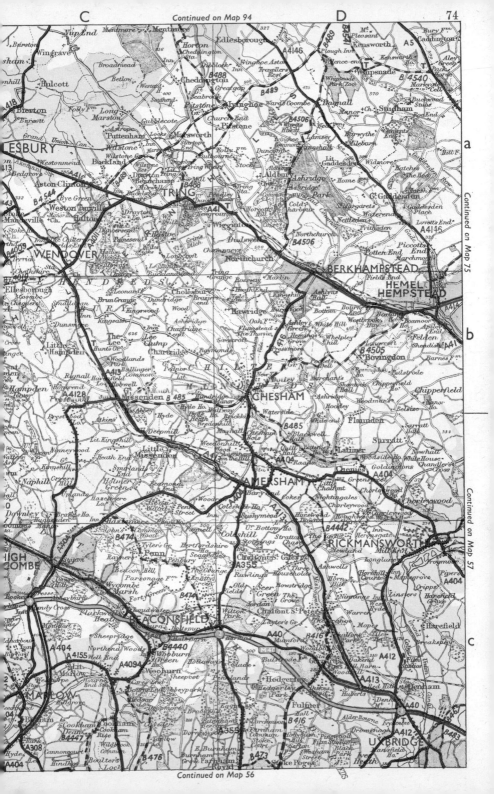

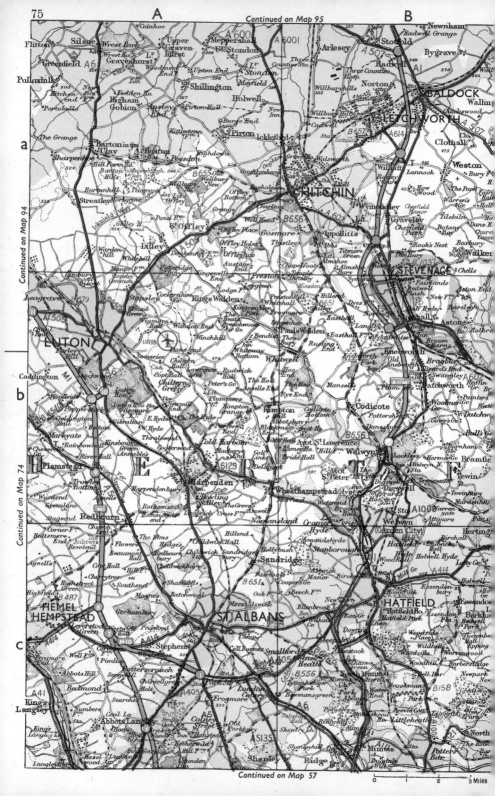

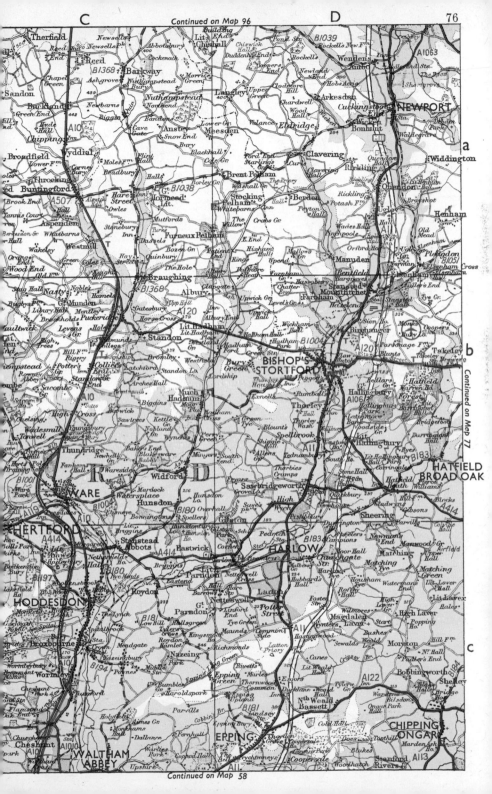

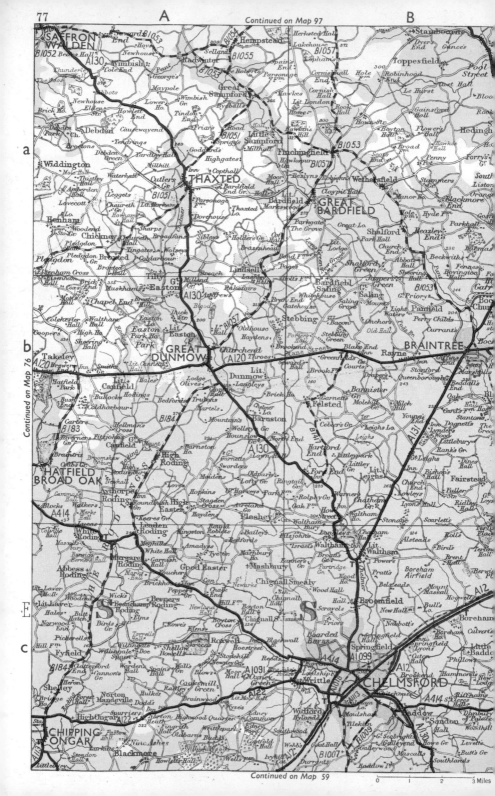

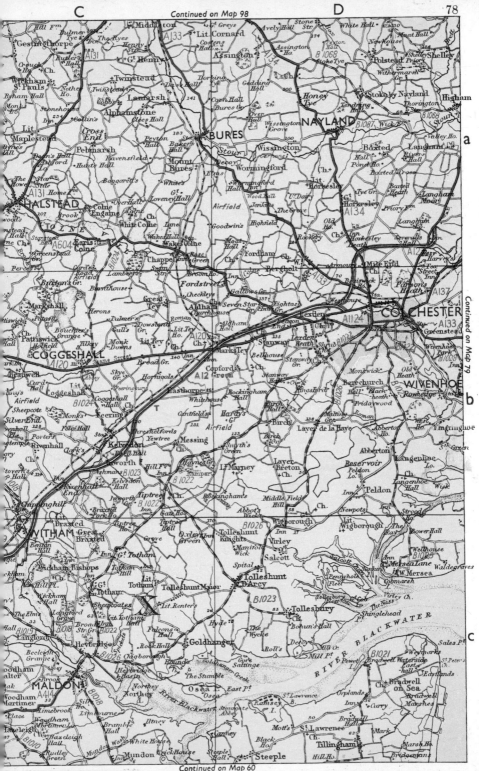

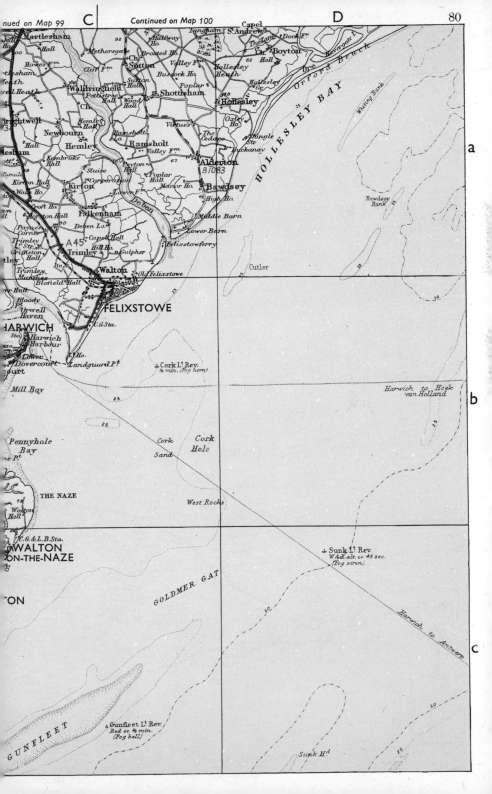

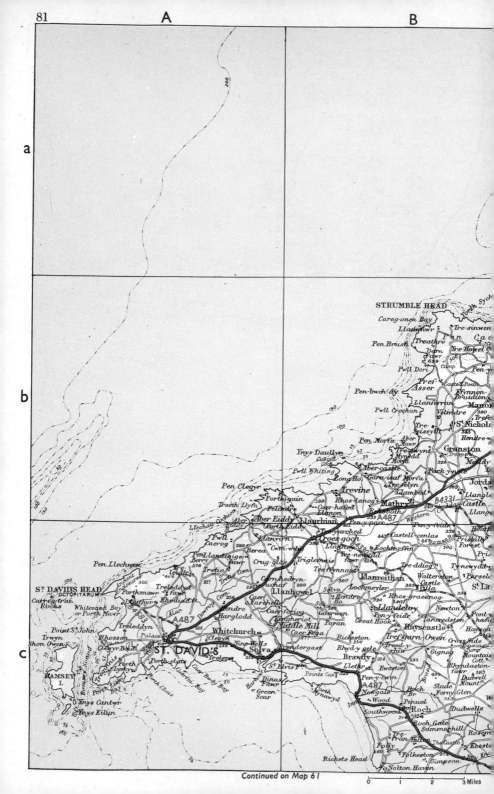

Continued on Map 61

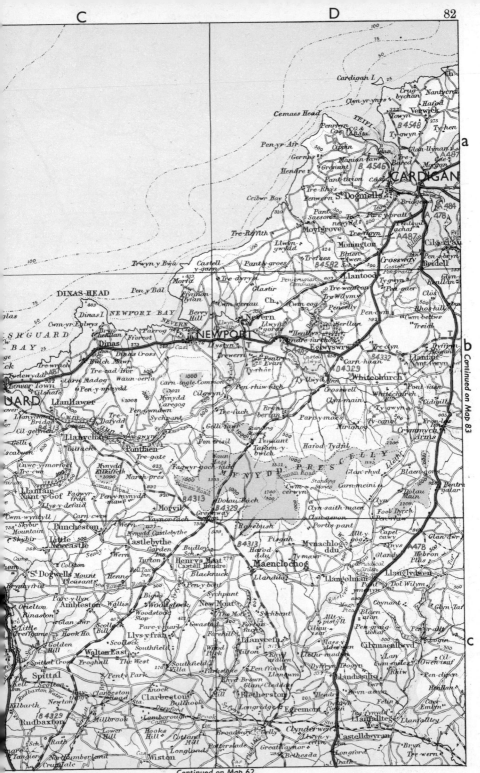

Continued on Map 83

Continued on Map 62

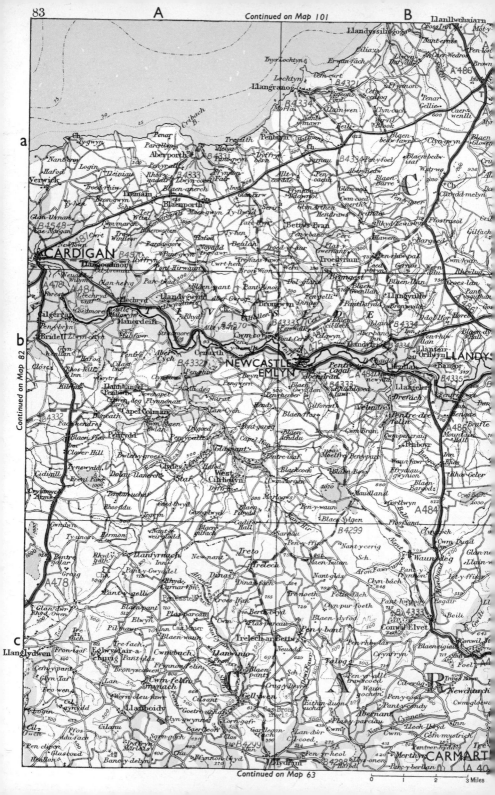

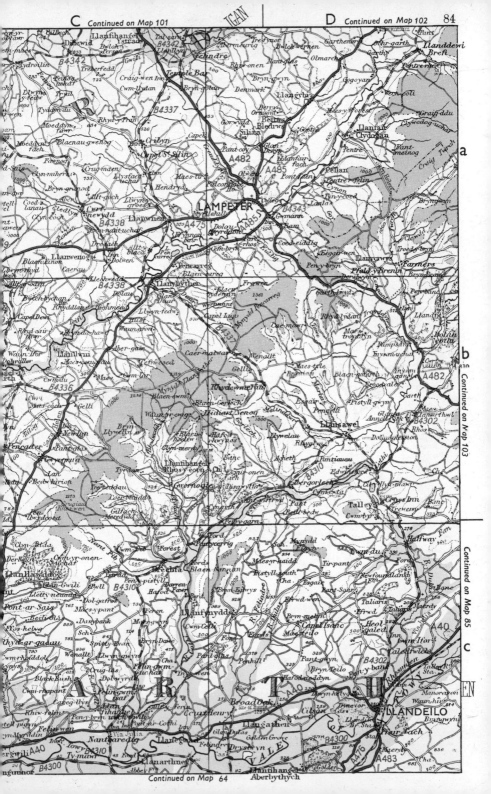

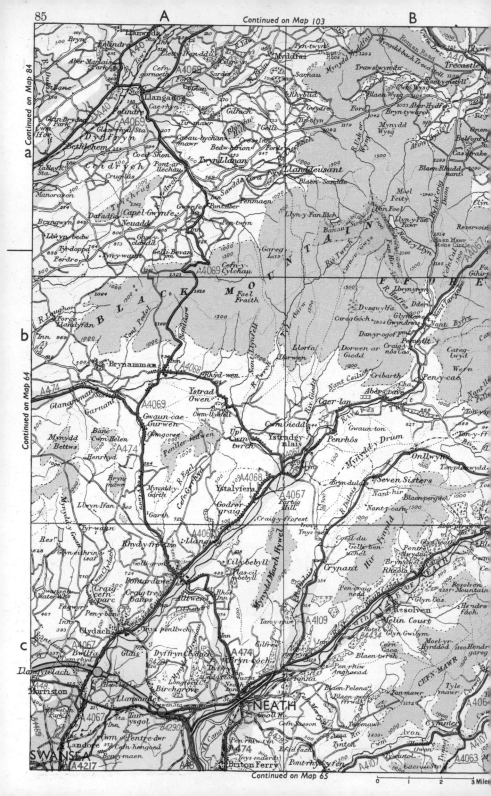

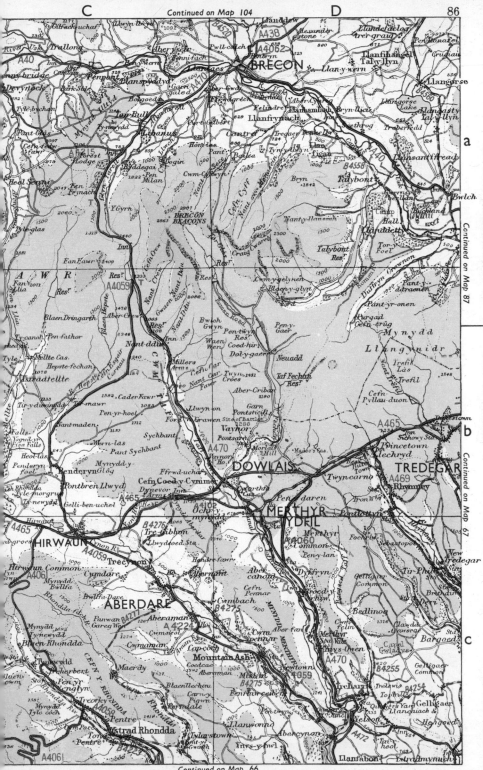
Continued on Map 87
Continued on Map 67

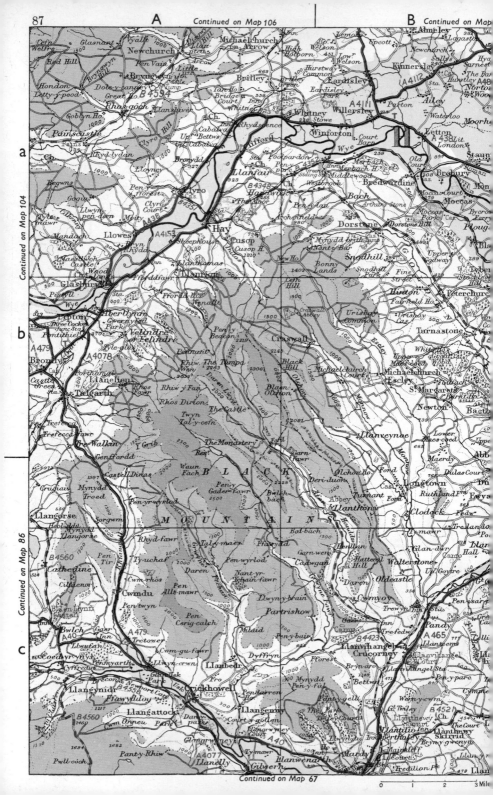

Continued on Map 104
Continued on Map 86

a

b

c

0   1   2   3 Mile

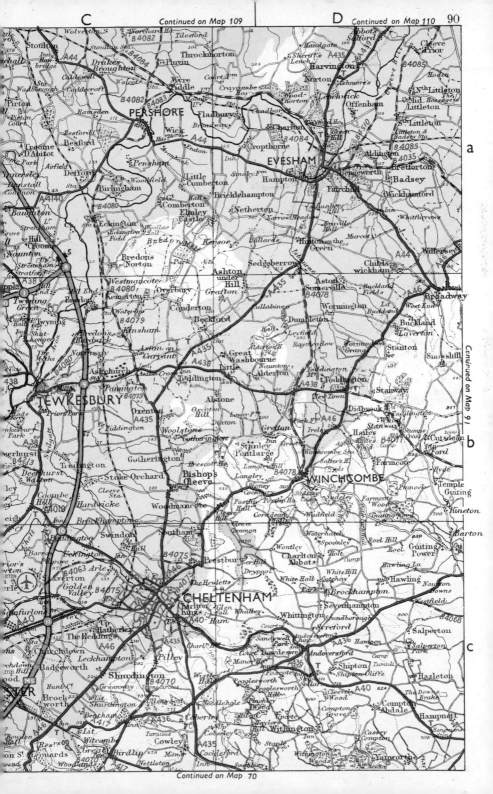

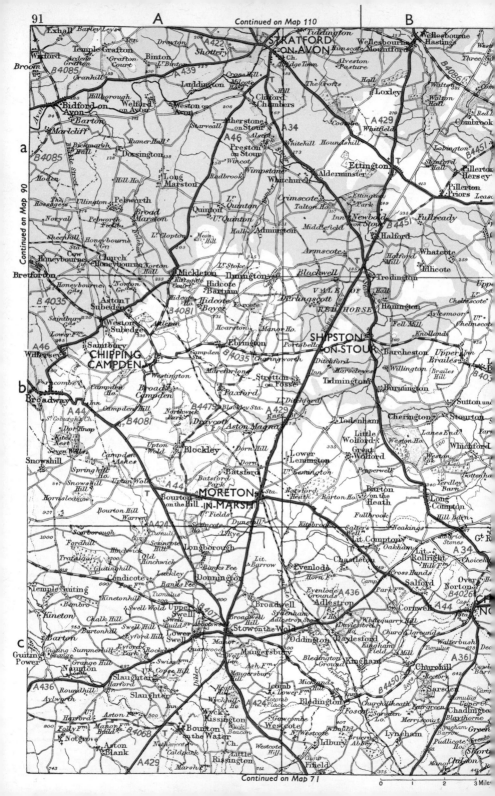

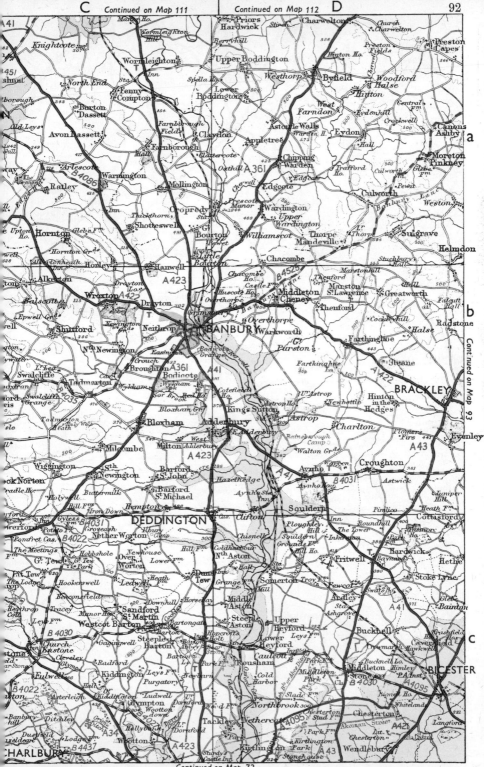

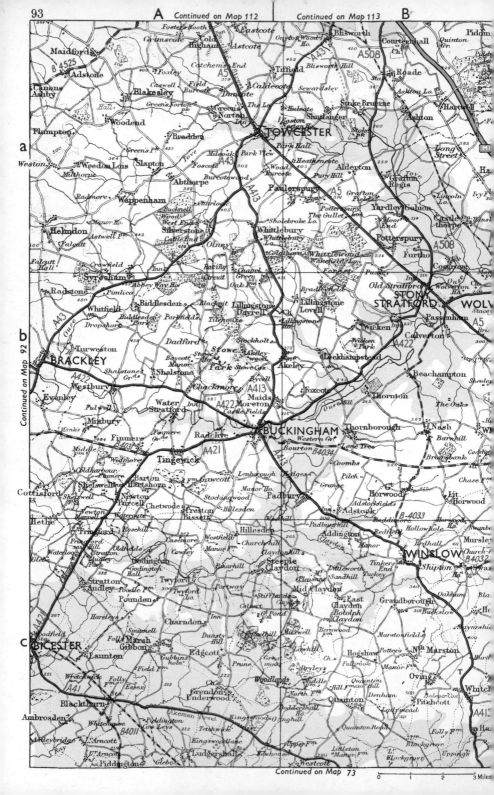

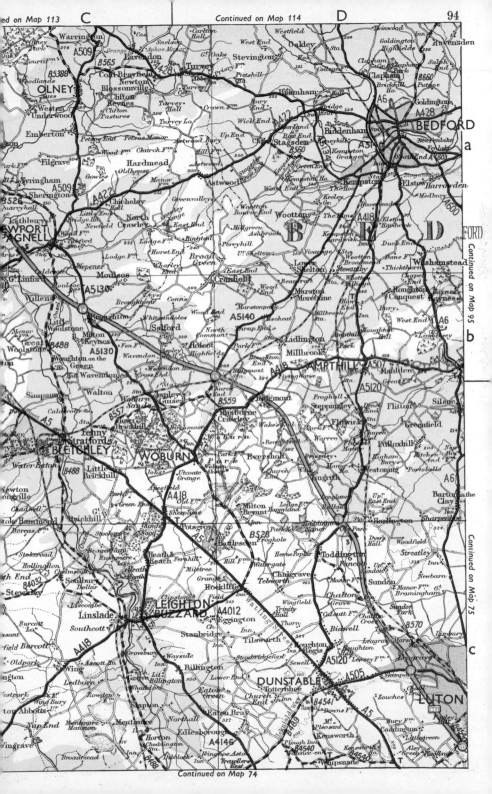

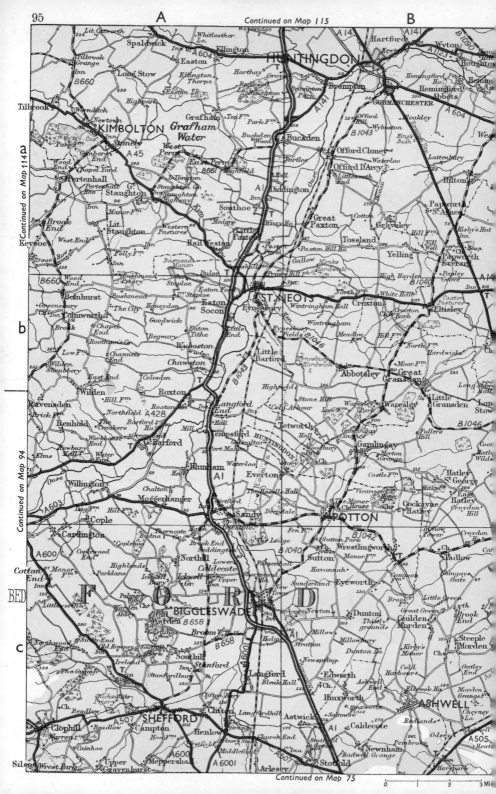

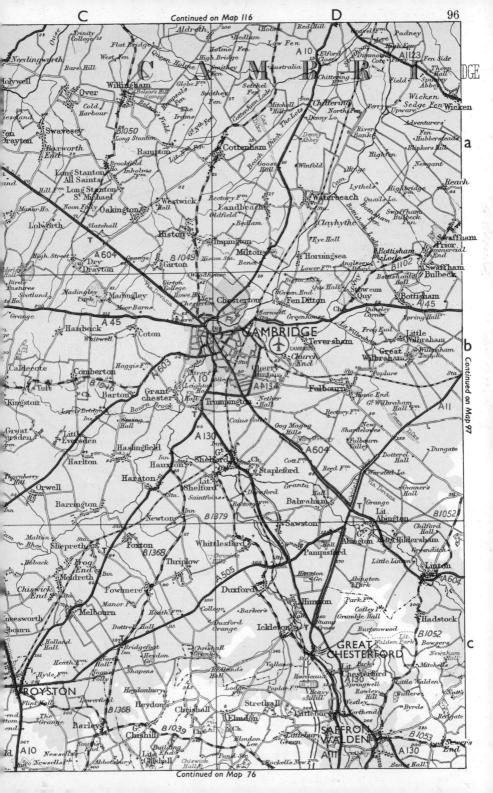

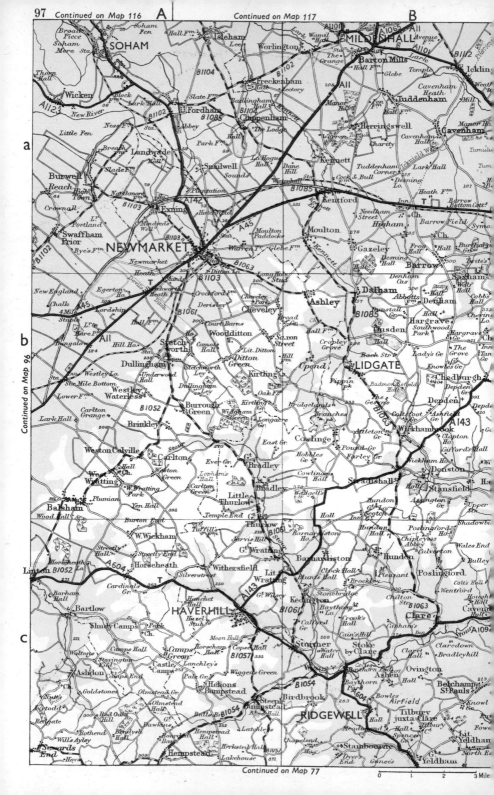

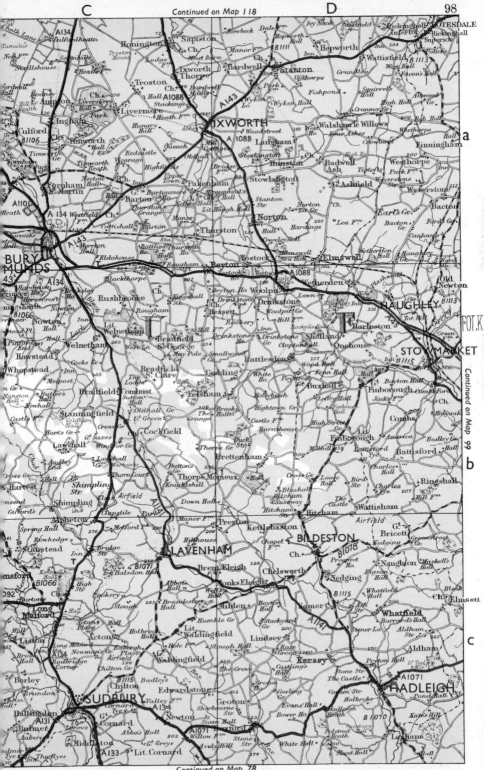

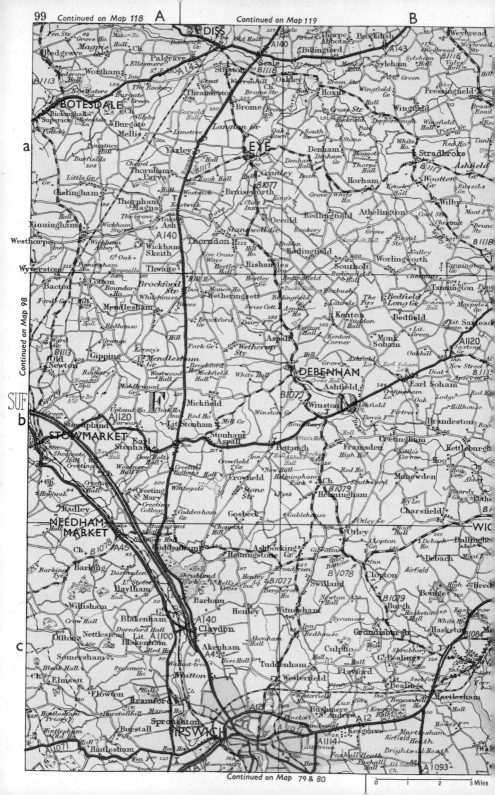

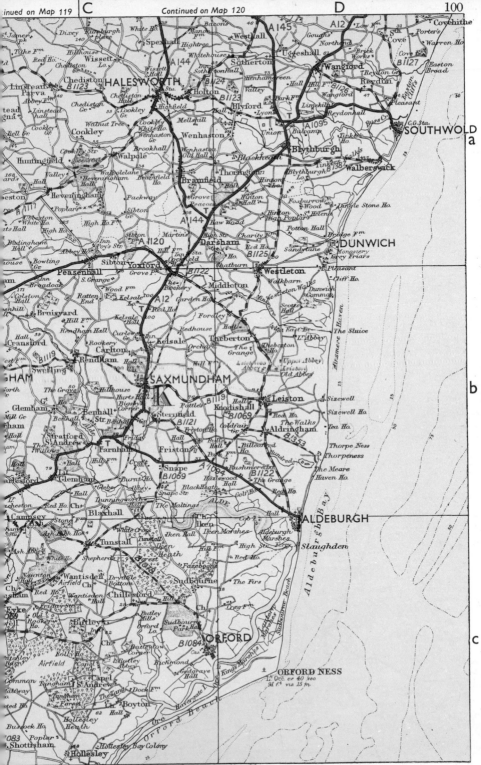

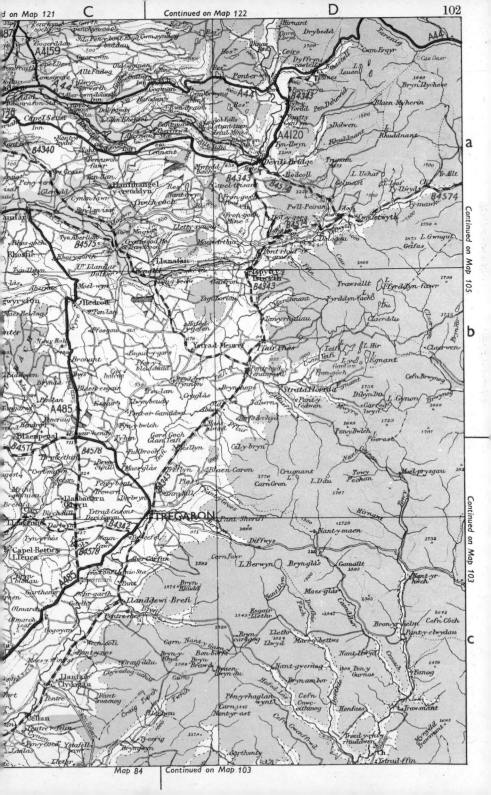

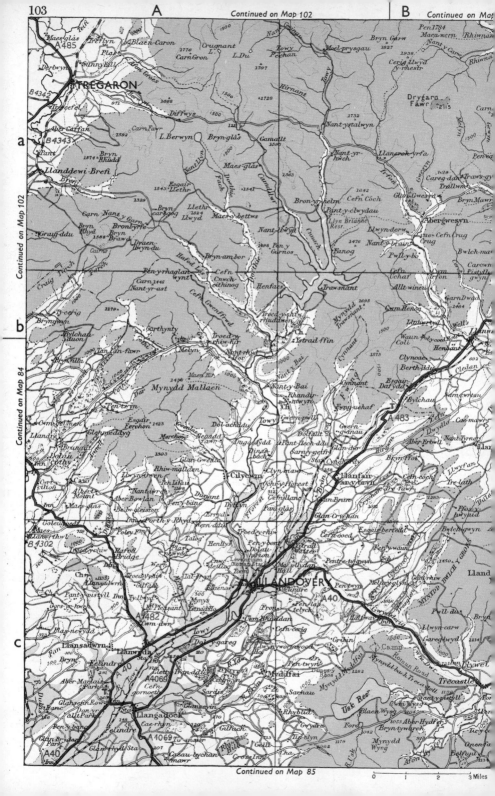

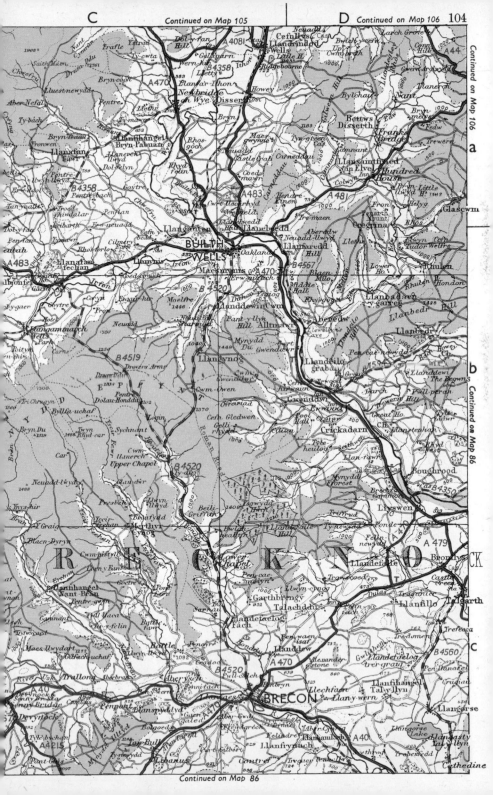

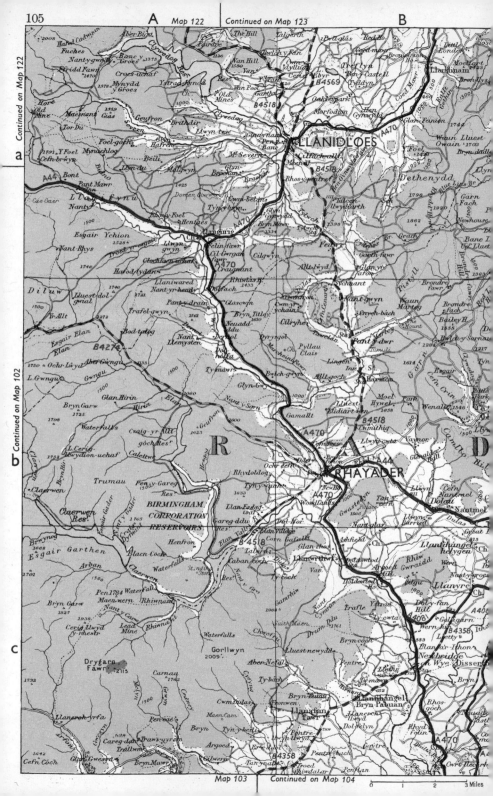

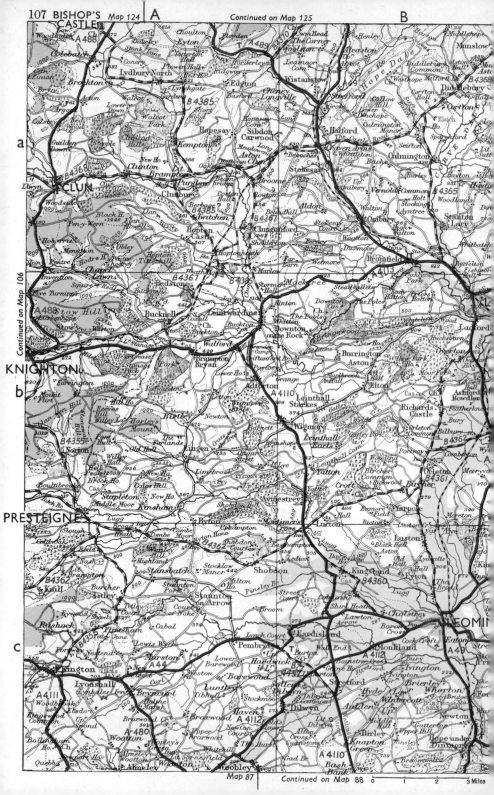

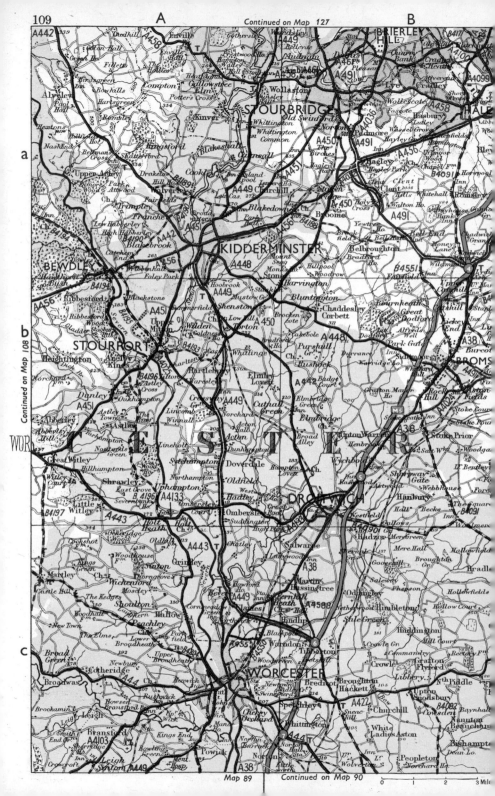

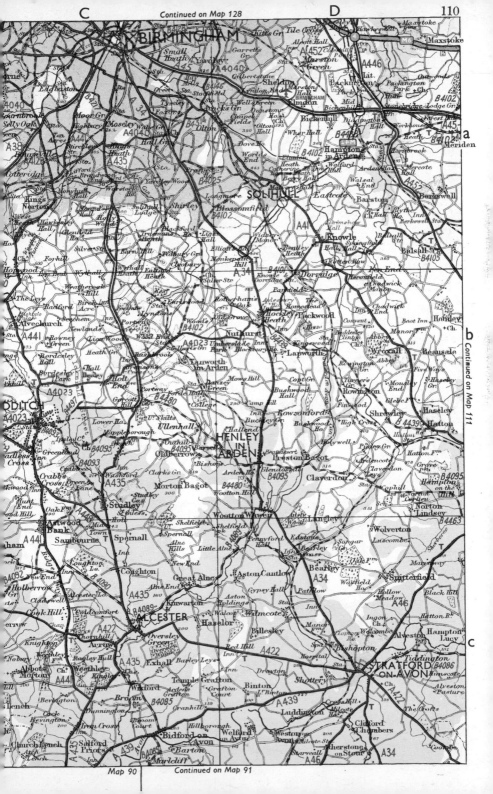

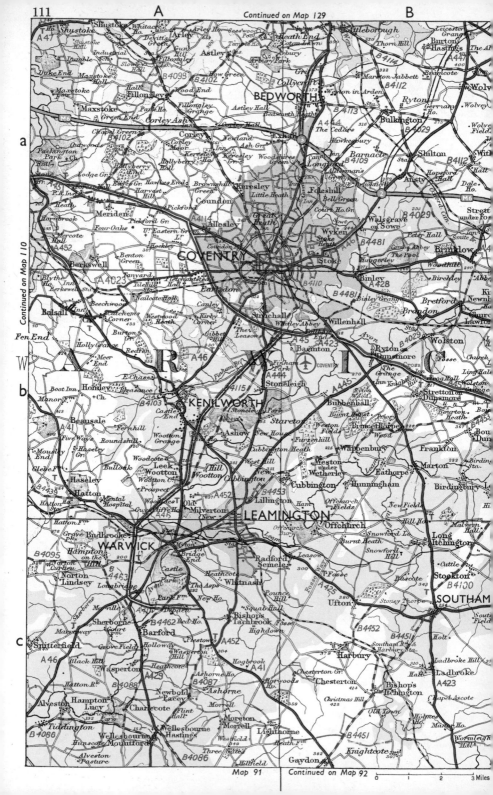

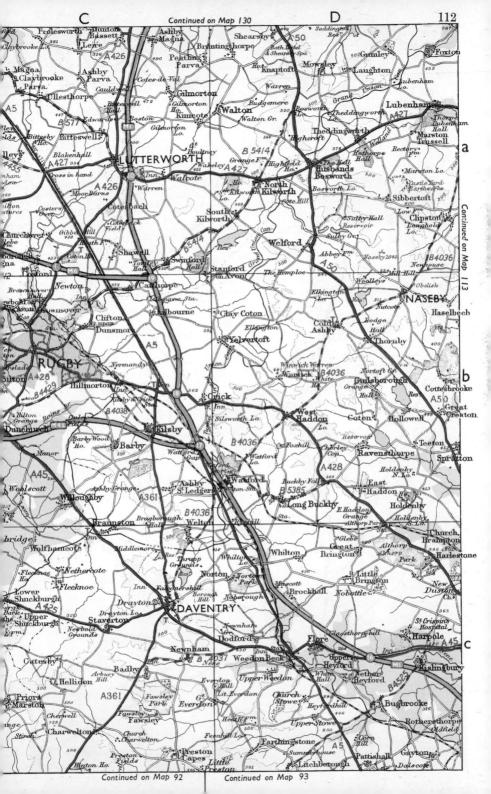

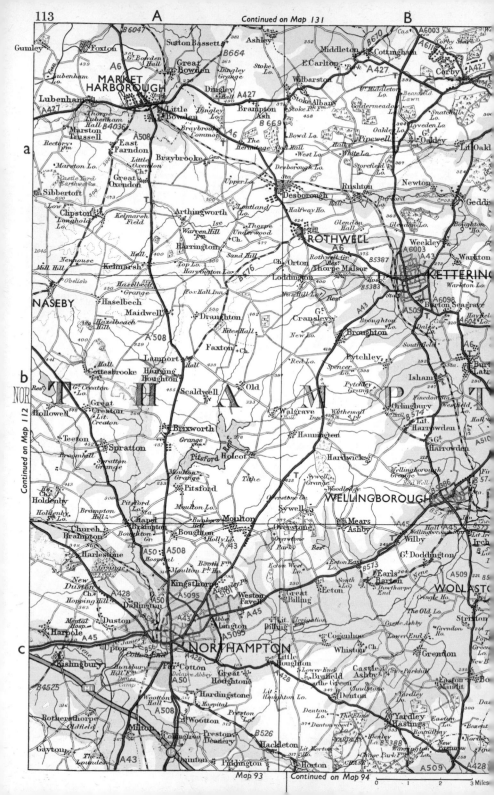

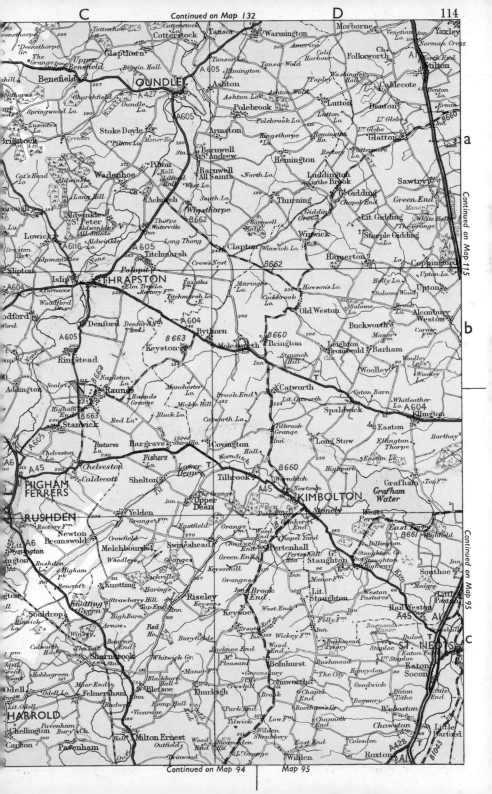

Continued on Map 115

Continued on Map 95

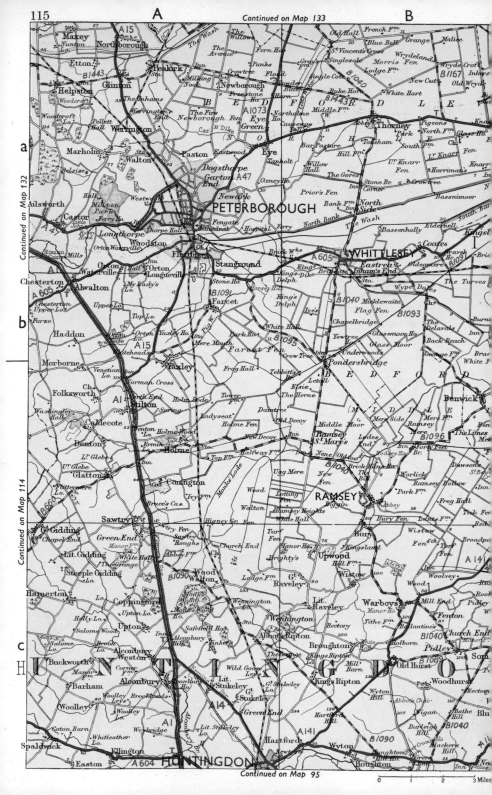

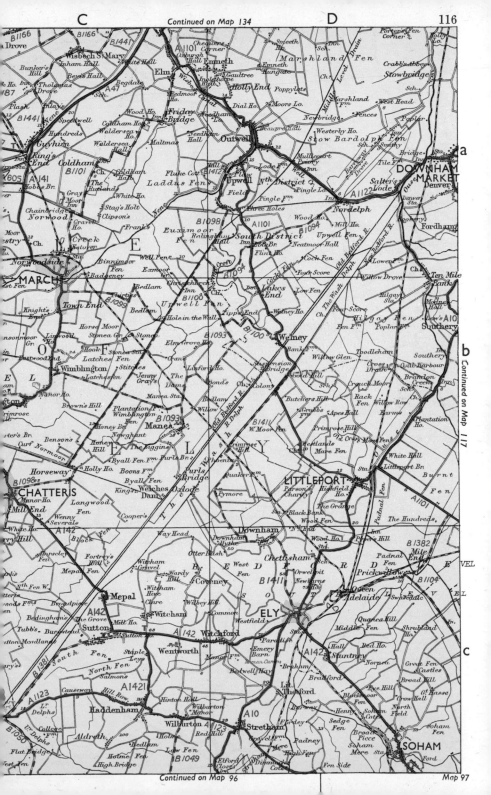

Map 97

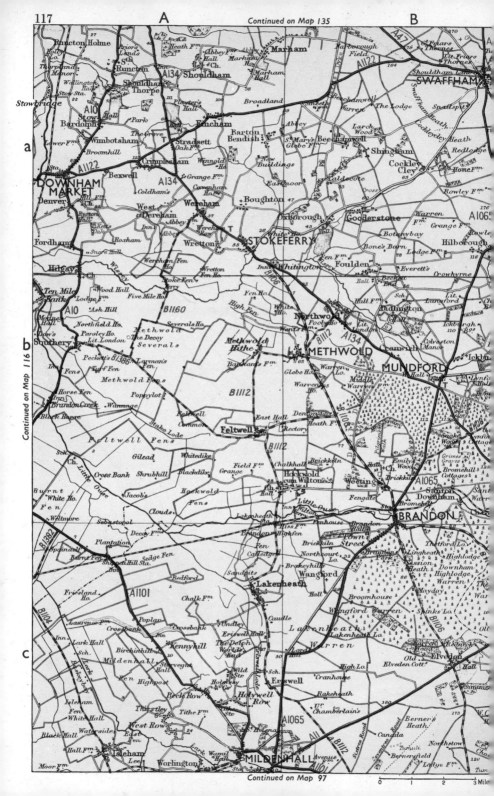

Continued on Map 135

A

B

Runcton Holme

Heath Fm

Marham

Narborough Field

A47

Fri Friars Thorpe

Lit. Friars Thorpe

Stowbridge

Abbey Fm
Ch.

Marham Hall

SWAFFHAM

St
Runcton

A134 Shouldham

Broadland

Beechamwell Warren

The Lodge

Snailspit

Swaffham Heath

Shouldham Thorpe

Player's Hall

Abbey

Larch Wood

Cockley Cley

Heath
Redlodge

a

Wimbotsham
Broomhill

Stradsett
Oak

St. Mary's Glebe Fm

Beechamwell

Shingham

Home Fm

A1122

Crimplesham

Winnold Ho.

New Buildings

Caldecote

Rowley Fm

DOWNHAM MARKET

Bexwell

Coldham's

Grange Fm

Eastmoor

Cross

A1065

Denver

Wereham

Boughton

Oxborough

Goodestone

Warren Fm

Grange Fm

West Dereham

White Ho.

STOKEFERRY

Bone's Barn

Hilborough

Fordham

Wretton

Whittington

Foulden

Everett's

Crowhyrne

Hilgay

Wereham Fen

Wretton Fen Ho.

Fen Ho.

Beckett End

Ten Mile Bank

Wood Hall

Five Mile Ho.

High Fen

White Ho.

Northwold

Lit. London

Ickburgh

b

Southery

B1386

Methwold
The Decoy
Severals

Methwold Hithe

METHWOLD

MUNDFORD

Feltwell Fens

B1112

Warren Lo.

Middle Warren

Poppylot

East Hall

Denton

Heath Fm

Feltwell

Rectory

B1112

Grimes Graves

Bromehill Cottages

Gilead

Whitedike

Blackdike

Chalkhall

Brickkeln

Weeting

Brickkiln

A1065

Santon Downham

Hockwold Fens

Hockwold cum Wilton

Fengate

Bromehill

Burnt White Ho. Fen

Sebastopol

Decoy Fm

Lakenheath

Little Ouse

BRANDON
Town Street

Thetford Lo.

Plantation

Brandon Fen

Hockten

Brickkiln

Northcourt

Brandon Park

Lingheath

Highlodge Heath

c

Friesland Ho.

A1101

Bedford

Sandhits

Brakeyhills

Wangford

Broomhouse

Wangford Warren

Spinks Lo.

Lakenheath

Mildenhall

Highpost

Wild Str.

Eriswell

Cranhouse

Lakenheath Warren

Elveden

West Row

Isleham

Worlington

MILDENHALL

A1065

Berner's Heath

Canada

Northstow

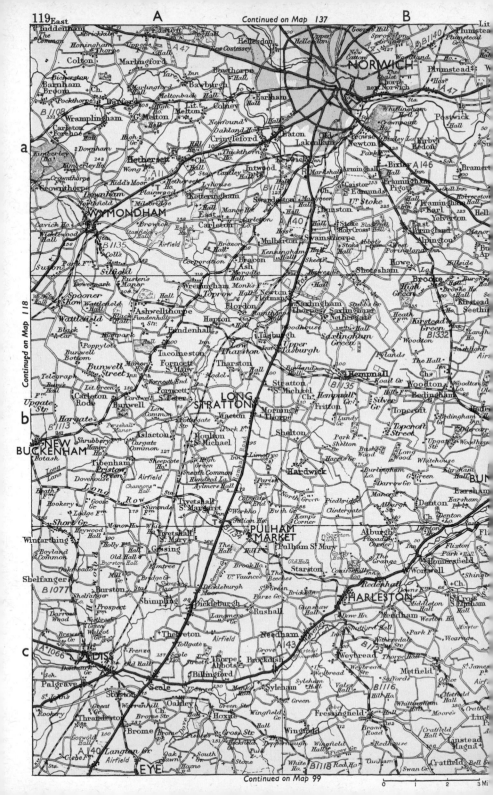

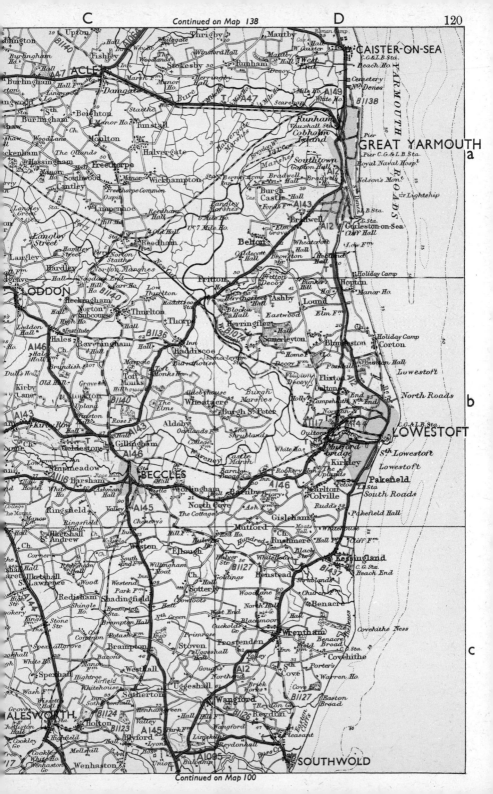

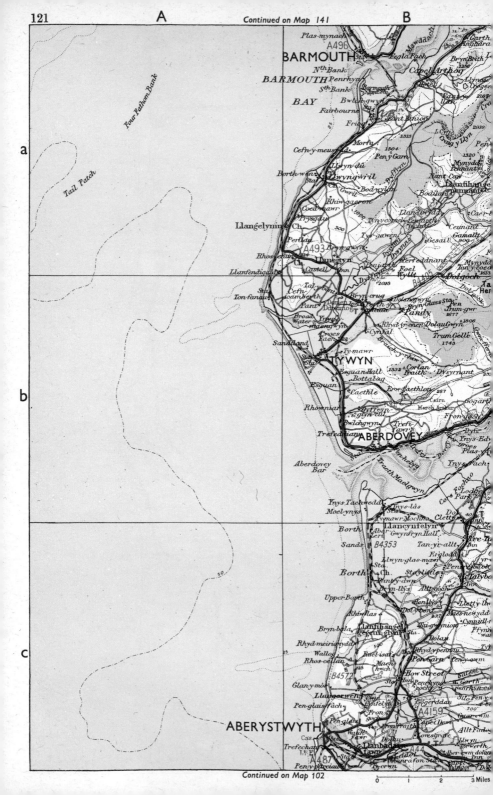

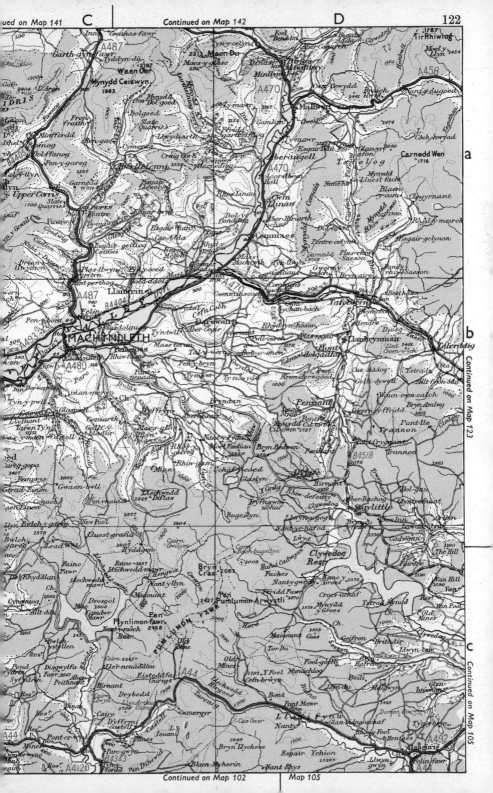

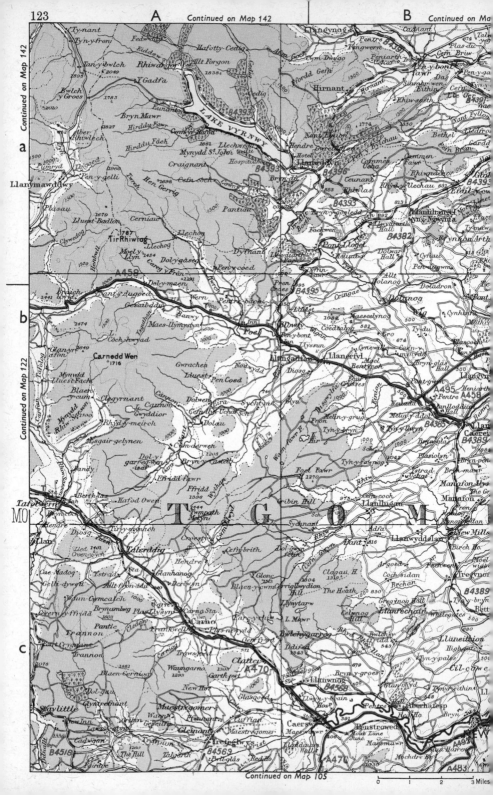

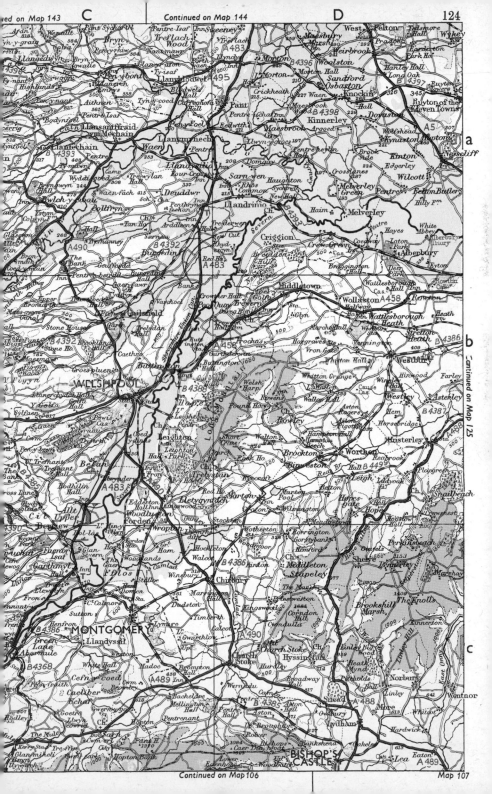

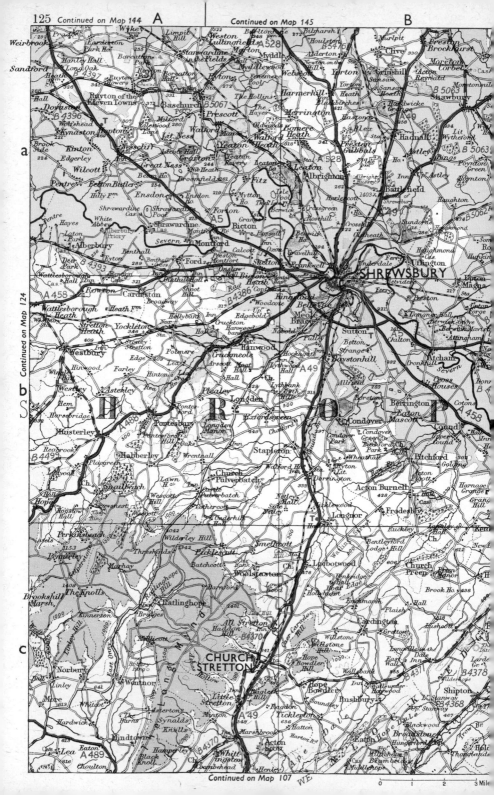

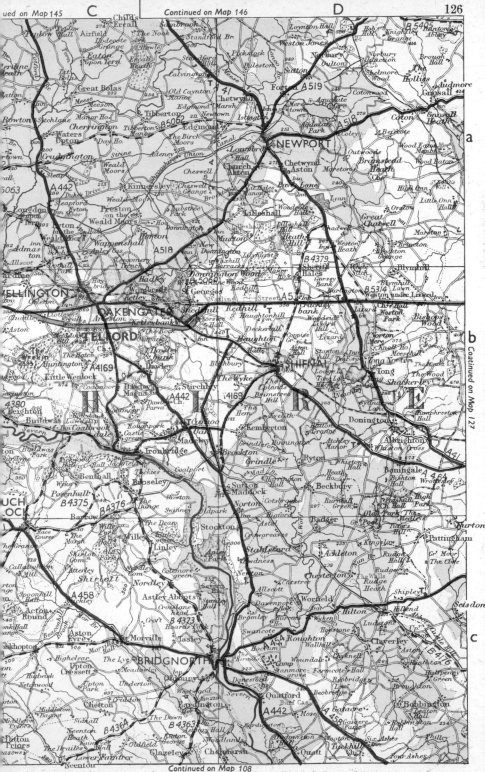
Continued on Map 145
Continued on Map 146
Continued on Map 127
Continued on Map 108

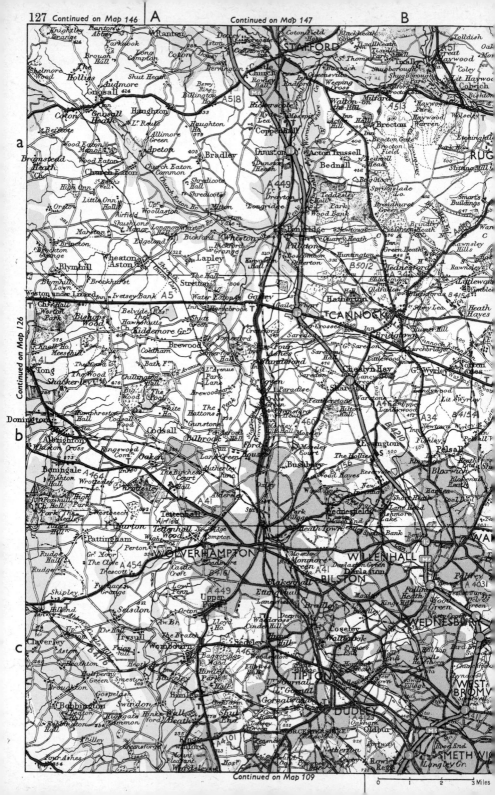

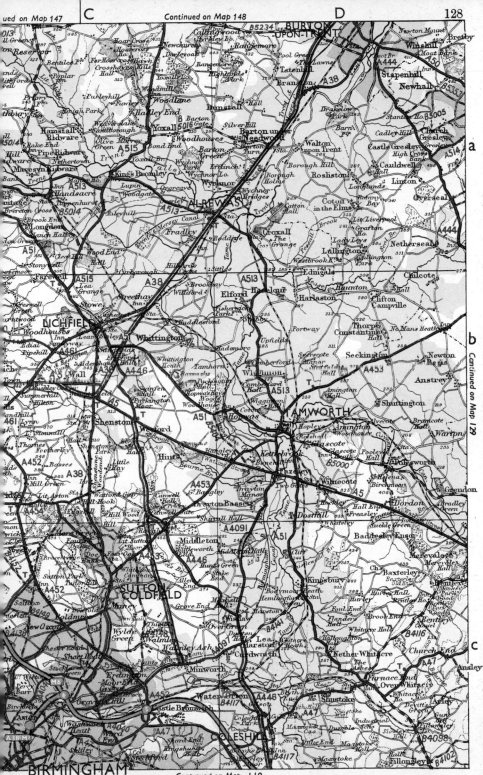

ued on Map 147

Continued on Map 129

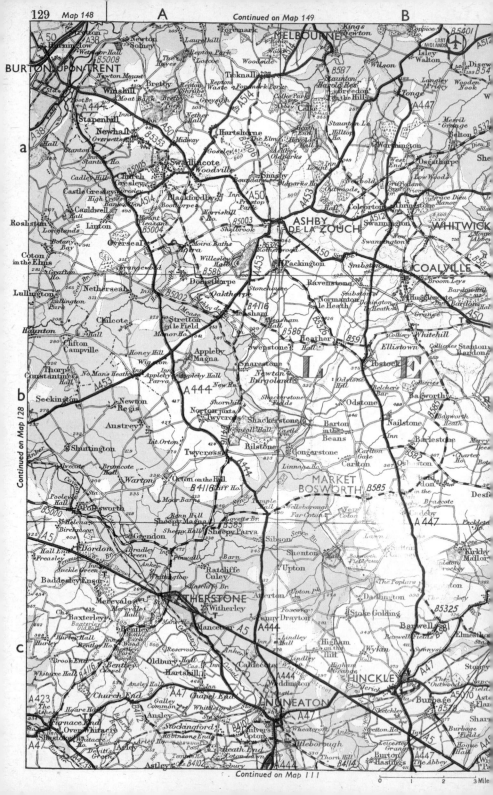

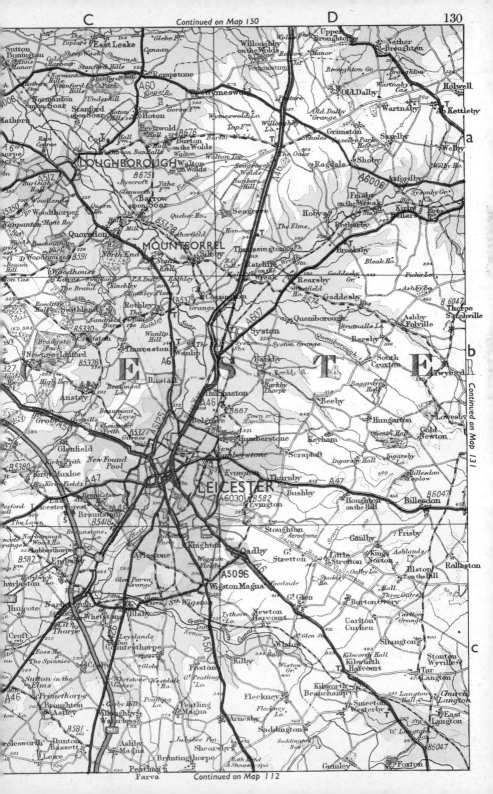

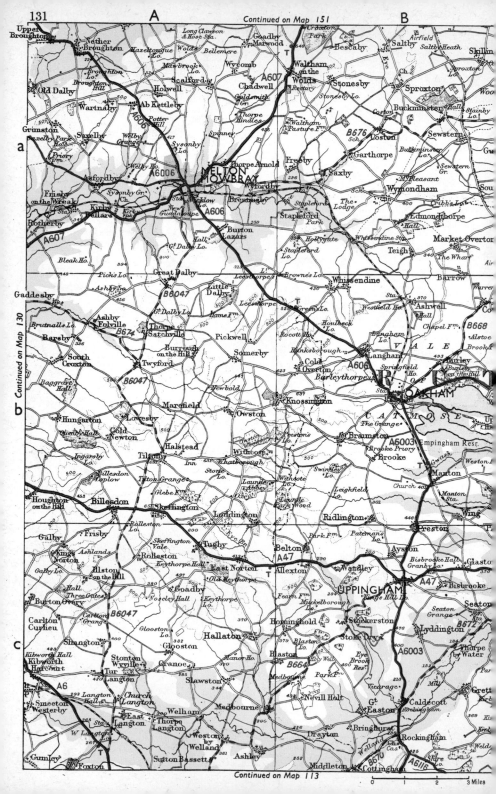

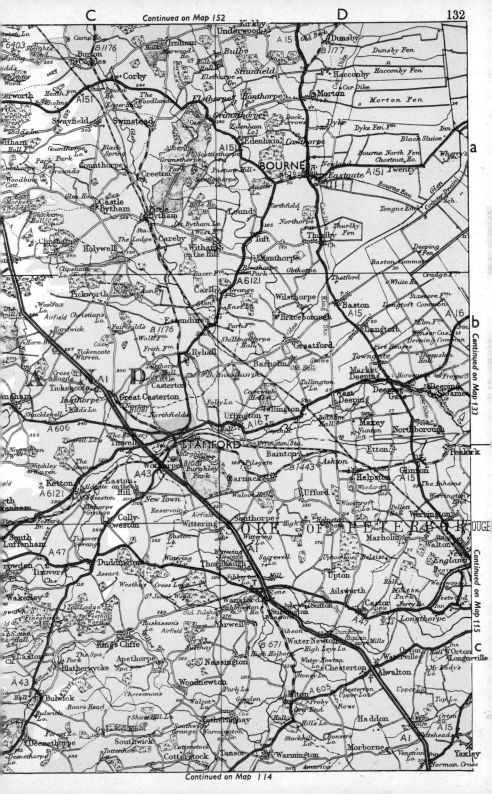

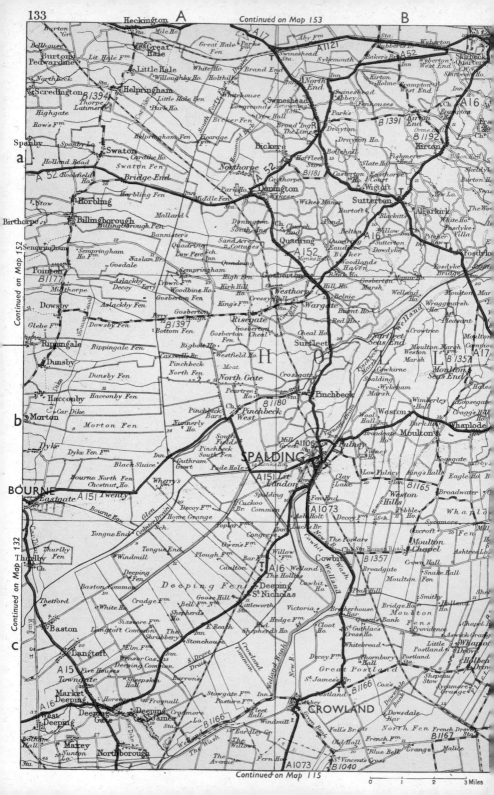

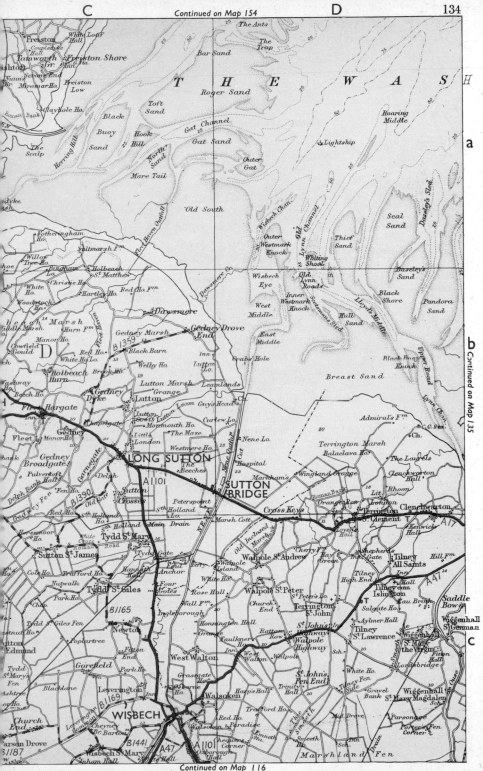

Continued on Map 154

THE WASH

The Ants
The Trap
Bar Sand
Roger Sand
Roaring Middle
White Loaf Hall
Freiston Shore
Freiston
Low
Tamworth
Scrane End
Miramar Ho.
Nunns
Br
Clayhole Ho.
Black
Buoy
Sand
Toft
Sand
Hook
Hill
North
Sand
Herring Hill
The Scalp
Mare Tail
Gat Channel
Gat Sand
Outer
Gat
Lightship
Daxeley's Sled
Old South
Seal
Sand
Daxeley's
Sand
Wisbech Chan.
Outer
Westmark
Knock
Whiting
Shoal
Thief
Sand
Black
Shore
Pandora
Sand
Fotheringham
Ho.
Saltmarsh Fm.
Willow
Tree Ho.
Bingham
Lo.
Christie Ho.
Holbeach
St Matthew
White
Ho.
Woodstock
Ho.
Hartley Ho.
Red Ho. Fm.
Fleet Haven Outfall
Dawsmere Cr.
Wisbech
Eye
Old
Lynn
Roads
Inner
Westmark
Knock
Freeman's Sled
Lynn Channel
Old Channel
Lloyd's
Channel
Black
Shore
Upper Road
Black Buoy
Knock
Continued on Map 135
Marsh
Hurn Fm.
Dawsmere
Gedney Drove
End
West
Middle
Hull
Sand
Manor
Ho.
Cowfield
Gould
D
Red Ho.
B1359
Black Barn
Welby Ho.
Inn
Lutton
Lo.
East
Middle
Crabs Hole
Breast Sand
Holbeach
Hurn
White Ho. Lo.
Brook Ho.
Gedney
Dyke
Lutton Marsh
Grange
Lutton
Leamlands
Admiral's Fm.
C.G. Sta.
Washway
Beech Ho.
Fleet Hargate
Inn
Chapelgate
Gedney
Manor Ho.
Little
London
Lutton
Gowts
Lutton
Monmouth Ho.
Lutton Leam
Guy's Head
Curlew Lo.
Ch.
Terrington Marsh
Balaclava Ho.
Ch.
The Laurels
Clenchwarton
Hall
Fleet
Gedney
Broadgate
Pulvertoft
Hall
The Maze
Westmere Ho.
The Beeches
Nene Lo.
Cut
Hospital
20
Wingland Grange
Markham's
Roman Bank
Orange Row
Rhoon
Lit.
London
Terrington
St Clement
Clenchwarton
A17
Delph Bank Ho.
Delph
A1101
LONG SUTTON
Petersport
Sth
Holland
Lo.
SUTTON
BRIDGE
Cross Keys
Loves
Hall
Kenwick
Hall
Bedney Fen
Red Ho.
Sutton
Crosses
Sth Holland
Ho.
Sth Holland
Main
Drain
Marsh Cott.
Old Inclosed
Marsh
Shepherd's
Gate
Tilney
All Saints
Inn
Hill Fm.
Horsemoor
Ho.
Tydd St Mary
Tydd Gote
Old Gate
Fairy
Cherry
Hay
Green
Tilney cum
Islington
Eau Brink
A47
Saddle
Bow
Sutton St James
Cole Ho.
Trafford Ho.
Nutwalk
Hannath
Hall
Peat
Anchor
Four
Gotes
Walpole
Island
White Ho.
Rose Hall
Walpole S¹ Andrew
Walpole S¹ Peter
S¹ Peter's Lo.
Tilney
High End
Tilney
St Lawrence
Salgate Fm.
Aybmer Hall
Wiggenhall
S¹ German
Park Ho.
Chap.
Tydd S¹ Giles
B1165
Newton
Ingleborough
Wall Fm.
Church
End
Terrington
S¹ John
S¹ John's Lo.
Sch.
White Ho.
Wiggenhall
S¹ Mary
the Virgin
Fitton
Hall
Lordsbridge
Tydd S¹ Giles Fen
Tydd S¹
Edmund
Poplartree
Faton
End
Park Ho.
Honnington Hall
Grange
Faulkner's
Inn
Ratten
Row
Walpole
Highway
Highway
S¹ John's
Pen End
White Ho.
Fen
Tilney
Fen Side
Gravel
Banks
Wiggenhall
S¹ Mary Magdalen
Sch.
Tydd
S¹ Mary's
Fen
Ashtree
Ho.
Gorefield
Blacklane
Leverington
B1169
Inn
West Walton
West
Walton
Grassgate
Ho.
Osborne
Ho.
Walsoken
Harp's Hall
S¹ John's
Trinity
Hall
Parsonage
Foster's Fen
Corner
Church
End
Parson Drove
B1187
Cheyney
Br. Barton
WISBECH
B1441
A47
A1101
Wisbech S¹ Mary
Inham Hall
Hall
Osborough
Hall
Walsoken
Red Ho.
Paradise
Emneth
Corner
Smeeth
Ho.
Chequers
Corner
Trafford Ho.
Mid Drove
Sch.
Marshland Fen

Continued on Map 116

a
b
c

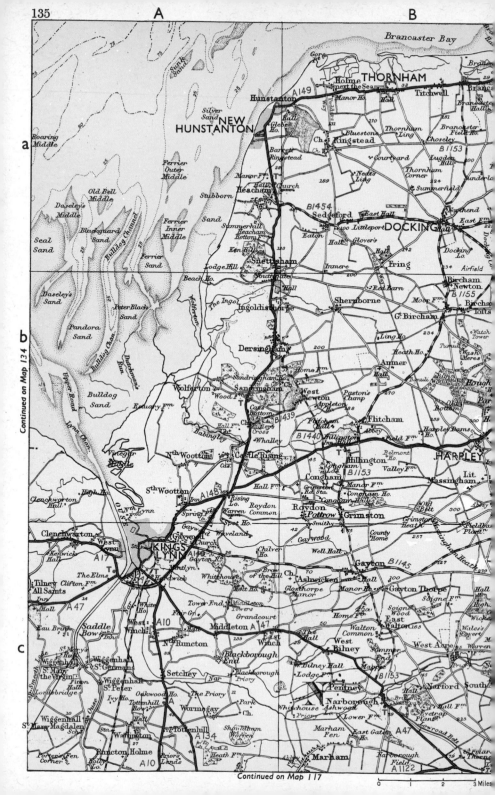

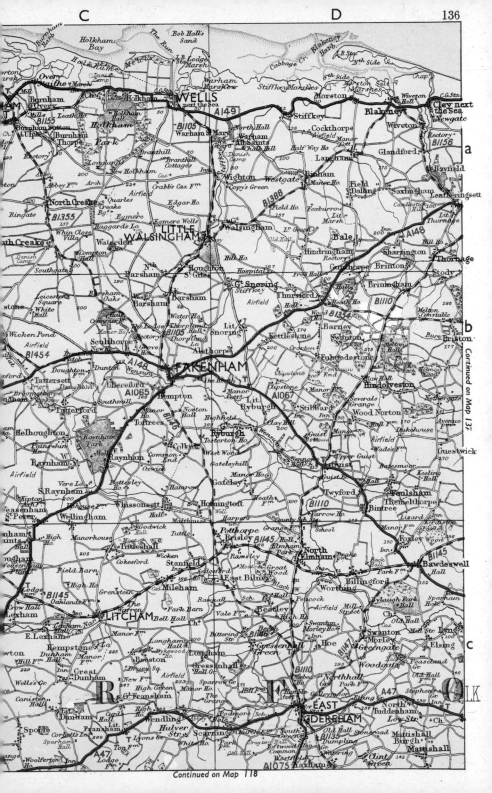

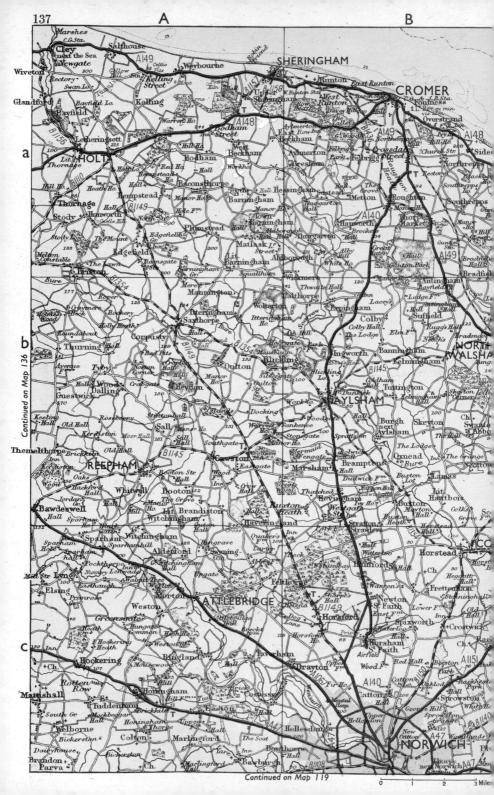

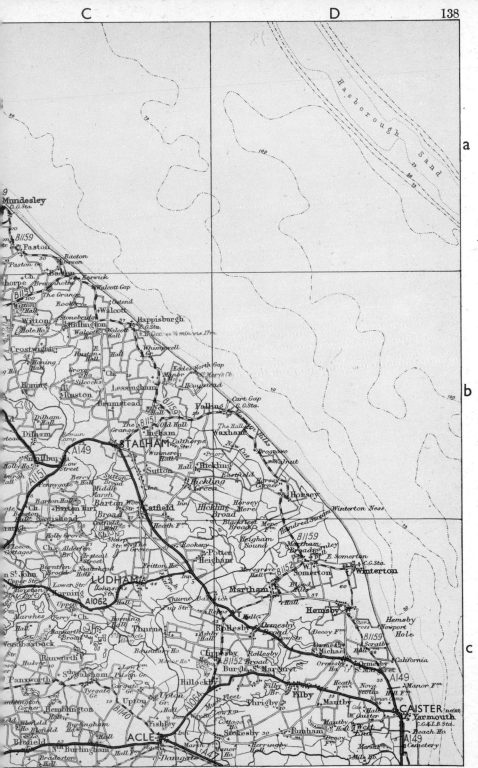

a

b

c

Hasborough Sand

Mundesley
C.G.Sta.

Paston
Bacton
Green
Bacton
Keswick
Walcott Gap
Ostend
Walcott
Happisburgh
Whimpwell
Eccles
North Gap
St. Mary's Ch.
Cart Gap
C.G.Sta.
STALHAM
Waxham
Sutton
Hickling
Hickling Green
Catfield
Barton Turf
Broad
Hickling Broad
Horsey Mere
Horsey
Winterton Ness
Heigham Sound
Potter Heigham
Martham
Somerton
W. Somerton
E. Somerton
Winterton
LUDHAM
Thurne
A1062
Horning
Repps
Bastwick
Hemsby
Rollesby
Ormesby
Ormesby Broad
Clippesby
B1152
Burgh
St. Margaret
Ormesby
St. Michael
Ormesby
St. Margaret
California
A149
Hilockin
Filby
Billockby
Upton
Fishley
B1140
ACLE
Stokesby
Runham
Maultby
Filby Br.
Thrigby
CAISTER
next
Yarmouth
C.G.&L.B.Std.

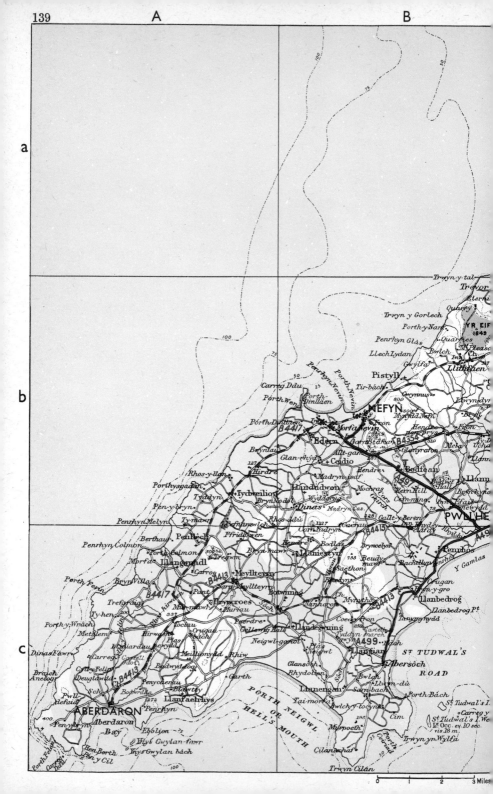

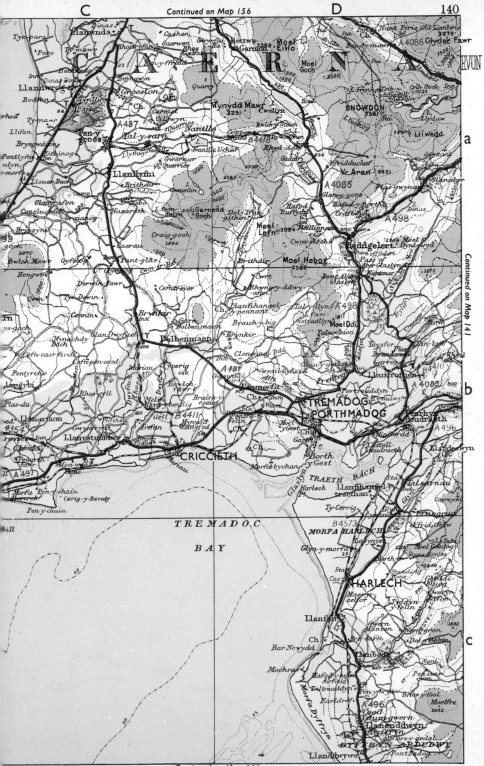

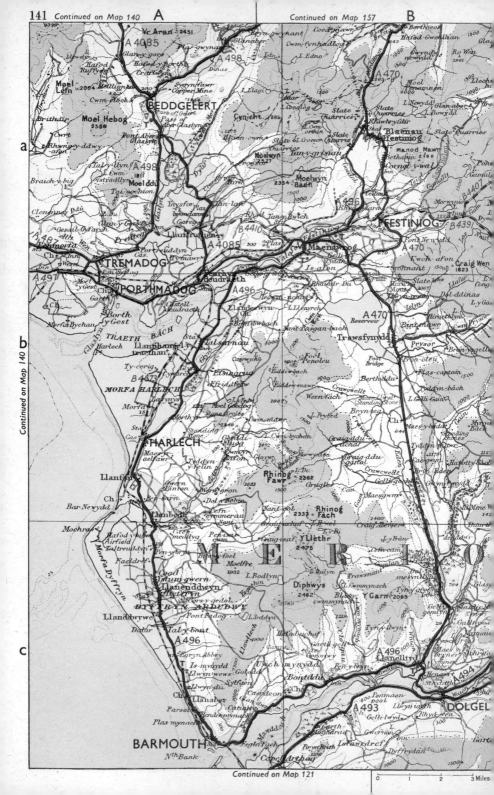

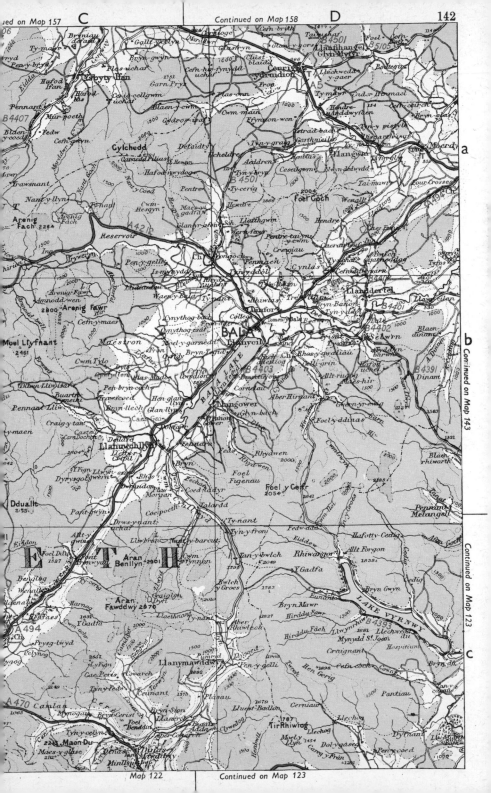

Map 122   Continued on Map 123

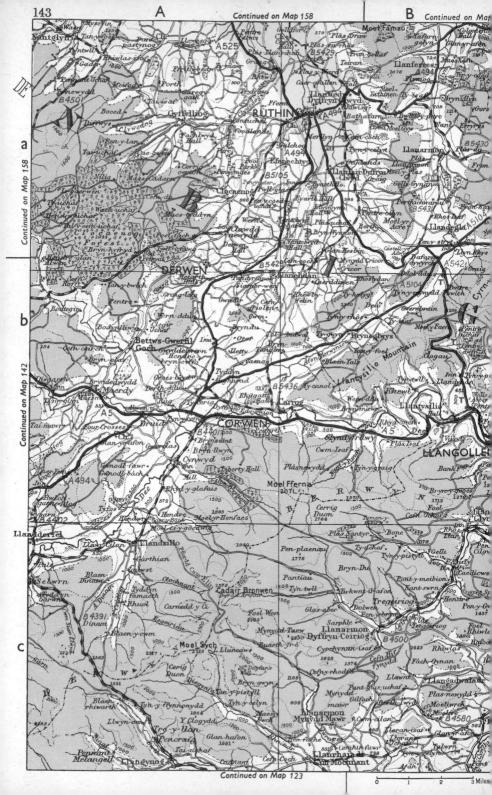

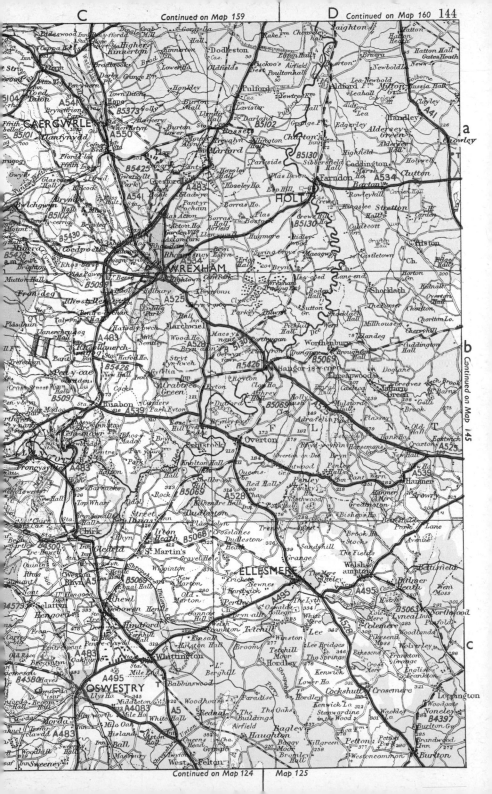

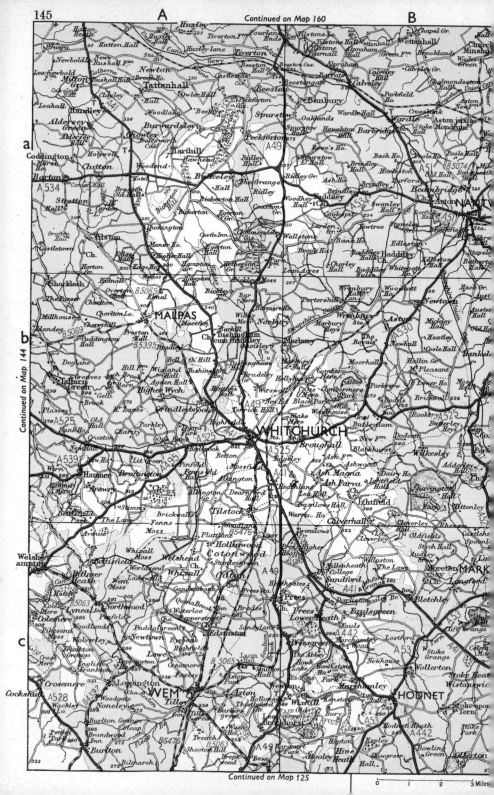

A

B

a

b

c

Continued on Map 144

Tattenhall

MALPAS

WHITCHURCH

WEM

NANT...

CHODNET

MARK...

3 Miles

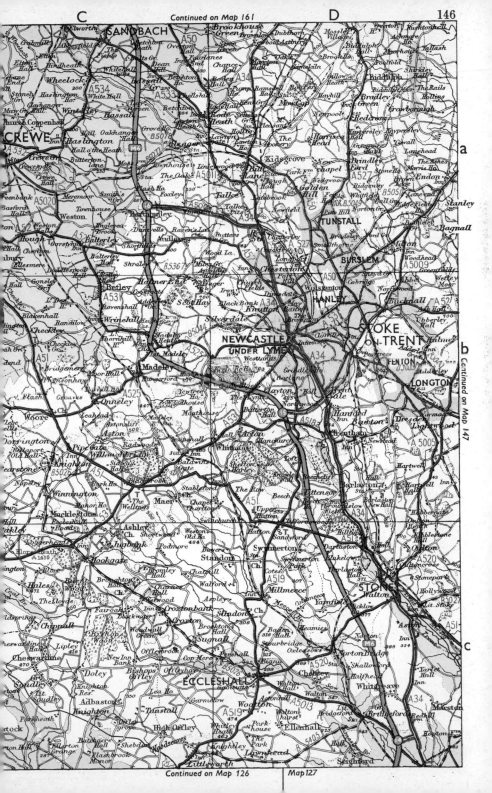

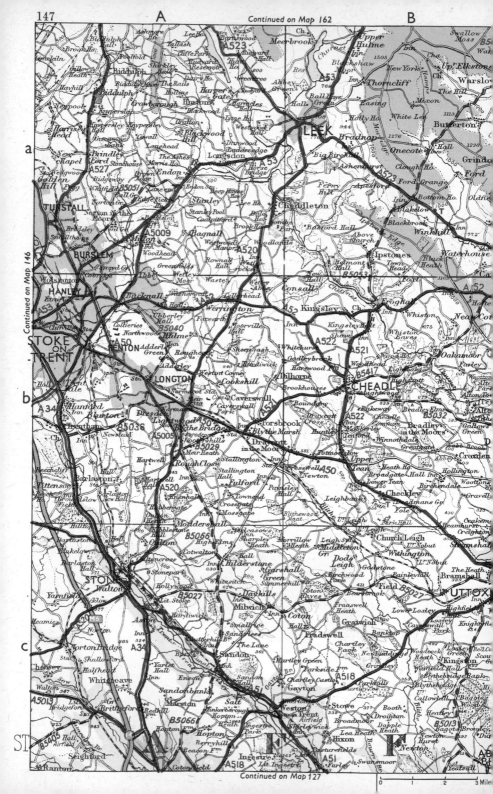

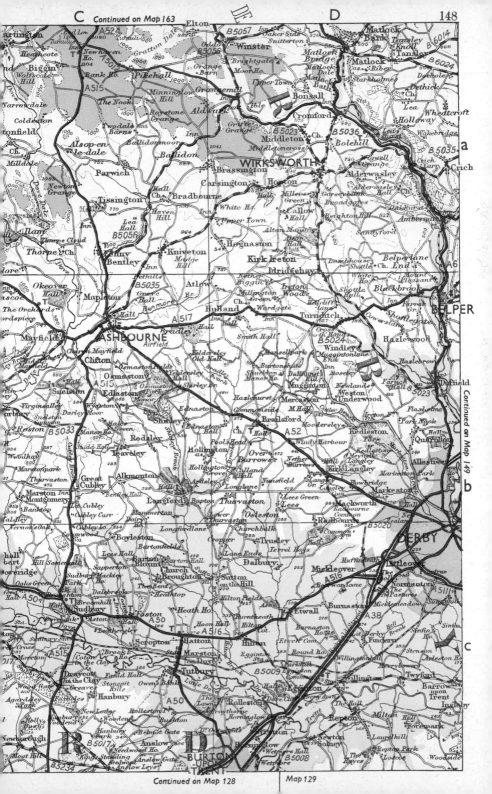

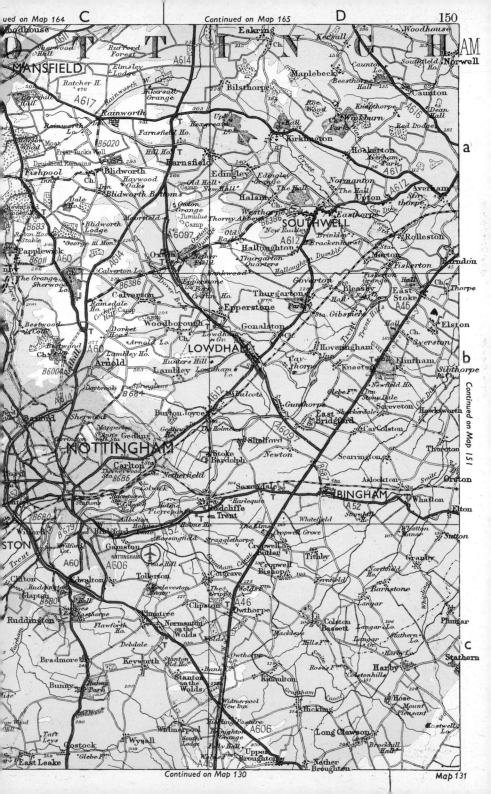

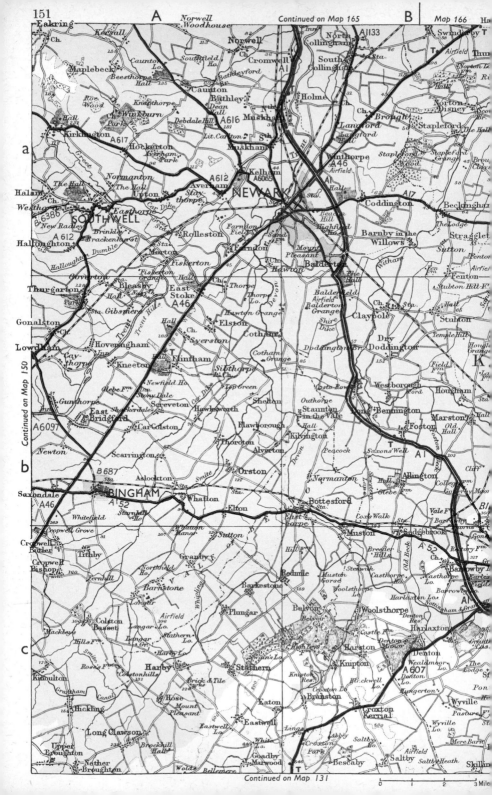

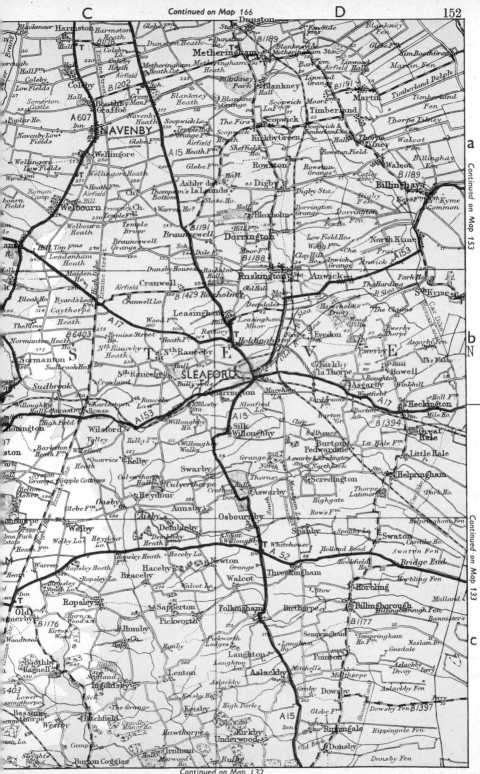
Continued on Map 153
Continued on Map 133

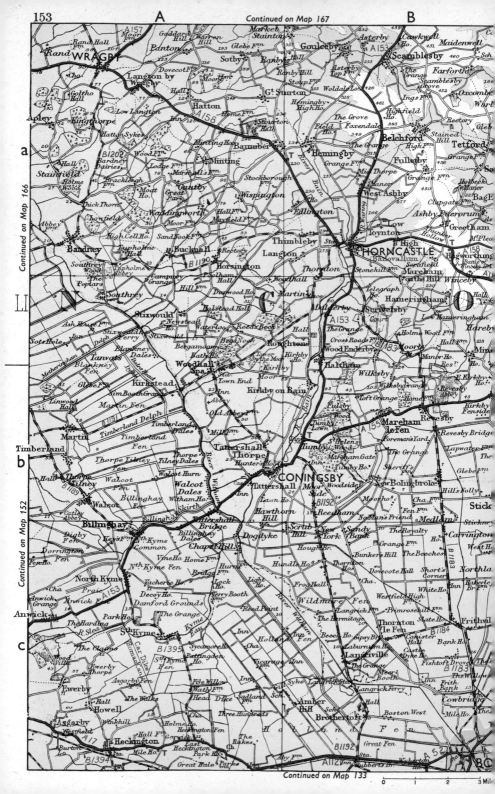

Continued on Map 168

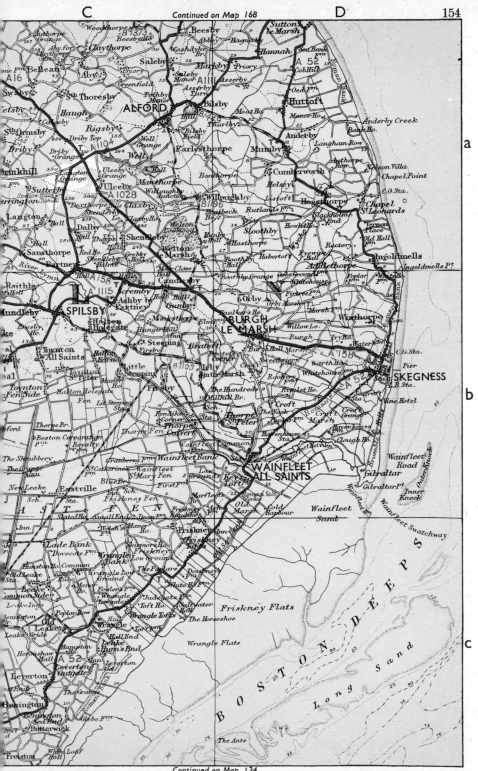

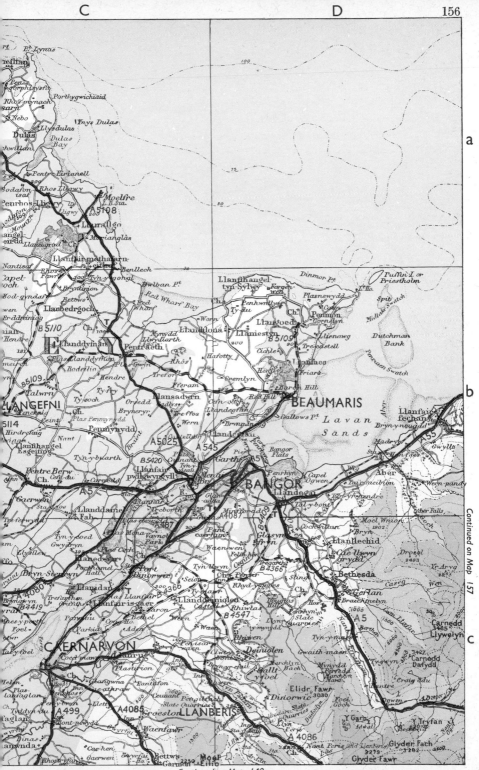

a

b

Continued on Map 157

c

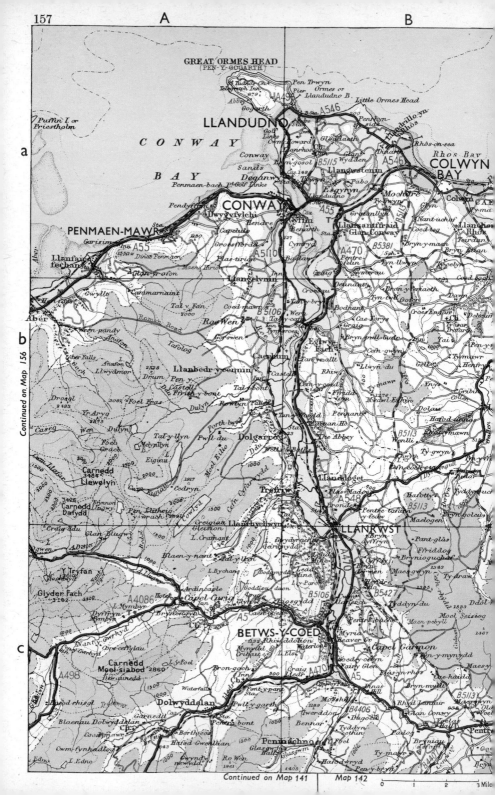

A   B

GREAT ORMES HEAD
(PEN-Y-GOGARTH)

St Tudno's Ch.
Telegraph Inn
Abbey
Gogarth

Pen Trwyn
Ormes or
Llandudno B.

Little Ormes Head

Puffin I. or
Priestholm

LLANDUDNO

Penrhyn-side

Hendrillo-yn-Rhos

Rhos-on-sea

C O N W A Y

Golf
Links

Craig-y-Don
Llanrhos

Gloddaeth

Craig
Wydden

Dinarth

Rhos Bay

Penmaen-bach Pt

Conway
Sands

Llys-faen

Bryn-gosol

Cas.148

Llangystenin

Pabo

Mochdre

COLWYN
BAY

B A Y

Deghwy

Golf Links

Esgyryn

Grafanllyn

Colwyn

A546

Pendyffryn

CONWAY

Henryd

Gyffin

Benarth

Mill

Cymryd

Llansantffraid
Glan Conway

Bryn-y-maen

Bryn-y-bain

Llandrillo

PENMAEN-MAWR

Llwyd-fylchu

Capelulo

Groeslonford

Plas-tirion

Maen Esgob

A55

Dinas Penmaen

Bodlew

Pentre-felin

B5381

Cymerau

A470

Coed-teg

Tyn-gwern

Llanfair-fechan

Aber

Llangelynin

Groes-lon

Coed-mawr

Tal-y-bryn

Croes

Bodhany

Cae-forys
Craig

Bryn-mill-bude

Croes Englan
Ch.
Tyddyn Isaf

Gwylts

Canmarnaint

Tal-y-Fan
2000

Tal-y-cafn

Defurant

Bron-y-maarch

Darn

Tyn-twll-Goch

Ro-Wen

Roewen

Tafolog

Llanbedr-y-cennin

Caerhun

Tai-r-yr-allt

Rhiw

Llwyn-du

Cefn-gwyn

Tai
1000

Ty-mawr
Henry

Drosgl

Pen-y-Castell

Ffridd-y-bont

Dulyn

Talybont

Rowen

Pen-yr-oedd

Ffridd
Lwyn

Mwdwl-Eithyn
1270

Ynys

Craig-

Carnedd
Llewelyn

Dolgarrog

Moel Eilio

Well

Baths

Maenan Ho.
The Abbey

Ty-gwyn

Rhos-
mawr

Dolas

Hafod-y-rhos

B5113

Carnedd
Dafydd

Cefn Cyfarwydd

Llanddoget

Plas Madoc

Hafotty's

Tyddyn-
côd

Craig-adu

Trefriw

Gwydir

A548

Penthe-tafarn-
y-fedw

Bryn-
ffordd

Maelogen

Creigiau Llanbychllwyn

LLANRWST

Pant-glâs

Bryniogwch

Tryfan

Leadd
Mine

Capel Curig

Biosgydd

B5106

Dolwyddelan

BETWS-Y-COED

A5

Capel Garmon

Carnedd
Moel-siabod 2860

Craig Ledr

A470

A498

A5

Continued on Map 156

a

b

c

Continued on Map 141   Map 142

0   1   2   3 Mile

Continued on Map 169

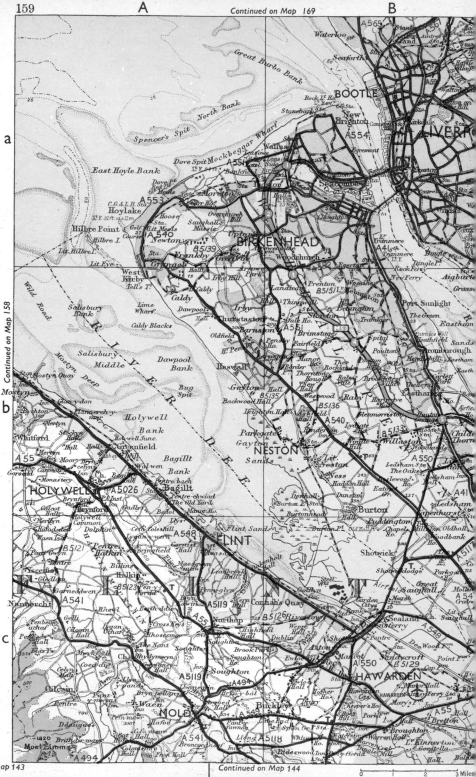

Continued on Map 158

Map 143

Continued on Map 144

nued on Map 169
Continued on Map 161

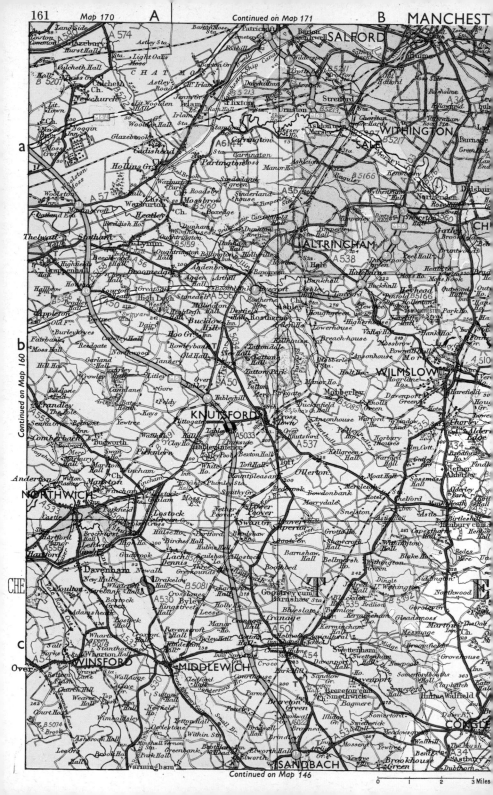

C   D

a

Continued on Map 165

b

c

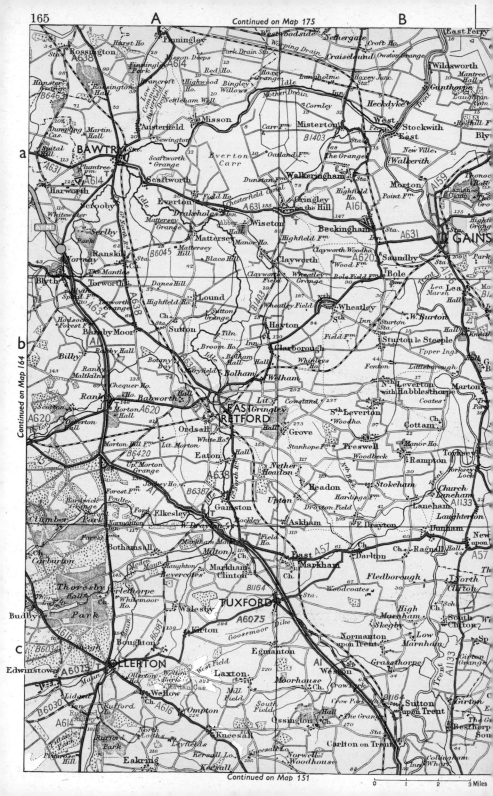

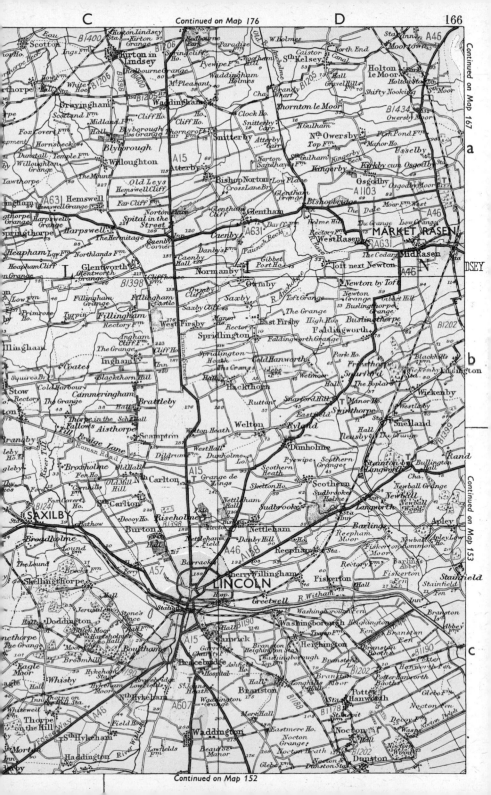

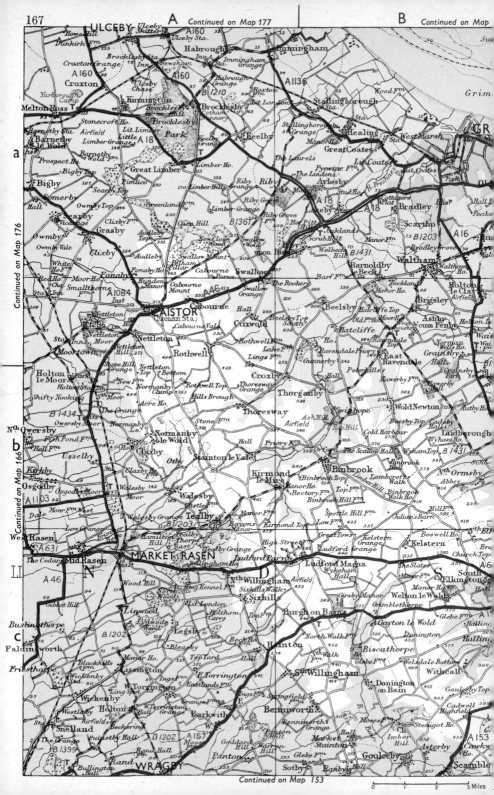

Continued on Map 176

Continued on Map 166

0   1   2   3 Miles

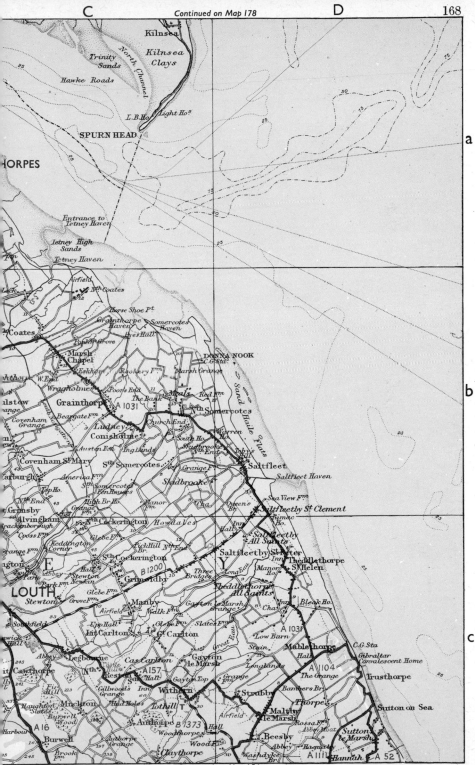

a

b

c

Kilnsea

Trinity
Sands

Kilnsea
Clays

North Channel

Hawke Roads

L.B.Ho.   Light Ho²

SPURN HEAD

HORPES

Entrance to
Tetney Haven

Tetney High
Sands

Tetney Haven

Airfield

Nth Coates

Horse Shoe Pt

Granthorpe
Haven

Somercotes
Haven

Coates

es Hall

Marsh
Chapel

Eskham

Rookery Fm

DONNA NOOK
C.G.Sta.

W.End

Wraghölme

Poors End

Marsh Grange

Grainthorpe

A 1031

The Bank

Meals

Red Fm

Nth Somercotes

ilstow

Beargate Fm

Ludney

Church End

Warren

Conisholme

Smith Ho.

Skidbrooke
Nth End

Austen Fm

Inglands

Covenham St Mary

Stⁿ Somercotes

America Fm

Sth
Somercotes
Penthouses

Grange Fm

Saltfleet

Covenham St Mary

arburgh

High Br Ho

Skidbrooke

Saltfleet Haven

Grimsby

Top Ho.

Manor
Fm

Sea View Fm

Alvingham

Grange
Fm

Nth Cockerington

Howdales

Queen's Br

Saltfleetby St Clement

rackenborough

Cross Fm

Glebe Fm

PickHill
Br.

Nth End

Hall

Rimac
Ho.

Keddington
Corner

Saltfleetby
All Saints

Sth Cockerington

Saltfleetby St Peter

E

Ball

B 1200

Three
Bridges

Long Eau

Manor
Ho.

Theddlethorpe
St Helen

Stewton Newton

Grimoldby

Theddlethorpe
All Saints

LOUTH

Glebe Fm

Manby

Grove Fm

Bleak Ho.

Stewton

Airfield

Walk Fm

Gayton le Marsh
Grange

Cha.

Southfield

Epp Hall

Glebe Fm

Slates Fm

A 1031

Low Barn

Int Carlton

Gt. Carlton

wick

Hall

Mablethorpe
Hall

C.G.Sta.

Legbourne

Cas Carlton

Great Eau

Stain

Gibraltar
Convalescent Home

Caythorpe

Nth

Reston

Gayton
le Marsh

Longlands

The Grange

A 1104

Trusthorpe

A 157

Gillwood's
Grange

Inn

Gayton Top

Grange
Fm

Banthorps Br

Withern

Strubby

Thorpe

Sutton on Sea

Muckton

Burwell
Wood

Tothill

Airfield

Maltby
le Marsh

Rossa Fm

Sutton
le Marsh

A 16

Authorpe

B 1373

Hall

Beesby

Abbey Moat

Burwell

Authorpe
Grange

Woodthorpe

Wood Fm

Abbey

Hagnaby

A 1111

Harbour

Brook
Fm

Claythorpe

Washdyke
Br.

Hannah   A 52

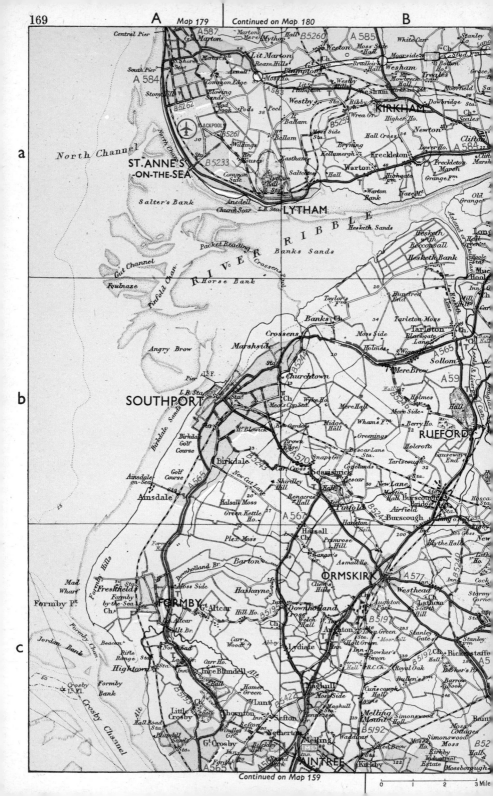

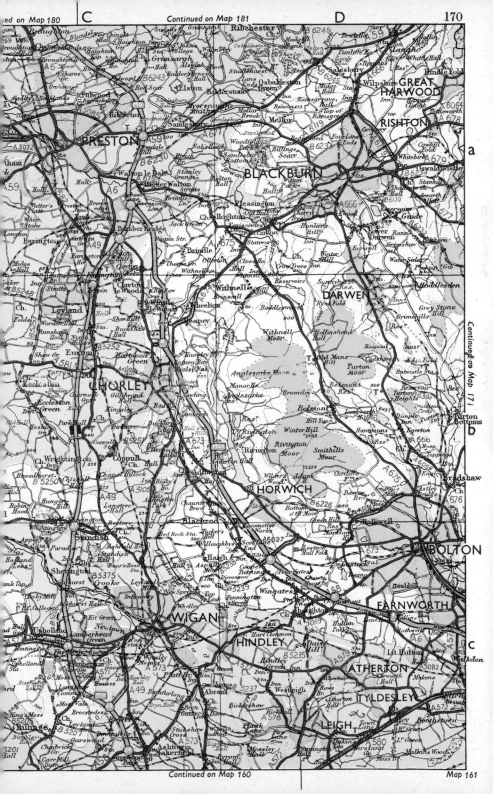

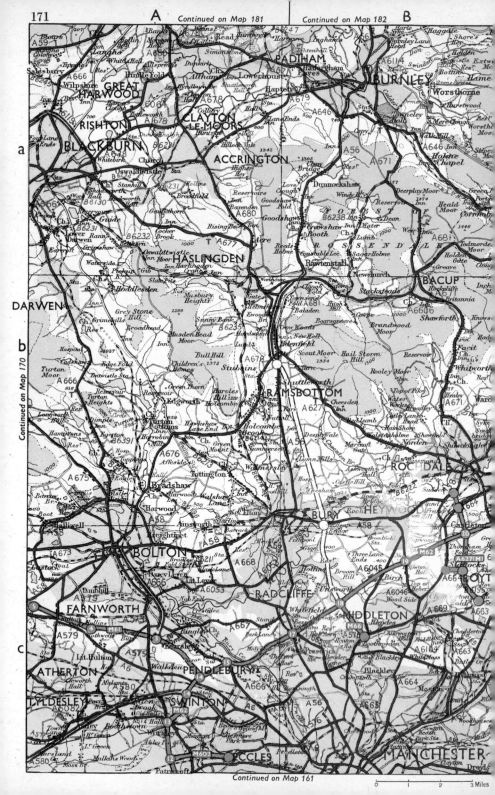

Continued on Map 162
Continued on Map 173

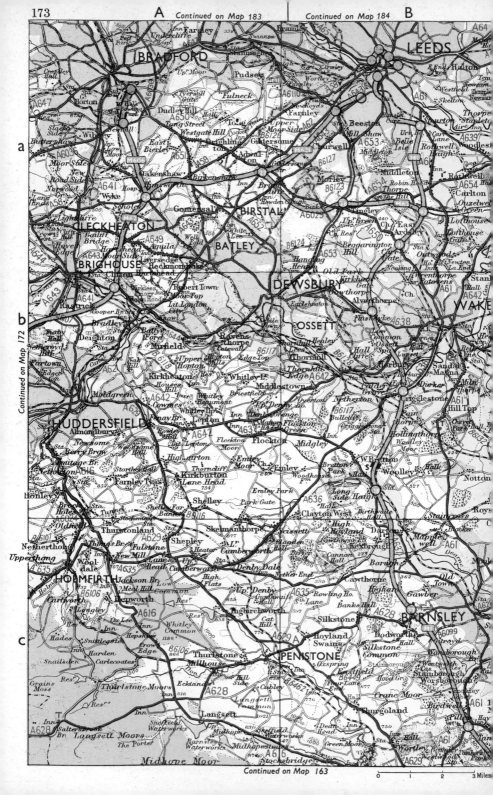

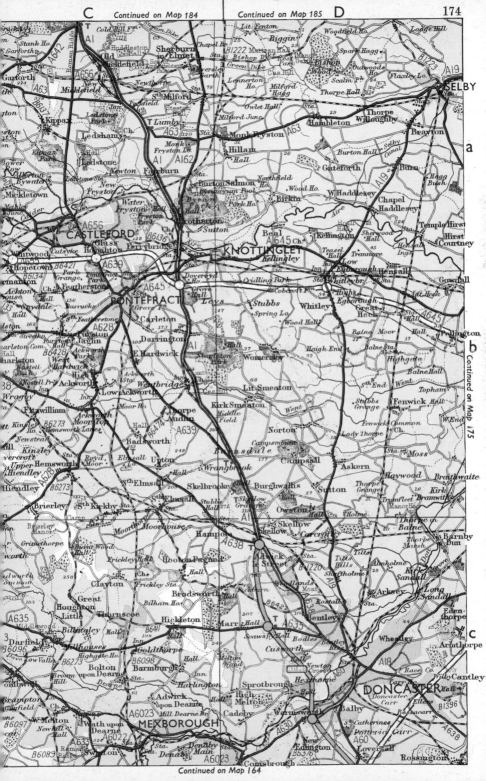

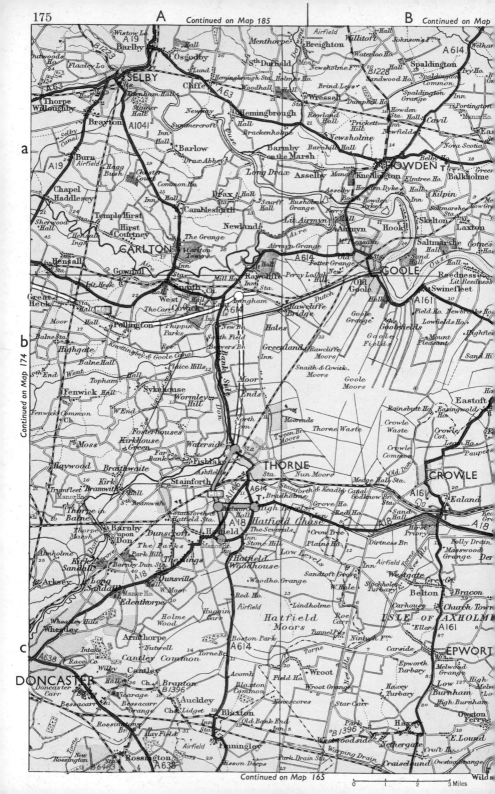

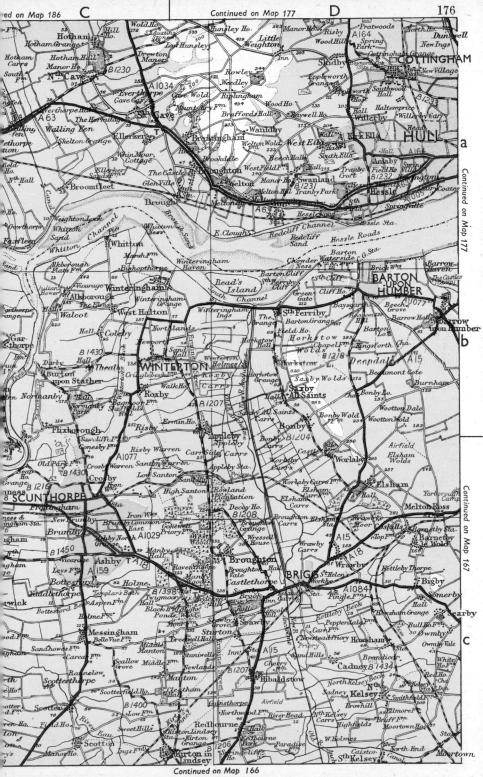

Continued on Map 188

A B

E A S T

R I D I N G

Middleton on the Wolds
Kilnwick
Lund
Thorpe
Holme on the Wolds
Kipling Cotes
Dalton Hall
South Dalton
Scorbrough
Etton
Cherry Burton
Gardham
Cherry Burton Wold
Bishop Burton
Walkington
Bentley
High Hunsley
Little Weighton
Rowley
Weedley
Riplingham
Brantingham
Wauldby
West Ella
Kirk Ella
Welton
Swanland
Hessle
Brough

BEVERLEY
Woodmansey
Thearne
Skidby
COTTINGHAM
Willerby
Anlaby

Watton
Beswick
Lockington
Alice
Leconfield
Arram
Tickton
Routh
Long Riston
Arnold
Skirlaugh
Wawne
Sutton

BRANDESBURTON
LEVEN
Catwick
Rise

HULL
KINGSTON UPON HULL
Marfleet
Paull

R I V E R   H U M B E R

New Holland
Goxhill Haven
Skitter Ness
Barton Waterside
BARTON-UPON-HUMBER
Barrow Haven
Barrow upon Humber
Goxhill
East Halton
Killingholme
South Killingholme

Read's Island
South Ferriby
Winteringham
Horkstow
Saxby Wolds
Saxby All Saints
Bonby
Appleby
Worlaby
Wootton
ULCEBY

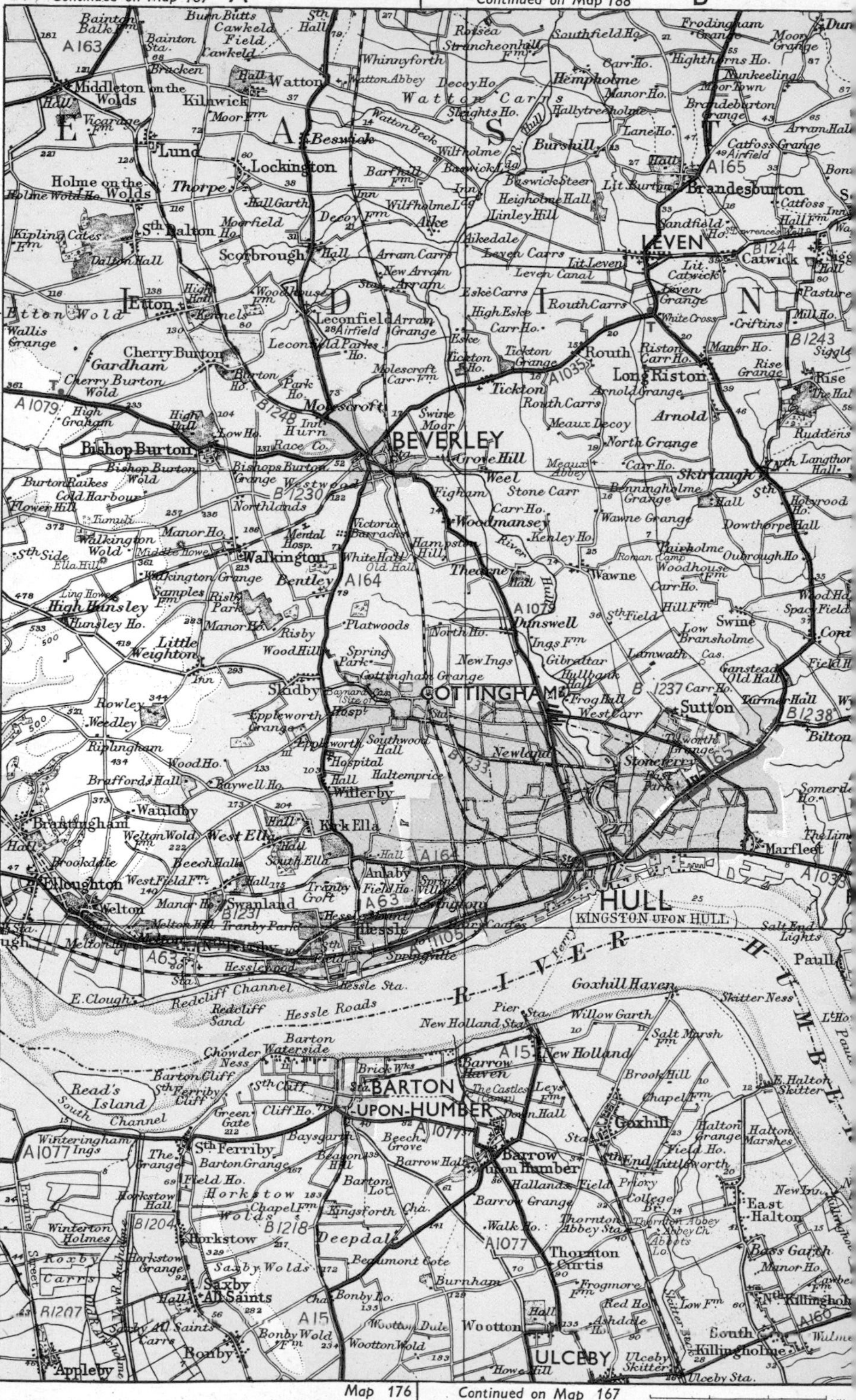

Map 176   Continued on Map 167

Continued on Map 186
Continued on Map 176

0   1   2   3 Mile

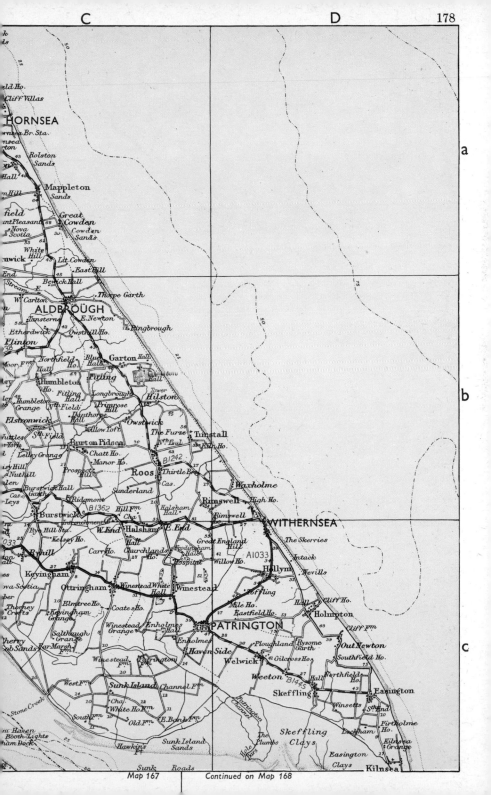

a

b

c

Cliff Villas

HORNSEA
nsea Br. Sta.
ton
Rolston
Sands
Hall
m Hill
Mappleton
Sands
field
untPleasant
Nova
Scotia
Great
Cowden
nwick
White
Hill
Cowden
Sands
End
Lit. Cowden
East Hill
Stream
Bewick Hall
W Carlton
Thorpe Garth
ALDBROUGH
Hansterne
E. Newton
Etherdwick
Owsthill Ho.
Ringbrough
Flinton
Moor Fm
Northfield
Blue
Hall
Garton
Hall
Humbleton
Ho.
Fitling
Humbleton
Grange
Fitling
Hall
Nth Field
Longbrough
Primrose
Hill
Tower
Hilston
Elstronwick
Winthorpe
Hall
Willow Toft
Owstwick
shuttes
St Field
Yorke
The Furze
Tunstall
Lelley Grange
Burton Pidsea
Nth Hull
Kiln Ho.
sy Hill
Nuthall
Chatt Ho.
Manor Ho.
Prospect
Hill
B1242
len
Roos
Thirtle Br
Burstwick Hall
Garth
Sunderland
Cas.
Leys
Ridgmont
Waxholme
Burstwick
B1362
Hill Fm
Cha.
Halsham
Hall
Rimswell
High Ho.
Rye Hill Sta.
W. End
Halsham
E. End
Rimswell
WITHERNSEA
033
Kelsey Ho.
Hall
The Skerries
ton
Ryhill
Carr Ho.
Churchlands
Ho.
Frodingham
Hall
Great England
Hill
A1033
Intack
Keyingham
Hospital
Willow Ho.
Hollym
Nevills
wa Scotia
Ottringham
Winstead
Hall
White
Hall
Winestead
Offling
Hall
Cliff Ho.
Holmpton
Thorney
Crofts
Elmtree Ho.
Coates Ho.
Mile Ho.
Eastfield Ho.
Cliff Fm
Keyingham
Grange
PATRINGTON
Salthaugh
Grange
Far Marsh
Fm
Winestead
Grange
Enholmes
Hall
Enholmes
Ploughland
Rysome
Garth
Out Newton
Southfield Ho.
herry
b Sands
Winestead
Fm
Patrington
Haven Side
Welwick
Gilcross Ho.
Northfield
Ho.
Easington
West Fm
Sunk Island
Channel Fm
Weeton
Hall
B1445
Stone Creek
Cha.
White Ho Fm
E. Bank Fm
Skeffling
Winsetts
Sth End
Firtholme
Ho.
m Haven
Booth Lights
am Dock
South Fm
Old Fm
Lockham
Kilnsea
Grange
Hawkin's
Pt
Sunk Island
Sands
Skeffling
Clays
The
Plumbs
Easington
Clays
Kilnsea
Sunk Roads

Map 167 Continued on Map 168

Continued on Map 192

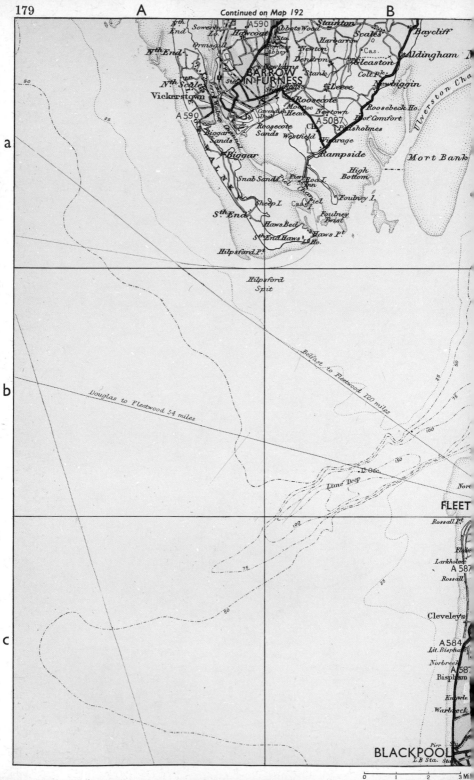

A

B

a

b

c

Nth End
Sowerby Lo.
Hawcoat
Abbots Wood
Stainton
Scales
Baycliff
A590
Nth End
Ormsgill
Harbarrow
Newton
Cas.
Aldingham
Abbey
Dendron
Gleaston
Newbarns
Stank
Nth Scale
sta.
BARROW IN FURNESS
Leece
Newbiggin
Vickerstown
Sheeps
Roosecote
Roosebeck Ho.
A 590
Cavendish Dock
Moo Doo Head
Newtown
A 5087
P. of Comfort
Roosecote Sands
Westfield
Pt.
Pleasholmes
Biggar Sands
CH.
Vicarage
Rampside
Biggar
Ulverston Cha
Snab Sands
Pier
Roa I.
High Bottom
Mort Bank
Sth End
Roo Inn
Piel
Foulney I.
Sheep I.
Cas. I.
Foulney Twist
Haws Bed
Haws Pt.
Sth End
Haws
Sth End Haws
Ho.
Hilpsford Pt.

Hilpsford Spit

Belfast to Fleetwood 120 miles

50
25
75
100

Douglas to Fleetwood 54 miles

Lt. Oée
Lune Deep

Nort

150

FLEET

Rossall Pt.
Flota
Larkholme
A 587
Rossall
25

Cleveleys

A 584
Lit. Bispha
Norbreck
A 587
Bispham
Knowle
Warbreck

BLACKPOOL
Pier
L.B Sta.
sta.

0   1   2   3 Mil

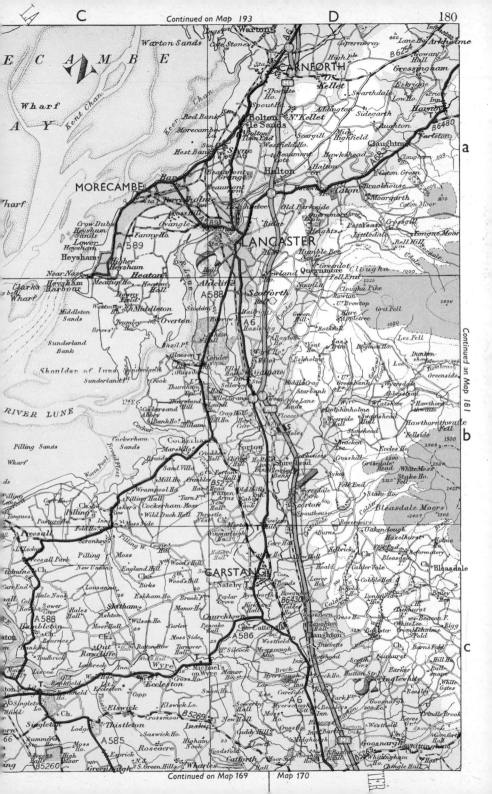

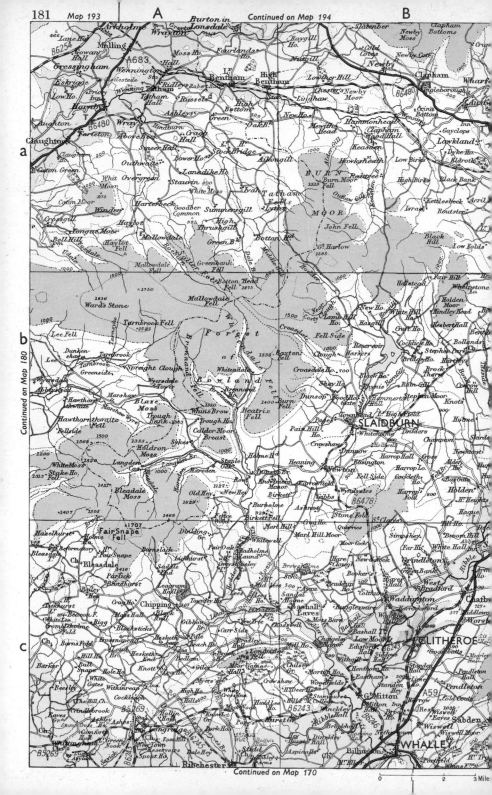

a

Continued on Map 182

b

c

Steal Moor   Ramsgill   Boothwaite   Kettlestang Shoot? Ho.   Dallow Ch.   Dallow   East Gill

Conistone Moor   Priest's Tarn   Rowgill Ho.   Colt Ho.   Gill Houses   Dallowgill Moor   Skell Gill

Grassington Moor   Stone Moor   Colt Ho. Gill   High & Low Holme Ho.   Skell B.

Gill Ho.   Ashfold Side   Heathfield Moor   W. Wood Ho.   Wath   Yeadon   PATELEY MOOR

Coalgrove Ho.   Reservoir   Appletreewick   Gate Up   Westfield Ho.   Goose Green   PATELEY BRIDGE

Grassington   Scar Top Ho.   Hebden   Moor   Hartcastle   Bewerley   Grassfield   Bewerley Hall   Heyshaw Moor   Heyshaw

Blythe   Thruskell Well   Craven   Fancarl Ho.   High Ravens Nest   Flat Moor

Thorpe   Burnsall   Woodhouse   Hartlington   Percival Hall   Pock Stones Moor   Humberstone Bank   Padside Hall   Dacre

Burnsall & Thorpe Fell   Appletreewick Pasture   High Skyreholme   Harden Moor   Padside

Drebley   Gamsworth   Earl Seat   Barden Fell   Rocking Moor   Lane Head   Thruscross   Thornthwaite   Dacre

Barden Moor   Barden Bn.   Rocking Hall   Low Moor   West End   Thruscross   Day Ash   Longscales

Rotten Park   Barden Broad Park   Hazlewood Moor   Burnt Ho.   Hanging Moor   Delves Ridge   Nessfield Ho.

Haugh   Halton Heights   Ridding   Park Ho.   Ker Gill Moor   Redshaw Hall   FOREST

Eastby   Stank   Intake   Friar Stones   Storiths   Blubberhouses   Fewston   Kettlesing

Embsay   Halton East   Abbey   Summerscale   Beamsley Moor   Blubberhouses Moor

Abbey   Halton Green   Bolton Abbey   The Devonshire Arms   Round Hall   Fewston Res.   Swinsty Res.   Whistle Ho.

Haw Park   Low Skibeden   Bolton Bridge   Langbar Moor   Sourby Fm.   Ellercarr   Timble   Scow Hall

Draughton   Fairfield   Langbar   Hardisty   Shaw Hall   High Snowden   Jack Hill

Skipton Moor   Addingham Low Moor Camp   Moor Ho.   High Denton   Askwith Moor   Dob Park

High Bradley Moor   Bank End   Addingham   Nesfield Ch.   Middleton   Denton   Scales   Norwood

High Bradley   Foster Cliff   Tivoli   Middleton Ho.   Denton Park   Whin Cas.   Town Head   Clifton   Farnley

Low Bradley   Cringles   Small Banks   Ford   Carr   New Br.   Leeds

Farnhill Moor   Craig Ho.   Addingham Side Moor   ILKLEY   Wheatley   Ben Rhydding   Greenholme   Weston   Hosp.

Kildwick   Silsden   ILKLEY MOOR   Burley in Wharfedale   Newall Park   Farnley

Eastburn   Up. Howden   High Moor   Mossville   Westbourne   OTLEY   The Chevin

Sutton Mill   Silsden Moor   Morton Moor   Burley Moor   M O O R   Menston   Chevin End   Carlton

Steeton   Whitley Head   Utley   Holden Gate   Moorcock   Upwood   West Morton East   Bingley Moor   Druidical Circle   Hawksworth Moor   Lunatic Asylum   Guiseley   Nun Royd

Upper Ho.   Redcar   Cliff Cas.   Beechcliffe   Prospect Ho.   Lane Head   Faweather   Hawksworth   Park Gate   Yeadon

Goose Eye   Braithwaite   Laycock   Hainworth   KEIGHLEY   Crossflats   Eldwick   Baildon   Esholt   Rawdon

Newsholme   Oakworth   Oak Bank   Hainworth   Harden   Moor Side   Tong Park   Tipper Esholt   London

Hewitt Hall   WHITE   BINGLEY   Harden   Gollinglith Carrs   Baildon Green   Charlestown   The Knoll   Thackley   Apperley

Stanbury   Oldfield   Cross Roads   Cullingworth   Wilsden   Saltaire   Idle

HAWORTH   Cullingworth Moor   Wilsden Stn.   SHIPLEY   Brighton   Eccleshill   Farsley

Marsh   Oxenhope   Hare Croft   Sandy Lane   Frizinghall   Wrose   Undercliffe

0   1   2   3 Miles

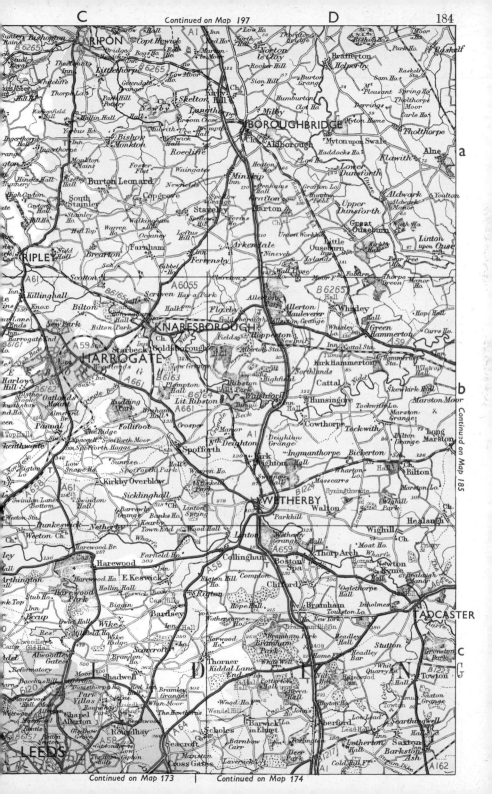

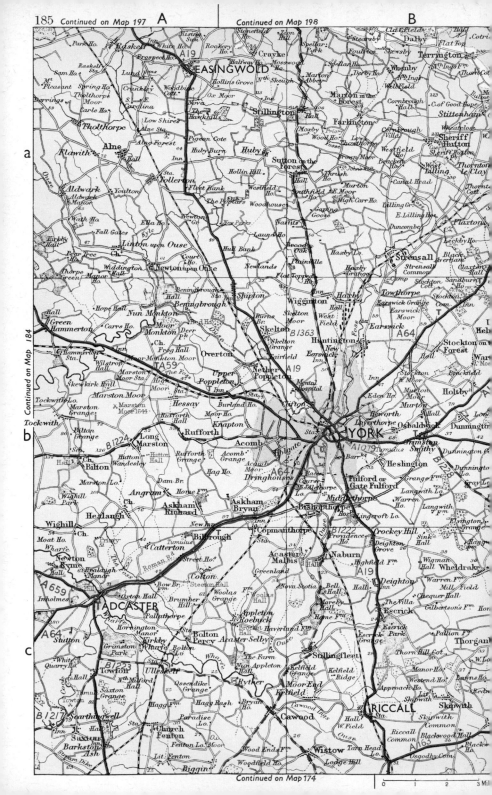

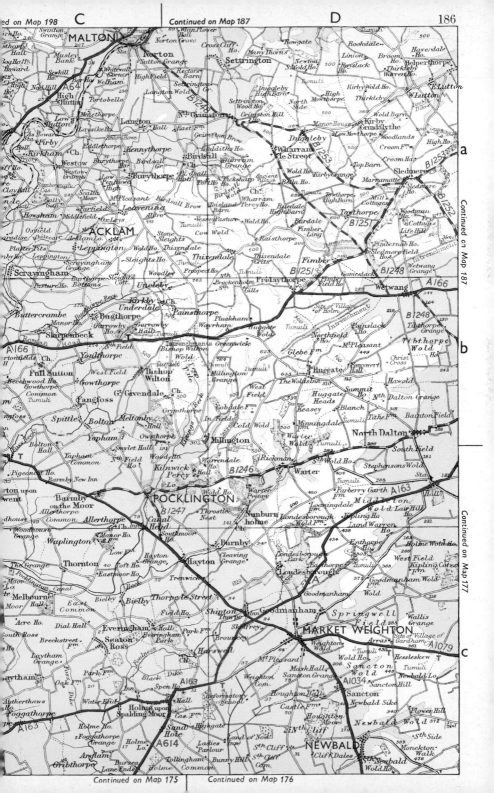

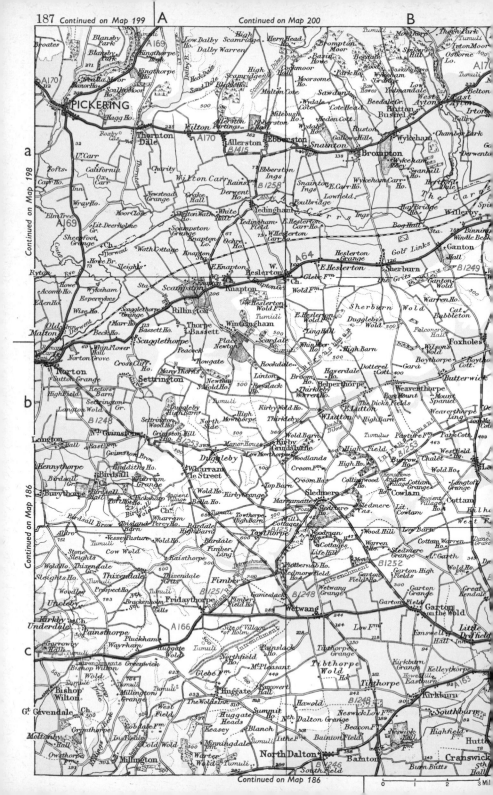

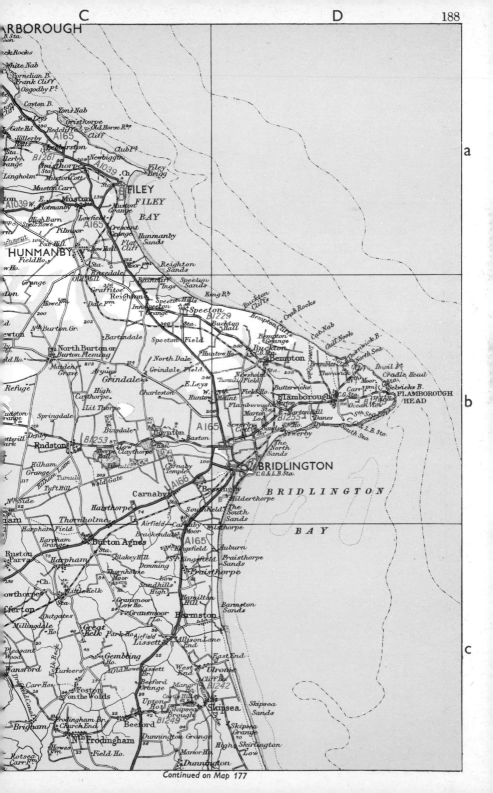

ARBOROUGH

a

b

c

FILEY

FILEY BAY

HUNMANBY

Speeton

Buckton

Bempton

FLAMBOROUGH
HEAD

Flamborough

B R I D L I N G T O N

BRIDLINGTON

B A Y

Rudston

Carnaby

Burton Agnes

Fraisthorpe

Barmston

Skipsea

Nth Frodingham

Continued on Map 177

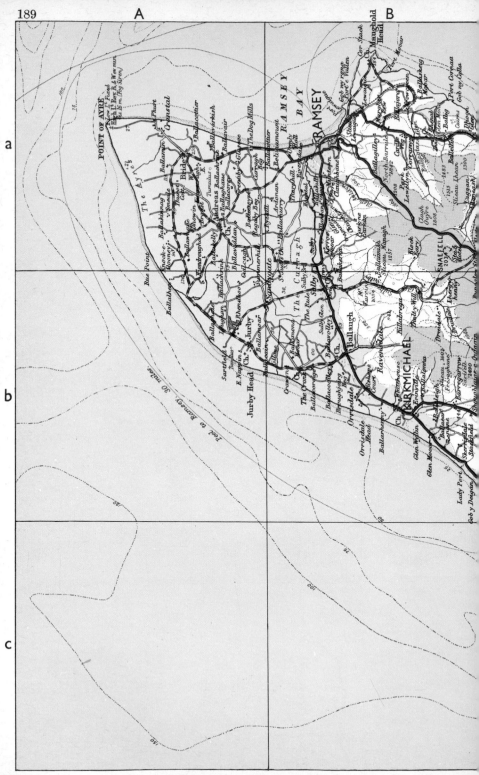

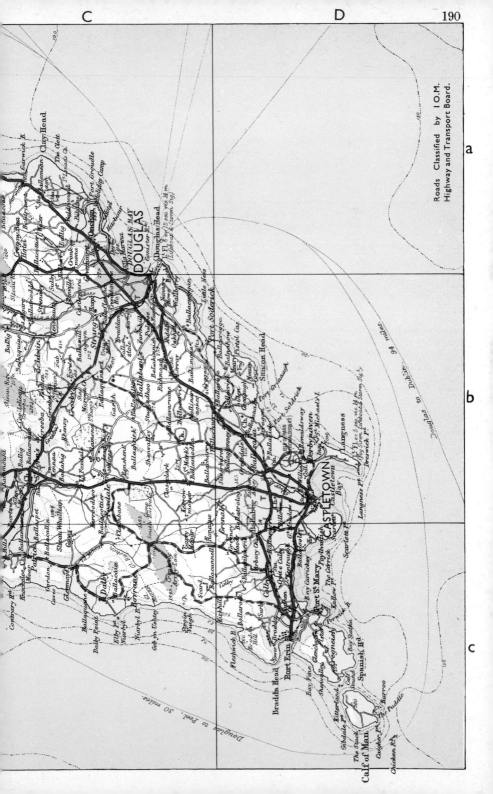

Continued on Map 201

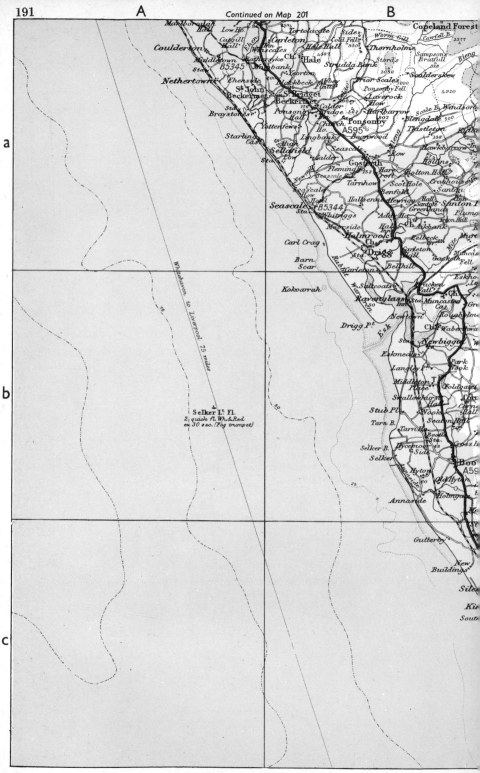

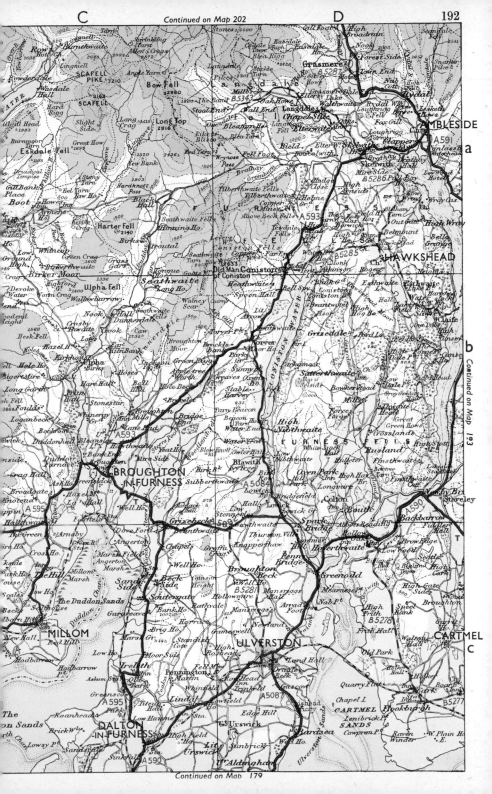

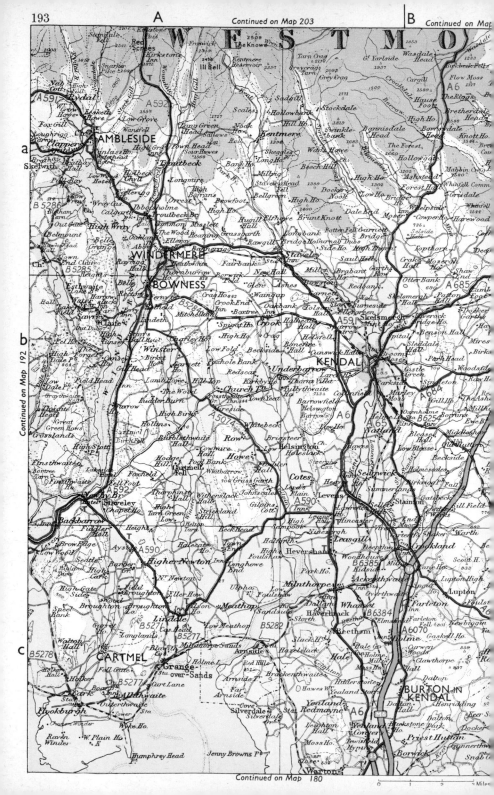

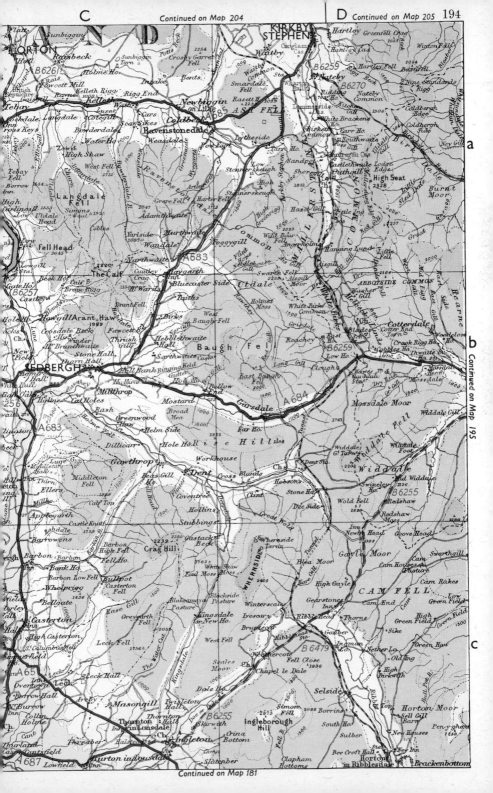

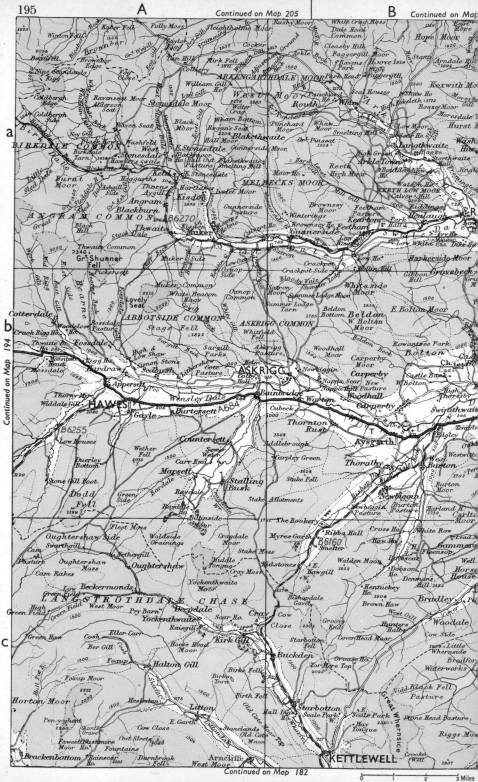

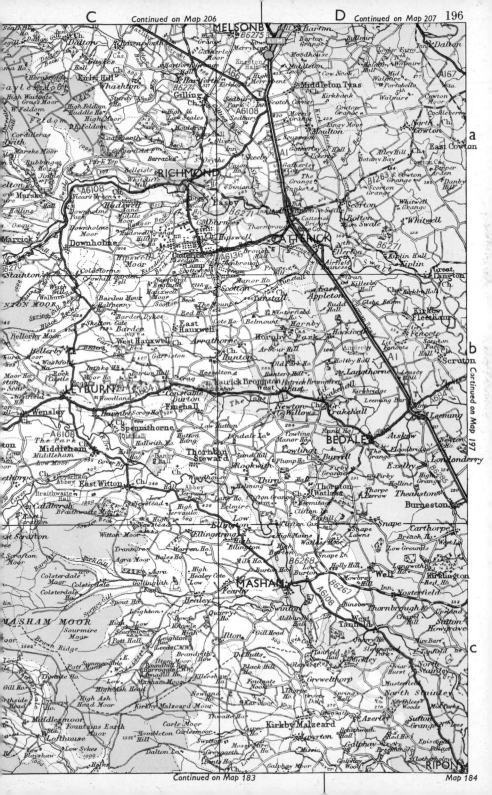

Continued on Map 197

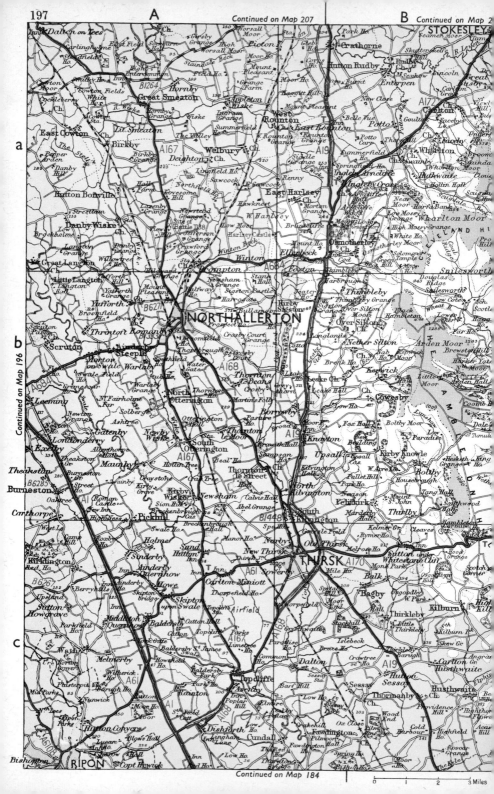

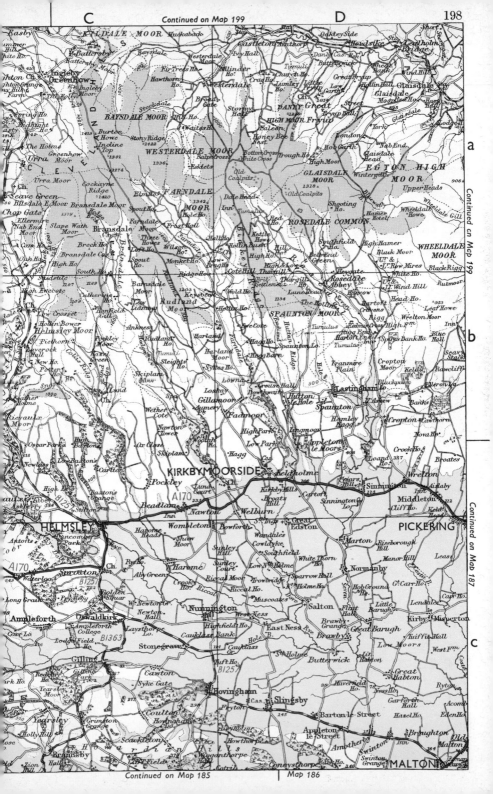
Continued on Map 199

Continued on Map 187

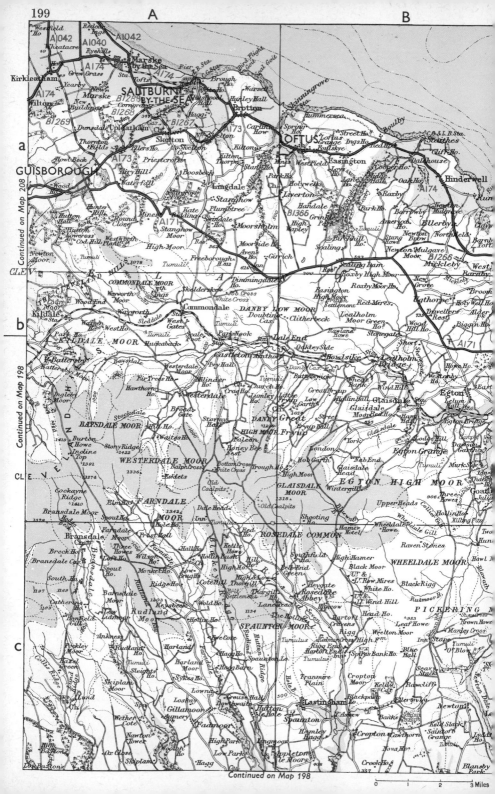

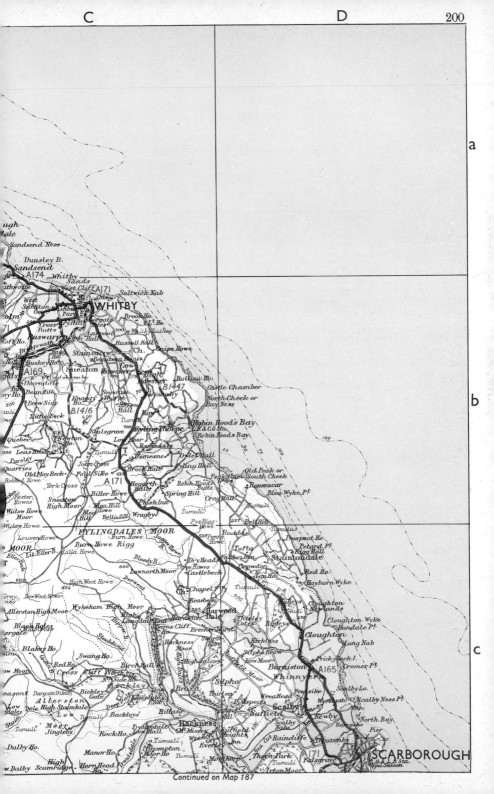

a

Sandsend Ness
Dunsley B.
Sandsend
A174 Whitby
Whitby Sands
West Cliff A171 Saltwick Nab
WHITBY
Ashby Park
Cross Butts
Ruswarp
Larpool Hall
Russell Hall
Caipe Howe
Ch.
Stainsacre
Hawsker
Castle Chamber
North Cheek or Bay Ness

b

A169
Sneaton
B1447
Deanhill
Brow Side
Knaggy Ho.
B1416
Rigg Hall
Ray
Castle Chamber
Little Beck
Robin Hood's Bay
L.B. & C.G. Sta.
Robin Hoods Bay
Fylingthorpe
Newton Ho.
Fyling Hall
Foul Sike
A171
Brock Hall
Old Peak or South Cheek
Quebec
York Cross
Hogarth Hall
Robin Hood's Butts
Ravenscar
Biller Howe
Spring Hill
Crag Hall
Bleu Wyke Pt.
Sneaton High Moor
Blea Hill
Phister Inn
Wragby
Widow Howe
Bellingill
Pye Rigg Howe
Bellfield

FYLINGDALES MOOR
Burn Howe Rigg
Juga Howe
Prospect Ho.
Petard Pt.
Rigg Hall
MOOR
Lit. Eller B.
Lilla Howe
Bloody B.
Dry Head
Tofta
Faddon Inn
Stainondale
High Woot Howe
Lownorth Moor
Three Howes
Castlebeck
Crowdon
Red Ho.
Derwent
Tan Ho.
Hayburn Wyke
Wykeham High Moor
Ch. Chapel Fm.
Keasbeck
Allerston High Moor
High Langdale End
Harwood Dale
Cloughton Newlands
Blakey Ho.
Barns Cliff
Breckenholme
Ripleys
Cloughton Wyke
Hundale Pt.
Long Nab
Swang Ho.
Hackness Moor
Kirklees
Cloughton
Red Ho.
Birch Hall
Highdales
Sylpho Brow
Prickybeck I.
Cromer Pt.
c
Cliff North
Low Moor
A165
Dargate Dikes
Allerston
Bickley
Gate
Broxa
Silpho
Barniston
Whinnyer
Scalby Lo.
Wrea Head
Scalby Ness Pt.
High Staindale
Low
Thirley
Aspect
Scalby
Newby
North Bay
Hackness
M! Misery
Suffield
Heights
Everley
Raincliffe
Barracks
Pier
Manor Ho.
Hern Head Ho.
Brompton Moor Ho.
Mowthorp
Thorn Park
Troxenby
SCARBOROUGH
Dalby Ho.
High Scamridge
Irton Moor
A171
Falsgrave
G. & L.B. Sta.
Spa Saloon

Continued on Map 187

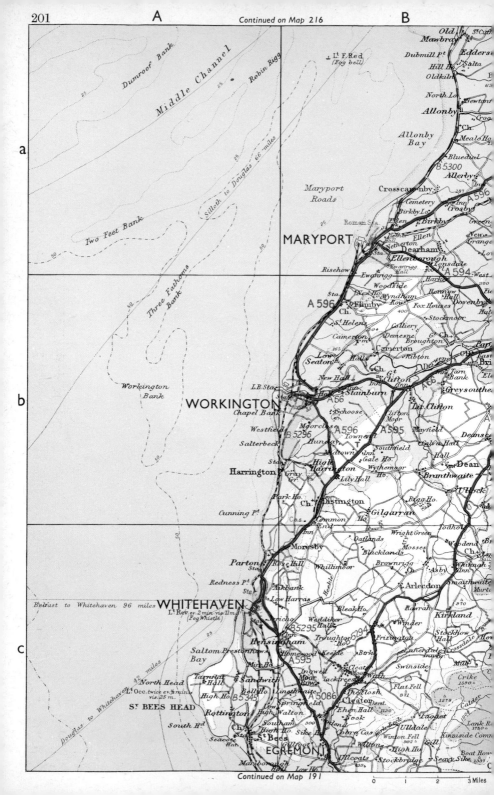

Continued on Map 216

A   B

a

b

c

Dumroof Bank

Middle Channel

Robin Rigg

25

45

25

Siloth to Douglas 66 miles

Two Feet Bank

50

Three Fathoms Bank

50

Workington Bank

50

Belfast to Whitehaven 96 miles

Douglas to Whitehaven 52 miles

Lt. F. Red (Fog bell)

Old
Mawbray
St. Cuth
Dubmill Pt
Edders
Hill Ho.
Salta
Oldkiln
North Lo.
Newtont
Allonby
Ch.
Groo
Allonby Bay
Mealo Ho.
Bluedial
B 5300
Allerby
Inn
Crosscanonby
A 596
Crosby
Green
Maryport Roads
Cemetery
Birkby Lo.
Birkby
New
Grange
Roman Sta.
Ellen
Ellen
New
Hall
Netherton
Dearham
Lo
MARYPORT
Sta.
Ellenborough
Ewanrigg
Lonsdale
Ha.
Risehow
Ewanrigg
Hall
A 594
West
Woodside
300
Harflo
Sta.
New Ho.
Wyndham
Row
Hennow
Hall
Dovenby
A 596
Flimby
400
Fox Houses
Hall
Ch.
St. Helens
Colliery
Stockmoor
Cameron
Demesne
Gt. Ch.
Pap
Fm.
Broughton
East
165
Camerton
Ch.
Bri
Low
Seaton
Hall
Ribton
Derwent
Tam
Bank
El
New Hall
Ch.
G.
Clifton
Inn
Greysouthe
L.B. Sta.
Stainburn
A 66
Lit. Clifton
WORKINGTON
Sta.
Schoose
Clifton
Moor
Mayfield
Deans
Chapel Bank
A 66
A 596
A 595
Westfield
Moorclose
Townend
T
Southfield
Calva
Hall
Hall
B 5296
Hundith
Inn
Gale Ho.
Dean
Salterbeck
Midtown
Wythemoor
Branthwaite
Sta.
High
Harrington
Lily Hall
Rigg Ho.
Ullock
Harrington
Gray
Gr.
Park Ho.
Ch.
Distington
Gilgarran
Todhol
Cunning Pt.
Cas.
Common
End
Inn
Oatlands
Wright Green
Mosses
Wodena
Ch.
Moresby
Blacklands
Brownrigg
Ch.
Asby
Whinnah
Inn
Parton
Rose Hill
Whillimoor
Heeke
Arlecdon
Smaithwaite
Sta.
Murt
Redness Pt.
Arkbank
Bleak Ho.
Rawrah
Kirkland
Sta.
Low Harras
Waddiker
Hall
Winder
Stockhow
Hall
WHITEHAVEN
Inn
B 5295
Troughton
A 594
Frizington
Linhardale
Crossdale
Ho
Lt. Rev. ev. 2 min. vis. 11 m. (Fog Whistle)
Hensingham
Homewood
Keele
Birks
Swinside
Mill
Saltom
Prestonhows
Bay
A 595
Moor
Row
Cleat
moor
Flat Fell
Crike
1596
Mine Ho.
Inawell
Blackree
Swith
871
North Head
Tarnflat
Hall
Sandwith
A 5086
Thwflosh
1278
Lank R.
1760
Lt. Occ. twice ev. ½ min. vis. 25 m.
Bell Ho.
Linethwaite
Springfield
Cleaton
Ehen Hall
250
Boat How
1537
High Ho.
B 5345
High Walton
Nook
St. **BEES HEAD**
Rottington
Low
High Walton
300
Heng
Ulldale
South H.
Southam
Winton Fell
502
Gill
Seacote
Ho.
St. **Bees**
Cas.
Whing
High Ho.
Seaz Sike
Ch.
Wilcoats
Stockbridge
EGREMONT
Marlboro
Low Ho.
450

Continued on Map 191

0   1   2   3 Miles

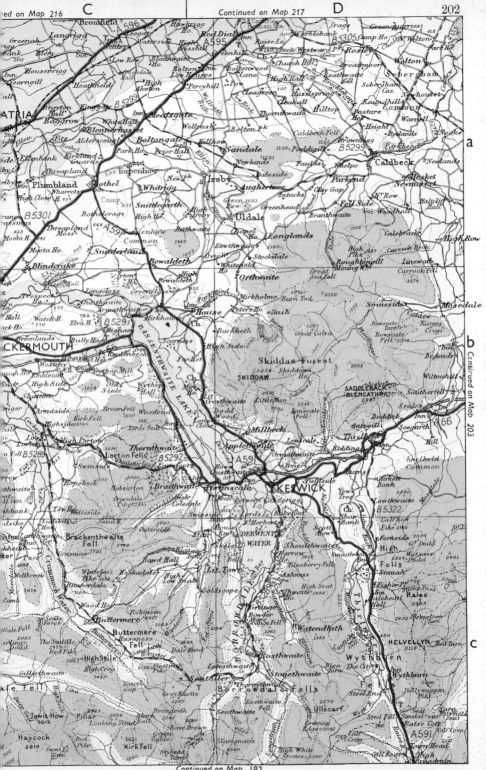

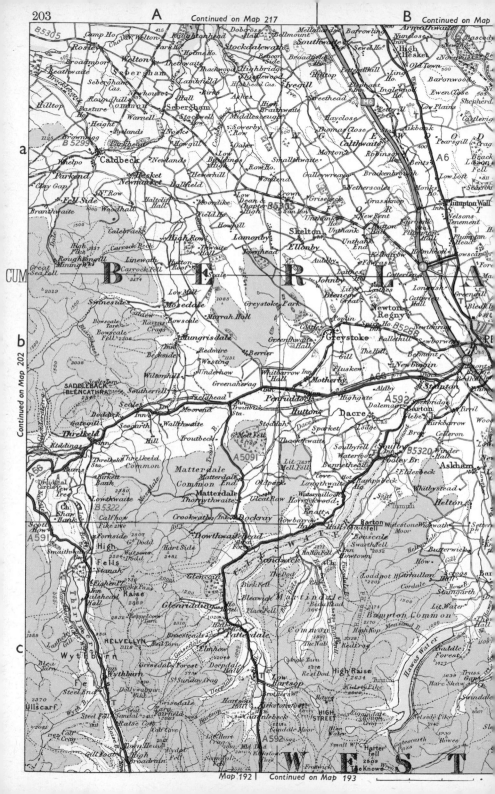

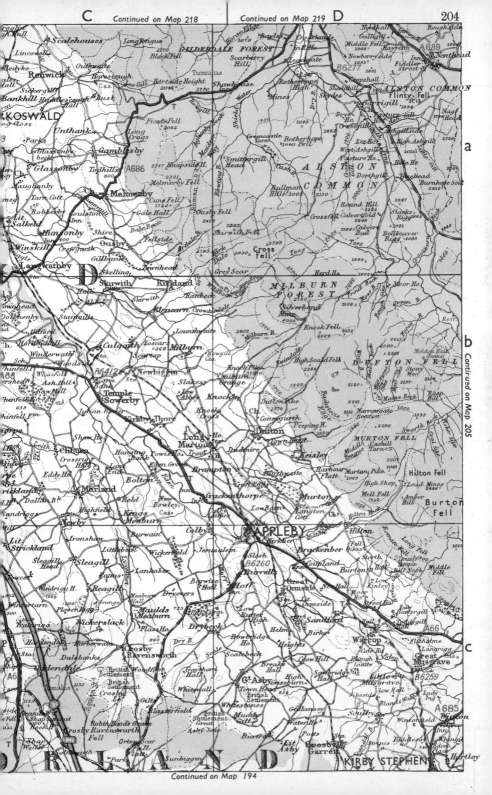

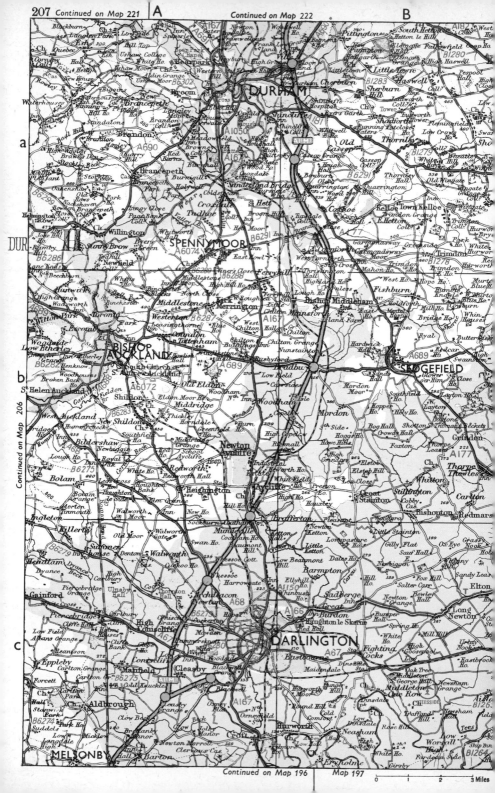

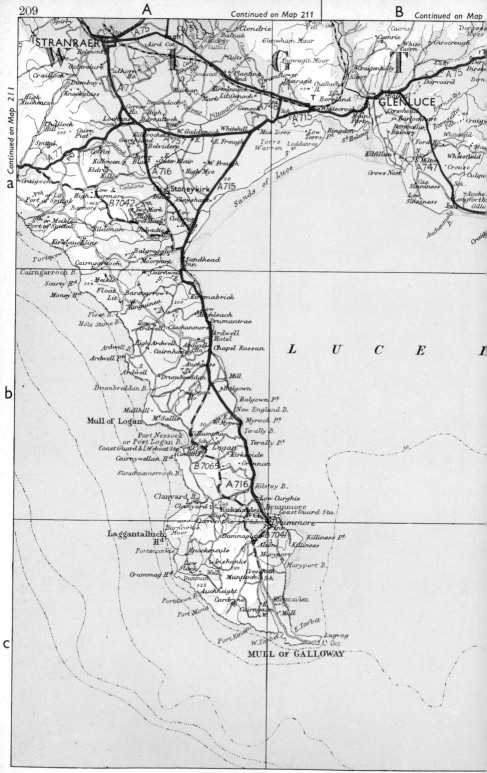

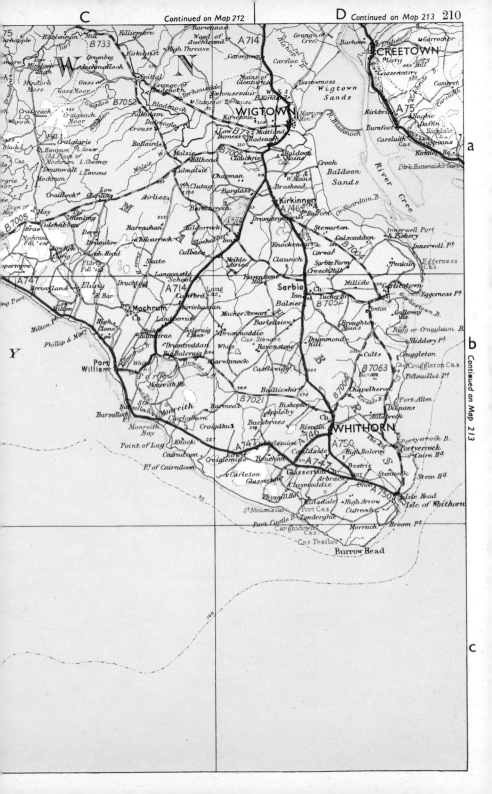

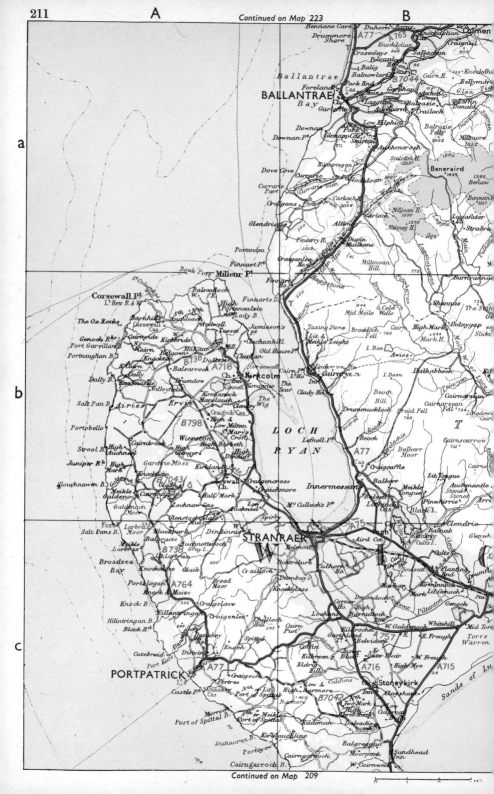

a

BALLANTRAE

Ballantrae
Bay

Beneraird

b

**LOCH
RYAN**

c

STRANRAER

PORTPATRICK

Stoneykirk

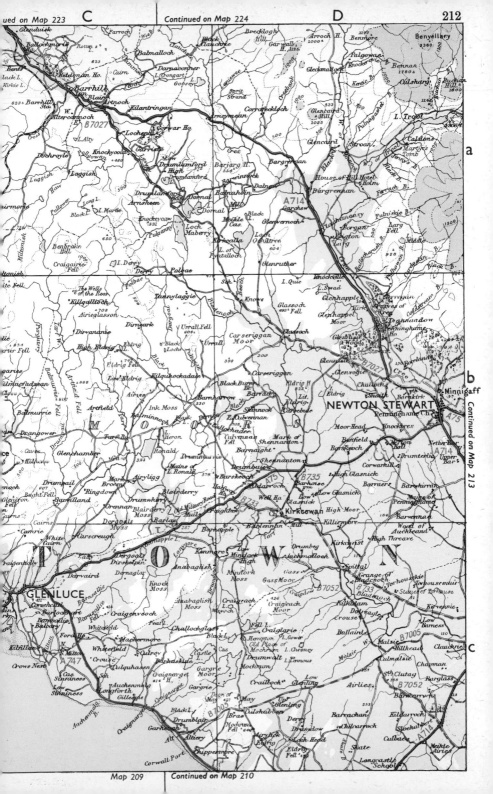

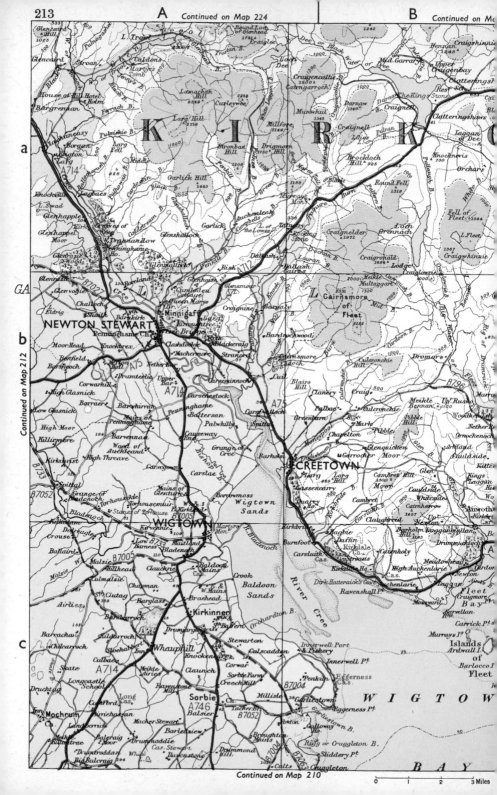

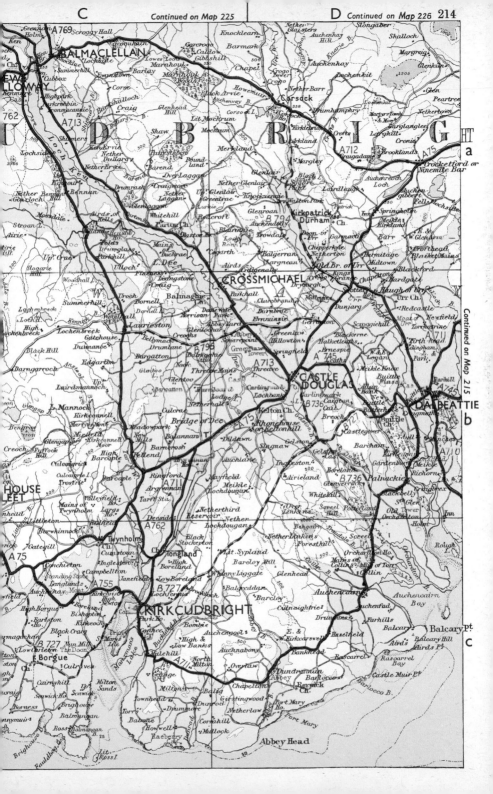

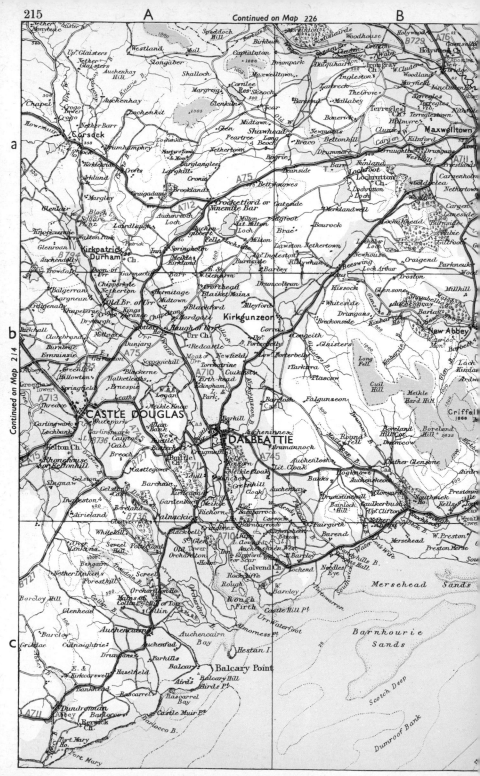

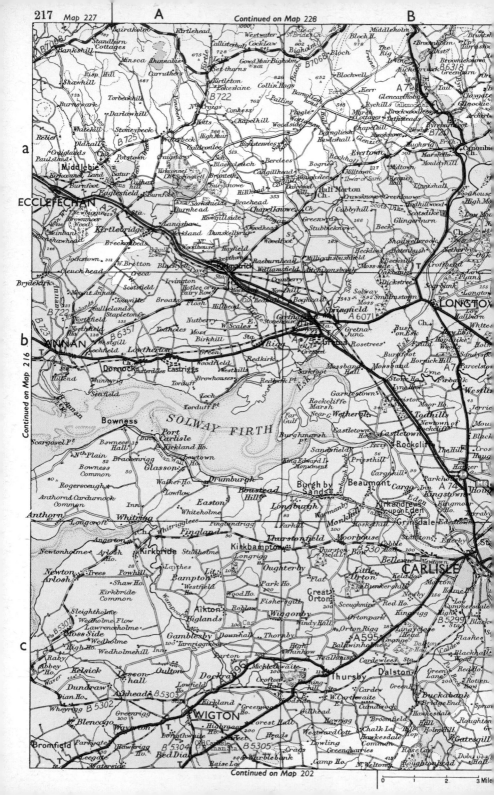

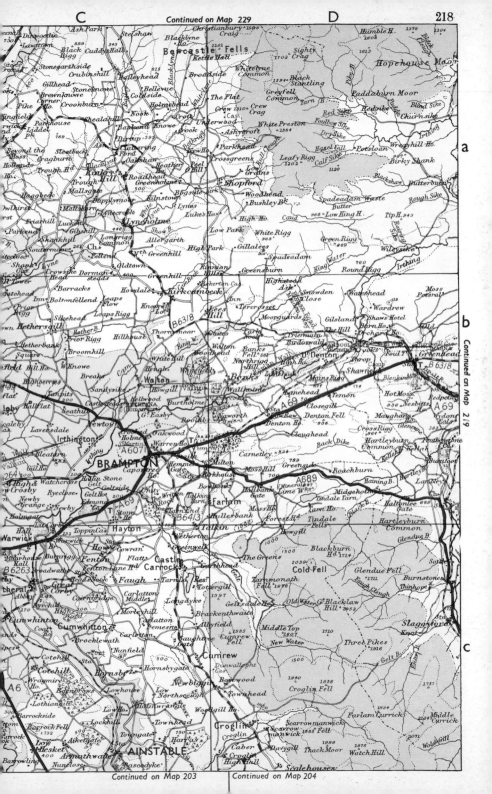

Continued on Map 218

HALTWHISTLE

PLENMELLER COMMON

ALSTON

WHITFIELD MOOR

Cold Fell

Hopehouse Moor

Thirlwall Common

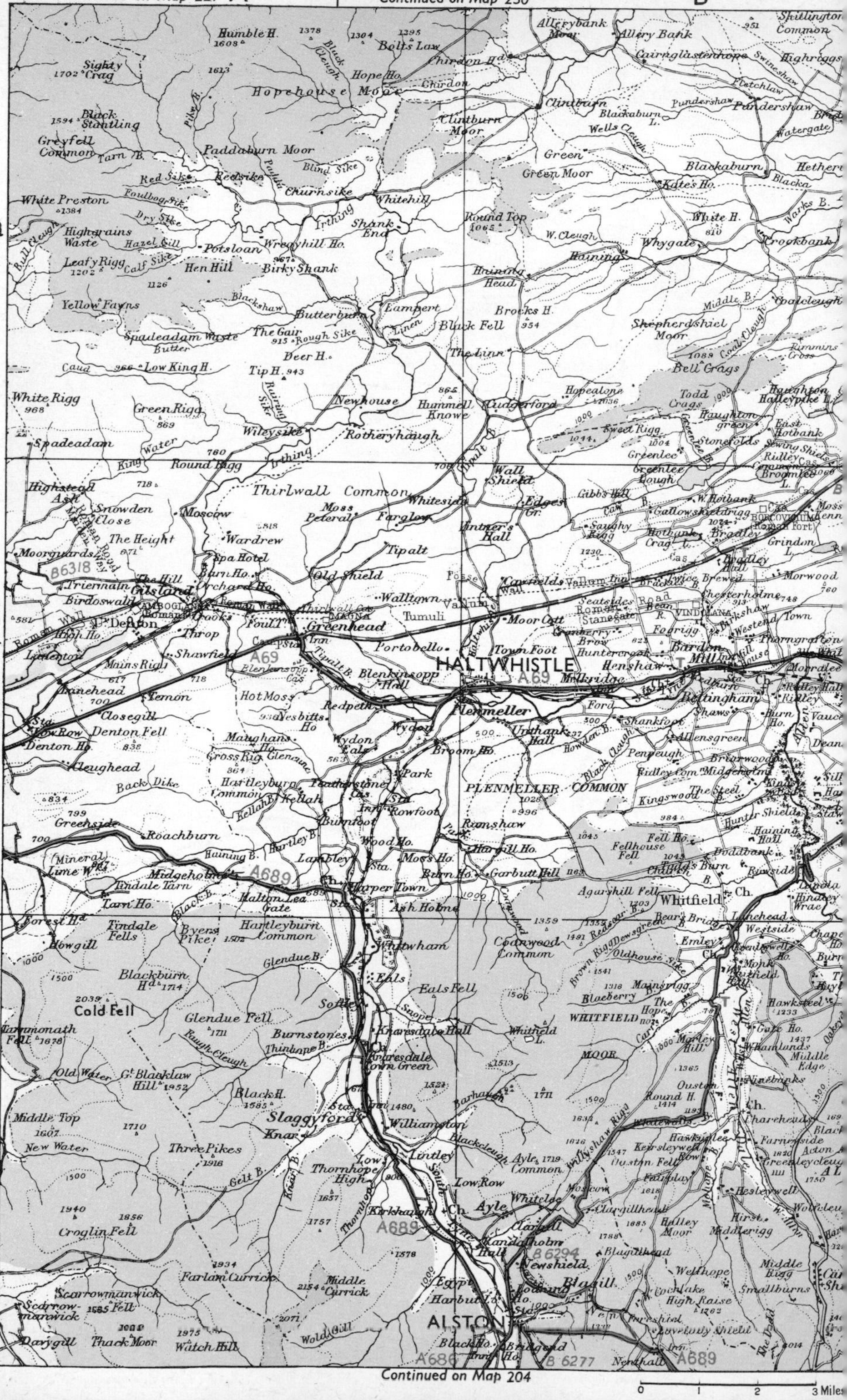

Gilsland

Slaggyford

Whitfield

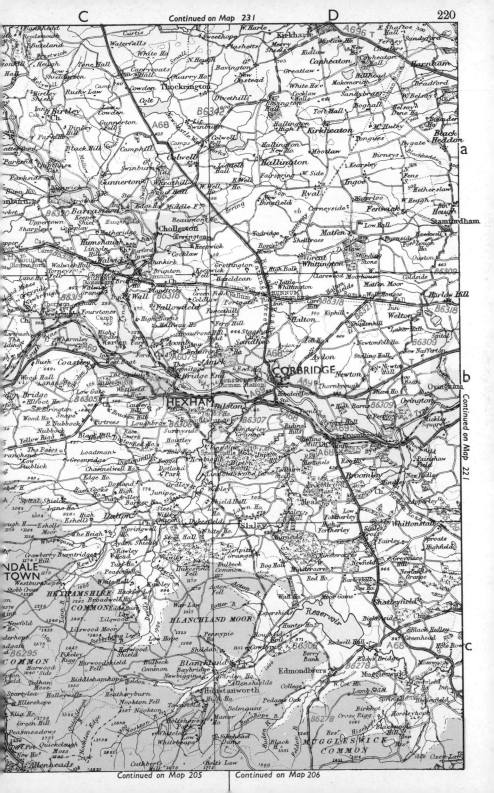

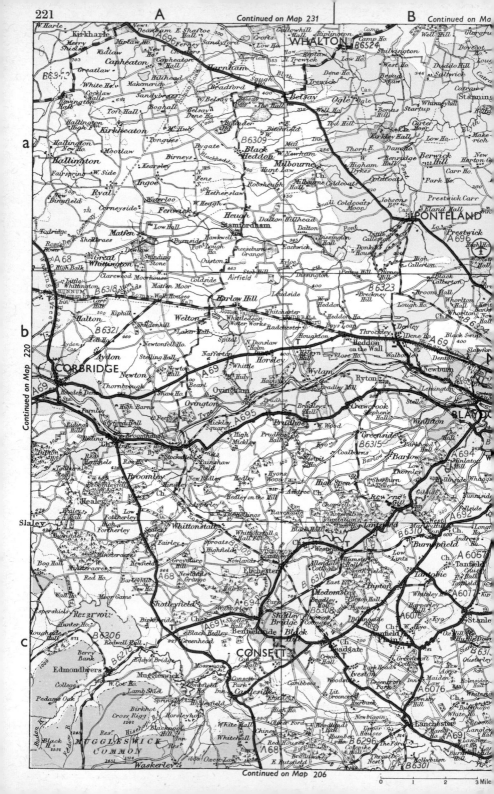

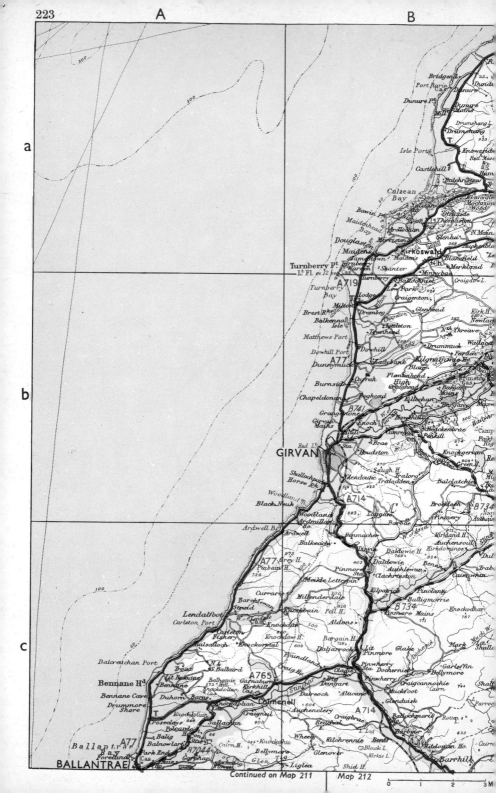

A   B

a

b

c

Bridgend
Port Carrie
Dunure P.
Dunure
Dunure
Castle
Drumshang
Knoweside
Red Moss
Isle Port
Castlehill
Colzean
Bay
Bawin
Maidenhead
Bay
Colzean
Ardlochan
Thomaston
N. Main
Glenhut
Douglaston
Morriston
Kirkoswald
Maidens
Jamestown
Maidens
Turnberry Pt
Turnberry
Warren
Shanter
Blanefield
Ch.
Merkland
Craigdow L.
L* Fl. ev 12 sec
Turnberry
Minnybae
Bogside
Low Park
A719
Turnberry
Bay
Lodge
Craigenton
Milton
Drambeg
Glenhead
Kirk H.
Newlan
Brest Rks
Balkenna
Isle
Chapelton
Littleton
Townhead
N* Threave
Matthews Port
Dowhill
Drummuck
Wallace
Dowhill Port
A77
Dowhill
Sauchbank
Farden
Kilgrammie
Dunnymuck
Blair
Plaininhead
High
Craighead
Killochan
Bargany
Mains
Bargany
Burnside
Ourah
Chapeldonan
Poghead
B741
Grangeston
Enoch
Hanchulie
Brackenbrae
Girvan
Mains
Conrennie
Knockgerran
Green
Red L*
Mill
Brae
GIRVAN
Sta.
Houdston
Shallochpark
Horse Rk.
Saugh H.
Glendoune
Bradord
Tralodden
Balclatchie
Woodland
Black Neuk
A714
Laggan
Barbae
Brockloch
B734
Pinwerry
Ardwell Bay
Woodland
Ardmillan
do.
Benmacher
Ardwell
Balkeachy
Dinvin
Kirdland H.
Auchensoul
Kirkdominae
Percy H.
Daldowie H.
Piabain
A77
Pinmore
Sta.
Daldowie
Auchlewan
Clachriston
Curnawan
Trab
Meikle Letterpin
Kilpatrick
Findlarty
Currarie
Strand
Millenderdale
Balligmorrie
Knockodhar
Bardelman
B734
Pinmore Mains
Lendalfoot
Knockbain
Fell H.
Aldons
Carleton Port
Knockdaw H.
Bargain H.
Daljarrock
Lit
Pinmore
Glake
Mark
Balsalloch
Knockorsnal
Houndland
Pinwherry
Sta.
Docherniel
Garleffin
Cairn
Balcreuchan Port
Traboch
N. &
S. Ballaird
Craig H.
Claqu
Dangart
Pinwherry
Craigannochie
Cairn
Bennane H*
Lit Bennane
Balhamie
Garnaburn
Kirkhill
Stinchar
Dairoch
Alacan
Muickfoot
Glenduisk
Duhorn
Barns
Knockdolian
Cas.
Colmonell
Auchencrory
A714
Barbour
Bennane Cave
Drummore
Shore
Knockdolian
Craignail
Craigbrae
Ballochgarrie
Roten
Croseclays
Sallochan
Reuthel
Balig
Balnowlart
Wheel
Kilchrennie
Benet
Kildavan Ho.
Cairn
Ballantrae
Bay
Foreland
A77
Balig
Park End
Cas.
Garphar
Cairn H.
Knockchu
Bellymore
Glenover
Black L.
Kirkie L.
A7044
BALLANTRAE
Liglea
Shid If.
Barrhill

0   1   2
3 M

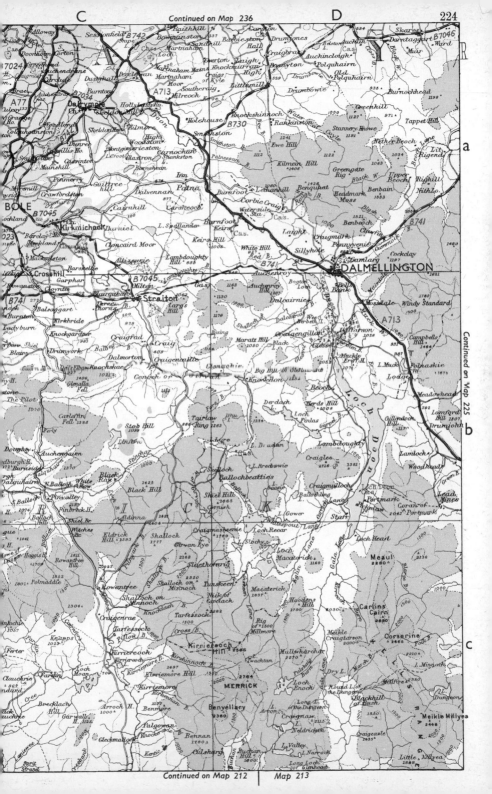

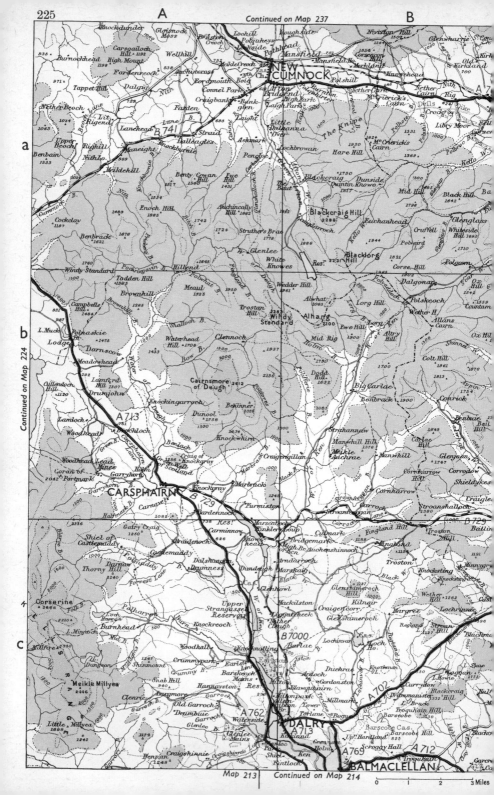

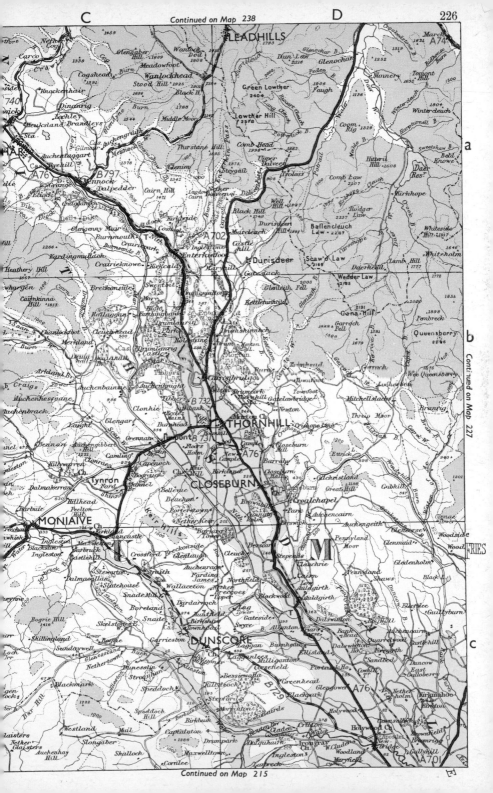

Continued on Map 238
Continued on Map 215
Continued on Map 227

LEADHILLS
Wanlockhead
Meadowfoot

A74

B797
B702
B732
B729

A76
A702
A701

MONIAIVE
THORNHILL
CLOSEBURN
DUNSCORE
Tynron
Durisdeer
Queensberry

Green Lowther
Lowther Hill
Comb Head
Upper Dalveen
Durisdeer Hill
Wedder Law
Gana Hill

Manner
Winterclough
Kirkhope
Whiteside Hill
Daer Res.

Continued on Map 215

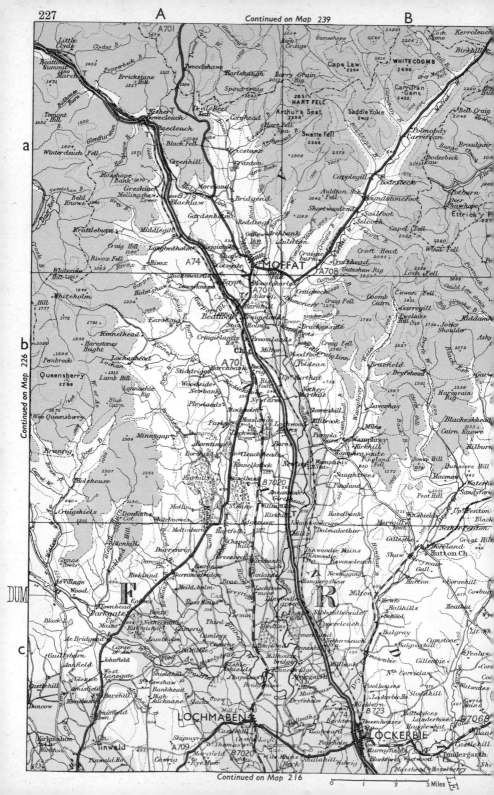

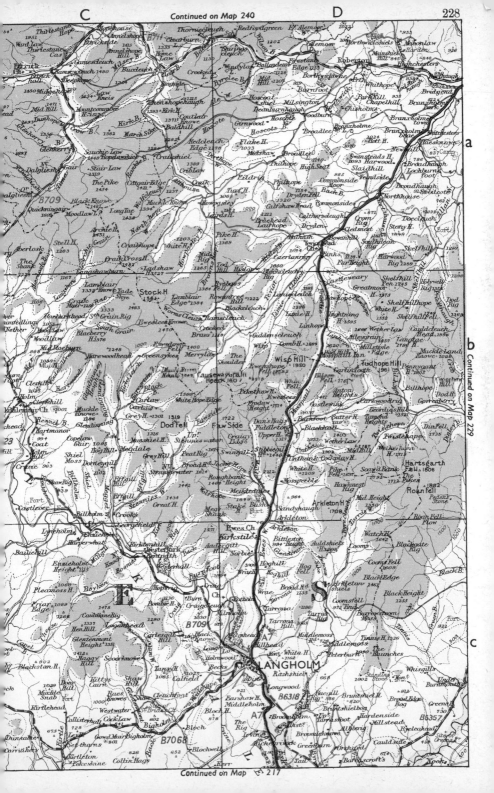

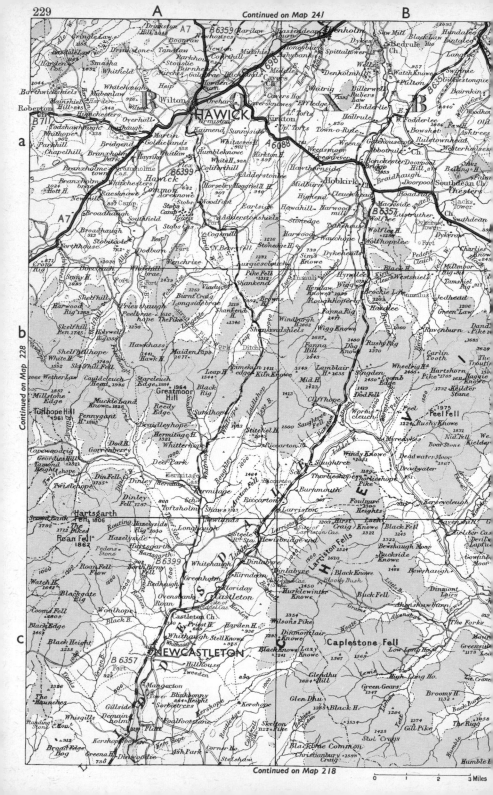

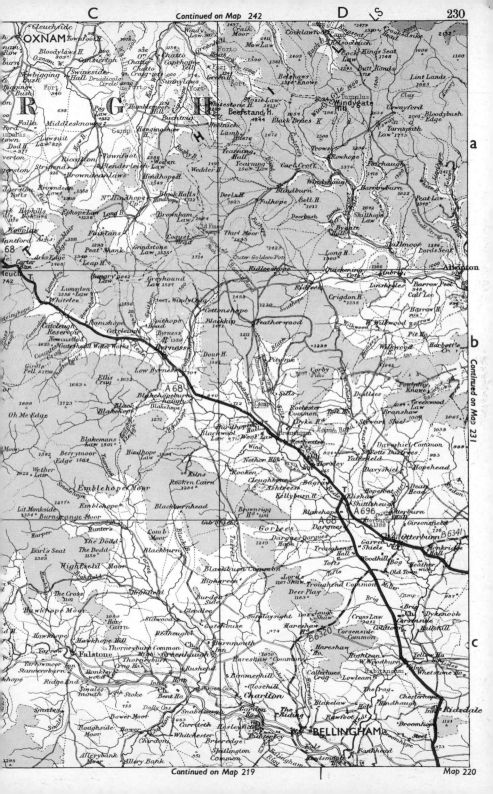

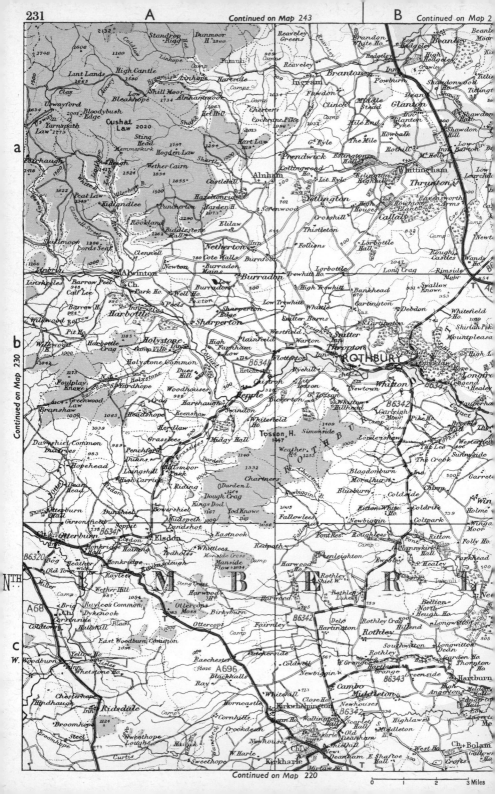

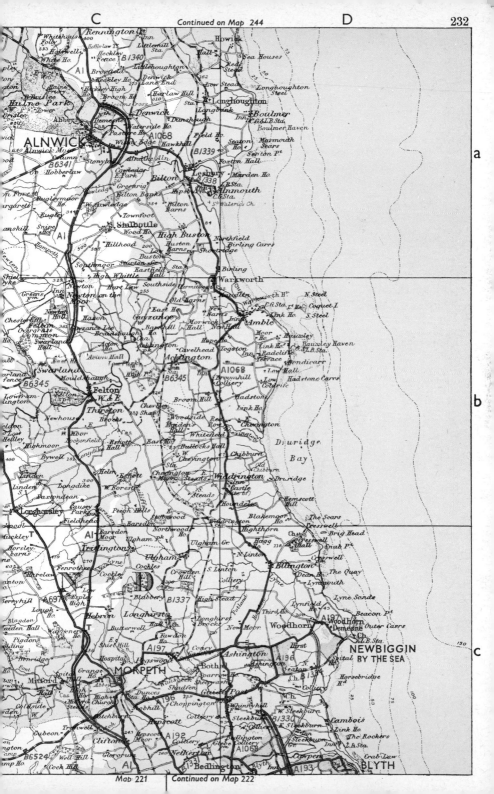

a

b

c

Map 221   Continued on Map 222

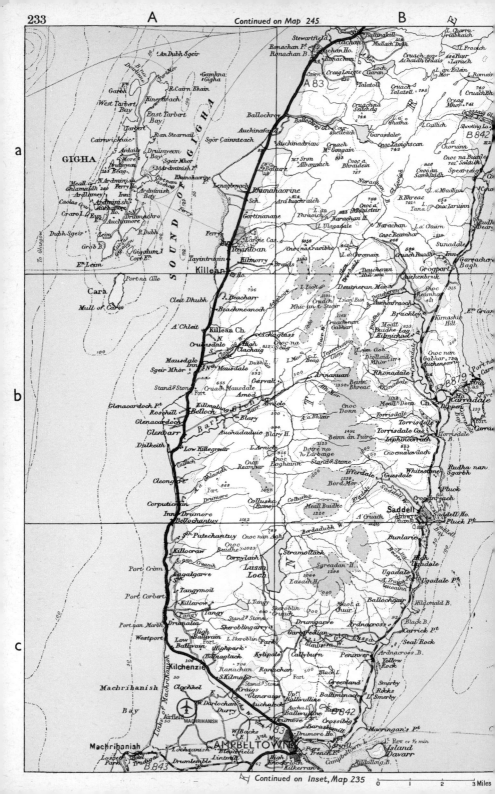

0   1   2   3 Miles

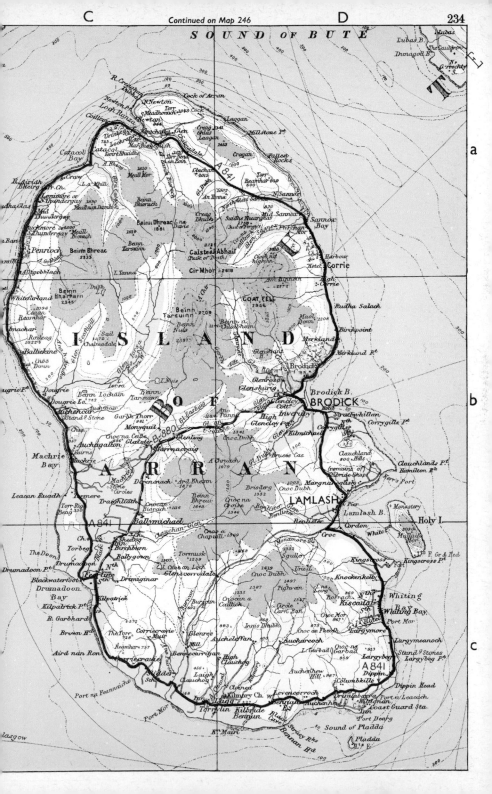

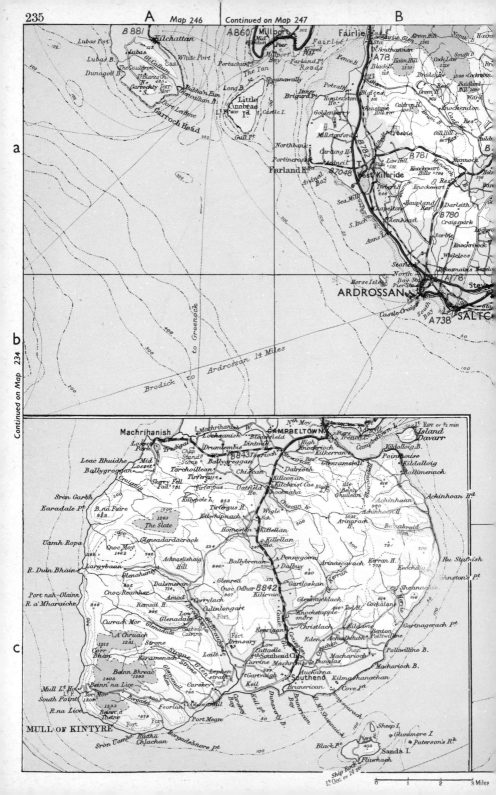

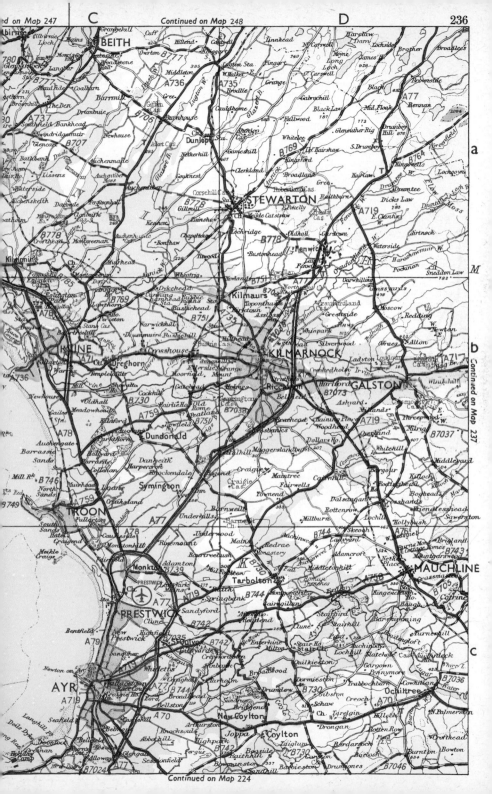

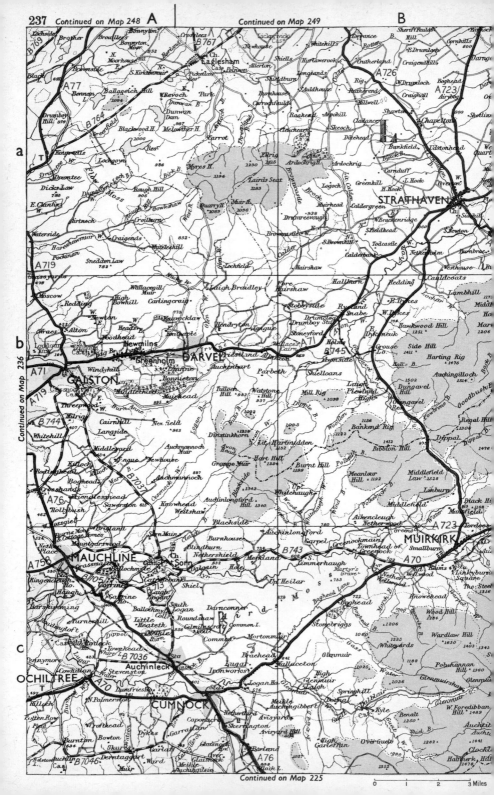

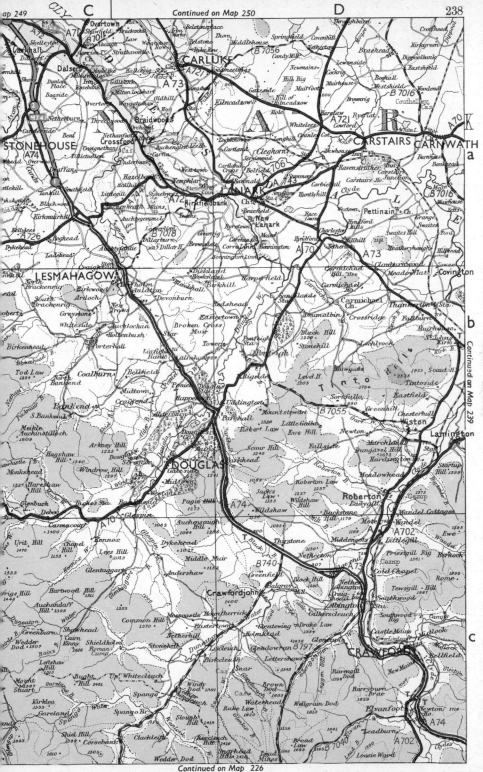

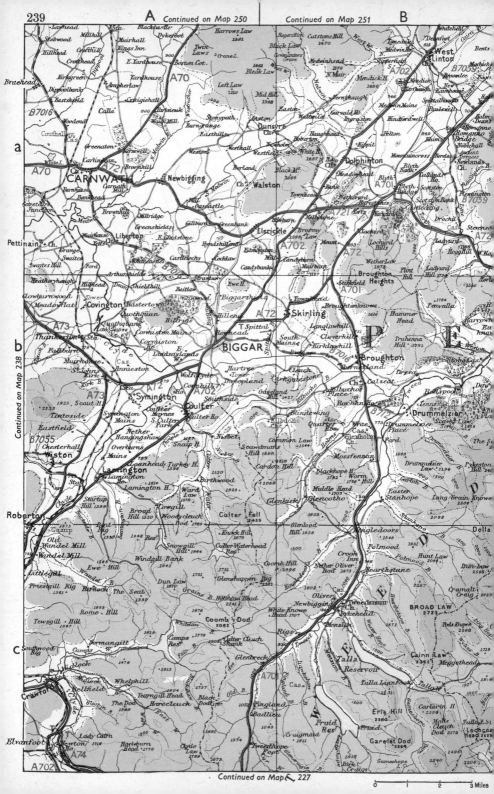

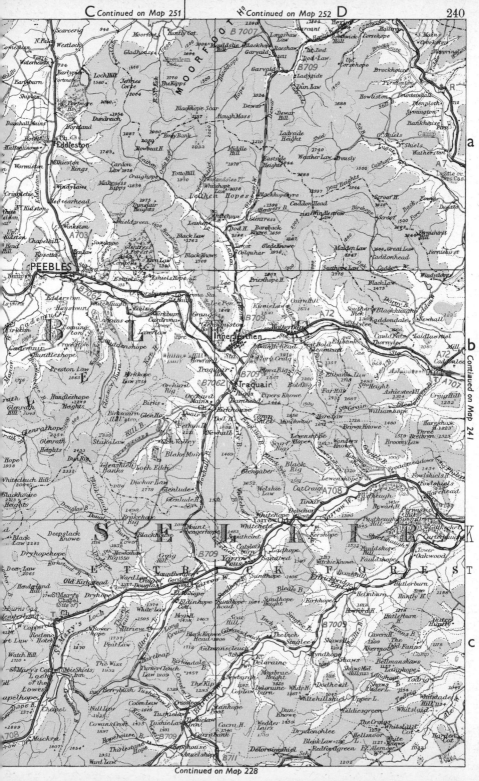

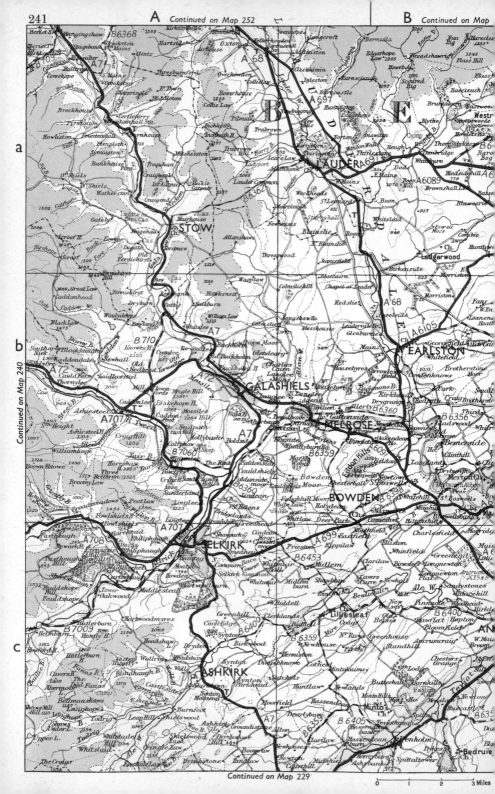

Continued on Map 252

Continued on Map

Continued on Map 240

Continued on Map 229

A

B

E

a

b

c

STOW

GALASHIELS

MELROSE

EARLSTON

BOWDEN

SELKIRK

ASHKIRK

LAUDER

0   1   2   3 Miles

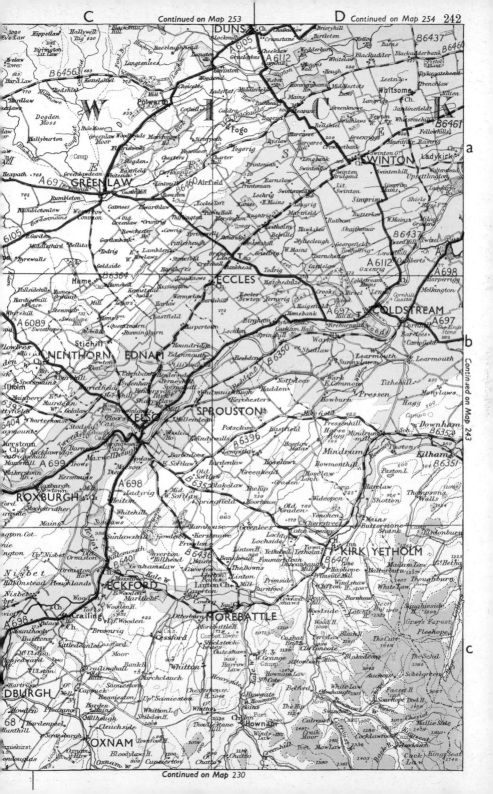

a

b

c

BERWICK UPON TWEED

COLDSTREAM

WOOLER

Norham

Ladykirk

Whitsome

Swinton

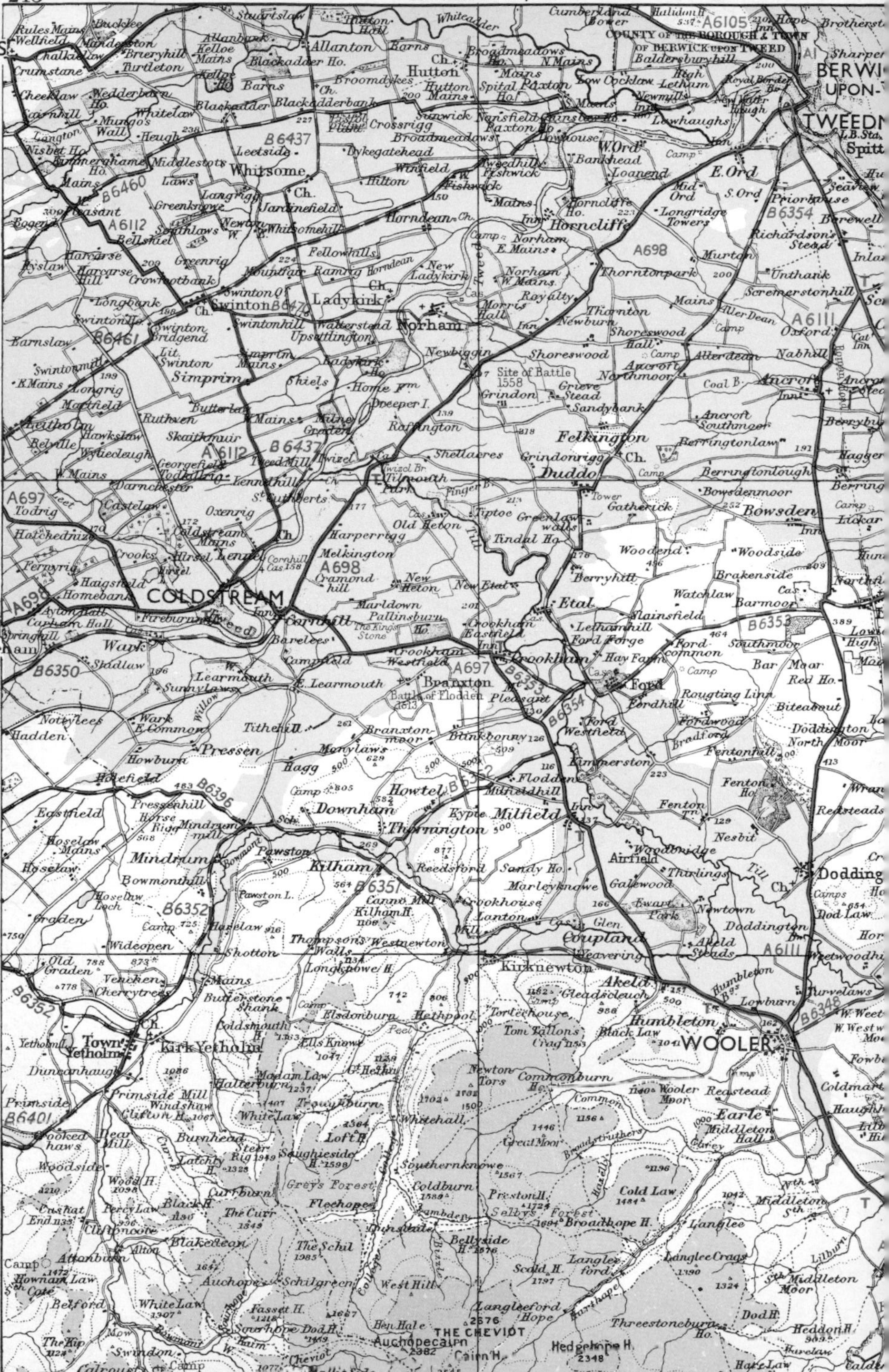

Simprim

Duddo

Bowsden

Ancroft

Etal

Ford

Milfield

Branxton

Crookham

Howtel

Downham

Kilham

Mindrum

Kirknewton

Humbleton

Earle

Town Yetholm

Kirk Yetholm

THE CHEVIOT
2676

Comb Fell

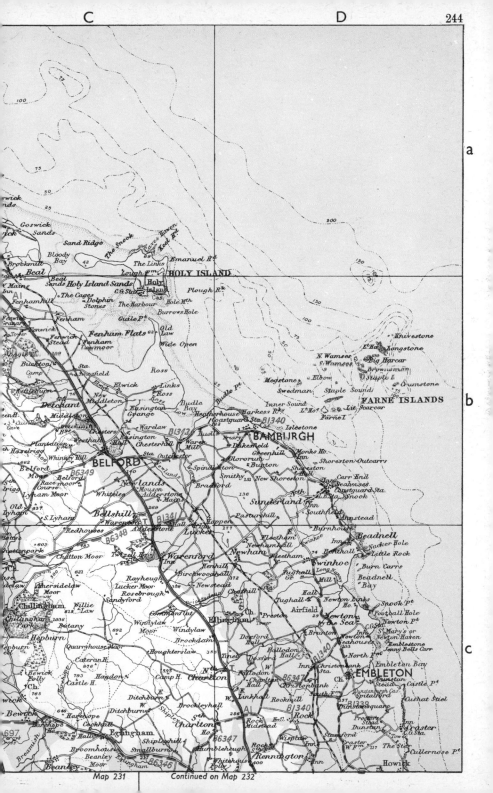

a

b

c

HOLY ISLAND

Holy Island Sands

Holy Island

The Harbour

Fenham Flats

Old Law

Wide Open

Ross

Links Ross

Budle Bay

N Wamses

S Wamses

Knivestone

Longstone

Big Harcar

Brownsman

Staple I.

Crumstone

FARNE ISLANDS

Megstone

Elbow

Swedman

Inner Sound

Staple Sound

Scarcar

Farne I.

BAMBURGH

Harkess Rks.

Coastguard Sta.

Islestone

Heatherhouse

Ware Mill

Dukesfield

Shoreston Outcarrs

Glororum

Greenhill

Monks Ho.

BELFORD

Chesterhill

Spindlestone

Burton

Shoreston

Carr End

Seahouses

Outchester

Smithy

New Shoreston

Coastguard Sta.

Newlands

Bradford

Nth.

Snook

Adderstone

Mousen

Sunderland

Southfield

Bellshill

Pasturehill

Innstead

Warenton

Hoppen

Burnhouse

Beadnell

Nacker Hole

Adderstone

Lucker

Fleetham

Swinhoe

Little Rock

Warenford

Newham

Fleetham

Benthall

Birchwoodhall

Fenhill

Tughall

Burn Carrs

Rayheugh

Newstead

Mill

Beadnell Bay

Lucker Moor

Rosebrough

Chathill

Tughall Hall

Newton Links

Snook Pt.

Sandyford

Preston

Airfield

Newton by the Sea

Football Hole

Chillingham

Ellingham

Brunton

Newton Pt.

St. Mary's or Newton Haven

Windylaw

Doxford Hall

Seahouses

Embleston

Jenny Bell's Carr

Brockdam

Houghterslaw

Tiree

North Fm.

Embleton Bay

Quarryhouse Moor

Doxford

Christonbank

EMBLETON

Castle H.

Camp H.

N. Charlton

Balloden Hall

Christonbank

Dunstanburgh Cas.

Preston

Castle Pt.

Bewick

Charlton Hall

Chollerton

South Fm.

Spitalford

Cushat Stiel

Ditchburn

Brockleyhall

Linkhall

Rock

Proctor's Stead

Craster

Eglingham

Charlton Ho.

Rock Midstead

Dunstan

Howick

Shipleyhill

Rock

Wisptan

Craster

The Star

Broomhouse

Smallburns

Humbleheugh

Rennington

Stamford

Cullernose Pt.

Beanley Moor

Whitehouse Folly

Howick

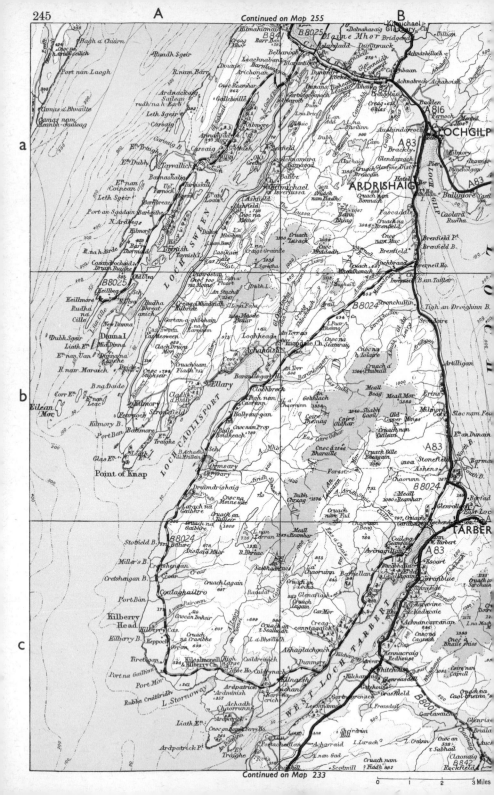

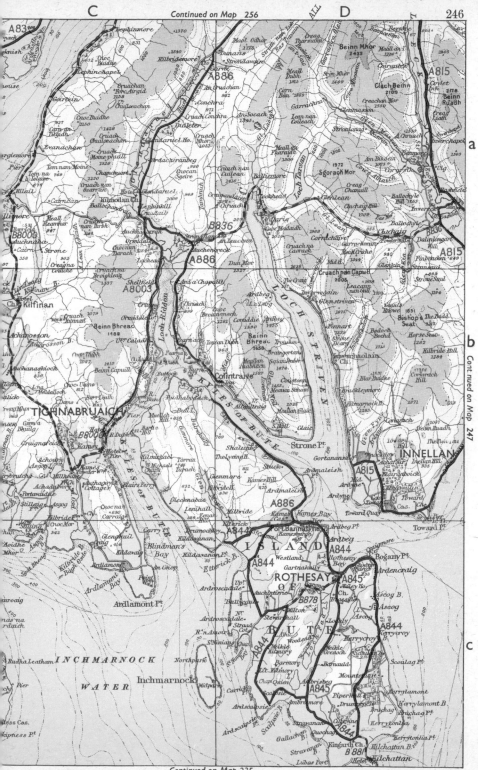

Continued on Map 246

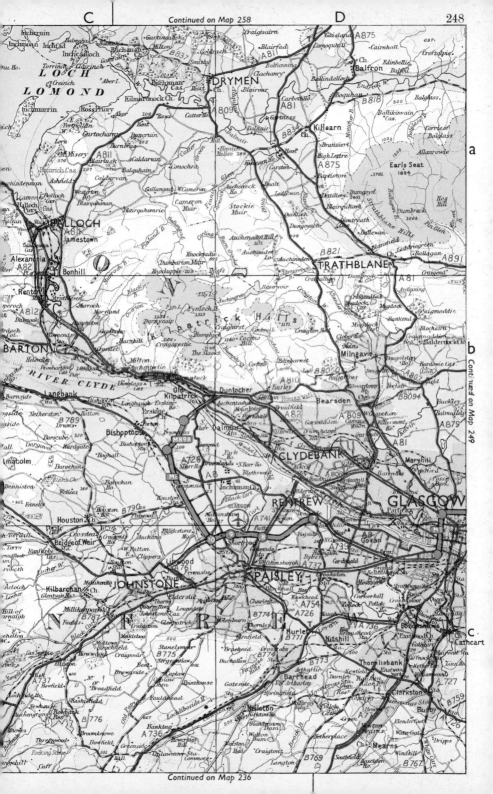

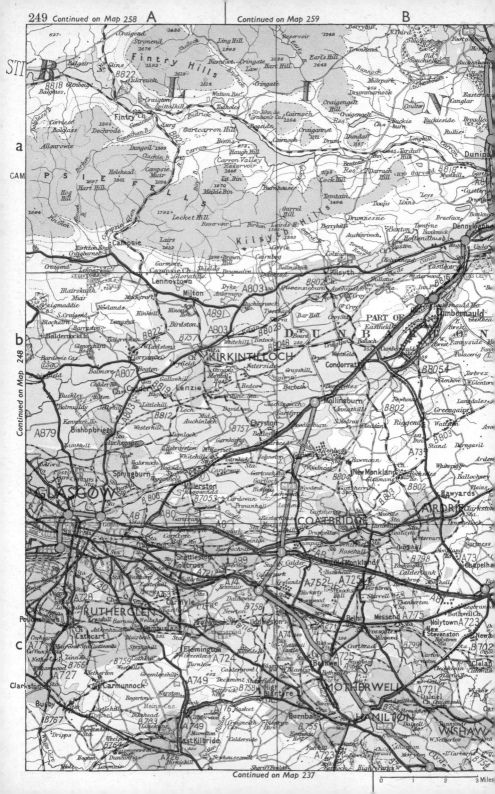

Continued on Map 258

Continued on Map 248

0   1   2   3 Miles

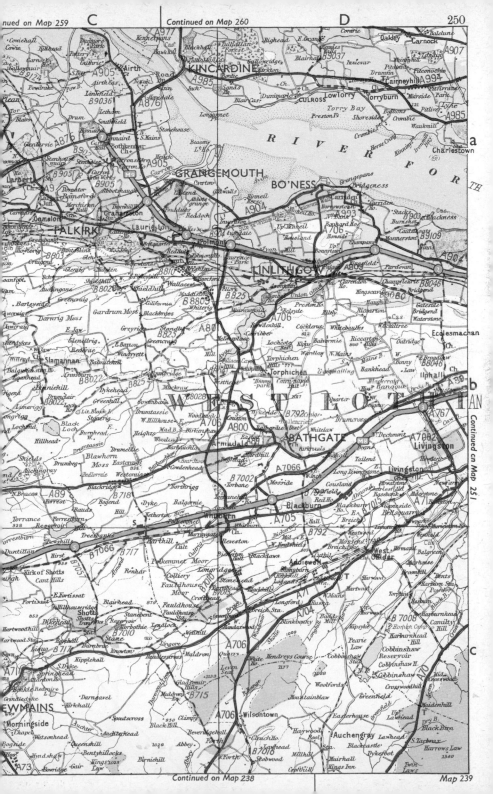

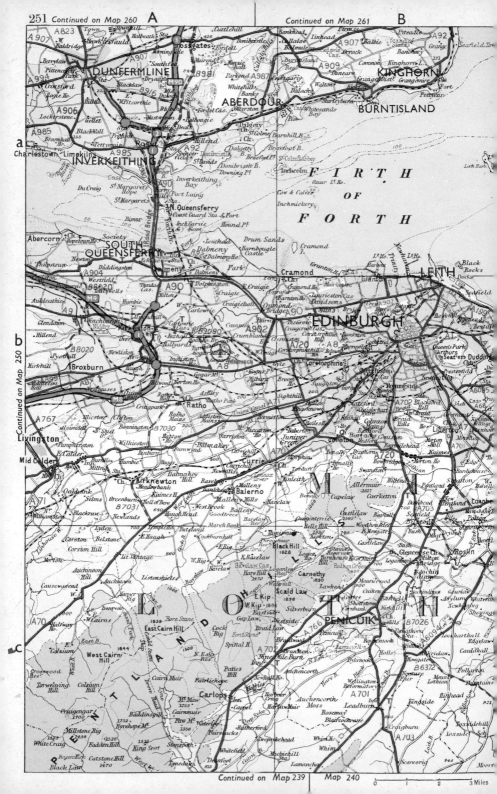

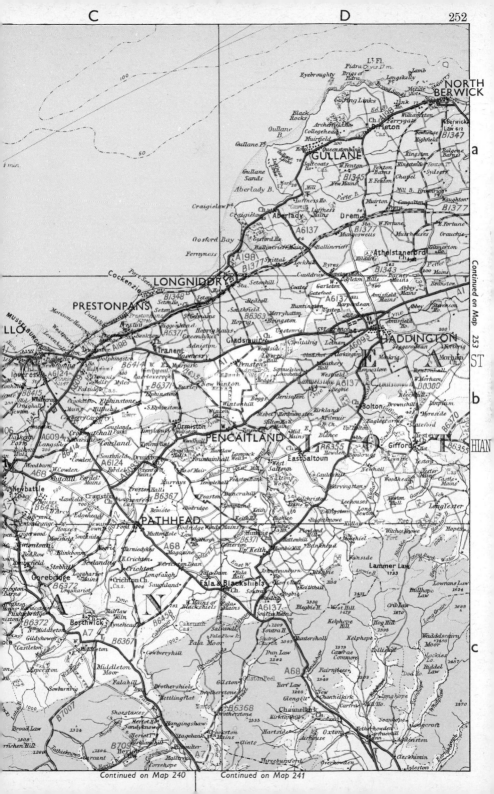

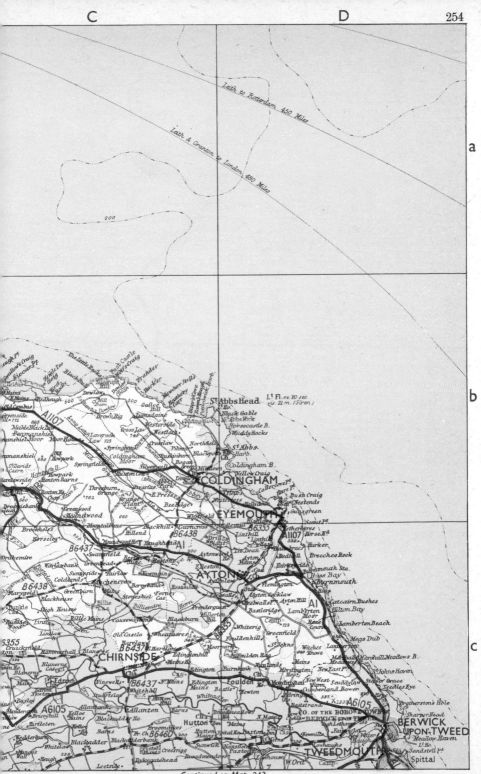

a

Leith to Rotterdam 450 Miles

Leith & Granton to London, 480 Miles

200

b

St. Abbs Head

Lt. Fl. ev. 10 sec.
vis. 21 m. (Siren)

Black Sable

Horsecastle B.

Widdy Rocks

St. Abbs

Harb.

Coldingham B.

Yellow Craig

COLDINGHAM

Callercoats

Bush Craig

Gunsgreen

EYEMOUTH

Westends

Nestends

Scout Pt.

B6355

Netherbrres

B6438

B1107

Hurker

B6437

A1

Breeches Rock

Eyemouth Sta.

AYTON

Gunsgreen Bay

Burnmouth

A1

Catcairn Bushes

Hilton Bay

Lamberton
Moor

Lamberton Beach

Megs Dub

B6438

Lamberton

Greenfield

St. Johns

Wiches
Knowe

Marshall Meadows B.

CHIRNSIDE

B6437

St. Johns Haven

Foulden

Staw of Grace

A6105

Needles Eye

New West

Gainslawland Bower

Hutton

BERWICK
UPON-TWEED

Fisher's Hole

Sharper Head

B6460

TWEEDMOUTH

Meadow Haven

Sandstell Pt.

Spittal

Continued on Map 243

c

OBAN

KILNINVER

KILMELFORD

KILMARTIN

Kilbride

Kilmore

Loch Feochan

LOCH MELFORT

Ford Inn

Seil

Easdale

Luing

Shuna

Scarba

Craignish

Kerrera

Insh

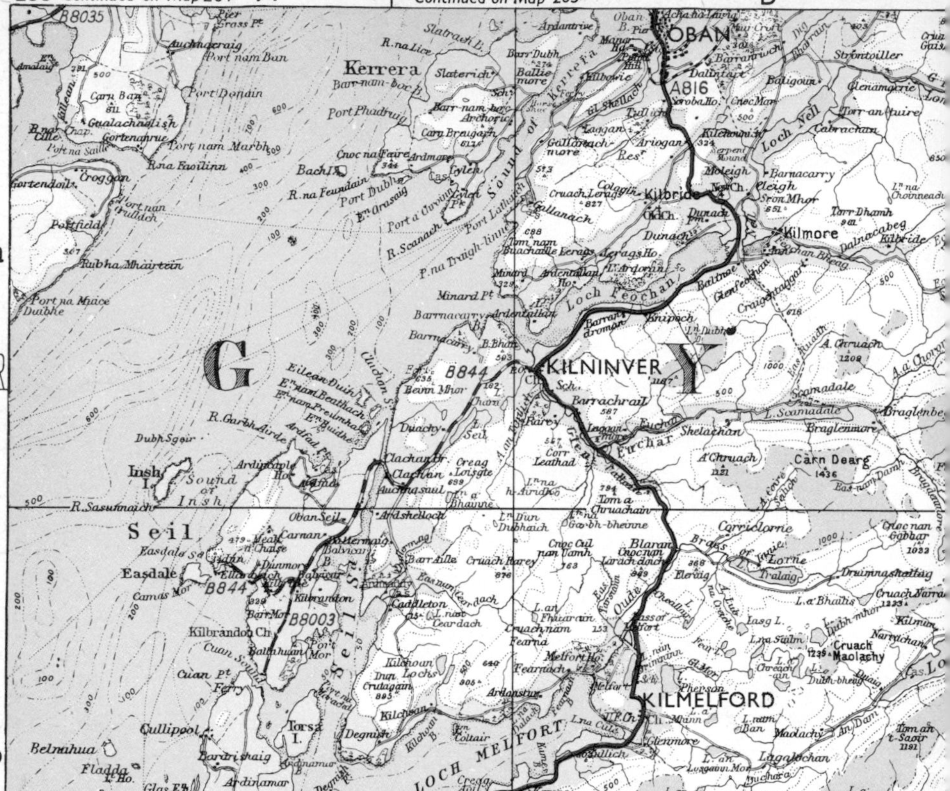

0   1   2   3 Miles

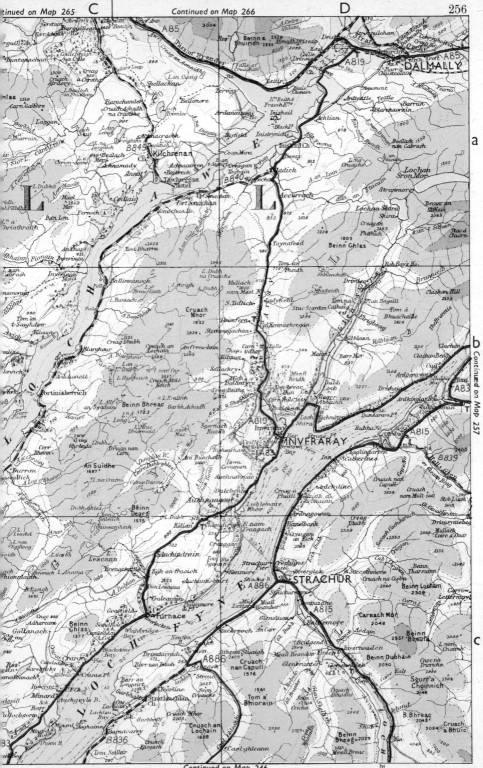

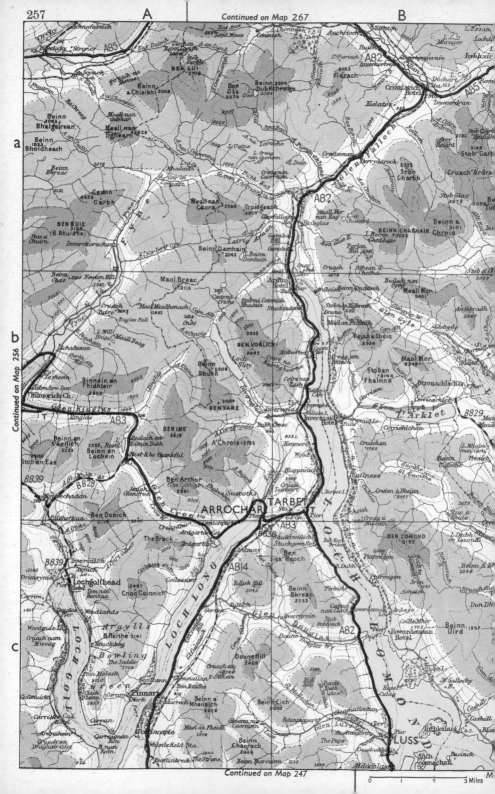

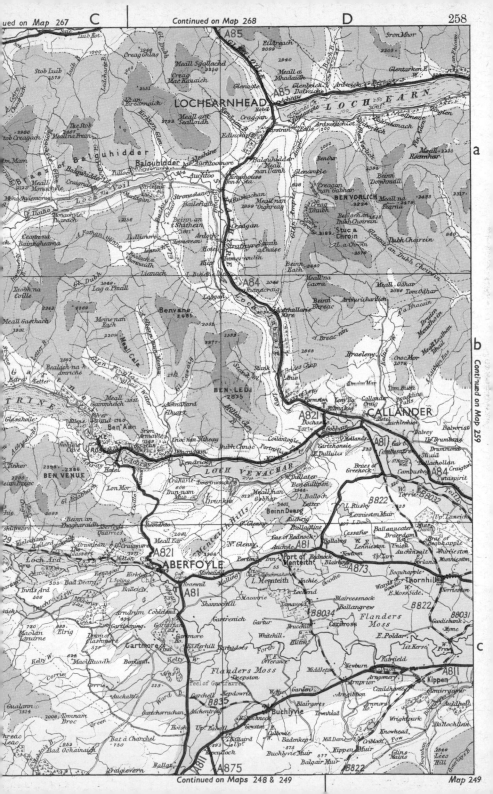

LOCHEARNHEAD

LOCH EARN

BEN VORLICH
·3224·

Stuc a
Chroin

BALQUHIDDER
Braes of Balquhidder

Benvane
·2685·

BEN LEDI
·2875·

Ben A'an

BEN VENUE

CALLANDER

A821

A81

LOCH VENACHAR

Menteith Hills

B822

A84

ABERFOYLE

A821

A81

Port of
Menteith

A873

THORNHILL

Flanders
Moss

B822

Flanders Moss

Buchlyvie

A875

A811

Kippen

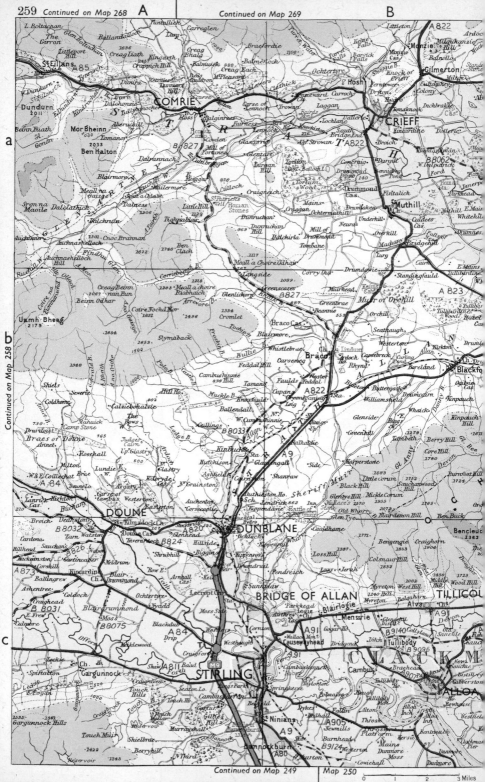

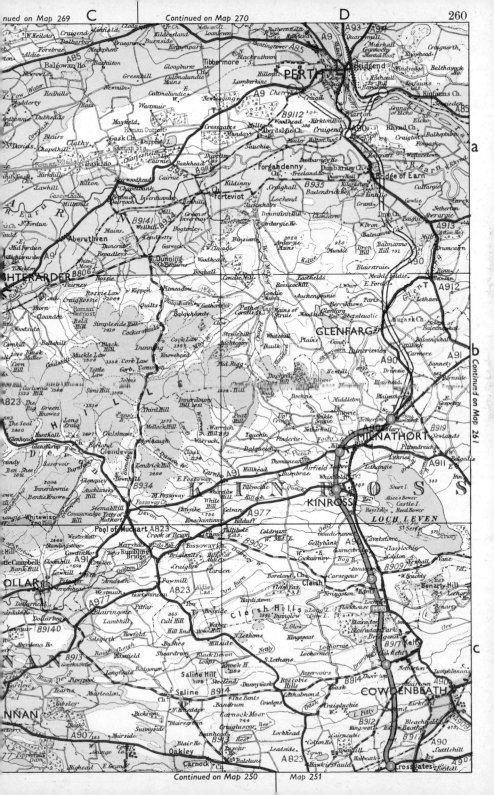

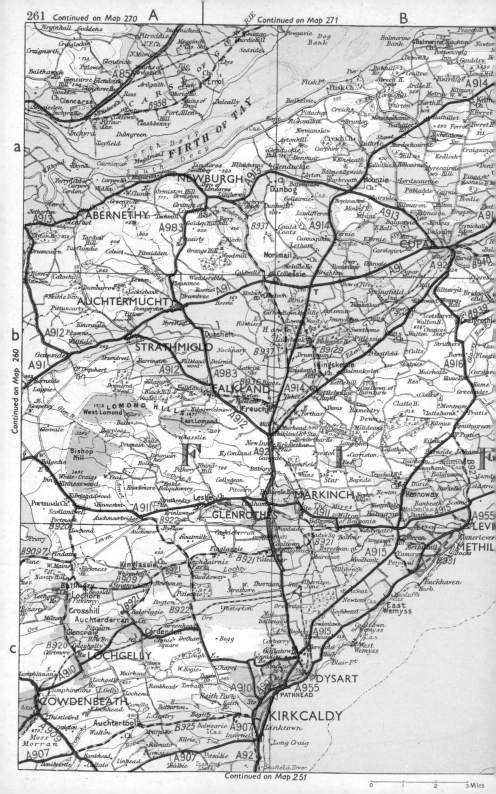

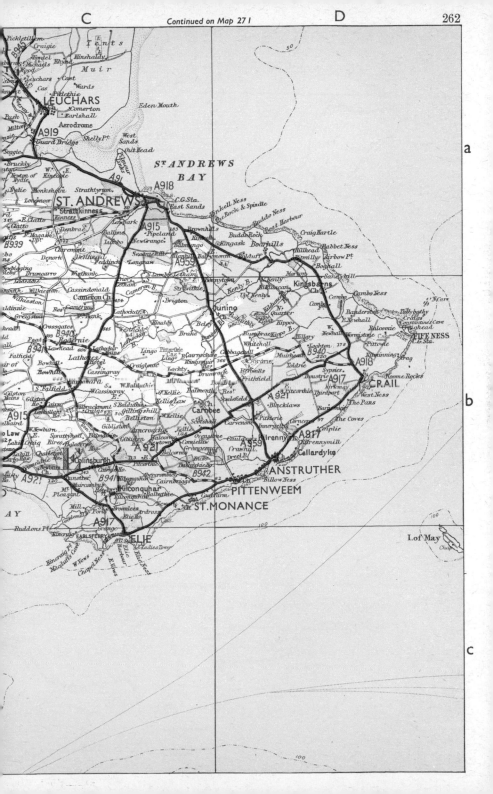

C
D
a
b
c

ST. ANDREWS BAY

LEUCHARS
A919
Guard Bridge
Aerodrome
Comerton
Earlshall
Eden Mouth
West Sands
Out Head
Shelly Pt.

A91
A918
ST. ANDREWS
A915
Strathkinness
East Sands
Kinkell Ness
The Rock & Spindle
Buddo Ness

B939
A959
Balmungo
Kingask
Boarhills
CraigHartle
Babbet Ness
Kirbow Pt.
Hillhead
Boghall

Cameron Ch.
Dunino
Kenly B.
Kingsbarns Ch.
Cambo Ness
Cambo

Brake
Kippo
Hillary
Lochton
B940
Toldrie
Sypsies
FIFE NESS
Fife Lt. Sta.
Boome Rocks

Lathones
A917
Kirkmay
Thirdpart
West Ness
The Coves
CRAIL
The Pans
Barnsmuir

A915
Craig
A921
Carnbee
A959
Kilrenny
Cellardyke
ANSTRUTHER

Colinsburgh
B941
B942
PITTENWEEM

Kilconquhar
A917
ELIE
EARLSFERRY
ST. MONANCE

I. of May

100
100
100

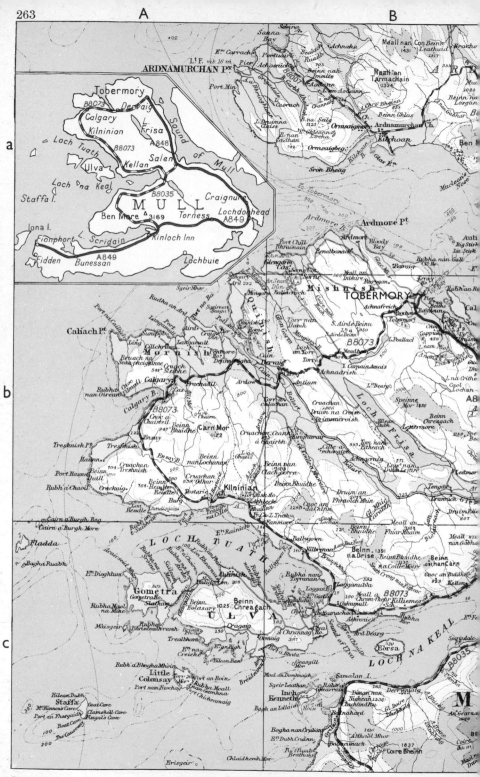

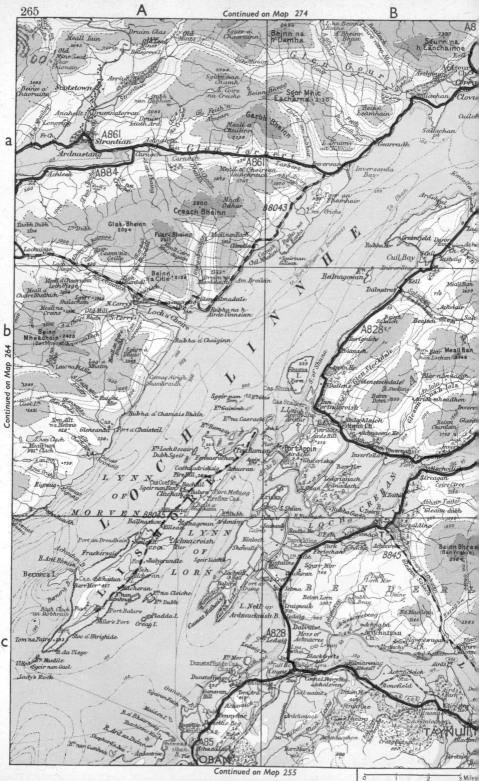

Continued on Map 264

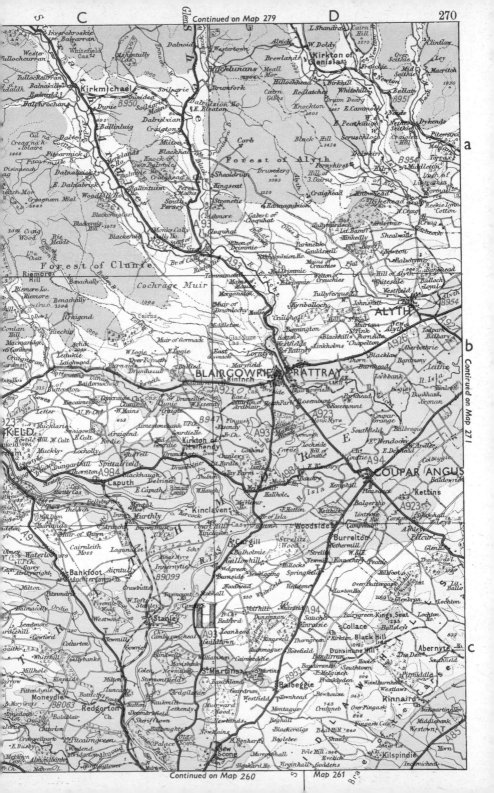

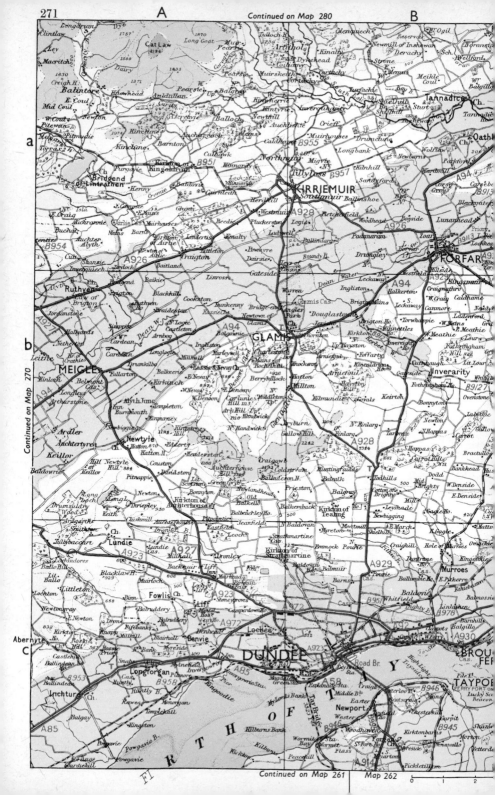

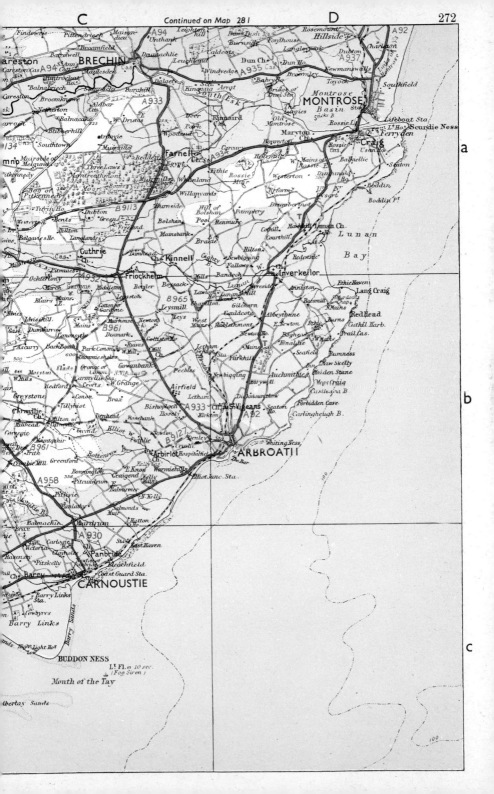

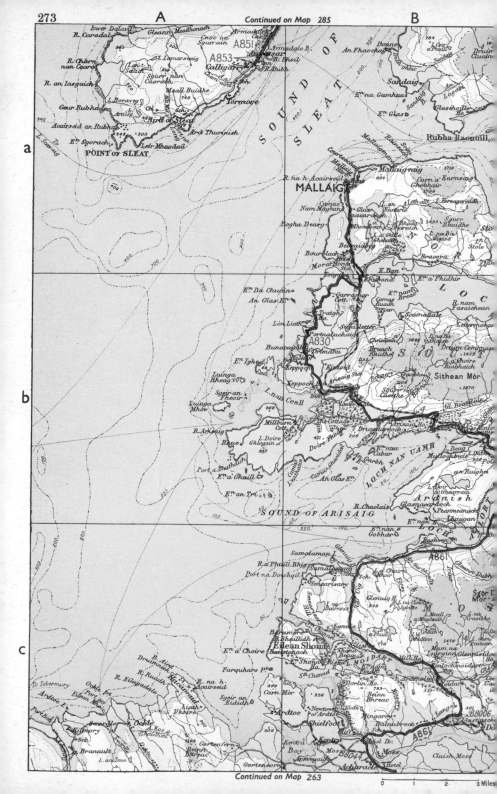

Continued on Map 285

A

B

a

b

c

SOUND OF SLEAT

POINT OF SLEAT

MALLAIG

Mallaigvaig

Rubha Raonuill

A851

A853

Calligary

Tormore

Ardvasar

Armadale Cas.

Armadale B.

An Fhaochag

Doune

Sandaig

Ard of Sleat

Ard Thurnish

Ard Thurnish

SOUND OF ARISAIG

Sithean Mòr

Eilean Shona

MOIDART

Arisaig

A830

A861

A861

Ardtoe

Shielfoot

Acharacle

Continued on Map 263

0   1   2   3 Miles

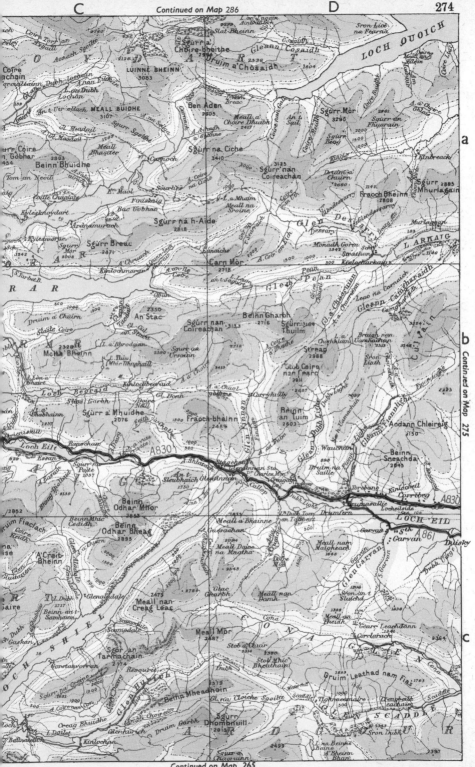

LOCH QUOICH

Sgurr a'
Choire-bheithe
Gleann Cosaidh
Sron Liac
na Fearna

Druim a'Chosaidh
2536
1604

LUINNE BHEINN
3083

Sgurr Mor
3290
Sgurr an
Fhuarain
2956

MEALL BUIDHE
3107

Ben Aden
2905

Meall a'
Choire Dhuibh
2417

An t.
Sail
Sgurr
Beag

Kinbreack

Sgurr Coire
n Gobhar
2863

Beinn Bhuidhe

Meall
Bhasiter

Sgurr na Ciche
3410

Sgurr'nan
Coireachan
3125

Druim a'
Chuirn
2680

Sgurr
Mhurlagain
2885

Fraoch Bheinn
2808

Sgurr na h-Aide
2818

Glen De
Dessarry

Kinlochmoran

Sgurr Breac
2371

Carn Mor
2718

Monadh Gorn

L. ARKAIG

Kinlocharkaig

R
A
R

Glen Pean

An Stac
2350

Beinn Gharbh
2776

Sgurr nan
Coireachan
3133

Gleann Camgharaidh

Sgurr
Thuilm

Streap
2988

Meith Bheinn
2328

Sgurr an
Ursainn

Gulb Coire
nan Gall
2911

Loch Beoraid

Sgurr a'Mhuidhe
2076

Fraoch-bhann
2489

Beinn
an Tuim
2503

Aodann Chleireig
2750

Beinn
Sneachda
2945

A830

Loch Eilt

An t
Sleubhaich
1750

Glenfinnan

Beinn
Odhar Mhor
3853

Beinn
Odhar Bheag
2895

LOCH EIL
A830

A861
Garvan

Dubisky

A'Chraig
Bheinn

Meall nan
Creag Leac
2471

Meall nam
Maigheach
1648

Glen Garvan

R

LOCH SHIEL

Meall Mor
2487

Stob a'Chuir
2314

Gorm Leachdann

Sgor an
Tarmachain
2774

Stob Mhic
Bheathain

Druim Leathad nam Fias
1763

Beinn Mheadhoin

Sgurr
Dhomhnuill
2915

GLEN SCADDLE

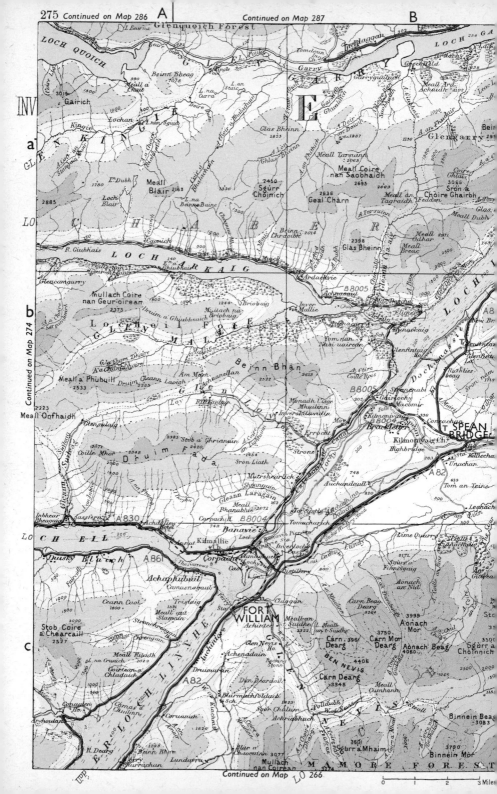

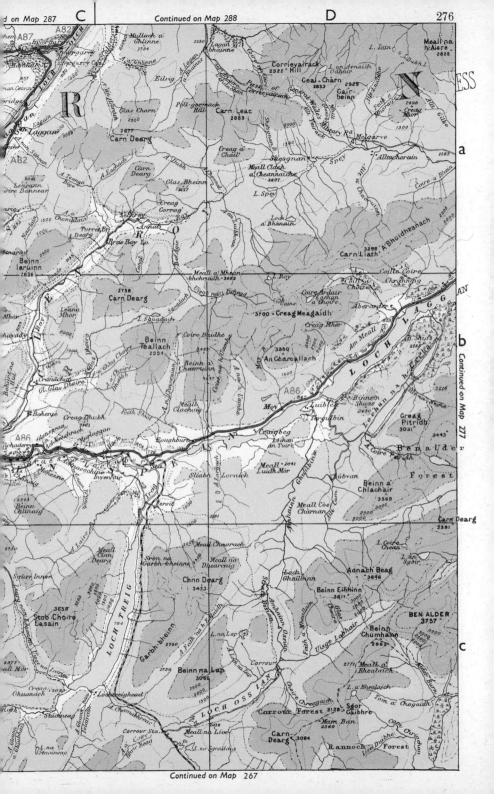

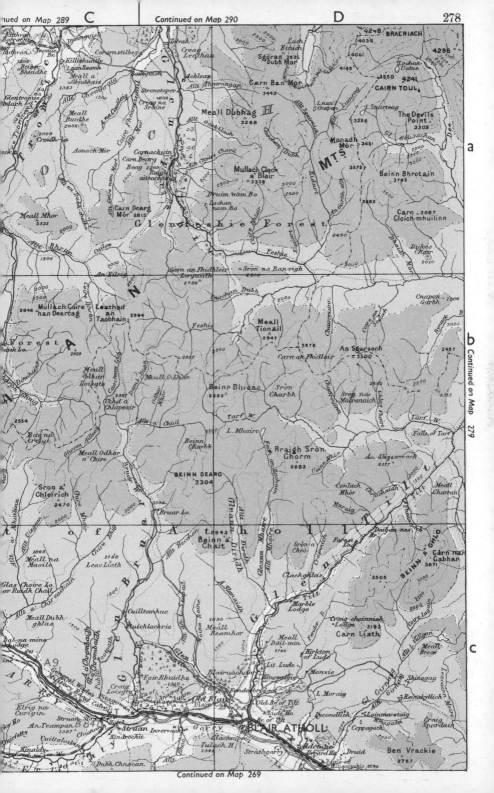

nued on Map 289
Continued on Map 290

Continued on Map 279

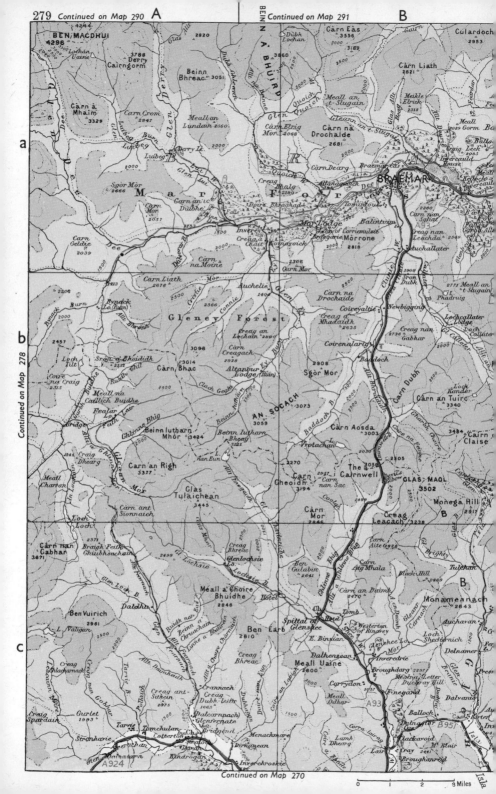

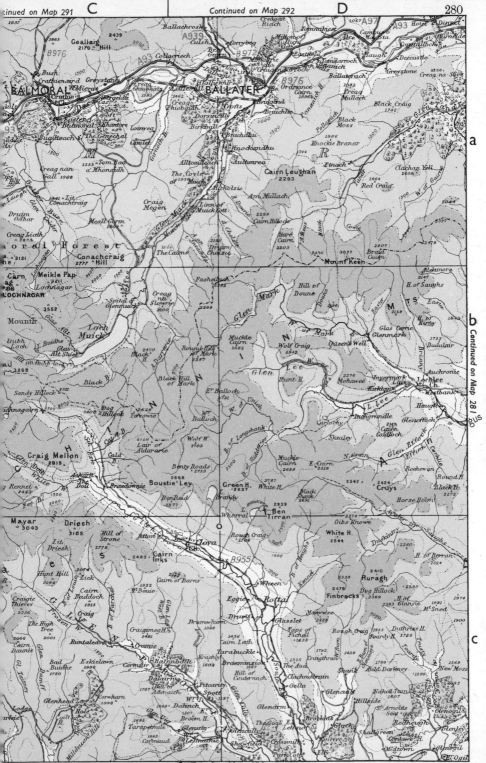

Continued on Map 281

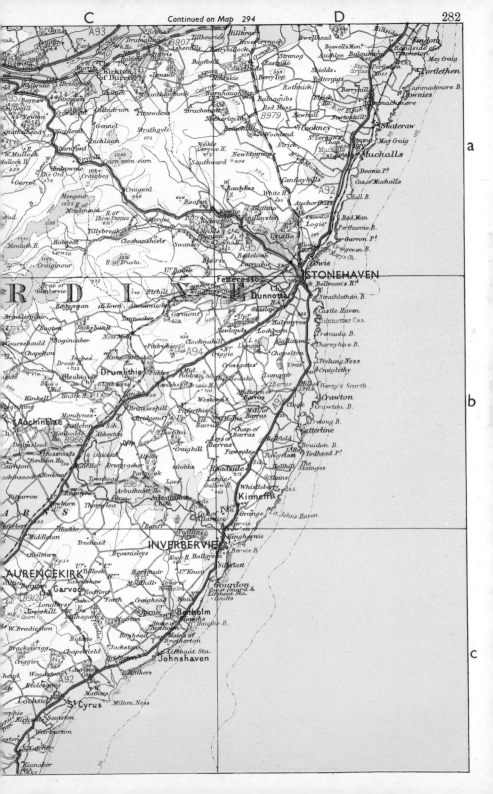

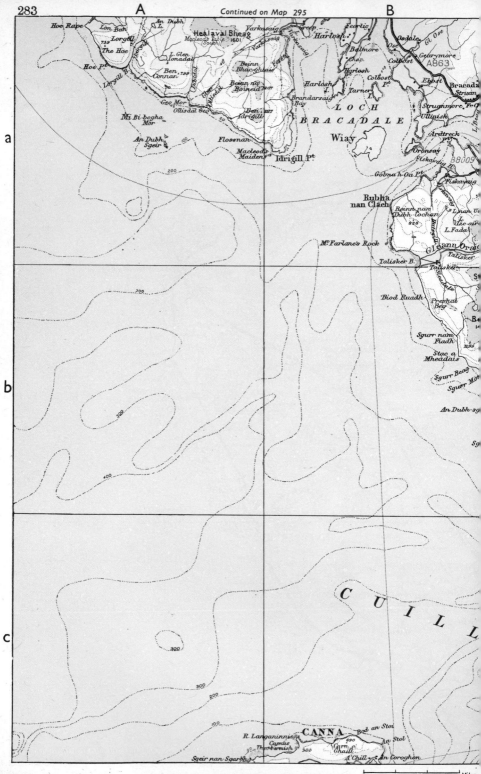

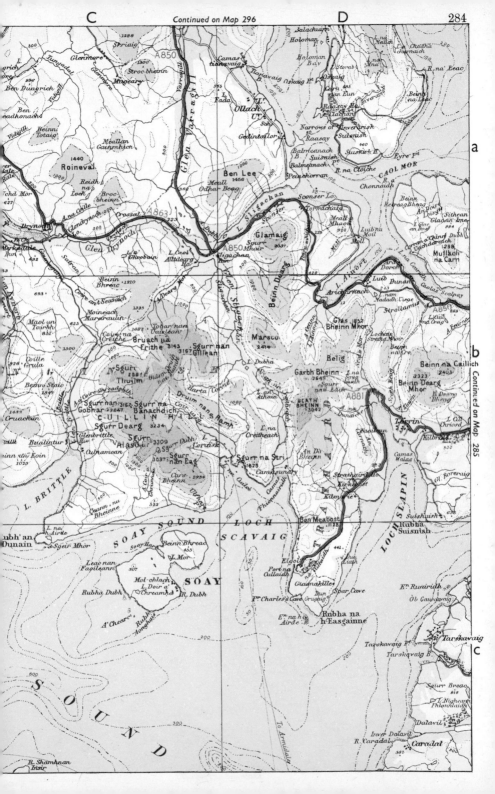

Continued on Map 285

a

b

c

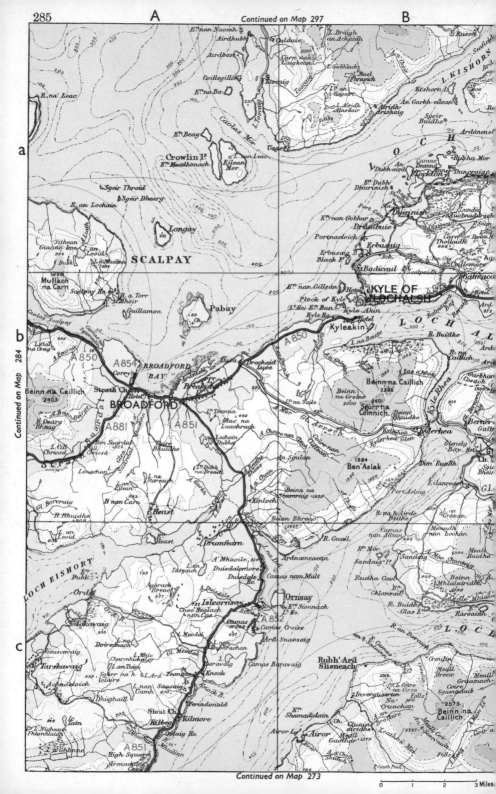

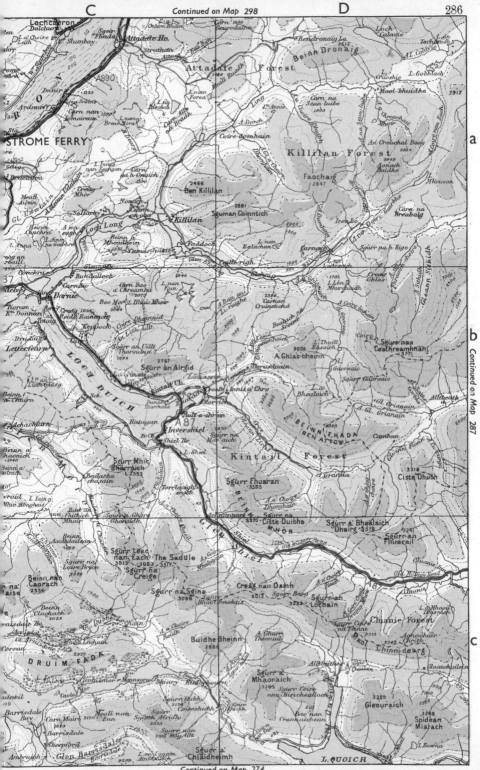

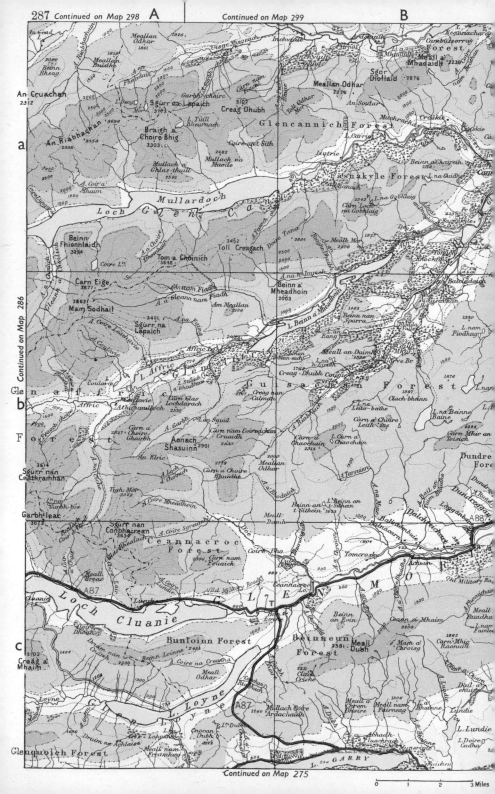

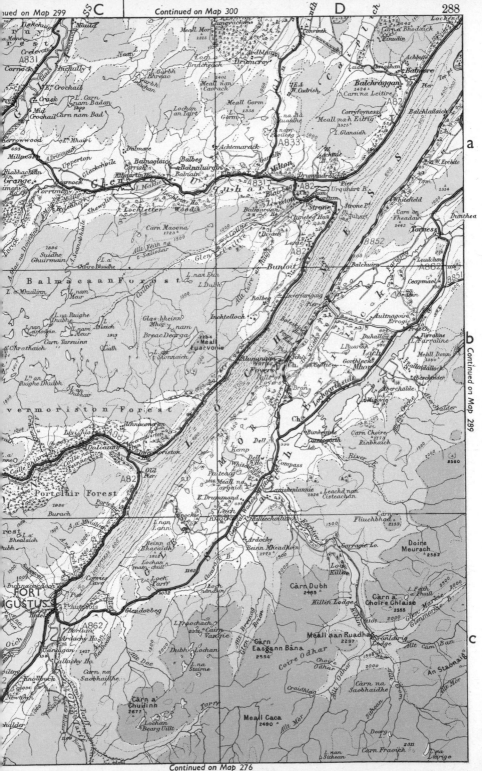
Continued on Map 289

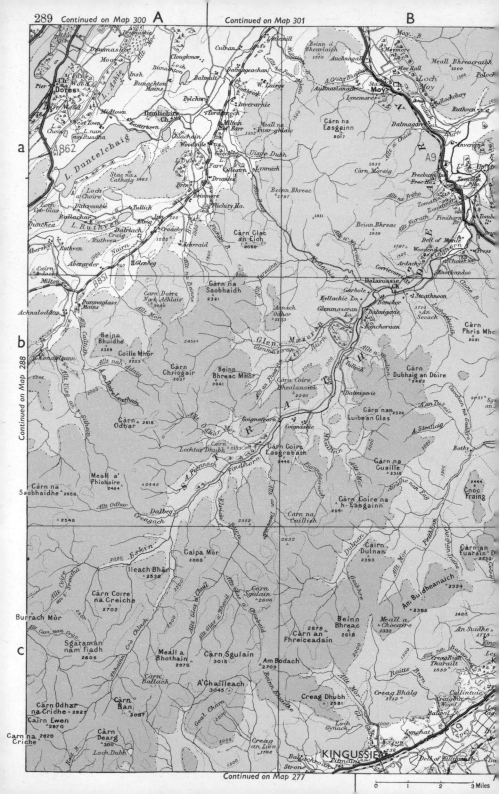

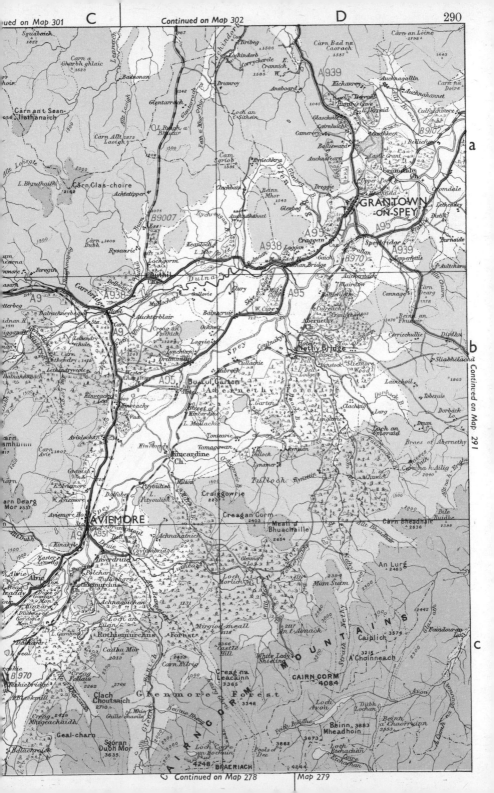

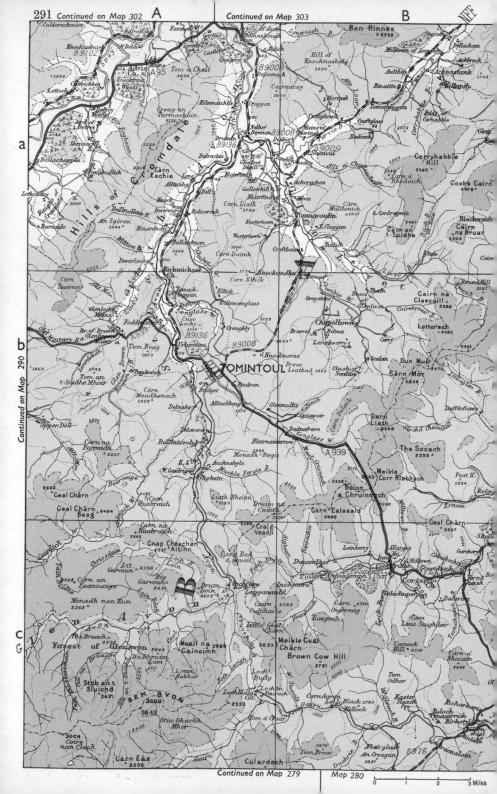

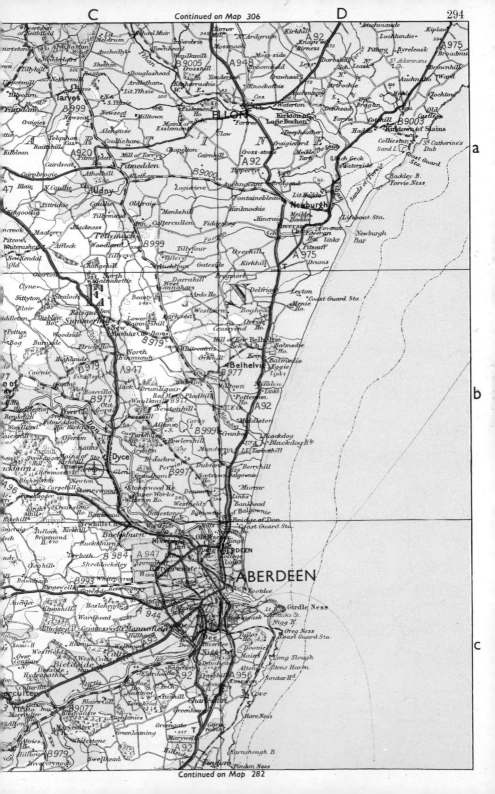

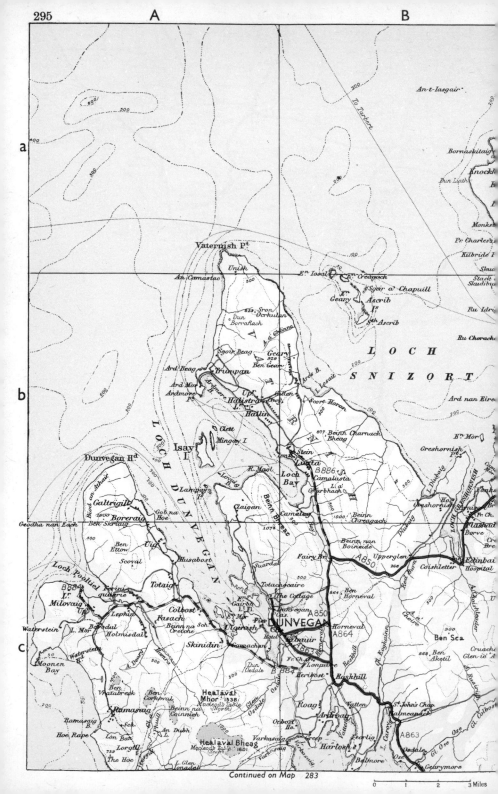

A   B

a

b

c

An-t-Iasgair

Bornaskitaig
Knockbl
Dun Liath
Monkst
Pr Charles's I
Kilbride I
Slaua
Stack
Skudibu
Ru Idri

Vaternish Pt
Unish
An Camastac
Eʳⁿ Iosal
Eʳⁿ Creagach
Sgeir a' Chapuill
Eʳⁿ Geary
Ascrib
Sⁱ Ascrib
Ru Chorachc

Sron Ochuilan
Dun Borrafiach
Sgeir Beag
Geary
Ben Gean
Ard'e B.
L O C H
S N I Z O R T
Ard nan Eire
Krumpan
Ard Beag
Ard Mor
Andmore Pt
Uigʳ
Hallistra
Hallin
L.
Glen
Score Horan
Eʳⁿ Mor
Greshornish
Ard nan Eire
Eʳⁿ Mor

Clett
Mingay I
Stein
Luata
Loch
Bay
Beinn Charnach
Bheag
Greshornish Pᵗ
Isay
I.
Dunvegan Hd
Camalusta
Lⁱ a'
Ghearbhach
Ho
Greshornish
Dhuboig
Fanks

Borerau
Bʳⁿ Skriaig
Ben Ettow
Uig
Scoval
Galtrigill
Geodha nan Each
Gob na
Hoe
Lampay's
R. Mool
Lovat
R. Mool
Claigan
Camatag
Beinn
Bhreac
1074
Beinn
Chreagach
1000
Beinn nan
Boineide
Fairy Brg
A850
Upperglen
Dhuboig
LOCH GRESHORNISH
Flashnil
Borve
Cre
Bre
Coishletter
Edinbai
Hospital

Husabost
Suardal
Totacascaire
The Cottage
Ben
Horneval
Mugʳⁿ Mʳⁿ
Cruache
Glen io'd
Ben Sca
Loch Pooltiel
Fiin
quarrie
B884
Milovaig
Waterstein
L. Mor
Lephin
Boʳⁿ dal
Holmisdal
Fasach
Beinn na Sch
Creiche
Colbost
Gairbh
L. F.
E.ⁿ Mor
Claigmish
Gauvegan
Cas
Pier
A850
DUNVEGAN
Hotel
A864
Fr. Ch.
Horneval
Borneval
Crᵗ Eoghainn
Ben
Aktil
Mon Mheadar
Ben
Hornaval
Cruache
Glen io'd

Moonen
Bay
Waterstein
Hd
A Dearg
Hamra
Skinidin
Camachan
Dun Osdale
B884
Fr. Ch.
Idrmuir
A863
Longmore
Heribost
Roskhill
Roag
Al Eoghainn
Ben Sca

Ramasaig
Ben
Vratabreck
Ben
Corkhval
Beinn na Cainnich
An Dubh
A L.
Healaval
Mhor 1538
Macleod's Table
(North)
Glen
Osdale
Roag
Orbost
Ho.
Arthroag
Vatten
St John's Chap
Balmcanach
Osdale
Gl Ose
A863
Gejurymore

Ramasaig
B.
Hoe Rape
Lon Ban
Lorgill
The Hoe
759
An Dubh
A L.
Healaval Bheag
Macleod's Table
(South) 1601
Varkasaig
Vatnagaig
Harlosh
Fearlia
Feorlig
L. Carˢⁱ
Osdale
Gl Ose
Gl Colbost

Continued on Map 283

0 1 2 3 Miles

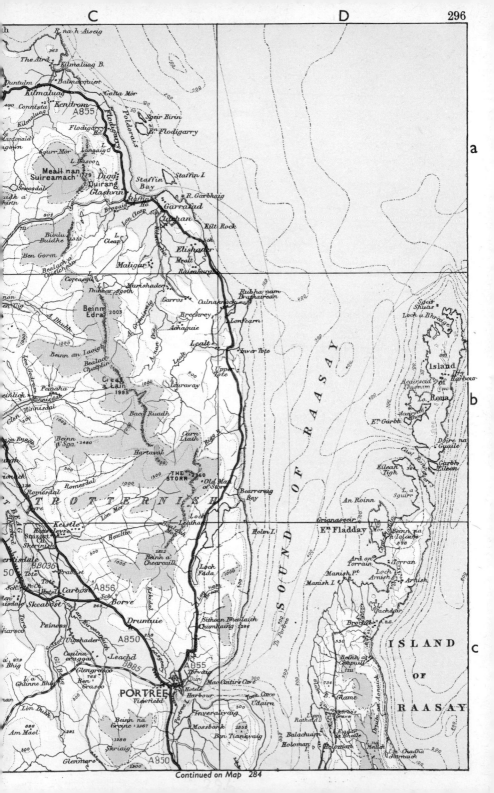

C

D

a

b

c

R. na h-Aiseig
The Aird
963
Duntulm
Kilmaluag B.
Balmaqueien
Kilmaluag
Connista
Kentroa
A855
Flodigarry
Kilmaluag
Calta Mor
Macdonald
gown
Flodigarry Ho.
Sgurr Mor
L. Langaig
L. Fasco
Foldorais
Sgeir Birin
Et Flodigarry
Meall nan
Suireamach
779
Digg
Sneosdal
Duirang
Glashvin
Staffin
Bay
Staffin I.
hirn
Brogaig
Bioda
Buidhe
Garrafad
R. Garbhaig
Ben Gorm
801
Achlan
Bealach a'
Choiichan
Ion Cleat
Ho.
Kilt Rock
Corcasgil
L. Cleap
Elishader
Maligar
Meall
Raisaburgh

Munshader
Thikar sgoth
Rubha nam
Brathairean
Beinn
Edra
2003
Garros
Brockrey
Culnacnock
Lonfearn
Ashaguie
A Grenvolg
Leolt
Inver Tote
Beinn an Laoigh
Bealach
Chaplin
Upper
Tote
Craig
a Lain
1995
Lauravay
Penaha
Baca Ruadh
Cairn
Liath
Hartaval
Rigg B.
Beinn
d' Sga
1480
Romesdal
Romesdal
THE
STORR
2360
Old Man
of Storr
Bearreraig
Bay
TROTTERNISH
Keistle
Bra
Loch
Leathan
An Roinn
Snizort
Skerinish
Grianasgeir
Haultin
Holm L.
Et Fladday
Ertisdale
A8036
Tote
Beinn a'
Chearcaill
1812
Fr Ch.
Tote
Hotel
Carbost
A856
Sch.
Borve
Loch
Fada
Skeabost
268
Ard an
Torrain
Manish Pt
Manish I.
Peiness
Drumuie
Loch
Arnish
Arnish
Uigshader
A850
Sithean Bheinlaich
Chumhaing
Uachdar
Brochel
Vensta
Leachd
Glengrasco
Ben Grasco
B.S.
Beinn na
Greine
1567
MacCaitir's Cave
Tom Cave
Udairn
Beinn a'
Chapuill
ISLAND
OF
RAASAY
PORTREE
Viewfield
Inveraivaig
Mossbank
Ben Tianavaig
Am Maol
Skriaig
Balachuirn
Holoman
B. Glame
Eigg a' Ghaile
Glenmore
A850
Holman I.
Holoman

SOUND
OF
RAASAY

Sgeir
Shuas
Loch a' Bhraige
Eilean
Island
of
Rona
Acairseid
or
Harbour
Et Garbh
Doire na
Guaile
Eilean
Tigh
Garbh
Eilean
L. a
Squirr
Beinn na'
h-Iolaire
626
Torran

Continued on Map 284

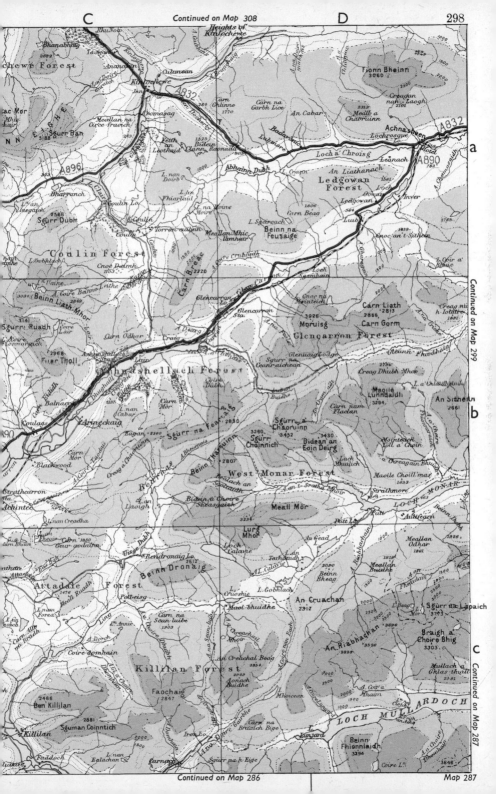

Continued on Map 308
Continued on Map 299
Continued on Map 287

Heights of Kinlochewe

Rha'Noin

Bhanabhaig
2892

chewe Forest

Anancaun
Kinlochewe

Taagan

Oulanean

A832

Meallan na Circe tranch

Meallan na Ghoir Luce

Fionn Bheinn
3060

Creagan nah Laogh
2101

ac Mor

Sgurr Ban
3188

NN

EIGHE

Feith an Leothaid

Bidein Clann Raonaild

Abhainn Dubh

Càrn Gliinne
1770

Càrn na Garbh Luce

An Cabar

Meall a Chaoruinn
2313

Achnasheen
Lochrosque
Sta Hotel

A832

A896

Loch a Chroisg

An Liathanach
1561

Leanach

A890

a

Bharranch

Coulin Lo

Coulin

L. nan Doirb

L. na Feine More

Abhainn Dubh

L. Craon

Ledgowan Forest

Loch Gowan

Ledgowan

Luib

Inver

Loch na Coir a Bhaic

Sgurr Dubh
2566

Torran cuilinn

Coulin

Meallan Mhic Iamhar

L. Sgeireach

Beinn na Feusaige

Càrn Beag
1806

Knoc an t Sithean

Coulin Forest

Cnoc Beinnh
1053

Loch Sgamhain

L. Grobhlach

Beinn Liath-Mhor
3034

A Coire Beinne Leithe

Glencarron Lo

Glencarron Sta.

Cnoc na Mointeich

Càrn Liath
2813

Creag nih Iotairc
1631

Sgurr Ruadh
3141

Coire Lair

Càrn Odhar

Craig

A Dearg

Moruisg
3026

Glencarron Forest

Càrn Gorm
2866

Fuar Tholl
2968

Coire Commorach

Loch Dughaill

Glenuaig Lodge

Sgurr na Ceann-aichean

Creag Dhubh Mhor

Reunn Fhodhaig

Coulags

Aghriskelloch Forest

Càrn Mòr

Lochan Buidhe

Achnashellach Forest

Maoile Lunndaidh
3294

L. a Chlaisleathain

An Sithean
2661

b

Aireagaig

Eagan
2100

Sgurr na Fear

Càrn nam Fiaclan

Mòinteach Toll a Choin

A Chore Thuill a Chein

Blackwood

A Coire Tladur

A Bhuc-meig

Sgurr a Chaoruinn
3452

Sgurr Choinnich
3260

Bidean an Eoin Deirg
3430

Loch Mhuilich

Maoile Choill mas
1853

LOCH MONAR

Beinne Dubh

Beinne Tharsuinn
2807

West Monar Forest

Strathmore

Patt Lo

Auldcearn

Bealach an Sgoltaidh

A n t Sratha Mhòr

Achintee

L. an Laoigh

Bidein a Choire Sheasgaich

Meall Mòr
3234

Patt

90

Strathcarron

Meallan Odhar
1861

Lurg Mhòr

Loch Calavie

L. an Tarneadh

An Gead

A L. Calavie

Meallan Buidhe
1819

Loch Monar

Uisg Dubh

Bendronaig Lo
2612

Beinn Bheag
2030

An Cruachan
2317

Meallan Buidhe

Beinn Dronaig

Crioshie

L. Gobhlach

A Fhaidain

Sgurr na Lapaich
3773

Attadale Forest

Pott-eisg

Maol bhuidhe

L Beag Mor

Braigh a Choire Bhig
3303

Meall Ruadh

Lung

Càrn na Scan luibe
1903

Oireachall Mhor

An Riabhachan
2825

Mullach na Ghlas thuill
2591

Coire-domhain

A Dorch

Gil a Chain

An Creachal Beag
2554

Aonach Buidhe

A Coir a Mhaim

Killilan Forest

Faochaig
2847

Loch Mullardoch

LOCH MULLARDOCH

Ben Killilan
2466

Sguman Coinntich
2881

Killilan

Faddoch

L. nan Eallachan

Carnach

Sgurr pa h Eige

Beinn Fhionnlaidh
3294

Coire L

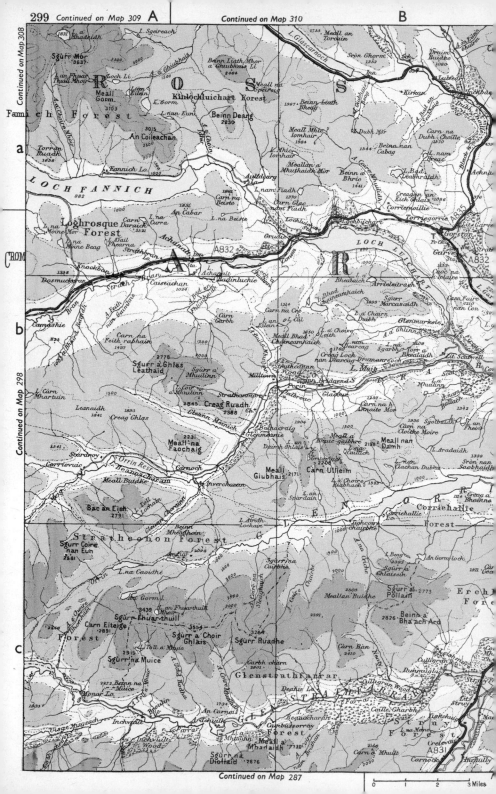

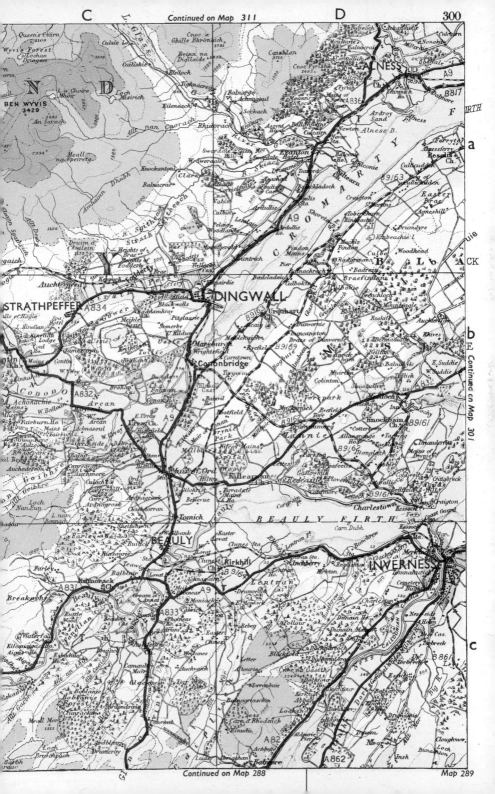
Map 289

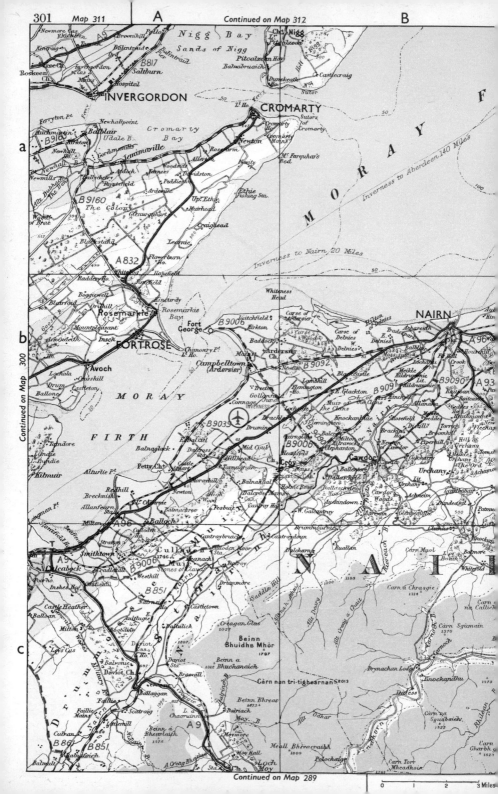

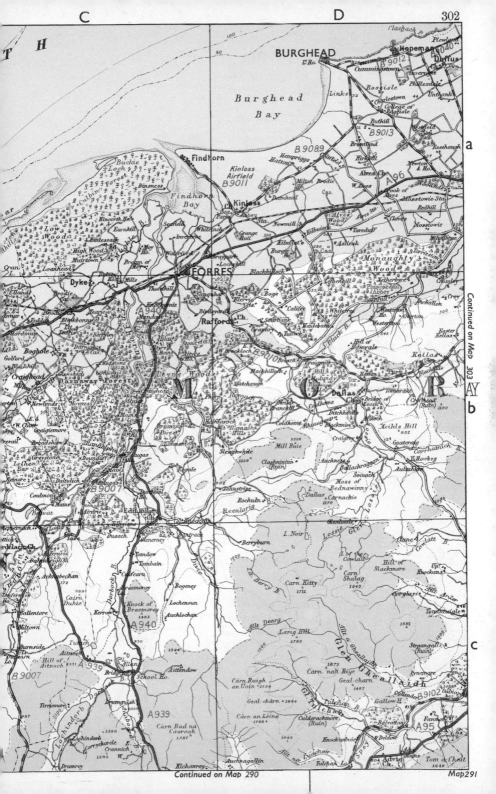

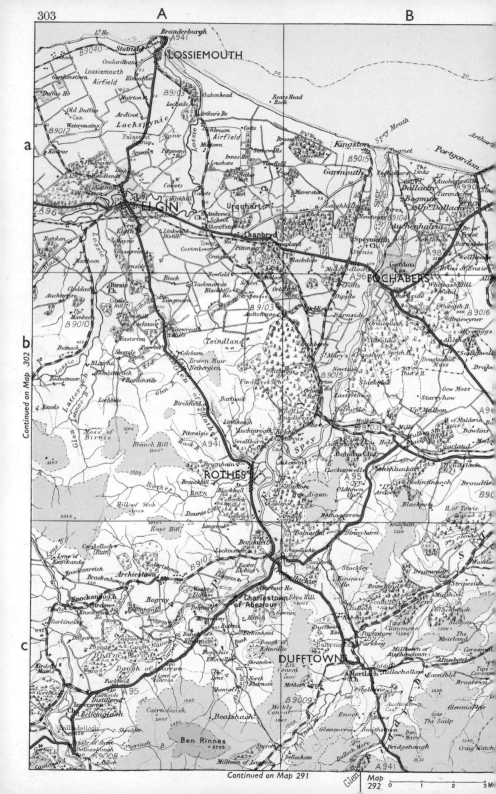

A   B

Lt Ho.
Branderburgh
A941
Stotfield
LOSSIEMOUTH
B9040
Coulardbank
Covesea
Gordonstown
Lossiemouth
Airfield
Kinneddar
Duffus Ho.
Muirton
Old Duffus Cas.
B9103
Oakenhead
Lochside
Arthur's Br.
Bears Head Rock
Spey Mouth
Watermains
Ardivot
Lochinver
Innes Ho.
Broomhill
Kingston
Tugnet
The Links
Portgordon
Palace of Spynie
Loch Spynie
Lossie
Salterhill
Airfield
Miltown
Stonewells
B9015
Garmouth
Auchengreggan
Tannachy
A990
Kinrae
Batchen
Woodlands
Bishopmill
Newmoss
W. Calcots
Essil
Meft
Mether
Mosstodloch
Maverston
Garmouth
Speymouth + Ch.
Dallachy
Bogmoor
Upr Dollachy
Br. of Enzie
Bryas of Enzie
Newlands
Burnside
Wellheads
ELGIN
A96
New Elgin
Mayne
Glassgreen
Burnside
Andrews School
Sheriffston
Kirkhill
Calcots
Urquhart
Lochs
Newton
Ayres
Gordon Cas.
FOCHABERS
Whiteashhill Wood
Whiteash H.
Braewynter
Myreggs
Linkwood Distill.
Coxtownend
Tower
Pittensier
Thanbryd
Craigland
Blackdam
A96
Coxton
Crofts
Dipple
Burnside
Ordiequish
Scotch H.
Aultonside
Mosstodloch
Douglashill Moss
Drake
Birnie Ch.
Clackmarras
Newfield
Blackhills Ho.
School
Strypes
Orbliston June.
Newton
b
Castle hill
Upr Manbeen
B9010
Longmorn
Thornhill
Cockmuir
Whitewreath
Easterton
Teindland
Brawn Muir
Nethergien
Coleburn
Whitedogs
Findlays
Orton Ho.
Newton
Orton Sta.
B9015
Easterstown
Blairlea
Glenlatterach
Boat of Brig
Bardenside
Lochbuie
Moss of Birnie
Branch Hill
Birchfield
Littlefolds
Littlehaugh
Auchenroath
Gow Moss
Starryhow
Upr Mulben
H. of Muldearie
Bowlins
Mulben Sta.
Blacksh.
Garland
Spey
Brumbain
Smallburn
Dundurcas
Tulchan
Dalvey
Boharm Ch.
Muchrachart
Myrrdilack
Broadfield
ROTHES
Braeshill
Blackhall
Aikenway
Clockanwells
Arndilly
Upr
Ardoch
Hodinfinnach
Blackpots
H. of Towie
Hill of Stob
Dounie Cott.
Rant Hill
Longcroft
Balnacoul
Dinnyhorn
Knockan
Daugh
S
Woodside
Carskellock (Ruin)
Lyne of Knockando
Robertstown
Danaleith
Lochinstoie
Craigellachie
June
Gauldwell
Stockley
Kinnivie
Ho.
Brawlands
Midthart
Stripeside
Archiestown
B9102
Easter Elchies
Logan
c
Bogray
Wester Elchies
Charlestown of Aberlour
Rhae Hill
Duffown
Tulloch
Climmore
Blackstack
The Meirland
Corsemill
Knockando Ch.
Curdow
Cairncrofts
Knockandhu
Ballintomb
Delnapot
Burnhead
Kingunnyre
Hilton
DUFFTOWN
Parkgreen
Parkbey
Milltown of Auchindown
Altnabrid
Garlinebeg
Dalgarven
Thomas
Carron Mains
Shandron
Daugh of Edinville
Mortlach
Tullochallum
Earlsfield
Braetown
Dildian
Woods
Daugh of Corsemill
Daugh of Carron
Eddich
Pittyvaich
Methereleary
Auchnarrow
Tips of Corsemill
The Scalp
Glenmarkie
Parkhead
Lyne of Carron
Dell
B95
Shenval
Burnside Distillery
Inveravon Ch.
Edinvillie
Cairn Guish
1607
Beathach
Enoch
Smithstown
Ben Maln
Craig Watch
Ballindalloch
Shoulder
Ben Rinnes
△ 2755
Glencorrie
Bridgehaugh
Bulloch More
Lynriach
B9008
Milltown of Lagmore
Dellacham
A941

Continued on Map 302

Continued on Map 291

Map 292

0   1   2   3 M.

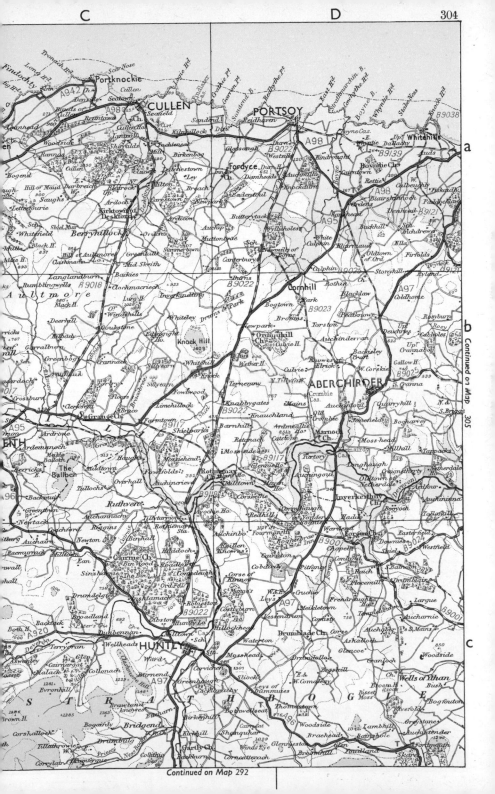

C

D

Portknockie

CULLEN

PORTSOY

Up.Whitehills

Fordyce

Boyndie Cha

A98

A95

Kirktown of
Deskford

Berryhillock

Cornhill

A97

Aultmore

Knock Hill 1409

ABERCHIRDER

Continued on Map 305

a

b

c

A95

Ruthven

Inverkeithny Cha

A96

Largue

HUNTLY

A97

Drumblade Ch.

Wells of Ythan

A920

S   T   R   A   T   H   B   O   G   I   E

A96

Bridgend

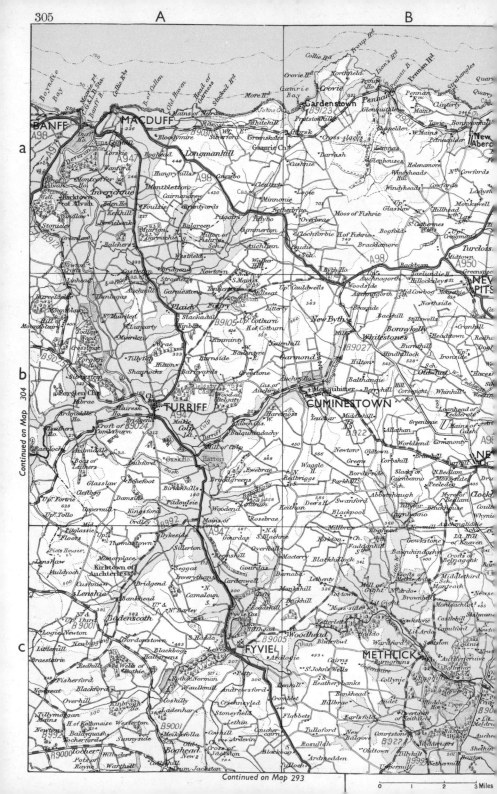

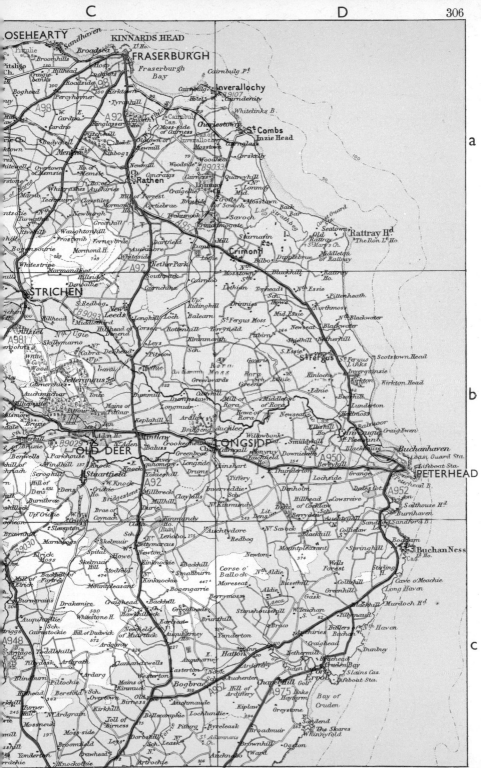

C

D

a

b

c

OSEHEARTY
KINNARDS HEAD
Lt. Ho.
FRASERBURGH
Broadsea
Pitullie
Sandhaven
Broomhills
Pitsligo
Ch.
Hillhead
Hosp.
Roadside
Fraserburgh
Bay
Cairnbulg Pt.
Boghead
Percyhorner
Kirktown
A98
A981
Craigie
banks
Cairnbulg
Inverallochy
Hotel
B9107
Whitelinks B.
Cardno
W.
Cardno
Kinglasser
A92
Tyranhill
Pitforth
Ho.
Cairnbulg
St Combs
Charlestown
Inzie Head
Bodychell
Nth.
Menzie
Ho. of
Memsie
Ch.
Bod I.
Oldtown of
Inverallochy
Mosstown
Carnglass
Overtown
of Memsie
Whitehill
Moss-side
of Garness
Rathen
Newmill
Woodside
Woodhead
Corskelly
B9033
Croftmorn
Whinny
rashes of
Auchiries
Curriess
Quarryhill
Lonmay
Rathen
Claystiles
Ho. of Forest
Craigellie
Lonmay
Mid.
Newburgh
Mormonth.
Croichill
Cortiebrae
Brydield
Crofts
of Savoch
Mosstown
Nth.
Rivehill
Waughton Hill
Forney brae
Dartfield
Broken Ho.
Savoch
L. of Strathbeg
Back
Bar
Bogensourie
Mormond H.
Whitestripe
Auchmore
Camp
Grimsdryhangate
Starnafin
Old
Rattray
St Mary's Ch.
Coast Guard
Sta.
Seatown
Rattray Hd.
The Ron Lt. Ho.
STRICHEN
Marmondside Hillside
Densallie
A92
Netherpark
Logie
Mill
Crimond
Bilbo
Dipplebrae
Middleton
or Rattray
Nether Mill
A98
Hillhead
S. Redbog
B9093
New Leeds
Middlewood
Longhill
Loch
Southpark
Cairnob
Carncuna
Up.
Ridinghill
Balean
Lothian
Mosstown
Blackhill
Rattray
Ch.
Drinnies
Tyrehead
Nth. Essie
Howe
Pittenheath
Hillhead of
Denend
Corses
Rottenhill
St Fergus Moss
Mid. Essie
Nyrthmoss
Nth. Blackwater
A981
Hiltzie
Skillymarno
Nth.
Terryneld
Newseat
Blackwater
Blackwater
Cabra
Denhead
Kirdrummie
Pitbirn
Shielhill
Netherhill
S. Essie
St Fergus
Fergus Links
Scotstown Head
White
Cruden
Wood
Pitsoe
Leys
Sch.
Gowrie
W.
Little
Einlochs
Kirkton
Invergquinzie
Kirkton Head
Cairneybues
Auchmachar
Toux
Rora
Moss
Greywards
Rora
Greens
Edrie
Braehill
Pitfour Ho.
Dunmill
Dronquetown
Longmuir
Mill of
Rora
Middleton
of Rora
Newseat
Balmoor
Craig Ewen
Keplandhill
Ardlaw
Howe of
Rora
Inv. Ougie
Aden Ho.
Mintlaw
Bradgend
Auchlee
Ellishall
Ho.
Mt. Pleasant
Blackhouse
Buchanhaven
Coast Guard Sta.
OLD DEER
Bruxie
Nth. Aden
Baluss
Crookeonhill
Chap.
Willowbunk
Smiddyhill
Berryhill
A950
Lifeboat Sta.
PETERHEAD
Stuartfield
W. Knock
Knock
Yokieshill
Longside
Greenbrae
LONGSIDE
Cuningall
Nonrny
Faichfield
Downieheds
Grange
Lochside
Dales Lot.
A952
Windhill
Gruine
Ho.
Bridgestone
Millbreck
Drums
Kinshart
Tiffery
Inverveddie
Thunderton
Berryhill
Denholm
Hillhead of
Cocklaw
Cowsrieve
Salthouse Hd.
Upr. Crichie
Brae of
Coynach
Clola
Durie
Nth. Kirmundy
Lit.
Dens
Dens of
Cocklaw
Sch.
Berrydens
Auchtiegall
Sandford
Sandford B.
Burnhaven
Slampton
Skelmuir
Kinmundy
Ho. (Ruin)
Lenabo
Auchtydore
Redbog
Nth. Savoch
Blackhill
Collielaw
Springhill
Buchan Ness
Lt. Ho.
B9030
Marnoch's
Spital
Howe
Newton
Backhill
Mountpleasant
Wells
Forest
Starling
H.
Cas.
Elrick
Moss
Skelmuir
Hill
Stodfold
Kinknockie
Smallburn
Corse o'
Balloch
Nth. Aldie
Bissethill
Greenhill
Collyhill
Cave o'Meachie
Long Haven
Backhill of
Fortree
Mountpleasant
Kinknockie
Bogengarrie
Moreseat
Aldie
Gask
S. Leuca
Whinnyfold
Drakemire
Craighead
Berrymoss
Greenheads
Brunthill
Stanshousehill
W. Teuchan
S.
Braco
Schivas
Dunbuy
Blackhill
Murdoch Hd.
Nth. Haven
Auquhaddie
Whitestone H.
Newfield of
Murdack
Auquharney
Yonderton
Bittlers
Buchan
A948
Cairnstockie
Hill of Dudwick
Ardgrain
Hatton
Ardiffery
Craighead
Cruden
Bay
Slains Cas.
Lifeboat Sta.
Tillydesk
E. Hatton
Auquhorties
Chapel Hill
Golf
Port
Errol
Ardarg
Sch.
Easterton
Westerton
Auchenter
Nth.
Hill of
Ardiffery
A975
Links
Hayburn
Bay of
Cruden
Ardgrain
Nth.
Overtown
Birness
Kirkhill
Bogbrae
Greystone
Sandend
Blindburn
Mains of
Kinmuck
Ota
Ardarg
Aucknaude
Kiplaw
E.
Sandend
The Skares
Toll of
Birness
Lenabo
Lochhundie
Whinnyfold
Pitlochie
Bereford
Hillhead
Lexs
Dorbshill
Nth.
Leask
St Adamnan's
Ch.
Broadmuir
Brownhill
Ward
Oggston
Mossneuk
Moss-side
Broomfield
Crawhead
Byreleask
Artrochie
Turner
Hall
Yonderton
Knockothie

Continued on Map 294

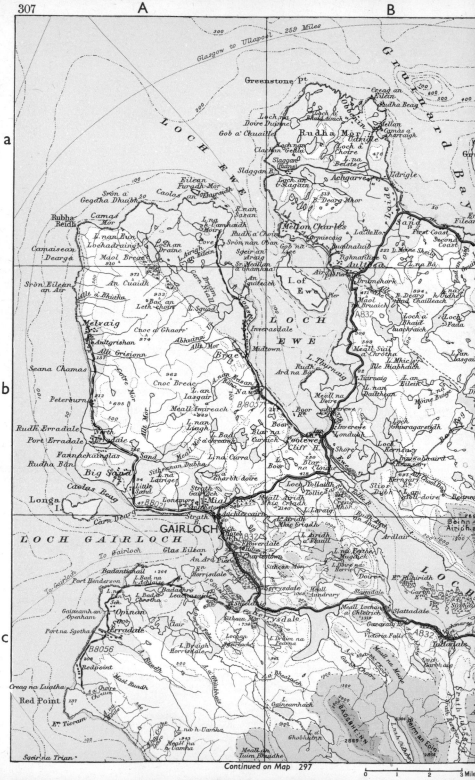

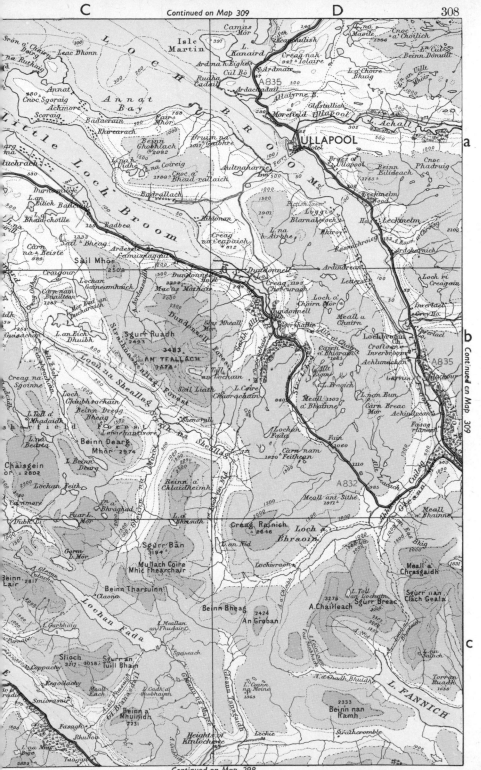

Isle Martin

Camas Mór

Scoraig

Sròn a' Chàirn Doire na Ruthan

Leac Bhonn

LOCH BROOM

L. Kanaird

Ardmair

Ardnah Eighe

Cùl Bò

Creag nak Iolaire

Scoraig Mùllach

Cnoc a' Choilich

Beinn Donaill

L.na Uilt Mhòr

Annat Bay

Annat

Cnoc Sgoraig

Achmore

Scoraig

Badacrain

Rhirearach

Fair Mhòr

A835

Ardachadail

Allt Airne B.

Morefield

Glastullich

Ullapool

L. Achall

Beinn Ghobhlach 2082

Bruich na Gabhre

ULLAPOOL

Brass of Ullapool

Cnoc Phadruig

L.na Uidhe

na Coireig

Cnoc a' Bhaad rallaich

Aultnaharrie

Inn

Braes of Ullapool

Beinn Eilideach 1755

Leckmelm Wood

Leckmelm

Little Loch Broom

Badralloch

Pictish Tower

L.na h-Airbhe

Lyggie Blarnalearoch

Rhiroy

Carn na Beiste

Sail Bheag

Radbea

Kildonan

Creag na Ceapaich

Rhoroin Roieig

Ardcharnich

Sàil Mhòr

Ardessie

Camisnagaul

Dundonnell Hotel

Dundonnell

Ardindrean

Letters

Loch ri Creagain

Craggay

Lochan Gaineamhach

Mac as Mathair

Creag Charcurach

Loch a' Chàirn Mòr

Inverlael

Grey Ho.

Càrn nan Bruailtean

Meall Red an Fhucharaich

Strathnasealg Forest

Glas Mheall Mòr

Sgurr Ruadh 2493

3483 AN TEALLACH 3474

Toll an Lochain

Glas Mheall

Sgùrr Fiona

Meall a' Chairn

Creag n' Bhiorain

Lochbroom

Croftown Inverbroom

Achlunachan

A835

Loch na Sheallag

Sàil Liath

L. Coire Chaorachain

Loch na Sheallag

Meall a' Bhainne

Allt Eighin

L. Bragich

Carn Breac Mòr

Achindrean

Fasag

Loch Chubhsachain

Beinn Dearg Bheag

Larachantivore

Shenavall

Da Sheallag

Lochan Fada

Carn nam Feithean 1820

Fain 1060

L.nan Eun

Beinn Dearg Mhòr 2974

L. na Bearta

L. Beinn Dearg

Reinn a' Chlaidheimh

Chaisgein mòr 2802

Lochan Feith

Meall an Sithe 1971

Meall a' Bhainne

Cammore

In a' Bhràghad

L. a

Fuar L. Mòr

Bunsath

Creag Rainich 2646

Loch a' Bhraoin

Drùbh m

Sgùrr Bàn 3194

L. an Nid

Meall a' Chrasgaidh

Gorm L. Mòr

Mullach Coire Mhic Fhearchair

Lochivraon

A. Chailleach

Sgurr nan Clach Geala 1831

Beinn Lair 2817

Beinn Tharsuinn

Claona

Beinn Bheag

An Groban 2424

Sgurr Breac

Lochan Fada

L. Garbhaig

L. Meallan an Fhudair

A. Chaidh Bhuidh

Lochan Fada

L. Toll an Lochain 3275

Sgeineach

L. an Saloch

Torran Ruadh 1656

Slioch 3217

Coppachy

Sgurr an Tuill Bhain 3058

Meall Each

L. Cadh' al Rubhaidh

L. Ceann na Moine 1365

Gleann Tanagaidh

L. FANNICH

Regoilachy

Smiorasair

Fasagh

Beinn a' Mhuinidh 2231

RhuNoa

Beinn nan Ramh 2333

Strahcromble

Heights of Kinlochewe

Leckie

Taagan

a

b

Continued on Map 309

c

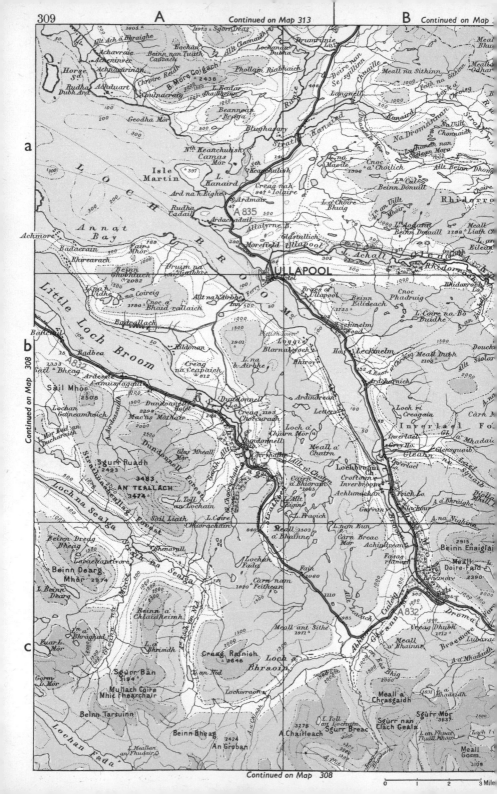

a

b

Continued on Map 308

c

ULLAPOOL

LOCH BROOM

Little Loch Broom

Isle Martin

Annat Bay

Achmore

A 835

A 832

Dundonnell Hotel

AN TEALLACH

Sgurr Ruadh

Beinn Dearg Mhòr

Beinn Tarsuinn

Sgùrr Bàn

Mullach Coire Mhic Fhearchair

Loch a' Bhraoin

Creag Rainich

An Groban

Beinn Bheag

A Chailleach

Sgùrr Breac

Sgùrr nan Clach Geala

Sgùrr Mòr

Meall a' Chrasgaidh

Lochan Fada

Loch na Sealga

Beinn Enaiglair

Braemore

Droma

A 832

Loggie

Leckmelm

Inverlael

Lochbroom

Beinn Dearg

Rhidorroch

0   1   2   3 Miles

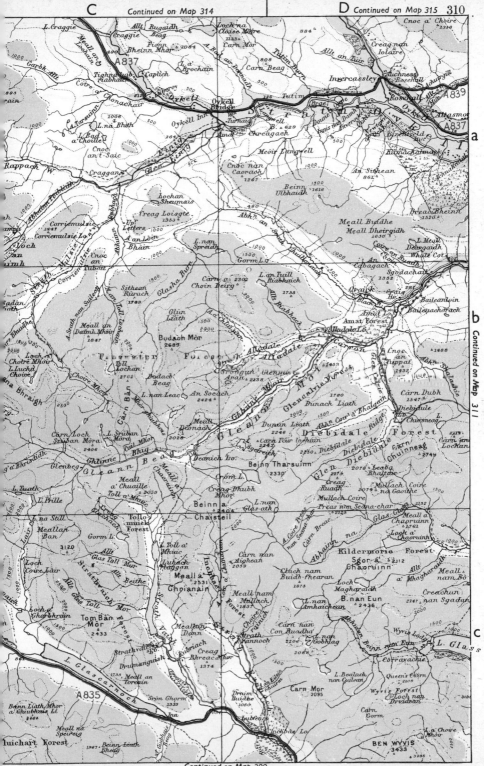

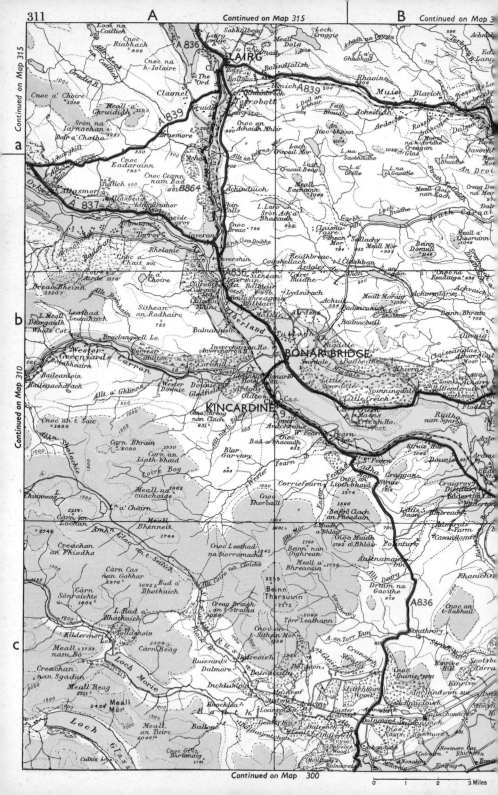

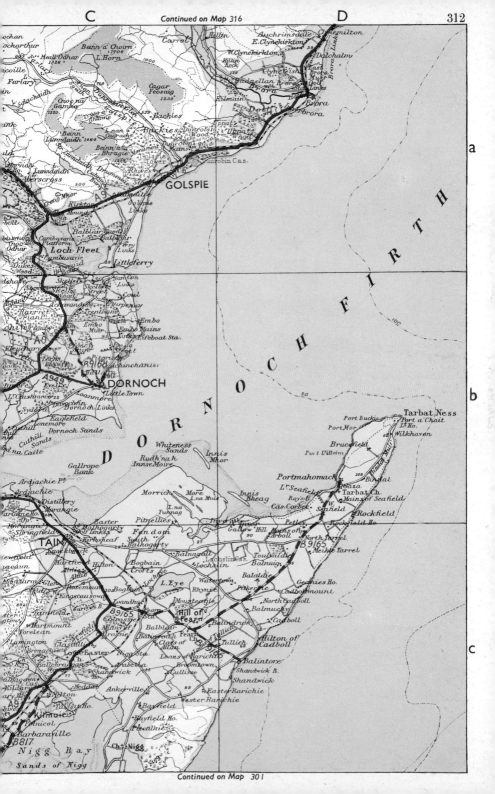

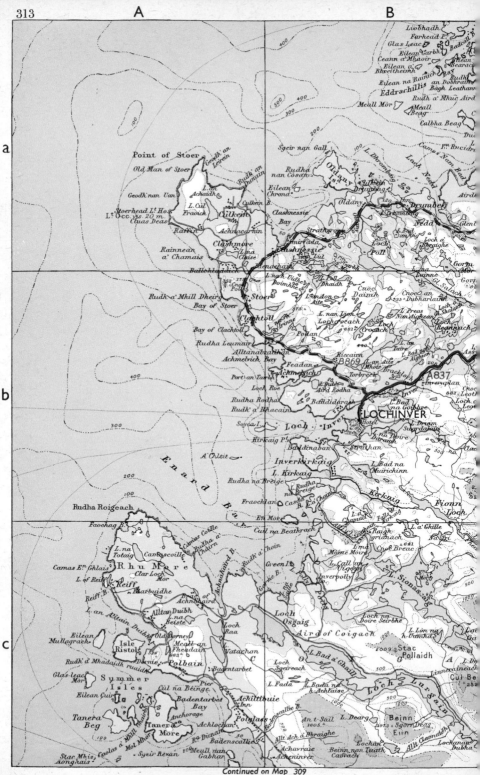

A

B

a

b

c

Point of Stoer
Old Man of Stoer
Geodh'nan Uan
Stoerhead L.t Ho.
L.t Occ. vis 20 m.
Cluas Deas
Raffin
Rainnean
a' Chamais
Clashmore
L.na
Claise
Balchladich
Rudh a' Mhill Dheirg
Bay of Stoer
Bay of Clachtoll
Rudha Leumair
Alltanabradhan
Achmelvich Bay
Port an Tairbh
Loch Roe
Rudha Rodhal
Rudh' a' Bhacain
Soyea I.
A' Chleit
Rudha Roigeach
Faochag I.
Camas En Ghlais
L. na
Totaig
Camascoille
Rudha Coille
Rudha a' Chàirn
Achnahaird B.
L. of Reiff
Reiff B.
Reiff
Garbuidhe
L. an Altan Duibh
Alltan Duibh
Bridge of
Achnahaird
Eilean
Mullagrach
Isle
Ristol
Old Dornie
Mcall an
Fheadain
Rudh' a' Mhadaidh
Polbain
Glas leac
Mór
Eilean Cuirn
Summer
Isles
Cùl na Beinge
Anchorage
Tanera
Beg
Mol Mhòr
Tanera
More
Badentarbet
Bay
Achlochan
Rd Diaval
Badenscallie
Stac Mhic
Aonghais
Caolas a' Mhill Bhàin
Sgeir Revan
Meull nan
Gabhar
Achiltibuie
Inn
Polglass
Benidorscallie B.
Achnahaird
Achavraie
An t-Sàil
Achenmver
Meall an Fheadain

I. an
Achaidh
L. Cùl
Fraoich
Culkein
Achnacarnin
Sgeir nan Gall
Rudha
nan Còsan
Eilean
Chrona
Clashnessie
Bay
Clashnessie
Strathan
Amnfada
L. na Cùl
Tarbh
Rudh' an
Dunain
Oldany Is.
L. Dhrombeg
L. Dròmbeg
Oldany
L. an
Ordain
Eddrachillis
Rudha a' Mhuc Aird
Meall Mór
Meall
Beag
Calbha Beag
Liobhadh
Farhead P.
Glas Leac
Ceann a' Mhaoir
Eilean a'
Bhreitheimh
Eilean na Rainich
Bay Leathan
Eilean Garbh
Rudha

Drumbeg
Nedd
Loch a'
Sheaighe
Glent

L. Drom
na Doire
draogh

Stoer
Clachtoll
Pollan
Feadan
Achmelvich
Baddidarroch
Kirkaig P.t
Baldinaban
Inverkirkaig
L. Kirkaig
Rudha na Breige
Rudha
na Breige
Casda
B. Eachainn
Fraochan
En Mór

Cùl na Beathrach
Rudha a' Choin
Green I.
Garbie B.
Rudha Castle

L. Roinebhat
Bhadh
Croc
Daimh
Croc an
Dubharlaid
L. nan Lion
Lochbreach
Croach
Riccaim
L. an dite
Mhoir
Torbreck
Brack Loch
Inverkirkaig
L. Bad
na Goblue
Strathan
L. Bad na
Muirchinn

Clochtoll
L. nan Aon
Aite

B869
LOCHINVER
Hotel
L. na Doire
draogh

L. Bad na
Muirchinn

1837
Inverquilan

Cùl na Beathrach
Inverpolly
L. Sionas

Loch
Osgaig
Aird of Coigach
Loch
Raa
Vatachan

L. Call an
Uigean
Maine Mour
Croc Breac
Raigh
griunach
L. a' Ghille
Na Uri

L. Lòin na
h-Uamhá
Stac
Pollaidh
A L. Dò
Cùl Be

Loch
Sgeireach
L. Bada na
h-Achlaise
L. Buta na
h-Achlaise

Loch Lurgain
Loch Dearg
Beinn
Sgorr Deas
Etin
Lochan
Dubha
Lochanan
Dubha

Beinn nan Tuath
Cabrach

B 869
Riccaim

Continued on Map 309

0   1   2   3 Miles

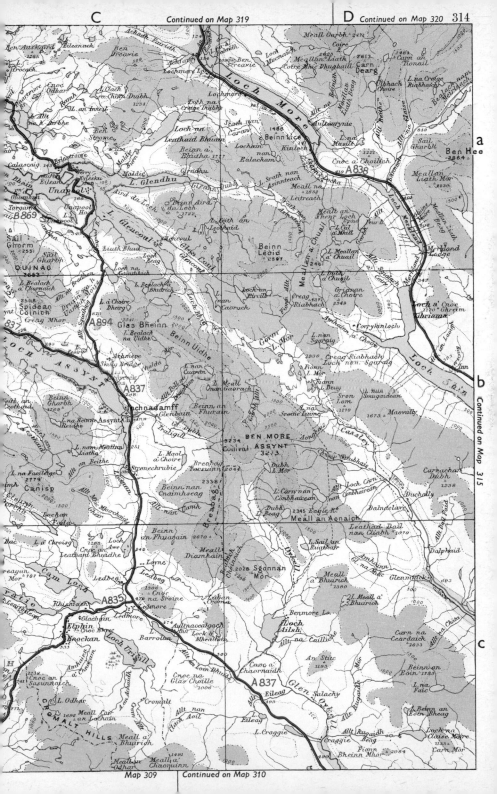

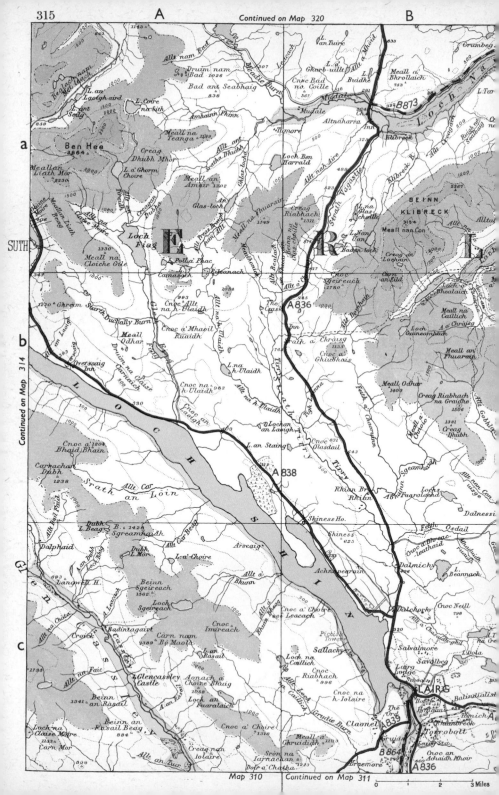

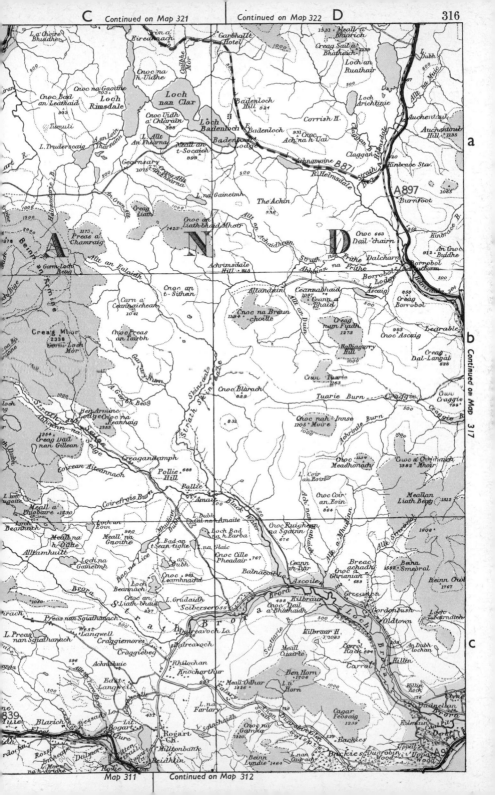

Continued on Map 322
Continued on Map

Continued on Map 322

Continued on Map 316

0   1   2   3 Miles

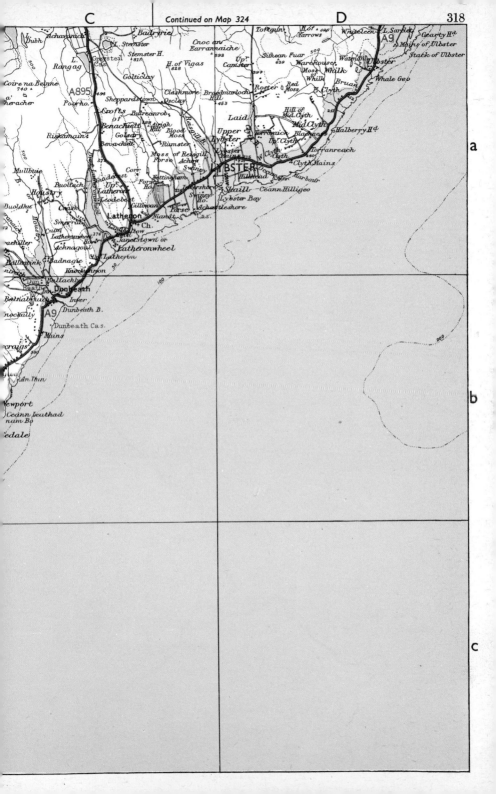

C

D

a

b

c

L. Dubh
Achavanich
Badryrie
L. Stemster
Stemster H.
Cnoc an Earrannaiche
Toftgun
H. of Yarrows
Whiteleen
L. Sarclet
Gearty H.d
Mains of Ulbster
Statk of Ulbster
Greystel Cas.
810
H. of Vigas
628
Up.r Canister
Sithean Fuar
630
509
Warehouse
Whilk
Watenan
Ulbster
Whale Geo
L. Rangag
Coire na Beinne
740
Golticlay
Clashmore
Broadmaloch
455
Roster
Red Moss
B. Clyth
Bruan
A895
494
Sheppardstown
Osclay
Hill of Mid. Clyth
255
Pourho.
Crofts
Buireanrob.
Irigh Hill
Laid
Upper Lybster
Mid Clyth
Halberry H.d
Benachielt
Golsary
Blood Moss
Terraneach
Blackness
Riskamain
Bevachielt
Rumster
Lybster Mains
Torranreach
Moss of Reisgill
Achow
Up. Clyth
Mullbuie
Corr
Nottingham
Clyth
Clyth Mains
Buoltach
Shaddest
Forse
Harshos
LYBSTER
Hill-head
Roster
Harbour
Houstry
Up. Latheron
Ho.
Marshos
Staill
Ceann Hilligeo
Leodebest
Gillowan
Inarshos
Smiley
Lybster Bay
Cnock
Swiney
Latheronwheel
Ho.
Latheron
Forse
Achastleshore
Smerral
Ch.
Wandt
Cairo
Latheronwheel
275
Langsetow
Ach-na-goul
W.r Latheron
Latheronwheel
Ballentink
Knockstanon
Dun
Ballachly
Braehungie
Inn
Dunbeath
Inver
A9
Dunbeath B.
Cnockally
Dunbeath Cas.
craigs
Mains
An Thin
Newport
Ceann Leuthad
nam Bo
dale

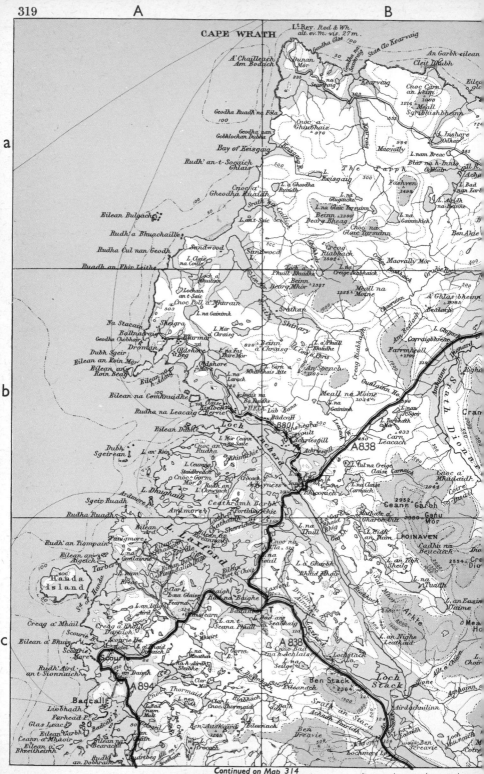

CAPE WRATH

Lt. Rev. Red & Wh.
alt. ev. m. vis. 27m.

A

B

a

b

c

Continued on Map 314

0   1   2   3 Miles

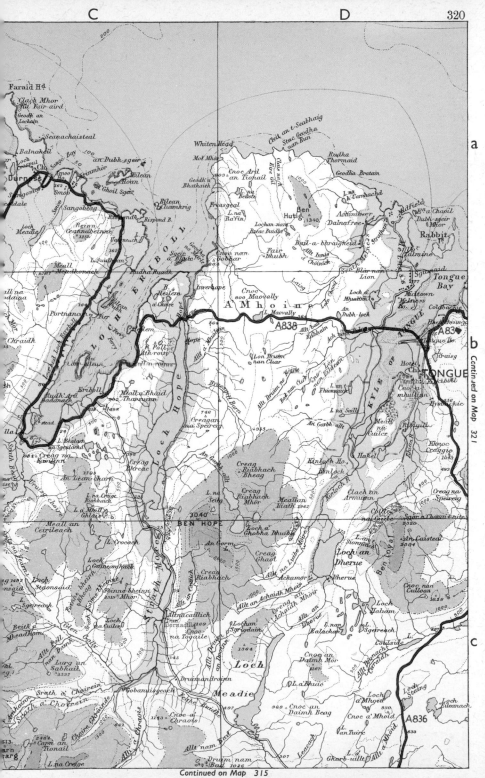

a

b

Continued on Map 321

c

Faraid Hᵈ

Clach Mhor
Rh' Fair-aird
Geodh an
Lochain

Seanachaisteal

Balnakeil

Durness

Sango Bay
an Dubh-sgeir

Whiten Head
Mol Mhor

Cleit an t-Seabhaig
Stac Geodha
nan Bun

Rudha
Thormaid

Geodha Bratain

Faraid Hᵈ

Sangomore
cdale

Smoo
Ho

Eilean
Hoan

Choil Sgeir

Geodh'a
Bhathaich

Cnoc Aird
an Tiohail

L. na
Ra'Fin

Ben
Hutig
1340

Ach'inmver

Midfield

Dubh-sgeir
Mhor

Sangobeag

Rispond

Rispond B.

Eilean
Cluamhrig

Friasgeal

Lochan nan
Breac Buidhe

Dalnafree

Rabbit

Reinn
Ceathabeinne
1253

Meall
Meadie

Varmeich

Cnoc nan
Gobhar

Fair
Dhubh

Buil-a-bhraghaid

Allt Innis
Choinich

Kalmine

Meall
Meudhonach

Rudha Ruadh

Inverhope

Cnoc nan
Choinich

Seil'a' Melness

Blàr nan
Lion

Tongue
Bay

LOCH ERIBOLL

Rudha
Heilem
a' Choire

Cnoc
Maovally

A Mhoine

L. Maovally

Laisg

Loch a'
Mhuilinn

Midtown
Bo.

Midtown
Melness

Coldbackie

Portnancon

Eriboll

Hope

Allt a' Mhuilinn

A838

Rhàbhain

Ach nam
Ba

An
Dubh-loch

A838

Ruadh'Aru
Badanach

Hope

Allt-rony

Lòn Drum
nan Clair

Bad nan Clar

Lòn Eildean

L. na
Fhionnaich

Hotel

TONGUE

Ribigill

Meall a' Bhaid
Thar-suinn

Dyke na Burn

Creagan
na Speirein
746

An Garbh-allt

L. na Saill

Meall
na Cuilce

Kinloch Ho.

Klenoc
Craggie

Creag
Dhreac

L. na Croige
Riabhach

Creag
Riabhach
Bheag

Creag
Riabhach
Mhor

Meallan
Liath

Kinloch
Lo.

Clach an
Armuinn

Creag na
Re'dinn

An Leathain

L. na
Seilg

BEN HOPE
3040

Loch a'
Chobha Dhuibh

An Gorm

Coille
na Gairbh

Sgor n'Choin-rite

Ard Caisteal

Meall an
Ceirileach

L. Crocach

Creag
Ghaol

Creag
Riabhach

Allt na Luibe More

Ackamor

Loch an
Dherue

Cnoc nan
Culdoon

Loch
Stansaid

Finne-bheinn
Mhor

Dherue

L. nan
Ealachan

Loch
Haluim

Coldside

Beith
Mheadhom

L. na Caled

Altnacaillich
Dornaq

Cnoc
na Togaile

Lochan
Sgriodain

Alltan
Dherue

Cnoc an
Daimh Mor

Lurg an
Sabhail

Druimandrann

Loch
MEADIE

Loch
a'Bhuic

Loch
a'Mhoid

Loch
Staing

Loch
Eileanach

Gobannaisgeach

Cnoc an
Daimh Beag

Cnoc a'Mhoid

A836

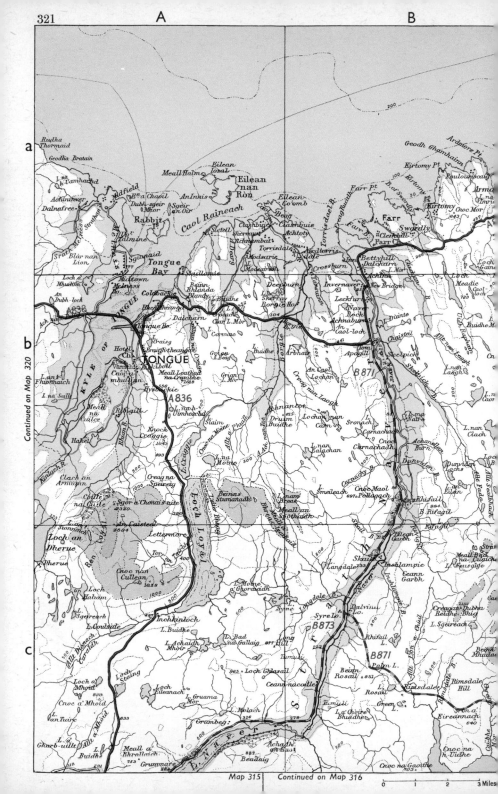

A   B

a

b

c

Continued on Map 320

Rudha
Thormaid

Geodha Bratain

L. na
h' Uamhachd

Achininver

Dalnafree

Midfield

E⁻ a' Chapil

Dubh-sgeir
a' Mhoir

Sgeir
an Oir

AnInnis

Rabbit Is.

Srath Melness

Strathan

Midtown

Ur Talmine

Blar nan
Lion

Sgunaid

Tongue
Bay

Stoillomie

Coldbackie

Loch a'
Mhuilinn

Midtown
McInnes

An
Dubh-loch

Ach nan

A838

Bhrachermie

Dalchuirn

Tongue Ho.

Ceannabeinne

Braigh
theanga

Hotel

KYLE OF TONGUE

Varrich
Ch.

TONGUE

Rhitongue

Cnoc a'
mhuilinn

A836

Melness
McInnes

Meall Leathad
na Craoibhe
1238

Hysbackie

Kinloch R.

Meall
na
Saule

Hakel

Rhingill

Rhian R.

L. nah'
Uamhachd

Slaim

Knock
Craggie
1043

993

Creag na
Speireig

Sgor a' Chonais' nite
2320

Chill'
na Guile

Clach an
Armuinn

Loch an
Dherue

Dherue

An Caisteal
2504

Lettermore

Torrisdale

Loch
Haluim

Cnoc nan
Cullean
1828

Inchkinloch

L. Sgeireach

L. Coulside

L. Buidhe

L. Achaidh
Mhoir

L. Bad
na Gallaig 977

Long
Hill

L. Staoing

Cnoc a' Mhoid
850

Loch a'
Mhoid

Cnoc na
Kileanach

L. Gruama
Mor

L.
van Tiare

L. a'
Gharb-uillt

L.
Buidhe

Meall a'
Bhrollaich
753

Grummore

Grumbeg

Allt Dhonach
Coraidh

Meall Halm

Eilean
Iosal

Eilean
nan
Ròn

Eilean
Co'omb

Caol Raineach

Beag

Sletell

Skerray

Achaembat

Torrisdale

Modsarie

L.
Modsarie

Beinn
Bhlanda
Blandy

Blaidhe

Clan L. Mor

Cornaag

Grian
L. Beag

L. Buidhe

Grian
L. Mor

Beinn's
Stumanadh

Coir na Moine

L. na
Moine

Allt a' Phuill

A 836 Road

L. nam
Breac

Bheil Chaillsgaisl

Meall an
Spothaidh

Moine a' Ghoraidh

Syre

L. Molach

Beadaig

Deesburn

L.
Sherray
Borgie Ho.

Crossburn

Leckfurin

Arbhair

Creag nan Laogh

Lochan nan
Cairn

Lochan nan
Carn

Smeileach

Cnoc Maol
Pollaqqch
691

Carnachadh

Skail

Langdale

Syre Lo.

B873

Rhifail

B871

Beinn
Rosail 851

L. Rosail

Rimsdale
Green

Tomuli

L. a' Choire
Bhuidhe

Naver

Clashbuie

Achtoty

Aultorrisdale

Invernaver

New Bridge

Nave
Rock

Achnaburn

An Caol-loch

Tom
Apgill

B871

Sronach

Carnachadh

Carnachy B.

Shiel B.

Bun

Dalvina
Lo.

Inchmuirk B.

Creagan Dubha
Beidhe Bhig

L. Sgeireach

B871

Rimsdale
Hill

Beinn
Mhadaidh

Farr Pt

B. er Sworrdy

Farr R.

Farr

Swordly

Clerkhill

Farr Ch.

Bettyhill
Dalchairn

Achina

Duntie

Chaisteil

Sronach

Cnoc
Carnachadh
Burn

Achanlochy
Burn

Dunviden
Lochs

Allt na
Fala

L. nan
Eilean

Rhifail

B. Rifagil

Rifagil

Allan Garbh

Meall Bad
na Fuaisiche
Reusaidhe

Loch
Meadie

Caol-loch

L. na
Caor

Uidh Raphail

Buidhe M.

Cn

L. nan
Laoigh

L. nan
Clach

Skullomie

Ardtore Pt

Geodh Ghamhainn

Kirtomy Pt

Foulourscaig

Kirtomy

Cnoc Mor
543

Arma

L. na
Muirie

Srath na
Eireannach
640

Cnoc na
h' Uidhe

Cashie

Strd

Stichichie B.

Slichichie B.

Map 315   Continued on Map 316

0   1   2   3 Miles

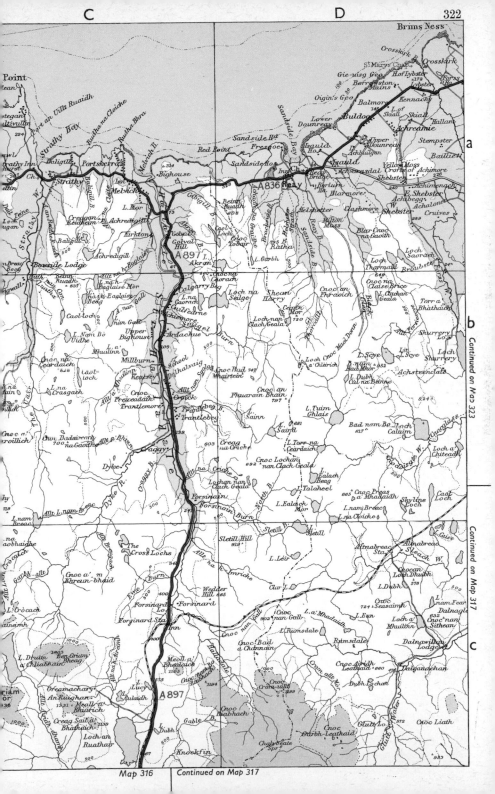

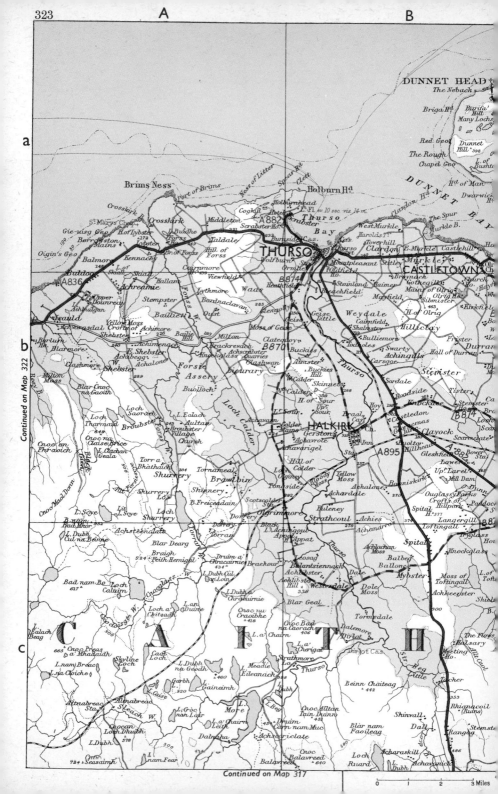

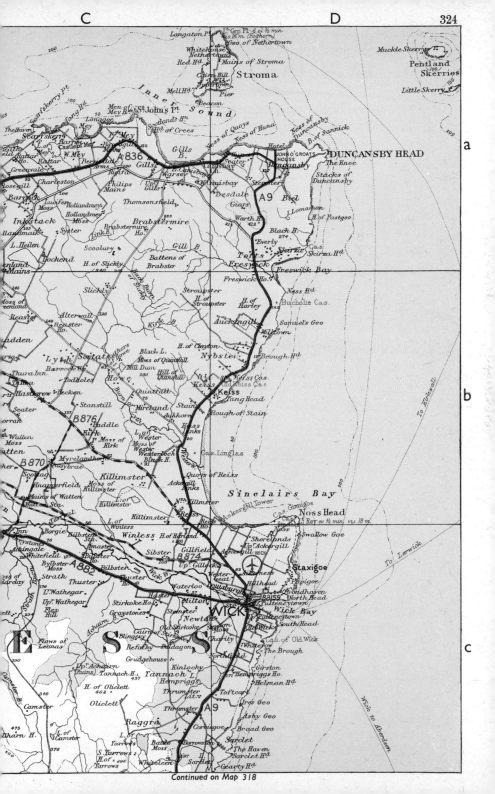

EXPLANATION OF INDEX

THE letters following the page number indicate the Map Square in which the place is situated. Large letters are shown at the top of the Map Section and small letters down the sides.

For Example **STRATFORD-ON-AVON**   Page **91**   Sq. **Aa**

is found on page 91 under square **A** and along square **a**.

WEATHER REGIONS

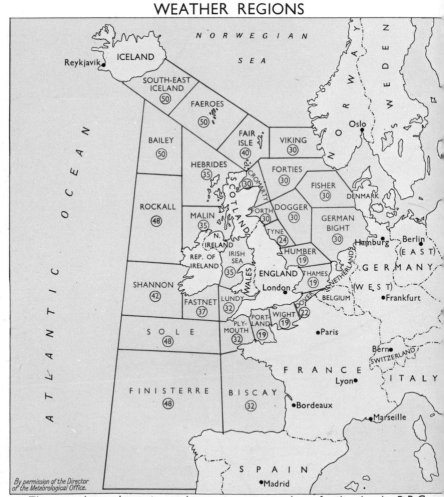

By permission of the Director of the Meteorological Office.

This map shows the various gale-warning areas made so familiar by the B.B.C.

The figures below each name indicate the average number of days a year on which a gale blows.

INDEX

COUNTY ABBREVIATIONS

Aber.	Aberdeen	Dors.	Dorset
Ang.	Anglesey	Dumb.	Dumbarton
Beds.	Bedford	Dumf.	Dumfries
Berks.	Berkshire	Dur.	Durham
Berw.	Berwick	E. Loth.	East Lothian
Brecon	Brecknock	Glam.	Glamorgan
Bucks.	Buckingham	Glos.	Gloucester
Caer.	Caernarvon	Hants.	Hampshire
Caith.	Caithness	Herefs.	Hereford
Cambs.	Cambridge	Herts.	Hertford
Card.	Cardigan	Hunts.	Huntingdon
Carm.	Carmarthen	Inver.	Inverness
Ches.	Cheshire	I.O.M.	Isle of Man
Corn.	Cornwall	Kinc.	Kincardine
Cumb.	Cumberland	Kinr.	Kinross
Den.	Denbigh	Kirk.	Kirkcudbright
Dev.	Devon	Lan.	Lanark

Lancs.	Lancashire	R. & C.	Ross & Cromarty
Leics.	Leicester	Rox.	Roxburgh
Lincs.	Lincoln	Rut.	Rutland
Mer.	Merioneth	Shrops.	Shropshire
M'sex.	Middlesex	Som.	Somerset
M. Loth.	Midlothian	Staffs.	Stafford
Mon.	Monmouth	Stir.	Stirling
Mont.	Montgomery	Suff.	Suffolk
Norf.	Norfolk	Sur.	Surrey
N'hants.	Northampton	Sus.	Sussex
N'land	Northumberland	Suth.	Sutherland
Notts.	Nottingham	War.	Warwick
Oxon.	Oxford	W. Loth.	West Lothian
Peeb.	Peebles	W'land.	Westmorland
Pem.	Pembroke	Wilts.	Wiltshire
Rad.	Radnor	Worcs.	Worcester
Renf.	Renfrew	Yorks.	Yorkshire

Name	PAGE	SQ.
ABBAS COMBE	35	Bb
Abberley	108	Db
Abberley Common	108	Db
Abberton, *Essex*	78	Db
Abberton, *Worcs.*	109	Bc
Abbess Roding	77	Ac
Abbey Cwmhir	105	Bb
Abbey Dore	87	Bb
Abbey St. Bathans	253	Bc
Abbey Town	216	Dc
Abbots Bickington	12	Ca
Abbots Bromley	147	Bc
Abbotsbury	17	Bb
Abbotsford	241	Bb
Abbotsham	29	Bc
Abbotskerswell	14	Cc
Abbots Langley	75	Ae
Abbots Leigh	50	Da
Abbots Lench	110	Cc
Abbotsley	95	Bb
Abbots Morton	110	Cc
Abbots Ripton	115	Bc
Abbots Salford	90	Da
Abbots Worthy	39	Ab
Abbotts Ann	38	Ca
Abdon	108	Ca
Aber	156	Db
Aberaman	86	Cc
Aberangell	122	Da
Aber Arad	83	Bb
Aberavon	65	Aa
Aberayron	101	Ab
Aberbargoed	67	Ab
Abercanaid	86	Dc
Abercarn	67	Ab
Aberchirder	304	Db
Abercorn	251	Aa
Abercrave	85	Bb
Abercych	83	Ab
Abercynon	66	Da
Aberdare	86	Cc
Aberdaron	139	Ac
Aberdeen	294	Db
Aberdour	251	Aa
Aberdovey	121	Bb
Aberedw	104	Db
Abererch	140	Cb
Aberfeldy	269	Ab
Aberffraw	155	Bc
Aberford	184	Dc
Aberfoyle	258	Cc
Abergavenny	67	Ba
Abergele	158	Ca
Abergorlech	84	Db
Abergwesyn	103	Ba
Abergwili	64	Ca
Abergwynfi	65	Ba
Abergynolwyn	121	Ba
Aberhafesp	123	Bc
Aberkenfig	65	Bb
Aberlady	252	Da
Aberlemno	272	Ca
Aberllefenni	122	Ca
Aberllynfi	87	Ab
Abernant, *Carm.*	83	Bc
Abernant, *Glam.*	86	Cc
Abernethy	261	Aa
Abernyte	270	Dc
Aberporth	83	Aa
Abercross	312	Ca
Aber-Soch	139	Bc
Abersychan	67	Ba
Abertillery	67	Aa

Name	PAGE	SQ.
Aberthin	66	Db
Aber-tridwr	66	Da
Aberuthven	260	Ca
Aberyscir	86	Ca
Aberystwyth	101	Ba
Abingdon	72	Db
Abinger	41	Bb
Abinghall	89	Ac
Abington, *Lan.*	238	Dc
Abington, *N'hants.*	113	Ac
Abington, Gt.	96	Dc
Abington, Lit.	96	Db
Abington Pigotts	95	Bc
Ab Kettleby	130	Da
Ablington	70	Da
Abney	163	Ab
Aboyne	281	Aa
Abram	170	Cc
Abridge	58	Da
Abson	51	Aa
Abthorpe	93	Aa
Aby	154	Ca
Acaster Malbis	185	Bc
Acaster Selby	185	Ac
Accrington	171	Aa
Achahoish	245	Ab
Achanalt	299	Aa
Achaphubuil	275	Ac
Acharacle	264	Ca
Acharn	268	Db
Achiltibuie	313	Ac
Achintee	298	Cb
Achintraid	285	Ba
Achnasheen	298	Da
Achnastank	291	Ba
Achreamie	322	Da
Achurch	114	Ca
Ackenthwaite	193	Bc
Acklam	186	Ca
Acklam, W.	208	Cc
Ackleton	126	Dc
Acklington	232	Cb
Ackton	174	Cb
Ackworth, High	174	Cb
Ackworth, Low	174	Cb
Ackworth Moor Top	174	Cb
Acle	120	Ca
Acocks Green	110	Da
Acol	46	Da
Acomb, *N'land.*	220	Cb
Acomb, *Yorks.*	185	Ab
Aconbury	88	Cb
Acre	171	Aa
Acrise	28	Ca
Acton, *Ches.*	160	Db
Acton, *Ches.*	145	Ba
Acton, *M'sex.*	57	Bb
Acton, *Staffs.*	146	Db
Acton, *Suff.*	98	Cc
Acton, *Worcs.*	109	Ab
Acton Beauchamp	89	Aa
Acton Burnell	125	Bb
Acton Green	89	Aa
Acton Round	126	Cc
Acton Scott	125	Ac
Acton Trussell	127	Ba
Acton Turville	69	Bc
Adbaston	146	Ca
Adber	35	Ab
Adderbury	92	Db
Adderley	145	Bb
Addiewell	250	Dc
Addingham	183	Ab

Name	PAGE	SQ.
Addington, *Bucks.*	93	Bc
Addington, *Kent*	43	Ba
Addington, *Sur.*	42	Da
Addington, Gt.	114	Cb
Addington, Lit.	114	Cb
Addlestone	41	Aa
Addlethorpe	154	Da
Adel	184	Cc
Adforton	107	Ab
Adisham	46	Cb
Adlestrop	91	Bc
Adlingfleet	176	Cb
Adlington	170	Cb
Admaston, *Shrop.*	126	Ca
Admaston, *Staffs.*	128	Ca
Admington	91	Aa
Adsborough	33	Bb
Adstock	93	Bb
Adstone	93	Aa
Adversane	23	Ba
Adwalton	173	Aa
Adwell	73	Bb
Adwick le Street	174	Dc
Adwick-on-Dearne	174	Cc
Affpuddle	18	Ca
Agglethorpe	196	Cb
Aigburth	159	Bb
Aike	177	Aa
Aikshead	217	Ac
Aikton	217	Ac
Ailey	87	Ba
Ailsworth	115	Aa
Ainderby Quernhow	197	Ac
Ainderby Steeple	197	Ab
Aingers Green	79	Bc
Ainsdale	169	Ab
Ainstable	218	Cc
Ainsworth	171	Ab
Aintree	169	Bc
Aird of Sleat	273	Aa
Airdrie	249	Bb
Airmyn	175	Ba
Airmyn, Lit.	175	Ba
Airor	285	Bc
Airth	250	Ca
Aisby	152	Cb
Aisholt	33	Bb
Aiskew	196	Db
Aislaby	207	Ba
Aisthorpe	166	Cb
Akeld	243	Bc
Akeley	93	Bb
Akenham	99	Ac
Alberbury	124	Da
Albert Street	144	Ca
Albourne	24	Cb
Albrighton, *Shrops.*	126	Db
Albrighton, *Shrops.*	125	Ba
Alburgh	119	Bb
Albury, *Herts.*	76	Cb
Albury, *Oxon.*	73	Ab
Albury, *Sur.*	41	Ab
Alcaston	107	Ba
Alcester	110	Cc
Alciston	25	Bc
Alcombe	48	Cb
Alconbury	115	Ac
Alconbury Weston	114	Db
Aldborough, *Norf.*	137	Ba
Aldborough, *Yorks.*	184	Da
Aldborough Hatch	58	Db
Aldborough, *Yorks.*	206	Dc

Name	PAGE	SQ.
Aldbrough, *Yorks.*	178	Ch
Aldbury	74	Da
Aldcliffe	180	Db
Aldclune	278	Dc
Aldeburgh	100	Dc
Aldeby	120	Cb
Aldenham	57	Aa
Alderbury	37	Bb
Alderford	137	Ac
Alderholt	37	Bc
Alderley	69	Bb
Alderley Edge	161	Bb
Aldermaston	55	Ab
Aldermaston Wharf	55	Ab
Alderminster	91	Ba
Aldersey Green	144	Da
Aldershot	56	Cc
Alderton, *Glos.*	90	Db
Alderton, *N'hants.*	93	Ba
Alderton, *Suff.*	80	Ca
Alderton, *Wilts.*	69	Bc
Alderwasley	148	Da
Aldford	144	Da
Aldham, *Essex*	78	Cb
Aldham, *Suff.*	79	Aa
Aldingbourne	23	Ac
Aldingham	179	Ba
Aldingham, Upr.	192	Dc
Aldington, *Kent*	28	Ca
Aldington, *Worcs.*	90	Da
Aldon	107	Ba
Aldreth	96	Cs
Aldridge	128	Cb
Aldringham	100	Db
Aldsworth	71	Aa
Aldwark, *Derby*	148	Ca
Aldwark, *Yorks.*	184	Da
Aldwick	23	Ac
Aldwinkle St. Peter	114	Ca
Aldworth	54	Da
Alethorpe	136	Db
Alexandria	248	Ca
Alfington	15	Ab
Alfold	41	Ac
Alford, *Aber.*	292	Db
Alford, *Lincs.*	154	Ca
Alford, *Som.*	35	Aa
Alfreton	149	Ba
Alfrick	108	Dc
Alfriston	25	Bc
Algarkirk	133	Ba
Alham, Higher	35	Ba
Alhampton	35	Ba
Alkborough	176	Cb
Alkerton	92	Cb
Alkham	28	Da
Alkington	128	Cb
Allaston	69	Aa
All Cannings	52	Db
Allendale Town	220	Cc
Allenheads	205	Ba
Allensmore	88	Cb
Aller	34	Cb
Allerby	201	Bu
Allerford	48	Cb
Allerston	187	Aa
Allerthorpe	186	Cb
Allerton, *Lancs.*	160	Ca
Allerton, *Yorks.*	172	Da
Allerton Bywater	174	Ca
Allerton Mauleverer	184	Db
Allesley	111	Aa
Allestree	148	Db

	PAGE	SQ.
Allexton .	131	Bc
Allhallows .	60	Cc
Allington, *Kent* .	44	Ca
Allington, *Lincs.*	151	Bb
Allington, *Wilts.*	37	Bb
Allington, *Wilts.*	52	Db
Allington, *Wilts.*	52	Ca
Allithwaite .	193	Ac
Alloa .	259	Bc
Allonby .	201	Ba
Allowenshay .	16	Da
All Saints and St. Nicholas.	119	Bc
All Stretton .	125	Ac
Alltmawr .	104	Db
Allt-wen .	85	Ac
Allweston .	35	Ac
Almeley .	87	Ba
Almer .	18	Da
Almington .	146	Cc
Almondbury .	172	Db
Almondsbury .	68	Dc
Alne .	184	Da
Alne, Gt. .	110	Cc
Alness .	300	Da
Alnham .	231	Aa
Alnmouth .	232	Ca
Alnwick .	232	Ca
Alperton .	57	Ab
Alphamstone .	78	Ca
Alpheton .	98	Cb
Alphington .	14	Da
Alpington .	119	Ba
Alport .	163	Ac
Alresford .	79	Ac
Alresford, New .	39	Ab
Alresfor Old .	39	Ab
Alrewas .	128	Ca
Alsager .	146	Ca
Alsop-en-le-dale .	148	Ca
Alston .	219	Bc
Alstone .	90	Db
Alstonfield .	148	Ca
Alston Sutton .	50	Cc
Altandow .	313	Ac
Altarnun .	7	Aa
Altcar, Gt. .	169	Aa
Altham .	171	Aa
Althorne .	60	Ca
Althorpe .	176	Cc
Altofts .	174	Ca
Alton, *Derby* .	163	Bc
Alton, *Hants.* .	39	Ba
Alton, *Staffs.* .	147	Bb
Alton Barnes .	53	Ab
Alton Pancras .	18	Ca
Alton Priors .	53	Ab
Altrincham .	161	Ba
Alva .	259	Bc
Alvanley .	160	Cb
Alvaston .	149	Ac
Alvechurch .	110	Cb
Alvediston .	36	Db
Alveley .	108	Da
Alverdiscott .	30	Cc
Alverston .	21	Bc
Alverthorpe .	173	Bb
Alverton .	151	Ab
Alvescot .	71	Bb
Alveston, *Glos.* .	69	Ac
Alveston, *War.* .	110	Dc
Alvingham .	168	Cc
Alvington .	68	Db
Alwalton .	115	Ab
Alwington .	29	Bc
Alwinton .	230	Da
Alwoodley Gates .	184	Cc
Alyth .	270	Db
Ambergate .	148	Da
Amber Hill .	153	Bc
Amberley, *Glos.* .	69	Bb
Amberley, *Sus.* .	23	Bb
Amble .	232	Db
Amblecote .	109	Ba
Ambleside .	192	Da
Ambleston .	82	Cc
Ambrosden .	93	Ac
Amcotts .	176	Cb
Amersham .	74	Db
Amesbury .	37	Ba
Amington .	128	Db
Amlwch .	155	Ba
Ammanford .	64	Da
Amotherby .	198	Dc
Ampfield .	38	Dc
Ampleforth .	198	Cc
Ampney Crucis .	70	Da
Ampney St. Mary .	70	Da
Ampney St. Peter .	70	Db
Amport .	38	Ca
Ampthill .	94	Db
Ampton .	98	Ca
Amroth .	62	Db
Amulree .	269	Bc
Amwell, Gt. .	76	Cc

	PAGE	SQ.
Amwell, Lit. .	76	Cc
Ancaster .	152	Cb
Ancroft .	243	Ba
Ancrum .	241	Dc
Anderby .	154	Da
Andersfield .	33	Bb
Anderson .	18	Da
Anderton .	160	Db
Andover .	38	Da
Andreas .	189	Aa
Angelbank .	108	Ca
Angersleigh .	33	Ac
Angle .	61	Bb
Anglesey .	155	Bb
Angmering .	23	Bc
Angram, *Yorks.* .	195	Aa
Angram, *Yorks.* .	185	Ab
Anick .	220	Cb
Anlaby .	176	Da
Anmer .	135	Bb
Annan .	216	Db
Annesley .	149	Ba
Annesley Wood-house .	149	Ba
Annfield Plain .	221	Bc
Ansford .	35	Ba
Ansley .	128	Dc
Anslow .	148	Cc
Anstey, *Hants.* .	39	Ba
Anstey, *Herts.* .	76	Ca
Anstey, *Leics.* .	130	Cb
Anstey, E. .	32	Ca
Anstey, W. .	32	Ca
Anston, N. .	164	Db
Anston, S. .	164	Db
Anstruther, Easter	262	Db
Anstruther, Wester	262	Db
Ansty, *Dors.* .	36	Db
Ansty, *War.* .	111	Ba
Anthorn .	216	Db
Antingham .	137	Bb
Anton, E. .	54	Cc
Antony .	8	Cc
Anwick .	152	Bb
Anwoth .	213	Bb
Apethorpe .	132	Cc
Apeton .	127	Aa
Apley .	153	Aa
Apperknowle .	164	Cb
Apperley .	90	Cb
Apperley Bridge .	183	Bc
Apperley, Lr. .	90	Cb
Appersett .	195	Ab
Appleby, *Lincs.* .	176	Db
Appleby, *W'land* .	204	Dc
Appleby Magna .	129	Ab
Applecross .	297	Ab
Appledore, *Dev.* .	30	Cb
Appledore, *Kent* .	27	Bb
Appledore Heath.	27	Bb
Appledram .	22	Da
Appleford .	72	Dc
Applegarth .	227	Bc
Appleshaw .	53	Bc
Applethwaite .	202	Db
Appleton, *Berks.* .	72	Cb
Appleton, *Ches.* .	160	Cb
Appleton, E. .	196	Db
Appleton-le-Moor	198	Db
Appleton-le-Street	198	Dc
Appleton Roebuck	185	Ac
Appleton Wiske .	197	Ba
Appletree .	92	Da
Appletreewick .	182	Db
Appley .	33	Ac
Apsley End .	75	Aa
Aquhythie .	293	Bb
Aquila .	173	Aa
Arbeadie .	281	Ba
Arbirlot .	272	Cb
Arborfield .	55	Bb
Arbroath .	272	Db
Archdeacon Newton .	207	Ac
Archiestown .	303	Ac
Ardbeg .	246	Dc
Ardeley .	76	Ca
Ardelve .	286	Cb
Ardentinny .	247	Aa
Ardeonaig .	268	Dc
Ardgour .	265	Ba
Ardingly .	24	Da
Ardington .	72	Cc
Ardlair .	292	Da
Ardleigh .	79	Ab
Ardler .	271	Ab
Ardley .	92	Dc
Ardlui .	257	Bb
Ardminish .	233	Aa
Ardmore .	263	Ba
Ardnastang .	265	Aa
Ardoyne .	293	Aa
Ardrishaig .	245	Ba
Ardroag .	295	Bc
Ardrossan .	235	Bb

	PAGE	SQ.
Ardsley .	174	Cc
Ardsley, E. .	173	Ba
Ardtalnaig .	268	Db
Ardtoe .	273	Bc
Areley Kings .	109	Ab
Arford .	40	Ca
Arglam .	186	Cc
Argoed .	67	Ab
Arinakaig .	298	Cb
Arkendale .	184	Da
Arkesden .	76	Da
Arkholme .	180	Da
Arkle Town .	195	Ba
Arksey .	174	Dc
Arkwright Town .	164	Cc
Arle .	90	Cc
Arlecdon .	201	Bc
Arlesey .	75	Ba
Arleston .	126	Cb
Arley .	128	Dc
Arley, Upr. .	108	Da
Arlingham .	69	Aa
Arlington, *Dev.* .	30	Da
Arlington, *Glos.* .	71	Ba
Arlington, *Sus.* .	25	Bb
Armadale, *Suth.* .	321	Ba
Armadale, *W.Loth.*	250	Cb
Armathwaite .	203	Ba
Arminghall .	119	Ba
Armitage .	128	Ca
Armitage Bridge .	172	Db
Armscote .	91	Ba
Armston .	114	Da
Arnaby .	174	Dc
Arncliffe .	182	Ca
Arne .	19	Ba
Arnesby .	130	Dc
Arnfield .	162	Da
Arnisdale .	286	Cc
Arnold, *Notts.* .	150	Cb
Arnold, *Yorks.* .	177	Ba
Arnside .	193	Ac
Arowry .	144	Db
Arpinge .	28	Ca
Arram .	177	Aa
Arrathorne .	196	Db
Arreton .	21	Bc
Arrington .	95	Bb
Arrochar .	257	Ab
Arrow .	110	Cc
Arthington .	184	Cc
Arthingworth .	113	Aa
Arundel .	23	Ac
Asby, Lit. .	204	Dc
Asby, Gt. .	204	Dc
Ascog .	246	Dc
Ascot (Royal) .	56	Cb
Ascott .	91	Bb
Ascot under Wych-wood .	71	Ba
Asenby .	197	Ba
Asfordby .	130	Da
Asgarby, *Lincs.* .	152	Db
Asgarby, *Lincs.* .	153	Bb
Ash, *Kent* .	43	Bc
Ash, *Kent* .	46	Cb
Ash, *Som.* .	33	Bc
Ash, *Som.* .	34	Dc
Ash, *Sur.* .	56	Cc
Ashampstead .	54	Da
Ashbocking, Gr. .	99	Bc
Ashbourne .	148	Cb
Ashbrittle .	33	Ac
Ashburton .	13	Bc
Ashbury, *Berks.* .	71	Bc
Ashbury, *Dev.* .	12	Db
Ashby, *Lincs.* .	176	Cc
Ashby, *Norf.* .	119	Ba
Ashby, *Suff.* .	120	Db
Ashby by Partney	154	Cb
Ashby-cum-Fenby	167	Bb
Ashby de la Launde	152	
Ashby-de-la-Zouch	129	Ba
Ashby Folville .	130	Db
Ashby Magna .	112	Ca
Ashby Parva .	112	Ca
Ashby Puerorum .	153	Ba
Ashby St. Ledgers	112	Cb
Ashchurch .	90	Cb
Ashcombe .	14	Db
Ashcott .	34	Da
Ashdon .	97	Ac
Ashe .	54	Dc
Asheldham .	60	Da
Ashen .	97	Bc
Ashendon .	73	Ba
Ashfield .	99	Bb
Ashfield Gr. .	99	Ba
Ashfield, Gt. .	98	Da
Ashford, *Dev.* .	30	Cb
Ashford, *Derby* .	163	Ac
Ashford, *Kent* .	27	Ba
Ashford, *M'sex.* .	56	Db
Ashford Bowdler	107	Bb
Ashford Carborell	107	Bb

	PAGE	SQ.
Ashford, South .	27	B
Ashill, *Dev.* .	15	Aa
Ashill, *Norf.* .	118	Cc
Ashill, *Som.* .	34	Cc
Ashingdon .	60	Cc
Ashington, *Sus.* .	23	Ba
Ashington, *N'land.*	232	Ba
Ashington, *Som.* .	35	Ac
Ashkirk .	241	Ac
Ashleworth .	89	Bb
Ashley, *Cambs.* .	97	Bb
Ashley, *Ches.* .	161	Bb
Ashley, *Hants.* .	38	Cb
Ashley, *Kent* .	46	Db
Ashley, *N'hants.* .	113	Aa
Ashley, *Staffs.* .	146	Cc
Ashley, *Wilts.* .	51	Ba
Ashley, *Wilts.* .	70	Cc
Ashley Green .	74	Db
Ashling .	22	Db
Ash Magna .	145	Bb
Ashmanhaugh .	138	Ca
Ashmansworth .	54	Cc
Ashmore .	36	Bb
Ashmore Green .	54	Db
Ashopton .	163	Ac
Ashover .	163	Bc
Ashover Hay .	149	Aa
Ashow .	111	Ab
Ash Parva .	145	Bb
Ashperton .	88	Da
Ashprington .	10	Ca
Ash Priors .	33	Ab
Ashreigney .	31	Ab
Ashridge .	74	Da
Ashtead .	41	Bb
Ashton, *Ches.* .	160	Cc
Ashton, *Corn.* .	2	Cc
Ashton, *Herefs.* .	107	Bb
Ashton, *N'hants.* .	114	Da
Ashton, *N'hants.* .	93	Ba
Ashton, *Renf.* .	247	Bb
Ashton Common .	52	Cb
Ashton, Higher .	14	Cb
Ashton in Maker-field .	170	Cc
Ashton Keynes .	70	Db
Ashton-u.-Hill .	90	Db
Ashton-u.-Lyne .	171	Bc
Ashton-on-Mersey	161	Ba
Ashton, W. .	52	Cb
Ashurst, *Sus.* .	24	Cb
Ashwater .	12	Cb
Ashwell, *Herts.* .	95	Bc
Ashwell, *Rut.* .	131	Bb
Ashwellthorpe .	119	Ab
Ashwick .	51	Ac
Ashwicken .	135	Bc
Askern .	174	Db
Askerswell .	17	Ab
Askett .	73	Bb
Askham, *Notts.* .	165	Bb
Askham, *W'land* .	203	Bb
Askham Bryan .	185	Ab
Askham Richard .	185	Ab
Askrigg .	195	Bb
Askwith .	183	Bb
Aslackby .	152	Bc
Aslacton .	119	Ab
Aslockton .	150	Db
Aspall .	99	Ab
Aspatria .	202	Ca
Aspenden .	76	Ca
Aspley Guise .	94	Cb
Asselby .	175	Ba
Assendon, Lr. .	73	Ba
Assendon, Mid .	73	Bc
Assington .	78	Da
Astbury .	161	Bc
Asterby .	153	Ba
Asterley .	124	Db
Asthall .	71	Ba
Asthall Leigh .	71	Ba
Astley, *Shrops.* .	125	Ba
Astley, *War.* .	111	Aa
Astley, *Worcs.* .	108	Db
Astley Abbotts .	126	Cc
Aston, *Ches.* .	145	Ab
Aston, *Derby* .	163	Ab
Aston, *Flint* .	159	Bc
Aston, *Herefs.* .	107	Bb
Aston, *Herts.* .	75	Bb
Aston, *Oxon.* .	71	Bb
Aston, *Shrops.* .	145	Ac
Aston, *Staffs.* .	146	Cb
Aston, *War.* .	128	Cc
Aston, *Yorks.* .	164	Cb
Aston Abbotts .	94	Cb
Aston Blank .	91	Ac
Aston Botterell .	108	Ca
Aston Cantlow .	110	Dc
Aston Clinton .	74	Cb
Aston, E. .	38	Da
Aston Eyre .	126	Cc

Name	Page	Sq
Aston Fields	109	Bb
Aston Flamville	129	Bc
Aston Ingham	89	Ac
Aston juxta Mondrum	145	Ba
Aston le Walls	92	Ba
Aston Magna	91	Ab
Aston, Mid.	92	Dc
Aston, N.	92	Dc
Aston-on-Carrant	90	Cb
Aston-on-Clun	107	Aa
Aston Rowant	73	Bb
Aston Sandford	73	Ba
Aston Somerville	90	Db
Aston Subedge	91	Ab
Aston Tirrold	72	Dc
Aston-upon-Trent	149	Bc
Aston Upthorpe	72	Dc
Astrop	92	Db
Astwick	95	Bc
Astwith	164	Cc
Astwood	94	Ca
Astwood Bank	110	Cb
Aswarby	152	Db
Aswardby	154	Ca
Atcham	125	Da
Athelhampton	18	Ca
Athelington	99	Ba
Athelney	34	Cb
Athelstaneford	252	Da
Atherington	30	Dc
Atherstone	129	Ac
Atherstone-on-Stour	91	Aa
Atherton	170	Dc
Atlow	148	Cb
Attadale	286	Ca
Attenborough	150	Cc
Atterby	166	Ca
Atterton	129	Ac
Attleborough, Norf.	118	Db
Attleborough, War.	111	Ba
Attlebridge	137	Ac
Atwick	178	Ba
Atworth	52	Ca
Auberrow	88	Ca
Auburn	152	Ca
Auchencairn	214	Dc
Auchencar	234	Cb
Auchengray	250	Dc
Auchenhalrig	303	Ba
Auchinblae	282	Cb
Auchinleck	237	Ac
Auchleven	293	Aa
Auchnagoul	256	Cb
Auchterarder	260	Cb
Auchterderran	261	Ac
Auchtermuchty	261	Ab
Auchterneed	300	Cb
Auchtertool	261	Ac
Auchtertyre	271	Ab
Auckingill	324	Db
Auckland, W.	206	Db
Auckley	175	Ac
Audlem	145	Bb
Audley	146	Ca
Audmore	126	Da
Audnam	109	Ba
Aughertree	202	Da
Aughton, Lancs.	169	Bc
Aughton, Wilts.	53	Bc
Aughton, Yorks.	186	Dc
Aughton, Yorks.	164	Ca
Auldearn	302	Cb
Aulden	107	Bc
Ault Hucknall	164	Cc
Aunsby	152	Cb
Aust	68	Dc
Austerfield	165	Aa
Austonley	172	Dc
Austrey	128	Db
Austwick	181	Ba
Authorpe	168	Cc
Avebury	52	Ca
Aveley	58	Db
Avening	70	Cb
Averham	150	Da
Aveton Gifford	9	Bb
Aviemore	290	Cb
Avington, Berks.	54	Cb
Avington, Hants.	39	Ab
Avoch	301	Aa
Avon, Hants.	19	Bb
Avon, Wilts.	52	Ca
Avonbridge	250	Cb
Avon Dassett	92	Ca
Avonmouth	68	Dc
Avon Wick	9	Ba
Awliscombe	15	Ab
Awre	69	Aa
Awsworth	149	Bb
Axbridge	50	Cb
Axford	53	Bb
Axminster	16	Cb
Axmouth	16	Cb
Aycliffe	207	Ab
Aydon	220	Db
Aylburton	68	Db
Ayle	219	Bc
Aylesbeare	15	Ab
Aylesbury	74	Ca
Aylesby	167	Ba
Aylesford	44	Ca
Aylestone	130	Cc
Aylmerton	137	Ba
Aylsham	137	Bb
Aylton	89	Ab
Aymestrey	107	Bb
Aynho	92	Db
Ayot St. Lawrence	75	Bb
Ayot St. Peter	75	Bb
Ayr	236	Cc
Aysgarth	195	Bb
Ayston	131	Bc
Aythorpe Roding	77	Ab
Ayton	254	Dc
Ayton, E.	187	Ba
Ayton, Gt.	208	Dc
Ayton, W.	187	Ba
Azerley	196	Dc
BABBACOMBE	10	Da
Babcary	35	Ab
Babington	51	Ac
Babraham	96	Db
Babworth	165	Ab
Bach	87	Ba
Backbarrow	192	Db
Backe	63	Aa
Backford	159	Bc
Backies	312	Ca
Backwell	50	Ca
Backworth	222	Ca
Baconsthorpe	137	Aa
Bacton, Herefs.	87	Bb
Bacton, Norf.	138	Cb
Bacton, Suff.	98	Da
Bacup	171	Bb
Badbea	317	Bb
Badbury	53	Aa
Badby	112	Cc
Baddesley Ensor	128	Dc
Baddesley, N.	38	Dc
Baddiley	145	Ba
Baddow, Gt.	77	Bc
Baddow, Lit.	77	Bc
Badenscoth	305	Ac
Badger	126	Dc
Badgeworth	90	Cc
Badgworth	50	Cc
Badicaul	285	Ba
Badingham	100	Cb
Badlesmere	45	Ab
Badley	99	Ab
Badminton, Gt.	69	Bc
Badminton, Lit.	69	Bc
Badryrie	318	Ca
Badsey	90	Ba
Badsworth	174	Cb
Badwell Ash	98	Da
Bagborough	33	Ab
Bagby	197	Bc
Bag Enderby	153	Ba
Bagendon	70	Da
Baggrow	202	Ca
Bagillt	159	Ab
Baginton	111	Bb
Bagley	144	Dc
Bagmore	39	Ba
Bagnall	146	Da
Bagnor	54	Cb
Bagshaw	162	Db
Bagshot	56	Cb
Bagstone	69	Ac
Bagthorpe, Norf.	135	Ba
Bagthorpe, Notts.	149	Ba
Bagworth	129	Bb
Baildon	183	Bc
Bailiff Bridge	172	Da
Baillieston	249	Ac
Bainbridge	195	Bb
Bainton, N'hants.	132	Db
Bainton, Oxon.	92	Dc
Bainton, Yorks.	187	Bc
Baker Street	59	Ab
Bakewell	163	Ac
Bala	142	Db
Balbeggie	270	Dc
Balblair	301	Aa
Balby	174	Dc
Balchraggan	288	Da
Balcombe	24	Da
Baldernock	248	Db
Baldersby	197	Ac
Balderstone	170	Da
Balderton	151	Ba
Baldock	75	Ba
Baldwin	190	Cb
Bale	136	Da
Balerno	251	Ab
Balfron	248	Da
Balgowan	277	Ba
Balhalgardy	293	Db
Balham	57	Bc
Balhinny	292	Ba
Balintore, Angus	271	Aa
Balintore, R. & C.	312	Dc
Balk	197	Bc
Balkholme	175	Ba
Balking	71	Bc
Ball	144	Ca
Ballabeg	190	Dc
Ballachulish	266	Ca
Ballachulish, N.	266	Ca
Ballantrae	211	Ba
Ballasalla	190	Db
Ballater	280	Ca
Ballathona	189	Ab
Ballaugh	189	Ab
Ballidon	148	Ca
Ballimore	246	Ca
Ballingdon	98	Cc
Ballingham	88	Db
Ballingry	261	Ac
Ballinluig	269	Ba
Balloch, Dumb.	248	Ca
Balloch, Inver.	301	Ab
Ballymichael	234	Cb
Balmacara	285	Da
Balmaclellan	214	Ca
Balmaghie	214	Da
Balmer Heath	144	Dc
Balmerino	261	Ba
Balmoral	280	Ca
Balmore	288	Da
Balnaguard	269	Ba
Balquhidder	258	Ca
Balsall	110	Da
Balscott	92	Cb
Balsham	97	Ab
Baltonsborough	35	Aa
Bamber Bridge	170	Ca
Bamburgh	244	Db
Bamford	103	Ab
Bamfurlong	90	Ca
Bampton, Devon.	32	Da
Bampton, Oxon.	71	Bb
Bampton, W'land.	203	Bc
Bampton, Lit.	217	Ac
Banavie	275	Ac
Banbury	92	Cb
Banchory	281	Ba
Banc-y-felin	63	Ba
Banc-y-ffordd	84	Cb
Bandodle	293	Ac
Banff	305	Aa
Banghurst	54	Db
Bangor, Caer.	156	Db
Bangor, Card.	83	Bb
Bangor-is-y-coed.	144	Db
Banham	118	Db
Bankend, Dumf.	216	Ca
Bankend, Lan.	238	Cb
Bankfoot	270	Cc
Bankhill	204	Ca
Bank Newton	182	Cb
Banks, Cumb.	218	Db
Banks, Lancs.	169	Bb
Banningham	137	Bb
Bannister Green	77	Bb
Bannockburn	259	Bc
Banstead	42	Ca
Banwell	50	Cb
Bapchild	44	Da
Barbaraville	312	Ca
Barber Booth	162	Db
Barby	112	Cb
Barcheston	91	Bb
Barcombe	25	Ab
Barden	196	Cb
Bardfield, Gt.	77	Ba
Bardfield, Lit.	77	Ba
Bardfield Saling	77	Bb
Bardney	153	Aa
Bardon	129	Bb
Bardon Mill	219	Bb
Bardsey	184	Cc
Bardwell	98	Ca
Bare	180	Ca
Barewood	107	Aa
Barford, Norf.	119	Aa
Barford, War.	111	Ac
Barford, Gt.	95	Ab
Barford, Lit.	95	Ab
Barford St. John	92	Cb
Barford St. Martin	37	Ab
Barford St. Michael	92	Cb
Barfreston	46	Cc
Bargoed	67	Ab
Barham, Hunts.	114	Db
Barham, Kent	46	Cc
Barham, Suff.	99	Ac
Barholm	132	Db
Barkby	180	Db
Barkby Thorpe	130	Db
Barkestone	151	Ac
Barkham	55	Bb
Barking, Essex	58	Cb
Barking, Suff.	99	Ac
Barking Side	58	Da
Barkisland	172	Db
Barkston, Lincs.	152	Cb
Barkston, Yorks.	184	Dc
Barkway	76	Ca
Barkwith, E.	167	Ac
Barkwith, W.	167	Ac
Barlaston	146	Db
Barlavington	23	Ab
Barlborough	164	Cb
Barlby	175	Aa
Barlestone	129	Bb
Barley, Herts.	96	Cc
Barley, Lancs.	182	Cc
Barleythorpe	131	Bb
Barling	60	Db
Barlings	166	Dc
Barlow, Derby	163	Bb
Barlow, Dur.	221	Bb
Barlow, Yorks.	175	Aa
Barmburgh	174	Cc
Barmby on the Marsh	175	Aa
Barmby on the Moor	186	Cb
Barmer	135	Bb
Barming, E.	44	Ca
Barmouth	121	Ba
Barmpton	207	Bc
Barnston	188	Cc
Barnack	132	Db
Barnacle	111	Ba
Barnard Castle	206	Cc
Barnardiston	97	Bc
Barnards Green	89	Ba
Barnby	120	Db
Barnby Dun	174	Dc
Barnby, E.	199	Ba
Barnby in the Willows	151	Ba
Barnby Moor	165	Ab
Barnby, W.	199	Ba
Barnet	57	Bb
Barnetby-le-Wold	176	Dc
Barney	136	Db
Barnham, Suff.	118	Cc
Barnham Broom	118	Da
Barningham, Suff.	118	Cc
Barningham, Yorks.	206	Cc
Barnoldby le Beck	167	Ba
Barnoldswick	182	Cc
Barns Green	23	Ba
Barnsley, Glos.	70	Da
Barnsley, Yorks.	173	Bb
Barnstaple	30	Db
Barnston, Ches.	159	Bb
Barnston, Essex	77	Ab
Barnston, Notts.	150	Dc
Barnt Green	110	Cb
Barnton	160	Dc
Barnwell All Saints	114	Ca
Barnwell St. Andrew	114	Ca
Barnwood	90	Cc
Barr	223	Bb
Barrasford	220	Ca
Barremman	247	Ba
Barrhead	248	Dc
Barrhill	212	Ca
Barrington, Cambs.	96	Cb
Barrington, Som..	34	Ca
Barrington, Gt.	71	Ba
Barrington, Lit.	71	Ba
Barrmill	236	Ca
Barrock	324	Ca
Barrow, Rut.	131	Bb
Barrow, Shrops.	126	Cc
Barrow, Suff.	97	Bc
Barrowby	151	Bc
Barrowden	132	Ca
Barrowford	182	Cc
Barrow, Gt.	160	Cc
Barrow Gurney	50	Da
Barrow Haven	176	Da
Barrow-in-Furness	179	Aa
Barrow, Lit.	160	Cc
Barrow, N.	35	Ab
Barrow, S.	35	Ab
Barrow Street	36	Ca
Barrow-u.-Humber	176	Db
Barrow-upon-Soar	130	Ca
Barrow-on-Trent	148	Dc
Barry, Angus	272	Cc
Barry, Glam.	49	Aa
Barsby	130	Db
Barsham	120	Cb
Barsham, E.	136	Cb
Barsham, W.	136	Cb
Barston	110	Da
Bartestree	88	Da

	PAGE	SQ
Barthomley	146	Ca
Bartley Green	110	Ca
Bartlow	97	Ac
Barton, *Cambs.*	96	Cb
Barton, *Ches.*	144	Da
Barton, *Dev.*	10	Da
Barton, *Glos.*	90	Dc
Barton, *Hants.*	20	Cb
Barton, *Lancs.*	169	Ac
Barton, *Oxon.*	72	Da
Barton, *War.*	91	Aa
Barton, *W'land.*	203	Bb
Barton, *Yorks.*	196	Ba
Barton Bendish	117	Aa
Barton Blount	148	Cc
Barton End	69	Bb
Barton Green	128	Ca
Barton, Gt.	98	Ca
Barton Hartshorn	93	Ab
Barton-in-Fabis	150	Cc
Barton-in-the-Beans	129	Bb
Barton-in-the-Clay	75	Aa
Barton-le-Street	198	Da
Barton-le-Willows	186	Ca
Barton Mills	97	Ba
Barton-on-the-Heath	91	Bb
Barton Seagrave	113	Bb
Barton Stacey	38	Da
Barton St. David	34	Db
Barton Town	30	Da
Barton Turf	138	Cb
Barton-under-Needwood	128	Da
Barton-u.-Humber	176	Db
Barton-on-Irwell	161	Ba
Barugh	173	Bc
Barugh, Gt.	198	Dc
Barwell	129	Bc
Barwick-in-Elmet	184	Dc
Baschurch	125	Aa
Basford	150	Cb
Basildon, *Berks.*	55	Aa
Basildon, *Essex*	59	Bb
Basildon, Upper	55	Aa
Basing	55	Ac
Basingstoke	55	Ac
Baslow	163	Bc
Bason Bridge	34	Ca
Bassaleg	67	Bc
Bass Garth	177	Bc
Bassingbourn	96	Cc
Bassingham	151	Ba
Bassingthorpe	152	Cc
Bassus Green	76	Ca
Baston	132	Db
Batchworth	57	Aa
Batcombe, *Dor.*	17	Ba
Batcombe, *Som.*	35	Ba
Bath	51	Bb
Bathampton	51	Ba
Bathealton	33	Ac
Batheaston	51	Ba
Bathford	51	Ba
Bathgate	250	Db
Bathpool	33	Bb
Bathway	50	Dc
Batley	173	Aa
Batsford	91	Ab
Battersby	198	Ca
Battersea	57	Bb
Battisford	98	Db
Battle, *Brecon*	104	Cc
Battle, *Sus.*	26	Db
Battlefield	125	Ba
Battlesbridge	59	Ba
Battlesden	94	Dc
Battye Ford	173	Ab
Baughton	90	Ca
Baumber	153	Aa
Baunton	70	Da
Baverstock	37	Ab
Bawburgh	119	Aa
Bawdeswell	136	Dc
Bawdrip	34	Ca
Bawdsey	80	Ca
Bawtry	165	Aa
Baxterley	128	Dc
Baycliff	179	Ba
Baydon	53	Ba
Bayfield	136	Da
Bayford, *Herts.*	76	Cc
Bayford, *Som.*	35	Ba
Baylham	99	Ac
Baynhall	90	Ca
Baysham	88	Db
Baystonhill	125	Bb
Bayton	108	Db
Beach	51	Aa
Beachampton	93	Bb
Beachley	68	Db
Beaconsfield	74	Cc
Beaconthorpe	167	Ba
Beadlam	198	Cb
Beadnell	244	Dc
Benford	31	Ab
Beal, *N'land.*	244	Ca
Beal, *Yorks.*	174	Da
Bealings, Gt.	99	Bc
Bealings, Lit.	99	Bc
Beambridge	145	Ba
Beaminster	16	Db
Beanacre	52	Ca
Beanley	231	Ba
Bearley	110	Dc
Bear Park	207	Aa
Bearsden	248	Db
Bearstead	44	Ca
Bearstone	146	Cb
Beattock	227	Ab
Beauchamp Roding	77	Ac
Beauchief	163	Bb
Beaufort	67	Aa
Beaulieu	20	Da
Beauly	300	Cc
Beaumaris	156	Da
Beaumont, *Cumb.*	217	Bb
Beaumont, *Essex*	79	Bb
Beausale	110	Db
Beauworth	39	Ab
Beaworthy	12	Db
Beazley End	77	Ba
Bebington, Higher	159	Bb
Bebington, Lower	159	Bb
Beccles	120	Cb
Beckbury	126	Db
Beckenham	58	Cc
Beckermonds	195	Ac
Beckfoot	216	Cc
Beckford	90	Cb
Beckingham,*Lincs.*	151	Ba
Beckingham,*Notts.*	165	Ba
Beckington	51	Bc
Beckley, *Oxon.*	72	Ca
Beckley, *Sus.*	26	Da
Beck Row	117	Ac
Beck Side	192	Cc
Becontree	58	Db
Becontree Heath	58	Db
Bedale	196	Db
Beddau	66	Db
Beddgelert	140	Da
Beddingham	25	Ab
Beddington	42	Ca
Bedfield	99	Bb
Bedhampton	22	Ca
Bedingfield	99	Ba
Bedingham	119	Bb
Bedlington	222	Da
Bedlinog	86	Dc
Bedminster Down	50	Ac
Bedmond	75	Ac
Bednall	127	Ba
Bedrule	229	Ba
Bedstone	107	Ab
Bedwas	67	Ac
Bedwellty	67	Ab
Bedworth	111	Ba
Bedwyn, Gt.	53	Bb
Bedwyn, Lit.	53	Bb
Beeby	130	Db
Beechamwell	117	Ba
Beechcliffe	183	Ac
Beech Hill	55	Bb
Beechingstoke	52	Db
Beedon	54	Da
Beedon Hill	54	Da
Beeford	188	Cc
Beeley	163	Bc
Beelsby	167	Bb
Beenham	54	Db
Beer	15	Bc
Beer Crocombe	34	Cc
Beer Hackett	35	Ac
Beesby	154	Da
Beeston, *Beds.*	95	Ac
Beeston, *Ches.*	145	Ba
Beeston, *Norf.*	136	Cc
Beeston, *Notts.*	150	Cc
Beeston, *Yorks.*	173	Ba
Beeston Regis	137	Ba
Beetham	193	Bc
Beetley	136	Dc
Begbroke	72	Da
Begelly	62	Db
Beggarington Hill	173	Ba
Beggearn Huish	33	Aa
Beguildy	106	Ca
Beighton, *Derby*	164	Cb
Beighton, *Norf.*	120	Ca
Beith	236	Ca
Bekesbourne	46	Cb
Belan	124	Cb
Belaugh	137	Bc
Belbroughton	109	Ba
Belchalwell	36	Cc
Belcham Otton	97	Bc
Belchamp St. Pauls	97	Bc
Belchamp Walter.	97	Bc
Belchford	153	Ba
Belford	244	Cb
Belgrave	130	Cb
Belhelvie	294	Db
Bellasize	176	Ca
Belleau	154	Ca
Bellehiglash	303	Ac
Bell End	109	Ba
Bellerby	196	Cb
Belle Vue, *Shrops.*	125	Bb
Belle Vue, *Yorks.*	173	Bb
Bellevue, *Cumb.*	217	Bc
Bellingham	230	Dc
Bell, Lower	44	Ca
Bellshill, *Lan.*	249	Bc
Bellshill, *N'land.*	244	Cb
Belmesthorpe	132	Cb
Belmont, *Lancs.*	170	Db
Belmont, *Sur.*	42	Ca
Belper	148	Db
Belperlane End	148	Da
Belsay	221	Ba
Belstead	79	Ba
Belstone	13	Aa
Beltinge	46	Ca
Beltingham	219	Bb
Beltoft	175	Bc
Belton, *Lincs.*	152	Cb
Belton, *Lincs.*	175	Bc
Belton, *Rut.*	131	Bc
Belton, *Suff.*	120	Da
Belvoir	151	Bc
Bembridge	22	Cb
Bemersyde	241	Bb
Bemerton	37	Bb
Bempton	188	Db
Benacre	120	Dc
Benefield	114	Ca
Benefield, Upper	114	Ca
Benenden	44	Cc
Benfieldside	221	Ac
Benfleet, N.	59	Bb
Benfleet, S.	59	Bb
Bengeo	76	Cb
Bengeworth	90	Da
Benhall	100	Cb
Benholm	282	Cc
Beningbrough	185	Ab
Benington	154	Cc
Benington Sea End	154	Cc
Bennington	76	Cb
Benniworth	167	Bc
Benson	73	Ac
Benthall	126	Cb
Bentham, High	181	Aa
Bentham, Lr.	181	Aa
Bentley, *Hants.*	40	Ca
Bentley, *Suff.*	79	Ba
Bentley, *War.*	128	Dc
Bentley, *Yorks.*	177	Ab
Bentley, *Yorks.*	174	Dc
Bentley, Gt.	79	Bc
Bentley, Lit.	79	Bb
Bentworth	39	Ba
Benvie	271	Ac
Benwick	115	Bb
Bepton	40	Cc
Berden	76	Da
Bere Alston	8	Cb
Berechurch	78	Db
Bere Regis	18	Da
Bergholt, E.	79	Ba
Bergholt, W.	78	Db
Berkeley	69	Ab
Berkhampstead	74	Da
Berkhampstead,Lit.	75	Ba
Berkley	51	Bc
Berkswell	110	Da
Bermondsey	58	Cb
Bernera	285	Bb
Berners Roding	77	Ac
Bernisdale	296	Cc
Berrick Salome	73	Ac
Berriedale	318	Cb
Berriew	124	Cc
Berrington	125	Bb
Berrington Heath	108	Cb
Berrow, *Som.*	49	Bc
Berrow, *Worcs.*	89	Bb
Berrow Green	108	Da
Berry Brow	172	Db
Berry Hill	68	Da
Berrynarbor	30	Ca
Berry Pomeroy	10	Ca
Bersted, N.	23	Ac
Bersted, S.	23	Ac
Berwick, *Dors.*	17	Ab
Berwick, *Sus.*	25	Bc
Berwick Bassett	52	Da
Berwick Hill	221	Ba
Berwick-on-Tweed	243	Ba
Berwick St. James	37	Aa
Berwick St. John.	36	Db
Berwick St. Leonard	36	Da
Bescaby	131	Ba
Besford	90	Ca
Bessels Leigh	72	Cb
Bessingby	188	Cb
Bessingham	137	Ba
Besthorpe, *Norf.*	118	Db
Besthorpe, *Notts.*	165	Bc
Beswick	177	Aa
Betchworth	42	Cb
Bethersden	27	Aa
Bethesda	156	Dc
Bethlehem	85	Aa
Bethnal Green	58	Cb
Betley	146	Cb
Betsham	59	Ac
Bettiscombe	16	Db
Bettisfield	144	Dc
Bettws, *Carm.*	64	Da
Bettws, *Glam.*	66	Ca
Bettws, *Mon.*	67	Bc
Bettws Bledrws	84	Da
Bettws Cedewain.	123	Bc
Bettws Disserth	104	Da
Bettws Evan	83	Ba
Bettws Garmon	140	Da
Bettws-Gwerfil-Goch	143	Ab
Bettws-newydd	67	Bc
Bettws-y-Coed	157	Bc
Bettws-y-crwyn	106	Da
Bettws-yn-Rhos	158	Ca
Bettyhill	321	Ba
Beverley	177	Aa
Beverstone	70	Cb
Bevington	69	Ab
Bewaldeth	202	Ca
Bewdley	108	Db
Bewholme	177	Ba
Bewick	244	Ca
Bexhill	26	Db
Bexley	58	Dc
Bexley Heath	58	Dc
Bexwell	117	Aa
Beyton	98	Da
Bibstone	69	Ab
Bibury	71	Ab
Bicester	92	Dc
Bickenhall	33	Bc
Bickenhill	110	Da
Bicker	133	Aa
Bickerstaffe	169	Bc
Bickerton	184	Db
Bickington, *Dev.*	14	Ca
Bickington, *Dev.*	30	Cb
Bickleigh, *Dev.*	8	Db
Bickleigh, *Dev.*	32	Db
Bicknacre	59	Ba
Bicknoller	33	Aa
Bicknor	44	Da
Bickton	37	Bc
Bicton, *Dev.*	15	Ac
Bicton, *Shrops.*	125	Aa
Bictor. Heath	125	Aa
Bidborough	43	Ab
Biddenden	27	Aa
Biddenham	94	Da
Biddisham	50	Cb
Biddlesden	93	Ab
Biddlestone	52	Ca
Biddulph	146	Cb
Bideford	30	Cc
Bidford	91	Aa
Bidston	159	Ba
Bidwell	94	Dc
Bielby	186	Cc
Bieldside	294	Ca
Bierley, E.	173	Aa
Bierton	74	Ca
Bigbury	9	Bb
Bigby	176	Da
Biggar, *Lan.*	239	Ab
Biggar, *Lancs.*	179	Ba
Biggin, *Derby*	148	Ca
Biggin, *Yorks.*	174	Da
Biggleswade	95	Ac
Bighetmet	171	Ac
Bighton	39	Bb
Biglands	217	Ac
Bignor	23	Ab
Bilborough	150	Cb
Bilbrook, *Som.*	48	Db
Bilbrook, *Staffs.*	127	Ab
Bilbrough	185	Ac
Bilby	165	Ab
Bildershaw	206	Db
Bildeston	98	Dc
Billericay	59	Ba
Billesdon	130	Db
Billesley	110	Dc
Billingborough	133	Aa
Billinge	170	Cc
Billingford, *Norf.*	136	Dc
Billingford, *Norf.*	99	Ba
Billing, Gt.	113	Bc

Name	PAGE	SQ
Billing, Lit.	113	Ac
Billingham	208	Cb
Billinghay	152	Da
Billingley	174	Cc
Billingshurst	23	Ba
Billingsley	108	Ba
Billington, Beds.	94	Cc
Billington, Lancs.	181	Ba
Billockby	138	Cc
Billy Row	206	Da
Bilsby	154	Ca
Bilsington	27	Da
Bilsthorpe	150	Da
Bilston	127	Bc
Bilstone	129	Ab
Bilton, N'land.	232	Ca
Bilton, War.	112	Cb
Bilton, Yorks.	177	Ab
Bilton, Yorks.	184	Db
Bilton, Yorks.	184	Db
Binbrook	167	Bb
Bincombe	17	Bb
Binegar	50	Dc
Binfield	56	Ca
Bingham	150	Db
Bingley, Lancs.	171	Ac
Bingley, Yorks.	183	Ac
Binham	130	Da
Binley, Hants.	54	Cc
Binley, War.	111	Bb
Binsey	72	Da
Binstead	21	Bb
Binsted, Hants.	40	Ca
Binsted, Sus.	23	Ac
Binton	91	Aa
Bintree	136	Db
Binweston	124	Db
Birch, Essex	78	Db
Birch, Lancs.	171	Bc
Bircham Newton	135	Bb
Bircham Tofts	135	Bb
Birchanger	76	Db
Birchencliffe	172	Db
Bircher	107	Bb
Birchgrove, Glam.	65	Aa
Birchgrove, Glam.	67	Ac
Birch Heath	160	Dc
Birchington	46	Da
Birch, Little	88	Cb
Birch, Much	88	Cb
Bircholt Court	28	Ca
Birchover	163	Ac
Birch Vale	162	Da
Birdbrook	97	Bc
Birdham	22	Da
Birdingbury	111	Bb
Birdlip	70	Ca
Birdsall	186	Ca
Birdsmoor Gate	16	Db
Birdwell	173	Bc
Birdwood	89	Bc
Birgham	242	Db
Birkby, Cumb.	201	Ba
Birkby, Yorks.	197	Aa
Birkdale	169	Ab
Birkenhead	159	Ba
Birkenshaw	173	Aa
Birkin	174	Da
Birley	107	Bc
Birley Carr	163	Ba
Birling	43	Ba
Birlingham	90	Ca
Birmingham	110	Ca
Birnam	270	Cb
Birse	281	Ba
Birstal	173	Aa
Birstall	130	Cb
Birstwith	183	Bb
Birthorpe	133	Aa
Birtley, Dur.	222	Cc
Birtley, Herefs.	107	Ab
Birtley, N'land.	220	Ca
Birtsmorton	89	Bb
Birts Street	89	Bb
Bisbrooke	131	Bc
Biscathorpe	167	Bc
Bisham	74	Cc
Bishampton	109	Bc
Bishop Auckland	206	Db
Bishopbridge	166	Da
Bishopbriggs	249	Db
Bishop Burton	177	Aa
Bishop Middleham	207	Bb
Bishop Monkton	184	Ca
Bishop Norton	166	Da
Bishopsbourne	46	Cb
Bishops Cannings	52	Db
Bishops Castle	106	Da
Bishops Caundle	35	Bc
Bishops Cleeve	90	Cb
Bishops Frome	89	Aa
Bishops Hull	33	Bc
Bishops Itchington	111	Ac
Bishops Lydeard	33	Bb
Bishops Norton	89	Bc
Bishops Nympton	31	Ba
Bishops Offley	146	Cb
Bishops Stortford	76	Db
Bishops Sutton	39	Db
Bishops Tachbrook	111	Ac
Bishops Tawton	30	Db
Bishopsteignton	14	Db
Bishopstoke	38	Dc
Bishopston	64	Dc
Bishopstone, Bucks.	73	Ba
Bishopstone, Herefs.	88	Ca
Bishopstone, Sus.	25	Aa
Bishopstone, Wilts.	37	Ab
Bishopstone, Wilts.	37	Ab
Bishopstrow	52	Cc
Bishop Sutton	50	Db
Bishops Waltham	39	Ac
Bishop's Wood	126	Db
Bishopsworth	50	Da
Bishop Thornton	184	Ca
Bishopthorpe	185	Bb
Bishopton, Dur.	207	Db
Bishopton, Renf.	248	Cb
Bishopton, War.	110	Dc
Bishopton, Yorks.	184	Da
Bishop Wilton	186	Db
Bishton	68	Cc
Bisley, Glos.	70	Ca
Bisley, Sur.	56	Cb
Bispham	179	Bc
Bitchfield	152	Ca
Bittadon	30	Ca
Bitterley	108	Ca
Bitterne	38	Dc
Bitteswell	112	Ca
Bittles Green	36	Cb
Bitton	51	Aa
Bix	73	Bc
Bixley	119	Ba
Blaby	130	Cc
Blackawton	10	Cb
Blackborough	15	Aa
Blackborough End	135	Ac
Black Bourton	71	Bb
Blackboys	25	Ba
Blackbrook, Derby.	148	Da
Black Brook, Lancs.	160	Da
Blackburn, Aber.	294	Cb
Blackburn, Lancs.	170	Da
Blackburn, W. Loth.	256	Db
Blackdown	16	Da
Blackdown	8	Da
Blacker Hill	173	Bc
Blackford, Perth.	259	Bb
Blackford, Shrops.	108	Ca
Blackford, Som.	35	Bb
Blackford, Som.	34	Ca
Blackfordby	129	Aa
Blackheath, Staffs.	109	Ba
Blackheath, Suff.	100	Da
Black Heddon	220	Da
Black Hill	221	Bc
Blackhorse	51	Aa
Blackland	52	Da
Blackley, Lancs.	171	Bc
Blackley, Yorks.	172	Db
Blackmanstone	27	Bb
Blackmere	77	Aa
Blackmoor	50	Cb
Black Moor Foot	172	Db
Blackmore End	77	Ba
Black Notley	77	Bb
Blackpool, Dev.	10	Db
Blackpool, Lancs.	179	Bc
Blackridge	250	Cb
Blackrod	170	Cb
Blackshaw	216	Cb
Blackston Junc.	250	Cb
Blackthorn	93	Ac
Blacktoft	176	Ca
Black Torrington	12	Da
Blacktown	67	Bc
Blackwater	21	Ac
Blackwaterfoot	234	Db
Blackwell, Derby.	149	Ba
Blackwell, War.	91	Ba
Blackwood	67	Ab
Blackwood Hill	147	Ba
Bladon, Oxon.	72	Ca
Bladon, Som.	34	Ca
Blaenau Ffestiniog	141	Ba
Blaenavon	67	Ba
Blaen-garw	66	Ca
Blaenpenal	102	Cb
Blaenporth	83	Aa
Blaen-Rhondda	86	Ca
Blaengwrach	85	Bc
Blagdon, Som.	33	Ba
Blagdon, Som.	50	Db
Blagill	219	Bc
Blaina	67	Aa
Blair Atholl	278	Dc
Blairgowrie	270	Db
Blairlogie	259	Ac
Blairmore	247	Aa
Blaisdon	89	Ac
Blakebrook	109	Aa
Blakedown	109	Aa
Blakeney, Glos.	69	Aa
Blakeney, Norf.	136	Da
Blakenham, Gt.	99	Ac
Blakenham, Lit.	99	Ac
Blakemere	87	Ba
Blakeshall	109	Aa
Blakesley	93	Aa
Blakethwaite	195	Aa
Blanchland	220	Dc
Blandford	36	Ca
Blandford St. Mary	36	Dc
Blankney	152	Da
Blantyre, High	249	Ac
Blashford	19	Ba
Blaston	131	Bc
Blatchington, E.	25	Ca
Blatchington, W.	24	Dc
Blatherwycke	132	Cc
Blawith	192	Db
Blaxhall	100	Cb
Blaxton	175	Ac
Blaydon	221	Bb
Bleadney	34	Da
Bleadon	49	Bb
Blean	45	Bb
Bleasby	150	Da
Bleasdale	180	Dc
Blechingley	42	Cc
Bleddfa	106	Db
Bledington	91	Bc
Bledlow	73	Bb
Blencarn	204	Cb
Blencogo	216	Dc
Blencow	203	Bb
Blendworth	39	Bc
Blennerhasset	202	Ca
Bletchenden	27	Aa
Bletchington	72	Ca
Bletchley, Bucks.	94	Cb
Bletchley, Shrops.	145	Bb
Bletherston	62	Da
Blewbury	72	Cc
Blickling	137	Ab
Blidworth	150	Ca
Blidworth Bottoms	150	Ca
Blindcrake	202	Ca
Blindley Heath	42	Db
Blisland	6	Da
Blisworth	93	Ba
Blithbury	128	Ca
Blockley	91	Ab
Blofield	120	Ca
Blo Norton	118	Dc
Blore	148	Ca
Blossomfield	110	Da
Blounts Green	147	Bc
Blowty	123	Bb
Bloxham	92	Cb
Bloxholm	152	Da
Bloxwich	127	Bb
Bloxworth	18	Da
Blubberhouses	183	Bb
Blue Anchor	48	Db
Blundeston	120	Db
Blunham	95	Ab
Blunsdon St. Andrew	71	Ac
Bluntington	109	Bb
Bluntisham	115	Bc
Blurton	146	Db
Blyborough	166	Ca
Blyford	100	Da
Blymhill	126	Db
Blyth, N'land.	222	Ca
Blyth, Notts.	165	Ab
Blythburgh	100	Da
Blythford	147	Ab
Blythemarsh	147	Ab
Blyton	165	Ba
Boarhills	262	Da
Boarhunt	21	Ba
Boarstall	73	Aa
Boat of Garten	290	Cb
Bobbing	44	Da
Bobbington	126	Dc
Bobbingworth	76	Dc
Bocking	77	Ba
Bocking Church-street	77	Bb
Bockleton	108	Cc
Bodden	51	Ac
Boddington	90	Cc
Boddington, Lr.	92	Da
Boddington, Upr.	92	Da
Bodedern	155	Bb
Bodenham, Herefs.	107	Bc
Bodenham, Wilts.	37	Bb
Bodenham Moor	88	Da
Bodewryd	155	Ba
Bodfari	158	Db
Bodfean	139	Bb
Bod-ffordd	155	Bb
Bodham	137	Aa
Bodham Street	137	Aa
Bodiam	26	Da
Bodicote	92	Cb
Bodle Street Green	26	Cb
Bodmin	6	Cb
Bodney	117	Bb
Bodsham Gr	45	Bc
Bogbrae	306	Cc
Boghead, New	293	Ba
Boghead, Old	293	Ba
Bogmuir	303	Ba
Bognor Regis	23	Ac
Bolam, Dur.	206	Db
Bolam, N'land.	231	Bc
Bolberry	9	Ba
Bolderston	163	Ba
Boldmere	128	Cc
Boldon, E.	222	Db
Boldon, W.	222	Cb
Boldre	20	Cb
Boldron	206	Cc
Bole	165	Ba
Bolehill, Derby	148	Ba
Bolehill, Yorks.	164	Cb
Bolham, Dev.	32	Db
Bolham, Notts.	165	Ab
Bollington	162	Cb
Bolney	24	Ca
Bolnhurst	95	Ab
Bolsover	164	Cc
Bolstone	88	Db
Boltby	197	Bb
Bolton, E. Loth.	252	Dh
Bolton, Lancs.	170	Dc
Bolton, N'land.	231	Ba
Bolton, W'land.	204	Cb
Bolton, Yorks.	186	Cb
Bolton Abbey	183	Ab
Bolton-by-Bowland	181	Bb
Boltongate	202	Ca
Bolton-le-Sands	180	Da
Bolton-on-Dearne	174	Cc
Bolton-on-Swale	196	Cb
Bolton Percy	185	Ac
Bolts Burn	205	Ba
Bomere Heath	125	Ba
Bonar Bridge	311	Bb
Bonawe	265	Bc
Bonby	176	Db
Bonchurch	21	Bc
Bondleigh	31	Bc
Bo'ness	250	Da
Bonhill	248	Ca
Boningale	126	Db
Bonkle	250	Cc
Bonnington	27	Ba
Bonnybridge	250	Da
Bonnyrigg	252	Cb
Bonnyton	293	Aa
Bonsall	140	Da
Bontddu	141	Bc
Bont-dolgadfan	122	Db
Bonvilston	66	Db
Bookham, Great	41	Ba
Bookham, Little	41	Ba
Boot	192	Ca
Booth	172	Ca
Boothby Graffoe	152	Ca
Boothby Pagnell	152	Cc
Boothstown	170	Dc
Booth Town	172	Ba
Bootle, Cumb.	191	Bb
Bootle, Lancs.	159	Ba
Booton	137	Ab
Boraston	108	Cb
Borden	44	Da
Border	85	Ba
Boreham	77	Bc
Boreham Street	26	Cb
Boreraig, Inver.	285	Ac
Boreraig, Inver.	295	Ab
Borgue, Caith.	318	Cb
Borgue, Kirk.	214	Cc
Borley	98	Cc
Boroughbridge	184	Da
Borough Green	43	Ba
Borrowash	149	Bc
Borrowby	197	Bb
Borstal	44	Ca
Borth	121	Bc
Borthwick	252	Cc
Borth-y-Gest	140	Db
Borwick	193	Bc
Bosbury	89	Aa
Boscastle	11	Ac
Boscaswell	1	Ab
Boscombe, Hants.	19	Bb
Boscombe, Wilts.	37	Ba
Boscombe, E.	37	Ba
Boscombe, W.	37	Ba
Bosham	22	Da
Bosherston	62	Cc
Bossall	186	Ca

Name	PAGE	SQ.
Bossingham	45	Bc
Bossington	48	Cb
Boston	133	Ba
Boston Spa	184	Dc
Boswinger	4	Da
Botcherby	217	Bc
Botesdale	98	Da
Bothal	232	Cc
Bothamsall	165	Ac
Bothel	202	Ca
Bothenhampton	16	Db
Bothenkennar	250	Ca
Bothwell	249	Bb
Botley, Berks.	72	Db
Botley, Bucks.	74	Db
Botley Hants.	39	Ac
Botolph Claydon	93	Bc
Botolphs	24	Cb
Bottesford, Leics.	151	Bb
Bottesford, Lincs.	176	Cc
Bottisham	96	Db
Bottisham Lode	96	Da
Botus Fleming	8	Cb
Boughrood	104	Db
Boughton,N'hants.	113	Ac
Boughton, Norf.	117	Aa
Boughton, Notts.	165	Ac
Boughton Aluph	45	Ac
Boughton Malherbe	44	Db
Boughton Monchelsea	44	Cb
Boughton Street	45	Bb
Bouldon	108	Ca
Boulge	99	Bc
Boulmer	232	Da
Boultham	166	Cc
Boulton	149	Ac
Bourn	96	Cb
Bournbrook	110	Ca
Bourne	132	Da
Bournemouth	19	Bb
Bournheath	109	Bb
Bournville	110	Ca
Bourton, Berks.	71	Bc
Bourton, Dors.	36	Ca
Bourton, Shrops.	126	Cc
Bourton, Som.	50	Cb
Bourton, Gt.	92	Ca
Bourton, Lit.	92	Ca
Bourton on Dunsmore	111	Bb
Bourton-on-the-Hill	91	Ab
Bourton-on-the-Water	91	Ac
Boustead Hill	217	Ac
Bouth	192	Db
Boveney	56	Ca
Boveridge	37	Ac
Boverton	66	Cc
Bovey, North	13	Bb
Bovey Tracey	14	Cb
Bovingdon	74	Db
Bovington	18	Db
Bow	31	Bc
Bow Brickhill	94	Cb
Bowbridge	70	Ca
Bowden	241	Bb
Bowden, Gt.	113	Aa
Bowden, Lit.	113	Aa
Bower Ashton	50	Da
Bower Chalke	37	Ab
Bowerhill	52	Cb
Bower Hinton	34	Dc
Bowermadden	324	Cb
Bowers Gifford	59	Bb
Bowertower	324	Cb
Bowes	206	Cc
Bowlers Green	40	Ba
Bowling	248	Cb
Bowling Alley	75	Ab
Bowness, Cumb.	216	Db
Bowness, W'land.	193	Ab
Bowsden	243	Bb
Bowspring	68	Db
Bow Street, Card.	121	Bc
Bow Street, Norf.	118	Db
Bowthorpe	119	Aa
Box	51	Ba
Boxbush	69	Ba
Boxford, Berks.	54	Ca
Boxford, Suff.	98	Dc
Boxgrove	23	Ac
Boxley	44	Ca
Boxted, Essex	78	Da
Boxted, Suff.	97	Bc
Botwell	69	Bb
Boxworth	96	Ca
Boxworth End	96	Ca
Boyleston	148	Cc
Boynton	188	Ca
Boyton, Corn.	12	Cc
Boyton, Suff.	99	Db
Boyton, Wilts.	36	Da
Bozeat	113	Bc
Brabourne	28	Ca
Bracadale	283	Ba
Braceborough	132	Db
Bracebridge	166	Cc
Braceby	152	Cc
Bracewell	182	Cb
Brackenber	204	Dc
Brackenbottom	182	Ca
Brackenfield Green	149	Aa
Brackenthwaite	184	Cb
Brackletter	275	Bb
Brackley	92	Db
Bracknell	56	Cb
Braco	259	Bb
Bracon Ash	119	Aa
Bradbury	207	Bb
Bradden	93	Aa
Braddock	6	Db
Bradenham	74	Cb
Bradenham, E.	118	Ca
Bradenham, W.	118	Ca
Bradenstoke	70	Db
Bradfield, Berks.	55	Aa
Bradfield, Essex	79	Bb
Bradfield, Norf.	137	Ba
Bradfield, Yorks.	163	Ba
Bradfield Combust	98	Cb
Bradfield St. Clare	98	Cb
Bradfield St. George	98	Cb
Bradford, Dev.	12	Da
Bradford, Yorks.	172	Da
Bradford Abbas	35	Ac
Bradford Leigh	51	Bb
Bradford-on-Avon	51	Bb
Bradford-on-Tone	33	Ba
Bradford Peverell	17	Ba
Bradford, W.	181	Bc
Brading	21	Bc
Bradley, Derby	148	Cb
Bradley, Hants.	39	Ba
Bradley, Lincs.	167	Ba
Bradley, Staff.	127	Aa
Bradley, Staff.	127	Bc
Bradley, Worcs.	109	Bc
Bradley, Yorks.	172	Da
Bradley, Yorks.	195	Bc
Bradley Green, Som.	33	Ba
Bradley Green, Staffs.	146	Da
Bradley, Gt.	97	Ab
Bradley-in-the-Moors	147	Bb
Bradley, Lit.	97	Ab
Bradley, Low	182	Db
Bradley, N.	52	Cb
Bradley, W.	35	Aa
Bradlow	89	Aa
Bradmore	150	Cc
Bradney	34	Ca
Bradninch	32	Dc
Bradnop	147	Ba
Bradpole	16	Cb
Bradshaw, Lancs.	170	Db
Bradshaw, Yorks.	172	Da
Bradway	163	Bb
Bradwell, Bucks.	94	Cb
Bradwell, Derby	163	Ab
Bradwell, Essex	78	Cb
Bradwell, Suff.	120	Da
Bradwell Juxta Mare	78	Dc
Bradstone	8	Ca
Bradworthy	12	Ca
Braehead	238	Da
Braemar	279	Ba
Brafferton, Dur.	207	Bb
Brafferton, Yorks.	184	Ba
Brafield-on-the-Green	113	Bc
Bragbury	75	Bb
Braidwood	238	Ca
Brailes, Lr.	91	Bb
Brailes, Upr.	91	Bb
Brailsford	148	Db
Braintree	77	Bb
Braiseworth	99	Aa
Braithwaite,Cumb.	202	Cb
Braithwaite, Yorks.	182	Dc
Braithwaite, Yorks.	174	Db
Braithwell	164	Da
Brakenhall	127	Ac
Brakin	175	Bc
Bramber	24	Cb
Bramcote	149	Bc
Bramdean	39	Bb
Bramerton	119	Ba
Bramfield, Herts.	75	Bb
Bramfield, Suff.	100	Ca
Bramford	79	Ba
Bramhall	162	Cb
Bramham	184	Dc
Bramhope	183	Bc
Bramley, Hunts.	55	Ac
Bramley, Sur.	41	Ab
Bramley, Yorks.	164	Ca
Bramley, Yorks.	173	Ba
Brampford Speke.	32	Dc
Brampton, Cumb.	218	Cb
Brampton, Herefs.	88	Cb
Brampton, Hunts.	95	Ba
Brampton, Lincs.	165	Bb
Brampton, Norf.	137	Bb
Brampton, Suff.	120	Cc
Brampton,W'land.	204	Db
Brampton, Yorks.	174	Cc
Brampton Abbotts	88	Db
Brampton Ash	113	Aa
Brampton Bryan.	107	Ab
Brampton-en-le-Morthen	164	Ca
Brampton, Lit.	107	Aa
Bramshall	147	Bc
Bramshaw	38	Cc
Brams Hill	55	Bb
Bramshott	40	Cb
Bramstead Heath	126	Da
Bramwell	34	Cb
Brancaster	135	Ba
Brancepeth	207	Aa
Brancepeth, New.	207	Aa
Branderburgh	303	Aa
Brandesburton	177	Ba
Brandeston	99	Bb
Brandiston	137	Ab
Brandon, Dur.	207	Aa
Brandon, Lincs.	151	Bb
Brandon, Suff.	117	Bb
Brandon, War.	111	Bb
Brandon Parva	118	Da
Brandsby	198	Cc
Branksome	19	Bb
Bransby	166	Cb
Branscombe	15	Bc
Bransdale	198	Ca
Bransford	109	Ac
Bransgore	20	Cb
Branston, Leics.	151	Bc
Branston, Lincs.	166	Da
Branston, Staffs.	128	Da
Brant Broughton.	151	Ba
Brantham	79	Bb
Branthwaite	201	Bb
Brantingham	176	Ca
Branton, N'land.	231	Ba
Branton, Yorks.	175	Ac
Branxton	243	Ac
Brassington	148	Da
Brasted	43	Aa
Bratoft	154	Cb
Brattleby	166	Cb
Bratton	52	Cc
Bratton Covelly	12	Cc
Bratton Fleming	30	Db
Bratton Seymour.	35	Ba
Braughing	76	Cb
Brauncewell	152	Ca
Braunston, Rut.	131	Bb
Braunston,N'hants.	112	Cb
Braunstone	130	Cb
Braunton	30	Cb
Brawby	198	Dc
Brawdy	61	Ba
Braxted, Gt.	78	Cc
Braxted, Lit.	78	Cc
Bray	56	Ca
Braybrooke	113	Aa
Braydon	70	Dc
Brayford	30	Db
Braythorn	184	Cb
Brayton	174	Da
Breadsall	149	Ab
Breadstone	69	Ab
Bread Town	53	Aa
Breage	2	Cc
Breakish, Lr.	285	Ab
Breakish, Upr.	285	Ab
Bream	68	Da
Bream Eaves	68	Da
Breamore	37	Bc
Brean	49	Bb
Brearton	184	Ca
Breaston	149	Bc
Brechfa	84	Cc
Brechin	272	Ca
Brechin, Lit.	281	Bc
Breckles	118	Cb
Brecon	86	Da
Brede	26	Db
Bredenbury	108	Cc
Bredfield	99	Bc
Bredgar	44	Da
Bredhurst	44	Ca
Bredicot	109	Bc
Bredon	90	Cb
Bredons Hardwick	90	Cb
Bredons Norton	90	Ca
Bredwardine	87	Ba
Breedon on the Hill	129	Ba
Breighton	175	Ba
Breinton	88	Ca
Bremhill	52	Ca
Bremhill Wick	52	Ca
Brenchley	43	Bb
Brendon	47	Ab
Brendon Hill	48	Bc
Brenkley	221	Ba
Brent, East	49	Bc
Brent Eleigh	98	Dc
Brentford	57	Ab
Brentingby	131	Aa
Brent Knoll	49	Bb
Brent Pelham	76	Da
Brentwood	59	Aa
Brenzett	27	Bb
Brereton	127	Ba
Brereton-cum-Smethwick	161	Bc
Brereton Green	161	Bc
Bressingham	118	Dc
Bretby	128	Da
Bretford	111	Bb
Bretforton	90	Da
Bretherton	169	Bb
Brettenham, Norf.	118	Cc
Brettenham, Suff.	98	Db
Bretton	159	Bc
Bretton, W.	173	Bb
Brewham, N.	35	Ba
Brewham, S.	35	Ba
Brewood	127	Ab
Bricett, Gt.	98	Dc
Brickhill, Gt.	94	Cb
Brickhill, Lit.	94	Cb
Bricklehampton	90	Da
Bride	189	Aa
Bridekirk	202	Cb
Bridell	82	Ba
Bridestowe	12	Dc
Bridford	14	Ca
Bridge	46	Cb
Bridge End, Dur.	206	Cc
Bridge End, Lincs.	133	Aa
Bridge End, Lincs.	152	Cb
Bridge End,N'land.	220	Cb
Bridgeford, Gt.	146	Dc
Bridgehampton	35	Ab
Bridgend, Aber.	304	Ca
Bridgend, Banff.	292	Cc
Bridgend, Glam.	66	Cb
Bridgend, Perth	260	Da
Bridgend of Lintrathen	271	Aa
Bridgeness	250	Da
Bridge of Allan	259	Ca
Bridge of Dee	214	Cb
Bridge of Earn	260	Da
Bridge of Weir	248	Cc
Bridgerule East	11	Bb
Bridge Sollers	88	Ca
Bridge Trafford	160	Ca
Bridge Yate	51	Aa
Bridgford, W.	150	Cc
Bridgham	118	Cc
Bridgnorth	126	Cc
Bridgtown	127	Bb
Bridgwater	34	Ca
Bridlington	188	Da
Bridport	16	Db
Bridstow	88	Dc
Brierfield	182	Cc
Brierley, Herefs.	107	Bc
Brierley, Yorks.	174	Cb
Brierley Hill	109	Ba
Brigg	176	Db
Brigham, Cumb.	201	Bb
Brigham, Yorks.	188	Ca
Brighouse	172	Da
Brighstone	21	Ac
Brighthampton	72	Cb
Brightling	26	Ca
Brightlingsea	79	Ac
Brighton	24	Cb
Brightons	250	Ca
Brights Leary	30	Db
Brightwalton	54	Ca
Brightwalton Gr.	54	Ca
Brightwell, Berks.	72	Dc
Brightwell, Suff.	80	Ca
Brightwell Baldwin	73	Ab
Brignall	206	Cc
Brinkley	167	Bb
Brigstock	114	Ca
Brill	73	Aa
Brilley	87	Aa
Brimfield	107	Bb
Brimington	164	Cb
Brimington Common	164	Cc
Brimpsfield	70	Ca
Brimpton	54	Db
Brimscombe	70	Cb
Brimshot	41	Aa
Brimstage	159	Cb

Name	Page	Sq.
Brindle	170	Ca
Brindley Ford	146	Da
Bringhurst	131	Bc
Brington	114	Db
Brington, Gt.	112	Dc
Brington, Lit.	112	Dc
Briningham	136	Db
Brinkhill	154	Ca
Brinkley	97	Ab
Brinklow	111	Ba
Brinkworth	70	Ca
Brinsea	50	Cb
Brinsley	149	Bb
Brinsop	88	Ca
Brinsworth	164	Ca
Brinton	136	Da
Brisco	217	Bc
Brisley	136	Dc
Brislington	51	Aa
Bristol	50	Da
Briston	136	Db
Britford	37	Bb
Briton Ferry	65	Ac
Britwell Salome	73	Ac
Brixham	10	Ca
Brixton, Dev.	8	Dc
Brixton, London	57	Bc
Brixton Deverill	36	Ca
Brixworth	113	Ab
Brize Norton	71	Ba
Broadbottom	162	Ca
Broad Campden	91	Ab
Broad Chalke	37	Ab
Broad Clyst	14	Da
Broadfield	76	Ca
Broadford	285	Ab
Broad Green, Beds.	94	Ca
Broad Green, Worcs.	108	Dc
Broad Heath	108	Db
Broadhembury	15	Aa
Broadhempston	10	Ca
Broad Hinton	53	Aa
Broadholme	166	Cc
Broadley	63	Bb
Broadmayne	18	Cb
Broadnymet	31	Bc
Broad Oak, Herefs.	88	Cc
Broadoak, Carm.	64	Dc
Broadoak, Kent	45	Bb
Broadstairs	40	Da
Broads, The	138	Cb
Broadstone, Dors.	19	Ab
Broadstone, Shrops.	125	Bc
Broadwas	108	Dc
Broadwater	24	Cc
Broadway, Carm.	63	Aa
Broadway, Dors.	17	Bb
Broadway, Som.	34	Ca
Broadway, Som.	51	Ac
Broadway, Worcs.	90	Db
Broadwell, Glos.	91	Ac
Broadwell, Oxon.	71	Bb
Broadwell, War.	111	Bc
Broadwindsor	16	Da
Broadwood Kelly	31	Ab
Broadwood Widger	12	Cc
Brobury	87	Ba
Brockdish	99	Ba
Brockenhurst	20	Da
Brockford Str.	99	Ab
Brockhall	112	Db
Brockham	41	Bb
Brockhampton, Glos.	90	Cb
Brockhampton, Glos.	90	Dc
Brockhampton, Herefs.	88	Db
Brock Holes	172	Db
Brocklesby	167	Aa
Brockley	98	Cb
Brockley Green	98	Cb
Brockton, Shrops.	106	Da
Brockton, Shrops.	124	Db
Brockton, Shrops.	125	Bc
Brockton, Shrops.	126	Db
Brockworth	90	Cc
Brocton	127	Ba
Brodick	234	Db
Brodsworth	174	Cc
Brokenborough	70	Cc
Bromborough	159	Bb
Brome	99	Aa
Bromeswell	100	Ca
Bromfield, Cumb.	202	Ca
Bromfield, Kent	44	Db
Bromfield, Shrops.	107	Ab
Bromham, Beds.	94	Ba
Bromham, Wilts.	52	Cb
Bromley, Kent	58	Cb
Bromley, London.	58	Cb
Bromley, Gt.	79	Ab
Bromley, Lit.	79	Ab
Brompton, Kent	59	Bc
Brompton, Yorks.	197	Aa
Brompton, Yorks.	187	Ba
Brompton, New	59	Bc
Brompton-on-Swale	196	Da
Brompton Ralph.	33	Ab
Brompton Regis	48	Cc
Bromsberrow	89	Bb
Bromsberrow Heath	89	Bb
Bromsgrove	109	Bb
Bromyard	108	Cc
Brongest	83	Bb
Brongwyn	83	Ab
Bronington	145	Ab
Bronllys	87	Ab
Brook, Carm.	63	Ab
Brook, Hants.	20	Dc
Brook, Kent	45	Bc
Brooke, Norf.	119	Bb
Brooke, Rut.	131	Bb
Brook End, Beds.	95	Aa
Brookend, Glos.	68	Db
Brook Foot.	172	Da
Brookhouse	164	Ca
Brookhouse Green	146	Ba
Brookland	27	Bb
Brooksby	130	Ca
Brooks Green	23	Ba
Brook Street	27	Aa
Brookthorpe	69	Ba
Brooms Ash	89	Ac
Brooms Green	89	Ab
Brora	312	Da
Broseley	126	Cb
Brothertoft	153	Bc
Brotherton	174	Ca
Brotton	199	Aa
Brough, Derby	163	Ab
Brough, Caith.	323	Ba
Brough, Notts.	151	Ba
Brough, Yorks.	176	Ca
Broughall	145	Bb
Brough Sowerby	205	Ac
Broughton, Bucks.	94	Cb
Broughton, Flint.	159	Bc
Broughton, Glam.	66	Cc
Broughton, Hants.	38	Cb
Broughton, Hunts.	115	Bc
Broughton, Lancs.	170	Ca
Broughton, Lincs.	176	Da
Broughton, N'hants.	113	Bb
Broughton, Oxon.	92	Cb
Broughton, Peebs.	239	Bb
Broughton, Yorks.	182	Db
Broughton, Yorks.	198	Ca
Broughton, Yorks.	198	Dc
Broughton Astley	130	Cc
Broughton Beck	192	Dc
Broughton Comm.	52	Cb
Broughton Gifford	52	Cb
Broughton Hackett	109	Ba
Broughton-in-Furness	192	Cb
Broughton Poggs.	71	Bb
Broughty Ferry	271	Bc
Brough-under-Stainmore	205	Ac
Brown Candover	39	Aa
Brownhills	128	Cb
Brownsover	112	Cb
Brownston	9	Bb
Brox	41	Aa
Broxa	200	Cc
Broxbourne	76	Cc
Broxburn	251	Ab
Broxholme	166	Cb
Broxted	77	Aa
Broxwood, Lr.	107	Ac
Broyle Side	25	Ab
Bruisyard	100	Cb
Brumby	176	Da
Brumstead	138	Cb
Brundall	119	Ba
Brundish	99	Ba
Brunstock	217	Bb
Bruntcliffe	173	Aa
Bruntingthorpe	112	Da
Brunton	53	Bc
Brushford, Dev.	31	Ba
Brushford, Som.	32	Ba
Bruton	35	Ba
Bryanston	36	Cc
Bryants Puddle	18	Ca
Brydekirk	216	Da
Brymbo	144	Ca
Brympton	34	Dc
Bryn, Glam.	67	Ab
Bryn, Glam.	65	Ba
Bryn, Shrops.	124	Ca
Brynamman	85	Ab
Bryncethin	66	Cb
Bryncroes	139	Ac
Bryncurl	107	Ac
Bryneglwys	43	Bb
Brynford	159	Ab
Bryngwran	155	Bb
Bryngwyn, Mon.	68	Ca
Bryngwyn, Rad.	87	Aa
Brynkir	140	Cb
Bryn-Mawr	67	Aa
Bryn Saddler	66	Db
Bryn Siencyn	156	Cc
Bubbenhall	111	Bb
Bubwith	185	Bc
Buchanan	248	Ca
Buchanhaven	306	Db
Buchlyvie	258	Dc
Buckabank	217	Bc
Buckden, Hunts.	95	Ba
Buckden, Yorks.	195	Bc
Buckenham	120	Ca
Buckenham, New	118	Db
Buckenham, Old	118	Db
Buckerell	15	Ab
Buckfast	10	Ca
Buckfastleigh	10	Ca
Buckhaven	261	Bc
Buckholt	88	Cc
Buckhorn Weston	36	Cb
Buckhurst Hill	58	Ca
Buckie	303	Ba
Buckingham	93	Ab
Buckland, Berks.	72	Cb
Buckland, Bucks.	74	Ca
Buckland, Dev.	30	Db
Buckland, Glos.	90	Db
Buckland, Herts.	76	Ca
Buckland, Kent	28	Da
Buckland, Sur.	42	Cb
Buckland Brewer.	29	Bc
Buckland Denham	51	Bc
Buckland-in-the-Moor	13	Bc
Buckland Monachorum	8	Db
Buckland Newton	18	Ca
Buckland Ripers	17	Bb
Buckland St. Mary	16	Ca
Bucklebury	54	Db
Bucklesham	80	Ca
Buckley	159	Bc
Bucklow Hill	161	Ab
Buckminster	131	Ba
Bucknall, Lincs.	153	Aa
Bucknall, Shrops.	107	Ab
Bucknell, Oxon.	92	Dc
Bucknell, Staffs.	146	Db
Bucksburn	294	Cc
Bucks Green	23	Ba
Bucks Mills.	29	Bc
Buckton	188	Db
Buckworth	114	Db
Budbrooke	111	Ac
Budby	164	Dc
Bude	11	Ba
Budleigh, East	15	Ac
Budleigh Salterton	15	Ac
Budock	2	Db
Budworth, Gt.	161	Ab
Budworth, Lit.	160	Dc
Buerton	146	Cb
Bugbrooke	112	Dc
Buglawton	161	Bc
Bugley	52	Cc
Bugthorpe	186	Cb
Buildwas	126	Cb
Builth Wells	104	Ca
Buittle	214	Db
Bulby	132	Da
Bulford	37	Ba
Bulkeley	145	Aa
Bulkington, War.	111	Ba
Bulkington, Wilts.	52	Cb
Bulldoo	322	Da
Bulley	89	Bc
Bullingham	88	Db
Bullingham, Lr.	88	Db
Bullington	38	Da
Bulmer, Essex	98	Cc
Bulmer, Yorks.	185	Ba
Bulphan	59	Ab
Bulwell	150	Cb
Bulwick	132	Cc
Bunbury	145	Ba
Bungay	119	Bb
Bunloit	288	Db
Bunny	150	Cc
Buntingford	76	Ca
Bunwell	119	Ab
Bunwell Street	119	Ab
Burbage, Derby	162	Dc
Burbage, Leics.	129	Bc
Burbage, Wilts.	53	Bb
Burchetts Green	56	Ca
Burcombe	37	Ab
Burcot, Oxon.	72	Db
Burcot, Worcs.	109	Bb
Burcott	94	Cc
Burdon, Gt.	207	Bc
Bures	78	Ca
Burford, Oxon.	71	Ba
Burford, Shrops.	108	Cb
Burgate	99	Aa
Burgess Hill	24	Db
Burgh	99	Bc
Burgh Apton	119	Ba
Burgh-by-Sands	217	Bb
Burgh Castle	120	Da
Burghclere	54	Dc
Burghead	302	Da
Burghfield	55	Ab
Burghill	88	Ca
Burgh-le-Marsh	154	Db
Burgh Muir	293	Bb
Burgh-next-Aylsham	137	Bb
Burgh-on-Bain	167	Bc
Burgh St. Margaret	138	Dc
Burgh St. Peter	120	Db
Burghwallis	174	Db
Burham	44	Ca
Buriton	40	Cc
Burleigh	56	Cb
Burlescombe	33	Ac
Burley	131	Bb
Burley Gate	88	Da
Burley-in-Wharfedale	183	Bc
Burlingham, N.	120	Ca
Burlingham, S.	120	Ca
Burlton	144	Dc
Burmarsh, Herefs.	88	Da
Burmarsh, Kent	28	Da
Burmington	91	Bb
Burn	174	Da
Burnage	161	Ba
Burnaston	148	Dc
Burnby	186	Dc
Burncross	163	Ba
Burneston	196	Db
Burnett	51	Aa
Burnham, Bucks.	56	Ca
Burnham, Essex	60	Da
Burnham, Som.	34	Ca
Burnham Deepdale	136	Ca
Burnham, Low	175	Bc
Burnham Norton	136	Ca
Burnham Overy	136	Ca
Burnham Thorpe	136	Ca
Burnham Westgate	136	Ca
Burniston	200	Dc
Burnley	171	Ba
Burnmouth	254	Dc
Burnopfield	221	Bc
Burnsall	182	Da
Burntisland	251	Ba
Burnt Yates	184	Ca
Burpham	23	Bb
Burradon	231	Ab
Burrells	204	Dc
Burrelton	270	Dc
Burrill	196	Db
Burringham	176	Cc
Burrington, Dev.	30	Dc
Burrington, Herefs.	107	Bb
Burrington, Som.	50	Cb
Burrough Green	97	Ab
Burrough-on-the-Hill	131	Ab
Burrowhill	56	Db
Burry Port	64	Cb
Burscough	169	Bb
Burscough Bridge	169	Bb
Bursea	175	Ba
Burshill	177	Ba
Bursledon	21	Aa
Burslem	146	Da
Burstall	79	Ba
Burstead, Gt.	59	Ba
Burstead, Lit.	59	Aa
Burstock	16	Da
Burston	119	Ac
Burstow	42	Cb
Burstwick	178	Cb
Burtersett	195	Ab
Burton, Ches.	159	Bb
Burton, Ches.	160	Cc
Burton, Lincs.	166	Cc
Burton, Pem.	62	Cb
Burton, Som.	33	Ba
Burton, Wilts.	36	Ca
Burton, Wilts.	69	Bc
Burton Agnes	188	Cc
Burton Bradstock	16	Dc

Place	Page	Sq.
Burton Coggles	132	Ca
Burton Dassett	92	Ca
Burton Hastings	111	Ba
Burton-in-Kendal	193	Bc
Burton-in-Lonsdale	181	Aa
Burton Joyce	150	Cb
Burton Latimer	113	Bb
Burton Lazars	131	Aa
Burton Leonard	184	Ca
Burton, N.	188	Cb
Burton-on-the-Wolds	130	Ca
Burton Overy	130	Dc
Burton Pedwardine	133	Aa
Burton Pidsea	178	Cb
Burton Salmon	174	Ca
Burton's Green	78	Cb
Burton-upon-Stather	176	Cb
Burton-upon-Trent	128	Da
Burton, W. Notts.	165	Bb
Burton, W. Sus.	23	Ab
Burton, W. Yorks.	195	Bb
Burtonwood	160	Ba
Burtree Ford	205	Ba
Burwardsley	145	Aa
Burwarton	108	Ca
Burwash	26	Ca
Burwell, Cambs.	97	Aa
Burwell, Lincs.	154	Ca
Bury, Hunts.	115	Bc
Bury, Lancs.	171	Bb
Bury, Som.	32	Da
Bury, Sus.	23	Ab
Bury Green	76	Db
Bury St. Edmunds	98	Ca
Burythorpe	186	Ca
Buscot	71	Bb
Busby	248	Dc
Busby, Gt.	197	Ba
Bush Bank	88	Ca
Bushbury	127	Bb
Bushby	130	Db
Bushey	57	Aa
Busheyheath	57	Aa
Bushley	90	Cb
Buslingthorpe	166	Db
Bussage	70	Ca
Buston, High	232	Ca
Butcombe	50	Db
Butleigh	34	Db
Butleigh Wootton	34	Db
Butlers Marston	91	Ba
Butley	100	Ca
Buttercrambe	186	Cb
Butterleigh	32	Db
Butterley	149	Ba
Buttermere, Cumb.	202	Cc
Buttermere, Wilts.	54	Ca
Buttershaw	172	Da
Butterton	147	Ba
Butterwick, Lincs.	154	Cc
Butterwick, Yorks.	187	Bb
Butterwick, Yorks.	198	Dc
Butterwick, E.	176	Cc
Butterwick, W.	176	Cc
Buttington	124	Cb
Butt Lane	146	Da
Buttonoak	108	Da
Buttsbury	59	Aa
Buxhall	98	Db
Buxted	25	Ba
Buxton, Derby	162	Dc
Buxton, Norf.	137	Bb
Buxton Heath	137	Bb
Bwlch	86	Da
Bwlch-gwyn	144	Ca
Bwlch-y-cibau	124	Ca
Bwlch-y-mynydd	64	Db
Bwlfa	64	Db
Byfield	92	Da
Byfleet	41	Aa
Byford	87	Ba
Bygrave	75	Ba
Byland Abbey	197	Bc
Byley	161	Ac
Bythorn	114	Cb
Byton	107	Ab
Byworth	23	Aa
CABOURNE	167	Ab
Cadbury	32	Dc
Cadbury, N.	35	Bb
Cadbury, S.	35	Bb
Cadder	249	Ab
Caddington	74	Da
Cadeby, Leics.	129	Bb
Cadeby, Yorks.	174	Dc
Cadeleigh	32	Db
Cadishead	161	Aa
Cadley	53	Bc
Cadmore End	73	Bc
Cadnam	38	Cc
Cadney	170	Dc
Cadoxton	49	Aa
Cae-llwyn-grydd	156	Dc
Caenby	166	Da
Caerau	49	Aa
Caergeiliog	155	Ab
Caergwrle	144	Ca
Caerhun	157	Ab
Caerleon	67	Bb
Caernarvon	156	Cc
Caerphilly	67	Ac
Caersws	123	Bc
Caerwent	68	Cb
Caerwys	158	Db
Cainscross	69	Ba
Caio	84	Db
Cairneyhill	250	Da
Cairnryan	211	Bb
Caister-next-Yarmouth	120	Da
Caister St. Edmunds	119	Ba
Caistor	167	Ab
Calbourne	21	Ac
Calcot	70	Da
Calcot Row	55	Aa
Calcutt	71	Ac
Caldbeck	202	Da
Cladbergh	196	Db
Caldecote, Beds.	95	Ac
Caldecote, Cambs.	96	Cb
Caldecote, Herts.	95	Bc
Caldecote, Hunts.	114	Da
Caldecote, N'hants.	93	Aa
Caldecote, War.	129	Ac
Caldecott, N'hants.	114	Cb
Caldecott, Rut.	131	Bc
Calderbank	249	Bc
Calderbrook	172	Cb
Caldercruix.	250	Cb
Calder Grove	173	Bb
Caldicot	68	Cc
Caldwell, Yorks.	206	Dc
Caldy	159	Ab
Calgary	263	Ab
Calke	129	Ba
Callaly	231	Ba
Callander	258	Db
Callestock	2	Da
Calligarry	273	Aa
Callington	7	Bb
Callingwood	128	Da
Callow, Derby	148	Da
Callow, Herefs.	88	Cb
Callow End	89	Ba
Calmsden	70	Da
Calne	52	Da
Calow	164	Cc
Calstock	8	Cb
Calstone Wellington	52	Da
Calthorpe	137	Bb
Calthwaite	203	Ba
Calton	148	Ca
Calveley	145	Ba
Calver	163	Ab
Calverley	183	Bc
Calverton, Bucks.	93	Bb
Calverton, Notts.	150	Cb
Calvo	216	Dc
Cam	69	Bb
Cam, Lower	69	Bb
Camberley	56	Cb
Camberwell	58	Cb
Camblesforth	175	Aa
Cambo	231	Bc
Cambois	232	Dc
Camborne	2	Cb
Cambridge, Cambs.	96	Db
Cambridge, Glos.	69	Bb
Cambus	259	Bc
Cambuslang	249	Ac
Cambusnethan	249	Bc
Camden Town	57	Bb
Camelford	11	Ac
Camelon	250	Ca
Camel, W.	35	Ab
Camely	50	Db
Camers Green	89	Bb
Camerton, Cambs.	2	Cb
Camerton, Cumb.	201	Bb
Camerton, Som	51	Ab
Cammeringham	166	Cb
Campbeltown	301	Ab
Campbeltown	233	Bc
Campsall	174	Db
Campsey Ash	100	Cb
Camps Green	97	Ac
Campsie	249	Aa
Campton	95	Ac
Camrose	61	Ba
Camserney	269	Ab
Canal Head	186	Cb
Candlesby	154	Cb
Cane End	55	Aa
Canewdon	60	Ca
Canfield, Gt.	77	Ab
Canfield Lit.	77	Ab
Canford Magna	19	Ab
Cannington	33	Ba
Cannock	127	Bb
Cannock Wood	127	Ba
Canonbie	217	Ba
Canon Bridge	88	Ca
Canon Frome	89	Aa
Canon Pyon	88	Ca
Canons Ashby	92	Da
Canterbury	45	Bb
Cantley, Norf.	120	Ca
Cantley Yorks.	174	Dc
Canton	49	Aa
Cantref	86	Da
Canvey I.	59	Bb
Canwick	166	Cc
Cap-coch	86	Cc
Capel, Kent	43	Bb
Capel, Sur.	41	Bc
Capel Arthog	121	Ba
Capel Bettws Lleuca	102	Cc
Capel Coch	156	Cb
Capel Colman	83	Ab
Capel Curig	157	Ac
Capel Garmon	157	Bc
Capel Gwynfe	85	Aa
Capel Hendre	64	Da
Capel-le-Ferne	28	Da
Capel Llanilltern	66	Db
Capel-mawr	155	Bb
Capel St. Andrew.	80	Da
Capel St. Mary	79	Aa
Capel St. Silin	84	Ca
Capel Sion	102	Ca
Capenhurst	159	Bb
Capheaton	220	Da
Capland	34	Cc
Capston	44	Ca
Capton	33	Aa
Caputh	270	Cb
Caradal	273	Aa
Carbost, Inver.	284	Ca
Carbost, Inver.	296	Cc
Carbrooke	118	Ca
Carburton	164	Dc
Car Colston	150	Db
Carcroft	174	Dc
Cardeston	125	Ab
Cardiff	49	Aa
Cardigan	82	Da
Cardington, Beds.	95	Ac
Cardington,Shrops.	125	Bc
Cardinham	6	Db
Cardle	189	Ba
Cardow	303	Ac
Cardross	248	Cb
Cardurnock	216	Db
Careby	132	Ca
Careston	272	Ca
Carew Cheriton	62	Cb
Carew Newton	62	Cb
Carfin	249	Bc
Cargill	270	Dc
Cargo	217	Bb
Carhampton	48	Cb
Carisbrooke	21	Ab
Cark	192	Dc
Carlaverock	216	Ca
Carlby	132	Cb
Carleton, Cumb.	191	Ba
Carleton, Cumb.	218	Cc
Carleton, Yorks.	174	Ca
Carleton, Yorks.	182	Db
Carleton, E.	119	Aa
Carleton Forehoe	118	Da
Carleton, Gt.	179	Bc
Carleton Rode	119	Ab
Carleton St. Peter	120	Ca
Carlingcott	51	Ab
Carlops	251	Ac
Carlton, Beds.	114	Cc
Carlton, Cambs.	97	Ac
Carlton, Dur.	207	Bb
Carlton, Leics.	129	Bb
Carlton, Notts.	150	Cb
Carlton, Suff.	100	Cb
Carlton, Yorks.	175	Aa
Carlton, Yorks.	173	Ba
Carlton, Yorks.	197	Ba
Carlton, Yorks.	173	Bc
Carlton, Yorks.	196	Cb
Carlton Colville	120	Db
Carlton Curlieu	130	Dc
Carlton, E.	113	Ba
Carlton, Gt.	168	Cc
Carlton Husthwaite	197	Bc
Carlton-le-Moorland	151	Ba
Carlton, Lit.	168	Cc
Carlton Miniott.	197	Ac
Carlton, N., Lincs.	166	Cb
Carlton in Lindrick	164	Db
Carlton-on-Trent	165	Bc
Carlton, S., Lincs.	166	Cb
Carlton, S., Notts.	164	Db
Carlton Scroop	152	Cb
Carluke	238	Ca
Carmarthen	63	Ba
Carmel	64	Da
Carmichael	238	Db
Carmunnock	249	Ac
Carmyle	249	Ac
Carnaby	188	Cb
Carnach	266	Ca
Carnbee	262	Cb
Carne	4	Ca
Carnforth	180	Da
Carno	123	Ac
Carnock	250	Da
Carnoustie	272	Cc
Carnwath	238	Da
Carperby	195	Bb
Carr	164	Da
Carradale	233	Bb
Carrbridge	290	Cb
Carreglefn	155	Ba
Carr Gate	173	Ba
Carriden	250	Da
Carrington, Ches.	161	Aa
Carrington, Lincs.	153	Bc
Carrington, M. Loth.	252	Cc
Carrog	143	Bb
Carron	250	Ca
Carronbridge	226	Db
Carr Shield	219	Bc
Carr Ville	207	Ba
Carshalton	42	Ca
Carsington	148	Da
Carsphairn	225	Ab
Carstairs	238	Da
Carthorpe	196	Dc
Cartmel	192	Dc
Cartworth	172	Dc
Cary Fitzpaine	35	Ab
Cascob	106	Db
Cashmoor	36	Dc
Cassington	72	Ca
Cassop	207	Ba
Casseldwyran	62	Da
Casterton	194	Cc
Casterton, Gt.	132	Cb
Casterton, Lit.	132	Cb
Castle Acre	135	Bc
Castle Ashby	113	Bc
Castle Bolton	195	Bb
Castle Bromwich	128	Cc
Castle Bytham	132	Ca
Castlebythe	82	Cc
Castle Caereinion.	124	Ca
Castle Campbell	260	Ca
Castle Camps	97	Ac
Castle Carlton	168	Cc
Castle Cary	35	Ba
Castle Carrock	218	Cc
Castle Church	127	Aa
Castle Combe	51	Ba
Castle Donington	149	Bc
Castle Douglas	214	Db
Castle Eaton	71	Ab
Castle Eden	208	Ca
Castleford	174	Ca
Castle Frome	89	Aa
Castle Gresley	128	Da
Castle Hedingham	78	Ca
Castlemartin	61	Bc
Castle Morris	81	Bb
Castlemorton	89	Bb
Castle Rising	135	Ab
Castleside	221	Ac
Castle Thorpe Bucks.	93	Ba
Castlethorpe,Lincs.	176	Dc
Castleton, Derby.	163	Ab
Castleton, Lancs.	171	Bb
Castleton, Mon.	67	Bc
Castleton, Rox.	229	Ac
Castleton, Yorks.	198	Ba
Castletown, Caith.	323	Ba
Castletown, Cumb.	217	Bb
Castletown, I.O.M.	190	Db
Castley	184	Cb
Caston	118	Cb
Castor	115	Aa
Catcliffe	164	Ca
Catcott	34	Ca
Catcott Burtle	34	Ca
Caterham	42	Da
Catesby	112	Cc
Catfield	138	Ca
Catforth	180	Dc
Cathcart	248	Ac
Cathedine	87	Ac
Catherine Slack	172	Da
Catherington	39	Ba

Name	PAGE	SQ.
Catherston Leweston	16	Cb
Catlowdy	218	Ca
Catmore	54	Da
Caton	180	Da
Catrine	286	Dc
Catsfield	26	Cb
Catshill	109	Bb
Cattal	184	Db
Catterall	180	Dc
Catterick	196	Da
Catterline	282	Ac
Catterton	185	Ac
Catthorpe	112	Cb
Cattistock	17	Ba
Catton, Norf.	137	Bc
Catton, N'land.	220	Cc
Catton, High	186	Cb
Catton, Low	185	Bb
Catwick	177	Ba
Catworth	114	Db
Caudley Green	70	Ca
Caulcott	92	Dc
Cauldon	147	Ba
Cauldwell	128	Da
Caundle Marsh	35	Bc
Caunsall	109	Aa
Caunton	150	Da
Causewayhead	259	Bc
Cave, N.	176	Ca
Cavendish	97	Bc
Cavenham	97	Ba
Cavers	229	Aa
Caversfield	92	Dc
Caversham	55	Ba
Caversham, Lr.	55	Ba
Caverswall	147	Ab
Cave, S.	176	Ca
Cavil	175	Ba
Cawdor	301	Bb
Cawkwell	153	Ba
Cawood	185	Ac
Cawsand	8	Cc
Cawston	137	Ab
Cawthorne	173	Bc
Cawthorpe	132	Da
Cawthorpe, Lit.	168	Cc
Cawton	198	Ca
Caxton	95	Bb
Caynham	108	Cb
Caythorpe, Lancs.	152	Cb
Caythorpe, Notts.	150	Da
Cayton	188	Ca
Cefn Coed-y-Cymmer	86	Cb
Cefn-cribwr	65	Bb
Cefnllys	104	Da
Cefn-mawr	144	Cb
Ceidio	139	Bb
Cellan	84	Da
Cellardyke	262	Db
Cemmaes, Ang.	155	Ba
Cemmaes, Mont.	122	Da
Cenarth	83	Ab
Ceres	261	Bb
Cerne Abbas	17	Ba
Cerney, N.	70	Da
Cerney, S.	70	Db
Cerney Wick	70	Db
Cerrigceinwen	155	Bb
Cerrig-ydrudion	142	Da
Chaceley	90	Ca
Chacewater	2	Da
Chackmore	93	Ab
Chadderton Fold	171	Bc
Chaddesden	149	Ac
Chaddesley Corbett	109	Bb
Chaddleworth	54	Ca
Chadlington	91	Bc
Chadshunt	92	Ca
Cadwell, Essex	59	Ab
Chadwell, Leics.	131	Aa
Cadwell Heath	58	Db
Chaffcombe	16	Ca
Chagford	13	Ba
Chailey	25	Aa
Chalbury	19	Aa
Chalcombe	92	Da
Chaldon	42	Ca
Chaldon Herring	18	Cb
Chale	21	Ac
Chalfield	52	Cb
Chalfont St. Giles	74	Dc
Chalfont St. Peter	74	Dc
Chalford, Glos.	70	Ca
Chalford, Wilts.	52	Cc
Chalgrave	94	Dc
Chalgrove	73	Ab
Chalk	59	Ac
Challacombe	47	Ab
Challock	45	Ac
Challow, E.	72	Cc
Challow, W.	72	Cc
Chalmington	17	Ba
Chalton	94	Dc
Chalvey	56	Da
Chalvington	25	Db
Chandlers Ford	38	Dc
Chantry	51	Ac
Chapel	78	Ca
Chapel Allerton, Som.	50	Cc
Chapel Allerton Yorks.	184	Cc
Chapel Amble	6	Ca
Chapel Brampton	113	Ab
Chapel End, Essex	77	Ab
Chapel End, War.	129	Ac
Chapel-en-le-Frith	162	Db
Chapel Haddlesey	174	Da
Chapelhall	249	Db
Chapel Hill, Lincs.	153	Ac
Chapel Hill, Mon.	68	Db
Chapel Knapp	52	Ca
Chapelknowe	217	Aa
Chapel Lawn	106	Db
Chapel, Lower	104	Dc
Chapel, North	23	Aa
Chapel of Garioch	293	Ba
Chapel St.Leonards	154	Da
Chapel Stile	192	Da
Chapelton	237	Ba
Chapeltown, Banff	291	Db
Chapeltown, Yorks.	163	Ba
Chapel, Upper	104	Cb
Chapmanslade	51	Bc
Chard	16	Ca
Chardstock	16	Ca
Charfield	69	Ab
Charfield Green	69	Ab
Charford, N.	37	Bc
Charing	45	Ac
Charlbury	72	Ca
Charlcombe	51	Ba
Charlcotte	108	Ca
Charlcutt	52	Da
Charlecote	111	Ac
Charles	30	Db
Charleston	294	Cc
Charlestown, R. & C.	300	Db
Charlestown, Aber.	306	Da
Charlestown, Corn.	6	Cc
Charlestown, Fife	250	Da
Charlestown, Mon.	67	Ab
Charlestown of Aberlour	303	Ac
Charlesworth	162	Ca
Charleton	10	Cc
Charlinch	33	Ba
Charlton, Berks.	72	Cc
Charlton, Glos.	68	Dc
Charlton, Hants.	38	Ca
Charlton, London.	58	Cb
Charlton, N'hants.	92	Db
Charlton, N'land.	230	Dc
Charlton, Som.	51	Ac
Charlton, Som.	33	Bb
Charlton, Sus.	40	Cb
Charlton, Wilts.	53	Ac
Charlton, Wilts.	37	Bb
Charlton, Wilts.	70	Cc
Charlton, Wilts.	36	Db
Charlton, Worcs.	90	Da
Charlton Abbots	90	Dc
Charlton Adam	35	Ab
Charlton Horethorne	35	Ab
Charlton Kings	90	Cc
Charlton Mackrell	34	Db
Charlton Marshall	18	Da
Charlton Musgrove	35	Ba
Charlton, N.	244	Dc
Charlton-on-Otmoor	72	Da
Charlton, S.	244	Dc
Charlwood	42	Cb
Charminster	17	Bb
Charmouth	16	Cb
Charndon	93	Ac
Charney Basset	72	Cb
Charsfield	99	Bb
Charterhouse	50	Db
Chartham	45	Bb
Chartridge	74	Cb
Chart Sutton	44	Cb
Charwelton	92	Da
Chase Terrace	127	Bb
Chasetown	128	Cb
Chastleton	91	Bc
Chatburn	181	Bc
Chatham	59	Bc
Chatham Green	77	Bb
Chatteris	116	Cb
Chattisham	79	Aa
Chatton	244	Cc
Chawleigh	31	Bb
Chawston	95	Ab
Chawton	39	Ba
Chaxhill	89	Bc
Cheadle, Ches.	161	Ba
Cheadle, Staffs.	147	Bb
Cheam	42	Ca
Cheapside	56	Cb
Chearsley	73	Ba
Chebsey	146	Da
Checkendon	55	Aa
Checkley, Ches.	146	Da
Checkley, Herefs.	88	Db
Checkley, Staffs.	147	Bb
Chedourgh	97	Bb
Cheddar	50	Cb
Cheddington, Bucks.	74	Ca
Cheddington, Dors.	16	Da
Cheddleton	147	Aa
Cheddon Fitzpaine	33	Bb
Cheddon Upr.	33	Bb
Chedglow	70	Cb
Chedgrave	120	Cb
Chediston	100	Ca
Chedworth	70	Da
Chedzoy	34	Ca
Chelborough, W.	35	Ac
Chelfham	30	Db
Chellaston	149	Ac
Chellington	114	Cc
Chelmarsh	108	Ca
Chelmondiston	79	Ba
Chelmorton	162	Dc
Chelmsford	77	Bc
Chelsham	42	Da
Chelsea	57	Bb
Chelsfield	43	Aa
Chelsworth	98	Dc
Cheltenham	90	Cc
Cheltisham	116	Dc
Chelveston	114	Cb
Chelvey	50	Ca
Chelwood	51	Ab
Chelworth	70	Cb
Chelynch	51	Ac
Cheney Longville	107	Ba
Chenies	74	Db
Chepstow	68	Db
Cherhill	52	Da
Cherington, Glos.	70	Cb
Cherington, War.	91	Bb
Cheriton, Glam.	64	Cc
Cheriton, Hants.	39	Ab
Cheriton, Kent	28	Ca
Cheriton, Pem.	62	Cc
Cheriton Bishop	14	Ca
Cheriton Cross	14	Ca
Cheriton Fitzpaine	32	Cb
Cheriton, N.	35	Bb
Cheriton, S.	35	Bb
Cherrington	126	Ca
Cherry Burton	177	Aa
Cherry Hinton	96	Db
Cherry Orchard	109	Ac
Cherry Willingham	166	Dc
Chertsey	56	Db
Cheselbourne	18	Ca
Chesham	74	Db
Cheshunt	76	Cc
Cheslyn Hay	127	Bb
Chessington	41	Ba
Chester	159	Bc
Chesterblade	35	Ba
Chesterfield	164	Cc
Chesterford, Gt.	96	Dc
Chesterford, Lit.	96	Dc
Chester-le-Street	222	Cc
Chesters	229	Ba
Chesterton, Cambs.	96	Db
Chesterton, Hunts.	115	Ab
Chesterton, Oxon.	92	Db
Chesterton, Shrops.	126	Dc
Chesterton, Staffs.	146	Da
Chesterton, War.	111	Bc
Cheswardine	146	Cc
Cheswick	243	Ba
Chetnole	35	Ac
Chettle	36	Dc
Chetton	126	Cc
Chetwode	93	Ab
Chetwynd	126	Da
Chetwynd Aston	126	Da
Cheveley	97	Ab
Chevening	43	Aa
Cheverell, Gt.	52	Db
Cheverell, Lit.	52	Db
Chevington	97	Bb
Chew Magna	50	Db
Chew Stoke	50	Db
Chewton Mendip	50	Dc
Chicheley	94	Ca
Chichester	22	Da
Chickerell	17	Bc
Chicklade	36	Da
Chickney	77	Aa
Chicksgrove	36	Da
Chiddingfold	41	Aa
Chiddingly	25	Bb
Chiddingstone	43	Ab
Chideock	16	Db
Chidham	22	Da
Chieveley	54	Da
Chignal	77	Ac
Chignal Smealy	77	Ac
Chigwell	58	Da
Chigwell Row	58	Da
Chilbolton	38	Da
Chilcomb	39	Ab
Chilcompton	51	Ac
Chilcote	128	Db
Childerditch Street	59	Ab
Childer Thornton	159	Bb
Child Okeford	36	Cc
Childrey	72	Cc
Child's Ercall	126	Ca
Childs Wickham	90	Da
Childwall	160	Ca
Chilfrome	17	Ba
Chilham	45	Bb
Chilhampton	37	Ab
Chillaton	12	Dc
Chillenden	46	Cb
Chillesford	100	Cc
Chillingham	244	Cc
Chillington, Dev.	10	Cb
Chillington, Som.	16	Ca
Chilmark	36	Da
Chilson	91	Bc
Chilstone	88	Ca
Chilsworthy	12	Ca
Chiltern Green	75	Ab
Chilthorne Domer	34	Dc
Chiltington, East	25	Ab
Chiltington, W.	23	Bb
Chilton, Berks.	72	Dc
Chilton, Bucks.	73	Aa
Chilton, Suff.	98	Cc
Chilton Candover	39	Ab
Chilton Cantelo	35	Ab
Chilton Foliat	53	Bb
Chilton Polden	34	Ca
Chilton Trinity	34	Ca
Chilvers Coton	129	Ac
Chilwell	149	Bc
Chilworth	38	Dc
Chimney	72	Cb
Chingford	58	Ca
Chinley	162	Db
Chinnock, East	16	Da
Chinnock, Middle	16	Da
Chinnock, West	16	Da
Chinnor	73	Bb
Chipley	33	Ac
Chippenham, Cambs.	97	Aa
Chippenham, Wilts.	52	Da
Chipperfield	74	Db
Chipping, Herts.	76	Ca
Chipping, Lancs.	181	Ac
Chipping Barnet	57	Ba
Chipping Campden	91	Ab
Chipping Norton	91	Bc
Chipping Ongar	76	Dc
Chipping Sodbury	69	Bc
Chipping Warden	92	Da
Chippinghill	78	Cb
Chipstable	33	Ab
Chipstead, Kent	43	Aa
Chipstead, Sur.	42	Ca
Chirbury	124	Dc
Chirk	144	Cc
Chirnside	254	Cc
Chirton	52	Da
Chiselborough	34	Dc
Chisenbury, E.	53	Ac
Chisenbury, W.	53	Ac
Chisnall, Gt.	96	Cc
Chishall, Lit.	76	Ca
Chisledon	53	Aa
Chislenampton	73	Ab
Chislehurst	58	Dc
Chislet	46	Ca
Chiswick	57	Bb
Chiswick End	96	Cc
Chithurst	40	Da
Chittering	96	Da
Chitterne All Saints	37	Aa
Chitterne St. Mary	37	Aa
Chittlehamholt	30	Dc
Chittlehampton	30	Dc
Chivelstone	10	Cc
Chobham	41	Aa
Cholderton	37	Ba
Cholderton, E.	38	Ca
Cholesbury	74	Cb
Chollerton	220	Ca
Cholsey	73	Ac
Cholstrey	107	Bc
Cholwell	50	Db
Chop Gate	198	Ca
Chorley, Ches.	161	Bb
Chorley, Lancs.	170	Cb
Chorley, Shrops.	108	Ca
Chorley, Staffs.	128	Cb
Chorleywood	74	Db
Chowley	144	Da

	PAGE	SQ.		PAGE	SQ.		PAGE	SQ.		PAGE	SQ
Chrishall	96	Cc	Clappersgate	192	Da	Clifton, Gt.	201	Bb	Coddington, Notts.	151	Ba
Christchurch, Hants.	19	Bb	Clapton, Glos.	71	Aa	Clifton Hampden.	72	Bb	Codford St. Mary.	36	Da
Christchurch, Mon.	67	Ca	Clapton, N'hants.	114	Da	Clifton, Lit.	201	Bb	Codford St. Peter.	36	Da
Christian Malford.	70	Cc	Clapton, Som.	51	Ab	Clifton, N.	165	Bc	Codicote	75	Bb
Christleton	160	Ca	Clapton-in-Gordano	50	Ca	Clifton, S.	165	Bc	Codnor	149	Bb
Chirston	50	Cb	Clapworthy	31	Ba	Clifton Reynes	94	Ca	Codrington	69	Ac
Christow	14	Ca	Clarbeston	62	Ca	Clifton-upon-Dunsmore	112	Cb	Codsall	127	Ab
Chryston	249	Ab	Clarborough	165	Bb	Clifton-upon-Teme	108	Dc	Coedana	155	Bb
Chudleigh	14	Ca	Clardon	323	Ba	Climping	23	Ac	Coedkernew	67	Bc
Chudleigh Knighton	14	Ca	Clare	97	Bc	Clint	184	Ca	Coed-poeth	144	Ca
Chulmleigh	31	Bb	Clarencefield	216	Ca	Clint Green	118	Da	Coed Talon	144	Ca
Chunal	162	Da	Clarkston	248	Dc	Clippesby	138	Cc	Coed Tre-castell	66	Db
Church	171	Aa	Clashmore, Suth.	313	Aa	Clipsham	132	Ca	Coed-yr-ynys	87	Ac
Churcham	89	Bc	Clashmore, Suth	312	Cb	Clipston, N'hants.	112	Da	Coed Ystumgwern	140	Dc
Church Aston	126	Da	Clashnessie	313	Ba	Clipston, Notts.	150	Cc	Coffinswell	14	Dc
Church Brampton	112	Dc	Clatford, Upr.	38	Ca	Clipstone	164	Dc	Cofton Hackett	110	Cb
Church Broughton	148	Da	Clatter	123	Ac	Clitheroe	181	Bc	Cogan	49	Aa
Church Cobham	41	Ba	Clatworthy	33	Ab	Clive	125	Ba	Cogenhoe	113	Bc
Church Coppenhall	146	Da	Claughton, Lancs.	180	Da	Clixby	167	Aa	Cogges, High	72	Ca
Church Crookham	55	Bc	Claughton, Lancs.	180	Dc	Clocaenog	143	Aa	Coggeshall	78	Cb
Churchdown	90	Cc	Claverdon	110	Db	Clockhill	305	Bb	Coggeshall, Lit.	78	Cb
Church Eaton	127	Aa	Claverham	50	Ca	Clodock	87	Bb	Coggs	72	Ca
Church End, Beds.	94	Dc	Clavering	76	Da	Cloford	51	Bc	Coity	66	Cb
Church End, Cambs.	134	Cc	Claverley	126	Dc	Clophill	95	Ac	Coker, E.	35	Ac
Church End, Hunts.	115	Bc	Claverton	51	Bb	Clopton	99	Bc	Colaton Raleigh	15	Ac
Church End, War.	128	Dc	Clawddnewydd	143	Aa	Closeburn	226	Db	Colbost	295	Ac
Churchend, Essex	77	Ab	Clawton	12	Ca	Closworth	35	Ac	Colburn	196	Da
Churchend, Essex	60	Da	Claxby, Lincs.	167	Ab	Clothall	75	Ba	Colbury	20	Da
Church Enstone	92	Cc	Claxby, Lincs.	154	Ca	Clotton	160	Dc	Colby, I.O.M.	199	Dc
Church Fenton	185	Ac	Claxton, Norf.	119	Ba	Clough Head	172	Db	Colby, Norf.	137	Bb
Churchgate Street	76	Dc	Claxton, Yorks.	185	Ba	Cloughton	200	Dc	Colby, W'land.	204	Ca
Church Gresley	128	Da	Claybrooke	112	Ca	Clovelly	29	Bc	Colchester	78	Db
Church Handboro'	72	Ca	Clay Coton	112	Db	Clovulin	265	Ba	Cold Ash	54	Bb
Church Honeybourne	91	Aa	Clay Cross	164	Cc	Clowne	164	Cb	Cold Ashby	112	Db
Churchill, Dev.	30	Da	Claydon, Oxon.	92	Ca	Clows Top	108	Db	Cold Ashton	51	Ba
Churchill, Oxon.	91	Bc	Claydon, Suff.	99	Ac	Clubworthy	11	Bc	Cold Brayfield	94	Ca
Churchill, Som.	50	Cb	Claydon, E.	93	Bc	Clun	106	Da	Coldham	116	Ca
Churchill, Worcs.	109	Aa	Claydon, Mid.	93	Bc	Clunbury	107	Aa	Cold Hanworth	166	Db
Churchill, Worcs.	109	Bc	Claygate	41	Ba	Clungunford	107	Aa	Cold Harbour	75	Ab
Churchingford	15	Ba	Claygate Cross	43	Ba	Clunton	107	Aa	Cold Hiendley	173	Bb
Church Knowle	19	Ac	Clayhidon	33	Ca	Clutton, Ches.	144	Da	Cold Higham	93	Aa
Church Laneham	165	Bb	Claypole	151	Bb	Clutton, Som.	51	Ab	Coldingham	254	Cb
Church Langton	130	Ca	Claythorpe	154	Ca	Clydach	67	Aa	Cold Kirby	197	Bb
Church Lawford	111	Bb	Clayton, Staffs.	146	Db	Clydach-on-Tawe	85	Ac	Cold Newton	130	Db
Church Leigh	147	Bc	Clayton, Sus.	24	Db	Clydebank	248	Db	Cold Norton	60	Ca
Church Lench	110	Cc	Clayton, Yorks.	174	Cc	Clydey	83	Ab	Cold Overton	131	Bb
Church Minshull	145	Ba	Clayton, Yorks.	172	Ba	Clynder	247	Ba	Coldred	46	Cc
Church Oakley	54	Dc	Clayton-le-Moors	171	Aa	Clynderwen	62	Da	Coldridge	31	Bb
Churchover	112	Ca	Clayton-le-Woods	170	Ca	Clynnog-fawr	140	Ca	Coldstream	242	Cb
Church Preen	125	Bc	Clayton West	173	Bb	Clyro	87	Ba	Coldwaltham	23	Bb
Church Pulverbatch	125	Ab	Clayworth	165	Ba	Clyst Honiton	14	Da	Coldwell	88	Cb
Church Row	51	Bb	Cleadon	222	Db	Clyst Hydon	15	Ab	Cold Weston	108	Ca
Churchstanton	15	Ba	Clearwell	68	Ca	Clyst St. George	14	Da	Cole	35	Ba
Church Stoke	124	Dc	Cleasby	207	Ac	Clyst St. Lawrence	15	Ab	Colebatch	106	Da
Churchstow	9	Bb	Cleatlam	206	Da	Clyst St. Mary	14	Da	Colebrooke	31	Bc
Church Stowe	112	Dc	Cleator	201	Bc	Clyth, Mid.	318	Db	Coleby, Lincs.	152	Ca
Church Street	45	Ba	Cleckheaton	173	Aa	Cnwch-coch	102	Ca	Coleby, Lincs.	176	Ca
Church Stretton	125	Ac	Clee	167	Ba	Coal Aston	163	Bb	Coleford, Dev.	31	Bc
Churchthorpe	168	Cb	Clee Hill	108	Cb	Coalbrookdale	126	Cb	Coleford, Mon.	68	Ca
Church Town, Lincs.	175	Bc	Clee St. Margaret.	108	Ca	Coalbrookvale	67	Cb	Coleford, Som.	51	Ac
Churchtown, Lancs.	169	Bb	Cleethorpes	168	Ca	Coalburn	238	Cb	Colemere	144	Dc
Churchtown, Lancs.	180	Dc	Cleeton	108	Ca	Coalcleugh	205	Aa	Colemore	39	Bb
Church Warsop	164	Dc	Cleeve, Berks.	55	Aa	Coaley	69	Bb	Cole Orton	129	Ba
Churston Ferrers	10	Da	Cleeve, Som.	50	Ca	Coalpit Heath	69	Ac	Colerne	51	Ba
Churwell	173	Ba	Cleeve Prior	90	Da	Coalville	129	Ba	Colesborne	70	Ca
Chute	53	Bc	Cleghorn	238	Da	Coastley	220	Cb	Coleshill, Berks.	71	Bc
Chwilog	140	Cb	Clehonger	88	Cb	Coat	34	Dc	Coleshill, Bucks.	74	Db
Cilcennin	101	Bb	Cleish	260	Dc	Coatbridge	249	Bc	Coleshill, War.	128	Dc
Cilfynydd	66	Da	Cieland	249	Bc	Coate	53	Aa	Colinsburgh	262	Cc
Cilgerran	82	Da	Clements Tump	68	Da	Coates, Cambs.	115	Ba	Colinton	251	Bb
Cilian Aeron	101	Bc	Clenchwarton	134	Db	Coates, Glos.	70	Cb	Colintraive	246	Db
Cilrhedyn	83	Ab	Clent	109	Ba	Coates, Lincs.	166	Ca	Colkirk	136	Cb
Cil-y-bebyll	85	Ac	Cleobury Mortimer	108	Da	Coates, Sus.	23	Ab	Collace	270	Dc
Cilycwm	103	Ab	Cleobury North	108	Ca	Coates, Gt.	167	Ba	Collessie	261	Ba
Cilymaenllwyd	62	Da	Clerkenwell	57	Bb	Coates, Lit.	167	Ba	Collfryn	124	Ca
Cinderford	69	Aa	Clevedon	50	Ca	Coates, N.	168	Cb	Colliers End	76	Cb
Cirencester	70	Db	Clewer, Berks.	56	Da	Coatham Mundeville	207	Ac	Collin	216	Cл
City, Bucks.	73	Bb	Clewer, Som.	50	Cc	Cobb	16	Cb	Collingbourne Ducis	53	Bc
City, Glam.	66	Cb	Cley	136	Da	Coberley	90	Cc	Collingbourne Kingston	53	Bc
Clachaig	246	Da	Cliburn	204	Cb	Cobham, Kent	59	Ac	Collingham	184	Bc
Clachamish	296	Ca	Cliddesden	55	Ac	Cobham, Sur.	41	Ba	Collingham, N.	151	Ba
Clachan	265	Ab	Cliff, N.	186	Dc	Cobholm Island	120	Da	Collingham, S.	151	Ba
Clachtoll	313	Ab	Cliffe, Kent	59	Bc	Cockayne Hatley.	95	Ac	Collington	108	Cc
Clackmannan	259	Bc	Cliffe, Yorks.	175	Aa	Cockburnspath	253	Bb	Collingtree	113	Ac
Clacton, Gt.	79	Bc	Cliffe Pypard	52	Ba	Cockenzie	252	Cc	Collycroft	111	Ba
Clacton, Lit.	79	Bc	Cliffe, West	46	Dc	Cockerham	180	Cb	Colly Weston	132	Ca
Clacton-on-Sea	79	Bc	Clifford, Herefs.	87	Bc	Cockerington, N.	168	Ca	Colmonell	211	Ba
Claife	192	Db	Clifford, Yorks.	184	Dc	Cockerington, S.	168	Cc	Colmworth	95	Ab
Claines	109	Ac	Clifford Chambers	91	Aa	Cockermouth	202	Cb	Colnbrook	56	Da
Clandon, E.	41	Ab	Cliffsend	46	Db	Cockfield, Dur.	206	Db	Colne, Hunts.	115	Bc
Clandon, W.	41	Ab	Clifton, Beds.	95	Ac	Cockfield, Suff.	98	Ca	Colne, Lancs.	182	Cc
Clandown	51	Ab	Clifton, Ches.	160	Cb	Cocking	40	Dc	Colne Engaine	78	Ca
Clanfield, Hants.	39	Bc	Clifton, Derby	148	Cb	Cockington	10	Da	Colne Green	97	Bc
Clanfield, Oxon.	71	Bb	Clifton, Lancs.	171	Ac	Cocklade	34	Da	Colney	119	Aa
Clannaborough	31	Bc	Clifton, Lancs.	169	Ba	Cockley Cley	117	Ba	Colney Hatch	57	Ba
Clanville	53	Bc	Clifton, N'land.	232	Cc	Cockpole Green	55	Ba	Colney Heath	75	Ba
Claonel	311	Aa	Clifton, Notts.	150	Aa	Cockshot	109	Ba	Colney Street	75	Ac
Clapham, Beds.	94	Da	Clifton, Oxon.	92	Dc	Cockslatt	144	Dc	Coln Rogers	70	Da
Clapham, London	57	Bc	Clifton, Som.	50	Da	Cockthorpe	136	Da	Coln St. Aldwyn	71	Ab
Clapham, Sus.	23	Bc	Clifton, W'land.	203	Bb	Coddenham	99	Ac	Coln St. Dennis	70	Da
Clapham, Yorks.	181	Ba	Clifton, Yorks.	183	Bb	Coddington, Ches.	144	Da	Colside	271	Bc
			Clifton, Yorks.	185	Bb	Coddington, Herefs.	89	Aa	Colsterworth	132	Ca
			Clifton, Yorks.	164	Da				Colston Bassett	150	Dc
			Clifton, Yorks.	172	Db				Coltishall	137	Ba
			Clifton Campville	128	Db						

Name	Page	Sq
Colton, *Lancs.*	192	Db
Colton, *Norf.*	119	Aa
Colton, *Staffs.*	128	Ca
Colton, *Yorks.*	185	Aa
Colton, *Yorks.*	173	Ba
Colva	106	Dc
Colvend	215	Ac
Colwall	89	Ba
Colwall Stone	89	Ba
Colwell	220	Ca
Colwich	127	Ba
Colwinston	66	Cb
Colwyn	157	Bb
Colwyn Bay	157	Bb
Colyford	15	Bb
Colyton	15	Bb
Combe, *Berks.*	54	Cb
Combe, *Oxon.*	72	Ca
Combe Down	51	Bb
Combe Florey	33	Ab
Combe Hay	51	Bb
Combeinteignhead	14	Da
Combe Martin	30	Da
Combe Raleigh	15	Ba
Comberbach	160	Db
Comberton	96	Cb
Comberton, Gt.	90	Ca
Comberton, Lit.	90	Ca
Combe St. Nicholas	16	Ca
Combpyne	16	Cb
Combrook	91	Ba
Combs, *Derby*	162	Db
Combs, *Suff.*	98	Db
Combwich	33	Ba
Comers	293	Ac
Commondale	199	Ab
Compass	34	Cb
Compstall	162	Ca
Compton, *Berks.*	54	Da
Compton, *Hants.*	40	Cc
Compton, *Hants.*	38	Bb
Compton, *Som.*	34	Db
Compton, *Staffs.*	109	Aa
Compton, *Sur.*	40	Da
Compton Abbas, *Dors.*	17	Ba
Compton Abbas *Dors.*	36	Cb
Compton Abdale	90	Dc
Compton Bassett,	52	Da
Compton Beauchamp	71	Bc
Compton Bishop	50	Cb
Compton Chamberlayne	37	Ab
Compton Dando	51	Ab
Compton Durville	34	Dc
Compton, E.	35	Aa
Compton, Lit.	91	Bc
Compton, Long	91	Bb
Compton Martin	50	Db
Compton Pauncefoot	35	Bb
Compton Valence	17	Ba
Compton,W.,*Berks.*	54	Da
Compton, W., *Som.*	50	Da
Compton Wyniates	91	Bb
Comrie	259	Aa
Conchan	190	Dc
Conderton	90	Db
Condicote	91	Ac
Condorrat	249	Bb
Condover	125	Bb
Coneysthorpe	186	Ca
Coney Weston	118	Cc
Conford	40	Db
Congerstone	129	Rb
Congham	135	Bb
Congleton	161	Bc
Congresbury	50	Cb
Coningsby	153	Bb
Conington	96	Ca
Conisbrough	164	Da
Coniscliffe, High	207	Ac
Coniscliffe, Low	207	Ac
Conisholme	168	Cb
Coniston, *Lancs.*	192	Cb
Coniston, *Yorks.*	177	Bb
Coniston Cold	182	Cb
Conistone	182	Da
Connah's Quay	159	Bd
Connel	265	Bc
Connington	115	Ab
Conon	300	Cb
Cononley	182	Dc
Consett	221	Bc
Constable Burton	196	Cb
Constantine	2	Dc
Contin	300	Cb
Conway	157	Aa
Conwil Elvet	83	Bc
Cookbury	12	Ca
Cookham	74	Cc
Cookham Dean	74	Cc
Cook Hill	110	Cc
Cookley, *Suff.*	100	Ca
Cookley, *Worcs.*	109	Aa
Cookley Green	73	Bc
Cookshill	147	Ab
Cooksmill Green	77	Ac
Cooling	59	Bc
Coombe	17	Ab
Coombe Bissett	37	Ab
Coombe Keynes	18	Db
Coombes	24	Cc
Coopersale	58	Da
Cootham	23	Bb
Copdock	79	Ba
Copford	78	Db
Copgrove	184	Ca
Cople	95	Ab
Copley	172	Ca
Copmanthorpe	185	Ac
Coppenhall	127	Aa
Copperhouse	2	Cb
Coppingford	114	Da
Coppleridge	36	Cb
Copston Magna	111	Ba
Copt Hewick	184	Ca
Copthorne	42	Cc
Copt Oak	130	Cb
Copythorne	38	Cc
Corbets Tye	59	Ab
Corbridge	220	Db
Corby, *Lincs.*	132	Ca
Corby, *N'hants.*	113	Da
Corby, Gt.	218	Cc
Coreley	108	Cb
Corfe	33	Bc
Corfe Castle	19	Ac
Corfe Mullen	19	Ab
Corfton	107	Ba
Corhampton	39	Bc
Corley	111	Aa
Corley Ash	111	Aa
Cornard, Gt.	98	Ca
Cornard, Lit.	78	Ca
Cornelly, N.	65	Bb
Cornelly, S.	65	Bb
Corner, The	107	Ba
Corney	191	Bb
Cornforth	207	Ba
Corngl-y-wal	141	Ba
Cornhill, *Banff*	304	Db
Cornhill, *N'land*	242	Db
Cornholm	171	Ba
Cornsay	206	Da
Corntown	66	Cb
Cornwell	91	Bc
Cornwood	9	Ca
Cornworthy	10	Ca
Corpach	275	Da
Corpusty	137	Ab
Corra	145	Ba
Corran	265	Ba
Corribeg	274	Da
Corrie	234	Da
Corringham, *Essex*	59	Ba
Corringham, *Lincs.*	166	Ca
Corris	122	Ca
Corscombe	17	Aa
Corse Lawn	89	Bb
Corsham	52	Ca
Corsley	51	Bc
Corsock	214	Da
Corston, *Som.*	51	Ab
Corston, *Wilts.*	70	Cc
Corstorphine	251	Ab
Corton, *Suff.*	120	Db
Corton, *Wilts.*	36	Da
Corton Denham	35	Bb
Corwen	143	Ab
Coryton	12	Dc
Cosford	112	Ca
Cosgrove	93	Ba
Cosheston	62	Cb
Coskills	176	Dc
Cossall	149	Bb
Cossington, *Leics.*	130	Cb
Cossington, *Som.*	34	Ca
Costessy	137	Ac
Costock	150	Cc
Coston, *Leics.*	131	Ba
Coston, *Norf.*	118	Da
Cote, *Oxon.*	72	Cb
Cote, *Som.*	34	Ca
Cote Brook	160	Dc
Cotehill	218	Cc
Cotes	193	Bb
Cotesbach	112	Ca
Cotgrave	150	Da
Cotham	151	Ab
Cothelstone	33	Bb
Cotheridge	108	Dc
Cotherstone	206	Cc
Cotleigh	15	Bb
Cotmanhay	149	Bb
Cotness	175	Ba
Coton, *Cambs.*	96	Cb
Coton, *N'hants*	112	Db
Coton, *Staffs.*	127	Aa
Coton, *Staffs.*	126	Da
Coton, *Staffs.*	147	Bc
Coton-in-the-Elms	128	Da
Cottam, *Notts.*	165	Ba
Cottam, *Yorks.*	187	Bb
Cottenham	96	Ca
Cottered	76	Ca
Cotteridge	110	Ca
Cotterstock	114	Ca
Cottesbrooke	112	Da
Cottesmore	131	Bb
Cottingham, *N'hants.*	113	Ba
Cottingham, *Yorks.*	176	Da
Cottingley	183	Ac
Cottingwith	185	Bc
Cottisford	92	Dc
Cotton	99	Ab
Cotton End, *Beds.*	95	Ac
Cotton End, *N'hants.*	113	Ac
Cottown	292	Da
Coughton	110	Cc
Coulderton	191	Aa
Coulsdon	42	Ca
Coulston	52	Cb
Coulter	239	Ab
Coulton	198	Cc
Cound	125	Bb
Coundon, *Dur.*	207	Ab
Coundon, *War.*	111	Aa
Countersett	195	Ab
Countesthorpe	130	Cc
Countisbury	47	Ab
Coupland	243	Bb
Counthorpe	132	Ca
Coupar Angus	270	Db
Courteenhall	93	Ba
Courtway	33	Bb
Cousleywood	43	Bc
Cove, *Dev.*	32	Da
Cove, *Dumb.*	247	Ba
Cove, *Hants.*	56	Cc
Cove, *Kinc.*	294	Db
Covehithe	100	Da
Coven	127	Ab
Coveney	116	Cc
Covenham St. Bartholomew	168	Cb
Covenham St. Mary	168	Cb
Coventry	111	Aa
Coverack	2	Dc
Cove, S.	100	Da
Covington, *Hunts.*	114	Db
Covington, *Lan.*	238	Cc
Cowarne, Lit.	88	Da
Cowbeech	26	Cb
Cowbit	133	Bc
Cowbridge, *Glam.*	66	Cb
Cowbridge, *Lincs.*	153	Bc
Cowden	42	Dc
Cowdenbeath	260	Dc
Cowden, Gt.	178	Cb
Cowes	21	Ab
Cowesby	197	Ba
Cowes, East	21	Ab
Cowfold	24	Ca
Cow Honeybourne	90	Da
Cowick, E.	175	Ab
Cowick, W.	175	Ab
Cowlam	187	Bb
Cowley, *Glos.*	90	Cc
Cowley, *M'sex*	56	Da
Cowley, *Oxon.*	72	Db
Cowling	196	Db
Cowlinge	97	Bb
Cowling Hill	182	Dc
Cowmes	173	Ab
Cowpen	222	Ca
Cowpen Bewley	208	Cb
Cowsden	109	Bc
Cowthorpe	184	Db
Cowton, E.	196	Da
Cowton, N.	196	Da
Coxbank	145	Bb
Coxbench	149	Ab
Coxhoe	207	Ba
Coxley	34	Da
Coxlodge	221	Bb
Coxwell, Gt.	71	Bc
Coxwell, Lit.	71	Bc
Coxwold	197	Bc
Coychurch	66	Cb
Coylton	236	Dc
Coylton, New	236	Dc
Coynach	292	Cc
Crabbs Cross	110	Cb
Crabtree	24	Ca
Crabtree Green	144	Cb
Crackenthorpe	204	Db
Crackleybank	126	Db
Cracoe	182	Db
Cradley, *Herefs.*	89	Ba
Cradley, *Worcs.*	109	Ba
Cradley Heath	109	Ba
Crafthole	8	Cc
Cragg	172	Ca
Craggan	290	Da
Craig	272	Da
Craig-cefn-parc	64	Db
Craigdam	294	Ca
Craigearn	293	Bb
Craigellachie	303	Ac
Craigendoran	247	Ba
Craighead	302	Cb
Craigneuk	249	Bc
Craignure	264	Dc
Craigo	281	Bc
Craigour	269	Ba
Craigrothie	261	Bb
Craigton, *Angus*	271	Aa
Craigton, *Angus*	272	Cb
Craig-tre-banos	85	Ac
Crail	262	Db
Crailing	242	Cc
Craiselound	165	Ba
Crakehall, Gt.	196	Db
Crakehall, Lit.	196	Db
Crambe	186	Ca
Cramlington	222	Ca
Cramond	251	Bb
Cranage	161	Ac
Cranborne	37	Ac
Cranbrook	44	Cc
Cranfield	94	Db
Cranford	57	Ab
Cranford St. Andrew	113	Bb
Cranford St. John	113	Bb
Cranham, *Essex*	59	Ab
Cranham, *Glos.*	70	Ca
Crank	170	Cc
Cranleigh	41	Ac
Cranmore	51	Ac
Cranoe	131	Ac
Cransford	100	Cb
Cranstal	189	Aa
Cranswick	187	Bc
Crantock	5	Ab
Cranwell	152	Cb
Cranwich	117	Bb
Cranworth	118	Da
Crarae	256	Cc
Craster	244	Dc
Craswall	87	Bb
Cratfield	100	Ca
Crathie, *Aber.*	280	Ca
Crathie, *Inver.*	277	Aa
Crathorne	197	Ba
Craven Arms	107	Ba
Crawcrook	221	Bb
Crawford	238	Dc
Crawfordjohn	238	Dc
Crawick	226	Ca
Crawley, *Hants.*	38	Db
Crawley, *Oxon.*	71	Ba
Crawley, *Sus.*	42	Cc
Crawley, N.	94	Ca
Crawley Side	206	Ca
Crawshaw Booth	171	Ba
Crawton	282	Dc
Cray, *Brecon*	85	Ba
Cray, *Yorks.*	195	Ac
Crayford	58	Dc
Crayke	185	Aa
Crays Hill	59	Ba
Creacombe	32	Ca
Creake, N.	136	Ca
Creake, S.	136	Ca
Creaton, Gt.	112	Db
Credenhill	88	Ca
Crediton	32	Cb
Cree Bridge	213	Ab
Creech St. Michael	33	Bb
Creed	4	Ca
Creeksea	60	Da
Creeting St. Mary.	99	Ab
Creeton	132	Ca
Creetown	210	Da
Cregrina	104	Da
Creigiau	68	Cb
Cressage	125	Bb
Cressbrook	163	Ac
Cresselly	62	Db
Cressing	78	Cb
Cressingham, Gt.	118	Ca
Cressingham, Lit.	118	Ca
Cresswell	62	Cb
Cresswell	164	Db
Cretingham	99	Bb
Crewe	146	Ca
Crew Green	124	Da
Crewkerne	16	Da
Crianlarich	257	Ba
Cribyn	84	Ca
Criccieth	140	Cb
Crich	148	Da

Name	PAGE	SQ.
Crichton	252	Cc
Crick, *Mon.*	68	Cc
Crick, *N'hants*	112	Cb
Crickadarn	104	Db
Cricket Malherbie	16	Ca
Cricket St. Thomas	16	Ca
Crickham	50	Cc
Crickhowell	87	Ac
Cricklade	70	Db
Crieff	259	Ba
Criggion	124	Da
Crigglestone	173	Bb
Crimchard	16	Ca
Crimond	306	Da
Crimplesham	117	Aa
Crimscote	91	Ba
Crinan	255	Ac
Cringleford	119	Aa
Crinow	62	Da
Cripplestyle	37	Ac
Croalchapel	226	Db
Crockenhill	58	Dc
Crockernwell	13	Ba
Crockerton	52	Cc
Crockerton Green	52	Cc
Crocketford	214	Da
Crockey Hill	185	Bc
Croes-goch	81	Bc
Croes-penmaen	67	Ab
Croes-y-ceiliog	67	Bb
Croes-y-mwyalch	67	Bb
Croft, *Leics.*	130	Cc
Croft, *Lincs.*	154	Db
Croft, *Yorks.*	207	Ac
Crofton, *Wilts.*	53	Bb
Crofton, *Yorks.*	173	Bb
Croglin	218	Dc
Croick	310	Da
Cromarty	301	Aa
Cromer, *Herts.*	75	Da
Cromer, *Norf.*	137	Ba
Cromer Hyde	75	Bc
Cromford	148	Da
Cromhall	69	Ab
Cromwell	151	Ba
Crondall	55	Bc
Crondon	59	Ba
Cronton	160	Ca
Crook, *Dur.*	206	Da
Crook, *W'land.*	193	Ab
Crooke	170	Cc
Crookham, *Hants.*	55	Bc
Crookham, *N'land.*	243	Bb
Crookland	193	Bc
Crook of Devon	260	Cc
Croome D'Abitot.	90	Ca
Cropredy	92	Ca
Cropston	130	Cb
Cropthorne	90	Da
Cropton	198	Db
Cropwell Bishop	150	Dc
Cropwell Butler	150	Dc
Crosby, *Cumb.*	218	Cb
Crosby, *Cumb.*	201	Ba
Crosby, *I.O.M.*	190	Cb
Crosby, *Lincs.*	176	Cb
Crosby Garrett	204	Dc
Crosby, *Gt.*	169	Ac
Crosby, *Lit.*	169	Ac
Crosby Ravensworth	204	Cc
Croscombe	50	Dc
Crosemere	144	Dc
Crosland, S.	172	Db
Cross	50	Cb
Cross Ash	88	Cc
Crosscanonby	201	Ba
Crossdale Street	137	Ba
Cross End	78	Ca
Crossens	169	Bb
Crossford, *Fife*	251	Aa
Crossford, *Lan.*	238	Ca
Crossgates, *Fife*	251	Aa
Cross Gates, *Yorks.*	173	Ba
Cross Hands, *Carm.*	64	Ca
Cross Hands, *Glos.*	68	Dc
Cross Hill, *Yorks.*	182	Dc
Crosshill, *Ayr*	224	Ca
Cross Houses	125	Bb
Cross-in-Hand	25	Ba
Cross Keys, *Norf.*	134	Db
Crosskeys, *Mon.*	67	Ab
Crosskirk	322	Da
Crossmichael	214	Db
Cross Roads	182	Dc
Cross Street	99	Ba
Cross Town	161	Bb
Crossway	88	Cc
Crossway Green	109	Ab
Croston	170	Cb
Crostwick	137	Bc
Crostwight	138	Cb
Crouch End	57	Bb
Croughton	92	Db
Crowan	2	Cb
Crowborough, *Staffs.*	146	Da
Crowborough. *Sus.*	43	Ac
Crowcombe	33	Ab
Crowdecote	162	Dc
Crowden	172	Dc
Crowdhill	39	Ac
Crowell	73	Bb
Crowfield	99	Ab
Crow Hill	88	Db
Crowhole	163	Bb
Crowhurst, *Sur.*	42	Db
Crowhurst, *Sus.*	26	Db
Crowland	133	Bc
Crowlas	1	Bb
Crowle, *Lincs.*	175	Bb
Crowle, *Worcs.*	109	Bc
Crowmarsh Gifford	73	Ac
Crownthorpe	118	Da
Crowshill	118	Ca
Crowthorne	56	Cb
Crowton	160	Db
Croxall	128	Da
Croxby	167	Bb
Croxdale	207	Aa
Croxden	147	Bb
Croxleygreen	57	Aa
Croxton, *Cambs.*	95	Bb
Croxton, *Lincs.*	167	Aa
Croxton, *Staffs.*	146	Cc
Croxtonbank	146	Cc
Croxton Kerrial	151	Bc
Croy	301	Bb
Croyde	30	Cb
Croydon, *Cambs.*	95	Bb
Croydon, *Sur.*	42	Ca
Cruckmeole	125	Ab
Crudgington	126	Ca
Crudwell	70	Cb
Crumlin	67	Ab
Crundale	45	Bc
Crunwear	62	Db
Crux Easton	54	Cc
Crwbin	64	Ca
Crymmych Arms.	82	Db
Crynant	85	Bc
Crystal Palace	58	Cc
Cubbington	111	Bb
Cubbington, New	111	Ab
Cubert	5	Ac
Cubley, *Gt.*	148	Cb
Cublington	94	Cc
Cuckfield	24	Da
Cuckingstool End	76	Da
Cucklington	36	Cb
Cuckney	164	Dc
Cuddesdon	73	Ab
Cuddington	73	Ba
Cudham	42	Da
Cudlipptown	8	Da
Cudworth	16	Ca
Cudworth, *Lr.*	174	Cc
Cudworth, *Upr.*	174	Cc
Culbone	47	Bb
Culcabock	301	Ac
Culford	98	Ca
Culgaith	204	Cb
Culham	72	Db
Culinish	263	Ac
Culkein	313	Aa
Culkerton	70	Cb
Cullaford	13	Ba
Cullen	304	Ca
Cullercoats	222	Ca
Cullingworth	183	Ac
Cullompton	15	Aa
Culmington	107	Ba
Culmstock	15	Aa
Culpho	99	Bc
Culross	250	Da
Culter	294	Cc
Cults, *Aber.*	294	Cc
Cults, *Aber.*	292	Aa
Culverthorpe	152	Cb
Culworth	92	Da
Cumberauld	249	Bb
Cumberworth	154	Da
Cumberworth, *Lr.*	173	Ac
Cumberworth, *Upr.*	173	Ac
Cuminestown	305	Bb
Cummertrees	216	Db
Cumnock	237	Ac
Cumnor	72	Cb
Cumrew	218	Cc
Cumwhinton	218	Cc
Cumwhitton	218	Cc
Cundall	197	Ac
Cupar	261	Ba
Curbar	163	Bb
Curbridge	71	Ba
Curdworth	128	Dc
Curland	33	Bc
Currie	251	Ab
Curry Load	34	Cb
Curry Malle...	34	Cc
Curry, N.	34	Cb
Curry Rivel	34	Cb
Cury	2	Cc
Cusop	87	Aa
Cusworth	174	Dc
Cutcombe	48	Cb
Cutlers Green	77	Aa
Cutnall Green	109	Ab
Cutsdean	90	Db
Cuxham	73	Ab
Cuxton	44	Ca
Cuxwold	167	Ab
Cwm, *Flint*	158	Da
Cwm, *Glam.*	65	Aa
Cwm, *Mon.*	67	Ac
Cwmaman	86	Cc
Cwm-avon	65	Ba
Cwmbach, *Carm.*	83	Ac
Cwmbach. *Glam.*	86	Dc
Cwmbran	67	Bb
Cwmbran, *Upr.*	67	Bb
Cwmcoy	83	Ab
Cwmdare	86	Cc
Cwmdu	87	Ac
Cwm-felin-mynach	83	Ac
Cwm-ffrwd	63	Ba
Cwm Giedd	85	Bb
Cwm Ifor	84	Dc
Cwm Llinau	122	Da
Cwmtillery	67	Aa
Cwrt-newydd	84	Ca
Cyffylliog	143	Aa
Cymmer	65	Ba
Cymyoy	87	Bc
Cynwyd	143	Ab
Daccombe	14	Dc
Dacre, *Cumb.*	203	Bb
Dacre, *Yorks.*	183	Ba
Dadford	93	Ab
Dadlington	129	Bc
Dafen	64	Cb
Daffy Green	118	Ca
Dagenham	58	Db
Daggons	37	Ac
Daglingworth	70	Da
Dagnall	74	Da
Daisy Hill	170	Dc
Dalavich	256	Cb
Dalbeattie	214	Db
Dalbury	148	Dc
Dalby, *I.O.M.*	190	Cc
Dalby, *Lincs.*	154	Ca
Dalby, *Yorks.*	185	Ba
Dalby, *Gt.*	131	Aa
Dalby, *Lit.*	131	Ab
Dalchreichart	287	Bc
Dalderby	153	Bb
Dale, *Cumb.*	204	Ca
Dale, *Derby*	149	Bb
Dalelea	273	Bc
Dalgety	251	Aa
Dalham	97	Bb
Dalkeith	252	Cb
Dallachy, Nether.	303	Ba
Dallachy, Upper	303	Ba
Dallas	302	Db
Dallinghoo	99	Bc
Dallington, *N'hants*	113	Ac
Dallington, *Sus.*	26	Db
Dallowgill	183	Ba
Dalmadilly	293	Bb
Dalmally	256	Da
Dalmellington	224	Da
Dalmeny	251	Aa
Dalmuir	248	Db
Dalry, *Ayr.*	236	Ca
Dalry, *Kirk.*	225	Bc
Dalrymple	224	Ca
Dalserf	238	Ca
Dalston, *Cumb.*	217	Bc
Dalston, *London*	58	Cb
Dalton, *Dumf.*	216	Ca
Dalton, *N'land*	220	Cb
Dalton, *Yorks.*	197	Bc
Dalton, *Yorks.*	196	Ca
Dalton	164	Ca
Dalton-in-Furness	192	Cc
Dalton-le-Dale	222	Dc
Dalton Magna	164	Ca
Dalton, N.	186	Db
Dalton-on-Tees	196	Da
Dalton Piercy	208	Cb
Dalton, S.	177	Aa
Dalwood	15	Bb
Dalziel	249	Bc
Damerham, S.	37	Ac
Damgate	120	Ca
Danbury	77	Bc
Danby Wiske	197	Aa
Dandaleith	303	Ac
Dane End	76	Da
Danesmoor	164	Cc
Dans Castle	206	Da
Darcy Lever	171	Ac
Darenth	58	Dc
Darenth, S.	58	Dc
Daresbury	160	Db
Darfield	174	Cc
Dargate	45	Bb
Darlaston	127	Bc
Darley, *Derby*	163	Bc
Darley, *Yorks.*	183	Bb
Darley Abbey	149	Ab
Darlingscott	91	Bb
Darlington	207	Ac
Darlton	165	Bc
Darngaber	237	Ba
Darowen	122	Db
Darracott	30	Ca
Darrington	174	Cb
Darsham	100	Ca
Dartford	58	Dc
Dartington	10	Ca
Dartmouth	10	Db
Darton	173	Bc
Darvel	237	Ab
Darwen	170	Db
Darwen, *Lr.*	170	Db
Datchet	56	Da
Datchworth	75	Bb
Datchworth Green	75	Bb
Daubhill	170	Dc
Dauntsey	70	Cb
Davenham	161	Ac
Davenport	161	Bc
Daventry	112	Cc
Davidstow	11	Ac
Daviot	293	Ba
Dawes Heath	60	Cb
Dawley	126	Cb
Dawleybank	126	Cb
Dawley Magna	126	Cb
Dawlish	14	Db
Dawsmere	134	Cb
Dayhills	147	Ac
Daylesford	91	Bc
Deal	46	Db
Deal, *Upr.*	46	Dc
Dean, *Cumb.*	201	Bb
Dean, *Dev.*	30	Ca
Dean, *Dev.*	10	Ca
Dean, *Hants.*	38	Db
Dean, *Oxon.*	92	Cc
Dean, *Som.*	51	Ac
Dean, *Wilts.*	53	Ab
Dean, E.	38	Cc
Deane	54	Dc
Dean, Little	69	Aa
Dean, *Lr.*	114	Cb
Dean Prior	10	Ca
Deanscales	201	Bb
Dean, *Upr.*	114	Cb
Dean, W. *Sus.*	40	Dc
Dean, W. *Wilts.*	38	Ca
Dearham	201	Ba
Debach	99	Bc
Debden	77	Aa
Debenham	99	Bb
Deddington	92	Cc
Dedham	79	Ab
Deene	132	Cc
Deenethorpe	132	Cc
Deepdale	195	Ac
Deeping Gate	132	Db
Deeping St. James	132	Db
Deeping St. Nicholas	133	Ac
Deerhurst	90	Cb
Deerhurst Walton	90	Cb
Defford	90	Ca
Deganwy	157	Aa
Deighton, *Yorks.*	197	Aa
Deighton, *Yorks.*	185	Bc
Deighton, *Yorks.*	172	Db
Deighton, N.	184	Db
Delamere	160	Dc
Delly End	72	Ca
Delph	172	Cc
Dembleby	152	Cc
Denaby	174	Cc
Denaby Main	174	Cc
Denbigh	158	Db
Denbury	14	Cc
Denby	149	Bb
Denby Dale	173	Ac
Denby, Upper, *Yorks.*	173	Ab
Denby, Upper, *Yorks.*	173	Ac
Denchworth	72	Cc
Denford	114	Cb
Denham, *Bucks.*	74	Dc
Denham, *Suff.*	99	Ba
Denham, *Suff.*	97	Bb
Denholm	229	Ba
Denholme	172	Da
Denholme Gate	172	Da
Dennington	99	Bb
Dennis	109	Ba

Place	PAGE	SQ
Denny	249	Ba
Dennyloanhead	249	Ba
Denshanger	93	Bb
Denshaw	172	Cc
Denston	97	Bb
Denstone	147	Bb
Dent	194	Cb
Denton, *Hunts.*	114	Da
Denton, *Kent*	46	Cc
Denton, *Lancs.*	162	Ca
Denton, *Lincs.*	151	Bc
Denton, *Norf.*	119	Bb
Denton, *N'hants.*	113	Bc
Denton, *Oxon.*	73	Ab
Denton, *Sus.*	25	Ac
Denton, *Yorks.*	183	Bb
Dentons Green	160	Ca
Denton, Upr.	218	Db
Denver	116	Da
Denwick	232	Ca
Deopham	118	Da
Deopham Green	118	Db
Depden	97	Bb
Deptford	58	Cb
Derby	148	Dc
Derbyhaven	190	Db
Dereham, W.	117	Aa
Deri	86	Dc
Derlwyn	82	Dc
Derringtone	46	Cc
Derry Hill	52	Ca
Derrythorpe	175	Bc
Dersingham	135	Ab
Derwen	143	Aa
Derwent	163	Aa
Desborough	113	Ba
Desford	129	Bb
Detchant	244	Cb
Dethick	148	Da
Detling	44	Ca
Dwanden	68	Cb
Devil's Bridge	102	Da
Devil's Elbow	279	Bb
Devizes	52	Db
Devonport	8	Cc
Devoran	2	Db
Dovynock	86	Ca
Dewchurch, Lit.	88	Db
Dewchurch, Much	88	Ca
Dewlish	16	Ca
Dewsall	88	Cb
Dewsbury	173	Bb
Deythur	124	Ca
Dibden	20	Da
Dicker, Lr.	25	Bb
Dicker, Upr.	25	Bb
Dickleburgh	119	Ac
Didbrook	90	Db
Didcot	72	Dc
Diddington	95	Ba
Diddlebury	107	Ba
Didling	40	Cc
Didlington	117	Bb
Didmarton	69	Bc
Didsbury	161	Ba
Digby	152	Da
Digg	296	Ca
Digswell	75	Bb
Dihewid	84	Ca
Dilham	138	Cb
Dilhorne	147	Bb
Dilston	220	Db
Dilton	52	Cc
Dilton Marsh	51	Bc
Dilwyn	107	Bc
Dinas, *Caer.*	139	Bb
Dinas, *Carm.*	83	Ac
Dinas, *Glam.*	66	Ca
Dinas, *Pem.*	82	Cb
Dinas Mawddwy	122	Da
Dinas Powis	49	Aa
Dinder	50	Dc
Dinedor	88	Db
Dingestow	68	Ca
Dingley	113	Aa
Dingwall	300	Db
Dinham	68	Cb
Dinmore	88	Ca
Dinnington, *N'land*	221	Ba
Dinnington, *Som.*	16	Ba
Dinnington, *Yorks.*	164	Ba
Dinorwic	156	Dc
Dinton, *Bucks.*	73	Ba
Dinton, *Wilts.*	37	Ab
Dipley	55	Bc
Diptford	10	Ca
Dipton	221	Bc
Dirleton	252	Ca
Dirtcar	173	Bb
Discoed	106	Dc
Diseworth	129	Ba
Disley	162	Cb
Dishforth	197	Ac
Diss	99	Aa
Disserth	104	Da
Distington	201	Bb
Ditchampton	37	Ab
Ditcheat	35	Aa
Ditchingham	119	Rb
Ditchling	24	Db
Ditteridge	51	Ba
Dittisham	10	Db
Ditton, *Kent*	44	Ca
Ditton, *Lancs.*	160	Cb
Ditton Green	97	Ab
Ditton Priors	126	Cc
Dixton	68	Da
Dob Cross	172	Cc
Dobwalls	7	Ab
Docking	135	Ba
Docklow	108	Cc
Dockray, *Cumb.*	203	Ab
Dockray, *Cumb.*	217	Ac
Doddington, *Cambs.*	116	Cb
Doddington, Gt.	113	Cb
Doddington, *Kent*	44	Ba
Doddington, *Lincs.*	166	Cc
Doddington, *N'land*	243	Bb
Doddington *Shrops.*	108	Ca
Doddiscombsleigh	14	Ca
Dodford	112	Dc
Dodford, Gt.	109	Bb
Dodington, *Glos.*	69	Bc
Dodington, *Som..*	33	Ba
Dodleston	144	Da
Dods Leigh.	147	Bc
Dodworth	173	Bc
Dogdyke	153	Ac
Dogmersfield	55	Bc
Dogsthorpe	115	Aa
Dolanog	123	Bb
Doley	146	Cc
Dolgarrog	157	Ab
Dolgelley	141	Bc
Dollar	260	Cc
Dolphinton	239	Ba
Dolton	31	Ab
Dolwyddelan	157	Ac
Dommett	33	Bc
Doncaster	174	Dc
Donhead, St. Andrew	06	Db
Donhead, St. Mary	36	Db
Donington, *Lincs.*	133	Aa
Donington, *Shrops.*	126	Db
Donington-on Bain	167	Bc
Donkey Street	28	Ca
Donnington, *Glos.*	91	Ac
Donnington, *Herefs.*	89	Ab
Donnington, *Shrops.*	126	Ca
Donnington, *Sus..*	22	Da
Donnington Wood	126	Cb
Donisthorpe	129	Ab
Donyatt	16	Ca
Dorchester *Dors..*	17	Bb
Dorchester *Oxon.*	72	Dc
Dordon	128	Db
Dore	163	Bb
Dores.	289	Aa
Dorking	41	Bb
Dormans Land	42	Db
Dormington	88	Da
Dormston	109	Bc
Dorney	56	Ca
Dornie	286	Cb
Dornoch	312	Cb
Dornock	216	Db
Dorridge	110	Db
Dorrington, *Lincs.*	152	Da
Dorrington, *Shrops.*	146	Cb
Dorsington	91	Aa
Dorstone	87	Ba
Dorton	73	Aa
Dosthill	128	Db
Dottery	16	Db
Douglas, *I.O.M.*	190	Cb
Douglas, *Lan.*	238	Cb
Douglastown	271	Bb
Doulting	51	Ac
Doune	259	Ab
Dovaston	124	Da
Dove Holes	162	Db
Dovenby	201	Bb
Dover	28	Da
Dovercourt	80	Cb
Dovercourt, Lr.	80	Cb
Doverdale	109	Ab
Doveridge	148	Cc
Dowally	269	Bb
Dowdeswell	90	Dc
Dowlais	86	Db
Dowland	31	Ab
Dowlish Wake	16	Ca
Down Ampney	70	Db
Down, E.	30	Da
Downe	42	Da
Downend, *Berks.*	54	Da
Downend, *Glos.*	51	Aa
Downham, *Cambs.*	116	Dc
Downham, *Essex*	59	Ba
Downham, *Lancs.*	181	Bc
Downham, *Norf.*	119	Aa
Downham, *N'land.*	242	Db
Downham Market	116	Da
Down Hatherley	90	Cc
Downhead, *Som.*	35	Ab
Downhead, *Som..*	51	Ac
Downholland Cross	169	Bc
Downholme	196	Ca
Downies	282	Da
Downley	74	Cb
Downside, *Som.*	51	Ac
Downside, *Som.*	50	Da
Down St. Mary	31	Bc
Down Thomas	8	Dc
Downton	37	Bc
Downton-on-the-Rock	107	Bb
Down, W.	30	Ca
Dowsby	133	Ab
Dowthwaitehead	203	Ac
Doynton	51	Ba
Draethen	67	Ac
Drakeholes	165	Aa
Drakes Broughton	90	Ca
Draughton, *N'hants*	113	Ab
Draughton, *Yorks.*	182	Db
Drax	175	Aa
Draycot Cerne	70	Cc
Draycot Foliat	53	Aa
Draycot Moor	72	Cb
Draycott, *Derby*	149	Bc
Draycott, *Som.*	35	Ab
Draycott, *Som.*	50	Cc
Draycott, *Worcs.*	91	Ab
Draycott, *Worcs..*	89	Ba
Draycott-in-the-Clay	148	Cc
Draycott-in-the-Moor	147	Ab
Drayton, *Berks.*	72	Dc
Drayton, *Leics.*	131	Bc
Drayton, *Norf.*	137	Bc
Drayton, *N'han's.*	112	Cc
Drayton, *Oxon.*	92	Cb
Drayton, *Som.*	34	Ca
Drayton, *Worcs.*	109	Ba
Drayton Bassett	128	Db
Drayton Beauchamp	74	Ca
Drayton, E.	165	Bb
Drayton, Lit.	145	Bc
Drayton Parslow	94	Cc
Drayton St. Leonard	73	Ab
Drayton, W.	165	Ab
Drebley	182	Db
Dreghorn	236	Cb
Drem	252	Da
Dresden	146	Db
Drewsteignton	13	Ba
Driby	154	Ca
Driffield	70	Db
Driffield, Gt.	187	Bc
Driffield, Lit.	187	Bc
Drigg	191	Ba
Drighlington	173	Aa
Drimpton	16	Ba
Dringhouses	185	Ab
Drinkstone	98	Db
Droitwich	109	Bb
Dronfield	163	Bb
Dronfield Woodhouse	163	Bb
Dronley	271	Ac
Droxford	39	Ac
Droylsden	171	Bc
Druid	143	Ab
Drumbeg	313	Ba
Drumbuie	285	Ba
Drumburgh	217	Ab
Drumchapel	248	Db
Drumfearn	285	Ac
Drumlithie	282	Cb
Drummelzier	239	Bb
Drummore	209	Bb
Drumuie	296	Cc
Drybeck	204	Cc
Drybrook	89	Ac
Dry Doddington	151	Bb
Dry Drayton	96	Ca
Drymen	248	Ca
Drynoch	284	Ca
Dryslwyn	64	Ca
Ducklington	72	Ca
Duckmanton	164	Cc
Dudbridge	69	Ba
Duddingston	251	Bb
Duddington	132	Cc
Duddo	243	Ba
Duddon	160	Cc
Dudleston	144	Ca
Dudley	127	Bc
Dudley Hill	173	Aa
Duffield	148	Db
Duffield, N.	185	Bc
Duffield, S..	175	Aa
Dufftown	303	Bc
Dufton	204	Db
Duggleby	186	Da
Duirinish	285	Ba
Duisky	274	Dc
Dulas.	87	Bb
Dulcote	50	Dc
Dull	269	Ab
Dullingham	97	Ab
Duloe	7	Bb
Dulverton	32	Da
Dulwich	58	Cc
Dumbarton	248	Cb
Dumbleton	90	Db
Dumfries	215	Ba
Dummer	39	Aa
Dunball	34	Ca
Dunbar	253	Ba
Dunbeath	318	Cb
Dunblane	259	Ac
Dunbog	261	Ba
Dunbridge	38	Cb
Duncansby	324	Da
Duncanston	292	Da
Dunchideock	14	Ca
Dunchurch	112	Cb
Duncote	93	Aa
Duncton	23	Ab
Dundee	271	Bc
Dundon	34	Db
Dundonald	236	Cb
Dundraw	216	Dc
Dundreggan	287	Bb
Dundrennan	214	Dc
Dundry	50	Da
Dunfermline	251	Aa
Dungeness	28	Cc
Dungworth	163	Ba
Dunham	165	Bc
Dunham, Gt.	136	Cc
Dunham, Lit.	136	Cc
Dunham-on-the-Hill	160	Cc
Dunholme	166	Db
Dunino	262	Db
Dunipace	249	Ba
Dunkeld	270	Cb
Dunkerton	51	Ab
Dunkeswell	15	Ba
Dunkeswick	184	Cb
Dunkirk	45	Bb
Dunley	108	Db
Dunlop	236	Ca
Dunmow, Gt.	77	Ab
Dunmow, Lit.	77	Ab
Dunnet	324	Ca
Dunnet, W.	323	Ba
Dunnichen	271	Bb
Dunning	260	Ca
Dunnington, *Yorks.*	177	Ba
Dunnington, *Yorks.*	185	Bb
Dunnockshaw	171	Ba
Dunoon	247	Ab
Duns	242	Cb
Dunsby	132	Da
Dunscore	226	Cc
Dunscroft	175	Ac
Dunsfold	41	Ac
Dunsford	14	Ca
Dunsforth, Lr.	184	Cb
Dunsforth, Upr.	184	Da
Dunshelt	261	Ab
Dunsley	200	Cb
Dunstable	94	Cb
Dunstall	128	Da
Dunster	48	Cb
Duns Tew	92	Cc
Dunston, *Lincs.*	152	Da
Dunston, *Norf.*	119	Bc
Dunstone	8	Dc
Dunswell	176	Da
Dunsyre	239	Aa
Dunterton	8	Ca
Duntisbourne Abbots	70	Ca
Duntisbourne Rouse	70	Ca
Duntish	35	Bc
Duntocher	248	Db
Dunton, *Beds.*	95	Bc
Dunton, *Bucks.*	93	Bc
Dunton, *Essex*	59	Ab
Dunton Bassett	112	Ca

	PAGE	SQ.
Dunvant	64	Dc
Dunvegan	295	Bc
Dunwear	34	Cb
Dunwich	100	Da
Durham	207	Aa
Durisdeer	226	Da
Durleigh	33	Bb
Durley	39	Ac
Durness	320	Ca
Durnford	37	Ba
Durno	293	Ba
Durrington	37	Bc
Dursley	69	Bb
Durston	33	Bb
Durweston	36	Cc
Duston	113	Ac
Duston, New	112	Dc
Dutton	160	Db
Dutton Diffeth	144	Da
Duxford	96	Dc
Dwygyfylchi	157	Aa
Dwyran	156	Cc
Dyce	294	Cb
Dyffryn, Glam.	66	Ca
Dyffryn, Glam.	86	Dc
Dyffryn, Mer.	140	Dc
Dyffryn, Mon.	67	Bc
Dyke	302	Cc
Dykehead	250	Cc
Dylife	122	Da
Dymchurch	28	Cb
Dymock	89	Ab
Dyrham	51	Ba
Dysart	261	Bc
Dyserth	158	Da
EAGLE	166	Cc
Eagle Moor	166	Cc
Eaglescliffe	207	Bc
Eaglesfield, Cumb.	201	Bb
Eaglesfield, Dumf.	216	Da
Eaglesham	237	Aa
Eakring	150	Da
Ealand	175	Bb
Ealing	57	Ab
Earby	182	Cc
Eardington	126	Cc
Eardisland	107	Bc
Eardisley	87	Ba
Eardiston	108	Db
Earith	116	Cc
Earle	243	Dc
Earlestown	160	Da
Earlham	119	Aa
Earlish	296	Cb
Earls Barton	113	Bc
Earls Colne	78	Ca
Earls Croome	90	Ca
Earlsdon	111	Ab
Earlsferry	262	Cc
Earl Shilton	129	Bc
Earl Soham	99	Bb
Earl Sterndale	162	Da
Earlston	241	Bb
Earl Stonham	99	Ab
Earnley	22	Db
Earsdon	222	Ca
Earsham	119	Bb
Earswick	185	Bb
Eartham	23	Ab
Easby, Yorks.	198	Ca
Easby, Yorks.	196	Da
Easebourne	23	Aa
Easenhall	111	Ba
Eashing	40	Da
Easington, Bucks.	73	Ba
Easington, Dur.	207	Ba
Easington, Oxon.	73	Ab
Easington, Yorks.	199	Ba
Easington, Yorks.	178	Dc
Easington Lane	222	Dc
Easingwold	185	Aa
Easole Street	46	Cb
Eastacombe	30	Cb
East Allington	10	Cb
East Beckham	137	Ba
East Bedfont	57	Ac
East Bilney	136	Dc
Eastbourne, Dur.	207	Ba
Eastbourne, Sus.	25	Bc
East Bridgford	150	Da
Eastbury	54	Ca
Eastby	182	Db
Eastchurch	45	Aa
Eastcombe, Glos.	70	Ca
East Combe, Som.	33	Ab
Eastcote, N'hants.	93	Aa
Eastcote, War.	110	Da
Eastcott	52	Db
Eastcourt	70	Da
Eastdean, Sus.	25	Bc
East Dean, Sus.	23	Ab
East Dereham	136	Dc
East End, Hants.	54	Cb
Eastend, Essex	60	Da
Easter Compton	68	Dc
Eastergate	23	Ac
Easter, Good	77	Ac
Easter, High	77	Ab
Easterton	52	Db
Eastertown	49	Ba
East Ferry	165	Ba
Eastfield	173	Bc
Eastgate, Dur.	205	Ba
Eastgate, Lincs.	132	Da
East Grinstead	42	Dc
Eastham, Ches.	159	Bb
East Ham, Essex	58	Cb
Easthampstead	56	Cb
Easthope	125	Bc
Easthorpe, Essex	78	Cb
Easthorpe, Leics.	151	Bb
Easthorpe, Notts.	150	Da
Eastington, Glos.	71	Aa
Eastington, Glos.	69	Ba
East Kilbride	249	Ac
East Langton	130	Dc
Eastleach Martin	71	Ab
Eastleach Turville	71	Ab
East Leicester Forest	130	Cb
Eastleigh, Dev.	30	Cb
Eastleigh, Hants.	38	Dc
Eastling	45	Ab
East Linton	253	Ba
East Markham	165	Bc
Eastney	22	Cb
Eastnor	89	Ab
East Norton	131	Ac
Eastoft	175	Bb
Easton, Cumb.	217	Ab
Easton, Dor.	18	Cc
Easton, Hants.	39	Ab
Easton, Hunts.	95	Aa
Easton, Lincs.	132	Ca
Easton, Norf.	119	Aa
Easton, Som.	34	Da
Easton, Suff.	99	Bb
Easton, Wilts.	53	Bb
Easton, Wilts.	52	Ca
Easton, Gt.	77	Ab
Easton Grey	70	Cc
Easton in Gordano	50	Da
Easton, Lit.	77	Ab
Easton Maudit	113	Bc
Easton-on-the-Hill	132	Cb
East Poringland	119	Ba
East Portlemouth	10	Cc
Eastrea	115	Ba
East Ruston	138	Cb
East Retford	165	Ba
Eastrington	175	Ba
Eastrop	71	Ba
East Rudham	136	Cb
East Runton	137	Ba
Eastry	46	Db
East Stoke, Notts.	150	Da
East Stoke, Som.	34	Dc
East Sutton	44	Db
East the Water	30	Cc
Eastville	154	Cc
East Walton	135	Bc
Eastwell, Kent	45	Ac
Eastwell, Leics.	151	Ac
Eastwick	76	Cc
East Winch	135	Ac
Eastwood, Essex	60	Cb
Eastwood, Notts.	149	Bb
Eastwood, Renf.	248	Bc
Eathorpe	111	Bb
Eaton, Berks.	72	Cc
Eaton, Ches.	161	Bc
Eaton, Ches.	160	Dc
Eaton, Herefs.	107	Bc
Eaton, Leics.	151	Ac
Eaton, Norf.	119	Ba
Eaton, Notts.	165	Ab
Eaton, Shrops.	125	Bc
Eaton Bishop	88	Ca
Eaton Bray	94	Dc
Eaton Constantine	125	Bb
Eaton Green	94	Cc
Eaton Hastings	71	Bb
Eaton, Lit.	149	Ab
Eaton Mascott	125	Bb
Eaton Socon	95	Ab
Eaton-upon-Tern	126	Ca
Ebberston	187	Aa
Ebbesborne Wake	36	Db
Ebbw-Vale	67	Aa
Ebchester	221	Ac
Ebenezer, Caer.	156	Dc
Ebenezer, Carm.	63	Ba
Ebford	14	Da
Ebrington	91	Ab
Ecchinswell	54	Db
Ecclefechan	216	Da
Eccles, Berw.	242	Db
Eccles, Kent	44	Ca
Eccles, Lancs.	171	Ac
Eccles, Norf.	118	Db
Ecclesall	163	Bb
Ecclesfield	163	Ba
Eccleshall	146	Dc
Eccleshill	183	Bc
Ecclesmachan	250	Db
Eccleston, Ches.	160	Cc
Eccleston, Lancs.	160	Ca
Eccleston, Lancs.	170	Cb
Eccleston, Gt.	180	Cc
Eccleston Green	170	Cb
Eccup	184	Cc
Echt	293	Bc
Eckford	242	Cc
Eckington, Worcs.	90	Ca
Eckington, Yorks.	164	Cb
Ecton	113	Bc
Edale	162	Db
Edburton	24	Cb
Edderside	201	Ba
Edderton	311	Bb
Eddistone	29	Ac
Eddleston	240	Ca
Edenbridge	42	Db
Edenfield	171	Bb
Edenhall	204	Cb
Edenham	132	Da
Edensor	163	Bc
Edenthorpe	175	Ac
Edeyrn	139	Bb
Edgbaston	110	Ca
Edgcote	92	Da
Edgcott, Bucks.	93	Ac
Edgcott, Som.	47	Bb
Edge	69	Ba
Edgefield	137	Aa
Edgeworth	70	Ca
Edgmond	126	Ca
Edgton	107	Aa
Edgware	57	Ba
Edgworth	171	Ab
Edinbain	295	Bc
Edinburgh	251	Bb
Edingale	128	Da
Edingley	150	Da
Edingthorpe	138	Cb
Edington, Som.	34	Ca
Edington, Wilts.	52	Cc
Edington Burtley	34	Ca
Edingworth	49	Bc
Edithmead	34	Ca
Edith Weston	132	Cb
Edlaston	148	Cb
Edlesborough	74	Da
Edlingham	231	Ba
Edlington, Lincs.	153	Ba
Edlington, Yorks.	164	Dc
Edmondbyers	220	Dc
Edmondsham	37	Ac
Edmondsley	222	Cc
Edmondthorpe	131	Ba
Edmonton	58	Ca
Ednam	242	Cb
Edrom	254	Cc
Edstaston	145	Ac
Edston, Gt.	198	Db
Edvin Loach	108	Cc
Edvin Ralph	108	Cc
Edwardstone	98	Cc
Edwinstowe	165	Ac
Edworth	95	Bc
Edzell	281	Bc
Efail-y-cwm	123	Ba
Efenechtyd	143	Ba
Effingham	41	Ba
Egbury	54	Cc
Egdean	23	Ab
Egerton	44	Db
Egg Buckland	8	Db
Eggington	94	Dc
Egginton	148	Dc
Eggleston	206	Cb
Egham	56	Db
Egleton, Herefs.	88	Ca
Egleton, Rut.	131	Bb
Eglingham	244	Cc
Egloshayle	6	Ca
Egloskerry	11	Bc
Eglwys-Brewis	66	Dc
Eglwys-Cymmyn.	63	Aa
Eglwys Fach	157	Bb
Eglwysfair-a-churig	83	Ac
Eglwyswrw	82	Db
Egmanton	165	Ac
Egremont, Carm.	62	Da
Egremont, Cumb.	201	Bc
Egton	199	Bb
Egypt	38	Dc
Eisey	71	Ab
Eisingrig	140	Db
Elberton	68	Dc
Elburton	8	Dc
Eldersfield	89	Bb
Eldon, Old	207	Ab
Eldridge	76	Da
Eldrig	210	Cb
Elerch	121	Bc
Elford	128	Db
Elgin	303	Aa
Elgol	284	Dc
Elham	28	Ca
Elie	262	Cc
Elkesley	165	Ab
Eling	38	Dc
Elkington, N.	167	Bc
Elkington, S.	167	Bc
Elkstone	70	Ca
Elkstone, Upr.	147	Ba
Elland	172	Db
Ellary	245	Ab
Ellastone	148	Cb
Ella, W.	176	Da
Ellel	180	Db
Ellenborough	201	Ba
Ellenbrook	170	Dc
Ellenhall	146	Dc
Ellerbeck	197	Ba
Ellerburn	187	Aa
Ellerby, Yorks.	199	Ba
Ellerker	176	Ca
Ellerton, Yorks.	186	Cc
Ellerton, Yorks.	196	Da
Ellerwater	192	Da
Ellesborough	74	Cb
Ellesmere	144	Dc
Ellesmere Port	160	Cb
Ellingham, Hants.	19	Ba
Ellingham, Norf.	120	Cb
Ellingham, N'land.	244	Dc
Ellingham, Gt.	118	Db
Ellingham, Lit.	118	Db
Ellingstring	196	Ca
Ellington, Hunts.	95	Aa
Ellington, N'land.	232	Dc
Ellington, Low	196	Db
Ellisfield	39	Ba
Ellistown	129	Bb
Ellon	294	Da
Ellough	120	Cc
Elloughton	176	Ca
Ellwood	68	Ca
Elm	116	Ca
Elmbridge	109	Bb
Elmdon, Essex	96	Dc
Elmdon, War.	110	Da
Elmesthorpe	129	Bc
Elm, Gt.	51	Bc
Elmley	45	Aa
Elmley Castle	90	Ca
Elmley Lovett	109	Ab
Elmore	89	Bc
Elmsall, N.	174	Cb
Elmsall, S.	174	Cb
Elmsett	98	Dc
Elmstead	79	Ba
Elmstead Market	79	Ab
Elmsted	45	Bc
Elmstone	46	Cb
Elmswell	98	Da
Elphin	314	Cc
Elsdon	231	Ac
Elsecar	174	Cc
Elsenham	76	Db
Elsfield	72	Ba
Elsham	176	Db
Elsing	136	Dc
Elslack	182	Dc
Elsrickle	239	Aa
Elstead	40	Da
Elsted	40	Cc
Elsthorpe	132	Da
Elston, Lancs.	170	Ca
Elston, Notts.	150	Db
Elstow	94	Ba
Elstree	57	Aa
Elstronwick	178	Cc
Elswick	180	Cc
Elsworth	95	Ba
Eltham	58	Cc
Eltisley	95	Bb
Elton, Ches.	160	Cb
Elton, Derby	148	Ca
Elton, Dur.	207	Bc
Elton, Herefs.	107	Bb
Elton, Hunts.	132	Dc
Elton, Lancs.	171	Ba
Elton, Notts.	150	Db
Elvanfoot	238	Dc
Elveden	117	Bc
Elvetham	55	Bb
Elvington	185	Bb
Elwick	208	Cb
Elworth	17	Bb
Elworthy	33	Ab
Ely, Cambs.	116	Dc
Ely, Glam.	49	Dc
Emberton	94	Ca
Embleton, Dur.	207	Rb
Embleton, N'land.	244	Dc

Name	Page	Sq
Emborough	50	Dc
Embsay	182	Db
Emley	173	Bb
Emley Moor	173	Ab
Emmer Green	55	Ba
Emmington	73	Bb
Empingham	132	Cb
Empshott	40	Cb
Emsworth	22	Ca
Enborne	54	Cb
Encombe	19	Ac
Enderby	130	Cc
Endon	146	Da
Enfield	58	Ca
Enford	53	Ac
Englefield	55	Aa
English Batch	51	Ab
English Bicknor	88	Dc
English Combe	51	Ab
Enmeth	116	Da
Enmore	33	Bb
Ensbury	19	Bb
Ensdon	125	Aa
Ensis	30	Dc
Enstone	92	Cc
Enterkinfoot	226	Ca
Enterpen	197	Ba
Enville	109	Aa
Epperstone	150	Db
Epping	76	Dc
Epping Green	76	Dc
Eppleby	206	Dc
Epsom	41	Ba
Epwell	92	Cb
Epworth	175	Bc
Erbistock	144	Cb
Erbusaig	285	Ba
Erdington	128	Cc
Erith	58	Db
Erlestoke	52	Cb
Ermington	9	Ba
Erpingham	137	Bb
Erradale, S.	307	Ac
Errol	261	Aa
Erswell	117	Ac
Erwarton	79	Bb
Erwood	104	Db
Eryholme	207	Bc
Escrick	185	Bc
Esh	206	Da
Esher	41	Ba
Esholt, Upr.	183	Bc
Eshton	182	Db
Eskdalemuir	228	Cb
Essendine	132	Cb
Essendon	75	Ba
Essington	127	Bb
Eston	208	Dc
Etal	243	Bb
Etchilhampton	52	Db
Etchingham	26	Ca
Etchinghill	28	Ca
Etherley, High	206	Db
Etherley, Low	206	Db
Eton	56	Da
Ettingshall	127	Ac
Ettington	91	Ba
Etton, *N'hants.*	132	Db
Etton, *Yorks*	177	Aa
Ettrick	228	Ca
Etwall	148	Dc
Euston	118	Cc
Euxton	170	Cb
Evanton	300	Da
Evedon	152	Db
Evenjobb	106	Dc
Evenley	92	Db
Evenlode	91	Bc
Evenwood	206	Db
Evercreech	35	Ba
Everdon, Gt.	112	Cc
Everingham	186	Ca
Everley	53	Ac
Eversden, Gt.	96	Cb
Eversden, Lit.	96	Cb
Eversholt	94	Db
Evershot	17	Ba
Eversley	55	Bb
Eversley Cross	55	Bb
Everthorpe	176	Ca
Everton, *Beds.*	95	Ab
Everton, *Hants.*	20	Cb
Everton, *Lancs.*	159	Ba
Everton, *Notts.*	165	Aa
Evertown	217	Ba
Evesbatch	89	Aa
Evesham	90	Da
Ewell, *Kent.*	28	Da
Ewell, *Sur.*	42	Ca
Ewelme	73	Ac
Ewen	70	Db
Ewenny	66	Cb
Ewerby	152	Db
Ewes	228	Ca
Ewhurst, *Sur.*	41	Bc
Ewhurst, *Sus.*	26	Da
Ewyas Harold	87	Bb
Exbourne	31	Ac
Exbury	21	Aa
Exebridge	32	Da
Exelby	196	Db
Exeter	14	Da
Exford	47	Bb
Exfordsgreen	125	Aa
Exhall, *War.*	91	Aa
Exhall, *War.*	111	Ba
Exminster	14	Da
Exmouth	14	Db
Exning	97	Aa
Exton, *Dev.*	14	Da
Exton, *Hants.*	39	Bc
Exton, *Rut.*	132	Cb
Exton, *Som.*	48	Cc
Exwick	14	Da
Eyam	163	Ab
Eyam Woodlands	163	Ab
Eydon	92	Da
Eye, *Herefs.*	107	Bc
Eye, *N'hants.*	115	Aa
Eye, *Suff.*	99	Aa
Eye Green	115	Aa
Eyemouth	254	Db
Eyhorne Street	44	Da
Eyke	100	Cc
Eyling Thorpe	200	Cb
Eynesbury	95	Ab
Eynsford	43	Aa
Eynsham	72	Ca
Eype	16	Db
Eythorne	46	Cc
Eyton, *Herefs.*	107	Bc
Eyton, *Shrops.*	107	Aa
Eyton, *Shrops.*	125	Aa
Eyton-on-the-Weald Moors	126	Ca
Eyworth	95	Bc
Faccombe	54	Cc
Faceby	197	Ba
Facit	171	Bb
Faddiley	145	Ba
Fadmoor	198	Db
Faintree, Lr.	108	Ca
Fairburn	174	Ca
Fairchild	90	Da
Fairfield, *Derby*	162	Db
Fairfield, *Kent*	27	Bb
Fairford	71	Ab
Fairlie	235	Ba
Fairlight	27	Ac
Fairmile	15	Ab
Fair Oak	39	Ac
Fairseat	43	Ba
Fairsted	77	Bb
Fakenham, *Norf.*	136	Cb
Fakenham, *Suff.*	110	Cc
Fala & Blackshiels	252	Dc
Faldingworth	166	Db
Falfield	69	Ab
Falkenham	80	Ca
Falkirk	250	Ca
Falkland	261	Ab
Fallings Heath	127	Bc
Fallowfield	220	Cb
Falmer	24	Dc
Falmouth	2	Db
Falstone	230	Cc
Fambridge, N.	60	Ca
Fambridge, S.	60	Ca
Fancott	94	Dc
Fangfoss	186	Cb
Far Cotton	113	Ac
Fareham	21	Ba
Farewell	128	Cb
Far Forest	108	Db
Farforth	153	Ba
Faringdon, *Berks.*	71	Bb
Faringdon, *Hants.*	39	Bb
Faringdon, Lit.	71	Bb
Farington	170	Ca
Farlam	218	Db
Farleigh	50	Ca
Farleigh, E.	44	Cb
Farleigh Hungerford	51	Bb
Farleigh, W.	44	Cb
Farleigh Wallop	39	Ba
Farlesthorpe	154	Ca
Farleton	193	Bc
Farley, *Sur.*	42	Ca
Farley, *Wilts.*	37	Bb
Farlington, *Hants.*	22	Ca
Farlington, *Yorks.*	185	Ba
Farlow	108	Ca
Farmborough	51	Ab
Farmcote	90	Da
Farmers	84	Da
Farmington	71	Aa
Far Moor	170	Cc
Farnborough, *Berks.*	54	Ca
Farnborough, *Hants.*	56	Cc
Farnborough, *Kent*	42	Da
Farnborough, *War.*	92	Ca
Farncombe	40	Da
Farndish	114	Cc
Farndon, *Ches.*	144	Da
Farndon, *Notts.*	150	Da
Farndon, E.	113	Aa
Farndon, W.	92	Da
Farnell	272	Ca
Farnham, *Dors.*	36	Dc
Farnham, *Essex*	76	Db
Farnham, *Suff.*	100	Cb
Farnham, *Sur.*	40	Ca
Farnham, *Yorks.*	184	Ca
Farnham Royal	56	Da
Farnhurst	23	Aa
Farningham	58	Dc
Farnley	183	Db
Farnley Tyas	172	Bb
Farnsfield	150	Ca
Farnworth, *Lancs.*	170	Da
Farnworth, *Lancs.*	160	Ca
Farr	321	Ba
Farringdon	14	Da
Farrington Gurney	51	Ab
Farthinghoe	92	Db
Farthingloe	28	Da
Farthingstone	112	Dc
Fartown	172	Bb
Farsley	173	Aa
Farway	15	Bb
Fasach	295	Ac
Fatfield	222	Cc
Fattingley	162	Ca
Faugh	218	Cc
Fauldhouse	250	Cc
Faulkbourne	77	Bb
Faulkland	51	Bb
Faulsgreen	145	Bc
Faversham	45	Ab
Fawdington	197	Bc
Faweather	183	Bc
Fawfieldhead	162	Dc
Fawkham	59	Ac
Fawler	72	Ca
Fawley, *Berks.*	54	Ca
Fawley, *Bucks.*	73	Bc
Fawley, *Hants.*	21	Aa
Fawley Chapel	88	Db
Fawley, S.	54	Ca
Fawsley	112	Cc
Faxfleet	170	Ca
Faxton	113	Ab
Fazeley	128	Db
Fearby	196	Dc
Fearn	312	Cc
Fearnan	268	Db
Featherstone	174	Cb
Feckenham	110	Cc
Feering	78	Cb
Feetham	195	Ba
Feizor	181	Ba
Felbrigg	137	Ba
Felden	74	Db
Felindre, *Card.*	84	Ca
Felindre, *Carm.*	85	Aa
Felindre, *Glam.*	64	Db
Felindre, *Rad.*	106	Ca
Felindref	64	Ca
Felin-foel	64	Cb
Feliskirk	197	Bb
Felixstowe	80	Cb
Felkington	243	Ba
Felling	222	Cc
Fell Side	202	Da
Felmersham	114	Ca
Felmingham	137	Bb
Felpham	23	Ac
Felsham	98	Db
Felsted	77	Bb
Feltham	57	Ac
Felthorpe	137	Ba
Felton, *Herefs.*	88	Da
Felton, *N'land.*	232	Cc
Felton, *Som.*	50	Db
Felton Butler	124	Da
Feltwell	117	Ab
Fenay Bridge	173	Ab
Fence	182	Cc
Fencot	72	Ca
Fencote, Gt.	196	Db
Fen Ditton	96	Cb
Fen Drayton	96	Ca
Fen End	110	Db
Feniton	15	Ab
Fenny Bentley	148	Ca
Fenny Compton	92	Ca
Fenny Drayton	129	Ac
Fenny Stratford	94	Cb
Fen Stanton	96	Ca
Fenton, *Cumb.*	218	Cc
Fenton, *Hunts.*	115	Bc
Fenton, *Lincs.*	165	Bb
Fenton, *Notts.*	165	Ba
Fenwick, *Ayr.*	236	Da
Fenwick, *N'land.*	220	Da
Fenwick, *Yorks.*	174	Db
Feock	2	Db
Feorline	234	Cc
Fern	271	Ba
Ferndale	66	Ca
Fernham	71	Bc
Fernhill Heath	109	Bc
Fernilea	284	Ca
Ferrensby	184	Ca
Ferriby, N.	176	Da
Ferriby, S.	176	Db
Ferring, W.	23	Bc
Ferrybridge	174	Ca
Ferrydon	272	Da
Ferry Hill	116	Cc
Ferryside	63	Ba
Fersfield	118	Dc
Festiniog	141	Ba
Fetcham	41	Ba
Fetterangus	306	Cb
Fettercairn	281	Bc
Fetteresso	282	Db
Feus of Caldhame	281	Bc
Fewston	183	Bb
Ffair-fach	84	Dc
Ffair-rhos	102	Db
Ffald y-Brenin	84	Da
Fforest	64	Db
Ffynnon-ddrain	83	Bc
Ffynnongroew	15s	Da
Fiddington	33	Ba
Field	147	Bc
Field Dalling	136	Da
Field Head	130	Cb
Fifehead Magdalen	36	Cb
Fifehead Neville	36	Cc
Fife Keith	304	Cb
Fifield, *Berks.*	56	Ca
Fifield, *Oxon.*	71	Ba
Fifield Bavant	37	Ab
Figheldean	37	Ba
Fighting Cocks	207	Bc
Filby	138	Dc
Filey	188	Ca
Filgrave	94	Ca
Filkins	71	Bb
Filleigh	30	Db
Fillingham	166	Cb
Fillongley	111	Aa
Filton	68	Dc
Fimber	186	Ba
Finborough, Gt.	98	Db
Finborough, Lit.	98	Db
Fincham	117	Aa
Finchampstead	55	Bb
Finchingfield	77	Ba
Finchley	57	Ba
Finchley, E.	57	Ba
Findern	148	Dc
Findhorn	302	Ca
Findochty	304	Ca
Findon, *Kinc.*	282	Da
Findon, *Sus.*	23	Bb
Finedon	113	Bb
Fingest	73	Bc
Finghall	196	Cb
Fingland	217	Ac
Finglesham	46	Db
Fingringhoe	78	Db
Finmere	93	Ab
Finningham	98	Da
Finningley	165	Aa
Finstock	72	Ca
Fintry	249	Aa
Firbeck	164	Da
Firby	186	Ca
Firle, West	25	Ab
Firsby	154	Cb
Firsby, E.	166	Db
Firsby, W.	166	Ca
Fishbourne, New	22	Da
Fishburn	207	Bb
Fisherrow	252	Db
Fisherstreet	23	Aa
Fisherton-de-la-Mere	37	Aa
Fishguard	82	Cb
Fishlake	175	Ab
Fishley	120	Ca
Fishpool	150	Ca
Fishtoft	134	Ca
Fiskerton, *Lincs.*	166	Dc
Fiskerton, *Notts.*	150	Da
Fitling	178	Cb
Fittleton	53	Ac
Fittleworth	23	Bb
Fitz	125	Aa
Fitzwilliam	174	Ca
Five Ashes	25	Ba
Fivehead	34	Cc
Five Oak Green	43	Bb
Five Oaks	23	Ba
Five Roads	64	Cb
Flackwell Heath	74	Cc

	PAGE	SQ.
Fladbury	90	Da
Flagg	162	Dc
Flamborough	188	Db
Flamstead	75	Ab
Flansham	23	Ac
Flasby	182	Db
Flash	162	Dc
Flaunden	74	Db
Flawborough	151	Ab
Flawith	184	Da
Flax Bourton	50	Da
Flaxby	184	Db
Flaxley	89	Ac
Flaxton	185	Dc
Fleckney	130	Dc
Flecknoe	112	Cc
Fledborough	165	Bc
Fleet, Dors.	17	Bc
Fleet, Hants.	55	Bc
Fleet, Lincs.	134	Cb
Fleet Hargate	134	Cb
Fleet Marston	73	Ba
Fleetwood	179	Bb
Flemingston	66	Cc
Flempton	97	Ba
Fletching	25	Aa
Fletton	115	Aa
Flimby	201	Bb
Flint	159	Ac
Flintham	150	Ac
Flinton	178	Cb
Flitcham	135	Bb
Flitton	75	Aa
Flitwick	94	Db
Flixborough	176	Cb
Flixton, Lancs.	161	Aa
Flixton, Suff.	119	Bc
Flixton, Suff.	120	Db
Flockton	173	Ab
Flockton Green	173	Bb
Flookburgh	192	Dc
Floore	112	Dc
Flordon	119	Ab
Flowton	79	Ba
Flushdyke	173	Bb
Flushing	2	Db
Flyford Flavell	109	Bb
Fobbing	59	Bb
Fochabers	303	Bb
Fockerby	176	Cb
Fodderty	300	Cb
Foddington	35	Aa
Foggathorpe	186	Cc
Fogo	242	Dc
Foleshill	111	Ba
Folkestone	28	Da
Folkingham	152	Dc
Folkington	25	Bc
Folksworth	114	Da
Folkton	188	Ca
Follifoot	184	Cb
Folly Gate	13	Aa
Fonaby	167	Aa
Fonthill Bishop	36	Ab
Fonthill Gifford	36	Da
Fontmell Magna	36	Cb
Foolow	163	Ab
Foots Cray	58	Dc
Ford, Argyll	255	Bc
Ford, Bucks.	73	Ba
Ford, Derby	164	Cb
Ford, Dev.	29	Bc
Ford, Glos.	90	Db
Ford, Herefs.	107	Bc
Ford, N'land.	243	Bb
Ford, Shrops.	125	Aa
Ford, Staffs.	147	Ba
Ford, Sus.	23	Ac
Ford, Wilts.	51	Ba
Forden	124	Cb
Ford End	77	Bb
Fordham, Cambs.	97	Aa
Fordham, Essex	78	Da
Fordham, Norf.	118	Da
Ford Houses	127	Ab
Fordingbridge	37	Bc
Fordon	188	Cb
Fordstreet	78	Cb
Fordwells	71	Ba
Fordwich	46	Cb
Fordyce	304	Da
Foremark	148	Dc
Forest Hill	73	Aa
Forest Row	42	Dc
Forfar	271	Ba
Forgan	271	Bc
Forgandenny	260	Da
Formby	169	Ac
Forncett St. Mary	119	Ab
Forncett St. Peter	119	Ab
Fornham All Saints	98	Ca
Fornham St. Martin	98	Ca
Forrabury	11	Ac
Forres	302	Ca
Forsbrook	147	Ab
Forscote	51	Bb
Forse	318	Ca
Forston	17	Ba
Fort Augustus	288	Cc
Forteviot	260	Ca
Fort George	301	Ab
Forth	250	Dc
Forthampton	90	Cb
Forth Bridge	251	Aa
Fortingal	268	Db
Forton, Hants.	38	Da
Forton, Som.	16	Ca
Forton, Staffs.	126	Da
Fortrose	301	Ab
Fort William	275	Ac
Fosbury	53	Bc
Foscot	91	Bc
Foscott	93	Bb
Fosdyke	133	Ba
Foss	269	Aa
Fostall	45	Bb
Fosterhouses	175	Bb
Foston, Leics.	130	Ca
Foston, Lincs.	151	Bb
Foston, Yorks.	185	Ba
Foston	148	Cc
Foston-on-the-Wolds	188	Cc
Fotherby	167	Bb
Fotheringhay	132	Dc
Foulby	174	Cb
Foulden, Berw.	254	Dc
Foulden, Norf.	117	Ba
Foulness	60	Dc
Foulridge	182	Cc
Foulsham	136	Db
Four Ashes	127	Ab
Four Crosses	140	Cb
Four Forks	33	Ba
Four Oaks	128	Cc
Fovant	37	Ab
Fowey	6	Dc
Fowlis	271	Ac
Fowlis Wester	259	Ba
Fowlmere	96	Cc
Fownhope	88	Db
Foxcott	38	Ca
Foxdale	190	Cb
Foxearth	98	Cc
Foxham	52	Da
Foxholes	187	Bb
Foxley, Norf.	136	Dc
Foxley Wilts.	70	Cc
Foxt	147	Bb
Foxton, Cambs.	96	Cc
Foxton, Leics.	112	Da
Foxton, Yorks.	197	Ba
Foyers	288	Db
Fradley	128	Ca
Fradswell	147	Bc
Fraisthorpe	188	Cc
Framfield	25	Ba
Framilode	69	Ba
Framingham Earl	119	Ba
Framingham Pigot	119	Ba
Framlingham	99	Bb
Frampton, Dor.	17	Ba
Frampton, Lincs.	133	Ba
Frampton Cotterell	69	Aa
Frampton Mansell	70	Ca
Frampton-on-Severn	69	Bc
Framsden	99	Bb
Franche	109	Aa
Frandley	160	Db
Frankby	159	Aa
Frankley	109	Ba
Franks Bridge	104	Da
Frankton	111	Bb
Frankwell	125	Ba
Fransham, Gt.	136	Cc
Fransham, Lit.	136	Cc
Frant	43	Bc
Fraserburgh	306	Ca
Frating	79	Ac
Freckenham	97	Aa
Freckleton	169	Ba
Freeby	131	Ba
Freefolk	54	Dc
Freeland	72	Ca
Freethorpe	120	Ca
Freiston	134	Ca
Freiston Shore	134	Ca
Fremington	30	Cb
Frenchay	51	Aa
Frensham	40	Ca
Freshfield	169	Ac
Freshford	51	Bb
Freshwater	20	Db
Fressingfield	99	Ba
Freston	79	Ba
Fretherne	69	Ba
Frettenham	137	Bc
Freuchie	261	Ab
Friday Bridge	116	Ca
Fridaythorpe	186	Db
Friendly	172	Ca
Friern Barnet	57	Ba
Friesthorpe	166	Db
Frieston	152	Cb
Frieth	73	Bc
Frilford	72	Cb
Frilsham	54	Da
Frimley	56	Cc
Frimley Green	56	Cc
Frindsbury	59	Bc
Fring	135	Ba
Fringford	93	Ac
Frinsted	44	Da
Frinton	80	Cc
Friockheim	272	Ca
Frisby - on - the - Wreak	130	Da
Friskney	154	Cc
Friskney Tofts	154	Cc
Friston, Suff.	100	Cb
Friston, Sus.	25	Bc
Fritchley	149	Aa
Frith Common	108	Db
Frithelstock	30	Cc
Frithelstock Stone	30	Cc
Frithville	153	Bc
Frittenden	44	Cc
Fritton, Norf.	119	Bb
Fritton, Suff.	120	Db
Fritwell	92	Dc
Frocester	69	Ba
Frodesley	125	Bb
Frodingham	176	Cb
Frodingham, N.	188	Cc
Frodsham	160	Cb
Frog End	96	Cc
Froggatt	163	Bb
Froghall	147	Bb
Frogham	37	Bc
Frogmore	10	Cb
Frolesworth	112	Ca
Frome	51	Bc
Fromes Hill	89	Aa
Frome St. Quintin	17	Ba
Frome Vauchurch	17	Ba
Fron	106	Cb
Fron Cysyllte	144	Cb
Frostenden	120	Dc
Frosterley	206	Ca
Froxfield, Hants.	39	Bb
Froxfield, Wilts.	53	Bb
Froyle	40	Ca
Froyle, Lr.	40	Ca
Fryerning	59	Aa
Fugglestone St. Peter	37	Ab
Fulbeck	152	Cb
Fulbourn	96	Db
Fulbrook	71	Ba
Fulford, Som.	33	Bb
Fulford, Staffs.	147	Ba
Fulford, Yorks.	185	Bb
Fulham	57	Bc
Fulletby	153	Ba
Fullready	91	Ba
Full Sutton	186	Cb
Fulmer	74	Dc
Fulmodeston	136	Db
Fulneck	173	Aa
Fulney	133	Bb
Fulstone	173	Ac
Fulstow	168	Cb
Fulwell, Dur.	222	Db
Fulwell, Oxon.	92	Cc
Fulwood, Lancs.	170	Ca
Fulwood, Yorks.	163	Bb
Fundenhall	119	Ab
Funtington	22	Da
Furnace	256	Cc
Furnace End	128	Dc
Furness Vale	162	Cb
Furneux Pelham	76	Ca
Furtho	93	Ba
Fyfield, Berks.	72	Cb
Fyfield, Essex	77	Ac
Fyfield, Glos.	71	Bb
Fyfield, Hants.	38	Ca
Fyfield, Wilts.	53	Ab
Fyvie	305	Ac
GADDESBY	130	Db
Gaddesden, Gt.	74	Da
Gaddesden, Lit.	74	Da
Gadshill	59	Bc
Gaerwen	156	Cb
Gailey	127	Ab
Gainford	206	Dc
Gainsborough	165	Ba
Gairloch	307	Ac
Galashiels	241	Ab
Galgate	180	Db
Galhampton	35	Ba
Gallowhill	270	Dc
Gallowstree Elm	109	Aa
Gallt-y-foel	156	Dc
Galmington	33	Bc
Galmpton, Dev.	9	Bb
Galmpton, Dev.	10	Da
Galphay	196	Dc
Galston	236	Dd
Galtrigill	295	Ad
Gamblesby, Cumb.	217	Da
Gamblesby, Cumb.	204	Ca
Gameldon	37	Bb
Gamesley	162	Ca
Gamlingay	95	Bb
Gammersgill	195	Bc
Gamston, Notts.	165	Ab
Gamston, Notts.	150	Ca
Ganarew	88	Dc
Ganthorpe	185	Ba
Ganton	187	Ba
Garboldisham	118	Dc
Gardenstown	305	Ba
Gardham	177	Aa
Gardner Street	26	Cb
Gare Hill	36	Ca
Garelochhead	247	Ba
Garford	72	Cb
Garforth	174	Ca
Garforth, W.	174	Ca
Gargrave	182	Db
Gargunnock	259	Ac
Garliestown	210	Db
Garlogie	293	Bc
Garmouth	303	Ba
Garnant	85	Ab
Garrafad	295	Ba
Garrigill	204	Da
Garsdon	70	Cc
Garshall Green	147	Ac
Garsington	72	Db
Garstang	180	Dc
Garston	160	Cb
Garston, E.	54	Ca
Garth, Caer.	156	Db
Garth, Den.	144	Cb
Garth, Glam.	65	Ba
Garth, Glam.	67	Ac
Garthbeibio	123	Ab
Garthbrengy	104	Dc
Garth-gyn-fawr	122	Cc
Garthmyl	124	Cc
Garthorpe, Leics.	131	Ba
Garthorpe, Lincs.	176	Cb
Gartmore	258	Cc
Gartocharn	248	Ca
Garton	178	Cb
Garton End	115	Aa
Garton - on - the - Wold	187	Bc
Garvald	253	Ab
Garvan, S.	274	Dc
Garve	299	Ba
Garveston	118	Da
Garway	88	Cc
Garway Hill	88	Cc
Gastard	52	Ca
Gasthorpe	118	Cc
Gatacre	126	Dc
Gatcombe	21	Ac
Gateacre	160	Ca
Gate Burton	165	Bb
Gateforth	174	Ba
Gate Helmsley	185	Bb
Gatehouse of Fleet	214	Cb
Gateley	136	Db
Gatenby	197	Ab
Gategill	217	Bc
Gateshead	222	Cb
Gateside	261	Ab
Gatley	161	Ba
Gatton	42	Ca
Gattonside	241	Bb
Gaulby	130	Dc
Gawber	173	Bc
Gawcott	93	Ab
Gawsworth	162	Cc
Gawthorpe	173	Bb
Gawthrop	194	Cb
Gaydon	92	Cc
Gayhurst	94	Ca
Gayle	195	Ab
Gayles	196	Ca
Gayton, Ches.	159	Ab
Gayton, Norf.	135	Bc
Gayton, N'hants.	112	Dc
Gayton, Staffs.	147	Bc
Gayton-le-Marsh	168	Cc
Gayton-le-Wold	167	Bc
Gayton Thorpe	135	Bc
Gaywood	135	Ac
Gazeley	97	Ba
Gedding	98	Db
Geddington	113	Ba
Gedling	150	Cb
Gedney	134	Cb
Gedney Broadgate	134	Cb
Gedney Drove End	134	Cb

Name	Page	Sq.
Gedney Dyke	134	Cb
Gedney Hill	133	Bc
Geldeston	120	Cb
Gellan	292	Db
Gelligaer	66	Da
Gellywen	83	Ac
Gelston	151	Bb
Gembling	188	Cc
George Green	56	Da
Georgeham	30	Cb
George Nympton	31	Ba
Gerlan	156	Dc
Germansweek	12	Db
Germoe	2	Ca
Gerrans	4	Cb
Gerrards Cross	74	Dc
Gerston	323	Bb
Gestingthorpe	78	Ca
Gibraltar	154	Db
Gibsmere	150	Db
Giddeahall	52	Ca
Gidding, Gt.	114	Ca
Gidding, Lit.	114	Ca
Gidleigh	13	Ba
Gifford	252	Db
Giggleswick	182	Ca
Gilberdike	175	Ba
Gilcrux	201	Ba
Gildersome	173	Aa
Gildingwells	164	Db
Gileston	66	Cc
Gilgarran	201	Bb
Gillamoor	198	Db
Gilling, Yorks.	196	Ca
Gilling, Yorks.	198	Cc
Gillingham, Dors.	36	Cb
Gillingham, Kent	59	Bc
Gillingham, Norf.	120	Cb
Gills	324	Ca
Gilmerton, M.Loth.	251	Bb
Gilmerton, Perth	259	Ba
Gilmonby	206	Cb
Gilmorton	112	Ca
Gilstead	183	Ac
Gilston	76	Db
Gilwern	67	Aa
Gimingham	138	Ca
Gipping	99	Da
Girton, Camb.	96	Ca
Girton, Notts.	165	Dc
Girvan	223	Bb
Gisburn	182	Cb
Gisleham	120	Db
Gislingham	99	Aa
Gissing	119	Ac
Gittisham	15	Bb
Givendale, Gt.	186	Cb
Gladestry	106	Dc
Gladsmuir	252	Db
Glais	85	Ac
Glaisdale	198	Da
Glamis	271	Bb
Glanamman	64	Da
Glandford	136	Ba
Glanton	231	Ba
Glapthorn	114	Ca
Glapton	150	Cc
Glapwell	164	Cc
Glasbury	87	Ab
Glascoed	67	Bb
Glascote	128	Db
Glascwm	104	Da
Glasgow	248	Db
Glashvin	296	Ca
Glaspant	83	Ab
Glasserton	210	Db
Glass Houghton	174	Ca
Glasson	217	Ab
Glassonby	204	Ca
Glaston	131	Bc
Glastonbury	34	Da
Glasynfryn	156	Dc
Glatton	114	Da
Glazebury	168	Da
Glazeley	164	Cb
Gleadless	179	Ba
Gledrid	144	Cc
Gleinant	123	Ac
Glemham, Gt.	100	Cb
Glemham, Lit.	100	Cb
Glemsford	98	Cc
Glenbarr	233	Ab
Glenboig	249	Bb
Glencairn	226	Cb
Glencaple	216	Cb
Glencarse	261	Aa
Glencoe	266	Ca
Glencorse	251	Bc
Glendevon	260	Cb
Gleneagles	260	Cb
Glenelg	285	Bb
Glenfarg	260	Db
Glenfield	130	Cb
Glengarnock	236	Ca
Glenholm	239	Bb
Glenluce	209	Ba
Glen of Newmill	304	Cb
Glenridding	203	Ac
Glenrothes	261	Ab
Glentham	166	Da
Glentworth	166	Ca
Glewstone	88	Dc
Glinton	115	Aa
Glooston	131	Ac
Globwll	123	Ba
Glossop	162	Ba
Gloucester	89	Bc
Glusburn	182	Dc
Glympton	92	Cc
Glynde	25	Ab
Glyn Dyfrdwy	143	Bb
Glyn Neath	85	Bb
Glyn-y-beudy	85	Ab
Gnosall	126	Da
Gnosall Heath	126	Da
Goadby	131	Ac
Goadby Marwood	131	Aa
Goathill	35	Bb
Goathland	199	Bb
Goathurst	33	Bb
Gobowen	144	Cc
Godalming	41	Ab
Godden Green	43	Aa
Godington	93	Ac
Godmanchester	95	Ba
Godmanstone	17	Ba
Godmersham	45	Bc
Godney, Lr.	34	Da
Godney, Upr.	34	Da
Godolphin Cross	2	Cb
Godre'r-graig	85	Ab
Godshill, Hants.	21	Bc
Godshill, Hants.	37	Bc
Godstone	42	Db
Golborne	160	Da
Golcar	172	Db
Goldcliff	67	Bc
Golden Hill	146	Da
Golden Valley	90	Cc
Golders Green	57	Bb
Goldhanger	78	Cc
Goldington	94	Da
Goldsborough, Yorks.	200	Ca
Goldsborough, Yorks.	184	Cb
Goldsithney	1	Bc
Goldthorpe	174	Cc
Golspie	312	Ca
Gomersal	173	Aa
Gomshall	41	Bb
Gonalston	150	Db
Gonerby, Gt.	151	Bc
Gooderstone	117	Ba
Goodleigh	30	Db
Goodmanham	186	Dc
Goodnestone, Kent	45	Bb
Goodnestone, Kent	46	Cb
Goodrich	88	Dc
Goodshaw	171	Ba
Goodwick	82	Cb
Goodworth Clatford	38	Da
Goolefields	175	Bb
Goonhavern	2	Da
Gooseham	11	Ba
Goosey	72	Cc
Goosnargh	180	Dc
Goostrey-cum-Barnshaw	161	Bc
Gorebridge	252	Cc
Gorefield	134	Cc
Goring, Oxon.	55	Aa
Goring, Sus.	23	Bc
Gorleston	120	Da
Gornalwood	127	Ac
Gorseinon	64	Db
Gorsley	89	Ac
Gorsley Common	89	Ab
Gorsty Common	88	Cb
Gorton	162	Ca
Gosbeck	99	Ab
Gosberton	133	Bb
Gosfield	77	Ba
Gosforth	191	Bb
Gosforth, S.	222	Cb
Gosmore	75	Ba
Gosport, Carm.	63	Aa
Gosport, Hants.	21	Ba
Gosport, Hants.	38	Dc
Gossington	69	Ab
Goswick	244	Ca
Gotham	150	Cc
Gotherington	90	Cb
Goudhurst	44	Cc
Goulceby	153	Ba
Gourdon	282	Ca
Gourock	247	Bb
Govan	248	Db
Goverton	150	Db
Govilon	67	Ba
Gowanbank	272	Cb
Gowdall	174	Db
Gowerton	64	Db
Gowthorpe	186	Cb
Goxhill, Lincs.	177	Ba
Goxhill, Yorks.	177	Ba
Goxhill Haven	177	Bc
Goytre	67	Ba
Gradbach	162	Cc
Grade	3	Bc
Graffham	23	Ab
Grafham	95	Aa
Grafton, Oxon.	71	Bb
Grafton, Shrops.	125	Ba
Grafton, Worcs.	90	Db
Grafton, Yorks.	184	Da
Grafton, E.	53	Bb
Grafton Flyford	109	Bc
Grafton Regis	93	Ba
Grafton Underwood	113	Ba
Grahamston	250	Ca
Grain	60	Cc
Grainthorpe	168	Cb
Grampound	6	Cc
Granby	150	Dc
Grandborough, Bucks.	93	Bc
Grandborough, War	112	Cb
Grange, Ches.	159	Aa
Grange, Cumb.	202	Dc
Grange, Inver.	288	Ca
Grange Mill	148	Da
Grangemouth	250	Ca
Grange over Sands	193	Ac
Grangetown	49	Da
Gransden, Gt.	95	Bb
Gransden, Lit.	95	Bb
Granston	81	Bb
Grantchester	96	Cb
Grantham	151	Bc
Granton	251	Bb
Grantown on Spey	290	Da
Grappenhall	160	Da
Grasby	167	Aa
Grasmere	192	Da
Grassington	182	Da
Grassmoor	164	Cc
Grassthorpe	165	Ba
Gratley	38	Ca
Gratwich	147	Bc
Grave	35	Ba
Graveley, Cambs.	95	Ba
Graveley, Herts.	75	Ba
Gravelly Hill	128	Cc
Graveney	45	Bb
Gravenhurst, Lr.	75	Aa
Gravenhurst, Upr.	75	Aa
Gravesend	59	Ac
Grayingham	166	Ca
Grays	59	Ab
Grayshott	40	Db
Grayswood	40	Db
Grazeley	55	Ab
Greasbrough	164	Ca
Greasby	159	Aa
Greasley	149	Bb
Great Barr	127	Bc
Great Bircham	135	Bb
Great Bolas	126	Ca
Great Chart	27	Ba
Great Chatwell	126	Da
Great Danegate	43	Bc
Great Easton	131	Bc
Greatford	132	Db
Great Glen	130	Dc
Greatham, Dur.	208	Cb
Greatham, Hants.	40	Cb
Greatham, Sus.	23	Bb
Great Hanwood	125	Ab
Great Hinton	52	Cb
Great Ness	125	Aa
Great Ridge	36	Da
Great Walsingham	136	Da
Great Warley Street	59	Aa
Great Wishford	37	Aa
Greatworth	92	Db
Great Wyrley	127	Bb
Great Yarmouth	120	Da
Green End, Hunts.	115	Ac
Green End, Hunts.	114	Da
Greenfield, Beds.	75	Aa
Greenfield, Flint.	159	Ab
Greenford	57	Ab
Greengairs	249	Bb
Greengate	136	Dc
Greenhalgh	180	Cc
Greenham	33	Ac
Green Hammerton	184	Db
Greenhaugh	230	Cc
Greenhead	218	Db
Greenhill, Derby	163	Bb
Greenhill, Dumf.	216	Ca
Greenhithe	59	Ac
Greenlaw	242	Ca
Greenloaning	259	Bb
Greenock	247	Bb
Greenodd	192	Dc
Green Ore	50	Dc
Greensgate	137	Ac
Greenside	221	Bb
Greens Norton	93	Aa
Greenstead	78	Db
Greensted	76	Dc
Green Street	45	Ab
Greenstreet Green	43	Aa
Greenway	34	Cc
Greenwich	58	Cb
Greenyards, Wester	311	Aa
Greet	108	Cb
Greetham, Lincs.	153	Ba
Greetham, Rut.	131	Bb
Greetland	172	Db
Greetwell	166	Dc
Greinton	34	Cb
Grenaby	190	Db
Grendon, N'hants.	113	Bc
Grendon, War.	128	Db
Grendon Bishop	108	Cc
Grendon Green	108	Cc
Grendon Underwood	93	Ac
Grenoside	163	Ba
Gresford	144	Ca
Gresham	137	Ba
Gressenhall	136	Dc
Gressenhall Green	136	Dc
Gressingham	180	Da
Gretna Green	217	Bb
Gretton, Glos.	90	Db
Gretton, N'hants.	131	Bc
Grewelthorpe	196	Dc
Grey Green	175	Bc
Greylake	34	Cb
Greysouthen	201	Bb
Greystoke	203	Bb
Greystone	272	Cb
Greywell	55	Bc
Gribthorpe	186	Cc
Griff	111	Bb
Griffithstown	67	Bb
Grimley	109	Ac
Grimoldby	168	Cc
Grimsargh	170	Ca
Grimsbury	92	Cb
Grimsby	167	Ba
Grimsby, Lit.	168	Cb
Grimscote	93	Aa
Grimscott	11	Ba
Grimstead, E.	37	Bb
Grimstead, W.	37	Bb
Grimsthorpe	132	Da
Grimston, Leics.	130	Da
Grimston, Norf.	135	Bb
Grimston, N.	186	Da
Grimston Smithy	185	Bb
Grimstone	17	Ba
Grindale	188	Cb
Grindle	126	Db
Grindleford Bridge	163	Ba
Grindleton	181	Bc
Grindleybrook	145	Ab
Grindlow	163	Ab
Grindon, Dur.	207	Db
Grindon, Staffs.	147	Ba
Grindsbrook Booth	162	Da
Gringley, Lit.	165	Ab
Gringley - on - the-Hill	165	Ba
Grinsdale	217	Bb
Grinshill	125	Ba
Grinton	195	Ba
Gristhorpe	188	Ca
Griston	118	Ca
Grittenham	70	Dc
Grittleton	70	Cc
Grizebeck	192	Cb
Grizedale	192	Db
Groby	130	Cb
Groeslon	156	Ca
Groeston	140	Ca
Groeswen	66	Da
Gronant	158	Da
Groombridge	43	Ac
Grosmont, Mon.	88	Cc
Grosmont, Yorks.	199	Bb
Groton	98	Cc
Grove, Berks.	72	Cc
Grove, Bucks.	94	Cc
Grove, Notts.	165	Bb
Grove Hill	177	Cb
Grundisburgh	99	Bb
Guestling	27	Ac
Guestling Green	26	Db
Guestwick	136	Db
Guide	170	Da
Guide Post	232	Dc

	PAGE	SQ.
Guilden Morden	95	Bc
Guilden Sutton	160	Da
Guildford	41	Ab
Guildsted	44	Da
Guilsborough	112	Db
Guilsfield	124	Cb
Guisborough	199	Aa
Guiseley	183	Bc
Guist	136	Db
Gulting Power	90	Dc
Guldeford, E.	27	Ab
Gullane	252	Ba
Gulval	1	Bb
Gumfreston	62	Db
Gumley	112	Da
Gunby, Lincs.	131	Ba
Gunby, Lincs.	154	Cb
Gun Hill	25	Bb
Gunn	30	Db
Gunnerside	195	Ba
Gunnerton	220	Ca
Gunness	176	Cb
Gunnislake	8	Ca
Gunthorpe, Lincs.	165	Ba
Gunthorpe, Norf.	136	Da
Gunthorpe, Notts.	150	Db
Gunton	120	Db
Gunville	21	Ab
Gunwalloe	2	Cc
Gurney Slade	51	Ac
Gussage All Saints	19	Aa
Gussage St. Michael	36	Dc
Guston	28	Da
Guthrie	272	Ca
Guyhirne	116	Ca
Guyzance	232	Cb
Gwaelod-y-garth	66	Db
Gwaenysgor	158	Da
Gwalchmai	155	Bb
Gwaun-cae-gurwen	85	Ab
Gweek	2	Dc
Gwenddwr	104	Db
Gwennap	2	Db
Gwenter	3	Bc
Gwernesney	68	Cb
Gwernogle	84	Cb
Gwinear	2	Cb
Gwithian	2	Cb
Gwyrgrug	84	Cb
Gwytherin	157	Bb
Gyffin	157	Ba
HABBERLEY	125	Ab
Habergham Eaves	171	Ba
Habrough	167	Aa
Habton, Gt.	198	Dc
Haccombe	14	Dc
Hacconby	132	Da
Haceby	152	Ca
Hacheston	100	Cb
Hackenthorpe	164	Cb
Hackford	118	Da
Hackforth	196	Db
Hackington	45	Bb
Hackleton	113	Ac
Hackness	200	Cc
Hackney	58	Cb
Hackthorn	166	Db
Hackthorpe	204	Cb
Haddenham, Bucks.	73	Ba
Haddenham, Cambs.	116	Cc
Haddington, E. Loth.	252	Db
Haddington, Lincs.	151	Ba
Haddiscoe	120	Cb
Haddlesey, W.	174	Da
Haddon	115	Ab
Haddon, E.	112	Db
Haddon, W.	112	Db
Hadfield	162	Da
Hadham, Lit.	76	Cb
Hadleigh, Essex	60	Cb
Hadleigh, Suff.	98	Dc
Hadley, Shrops.	126	Cb
Hadley, Worcs.	109	Ab
Hadley End	128	Ca
Hadlow	43	Bb
Hadlow Down	25	Ba
Hadnall	125	Ba
Hadstock	96	Dc
Hadzor	109	Bc
Hagbourne, E.	72	Cb
Hagbourne, W.	72	Dc
Bagley, Herefs.	88	Da
Hagley, Worcs.	109	Ba
Hagnaby	153	Bb
Hagworthingham	153	Ba
Haigh, Lancs.	170	Cc
Haigh, Yorks.	173	Bb
Hailes	90	Db
Hailey, Herts.	76	Cc
Hailey, Oxon.	72	Ca
Hailsham	25	Bb
Hail Weston	95	Aa

	PAGE	SQ.
Haine	46	Da
Hainford	137	Bc
Hainton	167	Bc
Hainworth	183	Ac
Halam	150	Da
Halberton	32	Db
Halcro	324	Cb
Hale, Ches.	161	Ba
Hale, Cumb.	191	Ba
Hale, Hants.	37	Bc
Hale, Lancs.	160	Cb
Hale, Sur.	56	Cc
Hale, W'land.	193	Bc
Halebarns	161	Ba
Hale End	58	Ca
Hale, Gt.	152	Db
Hale Green	25	Bb
Hale, Lit.	152	Bb
Hales, Norf.	120	Cb
Hales, Staffs.	146	Cc
Halesowen	109	Ba
Halesworth	100	Ca
Halewood	160	Ca
Half Morton	217	Ba
Halford, Shrops.	107	Ba
Halford, War.	91	Ba
Halifax	172	Da
Halistra, Lr.	295	Ab
Halistra, Upr.	295	Ab
Halkin	159	Ac
Halkirk	323	Bb
Hallaton	131	Ac
Hallatrow	51	Ab
Hall Cliffe	173	Bb
Hallen	68	Dc
Hallin	295	Ab
Halling	44	Ca
Hallingbury, Gt.	76	Db
Hallingbury, Lit.	76	Db
Hallington, Lincs.	167	Ba
Hallington, N'land.	220	Da
Halliwell	170	Da
Halloughton	150	Da
Hallow	109	Ac
Hallwood Green	89	Ab
Halmer End	146	Cb
Halmonds Frome	89	Aa
Halmore	69	Ab
Halnaker	23	Ab
Halsall	169	Bc
Halse	33	Ab
Halsham	178	Ca
Halstead, Essex	78	Ca
Halstead, Leics.	131	Ab
Halsted	43	Aa
Halstock	35	Ac
Halstow, High	59	Bc
Halstow, Lr.	60	Cc
Haltham	153	Bb
Halton, Bucks.	74	Ca
Halton, Ches.	160	Db
Halton, Lancs.	180	Da
Halton, N'land.	220	Db
Halton, Yorks.	173	Ba
Halton, E., Lincs.	177	Bc
Halton, E., Yorks.	182	Db
Halton Gill	195	Ac
Halton Holegate	154	Cb
Halton, W.	182	Cb
Haltwhistle	219	Bb
Halvergate	120	Ca
Halwell	10	Cb
Halwill	12	Db
Ham, Glos.	69	Ab
Ham, Kent.	46	Db
Ham, Som..	51	Ac
Ham, Sur.	57	Ac
Ham, Wilts.	54	Cb
Hamble	21	Aa
Hambledon, Bucks.	73	Bc
Hambledon, Hants.	39	Bc
Hambledon, Sur.	40	Da
Hambleton, Lancs.	180	Ca
Hambleton, Yorks.	174	Ba
Hambridge	34	Cc
Hambrook	69	Ac
Ham Common	36	Cb
Hameringham	153	Bb
Hamerton	114	Da
Hamilton	249	Bc
Hamlet	15	Bb
Hammersmith	57	Bb
Hammerwich	128	Cb
Hammoon	36	Cc
Hamp	34	Cb
Hampden, Gt.	74	Cb
Hampden, Lit.	74	Cb
Hampden Row	74	Cb
Hampnett	71	Aa
Hampole	174	Dc
Hampreston	19	Ba
Hampstead	57	Bb
Hampstead Heath	57	Bb
Hampstead Marshall	54	Cb

	PAGE	SQ.
Hampstead Norris	54	Da
Hampsthwaite	184	Cb
Hampton, M'sex.	57	Ac
Hampton, Shrops.	108	Da
Hampton Bishop.	88	Db
Hampton Gay	72	Da
Hampton, Gt.	90	Da
Hampton-in-Arden	110	Da
Hampton Lucy	110	Dc
Hampton-on-the-Hill	110	Db
Hampton Poyle	72	Da
Hamptons	43	Bb
Hamstall Ridware	128	Ca
Hamstead	128	Cc
Hamsterley	206	Db
Ham Street	27	Ba
Hamworthy	19	Ab
Hanbury, Staffs.	148	Cc
Hanbury, Worcs.	109	Bb
Handbridge	160	Cc
Handcross	24	Da
Handley, Ches.	144	Da
Handley, Dors.	37	Ac
Handley, Mid.	164	Cb
Handley, Nether	164	Cb
Handley, W.	164	Cb
Handsacre	128	Ca
Handsworth, War.	127	Bc
Handsworth, Yorks.	164	Ca
Hanford	146	Db
Hanging Heaton	173	Ba
Hanging Houghton	113	Ab
Hangleton	24	Cc
Hanham	51	Ab
Hankelow	145	Bb
Hankerton	70	Cb
Hankford	12	Ca
Hanley	146	Db
Hanley Castle	89	Ba
Hanley Child	108	Cb
Hanley William	108	Bb
Hanlith	182	Ca
Hanmer	144	Db
Hannah	154	Da
Hanney, E.	72	Cc
Hanney, W.	72	Cc
Hanningfield, E.	59	Ba
Hanningfield, S.	59	Ba
Hanningfield, W.	59	Ba
Hannington, Hants.	54	Dc
Hannington, N'hants.	113	Bb
Hannington, Wilts.	71	Ac
Hanslope	93	Ba
Hanthorpe	132	Da
Hanwell, M'sex.	57	Ab
Hanwell, Oxon.	92	Cb
Hanworth, M'sex.	57	Ac
Hanworth, Norf.	137	Ba
Happisburgh	138	Cb
Hapsford	160	Cb
Hapton, Lancs.	171	Aa
Hapton, Norf.	119	Ab
Harberton	10	Ca
Harbertonford	10	Ca
Harbledown	45	Bb
Harborne	110	Ca
Harborough Magna	112	Ca
Harbottle	231	Ab
Harbridge	19	Ba
Harbury	111	Bc
Harby, Leics.	150	Dc
Harby, Notts.	166	Cc
Harden	183	Ac
Hardenbuish	52	Ca
Hardham	23	Bb
Hardhorn	180	Cc
Hardingham	118	Da
Hardingstone	113	Ac
Hardington	51	Bc
Hardington Mandeville	35	Ac
Hardley	120	Ca
Hardmead	94	Ca
Hardraw	195	Ab
Hardres, Lr.	45	Bb
Hardres, Upr.	45	Bc
Hardstoft	164	Cc
Hardwick, Bucks.	73	Ba
Hardwick, Cambs.	96	Cb
Hardwick, Herefs.	107	Ac
Hardwick, Lincs.	166	Cb
Hardwick, N'hants.	113	Bb
Hardwick, Norf.	119	Bb
Hardwick, Oxon.	72	Cb
Hardwick, Oxon.	92	Cb
Hardwick, E.	174	Cb
Hardwick, W.	174	Cb
Hardwicke	69	Ba
Hardwicke	90	Cb
Hareby	153	Bb
Harefield	74	Dc
Harescombe	69	Ba

	PAGE	SQ.
Haresfield	69	Ba
Hare Street	76	Ca
Harewood	184	Cc
Harewood End	88	Db
Harford	9	Ba
Hargatewall	162	Db
Hargham	118	Db
Hargrave, Ches.	160	Cc
Hargrave, N'hants.	114	Cb
Hargrave, Suff.	97	Bb
Harkstead	79	Ba
Harlaston	128	Db
Harlaxton	151	Bc
Harlech	140	Dc
Harlesden	57	Bb
Harleston, Norf.	119	Bc
Harleston, Suff.	98	Cb
Harlestone	112	Dc
Harley	126	Cb
Harling, E.	118	Dc
Harlington, Beds.	94	Cb
Harlington, M'sex.	57	Ab
Harlington, Yorks.	174	Cc
Harling, W.	118	Cc
Harlosh	283	Ba
Harlow	76	Dc
Harlow Hill, N'land.	220	Db
Harlow Hill, Yorks.	184	Cb
Harlsey, E.	197	Ba
Harlthorpe	186	Cc
Harlton	96	Cb
Harmby	196	Cb
Harmerhill	125	Ba
Harmondsworth	56	Da
Harmston	152	Ca
Harnham	220	Da
Harnham, E.	37	Bb
Harnham, W.	37	Bb
Harnhill	70	Db
Harold Wood	58	Da
Haroldston	61	Ba
Haroldston St. Issels	62	Ca
Harome	198	Cc
Harpenden	75	Ab
Harpers Gate	147	Aa
Harpham	188	Cc
Harpit	71	Bc
Harpley, Norf.	135	Bc
Harpley, Worcs.	108	Dc
Harpole	112	Dc
Harpsden	55	Ba
Harpswell	166	Ca
Harpton, Lr.	106	Dc
Harptree, E.	50	Db
Harptree, W.	50	Db
Harpur Hill	162	Dc
Harrietsham	44	Db
Harrington, Cumb.	201	Bb
Harrington, Lincs.	154	Ca
Harrington, N'hants.	113	Aa
Harrington, High	201	Bb
Harringworth	131	Bc
Harrisea Head	146	Ca
Harrogate	184	Cb
Harrold	114	Cc
Harrop Dale	172	Cc
Harrowden	94	Da
Harrowden, Gt.	113	Bb
Harrowden, Lit.	113	Bb
Harrow-on-the-Hill	57	Ab
Harston, Camb.	96	Cb
Harston, Leics.	151	Bc
Harswell	186	Cc
Hart	208	Ca
Hartburn	231	Bc
Harteat	98	Cb
Hartfield	43	Ac
Hartford, Ches.	160	Dc
Hartford, Hunts.	95	Ba
Hartford, Som.	32	Da
Hartford End	77	Bb
Hartforth	196	Ca
Harthill, Ches.	145	Aa
Harthill, Lan.	250	Cc
Harthill, Yorks.	164	Db
Harting, South	40	Cc
Hartington	148	Ca
Hartland	29	Ac
Hartlebury	109	Ab
Hartlepool	208	Ca
Hartley, Kent.	43	Ba
Hartley, Kent.	44	Cc
Hartley, N'land.	222	Ca
Hartley, W'land.	194	Da
Hartley Mauditt	40	Ca
Hartley Row	55	Bc
Hartley Wespall	55	Bc
Hartlip	44	Da
Harton, Dur.	222	Db
Harton, Yorks.	185	Ba
Hartpury	89	Bc
Hartshead	173	Aa

343

	PAGE	SQ.		PAGE	SQ.		PAGE	SQ.		PAGE	SQ.
Hartshead Moor Side	172	Da	Havering Atte Bower	58	Da	Heather	129	Bb	Henham	76	Da
Hartshill	129	Ac	Haveringland	137	Ab	Heathfield, Som.	33	Ab	Henlade	33	Bc
Hartshorne	129	Ac	Haversham	94	Ca	Heathfield, Sus.	25	Ba	Henley, Som.	34	Cb
Hartsop, Low	203	Ac	Haverthwaite	192	Dc	Heath Hayes	127	Bb	Henley, Suff.	99	Ac
Hartwell, Bucks.	73	Ba	Havyatt	34	Da	Heath Hill	126	Da	Henley, Sus.	23	Aa
Hartwell, N'hants.	93	Ba	Haw	89	Bb	Heath House	34	Ca	Henley, Wilts.	53	Bb
Hartwood Green	170	Cb	Hawarden	159	Bc	Heath Town	127	Bc	Henley-In-Arden	110	Db
Harty	45	Aa	Hawcoat	179	Aa	Heatley	161	Aa	Henley-on-Thames	55	Ba
Harvel	43	Ba	Hawes	195	Ab	Hebburn	222	Cb	Henllan, Card.	83	Bb
Harvington, Worcs.	90	Da	Hawick	229	Aa	Hebden	182	Da	Henllan, Den.	158	Cb
Harvington, Worcs.	109	Bb	Hawkchurch	16	Cb	Hebden Bridge	172	Ca	Henllys	67	Bb
Harwell	72	Dc	Hawkedon	97	Bb	Hebing End	76	Cb	Henlow	95	Ac
Harwich	80	Cb	Hawkeridge	52	Cb	Hebron	232	Cc	Hennock	14	Cb
Harwood	171	Ab	Hawkerland	15	Ac	Heck	216	Ca	Henny, Gt.	78	Ca
Harwood Dale	200	Ca	Hawkesbury	69	Bc	Heckdyke	165	Ba	Henrys Moat	82	Cc
Harwood, Gt.	170	Aa	Hawkesbury Upton	69	Bc	Heckfield	55	Bb	Hensall	174	Db
Harworth	164	Da	Hawkhurst	26	Da	Heck, Gt.	174	Db	Hensingham	201	Bc
Hasbury	109	Ba	Hawkinge	28	Da	Heckingham	120	Cb	Henstead	120	Dc
Hascombe	41	Ac	Hawkley	40	Cb	Heckington	133	Aa	Hensting	39	Ac
Haselbech	112	Db	Hawkridge	47	Bc	Heckmondwike	173	Aa	Henstridge	35	Bh
Haselbury Bryan.	35	Bb	Hawkshead	192	Da	Heddington	52	Da	Henstridge Bowden	35	Ab
Haselbury Plucknett	16	Dc	Hawkswick	182	Da	Heddington Wick	52	Da	Henton, Oxon.	73	Bb
Haseley	110	Db	Hawksworth, Notts.	150	Db	Heddon-on-the-Wall	221	Bb	Henton, Som.	34	Da
Haseley, Gt.	73	Ab	Hawksworth, Yorks.	183	Bc	Hedenham	119	Bb	Henwood	7	Ba
Haseley, Lit.	73	Ab	Hawkwell	60	Ca	Hedgerley	74	Dc	Heol-fawr	66	Cb
Haselor	110	Cc	Hawley	56	Cc	Hedging	34	Cb	Heol-galed	84	Dc
Haselour	128	Da	Hawling	90	Dc	Hednesford	127	Ba	Heol-y-cyw	66	Cb
Hasfield	89	Bb	Hawnby	197	Bb	Hedon	177	Bb	Hepple	231	Ab
Hasguard	61	Bb	Haworth	182	Dc	Hedsor	74	Cc	Hepscott	232	Cc
Hasingham	120	Ca	Hawridge	74	Db	Hegdon Hill	108	Cc	Heptonstall	172	Ca
Haskayne	169	Ac	Hawsker, High	200	Cb	Heighington, Dur.	207	Ab	Hepworth, Suff.	98	Cb
Hasketon	99	Bc	Hawsker, Low	200	Cb	Heighington, Lincs.	166	Dc	Hepworth, Yorks.	172	Dc
Hasland	164	Cc	Hawstead	98	Cb	Heightington	108	Db	Herbrandston	61	Bb
Haslemere	40	Db	Hawthorn	208	Ca	Heights of Kinlochewe	298	Da	Hereford	88	Ca
Haslingden	171	Aa	Hawthorn Bush	108	Db	Hele	30	Ca	Hereford, Lit.	108	Cb
Haslingfield	96	Cb	Hawthornden	251	Bc	Helensburgh	247	Ba	Hergest, Lr.	106	Dc
Haslington	146	Ca	Hawthorn Hill	153	Ab	Helford	2	Dc	Heriot	240	Cb
Hassall Green	146	Ca	Hawthorpe	152	Cc	Helhoughton	136	Cb	Hermitage, Berks.	53	Bb
Hassop	163	Ac	Hawton	151	Ba	Helion Bumpstead	97	Ac	Hermitage, Dors.	35	Bc
Hastigrow	324	Cb	Haxby	185	Bb	Helland, Corn.	6	Db	Hermon	155	Bc
Hastingleigh	45	Bc	Haxey	175	Bc	Helland, Som.	34	Cc	Hernden	46	Cb
Hastings	26	Db	Hay	87	Aa	Hellesdon	119	Aa	Herne	46	Ca
Hastoe	74	Ca	Haydock	160	Da	Hellidon	112	Cc	Herne Bay	46	Ca
Haswell	207	Ba	Haydon	35	Bc	Hellifield	183	Cb	Hernehill	45	Bb
Hatch	36	Db	Haydon Bridge	220	Cb	Hellingly	25	Bb	Herner	30	Dc
Hatch Beauchamp	34	Cc	Hayes	57	Ab	Hellington	119	Ba	Herodsfoot	7	Ab
Hatch End	57	Aa	Hayfield	162	Da	Helmdon	92	Da	Heronzate	59	Aa
Hatch, W.	33	Bc	Hayfield, Lit.	162	Da	Helmingham	99	Bb	Herriard	39	Ba
Hatcliffe	167	Db	Hayle	1	Bb	Helmsdale	317	Bc	Herringfleet	120	Db
Hatfield, Herefs.	108	Cc	Hayling Island	22	Ca	Helmsdale, W.	317	Dc	Herringswell	97	Ba
Hatfield, Herts.	75	Bc	Hayling, Sth.	22	Cb	Helmsley	198	Ca	Herrington	222	Cb
Hatfield, Yorks.	175	Ac	Haynes	94	Db	Helmsley, Upr.	185	Bb	Hersham	41	Ba
Hatfield Broad Oak	76	Db	Hayscastle	81	Bc	Helperby	184	Da	Herstmonceux	26	Cb
Hatfield, etc.	178	Ca	Hayton, Cumb.	218	Cc	Helperthorpe	186	Da	Hertford	76	Cc
Hatfield Heath	76	Db	Hayton, Notts.	165	Ab	Helpringham	133	Aa	Hertingfordbury	75	Bc
Hatfield Hyde	75	Bc	Hayton, Yorks.	186	Cc	Helpston	115	Aa	Hesket, High	203	Ba
Hatfield Peverel	77	Bc	Haytonbent	107	Ba	Helsby	160	Cb	Hesket, Low	218	Cc
Hatfield Woodhouse	175	Aa	Haywards Heath	24	Da	Helsington	193	Bb	Hesket Newmarket	202	Da
Hatford	72	Cb	Haywood, Yorks.	163	Ba	Helston	2	Cc	Hesketh Bank	169	Ba
Hatherden	54	Cc	Haywood, Yorks.	174	Db	Helstone	6	Da	Hesleden, High	208	Ca
Hatherleigh	31	Ac	Haywood, Gt.	127	Ba	Helton	203	Bb	Heslerton, E.	187	Ba
Hatherley, Upr.	90	Cc	Haywood, Lit.	127	Ba	Helwith	196	Ca	Heslerton, W.	187	Ba
Hathern	130	Ca	Hazeleigh	78	Cc	Hemblington	120	Ca	Heslington	185	Bb
Hatherop	71	Ab	Hazelend	76	Db	Hemel Hempstead	75	Aa	Hessay	185	Ab
Hathersage	163	Ac	Hazeley	55	Bc	Hemingbrough	175	Aa	Hessenford	7	Bb
Hathersage Booths	163	Ac	Hazelgrove	162	Ca	Hemingby	153	Ba	Hessett	98	Db
Hatherton, Ches.	146	Cb	Hazlemere	74	Cb	Hemingford Abbots	95	Ba	Hessle	176	Da
Hatherton, Staffs.	127	Bb	Hazleton	90	Dc	Hemingford Grey	95	Ba	Heston	57	Ab
Hatley, E.	95	Bb	Hazlewood	148	Db	Hemingstone	99	Ac	Heswall	159	Ab
Hatley St. George	95	Bb	Heacham	135	Aa	Hemington, Leics.	149	Bc	Hethe	92	Dc
Hattersley	162	Ca	Headbourne Worthy	38	Db	Hemington, N'hants.	114	Da	Hethel	119	Aa
Hatton, Aber.	306	Dc	Headcorn	44	Db	Hemington, Som.	51	Ab	Hethersett	119	Aa
Hatton, Ches.	160	Db	Headingley	184	Cc	Hemley	80	Ca	Hethersgill	218	Cb
Hatton, Derby	148	Cc	Headington	72	Da	Hempnall	119	Bb	Hett	207	Aa
Hatton, Lincs.	153	Aa	Headington, New	72	Db	Hempnall Green	119	Bb	Hetton	182	Db
Hatton, M'sex.	57	Ac	Headlam	206	Dc	Hempstead, Essex	77	Aa	Hetton Downs	222	Dc
Hatton, War.	110	Db	Headless Cross	110	Cb	Hempstead, Norf.	137	Aa	Hetton-le-Hole	222	Dc
Hatton of Fintray	294	Ca	Headley, Hants.	54	Db	Hempsted	89	Bc	Hetton, S.	207	Ba
Haugh	154	Ca	Headley, Hants.	40	Ca	Hempton, Norf.	136	Cb	Heugh	220	Da
Haugham	168	Cc	Headley, Sur.	41	Ba	Hempton, Oxon.	92	Cb	Heveningham	100	Ca
Haughley	98	Db	Headon	165	Bb	Hemsby	138	Dc	Hever	43	Ab
Haughton, Lancs.	162	Ca	Heage	149	Ab	Hemswell	166	Ca	Heversham	193	Bc
Haughton Shrops.	126	Db	Healaugh, Yorks.	195	Ab	Hemsworth, Derby	164	Cb	Hevingham	137	Bb
Haughton, Shrops.	144	Dc	Healaugh, Yorks.	184	Db	Hemsworth, Yorks.	174	Cb	Hewelsfield	68	Db
Haughton, Staffs.	127	Aa	Heale, Som.	51	Ac	Hemsworth Lane Ends	174	Cb	Hewelsfield Com.	68	Db
Haughton-le-Skerne	207	Bc	Heale, Som.	34	Cb	Hemyock	15	Ba	Hewish	50	Cb
Haultwick	76	Cb	Healey, N'land.	220	Db	Henbury	68	Dc	Heworth	185	Bb
Haunton	128	Db	Healey, Yorks.	196	Cc	Henbury-cum-Pexall	161	Bc	Hexham	220	Cb
Hause	202	Cb	Healing	167	Ba	Hendon	57	Ba	Hexthorpe	174	Dc
Hauxton	96	Cb	Heanor	149	Bb	Hendre	66	Cb	Hexton	75	Aa
Hauxwell, E.	196	Cb	Heanton Punchardon	30	Cb	Hendred, E.	72	Cc	Heybridge	78	Cc
Hauxwell, W.	196	Cb	Heapey	170	Cb	Hendred, W.	72	Cc	Heydon, Cambs.	96	Cc
Havant	22	Ca	Heapham	166	Ca	Hendy	64	Db	Heydon Norf.	137	Ab
Haven	107	Ac	Heasley Mill	47	Ac	Heneglwys	155	Bb	Heydour	152	Cb
Haven Side	178	Cc	Heath, Derby	164	Cc	Henfield	24	Cb	Heyford, Lr.	92	Dc
Haven Street	21	Bb	Heath, Shrops.	108	Ca	Henfynyw	101	Ab	Heyford, Nether	112	Dc
Haverbrack	193	Bc	Heath, Yorks.	173	Bb	Hengoed, Radnor.	106	Dc	Heyford, Upr., N'hants.	112	Dc
Havercroft	174	Cb	Heath and Reach	94	Cb	Hengoed, Shrops..	144	Cc	Heyford, Upr., Oxon.	92	Dc
Haverfordwest	62	Ca	Heath End, Glos.	69	Ab	Hengrave	98	Ca	Heyhead	161	Bb
Haverhill	97	Ac	Heath End, Hants.	55	Ab				Heyhouses	181	Bc
Haverigg	192	Cc	Heath End, War.	111	Bb				Heyop	106	Db
									Heysham, Higher	180	Ca
									Heysham, Lower	180	Ca

Name	PAGE	SQ.
Heyshaw	183	Ba
Heyshott	23	Ab
Heytesbury	52	Cc
Heythrop	92	Cc
Heywood, *Lancs.*	171	Bb
Heywood, *Wilts.*	52	Cb
Hibaldstow	176	Dc
Hickleton	174	Cc
Hickling	138	Cb
Hickling Green	138	Cb
Hidcote Bartram	91	Ab
Hidcote Boyce	91	Ab
Hiendley, S.	174	Cb
Hiendley, Upr.	174	Cb
Higham, *Derby*	149	Aa
Higham, *Kent.*	59	Bc
Higham, *Lancs.*	182	Cc
Higham, *Suff.*	97	Ba
Higham, *Suff.*	78	Da
Higham, *Yorks.*	173	Bc
Higham Ferrers	114	Cb
Higham Gobion	75	Aa
Higham-on-the-Hill	129	Bc
Highampton	12	Db
Higham Upshire	59	Bc
High Bickington	30	Dc
High Bray	47	Ac
Highbridge	34	Ca
High Bullen	31	Ba
Highburton	173	Ab
Highbury	51	Ac
Highclere	54	Cb
High Cross	112	Ca
High Egborough	174	Db
High Ercall	125	Ba
Higher Kinnerton	144	Ca
Higher Odcombe	34	Dc
Higher Walton	170	Ca
Higher Wych	145	Ab
Highgate, *M'sex.*	57	Bb
Highgate, *Yorks.*	174	Db
High Green, *Norf.*	119	Bb
High Green, *Worcs.*	90	Ca
High Green, *Yorks.*	163	Ba
High Halden	27	Aa
High Ham	34	Db
High Hatton	126	Ca
High Hoyland	173	Bc
High Hunsley	177	Ab
Highlane, *Ches.*	162	Cb
Highlane, *Derby*	164	Cb
Highlaws	216	Dc
Highleadon	89	Bc
Highley	108	Da
High Littleton	51	Ab
High Melton	174	Dc
Highnam	89	Bc
High Offley	146	Cc
High Roding	77	Ab
Hightae	216	Ca
Hightown	169	Ac
Highway	52	Ba
Highwayside	145	Ba
Highweek	14	Cc
Highwood	147	Bc
Highworth	71	Ac
High Wych	76	Db
High Wycombe	74	Cc
Hilborough	117	Ba
Hildersham	96	Bc
Hilderstone	147	Ac
Hilfarrance	33	Ac
Hilgay	117	Aa
Hill	69	Ab
Hillam	174	Da
Hillbeck	205	Ac
Hill Croome	90	Ca
Hill Deverill	36	Ca
Hill Dyke	153	Bc
Hillesden	93	Ac
Hillfield	35	Bc
Hillingdon	57	Ab
Hillington	135	Bb
Hillmorton	112	Cb
Hill Ridware	128	Ca
Hillside, *Angus*	272	Da
Hillside, *Shrops.*	108	Ca
Hill Side, *Worcs.*	108	Dc
Hillsley	69	Bb
Hill Top, *Yorks.*	163	Bb
Hill Top, *Yorks.*	173	Bb
Hill Wootton	111	Ab
Hillworth	89	Bb
Hilmarton	52	Ba
Hilperton	52	Cb
Hilperton Marsh	52	Cb
Hilston	178	Cb
Hilton, *Derby*	148	Dc
Hilton, *Dors.*	18	Ca
Hilton, *Dur.*	206	Db
Hilton, *Hants.*	95	Bc
Hilton, *Shrops.*	126	Dc
Hilton, *W'land.*	204	Dc
Hilton, *Yorks.*	208	Cc
Hilton of Cadboll	312	Dc
Himbleton	109	Bc
Himley	127	Ac
Hinckley	129	Bc
Hinderclay	118	Dc
Hinderwell	199	Ba
Hindford	144	Cc
Hindhead	40	Db
Hindle Fold	170	Da
Hindley	170	Dc
Hindley Green	170	Dc
Hindlip	109	Bc
Hindolveston	136	Db
Hindon	36	Da
Hindringham	136	Da
Hingham	118	Da
Hinksey, S.	72	Db
Hinksey, N.	72	Db
Hinstock	146	Cc
Hintlesham	79	Aa
Hinton, *Glos.*	51	Aa
Hinton, *Herefs.*	87	Bb
Hinton, *N'hants.*	92	Da
Hinton Ampner	39	Ba
Hinton Blewett	50	Db
Hinton Charterhouse	51	Bb
Hinton-in-the-Hedges	92	Db
Hinton, Little	53	Ba
Hinton Martell	19	Aa
Hinton-on-the-Green	90	Da
Hinton Parva	19	Aa
Hinton St. George	16	Da
Hinton St. Mary	36	Cc
Hinton Waldrist	72	Cb
Hints, *Shrops.*	108	Cb
Hints, *Staffs.*	128	Cb
Hinwick	114	Cc
Hinxhill	27	Ba
Hinxton	96	Bc
Hinxworth	95	Bc
Hipperholme	172	Da
Hipswell	196	Ba
Hirn	293	Bc
Hirnant	123	Ba
Hirst Courtney	174	Da
Hirwaun	86	Cc
Hiscott	30	Cc
Histon	96	Ca
Hitcham	98	Db
Hitchin	75	Ba
Hittisleigh	13	Ba
Hixon	147	Bc
Hoarwithy	88	Db
Hoath	46	Cb
Hoathly, E.	25	Bb
Hobkirk	229	Ba
Hoby	130	Da
Hockering	137	Ac
Hockerton	150	Ca
Hockham	118	Ca
Hockley	60	Ca
Hockley Heath	110	Ba
Hockliffe	94	Dc
Hockwold-cum-Wilton	117	Bb
Hoddesdon	76	Ca
Hoddlesden	170	Db
Hoddom	216	Da
Hodgeston	62	Cc
Hodnet	145	Bc
Hoe	136	Dc
Hoff	204	Dc
Hoggeston	93	Bc
Hoghton	170	Da
Hognaston	148	Da
Hogshaw	93	Bc
Hogsthorpe	154	Da
Holbeach	134	Cb
Holbeach Drove	133	Da
Holbeach Hurn	134	Cb
Holbeck	164	Dc
Holberrow Green	110	Ca
Holbeton	9	Bb
Holbrook, *Derby*	149	Ab
Holbrook, *Suff.*	79	Ba
Holbrook Common	51	Aa
Holcombe, *Dev.*	14	Db
Holcombe, *Som.*	51	Ac
Holcombe Brook	171	Ab
Holcombe Burnell	14	Ca
Holcombe Rogus	33	Ac
Holcot, *Beds.*	94	Cb
Holcot, *N'hants.*	113	Ab
Holdenby	112	Db
Holdenhurst	19	Bb
Holdgate	125	Bc
Holdingham	152	Db
Holdsworth	172	Da
Holford	33	Aa
Holgate	185	Bb
Holkham	136	Ca
Hollacombe	12	Da
Hollandbush	249	Ba
Holland, Gt.	79	Bc
Holland, Lit.	79	Bc
Hollbrook	164	Cb
Hollesley	80	Da
Hollingbourne	44	Da
Hollingthorpe	173	Bb
Hollington, *Derby*	148	Cb
Hollington, *Sus.*	26	Db
Hollingworth	162	Ca
Hollins	171	Bc
Hollinsclough	162	Dc
Hollins End	164	Cb
Hollins Green	161	Aa
Hollinwood, *Lancs.*	171	Bc
Hollinwood, *Shrops.*	145	Ac
Holloway	148	Da
Hollowell	112	Db
Hollybush	89	Bb
Holly End	116	Da
Hollym	178	Dc
Holme, *Hunts.*	115	Ab
Holme, *Lincs.*	176	Cc
Holme, *Notts.*	151	Ba
Holme, *W'land.*	193	Bc
Holme, *Yorks.*	197	Ac
Holme, *Yorks.*	172	Db
Holme, *Yorks.*	172	Dc
Holme Chapel	171	Ba
Holme, East	18	Db
Holme Hale	118	Ca
Holme Lacy	88	Db
Holme-next-the-Sea	135	Ba
Holme-on-the-Wolds	177	Aa
Holmer	88	Ca
Holmer Green	74	Cb
Holmesfield	163	Bb
Holme-upon-Spalding Moor	186	Cc
Holme, West	18	Db
Holmfirth	172	Dc
Holmpton	178	Dc
Holmrook	191	Ba
Holne	13	Bc
Holsworthy	12	Cb
Holt, *Den.*	144	Da
Holt, *Dors.*	19	Aa
Holt, *Norf.*	137	Aa
Holt, *Wilts.*	52	Cb
Holt, *Worcs.*	109	Ab
Holtby	185	Bb
Holt End	110	Cb
Holt Heath	109	Ab
Holton, *Oxon.*	73	Aa
Holton, *Som.*	35	Bb
Holton, *Suff.*	100	Ca
Holton-le-Clay	167	Bb
Holton-le-Moor	166	Da
Holton St. Mary	79	Aa
Holt Street	46	Cc
Holwell, *Dors.*	35	Bc
Holwell, *Herts.*	75	Aa
Holwell, *Leics.*	130	Da
Holwell, *Oxon.*	71	Ba
Holwell, *Som.*	51	Ac
Holybourne	39	Ba
Holyhead	155	Ab
Holy Island	244	Cb
Holyport	56	Ca
Holystone	231	Ab
Holytown	249	Bc
Holywell, *Flint*	159	Ab
Holywell, *Hunts.*	96	Ca
Holywell, *Lincs.*	132	Ca
Holywell, *N'land.*	222	Ca
Holywell, *Som.*	33	Ac
Holywell Green	172	Db
Holywell Row	117	Ac
Holywood	215	Ba
Homer	126	Cb
Homersfield	119	Bc
Homington	37	Bb
Honeyborough	62	Cb
Honeychurch	31	Ac
Honey Tye	78	Da
Honiley	110	Db
Honing	138	Cb
Honingham	137	Ac
Honington, *Lincs.*	152	Ca
Honington, *Suff.*	98	Ca
Honington, *War.*	91	Bb
Honiton	15	Bb
Honley	172	Db
Hoo, *Kent*	59	Bc
Hoo, *Kent*	46	Ca
Hoo, *Suff.*	99	Bb
Hooe	26	Cb
Hoo Green	161	Ab
Hook, *Hants.*	55	Bc
Hook, *Sur.*	41	Ba
Hook, *Yorks.*	175	Ba
Hookgate	146	Cc
Hook Green	59	Ac
Hook Norton	92	Cb
Hoole	160	Cc
Hooton Pagnell	174	Cc
Hooton Roberts	164	Ca
Hope, *Derby*	163	Ab
Hope, *Flint*	144	Da
Hope, *Shrops.*	124	Db
Hope Baggot	108	Da
Hope Bowdler	125	Bc
Hopeman	302	Da
Hope Mansel	88	Dc
Hopesay	107	Aa
Hopesgate	124	Dh
Hopetown	174	Ca
Hope-under-Dinmore	107	Bc
Hopton, *Derby*	148	Da
Hopton, *Shrops.*	124	Da
Hopton, *Staffs.*	147	Ac
Hopton, *Suff.*	120	Db
Hopton, *Suff.*	118	Dc
Hopton Cangeford	108	Da
Hopton Castle	107	Aa
Hopton, Upr.	173	Bb
Hopton Wafers	108	Ca
Hopwas	128	Cb
Horam	25	Bb
Horbling	133	Da
Horbury	173	Bb
Hordle	20	Cb
Hordley	144	Dc
Horfield	50	Ba
Horham	99	Ba
Horkesley, Gt.	78	Da
Horkesley, Lit.	78	Da
Horkstow	176	Db
Horley, *Oxon.*	92	Ca
Horley, *Sur.*	42	Cb
Hormead	76	Ca
Hornblotton	35	Aa
Hornblotton Green	35	Aa
Hornby, *Lancs.*	180	Da
Hornby, *Yorks.*	197	Aa
Hornby, *Yorks.*	196	Db
Horncastle	153	Ba
Hornchurch	58	Db
Horncliffe	243	Ba
Horndean	243	Aa
Horndean, *Hants.*	39	Bc
Horndon	8	Da
Horndon-on-the-Hill	59	Ab
Horne	42	Cb
Horner	48	Cb
Horning	138	Cc
Horninghold	131	Bc
Horninglow	148	Dc
Horningsea	96	Da
Horningsham	36	Ca
Horningsheath	98	Cb
Horningtoft	136	Da
Hornsby	218	Cc
Hornsea	178	Ca
Hornsey	57	Ba
Hornton	92	Ca
Horrabridge	8	Da
Horrington, E.	50	Dc
Horrington, W.	50	Dc
Horsebridge	38	Ca
Horsecastle	50	Ca
Horseheath	97	Ac
Horse House	195	Bc
Horsell	41	Ba
Horsenden	73	Bb
Horsepath	72	Cb
Horsepool	52	Ca
Horsey	138	Db
Horsford	137	Bc
Horsforth	183	Bc
Horsham	24	Ca
Horsham St. Faith	137	Bc
Horsington, *Lincs.*	153	Aa
Horsington, *Som.*	35	Bc
Horsley, *Derby*	149	Ab
Horsley, *Glos.*	69	Bb
Horsley, *N'land.*	221	Ab
Horsley, E.	41	Bb
Horsley, W.	41	Ab
Horsley Woodhouse	149	Ab
Horsmonden	44	Cc
Horstead	137	Bc
Horsted Keynes	25	Aa
Horsted, Lit.	25	Ab
Horton, *Bucks.*	74	Ca
Horton, *Bucks.*	56	Da
Horton, *Dors.*	19	Aa
Horton, *Glam.*	64	Ca
Horton, *Glos.*	69	Bc
Horton, *N'hants.*	93	Da
Horton, *Oxon.*	73	Aa
Horton, *Shrops.*	126	Ca
Horton, *Staffs.*	147	Aa
Horton, *Wilts.*	52	Db
Horton, *Yorks.*	182	Cb

Name	Page	Sq.
Horton, Gt.	172	Da
Horton-in-Ribblesdale	182	Ca
Horton Kirby	58	Dc
Horwich	170	Db
Horwood	30	Cb
Horwood, Gt.	93	Bb
Horwood, Lit.	93	Bb
Hose	150	Dc
Hosh	259	Ba
Hotham	176	Ca
Hothfield	45	Ac
Hoton	130	Ca
Hough-on-the-Hill	151	Ba
Hougham, *Kent*	28	Da
Hougham, *Lincs.*	151	Bb
Hougham, West	28	Ca
Houghton, *Cumb.*	217	Db
Houghton, *Hunts.*	95	Ba
Houghton, *Pem.*	62	Cb
Houghton, *Sus.*	23	Ab
Houghton Conquest	94	Db
Houghton, Gt., *N'hants.*	113	Ac
Houghton, Gt., *Yorks.*	174	Cc
Houghton, Lit., *N'hants.*	113	Bc
Houghton, Lit., *Yorks.*	174	Cc
Houghton-le-Spring	222	Cc
Houghton, Long	232	Ca
Houghton-on-the-Hill	130	Db
Houghton Regis	94	Dc
Houghton St. Giles	136	Ca
Hound	21	Aa
Houndsmoor	33	Ab
Houndstreet	51	Ab
Houndwood	254	Cb
Hounslow	57	Ac
Houston	248	Cb
Houstry	318	Ca
Hove	24	Dc
Hove Edge	172	Ba
Hoveringham	150	Db
Hoveton St. John	138	Ca
Hovingham	198	Cc
How	218	Cc
How Caple	88	Db
Howden	175	Ba
Howden le Wear	206	Db
Howe, *Caith.*	324	Ca
Howe, *Cumb.*	193	Ab
Howe, *Norf.*	119	Ba
Howe, East	19	Bb
Howe, West	19	Bb
Howell	152	Db
Howick, *Lancs.*	170	Ca
Howick, *N'land.*	232	Da
Howlsike	198	Da
Hownam	242	Dc
Howsell, Lr.	89	Ba
Howsell, Upr.	89	Ba
Howsham, *Lincs.*	176	Dc
Howsham, *Yorks.*	186	Ca
How Street	77	Bb
Howtel	243	Ab
Hoxne	99	Ba
Hoxton	58	Cb
Hoylake	159	Aa
Hoyland Nether	173	Bc
Hoyland Swaine	173	Bc
Hubberston	61	Bb
Huby, *Yorks.*	185	Aa
Huby, *Yorks.*	184	Cb
Hucclecote	90	Cc
Hucking	44	Da
Hucklow, Gt.	163	Ab
Hucklow, Lit.	163	Ab
Hucknall Torkard	150	Db
Huddersfield	172	Db
Huddington	109	Bc
Hudnalls	68	Da
Hudswell	196	Ca
Huggate	186	Db
Hugglescote	129	Bb
Hughenden	74	Cb
Hughley	125	Bc
Huish, *Dev.*	31	Ab
Huish, *Wilts.*	53	Ab
Huish Champflower	48	Dc
Huish Episcopi	34	Cb
Hulcott	74	Ca
Hull	176	Da
Hulland	148	Db
Hullavington	70	Ca
Hullbridge	60	Cb
Hulme, *Lancs.*	161	Aa
Hulme, *Lancs.*	160	Ba
Hulme, *Staffs.*	146	Db
Hulme End	148	Ca
Hulme, Upr.	147	Ba
Hulton, Lit.	170	Dc
Hulver Street	136	Cc
Humber	108	Cc
Humberston	167	Ba
Humberstone	130	Db
Humbleton, *N'land.*	243	Dc
Humbleton, *Yorks.*	178	Cb
Humby	152	Cc
Hume	242	Cb
Humshaugh	220	Ca
Huna	324	Da
Huncoat	171	Aa
Huncote	130	Ca
Hunderthwaite	206	Cb
Hundleby	154	Cb
Hundleton	62	Cb
Hundon	97	Bc
Hundred House	104	Da
Hungarton	130	Db
Hungerford, *Berks.*	54	Cb
Hungerford, *Berks.*	54	Cb
Hungerford, *Hants.*	37	Bc
Hungerford, Lit.	54	Da
Hungerford Newtown	54	Ca
Hunmanby	188	Ca
Hunningham	111	Bb
Hunsdon	76	Cb
Hunsingore	184	Db
Hunsonby	204	Ca
Hunstanton	135	Aa
Hunstanworth	220	Dc
Hunston, *Suff.*	98	Ca
Hunston, *Sus.*	22	Da
Hunsworth	173	Aa
Hunter's Quay	247	Ab
Huntham	34	Cb
Huntingdon, *Herefs.*	106	Dc
Huntingdon, *Hunts.*	95	Ba
Huntingfield	100	Ba
Huntingford	36	Ca
Huntington, *Herefs.*	88	Ca
Huntington, *Yorks.*	185	Bb
Huntley	89	Bc
Huntly	304	Cc
Hunton, *Kent*	44	Cb
Hunton, *Yorks.*	196	Ba
Huntscott	48	Cb
Huntsham	32	Da
Huntshaw	30	Cc
Huntspill	34	Ca
Huntworth	34	Cb
Hunwick	206	Db
Hunworth	137	Aa
Hurcot	34	Cb
Hurdcott	37	Bb
Hurdsfield	162	Cb
Hurlet	248	Dc
Hurley	56	Ca
Hurlford	236	Db
Hursley	38	Db
Hurst, *Berks.*	55	Ba
Hurst, *Yorks.*	195	Ba
Hurstbourne Priors	38	Da
Hurstbourne Tarrant	54	Cc
Hurst Green, *Lancs.*	181	Bc
Hurst Green, *Sus.*	26	Ca
Hurst Hill	127	Ac
Hurstpierpoint	24	Db
Hurworth	207	Ca
Hury	205	Bc
Husbands Bosworth	112	Da
Husborne Crawley	94	Db
Husthwaite	197	Bc
Huthwaite, *Notts.*	149	Ba
Huthwaite, *Yorks.*	196	Ba
Huttoft	154	Da
Hutton, *Berw.*	243	Aa
Hutton, *Cumb.*	203	Bb
Hutton, *Dumf.*	227	Bc
Hutton, *Essex*	59	Aa
Hutton, *Lancs.*	170	Ca
Hutton, *Som.*	49	Bb
Hutton, *Yorks.*	187	Bc
Hutton Bonville	197	Ca
Hutton Bushel	187	Ba
Hutton Conyers	197	Ac
Hutton Henry	208	Ca
Hutton, High	186	Ca
Hutton-le-Hole	198	Db
Hutton, Low	186	Ca
Hutton Magna	206	Dc
Hutton Roof	193	Bc
Hutton Rudby	197	Ba
Hutton Sessay	197	Bc
Huxham	32	Dc
Huxham Green	35	Aa
Huxley	160	Ca
Huyton	160	Ba
Hyde, *Herefs.*	107	Bc
Hyde, *Ches.*	162	Ca
Hykeham, N.	166	Cc
Hykeham, S.	166	Cc
Hylton, N.	222	Dc
Hylton, S.	222	Dc
Hyssington	124	Dc
Hythe, *Hants.*	21	Aa
Hythe, *Kent*	28	Ca
Hythe, West	28	Ca
IBBERTON	36	Cc
Ibsley	19	Ba
Ibstock	129	Bb
Ibstone	73	Bc
Ibthorpe	54	Cc
Ibworth	54	Dc
Icelton	50	Cb
Ickburgh	117	Bb
Ickenham	57	Ab
Ickford	73	Aa
Ickham	46	Cb
Ickleford	75	Ac
Icklesham	27	Ac
Ickleton	96	Cc
Icklingham	97	Ba
Ickwell Green	95	Ac
Icomb	91	Ac
Idbury	91	Bc
Iddesleigh	31	Ab
Ideford	14	Cc
Iden	27	Ab
Iden Green	26	Cc
Idle	183	Bc
Idlicote	91	Ba
Idmiston	37	Ba
Idridgehay	148	Da
Idrigill	295	Bb
Idstone	71	Bc
Iffley	72	Db
Ifield	42	Cc
Iford, *Hants.*	19	Bb
Iford, *Sus.*	25	Ab
Ifton	68	Cc
Ifton Heath	144	Cc
Ightfield	145	Bb
Ightham	43	Ba
Iken	100	Cc
Ilam	148	Ca
Ilchester	34	Dc
Ilderton	243	Dc
Ilford	58	Cb
Ilfracombe	30	Ca
Ilkeston	149	Bb
Ilketshall St. Andrew	120	Cc
Ilketshall St. John	120	Cc
Ilketshall St. Lawrence	120	Cc
Ilketshall St. Margaret	120	Cc
Ilkley	183	Ab
Illey	109	Ba
Illington	118	Cb
Illingworth	172	Ba
Illogan	2	Ca
Ilston-on-the-Hill	130	Dc
Ilmer	73	Bb
Ilmington	91	Ba
Ilminster	16	Ca
Ilsington	14	Cc
Ilsley, E.	54	Da
Ilsley, W.	54	Da
Ilston	64	Dc
Ilton, *Som.*	34	Cc
Ilton, *Yorks.*	196	Dc
Imber	52	Cc
Immingham	167	Ba
Impington	96	Da
Ince, *Ches.*	160	Cb
Ince, *Lancs.*	170	Ca
Ince Blundell	169	Ac
Inch	209	Aa
Inchbare	281	Bc
Inchberry	300	Dc
Inchinnan	248	Db
Inchkeith	251	Ba
Inchmarnock	246	Cc
Inchnadamff	314	Cb
Inchture	271	Ac
Ingatestone	59	Aa
Ingbirchworth	173	Ac
Ingestre	147	Ac
Ingham, *Lincs.*	166	Cb
Ingham, *Norf.*	138	Ca
Ingham, *Suff.*	98	Ca
Ingleby	148	Dc
Ingleby Arncliffe	197	Ba
Ingleby Cross	197	Ba
Ingleby Greenhow	198	Ca
Inglesham	71	Aa
Inglesham, Upr.	71	Bb
Ingleton, *Dur.*	206	Dc
Ingleton, *Yorks.*	194	Dc
Inglewhite	180	Dc
Inglistown	293	Bb
Ingoe	220	Da
Ingoldisthorpe	135	Ab
Ingoldmells	154	Da
Ingoldsby	152	Cc
Ingram	231	Ba
Ingrave	59	Aa
Ingrow	183	Ac
Ingst	68	Dc
Ingthorpe	132	Cb
Ingworth	137	Bb
Inhurst	54	Db
Inkberrow	110	Cc
Inkpen	54	Cb
Innellan	246	Db
Innerleithen	240	Db
Innermessan	211	Bb
Innerwick, *E. Loth.*	253	Bb
Innerwick, *Perth*	268	Cb
Insch	293	Aa
Inskip	180	Cc
Instow	30	Cb
Intake	164	Cb
Intwood	119	Aa
Inver Alligin	297	Ba
Inverallochy	306	Da
Inverarity	271	Bb
Inveraray	256	Db
Inverbervie	282	Cc
Invercassley	310	Da
Inverchaolain	246	Db
Inveresk	252	Cb
Invergordon	301	Aa
Inverharity	279	Bc
Inverichnie	305	Aa
Inverie	273	Ba
Inverkeilor	272	Da
Inverkeithing	251	Aa
Inverkip	247	Ab
Inverkirkaig	313	Bb
Inverness	300	Dc
Invershiel	286	Cb
Inversnaid	257	Bb
Inverurie	293	Bb
Inwardleigh	31	Ac
Inworth	78	Cb
Iping	40	Cc
Ipplepen	10	Ca
Ippollitts	75	Ba
Ipsden	73	Ac
Ipstones	147	Ba
Ipswich	79	Ba
Irby	159	Ab
Irby-in-the-Marsh	154	Cb
Irby-upon-Humber	167	Ba
Irchester	113	Bc
Ireby	202	Ca
Ireleth	192	Cc
Ireshopeburn	205	Ba
Ireton Wood	148	Db
Irlam, Higher	161	Aa
Irlam, Lower	161	Aa
Irnham	132	Ca
Iron Acton	69	Ac
Ironbridge	126	Cb
Iron Cross	110	Cc
Irongray	215	Ba
Ironville	149	Ba
Irthington	218	Cb
Irthlingborough	114	Cb
Irvine	236	Cb
Isauld	322	Da
Isfield	25	Ab
Isham	113	Bb
Isle Abbotts	34	Cc
Isle Brewers	34	Cc
Iselham	97	Aa
Isle Ornsay	285	Ac
Isley Walton	129	Ba
Islington	57	Bb
Islip, *N'hants.*	114	Cb
Islip, *Oxon.*	72	Da
Itchen	21	Aa
Itchen Abbas	39	Ab
Itchenor, W.	22	Da
Itchen Stoke	39	Ab
Itchingfield	23	Ba
Itchington	69	Ac
Itchington, Long	111	Bc
Itteringham	137	Ab
Itton, *Dev.*	31	Bc
Itton, *Mon.*	68	Cb
Ivegill	203	Ba
Iver	56	Da
Iver Heath	56	Da
Iveston	221	Bc
Ivinghoe	74	Da
Ivybridge	9	Ba
Ivychurch	27	Bb
Iwade	60	Cc
Iwerne Courtney	36	Cc
Iwerne Minster	36	Cc
Ixworth	98	Da
Ixworth Thorpe	98	Ca
JACKSON BRIDGE	172	Dc

Place	Page	Sq.
Jacobstow	11	Bb
Jacobstowe	31	Ac
Jameston	62	Dc
Jamestown	248	Ca
Janetstown	323	Ab
Jarrow	222	Cb
Jaspers Green	77	Bb
Jeantown or Lochcarron	286	Ca
Jedburgh	242	Cc
Jefferysgreen	24	Da
Jeffreston	62	Db
Jemimaville	301	Aa
Jevington	25	Bc
Johnby	203	Bb
John O' Groat's House	324	Da
Johnshaven	282	Cc
Johnston	62	Cb
Johnstone, Dumf.	227	Ac
Johnstone, Renf.	248	Cc
Johns Town	63	Ba
Joppa	252	Cb
Jordanston	81	Bb
Joyford	68	Da
Jugbank	146	Cc
Jump	174	Cc
Juniper Green	251	Bb
Jurby	189	Ab
KABER	205	Ac
Kames	246	Cb
Kea	2	Da
Keal Coates	154	Cb
Keal, E.	154	Cb
Keal, W.	154	Cb
Kearsley	171	Ac
Kearton	195	Ba
Keddington	168	Cc
Kedington	97	Bc
Kedleston	148	Db
Keelby	167	Aa
Keevil	52	Cb
Kegworth	149	Bc
Keig	293	Ab
Keighley	183	Ac
Keillor	271	Ab
Keinton Mandeville	35	Aa
Keisby	152	Cc
Keiss	324	Db
Keith	304	Cb
Kelbrook	182	Cc
Kelby	152	Cb
Keid	195	Aa
Keldholme	198	Db
Kelfield	185	Bc
Kelham	151	Aa
Kelk, Gt.	188	Cc
Keilacott	12	Cc
Kellaways	52	Ca
Kellet, Nether	180	Da
Kellet, Over	180	Da
Kelleth	194	Ca
Kelling	137	Aa
Kellingley	174	Da
Kelling Stree	137	Aa
Kellington	174	Da
Kells	214	Ca
Kelly	8	Ca
Kelmarsh	113	Aa
Kelmscot	71	Bb
Kelsale	100	Cb
Kelsall	160	Cc
Kelsey, N.	176	Dc
Kelsey, S.	166	Da
Kelshall	76	Ca
Kelsick	216	Dc
Kelso	242	Cb
Kelstern	167	Bc
Kelston	51	Aa
Kelton, Dumf.	216	Ca
Kelton, Kirk.	214	Db
Kelty	260	Dc
Kelvedon	78	Cb
Kelvedon Hatch	59	Aa
Kemberton	126	Db
Kemble	70	Db
Kemerton	90	Cb
Kemeys Commander	67	Ba
Kemeys Inferior	68	Cb
Kemnay	293	Bb
Kempley	89	Ab
Kempley Green	89	Ab
Kempsey	90	Ca
Kempsford	71	Ab
Kempston	94	Da
Kempstone	136	Cc
Kempton	107	Aa
Kemsing	43	Aa
Kenardington	27	Ba
Kenchester	88	Ca
Kencott	71	Bb
Kendal	193	Bb
Kendrom	296	Ca
Kenfig	65	Bb
Kenfig Hill	65	Bb
Kenilworth	111	Ab
Kenley	125	Bc
Kenmore	268	Db
Kenn, Dev.	14	Da
Kenn, Som.	50	Ca
Kennerleigh	32	Cb
Kennett	97	Ba
Kennett, E.	53	Ab
Kennett, W.	53	Ab
Kennford	14	Da
Kenninghall	118	Dc
Kennington, Berks.	72	Db
Kennington, Kent	45	Ac
Kennington, London	57	Bb
Kennoway	261	Bb
Kennyhill	117	Ac
Kennythorpe	186	Ca
Kensalroag	295	Bc
Kensington	57	Bb
Kensworth	74	Da
Kentchurch	88	Cc
Kentford	97	Ba
Kentisbeare	15	Aa
Kentisbury	30	Da
Kentish Town	57	Bb
Kenton, Dev.	14	Db
Kenton, M'sex.	57	Aa
Kenton, N'land.	212	Bb
Kenton, Suff.	99	Bb
Kentra	273	Bc
Kent Street	43	Ba
Kents Green	89	Bc
Kenwyn	2	Da
Kenyon	160	Da
Kepwick	197	Bb
Keresley	111	Aa
Kerris	1	Bc
Kerry	106	Ca
Kersall	150	Da
Kersey	79	Aa
Kerswell	15	Aa
Kerswell Green	90	Ca
Kesgrave	79	Ba
Kessingland	120	Da
Kestle	4	Da
Keston	42	Da
Keston Mark	42	Da
Keswick, Cumb.	202	Db
Keswick, Norf.	119	Ba
Keswick, E.	184	Cc
Ketley	126	Cb
Ketleybank	126	Cb
Ketsby	154	Cb
Kettering	113	Ba
Ketteringham	119	Aa
Kettins	270	Db
Kettlebaston	98	Dc
Kettlebrook	128	Db
Kettleburgh	99	Bb
Kettleness	199	Ba
Kettleshulme	162	Cb
Kettlesing Bottom	183	Bb
Kettlestone	136	Db
Kettlethorpe	165	Bb
Kettlewell	182	Da
Ketton	132	Cb
Kew	57	Ab
Kewstoke	49	Bb
Kexbrough	173	Bc
Kexby, Lincs.	166	Cb
Kexby, Yorks.	185	Bb
Keyford	51	Bc
Keyham	130	Db
Keyhaven	20	Db
Keyingham	178	Cc
Keymer	24	Db
Keynsham	51	Aa
Keysoe	95	Aa
Keys Toft	154	Db
Keyston	114	Cb
Key Street	44	Da
Keyworth	150	Cc
Kibblesworth	222	Cc
Kibworth Beauchamp	130	Dc
Kibworth Harcourt	130	Dc
Kiddal Lane End	184	Dc
Kiddemore Green	127	Ab
Kidderminster	109	Aa
Kidlington	92	Cc
Kidlington	72	Da
Kidmore End	55	Ba
Kidsgrove	146	Da
Kidwelly	63	Bb
Kilbarchan	248	Cc
Kilbeg	285	Ac
Kilbirnie	236	Ca
Kilbride	255	Ba
Kilburn, Derby	149	Ab
Kilburn, London	57	Bb
Kilburn, Yorks.	197	Bc
Kilburn, High	197	Bc
Kilby	130	Dc
Kilcalmonell and Kilberry	245	Ac
Kilchattan	246	Dc
Kilchenzie	233	Ac
Kilchoan	263	Ba
Kilchrenan	256	Ca
Kilconquhar	262	Cb
Kilcot	89	Ac
Kilcreggan	247	Ba
Kildale	208	Dc
Kildwick	182	Bc
Kilfinan	246	Cb
Kilgetty	62	Db
Kilham, N'land.	242	Db
Kilham, Yorks.	188	Cb
Kilkhampton	11	Ba
Killamarsh	164	Cb
Killay	64	Dc
Killean	233	Aa
Killearn	248	Da
Killerby	206	Dc
Killichonan	268	Ca
Killiecrankie	269	Ba
Killilan	286	Ca
Killin	268	Cc
Killinghall	184	Cb
Killingholme, N.	177	Bc
Killingholme, S.	177	Bc
Killingworth	222	Ca
Kilmacolm	248	Cb
Kilmaluag	29	Ca
Kilmany	261	Ba
Kilmarnock	236	Db
Kilmaronock	248	Ca
Kilmartin	255	Bb
Kilmaurs	236	Db
Kilmelfort	255	Bb
Kilmersdon	51	Ac
Kilmeston	39	Ab
Kilmichael Glassary	245	Ba
Kilmington, Dev.	16	Cb
Kilmington, Wills.	36	Ca
Kilmington Common	36	Ca
Kilmington Street	36	Ca
Kilmodan	246	Ca
Kilmonivaig	275	Bb
Kilmorack	300	Cc
Kilmore, Argyll	255	Ba
Kilmore, Inver.	285	Ac
Kilmory, Argyll	245	Ab
Kilmory, Bute	234	Dc
Kilmster	324	Cb
Kilmuir, R. & C.	312	Cc
Kilmuir, R. & C.	301	Ab
Kilmuir, R. & C.	295	Bb
Kilmun	247	Aa
Kilncadzow	238	Da
Kilndown	44	Cc
Kilnhurst	164	Ca
Kilninian	263	Ab
Kilninver	255	Ba
Kilnsea	168	Ca
Kilnsey	182	Da
Kilnwick	177	Aa
Kilnwick Percy	186	Cb
Kilpatrick, Old	248	Cb
Kilpeck	88	Cb
Kilpin	175	Ba
Kilrenny	262	Db
Kilsby	112	Cb
Kilspindie	270	Db
Kilsyth	249	Ba
Kiltarlity	300	Cc
Kiltearn	300	Da
Kilton	33	Ba
Kilwinning	236	Ca
Kilworth, N.	112	Da
Kilworth, S.	112	Da
Kilvaxter	295	Ba
Kilve	33	Aa
Kilverstone	118	Cc
Kilvington	151	Bb
Kilvington, N.	197	Bb
Kilvington, S.	197	Bb
Kimberley, Norf.	118	Da
Kimberley, Notts.	149	Bb
Kimberworth	164	Ca
Kimble, Gt.	74	Cb
Kimble, Lit.	74	Cb
Kimblesworth	222	Cc
Kimble Wick	73	Ba
Kimbolton, Herefs.	107	Bc
Kimbolton, Hunts.	95	Aa
Kimcote	112	Ca
Kimmeridge	18	Dc
Kimpton, Hants.	38	Ca
Kimpton, Herts.	75	Ab
Kincardine, Fife	250	Ca
Kincardine, R. & C.	311	Ab
Kincardine O'Neil	293	Ac
Kinelaven	270	Db
Kincraig	289	Dc
Kineton, Glos.	90	Db
Kineton, War.	91	Ba
Kingarth	246	Dc
Kingcoed	68	Ca
Kincombe, Higher	17	Aa
Kincombe, Lower	17	Aa
Kingerby	166	Da
Kingham	91	Bc
Kingholm Quay	215	Ba
Kinghorn	251	Ba
Kinglassie	261	Ba
Kingsand	8	Cc
Kingsbarns	262	Da
Kingsbridge	10	Cb
King's Bromley	128	Cb
Kingsburgh	296	Cb
Kingsbury	128	Cb
Kingsbury Episcopi	34	Dc
Kingsbury Green.	57	Ab
King's Caple	88	Db
Kingsclere	54	Cb
Kings Cliffe	132	Cc
Kingscote	69	Bb
Kingscott	30	Cc
Kingsdon	34	Cb
Kingsdown, Kent.	43	Ba
Kingsdown, Kent.	44	Da
Kingsdown, Kent.	46	Dc
Kingsdown, Wilts.	71	Ac
Kingsdown, Wilts.	51	Ba
Kingsey	73	Bb
Kingsfold	41	Bc
Kingsford	109	Aa
Kings Green	89	Bb
Kings Heath	110	Ca
Kingskerswell	14	Cc
Kingskettle	261	Bb
Kingsland, Cambs.	115	Ba
Kingsland, Herefs.	107	Bc
Kings Langley	75	Ac
Kings Meaburn	204	Db
Kingsmuir	271	Bb
King's Newnham	111	Ba
Kings Newton	129	Ba
Kingsnorth	27	Ba
Kingsnorth Pound	27	Ba
Kings Norton, Leics.	130	Dc
Kings Norton, War.	110	Ca
Kings Nympton	31	Ab
Kings Pyon	88	Ca
Kings Ripton	115	Bc
Kings Somborne	38	Db
Kings Stanley	69	Bb
Kings Sutton	92	Ba
Kingsteignton	14	Cb
Kingsthorpe	113	Ac
Kingston, Cambs.	96	Cb
Kingston, Dev.	9	Bb
Kingston, Dors.	19	Ac
Kingston, Dors.	36	Cc
Kingston, Hants.	21	Ac
Kingston, Hants.	19	Ba
Kingston, Kent.	46	Dc
Kingston, Moray.	303	Ba
Kingston, Som.	33	Cb
Kingston, Staffs.	147	Bc
Kingston, Sus.	23	Bc
Kingston, Sus.	24	Dc
Kingston Bagpuze	72	Cb
Kingston Blount	73	Bb
Kingston-by-Sea	24	Cb
Kingstone Deverill	36	Ca
Kingstone, Herefs.	88	Cb
Kingstone, Som.	16	Ca
Kingston Lisle	71	Bb
Kingston-on-Thames	50	Bc
Kingston St. Mary	33	Bb
Kingston Seymour	50	Ca
Kingston-upon-Soar	149	Bc
Kingstown	217	Bb
King Street	55	Bb
Kings Walden	75	Ab
Kingswear	10	Db
Kingswinford	127	Ac
Kingswood, Glos.	51	Aa
Kingswood, Glos.	69	Bb
Kingswood, Sur.	42	Ca
Kings Worthy	38	Cb
Kingthorpe	153	Aa
Kington, Glos.	68	Db
Kington, Herefs.	106	Dc
Kington, Worcs.	109	Bc
Kington Langley	52	Ca
Kington Magna	36	Cb
Kington St. Michael	52	Ca

Name	Page	SQ
ington, W.	51	Ba
ingussie	289	Bc
ingweston	34	Db
inkry Hill	218	Ca
inloch	270	Db
inloch Bervie	319	Dc
inlochewe	298	Ca
inlochleven	266	Da
inloch Rannoch	268	Db
inloss	302	Da
innaird	270	Dc
inneff	282	Db
innell	272	Ca
innerley, *Herefs.*	87	Ba
innersley, *Shrops.*	126	Ca
innersley, *Worcs.*	90	Ca
innerton, Lr.	159	Bc
inoulton	150	Dc
inross	260	Db
insham, *Herefs.*	107	Ab
insham, *Worcs.*	90	Cb
insley	174	Cb
inson	19	Bb
intbury	54	Cb
inton	124	Da
intore	293	Bb
inver	109	Aa
inwarton	110	Cc
iplin	196	Ca
ippax	174	Ca
ippen	253	Dc
irbean	215	Bb
irby	197	Ba
irby, E.	149	Ba
irby Grindalythe	186	Da
irby Hill, *Yorks.*	196	Ca
irby Hill, *Yorks.*	184	Da
irby Knowle	197	Bb
irby-le-Soken	79	Bc
irby Muxloe	198	Dc
irby Row	120	Cb
irby Sigston	197	Ab
irby, Upr.	79	Bc
irby Wiske	197	Ab
iridford	23	Ba
irlandrews-upon-Eden	217	Bb
irkbampton	217	Ac
irk Braithwaite	174	Db
irkbride	216	Db
irkburn	187	Bc
irkburton	173	Ab
irkby	169	Bc
irkby-cum-Osgodby	166	Da
irkby, E.	153	Bb
irkby Fleetham	196	Db
irkby Green	152	Da
irkby-in-Ashfield	149	Ba
irkby-la-Thorpe	152	Db
irkby Lonsdale	194	Cc
irkby Malham	182	Ca
irkby Mallory	129	Bc
irkby Malzeard	196	Dc
irkby Moorside	198	Db
irkby-on-Bain	153	Bb
irkby Overblow	184	Cb
irkby, S.	174	Cb
irkby Stephen	194	Ca
irkby Thore	204	Cb
irkby Underdale	186	Cb
irkby Underwood	132	Da
irkby Wharfe	185	Ac
irkcaldy	261	Bc
irkcambeck	218	Cb
irkcolm	211	Ab
irkconnel	225	Ba
irkcowan	212	Db
irkcudbright	214	Cc
irkdale	159	Ba
irk Deighton	184	Da
irk Ella	176	Da
irkfieldbank	238	Cb
irk Gill	195	Ac
irkgunzeon	215	Ab
irk Hallam	149	Bb
irkham, *Lancs.*	169	Da
irkham, *Yorks.*	186	Ca
irkham Gate	173	Bb
irk Hammerton	184	Db
irkharle	220	Da
irkheaton,*N'land.*	220	Da
irkhenton,*Yorks.*	173	Ab
irkhill	300	Db
irkhill of Kennethmont	292	Da
irkhouse Green	175	Ab
irkinner	210	Da
irkintilloch	249	Ab
Kirk Ireton	148	Ba
Kirkland *Cumb.*	201	Bc
Kirkland *Cumb.*	204	Cb
Kirk Langley	148	Db
Kirkleatham	199	Aa
Kirk Leavington	208	Cc
Kirkley	120	Db
Kirklington, *Notts.*	150	Da
Kirklington, *Yorks.*	196	Da
Kirklinton	218	Cb
Kirkliston	251	Ab
Kirkmahoe	226	Dc
Kirkmaiden	209	Ab
Kirk Merrington	207	Ab
Kirkmichael, *Ayr.*	224	Ca
Kirkmichael, *Dumf.*	227	Ac
Kirkmichael, *I.O.M.*	189	Bb
Kirkmichael, *Perth*	270	Ca
Kirknewton, *M. Loth.*	251	Ab
Kirknewton, *N'land.*	243	Bc
Kirkney	292	Da
Kirk of Shotts	250	Cc
Kirkoswald, *Ayr*	223	Ba
Kirkoswald, *Cumb.*	204	Ca
Kirkpatrick	217	Aa
Kirkpatrick Durham	214	Da
Kirkpatrick Juxta	227	Ab
Kirk Sandall	174	Dc
Kirksanton	191	Bc
Kirk Smeaton	174	Db
Kirkstall	184	Cc
Kirkstead, *Derby.*	149	Ba
Kirkstead, *Lincs.*	153	Da
Kirkstile	228	Dc
Kirkthorpe	173	Bb
Kirkton, R. & C.	297	Dc
Kirkton, *Roz.*	229	Aa
Kirkton End	133	Ba
Kirkton-in-Lindsey	166	Ca
Kirkton of Auchterhouse	271	Ab
Kirkton of Auchterless	305	Ac
Kirkton of Culsalmond	293	Aa
Kirkton of Durris	282	Ca
Kirkton of Glenisla	270	Da
Kirkton of Kingoldrum	271	Aa
Kirkton of Lethendy	270	Cb
Kirkton of Lochalsh	285	Bb
Kirkton of Logie Buchan	294	Da
Kirkton of Menmuir	281	Ac
Kirkton of Slains	294	Da
Kirkton of Strathmartine	271	Bc
Kirkton of Tealing	271	Bb
Kirktown of Alvah	305	Aa
Kirktown of Bourtie	293	Ba
Kirktown of Clatt	292	Da
Kirktown of Deskford	304	Ca
Kirktown of Rayne	293	Aa
Kirkurd	239	Ba
Kirkwhelpington	231	Bc
Kirk Yetholm	242	Dc
Kirmington	167	Aa
Kirmond-le-Mire	167	Bb
Kirn	247	Ab
Kirriemuir	271	Ba
Kirstead	119	Bb
Kirstead Green	119	Bb
Kirtle Bridge	216	Da
Kirtling	97	Ab
Kirtlington	92	Dc
Kirtomy	321	Ba
Kirton, *Lincs.*	133	Ba
Kirton, *Notts.*	165	Ac
Kirton, *Suff.*	80	Ca
Kisdon	195	Aa
Kislingbury	112	Da
Kites Hardwick	112	Cb
Kittisford	33	Ac
Kitts Green	110	Da
Kittybrewster	294	Cc
Kiveton Park	164	Cb
Knapdale, N.	245	Ab
Knapdale, S.	245	Ab
Knaphill	41	Aa
Knapp	34	Cb
Knapp Hill	38	Db
Knaptoft	112	Da
Knapton, *Norf.*	138	Ca
Knapton, *Yorks.*	185	Ab
Knapton, *Yorks.*	187	Ab
Knapton Green	107	Bc
Knapwell	96	Ca
Knaresborough	184	Ca
Knayton	197	Bb
Kneadby	176	Cb
Knebworth	75	Bb
Knedlington	175	Ba
Kneesall	165	Ac
Kneesworth	96	Cc
Kneeton	150	Db
Knelston	64	Cc
Knettishall	118	Cc
Knightcote	92	Ca
Knighton, *Dors.*	35	Ac
Knighton, *Leics.*	130	Cc
Knighton, *Rad.*	106	Db
Knighton, *Som.*	33	Ba
Knighton, *Staffs.*	146	Cb
Knighton, *Staffs.*	146	Cc
Knighton, East	18	Cb
Knighton, West	18	Cb
Knights Enham	54	Cc
Knill	106	Dc
Knipton	151	Bc
Kniveton	148	Ca
Knockan	314	Cc
Knockdee	323	Bb
Knockdown	69	Bc
Knockhoe	295	Ba
Knockholt	43	Aa
Knockin	124	Da
Knoddishall	100	Db
Knole	34	Db
Knossington	131	Ba
Knotting	114	Cc
Knotting Green	114	Cc
Knottingley	174	Da
Knowbury	108	Cb
Knowle, *Dev.*	30	Cb
Knowle, *Glos.*	50	Ca
Knowle, *Som.*	34	Ca
Knowle, *War.*	110	Da
Knowlehill	56	Db
Knowle St. Giles	16	Ca
Knowle Top	163	Ba
Knowl Hill	56	Ca
Knowlton, *Dors.*	19	Aa
Knowlton, *Kent*	46	Cb
Knowsley	160	Ca
Knowstono	32	Ca
Knowstone, E.	32	Ca
Knoyle, E.	36	Da
Knoyle, W.	36	Da
Knutsford	101	Ab
Knutton	146	Db
Kyleakin	285	Bb
Kyle of Lochalsh	285	Bb
Kylerhea	285	Bb
Kyme, N.	152	Da
Kyme, S.	152	Db
Kynaston, *Herefs.*	88	Db
Kynaston, *Shrops.*	124	Da
LACEBY	167	Ba
Lacey Green	74	Ca
Lach Dennis	161	Ac
Lackford	97	Ba
Lacock	52	Ca
Ladbroke	111	Bc
Lade Bank	154	Cc
Ladock	5	Bc
Ladybank	261	Bb
Ladybarn	161	Ba
Ladykirk	242	Da
Laggan, S.	276	Ca
Lairg	311	Aa
Lake	30	Cb
Lake Lock	173	Ba
Lakenheath	117	Ac
Lakes End	116	Db
Laleham	56	Db
Laleston	65	Bb
Lamarsh	78	Ca
Lamas	137	Bb
Lamberhead Green	170	Ca
Lamberhurst	43	Bc
Lambeth	57	Bb
Lambley	150	Cb
Lambourn	54	Ca
Lambourn, Upr.	53	Ba
Lambourne	58	Da
Lambrook, E.	34	Dc
Lambrook, W.	34	Cc
Lambston	61	Ba
Lamerton	8	Ca
Lamesley	222	Cb
Lamington	238	Db
Lamlash	234	Db
Lamonby	203	Aa
Lamorran	4	Cb
Lampeter	84	Da
Lampeter Velfrey	62	Da
Lamphey	62	Cb
Lamport	113	Ab
Lampton	57	Ab
Lamyatt	35	Ba
Lana	12	Cb
Lanark	238	Da
Lanark, New	238	Da
Lancaster	180	Ca
Lancaut	68	Db
Lanchester	221	Bc
Lancing	24	Cc
Landbeach	96	Ca
Landcross	30	Cc
Landewednac	3	Bc
Landford	38	Cc
Landimore	64	Cc
Landkey	30	Db
Landkey Newland	30	Db
Landore	64	Dc
Landport	21	Ba
Landsend, *Wilts.*	52	Ca
Land's End, *Corn.*	1	Ac
Landshipping Ferry	62	Cb
Landulph	8	Cb
Landwade	97	Aa
Laneast	11	Bc
Lane End, *Bucks.*	73	Bc
Lane-end, *Corn.*	6	Cb
Lane End, *Dors.*	18	Db
Lane End, *Wilts.*	51	Ba
Laneham	165	Bb
Lane Head, *Lancs.*	160	Ca
Lane Head, *Yorks.*	173	Aa
Langbank	248	Cb
Langcliffe	182	Ca
Langdale	192	Da
Langdon, E.	46	Db
Langdon, W.	46	Dc
Langenhoe	78	Db
Langford, *Beds*	95	Ac
Langford, *Essex*	78	Cc
Langford, *Norf.*	117	Bb
Langford, *Notts.*	151	Ba
Langford, *Oxon.*	71	Bb
Langford, *Som.*	33	Bb
Langford Budville	33	Ac
Langford End	95	Ab
Langford, Lit.	37	Aa
Langford, Lr.	50	Cb
Langford, Upr.	50	Cb
Langham, *Dors.*	36	Cb
Langham, *Essex*	78	Ca
Langham, *Norf.*	136	Da
Langham, *Rut.*	131	Bb
Langham, *Suff.*	98	Ca
Langham Moor	78	Da
Langho	170	Da
Langholm	228	Dc
Langley, *Derby*	149	Bb
Langley, *Essex*	76	Da
Langley, *Hunts.*	21	Aa
Langley, *Kent*	44	Cb
Langley, *Norf.*	120	Ca
Langley, *Som.*	33	Ab
Langley, *War.*	110	Db
Langley, *Worcs.*	127	Bc
Langley Burrell	52	Ca
Langley Green	127	Bc
Langley Marsh	33	Ab
Langley Mill	149	Bb
Langley Street	120	Ca
Langport	34	Db
Langridge, *Dev.*	30	Dc
Langridge, *Som.*	51	Ba
Langrigg	202	Ca
Langrish	39	Bb
Langriville	153	Bc
Langsett	173	Ac
Langthorne	196	Db
Langthorpe	184	Da
Langthwaite	195	Ba
Langtoft, *Lincs.*	132	Db
Langtoft, *Yorks.*	187	Bb
Langton, *Dur.*	206	Dc
Langton, *Lincs.*	153	Ba
Langton, *Lincs.*	154	Ca
Langton, *Yorks.*	186	Ca
Langton-by-Wragby	153	Aa
Langton, Gt.	196	Aa
Langton Herring	17	Db
Langton, Lit.	197	Ab
Langton Long Blandford	36	De
Langton Matravers	19	Ac
Langtree	12	Ca
Langwathby	204	Ca
Langwith, Nether	164	Cb
Langwith, Upr.	164	Dc
Langworth	166	Db
Lanivet	6	Cb
Lanlivery	6	Db
Lanner	2	Db
Lanreath	7	Ac
Lansallos	6	Dc
Lanteglos, *Corn.*	6	Da

348

Place	Page	Sq
Lanteglos, *Corn.*	6	Bb
Lapford	31	Dc
Lapley	127	Aa
Lapworth	110	Db
Larbert	250	Ca
Largo	262	Cb
Largs	247	Ac
Larkhall	238	Ca
Larling	118	Cb
Laroch	266	Cc
Lartington	206	Ce
Lasborough	69	Bb
Lasham	39	Ba
Lassington	89	Bc
Lasswade	251	Bb
Lastingham	198	Db
Latcham	34	Da
Latchford	160	Da
Latchingdon	60	Ca
Latchley	8	Ca
Lathbury	94	Ca
Latheron	318	Ca
Latheronwheel	318	Ca
Lathom	169	Bc
Latimer	74	Db
Latteridge	69	Ac
Lattiford	35	Bb
Latton, *Essex*	76	Dc
Latton, *Wilts.*	70	Db
Lauder	241	Ba
Laugharne	63	Aa
Laughterton	165	Bb
Laughton, *Leics.*	112	Da
Laughton, *Lincs.*	165	Ba
Laughton, *Lincs.*	152	Dc
Laughton, *Sus.*	25	Bb
Laughton-en-le-Morthen	164	Da
Launcells	11	Bb
Launceston	12	Cc
Launton	93	Ac
Laurencekirk	282	Cc
Laurieston, *Kirk.*	214	Cb
Laurieston, *Stir.*	250	Ca
Lavant, E.	22	Da
Lavant, Mid.	22	Da
Lavendon	94	Ca
Lavenham	98	Cc
Laver, High	76	Dc
Laver, Lit.	76	Dc
Lavernock	49	Aa
Laverstock	37	Bb
Laverstoke	54	Dc
Laverthorpe	185	Bb
Laverton, *Glos.*	90	Db
Laverton, *Som.*	51	Bc
Laverton, *Yorks.*	196	Bc
Lavington, E.	23	Ab
Lavington W.. *Sus.*	23	Aa
Lavington, W. *Wilts.*	52	Db
Lawers	268	Db
Lawford	79	Ab
Lawford, Lit.	111	Bb
Lawford, Long	111	Bb
Lawhitton	12	Cc
Lawkland	181	Ba
Lawnhead	146	Dc
Lawrenny	62	Cb
Lawshall	98	Cb
Laxey	190	Ca
Laxfield	99	Ba
Laxton, *N'hants.*	132	Cc
Laxton, *Notts.*	175	Ac
Laxton, *Yorks.*	185	Ba
Layer Breton	78	Db
Layer-de-la-Haye	78	Db
Layer Marney	78	Da
Layham	79	Aa
Laymore	16	Da
Laysters	108	Cc
Laysters Pole	108	Cb
Layston	76	Ca
Laytham	186	Cc
Layton	179	Bc
Lazonby	204	Ca
Lea, *Herefs.*	89	Ac
Lea, *Lincs.*	165	Bb
Lea, *Wilts.*	70	Cc
Leadenham	152	Ca
Leaden Roding	77	Ac
Leadgate	221	Bc
Leadhills	226	Da
Leafield	71	Ba
Leagrave	75	Ab
Leake, *Yorks.*	197	Bb
Leake Common Side	154	Cc
Leake, E.	130	Ca
Leake Hurn's End	154	Cc
Leake, W.	150	Cc
Lealholm Bridge	198	Da
Lealt	296	Cb
Lea Marston	128	Dc
Leamington	111	Ac
Leamington Hastings	111	Bb
Leamside	222	Cc
Leasingham	152	Cb
Leatherhead	41	Ba
Leathley	183	Ba
Leaton	125	Ba
Lea Town	169	Ba
Leaveland	45	Ab
Leavening	186	Ca
Lebberston	188	Ca
Lechlade	71	Bb
Leck	194	Cc
Leckford	38	Da
Leckhampstead, *Berks.*	54	Ca
Leckhampstead, *Bucks.*	93	Bb
Leckhampton	90	Cc
Leckmelm	309	Db
Leckwith	49	Aa
Leconfield	177	Aa
Ledbury	89	Ab
Ledgerwood	241	Ba
Ledsham, *Ches.*	159	Bb
Ledsham, *Yorks.*	174	Ca
Ledstone	174	Ca
Ledwell	92	Cc
Lee, *Bucks.*	74	Cb
Lee, *Dev.*	30	Ca
Lee, *Kent*	58	Cc
Leebotwood	125	Dc
Lee Brockhurst	145	Ac
Leece	179	Ba
Lee Clump	74	Cb
Leeds, *Kent*	44	Db
Leeds, *Yorks.*	173	Ba
Leedstown	2	Cb
Leek	147	Ba
Leek Wootton	111	Ab
Leeming, *Yorks.*	172	Ca
Leeming, *Yorks.*	196	Db
Lees	148	Db
Lees Hill	218	Ub
Leeswood	144	Ca
Leftwich Green	161	Ac
Legbourne	168	Cc
Legsby	167	Ac
Leicester	130	Cb
Leigh, *Dors.*	35	Bc
Leigh, *Essex*	60	Cb
Leigh, *Glos.*	90	Db
Leigh, *Kent*	43	Ab
Leigh, *Lancs.*	170	Dc
Leigh, *Sur.*	42	Cb
Leigh, *Wilts.*	70	Db
Leigh Delamere	70	Cc
Leigh Green	27	Aa
Leighland Chapel	48	Cc
Leigh, Lit.	160	Db
Leigh, N.	72	Ca
Leigh, S.	72	Ca
Leigh Sinton	89	Ba
Leighs, Lit.	77	Rb
Leighterton	69	Bb
Leighton, *Mont.*	124	Cb
Leighton, *Shrops.*	126	Cb
Leighton, *Som.*	51	Ac
Leighton Bromswold	114	Db
Leighton Buzzard	94	Cc
Leigh-upon-Mendip	51	Ac
Leinthall Earls	107	Bb
Leinthall Starkes	107	Bb
Leintwardine	107	Ab
Leire	112	Ca
Leiston	100	Db
Leith	251	Bb
Lelley	178	Cb
Lemington, Lr.	91	Bb
Lenchwick	90	Da
Lendalfoot	223	Ac
Lenham	44	Db
Lennel	242	Db
Lennoxtown	249	Ab
Lenshie	305	Ac
Lenton, *Lincs.*	152	Cb
Lenton, *Notts.*	150	Cb
Lenzie	249	Ab
Leominster	107	Bc
Leonard Stanley	69	Ba
Leppington	186	Ca
Lepton	173	Cb
Lerryn	6	Dc
Lesbury	232	Ca
Leslie, *Aber.*	293	Aa
Leslie, *Fife*	261	Bb
Lesmahagow	238	Cb
Lesnewth	11	Cc
Lessingham	138	Cb
Lessonhall	216	Db
Leswalt	211	Ab
Letchmoreheath	57	Aa
Letchworth	75	Ba
Letcombe Basset	72	Cc
Letcombe Regis	72	Cc
Letham	272	Cb
Letheringham	99	Bb
Letheringsett	136	Da
Letter	293	Bb
Letterewe	308	Cc
Letterfearn	286	Cb
Letterston	82	Cc
Letton	87	Ba
Letton Green	118	Da
Letwell	164	Da
Leuchars	262	Ca
Leven, *Fife*	261	Bb
Leven, *Yorks.*	177	Ba
Levens	193	Bb
Levenshulme	161	Bb
Leverington	134	Cc
Lever, Lit.	171	Ac
Leverton	154	Cc
Leverton, N. with Habblesthorpe	165	Bb
Leverton Outgate	154	Cc
Leverton, S.	165	Bb
Levington	80	Ca
Levisham	199	Bc
Lew	71	Bb
Lewannick	7	Ba
Lewdown	12	Dc
Lewes	25	Ab
Lewisham	58	Cc
Lewiston	288	Da
Lewknor	73	Bb
Lewtrenchard	12	Dc
Lexden	78	Db
Lexham, E.	136	Cc
Lexham, W.	136	Cc
Leybourne	43	Ba
Leyburn	196	Cb
Leyland	170	Cb
Leylodge	293	Bb
Leymoor	172	Db
Leysdown-on-Sea	45	Aa
Leysmill	272	Cb
Ley Street	58	Bb
Leyton	58	Cb
Lezant	7	Ba
Llanbryd	303	Aa
Libanus	86	Ca
Libberton	239	Aa
Libbery	109	Bc
Liberton	251	Bb
Lichfield	128	Cb
Lickey End	109	Bb
Liddington, *Rut.*	131	Bc
Liddington, *Wilts.*	53	Aa
Lidgate	97	Bb
Lidgmoor	88	Ca
Lidlington	94	Db
Lidstone	92	Cc
Liff	271	Ac
Lifton	12	Cc
Lightcliffe	172	Da
Lighthazles	172	Cb
Lighthorne	91	Ba
Lightwood	146	Db
Lilbourne	112	Cb
Lillesdon	34	Cc
Lilleshall	126	Da
Lilley	75	Aa
Lilliesleaf	241	Bc
Lillingstone Dayrell	93	Ab
Lillingstone Lovell	93	Bb
Lillington, *Dors.*	35	Bc
Lillington, *War.*	111	Ab
Lilling, W.	185	Ba
Lilstock	33	Ba
Limber, Gt.	167	Aa
Limekilns	251	Aa
Limington	34	Dc
Limpenhoe	120	Ca
Limpley Stoke	51	Bb
Limpsfield	42	Db
Linby	150	Ca
Linch	40	Cb
Linchmere	40	Cb
Lincoln	166	Cc
Lindal	192	Cc
Lindale	193	Ac
Lindfield	24	Ba
Lindley	172	Db
Lindridge	108	Cb
Lindsell	77	Ac
Lindsey	79	Aa
Linford, Gt.	94	Ca
Linford, Lit.	94	Ca
Lingdale	199	Aa
Lingen	107	Ab
Lingfield	42	Db
Lingwood	120	Ca
Linkenholt	54	Cc
Linkinhorne	7	Ba
Linktown	261	Ib
Linley	126	C
Linley Green	108	D
Linlithgow	250	D
Linslade	94	C
Linstead Magna	100	C
Linstead Parva	100	C
Linsted	45	A
Linstock	218	Cb
Linthurst	109	B
Linthwaite	172	D
Linton, *Cambs.*	96	D
Linton, *Derby*	128	D
Linton, *Herefs.*	89	A
Linton, *Kent*	44	C
Linton, *Rox.*	242	C
Linton, *Yorks.*	182	D
Linton, *Yorks.*	184	D
Linton-upon-Ouse	184	D
Lintzford	221	B
Linwood, *Lincs.*	167	A
Linwood, *Renf.*	248	C
Liphook	40	C
Liscard	159	B
Liskeard	7	B
Liss	40	C
Lissett	188	C
Lissington	166	D
Listoke	34	C
Liston	98	C
Lisvane	67	A
Litcham	136	C
Litchborough	112	D
Litchfield	54	C
Litherland	159	B
Litlington, *Cambs.*	95	B
Litlington, *Sus.*	25	B
Little Barningham	137	A
Littleborough	172	C
Littlebourne	46	C
Little Bredy	17	B
Littlebury	96	D
Littlebury Green	96	D
Little Bytham	132	C
Little Chart	45	A
Little Chester	149	A
Little Down	54	C
Littleferry	312	C
Littleham, *Dev.*	15	A
Littleham, *Dev.*	30	C
Littlehampton	23	B
Little Hautbois	137	B
Littleheath	75	B
Littlehempston	10	C
Little Kineton	91	B
Little London, *Hants.*	54	C
Little London, *Lincs.*	133	B
Little London City	173	A
Little Lynturk	293	C
Littlemore	72	D
Little Ness	125	A
Littleover	148	D
Little Petherick	5	B
Littleport	116	D
Little Somborne	38	D
Little Stretton	125	A
Little Thorpe, *Leics.*	130	Cc
Littlethorpe, *Yorks.*	184	C
Littleton, *Ches.*	160	C
Littleton, *Hants.*	38	D
Littleton, *M'sex*	56	D
Littleton, *Som.*	34	D
Littleton, N.	90	D
Littleton, S.	90	D
Littleton, W.	51	B
Littleton Drew	69	B
Littleton-upon-Severn	68	D
Little Torrington	12	D
Little Town, *Cumb.*	202	D
Little Town, *Dur.*	207	B
Little Walsingham	136	C
Little Wenlock	126	C
Littlewick Green	56	C
Littleworth, *Berks.*	71	B
Littleworth, *Staffs.*	127	B
Littlewort, *Staffs.*	146	C
Litton, *Som.*	50	D
Litton, *Yorks.*	195	A
Litton Cheney	17	A
Livermere, Gt.	98	C
Liverpool	159	B
Liversedge	173	A
Liverton	199	B
Livingston	250	B
Lizard	3	B
Llan-march	67	A
Llanelhaiarn	140	C
Llanafan	102	C
Llanfanfawr	104	C
Llanafanfechan		

349

	PAGE	SQ.
Llanallgo	156	Ca
Llananno	106	Cb
Llanarmon, *Caer.*	140	Ca
Llanarmon, *Den.*	143	Ba
Llanarmon Dyffryn Ceiriog	142	Bc
Llanarmon Mynydd Mawr	143	Bc
Llanarth, *Card.*	101	Ac
Llanarth, *Mon.*	67	Ba
Llanarthney	64	Ca
Llanasa	158	Da
Llanbabo	155	Ba
Llanbadarnfawr	102	Ca
Llanbadarnfynydd	106	Ca
Llanbadarn Odwyn	102	Cb
Llanbadarn Trefeglwys	101	Bb
Llanbadarn-y-garreg	104	Db
Llanbadoc	67	Bb
Llanbadr	104	Db
Llanbadrig	155	Ba
Llanbedr, *Brecon*	87	Ac
Llanbedr, *Mer.*	140	Dc
Llanbedr Dyffryn Clwyd	143	Ba
Llanbedr-goch	156	Cb
Llanbedrog	139	Bc
Llanbedr-y-cennin	157	Ab
Llanberis	156	Dc
Llanbethery	66	Dc
Llanbeulan	155	Bb
Llanbister	106	Cb
Llanblethian	66	Cc
Llanboidy	83	Ac
Llanbradach	67	Ac
Llanbrynmair	122	Db
Llanbyther	84	Cb
Llancarfan	66	Dc
Llancayo	67	Ba
Llancilian	156	Ca
Llancillo	87	Bc
Llancynfelyn	121	Bc
Llandaff	49	Aa
Llandawke	63	Aa
Llanddaniel Fab	156	Cb
Llanddarog	64	Ca
Llanddeiniol	101	Ba
Llanddeiniolen	156	Cc
Llandderfel	142	Db
Llanddetty	86	Da
Llanddeusant, *Ang.*	155	Ba
Llanddeusant, *Carm.*	85	Ba
Llanddew	86	Da
Llanddewi	64	Cc
Llanddewi Aberarth	101	Db
Llanddewi Brefi	84	Da
Llanddewi Cwm	104	Db
Llanddewi Ystradenny	106	Cb
Llanddoget	157	Bb
Llanddona	156	Cb
Llanddulas	158	Ca
Llanddwywe	140	Dc
Llanddyfnan	156	Cb
Llandecwyn	140	Db
Llandefaelog Fach	104	Dc
Llandefaelog-trer-graig	86	Da
Llandefalle	104	Dc
Llandefeilog	63	Ba
Llandegai	156	Db
Llandegfan	156	Db
Llandegla	143	Ba
Llandegley	106	Cc
Llandegveth	67	Bb
Llandegwning	139	Bc
Llandeilo-graban	104	Db
Llandeilor Fan	103	Bc
Llandeloy	81	Bc
Llandenny	68	Cb
Llandevaud	68	Cb
Llandevenny	68	Cc
Llandewi Velfrey	62	Da
Llandilo	84	Dc
Llandilo Abercowin	63	Aa
Llandinabo	88	Db
Llandinam	105	Ba
Llandissilio	62	Da
Llandogo	68	Da
Llandough, *Glam.*	49	Aa
Llandough, *Glam.*	66	Cc
Llandovery	103	Ac
Llandow	66	Cc
Llandowror	63	Aa
Llandrillo	143	Ac
Llandrillo-yn-Rhos	157	Ba
Llandrindod	104	Da
Llandrindod Wells	104	Da

	PAGE	SQ.
Llandrinio	124	Da
Llandrygarn	155	Bb
Llandudno	157	Ba
Llandudwen	139	Bb
Llandulas	103	Bb
Llandwrog	140	Ca
Llandybie	64	Da
Llandyfodwg	66	Da
Llandyfriog	83	Bb
Llandyfrydog	155	Ba
Llandygwydd	83	Ab
Llandyrnog	158	Db
Llandysilio	124	Ca
Llandyssil	124	Cc
Llandyssiliogogo	83	Ba
Llandyssul	83	Bb
Llanedeyrn	67	Ac
Llanedwen	156	Cc
Llanedy	64	Db
Llanegryn	121	Ba
Llanegwad	84	Cc
Llanelian-yn-Rhos	157	Ba
Llanelidan	143	Bb
Llanelieu	87	Ab
Llanelltyd	141	Bc
Llanelly, *Brecon*	67	Aa
Llanelli, *Carm.*	64	Cb
Llanelon	67	Ba
Llanelwedd	104	Da
Llanenddwyn	140	Dc
Llanengan	139	Bc
Llanerch Aeron	101	Bc
Llanerchymedd	155	Ba
Llanerfyl	123	Bb
Llanfabon	66	Da
Llanfachraeth	155	Ab
Llanfachreth	141	Bc
Llanfaelog	155	Ba
Llanfaelrhys	139	Ac
Llanfaes	156	Db
Llanfaethlu	155	Ba
Llanfaglan	156	Cc
Llanfair	140	Dc
Llanfair-ar-y-bryn	103	Bb
Llanfair Caereinion	123	Bb
Llanfair Clydogan	84	Da
Llanfair Dyffryn Clwyd	143	Ba
Llanfairfechan	156	Bb
Llanfair-is-gaer	156	Cc
Llanfair mathafarneithaf	156	Ca
Llanfair Nant Gwyn	82	Db
Llanfair Nant-y-Gof	82	Cb
Llanfair Orllwyn	83	Bb
Llanfair-pwllgwyngyll	156	Cb
Llanfair Talhaiarn	158	Cb
Llanfair-y-cwmwd	156	Cc
Llanfairynghornwy	155	Ba
Llanfair-yn-Neubwll	155	Ab
Llanfallteg West	62	Da
Llanfaredd	104	Da
Llanfechain	124	Ca
Llanfechell	155	Ba
Llanferres	143	Ba
Llanfflewyn	155	Ba
Llanfihangel	84	Cc
Llanfihangel Aberbythych	64	Da
Llanfihangel-ar-arth	84	Cb
Llanfihangel Bachellaeth	139	Bc
Llanfihangel Bryn Pabuan	104	Ca
Llanfihangel Cilfargen	84	Dc
Llanfihangel Esgeifiog	156	Cb
Llanfihangel-gegeur-glyn	121	Bc
Llanfihangel Glyn Myfyr	142	Da
Llanfihangel-helygen	105	Bc
Llanfihangel Iledrod	102	Cb
Llanfihangel-Nantbran	104	Cc
Llanfihangel-nant Melan	106	Cc
Llanfihangel Penbedw	83	Ab
Llanfihangel Rhos-y-corn	84	Cb
Llanfihangel Rhydithon	106	Cb
Llanfihangel Tal-y-llyn	86	Da
Llanfihangel Trer. Beirdd	156	C

	PAGE	SQ.
Llanfihangel-tyn-Sylwy	156	Db
Llanfihangel-y-creuddyn	102	Ca
Llanfihangel-yng-Ngwynfa	123	Ba
Llanfihangel-yn-nhowyn	155	Bb
Llanfihangel-y-Pennant	121	Ba
Llanfihangel Ystrad	84	Ca
Llanfihangel-y-traethau	140	Db
Llanfillo	104	Dc
Llanfoist	67	Ba
Llanfor	142	Db
Llanfrechfa	67	Bb
Llanfrothen	140	Db
Llanfrynach	86	Da
Llanfugail	155	Bb
Llanfwrog	155	Aa
Llanfyllin	124	Ca
Llanfynydd, *Carm.*	84	Cc
Llanfynydd, *Flint*	144	Ca
Llanfyrnach	83	Ac
Llangadfan	123	Ab
Llangadock	85	Aa
Llangadwaladr, *Ang.*	155	Bc
Llangadwaladr, *Den.*	143	Bc
Llangaffo	156	Cc
Llangain	63	Ba
Llangammarch Wells	104	Cb
Llangan	66	Cb
Llanganten	104	Ca
Llangar	143	Ab
Llangarren	88	Dc
Llangasty Tal-y-llyn	86	Da
Llangathe	84	Dc
Llangattock	87	Ac
Llangattock Lingoed	87	Bc
Llangattock-nigh-Usk	67	Ba
Llangattock Vibon Avel	88	Cc
Llangedwyn	124	Ca
Llangefni	156	Cb
Llangeinor	66	Ca
Llangeinwen	156	Cc
Llangeitho	102	Cc
Llangeler	83	Bb
Llangelynin, *Caer.*	157	Ab
Llangelynin, *Mer.*	121	Ba
Llangendeirne	64	Ca
Llangenith	63	Bc
Llangennech	64	Cb
Llangenny	87	Ac
Llangerniew	157	Bb
Llangeview	68	Cb
Llangian	139	Bc
Llangibby	67	Bb
Llangiwg	85	Ac
Llanglydwen	82	Dc
Llangoed	156	Db
Llangoedmor	83	Aa
Llangollen	143	Bb
Llangolman	82	Dc
Llangorse	86	Da
Llangorwen	102	Ca
Llangoven	68	Ca
Llangower	142	Db
Llangranog	83	Ba
Llangristiolus	156	Cb
Llangrove	88	Dc
Llangwyney	87	Ac
Llangstone	67	Bc
Llangua	88	Cc
Llangunllo	106	Db
Llangunnor	64	Ca
Llangurig	105	Aa
Llangwinisaf	68	Cb
Llangwm, *Den.*	142	Da
Llangwm, *Mon.*	68	Cb
Llangwnadl	139	Ac
Llangwstenin	157	Ba
Llangwyfan, *Ang.*	155	Bb
Llangwyfan, *Den.*	158	Db
Llangwyllog	155	Bb
Llangwm	62	Db
Llangwyryfon	102	Cb
Llangybi, *Caer.*	140	Cb
Llangybi, *Card.*	84	Da
Llangyfelach	64	Db
Llangynhafal	158	Db
Llangynidr	87	Ac
Llangyniew	123	Bb
Llangynin	63	Aa
Llangynllo	83	Bb
Llangynog, *Brecon*	104	Cb

	PAGE	SQ.
Llangynog, *Carm.*	63	Ba
Llangynog, *Mont.*	123	Ba
Llangynwyd	65	Ba
Llanhamlach	86	Da
Llanharan	66	Cb
Llanharry	66	Cb
Llanhennock	67	Bb
Llanhilleth	67	Ab
Llanhowel	81	Bc
Llanidan	156	Cc
Llanidloes	105	Ba
Llaniestyn *Ang.*	156	Db
Llaniestyn, *Caer.*	139	Bc
Llanigon	87	Aa
Llanilar	102	Ca
Llanilid	66	Cb
Llanina	101	Ac
Llanishen, *Glam.*	67	Ac
Llanishen, *Mon.*	68	Ca
Llanlawddog	84	Cb
Llanllawer	82	Cb
Llanllechid	156	Dc
Llanlleonfel	104	Cb
Llanllowell	68	Cb
Llanllugan	123	Bb
Llanllwch	63	Ba
Llanllwchaiarn, *Card.*	83	Ba
Llanllwchaiarn, *Mont.*	123	Bc
Llanllwni	84	Cb
Llanllyfni	140	Ca
Llanlowdy	88	Cc
Llanmadoc	64	Cc
Llanmaes	66	Cc
Llanmartin	68	Cc
Llanmerewig	124	Cc
Llanmihangel	66	Cc
Llannefydd	158	Cb
Llannon	64	Cb
Llannor	139	Bc
Llanon	101	Bb
Llanover	67	Ba
Llanpumpsaint	84	Cb
Llanreath	62	Cb
Llanreithan	81	Bc
Llanrhaiadr	158	Db
Llanrhaiadr-ym-Mochnant	143	Bc
Llanrhidian	64	Cc
Llanrhwydrys	155	Ba
Llanrhychwyn	157	Ab
Llanrhuddlad	155	Ba
Llanrhystyd	101	Bb
Llanrian	81	Bb
Llanrothal	88	Cc
Llanrug	156	Cc
Llanrwst	157	Bb
Llansadurnen	63	Aa
Llansadwrn, *Ang.*	156	Cb
Llansadwrn, *Carm.*	103	Ac
Llansamlet	65	Aa
Llan-saint	63	Bb
Llansaintfraed in Elvel	104	Da
Llansannan	158	Cb
Llansannor	66	Cb
Llansantffraid	101	Bb
Llansantffraid Glan-Conway	157	Bc
Llansantffraid Glyn Ceiriog	143	Bb
Llansantffraid-ym-Mechain	124	Ca
Llansantffread	86	Da
Llansawel	84	Db
Llansilin	143	Bc
Llansoy	68	Ca
Llanspyddyd	86	Ca
Llanstadwell	62	Cb
Llanstephan	63	Ba
Llanthewy-Rytherch	67	Ba
Llanthewy Skirrid	87	Bc
Llanthewy Vach	68	Bb
Llanthony	87	Bb
Llantilio Crossenny	68	Ca
Llantilio Pertholey	87	Bc
Llantood	82	Db
Llantrisant, *Ang.*	155	Ba
Llantrisant, *Glam.*	66	Db
Llantrissent	68	Cb
Llantrithyd	66	Dc
Llantwit	66	Cb
Llantwit Fardre	66	Db
Llantwit Major	66	Cc
Llantysilio	143	Bb
Llanuwchllyn	142	Db
Llanvaches	68	Cb
Llanvair Discoed	68	Cb
Llanvair Waterine	106	Db
Llanvapley	67	B

Name	Page	Sq.
Llanvetherine	87	Bc
Llanveynoe	87	Bb
Llanvihangel Crucorney	87	Bc
Llanvihangel-Lantarnam	67	Bb
Llanvihangel-near-Roggiett	68	Cc
Llanvihangel-nigh-Usk	67	Ba
Llanvihangel Pontymoil	67	Bb
Llanvihangel-tor-y-mynydd	68	Cb
Llanvihangel Ystern-Llewern	68	Ca
Llanwarne	88	Db
Llanwddyn	123	Ba
Llanwenarth	67	Ba
Llanwenllwyfo	156	Ca
Llanwenog	84	Ca
Llanwern	67	Bc
Llanwinio	83	Ac
Llanwnda, Caer.	140	Ca
Llanwnda, Pem.	81	Bb
Llanwnen	84	Ca
Llanwnog	123	Bc
Llanwnws	102	Cb
Llanwonno	66	Da
Llanwrda	85	Aa
Llanwrin	122	Cb
Llanwrthwl	105	Bc
Llanwrtyd Wells	103	Bb
Llanwyddelan	123	Bc
Llanyblodwel	124	Ca
Llanybri	63	Ba
Llanycefn	62	Da
Llanychaer	82	Cb
Llanychaiarn	101	Ba
Llanycil	142	Db
Llanycrwys	84	Da
Llanymawddwy	123	Aa
Llanymynech	124	Ca
Llanynghenedl	155	Ab
Llanynis	104	Ca
Llanynys	158	Db
Llanyre	105	Bc
Llanystumdwy	140	Cb
Llanywern	86	Ba
Llawhaden	62	Da
Llawnt	144	Cc
Llechcynfarwydd	155	Bb
Llechfaen	86	Ba
Llechryd, Card.	83	Ab
Llechryd, Mon.	86	Db
Llechylched	155	Bb
Lletty Brongu	65	Ba
Llidiart Nenog	84	Db
Llithfaen	139	Bb
Llowes	87	Aa
Llwydarth	65	Ba
Llwyngwril	121	Ba
Llwyn-hendy	64	Cb
Llwyn-y-pia	66	Cb
Llynfaes	155	Bb
Llysfaen	157	Ba
Llyswen	104	Db
Llysworney	66	Ca
Llys-y-fran	62	Ca
Llywel	85	Ba
Loanhead	251	Bb
Lochaline	264	Cb
Lochcarron or Jeantown	286	Ca
Lochdonhead	264	Dc
Lochearnhead	258	Da
Lochee	271	Ac
Lochfoot	215	Ba
Lochgelly	261	Ac
Lochgilphead	245	Ca
Lochgoilhead	257	Ac
Lochinver	313	Bb
Lochmaben	227	Ac
Loch Ranza	234	Ca
Lochrutton	215	Ba
Lochside	282	Cc
Lochwinnoch	248	Cc
Lockerbie	227	Bc
Lockeridge	53	Ab
Lockerley	38	Cb
Locking	49	Bb
Lockinge, E.	72	Cc
Lockinge, W.	72	Cc
Lockington, Leics.	149	Bc
Lockington, Yorks.	177	Aa
Loddington, Leics.	131	Ab
Loddington, N'hants	113	Bb
Loddiswell	9	Bb
Loddon	120	Cb
Loders	16	Db
Lodsworth	23	Aa
Lofthouse, Yorks.	173	Ba
Lofthouse, Yorks.	196	Cc
Lofthouse Gate	173	Ba
Loftus	199	Ba
Logie	261	Ba
Logie Easter	312	Cc
Logie Pert	281	Bc
Logieralt	269	Ba
Lolworth	96	Ca
Londesborough	186	Dc
London	57	Bb
London Colney	75	Ac
Londonderry	196	Db
Londonthorpe	152	Cb
Long Ashton	50	Da
Long Bennington	151	Bb
Longbenton	222	Db
Longborough	91	Ac
Long Bredy	17	Db
Longbridge Deverill	36	Da
Long Buckby	112	Db
Longburgh	217	Bb
Long Burton	35	Bc
Long Clawson	150	Da
Longcot	71	Bc
Long Crendon	73	Ba
Long Crichel	19	Aa
Longden	125	Ba
Long Ditton	57	Ac
Longdon, Staffs.	128	Ca
Longdon, Worcs.	89	Bb
Longdon-upon-Tern	126	Ca
Long Drax	175	Aa
Long Eaton	149	Bc
Longfield	59	Ac
Longfleet	19	Ab
Longford, Derby	148	Dc
Longford, Glos.	89	Bc
Longford, M'sex.	56	Da
Longford, Shrops.	126	Da
Longford, War.	111	Ba
Longforgan	271	Ac
Longformacus	253	Bc
Longframlington	231	Bb
Longham, Dors.	19	Bb
Longham, Norf.	136	Cc
Long Handborough	72	Ca
Longhirst	232	Ca
Longhope	89	Ac
Longhorsley	232	Cb
Long Itchington	111	Bc
Longlands	202	Da
Longlane	54	Da
Longleavens	90	Cc
Long Load	34	Dc
Longmanhill	305	Aa
Long Marton	204	Cb
Long Newton, Dur.	207	Bc
Long Newton, Glos.	70	Cb
Longney	69	Ba
Longniddry	252	Cb
Longnor, Shrops.	125	Bb
Longnor, Staffs.	162	Dc
Longparish	38	Da
Long Preston	182	Cb
Longridge, Lancs.	181	Ac
Longridge, W. Loth.	250	Dc
Long Riston	177	Ba
Long Sandall	174	Dc
Longsdon	147	Aa
Longside	306	Db
Longslow	145	Bc
Long Stanton All Saints	96	Ca
Long Stanton St. Michael	96	Ca
Longstock	38	Ca
Longstone, Gt.	163	Ac
Longstone, Llt.	163	Ac
Long Stowe	95	Bb
Long Stratton	119	Ab
Long Street, Bucks.	93	Ba
Longstreet, Wilts.	53	Ac
Long Sutton, Bucks.	73	Aa
Long Sutton, Hants.	40	Ca
Long Sutton, Lincs.	134	Cb
Long Sutton, Som.	34	Db
Longthorpe	115	Aa
Longton, Lancs.	169	Ba
Longton, Staffs.	146	Db
Longtown, Cumb.	217	Bb
Longtown, Herefs.	87	Bb
Long Whatton	129	Ba
Longwick	73	Bb
Longwood	172	Db
Longworth	72	Cb
Looe, East.	7	Bc
Looe, West.	7	Bc
Loose	44	Cb
Loosley Row	74	Cb
Lopen	16	Da
Lopham, N.	118	Dc
Lopham, S.	118	Dc
Loppington	144	Dc
Loscoe	149	Bb
Lossiemouth	303	Aa
Lostock	170	Dc
Lostock Green	161	Ab
Lostwithiel	6	Db
Lothbeg	317	Ac
Lothersdale	182	Dc
Lotherton	184	Dc
Lottisham	35	Aa
Loughborough	130	Ca
Loughor	64	Db
Loughton, Bucks.	94	Cb
Loughton, Essex	58	Ca
Loughton, Shrops.	108	Ca
Louisburgh	324	Dc
Lound, Lincs.	132	Da
Lound, Notts.	165	Ab
Lound, Suff.	120	Db
Lound, E.	175	Bc
Louth	168	Cc
Loveacott	30	Cc
Loversall	174	Dc
Loveston	62	Db
Lovington	35	Aa
Lowbands	89	Bb
Low Bradfield	163	Ba
Low Common	173	Bb
Lowden	52	Ca
Lowdham	150	Db
Lowe	145	Ac
Low Egborough	174	Da
Lower Beeding	24	Ca
Lower Freystrop.	62	Ca
Lower Gornal	127	Bc
Lower Green	43	Bc
Lowerhouse	171	Aa
Lowesby	130	Cc
Lowestoft	120	Db
Loweswater	202	Cc
Lowfieldheath	42	Cc
Low Ham	34	Db
Lowick, Lancs.	192	Db
Lowick, N'hants.	114	Ca
Lowick, N'land	243	Bb
Low Leighton	162	Db
Low Moor	181	Bc
Lowsonford	110	Bc
Low Street	136	Dc
Low Tharston	119	Ab
Lowther	204	Cb
Lowtherton	217	Bb
Lowthorpe	188	Cc
Lowton, Dev.	31	Bc
Lowton, Lancs.	160	Da
Loxbear	32	Cc
Loxhore	30	Db
Loxhore, Lr.	30	Db
Loxley, War.	91	Ba
Loxley, Yorks.	163	Ba
Loxton	49	Bb
Loxwood	23	Bb
Lubberland	108	Ca
Lubenham	112	Da
Luccombe	48	Cb
Lucker	244	Cc
Luckett	8	Ca
Luckington	69	Bc
Lucton	107	Bb
Ludborough	167	Bb
Ludchurch	62	Db
Luddenden	172	Ca
Luddenden Foot	172	Ca
Luddenham	45	Ab
Luddesdown	43	Ba
Luddington, Lincs.	176	Cb
Luddington, War.	91	Aa
Luddington-in-the-Brook	114	Da
Ludford Magna	167	Bc
Ludford Parva	167	Ac
Ludgershall, Bucks.	73	Aa
Ludgershall, Wilts.	53	Bc
Ludgvan	1	Bb
Ludham	138	Cc
Ludlow	107	Bb
Ludney	168	Cb
Ludwell	36	Db
Luffincott	12	Cb
Lufton	34	Dc
Lugwardine	88	Da
Lulham	88	Ca
Lullingstone	43	Aa
Lullington, Derby.	128	Da
Lullington, Som.	51	Bc
Lullington, Sus.	25	Bc
Lulsley	108	Dc
Lulworth, East	18	Db
Lulworth, West	18	Db
Lumb	172	C
Lumby	174	C
Lumley, Gt.	222	C
Lumphanan	293	A
Lumphinnans	260	D
Lumsden	292	D
Lund	177	A
Lundie	271	A
Lunt	169	A
Luntley	107	A
Luppitt	15	B
Lupton	193	B
Lurgashall	23	A
Lusby	153	B
Luss	257	B
Lustleigh	14	C
Luston	107	B
Luton, Beds.	75	A
Luton, Dev.	14	D
Luton, Kent	44	C
Lutterworth	112	C
Lutton, Dev.	8	D
Lutton, Lincs.	134	C
Lutton, N'hants	114	D
Lutton, Yorks.	186	A
Luxborough	48	C
Luxulian	6	C
Lybster	318	Da
Lybster, Upr.	318	Da
Lydbury, North	107	Aa
Lydd	27	Bb
Lydden	46	Cc
Lydeard, E.	33	Dc
Lydeard St. Lawrence	33	Aa
Lydford	12	Dc
Lydford, E.	35	Aa
Lydford, W.	35	Aa
Lydford Fair Place	35	Aa
Lydham	124	Dc
Lydiard Millicent.	70	Dc
Lydiard Tregoze	70	Dc
Lydiate	169	Bc
Lydlinch	35	Bc
Lydney	69	Aa
Lydstep	62	Db
Lye, Bucks.	74	Db
Lye, Worcs.	109	Ba
Lyes Green	51	Bc
Lyford	72	Cc
Lyme Regis	16	Cb
Lyminge	28	Ca
Lymington	20	Db
Lyminster	23	Bc
Lymm	161	Aa
Lympne	28	Ca
Lympsham	14	Db
Lympstone	14	Db
Lyncombe, S.	51	Bb
Lyndhurst	20	Da
Lyndon	131	Bc
Lyne, Peeb.	239	Ba
Lyne, Sur.	56	Db
Lyneal	144	Cc
Lyneham, Oxon.	91	Bc
Lyneham, Wilts.	0	Dc
Lyneholme	218	Ca
Lyne of Skene	293	Bb
Lyng, Norf.	136	Cc
Lyng, Som.	34	Cb
Lyng, W.	34	Cb
Lynmouth	47	Ab
Lynton	47	Ab
Lyons	222	Dc
Lyonshall	107	Ac
Lytchett Matravers	19	Ab
Lytchett Minster.	19	Ab
Lytham	169	Bb
Lythe	200	Ca
MABE	2	Db
Mablethorpe	168	Dc
Macclesfield	162	Cc
Macduff	305	Ac
Machen	67	Ac
Machen, Upr.	67	Ac
Machrihanish	233	Ac
Machynlleth	122	Cb
Mackworth	148	Db
Maclunans	270	Da
Maddington	37	Aa
Madehurst	23	Ab
Madeley, Shrops.	126	Cb
Madeley, Staffs.	146	Cb
Madingley	96	Cb
Madjeston	36	Cb
Madley	88	Cb
Madresfield	89	Ba
Madron	1	Bb
Maenclochog	82	Dc
Maentwrog	141	Ba

Place	Page	Sq.
Maer	146	Cb
Maerdy, *Glam.*	86	Cc
Maerdy, *Mer.*	142	Da
Maesbury Marsh	124	Da
Maesmynis	104	Ca
Maesteg	65	Ba
Maestregomer	123	Ac
Maes-y-bont	64	Da
Maes-y-cymmer	67	Ab
Magdalen Laver	76	Dc
Maghull	169	Bc
Magor	68	Cc
Magpie Green	99	Aa
Maiden Bradley	36	Ca
Maidenhead	56	Ca
Maiden Newton	17	Ba
Maidenwell	153	Ba
Maidford	93	Aa
Maids Moreton	93	Ab
Maidstone	44	Ca
Maidwell	113	Ab
Maindee	67	Bc
Mainsforth	207	Bb
Maisemore	89	Bc
Makerstoun	242	Cb
Malborough	9	Bc
Malden	57	Bc
Maldon	78	Cc
Malham	182	Ca
Maligar	206	Ca
Mallaig	273	Ba
Mallaigvaig	273	Ba
Malling, E.	44	Ca
Malling, South	25	Ab
Malling, W.	43	Ba
Mallwyd	122	Da
Malmesbury	70	Cc
Malpas, *Ches.*	145	Ab
Malpas, *Mon.*	67	Bc
Maltby, *Yorks.*	208	Cc
Maltby, *Yorks.*	164	Da
Maltby-le-Marsh	168	Dc
Malton	186	Ca
Malton, Old	187	Ab
Malvern, Gt.	89	Ba
Malvern, Lit.	89	Ba
Malvern, W.	89	Ba
Malvern Link	89	Ba
Malvern Wells	89	Ba
Mamble	108	Db
Mamhead	14	Db
Mamhilad	67	Bc
Manacean	2	Dc
Manafon	123	Bb
Manaton	13	Bb
Manby	168	Cc
Mancetter	129	Ac
Manchester	161	Ba
Manea	116	Cb
Maney	128	Cc
Manfield	207	Ac
Mangerton	16	Db
Mangotsfield	51	Aa
Manningford Abbots	53	Ac
Manningford Bruce	53	Ac
Mannings Heath	24	Ca
Mannington, *Dors.*	19	Ba
Mannington, *Norf.*	137	Ab
Manningtree	79	Ab
Mannofield	294	Cc
Manorbier	62	Dc
Manordeifi	83	Ab
Manorowen	81	Bb
Mansell Gamage	88	Ca
Mansell Lacy	88	Ca
Mansergh	194	Cc
Mansfield	150	Ca
Manson Green	118	Da
Manston, *Dors.*	36	Cc
Manston, *Kent*	46	Da
Manswood	19	Aa
Manthorpe, *Lincs.*	151	Bc
Manthorpe, *Lincs.*	132	Da
Manton, *Lincs.*	176	Cc
Manton, *Rut.*	131	Bb
Manton, *Wilts.*	53	Ab
Manuden	76	Da
Maperton	35	Bb
Maplebeck	150	Da
Maplederwell	55	Ac
Mapledurham	55	Aa
Maplestead, Gt.	78	Ca
Maplestead, Lit.	78	Ca
Mapperley	149	Bb
Mapperton, *Dors.*	17	Aa
Mapperton, *Dors.*	18	Da
Mappleton, *Derby*	148	Cb
Mappleton, *Yorks.*	178	Da
Mapplewell	173	Bc
Mappowder	35	Bc
Marazion	1	Bc
Marbury	145	Bb
March	116	Cb
Marcham	72	Db
Marchamley	145	Bc
March Baldon	72	Db
Marchington	148	Cc
Marchington Woodlands	148	Cc
Marchwiel	144	Cb
Marchwood	20	Da
Marcle, Lit.	89	Ab
Marcle, Much	89	Ab
Marcross	66	Cc
Marden, *Herefs.*	88	Da
Marden, *Kent*	44	Cb
Marden, *Wilts.*	52	Db
Marden, E.	40	Cc
Marden, N.	40	Cc
Marden, Up.	40	Cc
Marden, W	40	Cc
Mardy	87	Bc
Marefield	131	Aa
Mare Green	34	Cb
Mareham-le-Fen	153	Bb
Mareham-on-the-Hill	153	Ba
Marehay	149	Bb
Maresfield	25	Aa
Marfleet	177	Bb
Marford	144	Da
Margaret Marsh	36	Cb
Margaret Roding	77	Ac
Margaretting	59	Ba
Margate	46	Da
Marham	117	Aa
Marhamchurch	11	Db
Marholm	115	Aa
Mariansleigh	31	Ba
Mark	34	Ca
Markby	154	Da
Mark Causeway	34	Ca
Mark Cross	25	Ba
Markeaton	148	Db
Market Bosworth	129	Bb
Market Deeping	132	Db
Market Drayton	145	Bc
Market Harborough	113	Aa
Market Lavington	52	Db
Market Overton	131	Ba
Market Rasen	166	Da
Market Stainton	153	Aa
Market Weighton	186	Dc
Market Weston	119	Dc
Markfield	130	Cb
Markham Clinton	165	Ac
Markinch	261	Bb
Markington	184	Da
Marksbury	51	Ab
Markshall	78	Ca
Marks Tey	78	Db
Markyatestreet	75	Da
Marlborough	53	Ab
Marlcliff	91	Aa
Marldon	10	Da
Marlesford	100	Cb
Marlingford	119	Aa
Marloes	61	Ab
Marlow	74	Cc
Marlow, Lit.	74	Cc
Marlpool	149	Bb
Marnham, High	165	Bc
Marnham, Low	165	Bc
Marnhull	36	Cb
Marple	162	Ca
Marr	174	Dc
Marrick	196	Ca
Marros	63	Ab
Marsden, *Dur.*	222	Db
Marsden, *Yorks.*	172	Db
Marsden, Lit.	182	Cc
Marsett	195	Ab
Marsh	182	Dc
Marshalls Elm	34	Da
Marsham	137	Bb
Marsh Benham	54	Cb
Marsh Chapel	168	Cb
Marshfield, *Glos.*	51	Ba
Marshfield, *Mon.*	67	Ac
Marsh Gibbon	93	Ac
Marsh Green	42	Db
Marsh Lane	164	Cb
Marshside	169	Ab
Marsh Street	48	Cb
Marshwood	16	Cb
Marske, *Yorks.*	199	Aa
Marske, *Yorks.*	196	Ca
Marston, *Ches.*	161	Ab
Marston, *Herefs.*	107	Ac
Marston, *Lincs.*	151	Bb
Marston, *Oxon.*	72	Da
Marston, *Staffs.*	146	Dc
Marston, *Wilts.*	52	Cb
Marston Bigot	51	Bc
Marston, Broad	91	Aa
Marston Green	110	Da
Marston, Long, *Glos*	91	Aa
Marston, Long, *Herts.*	74	Ca
Marston, Long, *Yorks.*	184	Db
Marston Magna	35	Ab
Marston Meysey	71	Ab
Marston Montgomery	148	Cb
Marston Moor	184	Db
Marston Moretaine	94	Db
Marston, N.	93	Bc
Marston-on-Dove	148	Cc
Marston St. Lawrence	92	Db
Marston Stannett	108	Cc
Marston Trussell	112	Da
Marstow	88	Dc
Marsworth	74	Ca
Marten, *War.*	111	Bb
Marten, *Wilts.*	53	Bb
Martham	138	Dc
Martin, *Hants.*	37	Ac
Martin, *Lincs.*	153	Bb
Martin, *Lincs.*	152	Da
Martin, E.	37	Ac
Martinhoe	30	Da
Martin Hussingtree	109	Dc
Martin Mill	80	Ca
Martlesham	62	Cb
Martletwy	108	Dc
Martley	108	Dc
Martock	34	Dc
Marton, *Ches.*	161	Bc
Marton, *Lincs.*	165	Bb
Marton, *Shrops.*	125	Aa
Marton, *Shrops.*	124	Db
Marton, *Yorks.*	177	Bb
Marton, *Yorks.*	208	Cc
Marton, *Yorks.*	184	Da
Marton, *Yorks.*	198	Dc
Marton, E.	182	Cb
Marton-in-the-Forest	185	Ba
Marton, Lit.	169	Aa
Marton, W.	182	Cb
Martyr Worthy	20	Ab
Marwood	30	Cb
Maryburgh	300	Cb
Maryculter	294	Cc
Maryhill	248	Db
Marykirk	281	Bc
Maryport	201	Ba
Marystow	12	Da
Mary Tavy	8	Da
Marywell	281	Ba
Masham	196	Dc
Mashbury	77	Ac
Masongill	194	Cc
Massingham, Gt.	135	Bb
Massingham, Lit.	135	Bb
Mastin Moor	164	Cb
Matching	76	Dc
Matching Green	70	Dc
Matching Tye	76	Dc
Matfen	220	Da
Matfield Green	43	Bb
Mathern	68	Db
Mathon	89	Aa
Mathry	81	Bb
Matlask	137	Aa
Matlock	148	Da
Matlock Bank	148	Da
Matlock Bath	148	Da
Matlock Bridge	148	Da
Matson	89	Bc
Matterdale	203	Ab
Mattersey	165	Aa
Mattingley	55	Bc
Mattishall	118	Da
Mattishall Burgh.	118	Da
Mauchline	236	Dc
Maugersbury	91	Ac
Maulden	94	Db
Maulds Meaburn	204	Cc
Maunby	197	Ab
Maund Bryan	88	Da
Maundon	33	Ab
Mautby	120	Da
Mavesyn Ridware	128	Ca
Mavis Enderby	154	Cb
Mawbray, New	216	Cc
Mawdesley	170	Cb
Mawdlam	65	Bb
Mawgan	2	Dc
Mawnan	2	Dc
Mawthorpe	154	Ca
Maxey	115	Aa
Maxstoke	110	Da
Maxton	241	Bb
Maxwelltown	215	Ba
Maybole	224	Ca
Mayfield, *Derby*	148	Cb
Mayfield, *Sus.*	25	Ba
Maynard's Green	25	Bb
Maypole, *Kent*	46	Ca
Maypole, *Mon.*	88	Cc
Mead End	37	Ab
Meadgate	51	Ab
Meadle	73	Bb
Mealsgate	202	Ca
Meare	34	Da
Mearns	248	Dc
Means Ashby	113	Bb
Measham	129	Ab
Meathop	193	Ac
Meavy	8	Db
Medbourne	131	Ac
Meddon	11	Ba
Medlam	153	Bb
Medmenham	73	Bc
Medomsley	221	Bc
Medstead	39	Ba
Meerbrook	147	Ba
Meesden	76	Da
Meeth	31	Ab
Meigle	271	Ab
Meikleour	270	Db
Meikle Warthill	293	Ba
Meinciau	64	Ca
Melbourn	96	Cc
Melbourne, *Derby*	129	Ba
Melbourne, *Yorks.*	186	Cc
Melbury	29	Bc
Melbury Abbas	36	Db
Melbury Bubb	35	Ac
Melbury Osmond	35	Ac
Melbury Sampford	35	Ac
Melchbourne	114	Cc
Meldon	231	Bc
Meldreth	96	Cc
Melford, Long	98	Cc
Meliden	158	Da
Melin-court	85	Bc
Melkinthorpe	204	Cb
Melksham	52	Cb
Melksham Forest	52	Cb
Melling, *Lancs.*	181	Aa
Melling, *Lancs*	169	Bc
Melling Mount	169	Bc
Mellis	99	Aa
Mellon Charles	307	Ba
Mellor, *Derby*	162	Ca
Mellor, *Lancs.*	170	Da
Mells	51	Bc
Melmerby, *Cumb.*	204	Ca
Melmerby, *Yorks.*	197	Ac
Melmerby, *Yorks.*	196	Db
Melness	320	Db
Melrose	241	Bb
Melsonby	196	Da
Meltham	172	Dc
Melton, *Suff.*	99	Bc
Melton, *Yorks.*	176	Da
Meltonby	186	Cb
Melton, Gt.	119	Aa
Melton, Lit.	119	Aa
Melton Mowbray	131	Aa
Melton Ross	176	Db
Melton, W.	174	Cc
Melvaig	307	Ab
Melverley	124	Da
Melverley Green	124	Da
Melvich	322	Ca
Membury	16	Ca
Menai Bridge	156	Cb
Mendham	119	Bc
Mendlesham	99	Ab
Mendlesham Gr.	99	Ab
Menheniot	7	Bb
Mennock	226	Ca
Menston	183	Bc
Menstrie	259	Bc
Menthorpe	175	Aa
Mentmore	74	Ca
Meole Brace	125	Bb
Meon, E.	39	Bc
Meon, W.	39	Bb
Meonstoke	39	Bc
Meopham	43	Ba
Meopham Green	43	Ba
Mepal	116	Cc
Meppershall	75	Aa
Mercaston	148	Db
Merchiston	251	Bb
Mere	36	Ca
Mere Brow	169	Bb
Mere Green	128	Cc
Merevale	128	Dc
Mereworth	43	Bb
Meriden	110	Da
Merkinch	300	Dc
Merlin's Bridge	61	Ba
Merridge	33	Bb
Merrington	125	Ba
Merriott	16	Da
Merrow	41	Ab
Mersea, E.	79	Ac
Mersea Lane	78	Dc
Mersea, W.	78	Dc

Name	PAGE	SQ.
Mersham	27	Ba
Merstham	42	Cb
Merston	22	Da
Merstone	21	Bc
Merther	4	Ca
Merthyr	63	Ba
Merthyr Cynog	104	Cb
Merthyr Difan	66	Dc
Merthyr-mawr	65	Bb
Merthyr Tydfil	66	Db
Merton, Berw.	241	Bb
Merton, Dev.	12	Da
Merton, Norf.	118	Cb
Merton, Oxon.	72	Da
Meshaw	31	Ba
Messing	78	Cb
Messingham	176	Cc
Metfield	100	Ca
Metheringham	152	Da
Methil	261	Bc
Methley	174	Ca
Methlick	305	Bc
Methven	270	Cc
Methwold	117	Bb
Methwold Hithe	117	Ab
Mettingham	120	Cb
Metton	137	Ba
Mevagissey	4	Da
Mexborough	174	Cc
Meyllteyrn	139	Ac
Meysey Hampton	71	Ab
Michaelchurch	88	Dc
Michaelchurch Escley	87	Bb
Michaelchurch-on-Arrow	87	Aa
Michaelston-le-Pit	49	Aa
Michaelston-super-Ely	66	Db
Michaelston-y-Vedw	67	Bc
Michaelstow	6	Da
Michelmarsh	38	Ca
Mickfield	99	Ab
Micklebring	164	Ba
Mickleby	199	Ba
Micklefield, New	174	Ca
Micklefield, Old	174	Ca
Mickleham	41	Ba
Micklehurst	172	Cc
Mickleover	148	Dc
Mickleton, Glos.	91	Aa
Mickleton, Yorks.	206	Cb
Mickletown	174	Ca
Mickle Trafford	160	Cc
Mickley	196	Dc
Mid Calder	251	Ab
Middle	125	Aa
Middlebie	216	Da
Middleham	196	Cb
Middle Mill	81	Bc
Middlesbrough	208	Cd
Middlesmoor	196	Cc
Middlestone	207	Ab
Middlestown	173	Bb
Middlethorpe	185	Bb
Middleton, Derby.	163	Ac
Middleton, Derby.	148	Da
Middleton, Essex	78	Ca
Middleton, Glam.	64	Cc
Middleton, Hants.	38	Ba
Middleton, Lancs.	171	Bc
Middleton, Lancs.	180	Cb
Middleton, Norf.	135	Ac
Middleton, N'hants.	113	Ba
Middleton, N'land.	231	Bc
Middleton, Shrops.	124	Dc
Middleton, Suff.	100	Db
Middleton, Sus.	23	Ac
Middleton, War.	128	Cc
Middleton, W'land.	194	Cb
Middleton, Yorks.	173	Ba
Middleton, Yorks.	183	Bb
Middleton, Yorks.	198	Bb
Middleton Cheney	92	Db
Middleton Green	147	Bc
Middleton-in-Teesdale	205	Bb
Middleton One Row	207	Bc
Middleton-on-the-Hill	107	Bb
Middleton-on-the-Wolds	177	Aa
Middleton Scriven	108	Da
Middleton Stoney	92	Dc
Middleton Tyas	196	Ba
Middleton Quernhow	197	Ac
Middletown, Mont.	124	Da
Middletown, Som.	50	Ca
Middlewich	161	Ac
Middlewood	125	Aa
Middlezoy	34	Cb
Middridge	207	Ab
Midford	51	Bb
Midgley, Yorks.	173	Bb
Midgley, Yorks.	172	Ca
Midhopestones	173	Ac
Midhurst	23	Aa
Midlem	241	Bc
Midsomer Norton	51	Ab
Migvie	292	Cc
Milborne Port	35	Bb
Milborne St Andrew	18	Ca
Milborne Stileham	18	Ca
Milborne Wick	35	Bb
Milbourne, N'land.	221	Ba
Milbourne, Wilts.	70	Ca
Milburn	204	Cb
Milbury Heath	69	Ab
Milby	184	Da
Milcombe	92	Cb
Milden	98	Dc
Mildenhall, Suff.	97	Cb
Mildenhall, Wilts.	53	Bb
Milebush	44	Cb
Mile End, Cambs.	116	Dc
Mile End, Essex	78	Da
Mile End, Glos.	68	Da
Mileham	136	Cc
Milfield	243	Bb
Milford, Derby.	149	Ab
Milford, Dev.	29	Ac
Milford, Dev.	12	Da
Milford, Hants.	20	Db
Milford, Staffs.	127	Ba
Milford, Sur.	40	Da
Milford Haven	61	Bb
Milford, S.	174	Ca
Mill Bank	172	Cb
Millbeck	202	Db
Millbridge	40	Da
Millbrook, Beds.	94	Db
Millbrook, Ches.	172	Cc
Millbrook, Corn.	8	Cc
Millbrook, Hants.	38	Dc
Mill Prow	162	Ca
Mill End, Cambs.	116	Cb
Mill End, Herts.	74	Dc
Millerston	249	Ab
Millhill	57	Ba
Millhouse	173	Ac
Millhouses, Yorks.	163	Bb
Millhouses, Yorks.	174	Ca
Millikenpark	248	Cc
Millington	186	Db
Millmeece	146	Db
Millom	192	Cc
Millport	235	Ba
Mill Shaw	173	Ba
Millthorpe	163	Bb
Millthrop, Yorks.	194	Cb
Milltimber	288	Da
Milltown	293	Ac
Millwall	68	Da
Milnathort	260	Db
Milngavie	248	Da
Milnrow	172	Cb
Milnthorpe, Yorks.	173	Bb
Milnthorpe, W'land.	193	Bc
Milovaig, Lr.	295	Ac
Milovaig, Upr.	295	Ac
Milson	108	Cb
Milsted	44	Da
Milston	87	Ba
Milton, Berks.	72	Dc
Milton, Cambs.	96	Da
Milton, Derby.	162	Db
Milton, Derby.	148	Dc
Milton, Hants.	20	Cb
Milton, Kent	45	Bb
Milton, Kent	44	Da
Milton, Mon.	67	Bc
Milton, N'hants.	113	Ac
Milton, Notts.	165	Ac
Milton, Oxon.	92	Cb
Milton, Pem.	62	Cb
Milton, Som.	34	Dc
Milton, Som.	49	Bb
Milton, Staffs.	146	Da
Milton, Stir.	249	Ab
Milton Abbas	25	Bc
Milton Abbot	8	Ca
Milton Bryant	94	Bb
Milton Damerel	12	Ca
Milton Ernest	114	Cc
Milton Green	144	Da
Milton, Gt.	73	Ab
Milton Keynes	94	Cb
Milton Lilbourne	53	Ab
Milton, Lit.	73	Ab
Milton-of-Clova	280	Cc
Milton-on-Stour	36	Cb
Milton-under-Wychwood	71	Ba
Milverton, Som.	33	Ab
Milverton, War.	111	Ab
Milwich	147	Ac
Mimms, N.	75	Bc
Mimms, S.	75	Bc
Minchinhampton	70	Cb
Mindrum	242	Db
Minehead	48	Cb
Minera	144	Ca
Minety	70	Db
Miningsby	153	Bc
Minllyn	122	Da
Minnigaff	212	Db
Minskip	184	Da
Minstead	20	Da
Minster, Kent	45	Aa
Minster, Kent	46	Aa
Minsterley	124	Db
Minster Lovell	71	Ba
Minsterworth	89	Bc
Minterne Magna	17	Ba
Minterne Parva	17	Ba
Minting	153	Aa
Mintlaw	306	Cb
Minto	241	Bc
Minwear	62	Ca
Minworth	128	Cc
Mireland	324	Cb
Mirfield	173	Ab
Miserden	70	Ca
Miskin, Glam.	66	Da
Miskin, Glam.	66	Db
Missenden, Gt.	74	Cb
Missenden, Lit.	74	Cb
Misson	165	Aa
Misterton, Leics.	112	Ca
Misterton, Notts.	165	Aa
Misterton, Som.	16	Da
Mistley	79	Bb
Mitcham	57	Bc
Mitcheldean	89	Ac
Mitchell	5	Bc
Mitchel Troy	68	Ca
Mitford	232	Cc
Mithian	2	Ac
Mitton, Gt.	181	Bc
Mitton, Upr.	109	Ab
Mixbury	93	Ab
Mixenden	172	Ca
Mobberley	161	Bb
Mobley	69	Ab
Mochdre, Den.	157	Ba
Mochdre, Mont.	105	Ba
Mochrum	210	Cb
Mockerkin	201	Bb
Modbury	9	Bb
Moddershall	147	Ab
Moelfre	156	Ca
Moffat	227	Aa
Moggerhanger	95	Ab
Molash	45	Ab
Mold	159	Ac
Moldgreen	172	Db
Molescroft	177	Aa
Molesey, E.	57	Ac
Molesey, W.	57	Ac
Molesworth	114	Db
Molland	32	Ca
Mollinburn	249	Bb
Mollington	92	Ca
Molton, North	31	Ba
Molton, South	31	Ba
Monewden	99	Bb
Moneydie	270	Cc
Mongeham	46	Dc
Mongewell	73	Ac
Moniaive	226	Cb
Monifieth	271	Bc
Monimail	261	Ba
Monington	82	Da
Monk Bretton	173	Bc
Monken Hadley	57	Ba
Monkerton	14	Da
Monk Fryston	174	Da
Monk Hesleden	208	Ca
Monkhide	88	Da
Monkhill	217	Bb
Monkhopton	126	Cc
Monkland	107	Bc
Monkland, New	249	Bb
Monkland, Old	249	Bc
Monkleigh	30	Cc
Monknash	66	Cc
Monkokehampton	31	Ac
Monks Coppenhall	146	Ac
Monkseaton	222	Ca
Monks Eleigh	98	Dc
Monk Sherborne	55	Ac
Monksilver	33	Aa
Monks Kirby	111	Ba
Monk Soham	99	Bb
Monks Risborough	73	Bb
Monksthorpe	154	Cb
Monkswood	67	Ba
Monkton, Ayr	236	Cc
Monkton, Dev.	15	Da
Monkton, Dur.	222	Cb
Monkton, Kent	46	Ca
Monkton, Pem.	62	Cb
Monkton Combe	51	Bb
Monkton Deverill	36	Ca
Monkton Farleigh	51	Bb
Monkton Up Wimborne	37	Ac
Monmore Green	127	Bc
Monmouth	68	Ca
Monnington-on-Wye	87	Ba
Monreith	210	Cb
Montacute	34	Dc
Montford	125	Aa
Montgomery	124	Cc
Montrose	272	Da
Monxton	38	Cb
Monyash	163	Ac
Monymusk	293	Bc
Monzie	259	Ba
Moonzie	261	Ba
Moorby	153	Bb
Moordown	19	Db
Moore	160	Db
Moor End	73	Bb
Moor End Green	128	Cc
Moor Ends	175	Ac
Moorgate	172	Cc
Moor Green	52	Ca
Moorhampton	87	Ba
Moorhole	164	Cb
Moorhouse, Cumb.	217	Bc
Moorhouse, Notts.	165	Bc
Moorhouse, Yorks.	174	Ca
Moorland	34	Cb
Moorlinch	34	Cb
Moor Monkton	185	Da
Moorsholm	199	Aa
Moor Side, Lincs.	153	Bc
Moor Side, Yorks.	172	Ba
Moorside, Lancs.	172	Ca
Moorsley, Low	222	Cc
Moorthorpe	174	Ca
Moorton	72	Cb
Moor Top	173	Bb
Moortown	166	Da
Moorwinstow	11	Ba
Morborne	114	Da
Morchard Bishop	31	Bb
Morcott	131	Bc
Morda	144	Cc
Morden, Dors.	18	Da
Morden, Sur.	57	Bc
Morden, East	18	Da
Morden, West	18	Da
Mordiford	88	Db
Mordington	254	Cc
Mordon	207	Bb
More	124	Dc
Morebath	32	Da
Morebattle	242	Dc
Morecambe	180	Ca
Morecombelake	16	Db
More Crichel	19	Aa
Morefield	309	Aa
Moreleigh	10	Cb
Moresby	201	Bb
Morestead	39	Ab
Moreton, Ches.	159	Aa
Moreton, Dors.	18	Cb
Moreton, Essex	76	Da
Moreton, Oxon.	73	Bb
Moreton, Som.	50	Db
Moreton Corbet	125	Ba
Moreton Hampstead	13	Da
Moreton-in-Marsh	91	Ab
Moreton Jeffries	88	Da
Moreton Morrell	111	Ac
Moreton, N.	72	Db
Moreton-on-Lugg.	88	Ca
Moreton Pinkney	92	Da
Moreton, S.	72	Dc
Moreton Say	145	Bc
Moreton Valence	69	Ba
Morfa Nevin	139	Bb
Morganstown	66	Db
Mork	68	Db
Morland	204	Cb
Morley, Derby.	149	Ab
Morley, Dur.	206	Db
Morley, Yorks.	173	Ba
Morley St. Botolph	118	Ca
Morningside, Lan.	250	Cc
Morningside, M'loth.	251	Bb
Morning Thorpe	119	Bb
Morpeth	232	Cc
Morriston	64	Db
Morston	136	Da
Mortehoe	30	Ca
Morthen	164	Ca
Mortimers Cross	107	Bb
Mortlake	57	Bc

Place	Page	Sq.
Morton, *Derby*	149	Ba
Morton, *Glos.*	69	Ab
Morton, *Lincs.*	165	Ba
Morton, *Lincs.*	166	Cc
Morton, *Lincs.*	132	Da
Morton, *Norf.*	137	Ac
Morton, *Notts.*	150	Da
Morton, *Shrops.*	124	Da
Morton Bagot	110	Cb
Morton, E.	183	Ac
Morton-on-Swale	197	Ab
Morton, W.	183	Ac
Morval	7	Bc
Morvil	82	Cb
Morville	126	Cc
Mosbrough	164	Cb
Mosbrough, W.	164	Cb
Mosedale	202	Db
Moseley *Staffs.*	127	Bb
Moseley, *War.*	110	Ca
Mossbrow	161	Aa
Mossend	249	Bc
Mosser	201	Bb
Mossley	172	Cc
Mosterton	16	Da
Moston	171	Bc
Mostyn	158	Da
Motcombe	36	Cb
Motherby	203	Bb
Motherwell	249	Bc
Mottingham	58	Cc
Mottisfont	38	Cb
Mottistone	21	Ac
Mottram-in-Longdendale	162	Ca
Moulin	269	Ba
Moulsford	55	Aa
Moulton, *Ches.*	161	Ac
Moulton, *Lincs.*	133	Bb
Moulton, *Norf.*	120	Ca
Moulton, *N'hants.*	113	Ab
Moulton, *Suff.*	97	Ba
Moulton, *Yorks.*	196	Da
Moulton Chapel	133	Bc
Moulton St Michael	119	Ab
Moulton Seas End	133	Bb
Mountain	172	Da
Mountain Ash	86	Dc
Mount Bures	78	Ca
Mountfield	20	Ca
Mountgarrie	292	Db
Mountnessing	59	Aa
Mounton	68	Db
Mountsorrel	130	Ca
Mount Tabor	172	Da
Mousehole	1	Bc
Mousewald	216	Ca
Mow Cop	146	Da
Mowsley	112	Da
Moy	289	Ba
Moylgrove	82	Da
Muchalls	282	Da
Much Cowarne	88	Da
Muchelney	34	Db
Muchelney Ham	34	Dc
Much Hadham	76	Cb
Much Hoole	169	Ba
Much Wenlock	126	Cc
Muckart	260	Da
Mucking	59	Bb
Muckleford	17	Ba
Mucklestone	146	Cb
Muckton	168	Cc
Muddiford	30	Cb
Mudeford	20	Cb
Mudford	35	Ab
Mudgley	34	Db
Mugginton	148	Db
Muggleswick	220	Dc
Muie	311	Ba
Muirdrum	272	Cb
Muirhead	249	Ab
Muirkirk	237	Bc
Muir of Ord	300	Cb
Muker	195	Aa
Mulbarton	119	Aa
Mullion	2	Cc
Mumbles	64	Dc
Mumby	154	Da
Munden, Gt.	76	Cb
Munden, Lit.	76	Cb
Munderfield Row	89	Aa
Munderfield Stocks	89	Aa
Mundesley	138	Ca
Mundford	117	Bb
Mundham	119	Bb
Mundham, N.	22	Da
Mundham, S.	22	Da
Mundon	60	Ca
Mungrisdale	203	Ab
Munlochy	300	Da
Munsley	89	Aa
Munslow	107	Ba
Munslow Aston	107	Ba
Murcot	73	Aa
Murroes	271	Bc
Murrow	116	Ca
Mursley	93	Bc
Murston	44	Da
Murthly	270	Cb
Murton, *Dur.*	222	Dc
Murton, *N'land.*	222	Ca
Murton, *W'land.*	204	Db
Murton, *Yorks.*	185	Bb
Musbury	16	Cb
Musgrave, Gt.	204	Dc
Musgrave, Lit.	204	Dc
Muskham, N.	151	Aa
Muskham, S.	151	Aa
Musselburgh	252	Cb
Muston, *Leics.*	151	Ba
Muston, *Yorks.*	188	Ca
Mutford	120	Db
Mutfordbridge	120	Db
Muthill	259	Ba
Muxton	126	Ca
Mybster	323	Bc
Myddfai	85	Aa
Mydrim	63	Aa
Myerscough	170	Ca
Mylor	2	Db
Mynachlog-ddu	82	Dc
Mynydd-bach	68	Cb
Mytholmroyd	172	Ca
Myton-upon-Swale	184	Da
NABURN	185	Bc
Nackington	45	Bb
Nacton	79	Ba
Nafferton	188	Cc
Nailbridge	89	Ac
Nailsbourne	33	Cb
Nailsea	50	Ca
Nailstone	129	Bb
Nailsworth	69	Bb
Nairn	301	Bb
Nannerch	159	Ac
Nanpean	6	Cc
Nant	104	Da
Nantcwnlle	101	Bc
Nant-ddu	86	Cb
Nantgaredig	84	Cc
Nantgarw	66	Db
Nantglyn	142	Aa
Nant-gwym	105	Bb
Nantlle	140	Ca
Nantmel	105	Bb
Nantwich	145	Ba
Nant-y-caws	64	Ca
Nantyffyllon	65	Ba
Nant-y-glo	67	Aa
Nant-y-moel	66	Ca
Naphill	74	Cb
Napton-on-the-Hill	112	Cc
Narberth	62	Da
Narborough, *Leics.*	130	Cc
Narborough, *Norf.*	135	Bc
Narford	135	Bc
Naseby	112	Db
Nash, *Bucks.*	93	Bb
Nash, *Glam.*	66	Cc
Nash, *Mon.*	67	Bc
Nash, *Shrops.*	108	Cb
Nash, Lr.	62	Cb
Nassington	132	Dc
Nasty	76	Cb
Nateby, *Lancs.*	180	Dc
Nateby, *W'land*	194	Da
Nately Scures	55	Bc
Nately, Up.	55	Ac
Natland	193	Bb
Naughton	98	Dc
Naunton, *Glos.*	91	Ac
Naunton, *Worcs.*	90	Ca
Naunton Beauchamp	109	Bc
Navenby	152	Ca
Navestock	58	Da
Nawton	198	Cb
Nayland	78	Da
Nazeing	76	Cc
Near Cotton	147	Bb
Neasden	57	Bb
Neasham	207	Bc
Neath	65	Aa
Neatishead	138	Cb
Necton	118	Ca
Nedd	313	Ba
Nedging	98	Dc
Needham	119	Da
Needham Market.	99	Ac
Needingworth	96	Ca
Neen Savage	108	Da
Neen Sollars	108	Cb
Neenton	108	Ca
Neilston	248	Dc
Neithrop	92	Cb
Nelson, *Glam.*	66	Dc
Nelson, *Lancs.*	182	Cc
Nempnett Thrubwell	50	Db
Nenthead	204	Da
Nenthorn	242	Cb
Nerquis	143	Ba
Nesfield	183	Ab
Ness	159	Bb
Nesscliff	124	Ca
Ness, E.	198	Dc
Neston, *Ches.*	159	Bb
Neston, *Wilts.*	52	Ca
Neston, Lit.	159	Bb
Nether Alderley	161	Bb
Netheravon	53	Ac
Nether Broughton	130	Da
Netherbury	16	Cb
Netherby	134	Cc
Nether Cerne	17	Ba
Nether Compton	35	Ab
Nethercote	112	Cc
Netherend	68	Db
Nether Exe	32	Dc
Netherfield, *Notts.*	150	Cb
Netherfield, *Sus.*	26	Cb
Nethergate	165	Ba
Nether Green	164	Cb
Netherhampton	37	Ab
Nether Haugh	164	Ca
Nether Headon	165	Bb
Nether Heage	149	Aa
Netherseal	128	Da
Nether Shire Green	163	Ba
Nether Silton	197	Bb
Nether Stowey	33	Ba
Nether Street	52	Db
Netherthong	172	Dc
Nether Thorpe, *Yorks.*	164	Db
Netherthorpe, *Yorks.*	164	Cb
Netherton, *Berks.*	72	Cb
Netherton, *Ches.*	160	Cb
Netherton, *Dev.*	14	Dc
Netherton, *Hants.*	54	Cc
Netherton, *Lan.*	249	Bc
Netherton, *Lancs.*	169	Ac
Netherton, *N'land*	291	Aa
Netherton, *N'land*	222	Ca
Netherton, *Worcs.*	127	Bc
Netherton, *Worcs.*	90	Da
Netherton, *Yorks.*	173	Bb
Netherton, *Yorks.*	172	Db
Nethertown	191	Aa
Nether Wallop	98	Ca
Nether Whitacre	128	Dc
Netherwitton	231	Bc
Nethybridge	290	Db
Nettleswell	76	Dc
Nettlebed	73	Bc
Nettlebridge	51	Ac
Nettlecombe	17	Aa
Nettlecombe	33	Aa
Nettlestead, *Kent*	43	Bb
Nettlestead, *Suff.*	99	Ac
Nettleton, *Lincs.*	167	Ab
Nettleton, *Wilts.*	69	Bc
Netton	37	Bb
Neuadd	85	Aa
Nevendon	59	Ba
Nevern	82	Db
Nevill Holt	131	Bc
Nevin	139	Bb
New Abbey	215	Bb
New Aberdour	305	Ba
Newall	183	Bc
New Annesley	149	Ba
Newark, *N'hants.*	115	Aa
Newark, *Notts.*	151	Ba
Newarthill	249	Bc
Newbald, N.	186	Dc
Newbald, S.	186	Dc
Newball	166	Db
Newbattle	252	Cb
Newbiggin, *Cumb.*	203	Bb
Newbiggin, *Cumb.*	218	Cc
Newbiggin, *Dur.*	205	Bb
Newbiggin, *Lancs.*	180	Db
Newbiggin, *W'land*	191	Bb
Newbiggin, *W'land*	194	Ca
Newbiggin, *W'land*	204	Db
Newbiggin, *Yorks.*	195	Bb
Newbiggin-by-the-Sea	232	Dc
Newbigging	239	Aa
Newbold	163	Bc
Newbold-on-Avon	112	Cb
Newbold-on-Stour	91	Ba
Newbold Pacey	111	Ba
Newbold Verdon	129	Bb
New Bolingbroke	153	Bb
Newborough, *Ang.*	155	Bc
Newborough, *N'hants.*	115	Aa
Newborough, *Staffs.*	148	Cc
Newbottle	222	Cc
Newbourn	80	Ca
New Brampton	163	Bc
Newbridge, *Corn.*	1	Ac
Newbridge, *Hants.*	21	Ab
Newbridge, *Oxon.*	72	Cb
Newbridge Hill	51	Ba
Newbridge-on-Wye	104	Ca
New Brighton	159	Ba
Newbrough.	220	Cb
Newburgh, *Aber.*	294	Da
Newburgh, *Fife*	261	Aa
Newburgh, *Lancs.*	169	Bb
Newburn	221	Bb
Newbury, *Berks.*	54	Db
Newbury, *Som.*	51	Ac
Newbury, *Wilts.*	36	Ca
Newby, *W'land*	204	Cb
Newby, *Yorks.*	181	Ba
Newby, *Yorks.*	182	Cc
Newby, *Yorks.*	208	Cc
Newby Bridge	192	Db
Newbyth	305	Bb
Newby Wiske	197	Ab
Newcastle	106	Da
Newcastle Emlyn	83	Bb
Newcastle, Lit.	82	Cc
Newcastle-under-Lyme	146	Da
Newcastle-upon-Tyne	222	Cb
Newcastleton	229	Ac
New Chapel	146	Da
Newchurch, *Carm.*	83	Bc
Newchurch, *Hants.*	21	Bc
Newchurch, *Kent.*	27	Bb
Newchurch, *Lancs.*	161	Aa
Newchurch, *Lancs.*	171	Ba
Newchurch, *Lancs.*	182	Cc
Newchurch, *Mon.*	68	Cb
Newchurch, *Rad.*	87	Aa
New Cross	34	Dc
New Cumnock	225	Aa
New Deer	305	Bb
New Delph	172	Cc
Newdigate	41	Ba
New Duffus	302	Da
New Eastwood	149	Bb
New Edlington	174	Dc
New Elgin	303	Aa
Newenden	26	Da
New England	115	Aa
Newent	89	Ac
New Farnley	173	Ba
Newfield	206	Da
New Fryston	174	Ca
New Galloway	214	Ca
Newgate	136	Da
Newhall	128	Ca
Newham	244	Dc
Newhaven	25	Ac
Newhaven	251	Ba
Newhaw	41	Aa
New Hedges	62	Db
New Hey	172	Cb
New Holland	177	Bc
Newholm	200	Cb
New Houghton	135	Bb
New Humberstone	130	Db
New Hunstanton.	135	Aa
Newick	25	Aa
Newington, *Kent.*	28	Ca
Newington, *Kent.*	44	Da
Newington, *M'loth.*	251	Bb
Newington, *Oxon.*	73	Ab
Newington, *Yorks.*	176	Da
Newington Bagpath	69	Bb
Newington, N.	92	Cb
Newington, S.	92	Cb
New Inn	84	Cb
Newland, *Glos.*	68	Da
Newland, *Oxon.*	72	Ca
Newland, *Worcs.*	89	Ba
Newland, *Yorks.*	175	Aa
Newland, *Yorks.*	177	Bb
Newlands, *N'land*	244	Ca
Newlands, *Peeb.*	239	Ba
New Leeds	306	Ca
New Luce	212	Cb
Newlyn East	5	Bc
Newmains	250	Cc
New Malden	57	Bc
Newmarket, *Suff.*	97	Aa
New Mill, *Yorks.*	172	Dc
Newmill, *Banff*	304	Cb
New Mills, *Derby.*	162	Ca
New Mills, *Mont.*	123	Bc
Newmilns	237	Ab
New Moat	82	Dc

	PAGE	SQ.
Newnham, *Glos.*	69	Aa
Newnham, *Hants.*	55	Bc
Newnham, *Herts.*	75	Ba
Newnham, *Kent*	45	Ab
Newnham, *N'hants.*	112	Cc
Newnham, *Worcs.*	108	Cb
Newnham Murren	73	Ac
Newton, N.	53	Ac
New Oscott	128	Cc
New Pitsligo	305	Bb
Newport, *Dev.*	30	Db
Newport, *Essex*	76	Da
Newport, *Fife*	271	Bc
Newport, *Glos.*	69	Ab
Newport, *I. of W.*	21	Ab
Newport, *Mon.*	67	Bc
Newport, *Pem.*	82	Cb
Newport, *Shrops.*	126	Da
Newport Pagnell	94	Ca
New Quay, *Card.*	101	Ac
Newquay, *Corn.*	5	Ab
New Road Side, *Yorks.*	172	Da
New Road Side, *Yorks.*	182	Da
New Romney	27	Bb
Newsam Green	173	Ba
Newsham, *Dur.*	206	Dc
Newsham, *Yorks.*	197	Ab
New Sharlston	174	Cb
Newsholme, *Yorks.*	175	Ab
Newsholme, *Yorks.*	182	Dc
Newsome	172	Db
Newstead	149	Ba
New Stevenston	249	Bc
Newthorpe	149	Bb
Newtimber	24	Cb
Newton, *Caith.*	324	Cc
Newton, *Camb.*	96	Cb
Newton, *Cambs.*	134	Cc
Newton, *Ches.*	145	Aa
Newton, *Ches.*	160	Db
Newton, *Derby*	149	Ba
Newton, *Dors.*	36	Cc
Newton, *Dumf.*	227	Bb
Newton, *Glam.*	65	Bb
Newton, *Glam.*	64	Dc
Newton, *Herefs.*	87	Bb
Newton, *Herefs.*	107	Bc
Newton, *Lancs.*	169	Ba
Newton, *Lancs.*	180	Cc
Newton, *Lincs.*	152	Cc
Newton, *N'hants.*	113	Ba
Newton, *Norf.*	136	Cc
Newton, *N'land*	220	Db
Newton, *Notts.*	150	Db
Newton, *R. & C.*	301	Aa
Newton, *Staffs.*	147	Bc
Newton, *Suff.*	98	Cc
Newton, *War.*	112	Cb
Newton, *Yorks.*	199	Bc
Newton, *Yorks.*	208	Dc
Newton, *Yorks.*	174	Ca
Newton Abbot	14	Cc
Newton Arlosh	216	Dc
Newton Bewley	208	Cb
Newton Blossomville	94	Ca
Newton Bromswold	114	Cc
Newton Burgoland	129	Ab
Newton-by-the-Sea	244	Dc
Newton-by-Toft	166	Db
Newton Ferrers	8	Dc
Newton Flotman	119	Bb
Newton Harcourt	130	Dc
Newton, Higher	193	Ac
Newton Kyme	184	Dc
Newton-le-Willows	196	Db
Newton-le-Willows, *Lancs.*	160	Da
Newton Longville	94	Cb
Newton Mearns	248	Dc
Newtonmore	277	Ba
Newton, N.	34	Cb
Newton, Old	98	Db
Newton-on-the-Moor	232	Cb
Newton Peveril	18	Da
Newton Poppieford	15	Ac
Newton Purcell	93	Ab
Newton Regis	128	Db
Newton Regny	203	Bb
Newton, S.	37	Ab
Newton St. Cyres	32	Cc
Newton St. Faith	137	Bc
Newton St. Loe	51	Ab
Newton St. Petrock	12	Da
Newton Solney	148	Dc
Newtonstewart	212	Db
Newton Tony	37	Ba
Newton Tracey	30	Cc
Newton-upon-Derwent	186	Cb
Newton-upon-Ouse	185	Aa
Newton-upon-Trent	165	Bc
Newton Valence	39	Bb
Newton, W., *Cumb.*	202	Ca
Newton, W., *Som.*	33	Bb
Newton, W., *Yorks.*	178	Dc
New Town, *N'hants.*	132	Cb
Newtown, *Berks.*	72	Db
Newtown, *Ches.*	145	Bb
Newtown, *Cumb.*	202	Ac
Newtown, *Derby*	162	Cb
Newtown, *Dors.*	19	Bb
Newtown, *Hants.*	21	Ab
Newtown, *Hants.*	38	Cb
Newtown, *Hants.*	54	Db
Newtown, *Lancs.*	170	Cc
Newtown, *Mont.*	123	Bc
Newtown, *Shrops.*	145	Ac
Newtown, *Wilts.*	36	Db
Newtown Limford	130	Cb
Newtown Unthank	130	Cb
New Tredegar	67	Aa
Newtyle	271	Ab
New Yatt	72	Cb
New York	153	Bc
Neyland	62	Cb
Nibley, N.	69	Bb
Nibthwaite, High	192	Db
Nicholaston	64	Cc
Nigg	301	Ba
Nine Ashes	77	Ac
Ninfield	26	Cb
Nisbet	242	Cc
Niton	21	Ac
Nitshill	248	Dc
Noak Hill	58	Da
Nocton	166	Dc
Noke	72	Dc
Nolton	61	Ba
Nomansland	75	Bb
Noneley	144	Dc
Nonington	46	Cb
Norbiton	57	Ac
Norbury, *Ches.*	145	Bb
Norbury, *Derby*	148	Cb
Norbury, *Shrops.*	124	Dc
Norbury, *Staffs.*	126	Da
Norby	197	Bc
Nordelph	116	Da
Norden	171	Bb
Nordley	126	Cc
Norham	243	Aa
Norland	172	Db
Norley	160	Dc
Normanby, *Lincs.*	166	Cb
Normanby, *Lincs.*	176	Cb
Normanby, *Lincs.*	166	Da
Normanby, *Yorks.*	198	Dc
Normanby, *Yorks.*	208	Dc
Normanby-le-Wold	167	Ab
Normandy	56	Cc
Normanton, *Derby*	148	Dc
Normanton, *Leics.*	151	Bb
Normanton, *Lincs.*	152	Cb
Normanton, *Notts.*	150	Da
Normanton, *Yorks.*	174	Cb
Normanton-le-Heath	129	Bb
Normanton-on-the-Wolds	150	Dc
Normanton Spring	164	Cb
Normanton-upon-Soar	130	Ca
Normanton-upon-Trent	165	Bc
Nornay	165	Aa
Northallerton	197	Ab
Northam, *Dev.*	30	Cb
Northam, *Hants.*	38	Dc
Northampton	113	Ac
Northaw	75	Bc
North Barningham	137	Aa
North Barsham	136	Ca
North Berwick	252	Da
Northborough	115	Aa
Northbourne	46	Cb
North Brenton	8	Ca
Northchurch	74	Da
Northcott	12	Cc
North Cove	120	Db
North Cray	58	Dc
North Down	46	Da
Northedge	163	Bc
Northend, *Bucks.*	73	Bc
North End, *Lincs.*	133	Ba
North End, *Som.*	33	Bb
North End, *War.*	92	Ca
Northenden	161	Ba
North Elmham	136	Dc
North Evington	130	Db
Northfield, *Som.*	33	Bb
Northfield, *War.*	110	Ca
Northfleet	59	Ac
North Gate	133	Ab
Northhall Green	136	Dc
North Hill, *Corn.*	7	Ba
North Hill, *M'sex.*	57	Bb
North Huish	9	Ba
Northiam	26	Da
Northill	95	Ac
Northington	39	Aa
Northlands	153	Bc
Northleach	71	Aa
Northleigh, *Dev.*	15	Bb
Northleigh, *Dev.*	30	Ca
Northlew	12	Db
North Luffenham	132	Cb
Northmoor	72	Cb
Northmuir	271	Aa
Northney	22	Ca
Northolt	57	Ab
Northop	159	Ac
Northorpe, *Lincs.*	133	Ca
Northorpe, *Lincs.*	166	Ca
Northover, *Som.*	34	Da
Northover, *Som.*	34	Dc
Northowram	172	Da
North Petherton	34	Cb
Northport	18	Dc
Northrepps	137	Ba
North Runcton	135	Ac
North Scale	179	Aa
North Shields	222	Dc
North Street	55	Aa
North Tuddenham	136	Dc
North Walsham	137	Bb
Northway	90	Cb
Northwich	161	Ab
Northwick, *Glos.*	68	Dc
Northwick, *Som.*	34	Ca
North Witham	132	Ca
Northwold	117	Bb
Northwood, *Derby*	163	Bc
Northwood, *Hants.*	21	Ab
Northwood, *M'sex.*	57	Ac
Northwood, *Shrops.*	144	Dc
Northwood Green	89	Ac
North Wootton, *Dors.*	35	Bc
North Wootton, *Norf.*	135	Ab
Norton, *Ches.*	160	Db
Norton, *Dur.*	208	Cb
Norton, *Glam.*	64	Dc
Norton, *Glos.*	90	Cc
Norton, *Herts.*	75	Ba
Norton, *Kent*	45	Ac
Norton, *N'hants.*	112	Dc
Norton, *Notts.*	164	Bc
Norton, *Rad.*	106	Db
Norton, *Shrops.*	126	Db
Norton, *Som.*	49	Bb
Norton, *Suff.*	98	Da
Norton, *Sus.*	23	Ac
Norton, *Sus.*	25	Ac
Norton, *Wilts.*	70	Cc
Norton, *Worcs.*	109	Ac
Norton, *Worcs.*	109	Ba
Norton, *Worcs.*	90	Ca
Norton, *Yorks.*	163	Bb
Norton, *Yorks.*	186	Ca
Norton, *Yorks.*	174	Db
Norton Bavant	52	Cc
Norton Bridge	146	Dc
Norton Canes	127	Bb
Norton Canon	87	Ba
Norton Disney	151	Ba
Norton Ferris	36	Ca
Norton Fitzwarren	33	Bb
Norton-in-Hales	146	Cb
Norton-in-the-Moors	146	Da
Norton-juxta-Twycross	129	Ab
Norton-le-Clay	184	Da
Norton Lindsey	110	Db
Norton, Lit.	163	Bb
Norton Malreward	50	Db
Norton Mandeville	77	Ac
Norton St. Philip	51	Bb
Norton Subcourse	120	Cb
Norton-sub-Hamdon	34	Dc
Norton Wood	87	Ba
Norton Woodseats	163	Bb
Norwell	150	Da
Norwell Woodhouse	150	Da
Norwich	119	Ba
Norwood Green	172	Da
Norwoodside	116	Ca
Norwood, South	58	Cc
Norwood, Upr.	58	Cc
Noss Mayo	8	Dc
Nosterfield	196	Dc
Nottage	65	Bb
Nottingham	150	Cb
Nottington	17	Db
Notton, *Wilts.*	52	Ca
Notton, *Yorks.*	173	Bb
Nowton	98	Cb
Nuffield	73	Ac
Nunburnholme	186	Db
Nuneaton	129	Bc
Nuneham Courtenay	72	Db
Nun Monkton	185	Ab
Nunney	51	Bc
Nunnington, *Herefs.*	88	Da
Nunnington, *Yorks.*	198	Cc
Nunthorpe	208	Cc
Nunton	37	Bb
Nup End, *Bucks.*	74	Ca
Nupend, *Glos.*	69	Ba
Nursling	38	Cc
Nurstead	59	Ac
Nurton	126	Dc
Nutbourne, *Sus.*	23	Bb
Nutbourne, *Sus.*	22	Da
Nutfield	42	Cb
Nuthall	149	Bb
Nuthampstead	76	Ca
Nuthurst, *Sus.*	24	Ca
Nuthurst, *War.*	110	Cb
Nutley, *Hants.*	39	Ba
Nutley, *Sus.*	25	Aa
Nybster	324	Db
Nyetimber	22	Db
Nymet Rowland	31	Bb
Nympsfield	69	Bb
Nynehead	33	Ac
Nynehead, E.	33	Ac
Nythe	34	Db
OADBY	130	Dc
Oad Street	44	Db
Oakamoor	147	Bb
Oake	33	Ab
Oaken	127	Ab
Oakengates	126	Cb
Oakenshaw	173	Aa
Oakes	172	Db
Oakford, *Card.*	101	Ac
Oakford, *Dev.*	32	Ca
Oakfordbridge	32	Da
Oakham	131	Bb
Oakhill, *Som.*	51	Ac
Oakhill, *Wilts.*	53	Bb
Oakington	96	Ca
Oakley, *Beds.*	94	Ba
Oakley, *Bucks.*	73	Aa
Oakley, *Fife*	260	Cc
Oakley, *Norf.*	99	Ba
Oakley, *Oxon.*	73	Bb
Oakley, *Staffs.*	146	Cc
Oakley, Gt., *Essex*	79	Cb
Oakley, Gt., *N'hants.*	113	Ba
Oakley Green	56	Ca
Oakley, Lit., *Essex*	79	Cb
Oakley, Lit., *N'hants.*	113	Ba
Oakley, N.	54	Dc
Oaks	206	Db
Oaksey	70	Db
Oakworth	182	Dc
Oare, *Berks.*	54	Da
Oare, *Kent*	45	Ac
Oare, *Som.*	47	Bb
Oare, *Wilts.*	53	Ab
Oareford	47	Bb
Oasby	152	Cb
Oath	34	Cb
Oathlaw	271	Ac
Oatlands Mount	184	Cb
Oban	255	Ba
Oborne	35	Bb
Occold	99	Aa
Ochiltree	236	Dc
Ochr-y-mynydd	86	Cb
Ockbrook	149	Bc
Ockendon, N.	59	Ab
Ockendon, S.	59	Ab
Ockham	41	Aa
Ockle	273	Ac
Ockley	41	Bc
Ocle Pychard	88	Da
Odd Down	51	Bb
Oddendale	204	Cc
Oddingley	109	Bc
Oddington, *Glos.*	91	Bc
Oddington, *Oxon.*	72	Da
Odell	114	Cc
Odiham	55	Bc
Odstock	37	Bb
Odstone	129	Bb
Offchurch	111	Bc
Offenham	90	Da
Offham, *Kent*	43	Ba
Offham, *Sus.*	25	Ab
Offley, Gt.	75	Aa
Offord Cluney	95	Ba
Offord Darcy	95	Ba
Offton	99	Ab

Name	PAGE	SQ.
Offwell	15	Bb
Ogbourne St. Andrew	53	Aa
Ogbourne St. George	53	Ba
Ogden	172	Da
Ogle	221	Ba
Ogmore Vale	66	Ca
Ogwell, East	14	Cc
Ogwell, West	14	Cc
Okeford Fitzpaine	36	Cc
Okehampton	13	Aa
Okeover	148	Cb
Old	113	Ab
Old Aberdeen	294	Cc
Oldberrow	110	Cb
Old Blair	278	Ca
Old Bolingbroke	154	Cb
Old Brampton	163	Bb
Oldbury, Shrops.	126	Cc
Oldbury, War.	129	Ac
Oldbury, Worcs.	127	Bc
Oldbury-upon-Severn	68	Db
Old Byland	198	Da
Oldcastle	87	Bc
Old Church Stoke	124	Dc
Old Cleeve	48	Db
Oldcoates	164	Ba
Old Dalby	130	Da
Old Dam	162	Db
Old Deer	306	Cb
Old Ellerby, Yorks.	177	Bb
Oldfield, Worcs.	109	Ab
Oldfield, Yorks.	172	Dc
Old Flinder	293	Aa
Oldford	51	Bc
Old Goole	175	Bb
Oldham	172	Cc
Oldhamstocks	253	Bb
Old Hurst	115	Bc
Old Lakenham	119	Ba
Oldland	51	Aa
Old Leake	154	Cc
Old Mawbray	201	Ba
Old Meldrum	293	Ba
Old Rayne	293	Aa
Old Romney	27	Bb
Old Sarum	37	Bb
Old Town, Yorks.	173	Bc
Old Town, Yorks.	172	Ca
Old Windsor	56	Da
Old Woking	41	Aa
Ollach, Lr.	284	Da
Ollach, Upr.	284	Da
Ollerton, Ches.	161	Bb
Ollerton, Notts.	165	Aa
Ollerton, Shrops.	145	Bc
Olney, Bucks.	94	Ca
Olney, N'hants.	93	Aa
Olton	110	Ca
Olveston	68	Dc
Ombersley	109	Ab
Ompton	165	Ac
Onecote	147	Ba
Onehouse	98	Db
Ongar, High	77	Ac
Onibury	107	Ba
Onllwyn	85	Bb
Onneley	146	Cb
Openshaw	162	Ca
Orby	154	Db
Orchard, E.	36	Cb
Orchardleigh	51	Bc
Orchard Portman	33	Bc
Orchard, W.	36	Cb
Orcheston St. George	37	Aa
Orcheston St. Mary	37	Aa
Orcop	88	Cc
Ord	285	Ac
Ord, E.	243	Ba
Ordie	292	Dc
Ordsall	165	Ab
Ord, W.	243	Ba
Ore	26	Db
Oreton Common	108	Ca
Orford	100	Cc
Orlestone	27	Ba
Orleton, Heref s.	107	Bb
Orleton, Worcs.	108	Db
Orlingbury	113	Bb
Ormesby	208	Cc
Ormesby St. Margaret	138	Dc
Ormesby St. Michael	138	Dc
Ormiston	252	Cb
Ormsaigmore	263	Ba
Ormsby, N.	167	Bb
Ormsby, S.	154	Ca
Ormside, Gt.	204	Dc
Ormskirk	169	Bc
Orpington	43	Aa
Orrisdale	189	Bb

Name	PAGE	SQ.
Orsett	59	Ab
Orston	150	Db
Orthwaite	202	Db
Orton, N'hants.	113	Ba
Orton, W'land.	194	Ca
Orton, Gt.	217	Bc
Orton, Lit.	217	Bc
Orton Longueville	115	Aa
Orton-on-the-Hill	129	Ab
Orton Waterville	115	Aa
Orwell	96	Cb
Osbaldeston Green	170	Da
Osbaldwick	185	Bb
Osbaston, Leics.	129	Bb
Osbaston, Shrops.	124	Da
Osborne	21	Ab
Osbournby	152	Db
Oscroft	160	Cc
Osgathorpe	129	Ba
Osgodby, Lincs.	166	Da
Osgodby, Yorks.	175	Aa
Osgodby, Yorks.	188	Ca
Osleston	148	Db
Osmaston, Derby	149	Ac
Osmaston, Derby	148	Cb
Osmington	18	Cb
Osmotherley	197	Ba
Ospringe	45	Ab
Ossett	173	Bb
Ossett Spa	173	Bb
Ossington	165	Bc
Ostend	60	Da
Oswaldkirk	198	Cc
Oswaldtwistle	170	Da
Oswestry	144	Cc
Otford	43	Aa
Otham	44	Cb
Othery	34	Cb
Otley, Suff.	99	Bc
Otley, Yorks.	183	Bc
Otterbourne	38	Dc
Otterburn, N'land.	230	Dc
Otterburn, Yorks.	182	Cb
Otter Ferry	246	Ca
Otterford	15	Ba
Otterham	11	Bc
Otterhampton	33	Ba
Otterington, N.	197	Ab
Otterington, S.	197	Ab
Ottershaw	41	Aa
Otterton	15	Ac
Ottery St. Mary	15	Ab
Ottinge	28	Ca
Ottringham	178	Cc
Oughterby	217	Ac
Oughtershaw	195	Ac
Oughterside	202	Ca
Oughtibridge	163	Ba
Oulston	198	Cc
Oulton, Cumb.	217	Ac
Oulton, Norf.	137	Ab
Oulton, Staffs.	146	Dc
Oulton, Suff.	120	Db
Oulton, Yorks.	173	Ba
Oundle	114	Ca
Ousby	204	Ca
Ousden	97	Bb
Ouseburn, Gt.	184	Da
Ouseburn, Lit.	184	Da
Ousefleet	176	Ca
Ouston	222	Cc
Outhgill	194	Da
Outlane	172	Db
Outlane Moor	172	Db
Out Newton	178	Dc
Out Rawcliffe	180	Cc
Outwell	116	Ba
Outwood	173	Ba
Ouzelwell Green	173	Ba
Ovenden	172	Da
Over, Cambs.	96	Ca
Over, Ches.	160	Dc
Over Burrows	148	Db
Overbury	90	Cb
Over Compton	35	Ac
Over Green	128	Ca
Over Haddon	163	Ac
Overleigh	34	Cb
Over Norton	91	Bc
Overpool	159	Bb
Overseal	128	Cb
Over Silton	197	Bb
Oversland	45	Bb
Oversley Green	110	Cc
Overstone	113	Bc
Over Stowey	33	Ba
Overstrand	137	Ba
Overthorpe	92	Db
Overton, Ches.	160	Db
Overton, Flint	144	Db
Overton, Glam.	64	Cc
Overton, Hants.	54	Dc
Overton, Lancs.	180	Cb
Overton, Shrops.	107	Ba

Name	PAGE	SQ.
Overton, Yorks.	185	Ab
Overton, W.	53	Ab
Overtown	238	Ca
Over Wallop	38	Ca
Over Whitacre	128	Dc
Overy Staithe	136	Ca
Oving, Bucks.	93	Bc
Oving, Sus.	23	Ac
Ovingdean	24	Dc
Ovingham	220	Da
Ovington, Essex	97	Bc
Ovington, Hants.	39	Ab
Ovington, Norf.	118	Ca
Ovington, N'land.	220	Da
Ovington, Yorks.	206	Dc
Ower	21	Ca
Owermoigne	18	Cb
Owersby, N.	166	Da
Owinby	166	Db
Owlerton	163	Ba
Owlpen	69	Bb
Owlswick	73	Bb
Owmby	176	Dc
Owslebury	39	Ab
Owston, Leics.	131	Ab
Owston, Lincs.	175	Bc
Owston, Yorks.	174	Db
Owstwick	178	Cc
Owthorpe	150	Dc
Oxborough	117	Ca
Oxcombe	153	Ba
Oxendon, Gt.	113	Ac
Oxenhall	89	Ab
Oxenhope	172	Ca
Oxen Park	192	Db
Oxenton	90	Cb
Oxenwood	53	Bb
Oxford	72	Da
Oxhey	57	Aa
Oxhill	91	Ba
Oxley Green	78	Cc
Oxlode	116	Cb
Oxnam	230	Ca
Oxnead	137	Bb
Oxney Green	77	Ac
Oxshott	41	Ba
Oxted	42	Db
Oxton, Berw.	241	Aa
Oxton, Notts.	150	Ca
Oxton, Yorks.	185	Ac
Oxwich	64	Cc
Oykell Bridge	310	Ca
Oyne	293	Aa
Ozleworth	69	Bb
PACKINGTON	129	Ba
Packington, Lit.	110	Da
Packwood	110	Db
Padbury	93	Bb
Paddlesworth	28	Ca
Pademoor	175	Bb
Padfield	162	Da
Padiham	171	Aa
Padside	183	Bb
Padstow	5	Ba
Padworth	55	Ab
Pagham	22	Db
Paglesham	60	Ca
Paignton	10	Da
Pailton	112	Ca
Painscastle	87	Aa
Painswick	70	Ca
Painthorpe	173	Bb
Paisley	248	Dc
Pakefield	120	Db
Pakenham	98	Ca
Palfrey	127	Bc
Palgrave	99	Aa
Palling	138	Cb
Palnackie	214	Db
Palterton	161	Cc
Pamington	90	Cb
Pamphill	19	Aa
Pampisford	96	Dc
Panborough	34	Da
Panbride	272	Cc
Pancrasweek	11	Ba
Pandy, Mer.	121	Bb
Pandy, Mon.	87	Ba
Panfield	77	Bb
Pangbourne	55	Aa
Pannal	184	Cb
Panteg	67	Ba
Panton	153	Aa
Pant-y-dwr	105	Bb
Panxworth	138	Cc
Papcastle	201	Bb
Papplewick	150	Ca
Papworth Everard	95	Ba
Papworth St. Agnes	95	Ba
Parbold	170	Cb
Parbrook	35	Ab
Pardshaw	201	Bb
Parham	100	Cb

Name	PAGE	SQ.
Park Corner	73	Bc
Parkend, Cumb.	202	Da
Parkend, Glos.	68	Da
Parkgate, Ches.	159	Bb
Parkgate, Dumf.	227	Ac
Park Gate, Yorks.	164	Ca
Parkham	29	Bc
Parkhead	249	Ac
Park Lane	175	Ac
Parkstone	19	Ab
Park Villas	184	Cc
Parley, West	19	Bb
Parndon, Gt.	76	Cc
Parndon, Lit.	76	Cc
Parracombe	30	Da
Parson Drove	116	Ca
Parsons Heath	78	Db
Partick	248	Db
Partington	161	Aa
Partney	154	Ca
Parton, Cumb.	201	Ac
Parton, Kirk.	214	Ca
Parwich	148	Ca
Passenham	93	Bb
Paston, Norf.	138	Ca
Paston, N'hants.	115	Aa
Patcham	24	Db
Patching	23	Bc
Patchway	68	Dc
Pateley Bridge	183	Ba
Pathe	34	Cb
Pathhead, Ayr	225	Aa
Pathhead, Fife	261	Bc
Pathhead, M.Loth.	252	Cb
Patna	224	Ca
Patney	52	Db
Patrick Brompton	196	Db
Patricroft	161	Aa
Patrington	178	Dc
Patrixbourne	46	Cb
Patterdale	203	Ac
Pattingham	126	Da
Pattishall	112	Dc
Pattiswick	78	Cb
Paul	1	Bc
Paulerspury	93	Ba
Paulton	51	Ba
Pauntley	89	Bb
Pave Lane	126	Da
Pavenham	114	Cc
Pawlett	34	Ca
Paxford	91	Ab
Paxton, Gt.	95	Ba
Paxton, Lit.	95	Aa
Payhembury	15	Ab
Paythorne	182	Cb
Peacehaven	25	Ca
Peacemarsh	36	Cb
Peachley	109	Ac
Peak Forest	162	Db
Peakirk	115	Aa
Pean	28	Ca
Peasedown	51	Ab
Peasemore	54	Da
Peasenhall	100	Cb
Peaslake	41	Bb
Peasmarsh	27	Ca
Peatling Magna	130	Cc
Peatling Parva	112	Ca
Pebmarsh	78	Ca
Pebworth	91	Ca
Pecket Well	172	Ca
Peckforton	145	Ca
Peckham, W.	43	Bb
Peckleton	129	Bc
Pedlinge	28	Ca
Pedmore	109	Ba
Pedwell	34	Db
Peel	190	Cc
Peebles	240	Cb
Pegsdon	75	Aa
Pegswood	232	Cc
Pegwell	46	Cb
Peldon	78	Db
Peisall	127	Bb
Pelton	222	Cc
Pelutho	216	Dc
Pelynt	7	Ac
Pembroke	62	Cb
Pembroke Dock	62	Cb
Pembridge	107	Ac
Pembrey	63	Bb
Pembury	43	Bc
Penallt	68	Da
Penally	62	Cb
Penarth	49	Aa
Penarth, Lr.	49	Aa
Penboyr	83	Bb
Penbryn	83	Aa
Pencader	84	Cb
Pencaitland	252	Db
Pencairdg	84	Ca
Pen-clawdd	64	Cc
Pencoed	66	Cb

356

Name	PAGE	SQ.
Pencombe	108	Cc
Pencoyd	88	Cc
Pencraig, *Herefs.*	88	Dc
Pencraig, *Mont.*	143	Ac
Penderyn	86	Cb
Pendine	63	Ab
Pendlebury	171	Ac
Pendleton	181	Bc
Pendock	89	Bb
Pendomer	35	Ac
Pendoylan	66	Db
Penegoes	122	Cb
Pengam	67	Ab
Pen Garn	121	Bc
Penhow	68	Cb
Penhurst	26	Cb
Penicuik	251	Bc
Penistone	173	Bc
Penketh	160	Da
Penkridge	127	Ba
Penley	144	Db
Penllech	139	Ac
Penlline	66	Cb
Penmachno	141	Ba
Penmaen	64	Cc
Penmaenmawr	157	Ab
Penmaenrhos	157	Ba
Penmark	66	Dc
Penmon	156	Db
Penmorfa	140	Db
Penmynydd	156	Cb
Penn	74	Cc
Pennal	122	Cb
Pennant	122	Db
Pennant Melangell	142	Db
Pennard, E.	35	Aa
Pennard, W.	35	Aa
Pennerley	124	Bc
Penninghame	212	Db
Pennington	192	Cc
Penny Bridge	192	Dc
Penperlleni	67	Ba
Penpont, *Brecon.*	86	Ca
Penpont, *Corn.*	6	Da
Penpont, *Dumf.*	226	Cb
Penrhos, *Brecon.*	85	Bb
Penrhos, *Caer.*	139	Bc
Penrhos, *Mon.*	68	Ca
Penrhos Lligwy	156	Ca
Penrhyn-deudraeth	140	Db
Penrice	64	Cc
Penrith	203	Bb
Penruddock	203	Bb
Penrydd	82	Ab
Penryn	2	Db
Pensarn, *Ang.*	156	Ca
Pensarn, *Den.*	158	Ca
Pensax	108	Db
Penselwood	36	Ca
Pensford	51	Ab
Pensham	90	Ca
Penshaw	222	Cc
Penshurst	43	Ab
Penstone	32	Cc
Pentewan	6	Cc
Pentlow	97	Bc
Pentney	135	Bc
Penton Mewsey	53	Bc
Pentraeth	156	Cb
Pentre, *Den.*	158	Db
Pentre, *Glam.*	66	Ca
Pentre, *Mon.*	68	Ca
Pentre, *Shrops.*	124	Da
Pentreberw	156	Ca
Pentre-cagl	83	Bb
Pentre-chwyth	64	Dc
Pentre-dre-felin	83	Bb
Pentre-dwr	65	Aa
Pentrefoelas	157	Bc
Pentre Halkin	159	Ac
Pentrepoeth	67	Bc
Pentrich	149	Aa
Pentridge	37	Ac
Pentwyn	68	Da
Pentyrch	66	Db
Penwood	54	Cb
Penwortham	170	Ca
Pen-y-banc	84	Dc
Penybont, *Carm.*	83	Bc
Penybont, *Rad.*	106	Cc
Pen-y-bont, *Den.*	124	Ca
Pen-y-bont-fawr	123	Ba
Pen-y-cae, *Brecon*	85	Bb
Pen-y-cae, *Den.*	144	Cb
Pen-y-clawdd	68	Ca
Pen-y-daren	86	Db
Pen-y-garn	66	Db
Pen-y-graig	66	Ca
Penygroes, *Caer.*	140	Ca
Pen-y-groes, *Carm.*	64	Da
Pen-yr-englyn	66	Ca
Pen-yr-heol	68	Ca
Penzance	1	Bc
Peopleton	109	Bc
Peover, Lr.	161	Ba
Peover Superior	161	Bb
Peper Harow	40	Da
Peplow	126	Ca
Perivale	57	Ab
Perkhill	292	Dc
Perkinsbeach	124	Dc
Perlethorpe	165	Ac
Perranarworthal	2	Db
Perranporth	2	Da
Perranuthnoe	1	Bc
Perranzabuloe	2	Da
Perrott, North	16	Da
Perrott, South	16	Da
Perry, E.	95	Aa
Perry Green	33	Ba
Perry, W.	95	Aa
Pershore	90	Ca
Pertenhall	95	Aa
Perth	260	Cb
Perthy	144	Dc
Pertwood	36	Da
Peterborough	115	Aa
Peterchurch	87	Bb
Peterculter	294	Cc
Peterhead	306	Db
Peterlee	208	Ca
Petersfield	40	Cb
Petersham	57	Ac
Peterston-super-Ely	66	Db
Peterstone Wentlloog	67	Bc
Peterstow	88	Dc
Petertavy	8	Da
Petham	45	Bc
Petherton, Sth.	34	Dc
Petherwin, North	12	Cc
Petherwin, South.	7	Ba
Petrockstow	12	Da
Pett	27	Ac
Pettaugh	99	Bb
Pettinain	238	Da
Pettistree	99	Bc
Petton, *Dev.*	32	Da
Petton, *Shrops.*	144	Dc
Pettymuck	294	Ca
Petworth	23	Aa
Pevensey	26	Cc
Pewsey	53	Ab
Philham	29	Ac
Phillack	1	Bb
Philleigh	4	Ca
Phocle Green	88	Dc
Pibsbury	34	Db
Piccotts End	74	Da
Pickenham, N.	118	Ca
Pickenham, S.	118	Ca
Pickering	187	Aa
Pickhill	197	Ab
Picklescott	125	Ac
Pickmere	161	Ab
Pickwell	131	Ab
Pickwick	52	Ca
Pickworth, *Lincs.*	152	Cc
Pickworth, *Rut.*	132	Cb
Picton	197	Aa
Piddinghoe	25	Ac
Piddington, *N'hants.*	93	Ba
Piddington, *Oxon.*	73	Ba
Piddle, N.	109	Bc
Piddlehinton	18	Ca
Piddletrenthide	18	Ca
Pidley	115	Bc
Piercebridge	206	Da
Pightley	33	Bb
Pig Street	139	Bc
Pikehall	148	Ca
Pilcot	55	Bc
Pilham	166	Ca
Pill	50	Da
Pillaton, *Corn.*	7	Bb
Pillaton, *Staffs.*	127	Ba
Pillerton Hersey	91	Ba
Pillerton Priors	91	Ba
Pilleth	106	Db
Pilley	173	Bc
Pilling	180	Cb
Pillowell	69	Aa
Pilsdon	16	Db
Pilsley, *Derby*	163	Ac
Pilsley, *Derby*	149	Ba
Pilton, *Dev.*	30	Cb
Pilton, *N'hants.*	114	Ca
Pilton, *Rut.*	131	Bc
Pilton, *Som.*	35	Aa
Pimperne	36	Dc
Pinchbeck	133	Bb
Pinchbeck West	133	Ab
Pinfold	169	Bb
Pinhoe	14	Da
Pinmill	79	Ba
Pinner	57	Aa
Pinvin	90	Ca
Pinxton	149	Ba
Pinxton Green	149	Ba
Pipe and Lyde	88	Ca
Pipe Gate	146	Cb
Pipe Ridware	128	Ca
Pipewell	113	Ba
Pipton	87	Ab
Pirbright	56	Dc
Pirton, *Herts.*	75	Aa
Pirton, *Worcs.*	90	Ca
Pishill	73	Bc
Pistyll	139	Bb
Pitcairn	269	Ab
Pitcairngreen	270	Cc
Pitchard Green	162	Db
Pitchcombe	69	Ba
Pitchcott	93	Bc
Pitchford	125	Bb
Pitcombe	35	Ba
Pitlochry	269	Ba
Pitminster	33	Bc
Pitney	34	Db
Pitsea	59	Bb
Pitsford	113	Ab
Pitstone	74	Ca
Pitt	38	Db
Pittenweem	262	Db
Pittington	207	Ba
Pittodrie	293	Aa
Pitton	37	Bb
Pittulie	306	Ca
Pitway	34	Dc
Pixley	89	Aa
Plains	249	Bb
Plainsfield	33	Bb
Plaistow, *Derby*	149	Aa
Plaistow, *Sus.*	23	Aa
Plaitford	38	Cc
Platt Bridge	170	Cc
Plawsworth	222	Cc
Plaxtol	43	Bb
Playden	27	Ab
Playford	99	Bc
Plealey	125	Ab
Plean	250	Ca
Pleasington	170	Da
Pleasley	164	Bc
Pledgdon	76	Da
Plemstall	160	Cc
Plenmeller	219	Bb
Pleshey	77	Ab
Plockton	285	Ba
Ploughfield	87	Ba
Pluckley	44	Db
Plumbland	202	Ca
Plumpton, *N'hanis.*	93	Aa
Plumpton, *Sus.*	24	Db
Plumpton, Gt.	169	Ba
Plumstead, *London*	58	Db
Plumstead, *Norf.*	137	Aa
Plumstead, Gt.	119	Ba
Plumstead, Lit.	119	Ba
Plumtree	150	Cc
Plungar	150	Dc
Plush	18	Ca
Plymouth	8	Dc
Plympton	8	Dc
Plymstock	8	Dc
Plymtree	15	Aa
Pockley	198	Cb
Pocklington	186	Cb
Podimore	35	Ab
Podington	114	Cc
Poffley End	72	Ca
Pointon	133	Aa
Polbain	313	Ac
Polebrook	114	Ca
Polesworth	128	Dc
Polglass	313	Ac
Polgooth	6	Cc
Poling	23	Ac
Pollington	174	Db
Pollokshaws	248	Dc
Polmont	250	Ca
Polruan	6	Dc
Polsham	34	Da
Polstead	78	Da
Poltesco	3	Bc
Poltimore	14	Da
Polton	251	Bb
Polwarth	242	Ca
Polyphant	7	Ba
Pondersbridge	115	Bb
Ponders End	58	Ca
Ponsanooth	2	Db
Ponsonby	191	Ba
Pontamman	64	Da
Pont-Antwn	64	Ca
Pontardawe	85	Ac
Pont-ar-Sais	84	Cc
Pont Clun	66	Db
Pontefract	174	Db
Ponteland	221	Ba
Pontesbury	125	Ab
Pont Henry	64	Ca
Pont-llan-fraith	67	Ab
Pont Llogel	123	Ab
Pontlottyn	86	Db
Pont Nedd Fechan	85	Bb
Pontnewydd	67	Bb
Pontnewynydd	67	Bb
Ponton, Gt.	152	Cc
Ponton Lit.	151	Bc
Pont-rhyd-y-fen	65	Ba
Pontrhydyrun	67	Bb
Pontrilas	88	Cb
Pont Robert	123	Ab
Pontshill	88	Dc
Pont Walby	86	Cb
Pont-Yates	64	Cb
Pont-y-berem	64	Ca
Pont-y-cymmer	66	Ca
Pontypool	67	Bb
Pontypridd	66	Da
Pont-y-rhyll	66	Ca
Pont-y-waun	67	Ab
Pool, *Corn.*	2	Cb
Pool, *Yorks.*	183	Bc
Poole	19	Ab
Poole Keynes	70	Db
Poolewe	307	Bb
Poolhill	89	Ab
Pool Quay	124	Cb
Poolsbrook	164	Cc
Pool Street	77	Ba
Poorton, North	17	Aa
Popham	39	Aa
Poppleton, Nether	185	Ab
Poppleton, Upr.	185	Ab
Porchester	21	Ba
Porlock	47	Bb
Porlock, W.	47	Bb
Port Appin	265	Bb
Port Bannatyne	246	Dc
Portbury	50	Ca
Port Dinorwic	156	Cc
Port Elphinstone	293	Dc
Port Erin	190	Dc
Port Errol	306	Cc
Portessie	304	Ca
Port Eynon	64	Cc
Portfield	22	Da
Port Glasgow	247	Bb
Portgordon	303	Ba
Portgower	317	Cc
Porth	66	Ca
Porthallow	2	Dc
Porthcawl	65	Bb
Porthkerry	66	Dc
Porthleven	2	Cc
Porth-y-rhyd	64	Ca
Portincaple	257	Ac
Portinnisherrich	256	Cb
Portinscale	202	Db
Port Isaac	6	Ca
Portisham	17	Bb
Portishead	50	Ca
Portknockie	304	Ca
Portland, Isle of	18	Cc
Portlethen	282	Da
Portloe	4	Ca
Port Logan	209	Ab
Portmadoc	140	Da
Portmahomack	312	Db
Portmellon	4	Ca
Portnacroish	265	Bb
Portobello, *M. Loth.*	251	Bb
Portobello, *Staffs.*	127	Bb
Port of Menteith	258	Dc
Porton	37	Bc
Portpatrick	211	Ac
Portquin	6	Ca
Port Ramsay	265	Ab
Portreath	2	Ca
Portree	296	Cc
Port St. Mary	190	Dc
Port Seton	252	Cb
Portskerra	322	Ca
Portskewett	68	Cc
Portslade	24	Cc
Portslade-by-Sea	24	Cc
Portsmouth	22	Da
Port Soderick	190	Cb
Port Sonachan	256	Ca
Portsoy	304	Da
Port Sunlight	159	Bb
Port Talbot	65	Aa
Port William	210	Cb
Portyerrock	210	Db
Posenhall	126	Cb
Poslingford	97	Bc
Postbridge	13	Bb
Postcombe	73	Bb
Postling	28	Ca
Postwick	119	Ba
Potsgrove	94	Cc
Potten End	74	Da
Potter Hanworth	166	Dc

Name	Page	Sq.
Potter Heigham	138	Cc
Potterne	52	Db
Potterne Wick	52	Db
Potters Bar	57	Ba
Potterscrouch	75	Ac
Potters Marston	129	Bc
Potterspury	93	Ba
Potter Street	76	Dc
Potthorpe	136	Dc
Potto	197	Ba
Potton	95	Bb
Pottrow	135	Bb
Poughill, *Corn.*	11	Ba
Poughill, *Dev.*	32	Cb
Poulner	19	Ba
Poulshot	52	Cb
Poulton, *Ches.*	144	Da
Poulton, *Glos.*	70	Db
Poulton-le-Fylde	180	Cc
Pound	65	Bb
Pound Hill	42	Cb
Poundon	93	Ac
Poundsgate	13	Bc
Poundstock	11	Bb
Pounsley	25	Ba
Powderham	14	Db
Powerstock	17	Aa
Powick	109	Ac
Poxwell	18	Cb
Poynings	24	Db
Poyntington	35	Bb
Poynton	162	Cb
Poynton Green	162	Cb
Prees	145	Bc
Preesall	180	Cc
Preesgreen	145	Bc
Prees Lower Heath	145	Bc
Prendergast	62	Ca
Prendwick	231	Ba
Pren-gwyn	84	Cb
Prenteg	140	Db
Prescot	160	Ca
Prescott	125	Aa
Preshute	53	Ab
Prestatyn	158	Da
Prestbury, *Ches.*	162	Cb
Prestbury, *Glos.*	90	Cb
Presteigne	106	Dc
Prestleigh	35	Ba
Preston, *Den.*	14	Cb
Preston, *Dors.*	18	Cb
Preston, *E. Loth.*	253	Aa
Preston, *Glos.*	89	Ab
Preston, *Glos.*	70	Db
Preston, *Herts.*	75	Ab
Preston, *Kent*	45	Ab
Preston, *Kent*	46	Cb
Preston, *Lancs.*	170	Ca
Preston, *Rut.*	131	Bc
Preston, *Suff.*	98	Dc
Preston, *Sus.*	24	Dc
Preston, *Wilts.*	70	Db
Preston, *Wilts.*	53	Ba
Preston, *Yorks.*	178	Cb
Preston Bagot	110	Db
Preston Bissett	93	Ab
Preston Bowyer	33	Ab
Preston Brockhurst	125	Ba
Preston Candover	39	Ba
Preston Capes	92	Da
Preston Deanery	113	Ac
Preston, E.	23	Bc
Preston, Gt.	174	Ca
Preston Gubbals	125	Ba
Preston, Lit.	174	Ca
Preston-on-Stour	91	Aa
Preston-on-the-Hill	160	Db
Preston-on-the-Weald Moors	126	Ca
Preston-on-Wye	87	Ba
Prestonpans	252	Cb
Preston Plucknett	34	Dc
Preston-under-Scar	196	Cb
Preston Wynne	88	Da
Prestwich	171	Bc
Prestwick, *Ayr*	236	Cc
Prestwick, *N'land*	221	Ba
Prestwold	130	Ca
Prestwood	74	Cb
Prickwillow	116	Dc
Priddy	35	Ac
Priestcliffe	163	Ac
Priest Hutton	193	Bc
Primethorpe	130	Cc
Princes Pier	247	Bb
PrincesRisborough	73	Bb
Princethorpe	111	Bb
Princetown	8	Da
Prinsted	22	Ca
Priors Dean	40	Cb
Priors Hardwick	92	Da
Priors Marston	112	Cc
Priors Norton	90	Cc
Prisk	66	Cc
Priston	51	Ab
Pristow Green	119	Ab
Prittlewell	60	Cb
Privett	39	Bb
Probus	4	Ca
Providence	50	Da
Prudhoe	221	Bb
Publow	51	Ab
Puckeridge	76	Cb
Puckington	34	Ca
Pucklechurch	51	Ab
Puddington, *Ches.*	159	Bc
Puddington, *Dev.*	32	Cb
Puddletown	18	Ca
Pudleston	108	Cc
Pudsey	173	Aa
Pulborough	23	Bb
Pulford	144	Da
Pulham	35	Bc
Pulham St. Mary Magdalene	119	Ac
Pulham St. Mary the Virgin	119	Ac
Pulloxhill	75	Aa
Puncheston	82	Cc
Puncknowle	17	Ab
Puriton	34	Ca
Purleigh	60	Ca
Purley, *Berks.*	55	Aa
Purley, *Sur.*	42	Ca
Purlogue	106	Db
Purlpit	52	Ca
Puris Bridge	116	Cb
Purse Caundle	35	Ba
Purshull Green	109	Bb
Purslow	107	Aa
Purston	92	Db
Purston Jaglin	174	Cb
Purton, *Glos.*	69	Aa
Purton, *Wilts.*	70	Dc
Pusey	72	Cb
Putford	12	Ca
Putley	89	Ab
Putney	57	Bc
Putsborough	30	Ca
Putson	88	Cb
Puttenham, *Herts.*	74	Ca
Puttenham, *Sur.*	40	Da
Puxton	50	Db
Pwll	64	Cb
Pwllcrochan	61	Bb
Pwllheli	139	Bb
Pwll Meyric	68	Db
Pwll-trap	63	Aa
Pyecombe	24	Db
Pyle	65	Bb
Pylle	35	Ba
Pymore	16	Db
Pyrford	41	Aa
Pyrton	73	Ab
Pytchley	113	Db
Pyworthy	12	Cb
QUADRING	133	Ba
Quainton	93	Bc
Quantockshead, E.	33	Aa
Quantockshead, W.	33	Aa
Quarley	38	Ca
Quarndon	148	Db
Quarr	36	Cb
Quarrington	152	Db
Quarry Bank	109	Ba
Quatford	126	Dc
Quatt	108	Da
Quedgeley	69	Ba
Queen Adelaide	116	Dc
Queenborough	60	Cc
Queen Camel	35	Ab
Queen Charlton	51	Ab
Queenhill	90	Cb
Queensbury	172	Da
Queensferry	159	Bc
Queensferry, N.	251	Aa
Queensferry, S.	251	Aa
Quemerford	52	Da
Quendon	76	Da
Queniborough	130	Db
Quenington	71	Ab
Quernmore	180	Ca
Quethiock	7	Bb
Quidenham	118	Da
Quidhampton	37	Ab
Quinton, *Glos.*	91	Aa
Quinton, *N'hants.*	113	Ac
Quoditch	12	Cb
Quorndon	130	Ca
Radcot	71	Bb
Raddington	48	Dc
Radford, *Notts.*	150	Cb
Radford, *War.*	111	Ac
Radford Semele	111	Ac
Radipole	17	Ca
Radlett	57	Aa
Radley	72	Db
Radnage	73	Bb
Radnor, New	106	Dc
Radnor, Old	106	Dc
Radstock	51	Ab
Radstone	92	Db
Radway	92	Ca
Radwell	75	Ba
Radwinter	77	Aa
Radyr	66	Db
Rafford	302	Db
Ragdale	130	Da
Raglan	68	Ca
Ragnall	165	Bc
Rails	163	Ba
Rainford	169	Bc
Rainham, *Essex*	58	Db
Rainham, *Kent*	44	Ca
Rainham, Lr.	60	Cb
Rainhill	160	Ca
Rainton	197	Ac
Rainton, E.	222	Cc
Rainton, W.	222	Cc
Rainworth	150	Ca
Raisbeck	194	Ca
Raithby, *Lincs.*	154	Cb
Raithby, *Lincs.*	168	Cb
Rake	40	Cb
Ramasaig	295	Ac
Rame	8	Cc
Rampisham	17	Aa
Rampside	179	Ba
Rampton, *Cambs.*	96	Ca
Rampton, *Notts.*	165	Bb
Ramsbottom	171	Ba
Ramsbury	53	Ba
Ramscraigs	318	Cb
Ramsdean	39	Bc
Ramsdell	55	Ac
Ramsden	72	Ca
Ramsden Bellhouse	59	Ba
Ramsden Crays	59	Ba
Ramsden Heath	59	Ba
Ramsey, *Essex*	79	Bb
Ramsey, *Hunts.*	115	Db
Ramsey, *I.O.M.*	109	Ba
Ramsgate	46	Da
Ramsgill	183	Aa
Ramsholt	80	Ca
Ranby, *Lincs.*	153	Aa
Ranby, *Notts.*	165	Ab
Rand	153	Aa
Randwick	69	Ba
Rangemore	128	Da
Rangeworthy	69	Ac
Ranskill	165	Aa
Ranton	127	Aa
Ranworth	138	Cc
Rasen, Mid	166	Ba
Rasen, W.	166	Ba
Raskelf	184	Da
Rassa	67	Aa
Rastrick	172	Db
Ratby	130	Cb
Ratcliffe	164	Db
Ratcliffe Culey	129	Ac
Ratcliffe-on-the-Wreak	130	Da
Ratcliffe-upon-Soar	149	Bc
Rathen	306	Ca
Rathmell	182	Cb
Ratho	251	Ab
Rathven	304	Ca
Ratlake	38	Db
Ratley	92	Ca
Ratling	46	Cb
Ratlinghope	125	Ac
Rattery	10	Ca
Rattlesden	98	Db
Rattray	270	Da
Rauceby, N.	152	Cb
Rauceby, S.	152	Cb
Raunds	114	Cb
Raveley, Gt.	115	Bc
Raveley, Lit.	115	Bc
Ravendale, E.	167	Ba
Ravenfield	164	Ca
Ravenglass	191	Bb
Raveningham	120	Cb
Ravensdale	189	Bb
Ravensden	94	Ba
Ravenshaw	182	Db
Ravensthorpe, *N'hants.*	112	Db
Ravensthorpe, *Yorks.*	173	Ab
Ravenstone, *Bucks.*	94	Ca
Ravenstone, *Leics.*	129	Bb
Ravenstonedale	194	Ca
Ravensworth	196	Ca
Rawcliffe Bridge	175	Bb
Rawdon	183	Bc
Rawmarsh	164	Ca
Rawreth	59	Ba
Rawtenstall	171	Ba
Rawyards	249	Bb
Raydon	79	Ba
Rayleigh	59	Ba
Rayne	77	Ba
Raynham, E.	136	Cb
Raynham, W.	136	Cb
Read	171	Aa
Reading	55	Aa
Reagill	204	Cc
Rearsby	130	Db
Reasby	166	Db
Reay	322	Da
Reculver	46	Ca
Redberth	62	Db
Redbourn	75	Ab
Redbourne	176	Dc
Redbridge	38	Dc
Redbrook	68	Da
Redbrook Street	27	Aa
Redcar	208	Dc
Redcastle	300	Db
Redcross	146	Ca
Red Dial	202	Da
Redding	250	Ca
Reddings, The	90	Cc
Reddish	162	Ca
Redditch	110	Cb
Rede	97	Bb
Redenhall	119	Bc
Redenham	53	Bc
Redgorton	270	Cc
Redgrave	99	Aa
Redhill, *Notts.*	150	Cb
Redhill, *Shrops.*	126	Cb
Redhill, *Som.*	50	Db
Redhill, *Sur.*	42	Cb
Redisham	120	Cc
Redlingfield	99	Ba
Redlynch, *Som.*	35	Ba
Redlynch, *Wilts.*	37	Bc
Redmain	202	Cb
Redmarley D'Abitot	89	Bb
Redmarshall	207	Bb
Redmire	195	Db
Rednal, *Shrops.*	144	Ca
Rednal, *Worcs.*	110	Ca
Red Roses	63	Aa
Redruth	2	Db
Red Street	146	Ba
Redwick, *Glos.*	68	Dc
Redwick, *Mon.*	68	Cc
Redworth	207	Ab
Reed	76	Ca
Reedham, *Lincs.*	153	Ba
Reedham, *Norf.*	120	Cb
Reedness	175	Ba
Reedy	14	Ca
Reepham, *Lincs.*	166	Dc
Reepham, *Norf.*	137	Aa
Reeth	195	Ba
Reiff	313	Ac
Reigate	42	Cb
Reighton	188	Cb
Remenham	73	Bc
Rempstone	130	Ca
Rendcomb	70	Da
Rendham	100	Da
Rendlesham	100	Cc
Renfrew	248	Ab
Renhold	95	Ab
Renishaw	164	Cb
Rennington	232	Ca
Renton	248	Cb
Renwick	204	Ca
Repton	148	Db
Rerwick	214	Dc
Resolis	300	Da
Resolven	85	Bc
Reston, N.	168	Cb
Reston, S.	168	Cc
Restormel	6	Db
Rettendon	59	Ba
Revelstoke	8	Ca
Revesby	153	Bb
Rewe	32	Bc
Reydon	100	Da
Reymerston	118	Da
Reynalton	62	Db
Reynoldston	64	Cb
Rezare	7	Ba
Rhayader	105	Bb
Rheola	85	Bc
Rhewl, *Den.*	143	Bb
Rhewl, *Shrops.*	144	Cc
Rhiconich	319	Bb
Rhiwargor	123	Aa

	PAGE	SQ.
Rhiwderin	67	Ac
Rhodes	171	Bc
Rhondda	66	Ca
Rhonehouse	214	Db
Rhoose	66	Dc
Rhosbeirio	155	Ba
Rhoscolyn	155	Ab
Rhoscrowther	61	Bb
Rhos Dinas	82	Cb
Rhos-goch	87	Aa
Rhos-llanerch-rugog	144	Cb
Rhosmaen	84	Dc
Rhosnesney	144	Ca
Rhossili	63	Bc
Rhostie	102	Cb
Rhostyllen	144	Cb
Rhosybol	155	Ba
Rhos-y-brithdir	124	Ca
Rhu	247	Ba
Rhuddlan	158	Ca
Rhulen	104	Da
Rhunahaorine	233	Aa
Rhyd-ar-gaeau	84	Cc
Rhyd-cymmerau	84	Db
Rhydtalog	144	Ca
Rhydwaedlyd	67	Ac
Rhyd-y-fro	85	Ac
Rhyl	158	Ca
Rhymney	86	Db
Rhynie	292	Da
Ribbesford	108	Db
Ribbleton	170	Ca
Ribchester	170	Da
Ribston, Lit.	184	Db
Riby	167	Aa
Riccall	185	Bc
Riccarton	236	Db
Richards Castle	107	Bb
Richmond, Sur.	57	Ac
Richmond, Yorks.	196	Ca
Rickby	217	Bc
Rickerscote	127	Aa
Rickinghall	98	Da
Rickling	76	Da
Rickmansworth	74	Dc
Riddings, Cumb.	217	Ba
Riddings, Derby	149	Ba
Riddlecombe	31	Ab
Riddlesworth	118	Cc
Ridge, Herts.	57	Ba
Ridge, Wilts.	36	Da
Ridgeway, Derby	164	Cb
Ridgeway, Dev.	8	Dc
Ridgeway, Glos.	68	Dc
Ridgeway, Som.	51	Pc
Ridgeway Moor	164	Cb
Ridgewell	97	Bc
Ridgmont	94	Db
Riding Gate	35	Ba
Ridley	43	Ba
Ridlington, Norf.	138	Cb
Ridlington, Rut.	131	Bb
Ridsdale	230	Dc
Rievaulx	198	Cb
Rigg	217	Ab
Rigsby	154	Ca
Rigton, Yorks.	184	Cb
Rigton, Yorks.	184	Cc
Rilla Mill	7	Ba
Rillington	187	Ab
Rimington	182	Cc
Rimpton	35	Ab
Rimswell	178	Db
Ringinglow	163	Bb
Ringland	137	Ac
Ringley	171	Ac
Ringmer	25	Ab
Ringmore	9	Bb
Rings End	116	Ca
Ringsfield	120	Cb
Ringshall	98	Db
Ringstead, Norf.	135	Ba
Ringstead, N'hants.	114	Cb
Ringwold	46	Dc
Ringwood	19	Ba
Ripe	25	Bb
Ripley, Derby	149	Ba
Ripley, Hants.	19	Bb
Ripley, Sur.	41	Aa
Ripley, Yorks.	184	Ca
Ripon	184	Ca
Rippingale	133	Ab
Ripple, Kent	46	Dc
Ripple, Worcs.	90	Cb
Ripponden	172	Cb
Risbury	108	Cc
Risby, Lincs.	176	Ca
Risby, Suff.	97	Ba
Risca	67	Ab
Rise	177	Ba
Risegate	133	Ab
Riseholme	166	Cb
Riseley	114	Cc
Rishangles	99	Aa
Rishton	170	Da
Rishworth	172	Cb
Risley	149	Bc
Rissington, Gt.	71	Aa
Rissington, Lit.	91	Ac
Rivenhall	78	Cb
Rivenhall End	78	Cb
Riverhead	43	Aa
Rivertown	159	Bc
Rivington	170	Db
Road, Som.	33	Bb
Road, Som.	51	Bb
Roade	93	Ba
Roadside	282	Db
Roadwater	48	Cb
Roag	295	Bc
Roath	49	Aa
Roberton, Lan.	238	Db
Roberton, Rox.	228	Da
Robertsbridge	26	Ca
Roberts End	89	Ba
Robert Town	173	Ab
Robeston	61	Bb
Robeston Wathen	62	Ba
Robin Hood's Bay	200	Ca
Roborough	30	Dc
Rocester	148	Cb
Roch	61	Ba
Rochdale	171	Ba
Roche	6	Cb
Rochester	59	Bc
Rochford, Essex	60	Cb
Rochford, Worcs.	108	Cb
Rochford, Upr.	108	Cb
Rock, Mon.	67	Ab
Rock. N'land.	244	Dc
Rock, Worcs.	108	Db
Rockbourne	37	Ac
Rockcliffe	217	Bb
Rockfield, Mon.	68	Cb
Rockfield, R. & C.	312	Db
Rockhampton	69	Ab
Rock Hill	109	Bb
Rockingham	131	Bc
Rockland All Saints	118	Db
Rockland St Mary	119	Ba
Rockland St Peter	118	Db
Rockleaze	50	Da
Rockley	53	Aa
Rockwell Green	33	Ac
Rodborough	69	Ba
Rodbourne	70	Cc
Rodbourne Cheney	71	Ac
Rodden, Dors.	17	Bb
Rodden, Som.	51	Bc
Rode Heath	146	Da
Rode. N.	162	Cc
Rodford	69	Ac
Rodgrove	35	Bb
Rodhuish	48	Cb
Rodington	125	Ba
Rodley	183	Bc
Rodmarton	70	Cb
Rodmell	25	Ac
Rodmersham	44	Da
Rodney Stoke	50	Cc
Rodsley	148	Cb
Rodway	33	Ba
Roecliffe	184	Ca
Roe Wen	157	Ab
Rogart	312	Ca
Rogate	40	Cb
Rogerstone	67	Bc
Roke	73	Ac
Rokeby	206	Cc
Rolleston, Leics.	130	Dc
Rolleston, Notts.	150	Da
Rolleston, Staffs.	148	Dc
Rollestone	37	Aa
Rollright, Gt.	91	Bc
Rollright, Lit.	91	Bc
Rolston	178	Ca
Rolstone	50	Cb
Rolstone E.	50	Cb
Rolvenden	26	Da
Romanby	197	Ab
Romanno Bridge	239	Ba
Romansleigh	31	Ba
Romford, Dors.	19	Ba
Romford, Essex	58	Db
Romiley	162	Ca
Romsey	38	Cc
Romsley	109	Ba
Ronaldkirk	206	Cb
Rooks Bridge	50	Cc
Rookwith	196	Db
Roos	178	Cb
Roosecote	179	Ba
Ropley	39	Bb
Ropsley	152	Cc
Rose	2	Ba
Roseacre	180	Cc
Rose Ash	32	Ca
Rosedale Abbey	198	Db
Rosehall	310	Da
Rosehearty	306	Ca
Rosemarket	62	Cb
Rosemarkie	301	Ab
Rosgill	204	Cc
Rosley	202	Ba
Roslin	251	Bc
Rosliston	128	Da
Rosneath	247	Ba
Ross-on-Wye	88	Dc
Rossett	144	Ca
Rossington	165	Aa
Ross Priory	248	Ca
Rostherne	161	Ba
Rosthwaite	202	Dc
Roston	148	Cb
Rosyth	251	Aa
Rothbury	231	Bb
Rotherby	130	Da
Rotherfield	25	Ba
Rotherfield Greys	55	Ba
Rotherfield Peppard	55	Ba
Rotherham	164	Ca
Rothersthorpe	112	Dc
Rotherwick	55	Bc
Rothes	303	Ab
Rothesay	246	Dc
Rothley, Leics.	130	Cb
Rothley, N'land.	231	Bc
Rothney	293	Aa
Rothwell, Lincs.	167	Ab
Rothwell, N'hants.	113	Ba
Rothwell, Yorks.	173	Ba
Rothwell Haigh	173	Ba
Rottal	280	Dc
Rotten Row	118	Da
Rottingdean	24	Dc
Rottington	201	Ac
Roudham	118	Cc
Rougham	136	Cc
Rough Close	147	Ab
Roughlee	182	Cc
Roughton, Lincs.	153	Bb
Roughton, Norf.	137	Ba
Roughton, Shrops.	126	Dc
Roundhay	184	Cc
Round Oak	55	Ab
Roundway	52	Db
Rounton, E.	197	Ba
Rounton, W.	197	Ba
Rousdon	16	Cb
Rousham	92	Dc
Rous Lench	110	Cc
Routh	177	Ba
Routs Green	73	Bb
Row, Corn.	6	Da
Row. W'land.	193	Ab
Row, Yorks	200	Cb
Rowardennan	257	Bc
Rowarth	162	Da
Rowberrow	50	Cb
Rowde	52	Cb
Row Farms	51	Bb
Rowhedge	79	Ac
Rowington	110	Db
Rowledge	40	Ca
Rowley	124	Db
Rowley Regis	127	Bc
Rowner	21	Ba
Rowsham	74	Ca
Rowsley Gt.	163	Bc
Rowsley. Lit.	163	Bc
Rowston	152	Da
Rowthorn	164	Cc
Rowton, Ches.	160	Cc
Rowton, Shrops.	126	Ca
Row Town	41	Aa
Roxburgh	242	Cb
Roxby	176	Cb
Roxholm	152	Db
Roxton	95	Ab
Roxwell	77	Ac
Roydon, Essex	76	Cc
Roydon, Norf.	135	Bb
Roydon, Norf.	118	Dc
Royston, Herts.	96	Cc
Royston, Yorks.	173	Bb
Royton	171	Bc
Ruabon	144	Cb
Ruan Lanihorne	4	Ca
Ruan Major	3	Bc
Ruan Minor	3	Bc
Ruardean	88	Dc
Rubery	109	Ba
Ruckcroft	203	Ba
Ruckinge	27	Ba
Ruckland	153	Ba
Rudbaxton	62	Ca
Rudby	197	Ba
Ruddington	150	Cc
Rudford	89	Bc
Rudge	51	Bc
Rudgwick	41	Bc
Rudry	67	Ac
Rudston	188	Cb
Rufford	169	Bb
Rufforth	185	Ca
Rugby	112	Cb
Rugeley	127	Ba
Ruishton	33	Bc
Ruislip	57	Ab
Rumbling Bridge	260	Cc
Rumboldswhyke	22	
Rumburgh	120	Cc
Rumney	67	Ac
Runwell	33	Bc
Runcorn	160	Cb
Runcton Holme	117	Aa
Runcton, S.	117	Aa
Runhall	118	Da
Runham	120	Da
Runnington	33	Ac
Runswick	199	Ba
Runton	137	Ba
Ranwell	59	Ba
Rushall, Herefs.	89	Ab
Rushall, Norf.	119	Ac
Rushall, Staffs.	127	Bb
Rushall, Wilts.	53	Cb
Rushbrooke	98	Cb
Rushbury	125	Cb
Rushden, Herts.	76	Ca
Rushden, N'hants.	114	Cb
Rushford	118	Cc
Rushlake Green	26	Cb
Rushmere, Suff.	79	Ba
Rushmere, Suff.	120	Da
Rushock, Herefs.	106	Dc
Rushock, Worcs.	109	Bb
Rushton, Ches.	160	Cb
Rushton, N'hants.	113	Ba
Rushton, Shrops.	126	Cb
Ruskington	152	Db
Rusland	192	Db
Rusper	41	Bc
Ruspidge	69	Aa
Rustington	23	Bc
Ruston Parva	188	Cc
Ruswarp	200	Cb
Rutherglen	249	Ba
Ruthin	143	Ba
Ruthven, Aber.	304	Cc
Ruthven, Angus	271	Ab
Ruthwell	216	Cb
Ruyton of the Eleven Towns	124	Da
Ryal	220	Da
Ryall, Dors.	16	Db
Ryall Worcs.	90	Ca
Ryarsh	43	Ba
Ryburgh, Gt.	136	Db
Ryburgh. Lit.	136	Db
Rydal	192	Da
Ryde	21	Bb
Rye	27	Ab
Ryecroft	164	Ca
Rye Foreign	27	Ab
Rye Harbour	27	Ac
Rye Street	89	Bb
Ryhall	132	Cb
Ryhill, Yorks.	174	Cb
Ryhill Yorks.	178	Cc
Ryhope	222	Dc
Ryland	166	Db
Rylstone	182	Db
Ryme Intrinseca	35	Ac
Ryther	185	Ac
Ryton, Dur.	221	Bb
Ryton, Glos.	89	Bb
Ryton, Shrops.	126	Db
Ryton, War.	111	Ba
Ryton-on-Dunsmore	111	Bb
SABDEN	181	Bb
Sacombe	76	Cb
Sacombe Green	76	Cb
Sacriston	222	Ca
Sadberge	207	Ba
Saddell	233	Bb
Saddington	130	Dc
Saddle Bow	134	Dc
Saddleworth	172	Cc
Saffron Walden	77	Aa
Sageston	62	Cb
Saham Toney	118	Ca
Saighton	144	Da
St Agnes	2	Da
St. Albans	75	Ac
St. Allen	2	Da
St. Andrew Auckland	207	Ab
St. Andrews	262	Ca
St. Andrews Major	49	Aa
St. Annes on the Sea	169	Aa
St. Arvans	68	Db
St. Asaph	158	Da
St. Athan	66	Db

Name	Page	Sq.
St. Austell	6	Cc
St. Bees	201	Ac
St. Blazey	6	Dc
St. Boswells	241	Bb
St. Breock	6	Cb
St. Breward	6	Da
St. Briavels	68	Da
St. Bride's	61	Bb
St. Brides Major	66	Cc
St. Brides Netherwent	68	Cc
St. Brides super Ely	66	Db
St. Brides Wentlloog	67	Bc
St. Bridget Beckermet	191	Ba
St. Budeaux	8	Cb
St. Saintbury	91	Ab
St. Buryan	1	Ac
St. Catherine	51	Ba
St. Clears	63	Aa
St. Cleer	7	Bb
St. Clether	11	Bc
St. Columb Major	5	Bb
St. Columb Minor	5	Bb
St. Columb Porth	5	Bb
St. Combs	306	Da
St. Cross S. Elmham	119	Bc
St. Cyrus	282	Cc
St. Davids	61	Aa
St. Day	2	Db
St. Decumans	33	Aa
St. Dennis	6	Cc
St. Denys	38	Dc
St. Devereux	88	Cb
St. Dogmells	82	Da
St. Dogwells	82	Cc
St. Dominick	8	Cb
St. Donat's	66	Cc
St. Endellion	6	Ca
St. Enoder	5	Bc
St. Erme	5	Bc
St. Erth	5	Bb
St. Ervan	5	Bb
St. Eval	5	Bb
St. Ewe	4	Da
St. Fagans	49	Aa
St. Fergus	306	Db
St. Fillans	259	Aa
St. Florence	62	Db
St. Gennys	11	Ab
St. George	159	Ca
St. Georges	126	Cb
St. Germans	7	Bb
St. Giles-in-the-Wood	30	Cc
St. Giles-on-the-Heath	12	Cc
St. Gluvias	2	Db
St. Goran	4	Da
St. Harmon	105	Bb
St. Helen Auckland	206	Bd
St. Helens, Hants.	21	Bb
St. Helens, Lancs.	160	Ca
St. Hilary, Corn.	1	Bb
St. Hilary, Glam.	66	Cc
St. Ishmael's	61	Bb
St. Issey	5	Bb
St. Ive	7	Bb
St. Ives, Corn.	1	Bb
St. Ives Hunts.	95	Ba
St. James S. Elmham	119	Bc
St. John Beckermet	191	Aa
St. John's, Corn.	8	Cc
St. John's, I.O.M.	190	Cb
St. John's, Kent	43	Aa
St. John's Chapel	205	Ba
St. John's Common	24	Db
St. John's Fen End	134	Dc
St. John's Highway	134	Dc
St. John's Wood	57	Bb
St. Just, Corn.	1	Ac
St. Just Corn.	4	Cb
St. Kevern	2	Dc
St. Kew	6	Ca
St. Keyne	7	Bb
St. Lawrence. Essex	78	Dc
St. Lawrence. Hants.	21	Dc
St. Lawrence, Kent	46	Da
St. Lawrence, Pem.	81	Bc
St. Levan	1	Ac
St. Leonards	26	Db
St. Mabyn	6	Ca
St. Margaret	87	Bb
St. Margaret at Cliffe	46	Dc
St. Margaret S. Elmham	119	Bc
St. Martin. Corn.	2	Db
St. Martin, Corn.	7	Bc
St. Martin's, Perth	270	Dc
St. Martin's, Shrops.	144	Cc

Name	Page	Sq.
St. Mary Bourne	54	Cc
St. Mary Church, Devon	10	Da
St. Mary Church, Glam.	66	Cc
St. Mary Cray	58	Dc
St. Mary Hill	66	Cb
St. Marys Hoo	59	Bc
St.-Mary-in-the-Marsh	27	Bb
St. Marys	115	Bb
St. Maughan	88	Cc
St. Mawes	4	Cb
St. Mawgan	5	Bb
St. Mellion	8	Cb
St. Mellons	67	Ac
St. Merryn	5	Ba
St. Mewan	6	Cc
St. Michael Caerhays	4	Da
St. Michael Penkevel	4	Cb
St. Michael S. Elmham	120	Cc
St. Michael's-on-Wyre	180	Cc
St. Minver	6	Ca
St. Monans	262	Cb
St. Mungo	216	Da
St. Neot	6	Db
St. Neots	95	Ab
St. Nicholas, Dev.	14	Dc
St. Nicholas, Glam.	66	Db
St. Nicholas, Pem.	81	Bb
St. Nicholas-at-Wade	46	Ca
St Ninians	259	Bc
St. Osyth	79	Bc
St. Owens Cross	88	Dc
St. Pauls Cray	58	Dc
St. Pauls Walden	75	Bb
St. Peters	46	Da
St. Peter S. Elmham	119	Bc
St. Petrox	62	Cc
St. Pinnock	7	Ab
St. Quivox	236	Cc
St. Sampson	6	Dc
St. Stephen, Corn.	6	Cc
St. Stephen, Corn.	12	Cc
St. Stephens, Corn.	8	Cb
St. Stephens, Herts.	75	Ac
St. Teath	6	Ca
St. Tudy	6	Ca
St. Twynnell	62	Cc
St. Veep	6	Dc
St. Vigeans	272	Db
St. Wenn	6	Cb
St. Weonards	88	Cc
St. Winnow	6	Dc
Salcombe	10	Cc
Salcombe Regis	15	Cc
Salcott	78	Dc
Sale	161	Ba
Saleby	154	Ca
Sale Green	109	Ba
Salehurst	26	Ca
Salen, Argyll	264	Ca
Salen, Argyll	264	Cc
Salesbury	170	Ba
Salford, Beds.	94	Cb
Salford, Lancs.	161	Ba
Salford, Oxon.	91	Bc
Salford Priors	110	Ca
Salhouse	138	Cc
Saline	260	Cc
Saling, Gt.	77	Bb
Salisbury	37	Bb
Salkeld, Gt.	204	Ca
Salkeld, Lit.	204	Ca
Sall	137	Ab
Salmonby	153	Ba
Salperton	90	Dc
Salsburgh	250	Cc
Salt	147	Ac
Saltaire	183	Bc
Saltash	8	Cb
Saltburn by the Sea	199	Da
Saltby	131	Ba
Saltcoats	235	Bb
Salterforth	182	Cc
Salters Lode	116	Da
Saltfleet	168	Db
Saltfleetby All Saints	168	Dc
Saltfleetby St. Clement	168	Dc
Saltfleetby St. Peter	168	Dc
Saltford	51	Aa
Salthouse	137	Aa
Saltmarshe	175	Ba
Saltney	159	Bc
Salton	198	Dc
Salton, E.	252	Db
Saltwood	28	Ca

Name	Page	Sq.
Salwarpe	109	Bc
Salway Ash	16	Db
Sambourn	110	Dc
Sambrook	126	Ca
Samlesbury	170	Ba
Sampford Arundel	33	Ac
Sampford Brett	33	Aa
Sampford Courtenay	31	Ac
Sampford, Gt.	77	Aa
Sampford, Lit.	77	Aa
Sampford Peverell	15	Aa
Sampford Spiney	8	Da
Sancreed	1	Ac
Sancton	186	Dc
Sand	34	Da
Sandaig	273	Ac
Sandale	202	Da
Sandal Magna	173	Bb
Sandbach	146	Ca
Sandbank	247	Aa
Sanderstead	42	Da
Sandford, Den.	32	Cc
Sandford, Hants.	21	Bc
Sandford, Shrops.	145	Cc
Sandford, Shrops.	124	Da
Sandford, Som.	50	Cb
Sandford, W'land.	204	Dc
Sandford-on-Thames	72	Db
Sandford Orcas	35	Bb
Sandford St. Martin	72	Cc
Sandgate	28	Da
Sandhaven	306	Ca
Sandhoe	220	Db
Sand Hole	186	Cc
Sandholme	176	Ca
Sandhurst, Berks.	56	Cb
Sandhurst, Glos.	89	Bc
Sandhurst, Kent	26	Da
Sand Hutton, Yorks.	197	Ac
Sand Hutton, Yorks.	186	Cc
Sandiacre	149	Bc
Sandley	36	Cb
Sandon, Essex	77	Dc
Sandon, Herts.	76	Ca
Sandon, Staffs.	147	Ac
Sandonbank	147	Ac
Sandown	21	Bc
Sandridge, Herts.	75	Ac
Sandridge, Wilts.	52	Cb
Sandringham	135	Ab
Sandsend	200	Ca
Sand Side	192	Cc
Sandwich	46	Db
Sandwick	203	Bc
Sandwith	201	Ac
Sandy	95	Ab
Sandy Bank	153	Bc
Sandycroft	159	Bc
Sandygate, I.O.M.	189	Bb
Sandygate, Yorks.	163	Ba
Sandy Lane	52	Ca
Sandypark	13	Ba
Sandyway	88	Cc
Sankey, Gt.	160	Da
Sanquhar	226	Ca
Santon	117	Bb
Santon Bridge	191	Ba
Santon Downham	117	Bb
Sapcote	130	Cc
Sapey Common	108	Db
Sapey Upr.	108	Dc
Sapiston	98	Ca
Sapperton Glos.	70	Ca
Sapperton, Lincs.	152	Cc
Sarclet	324	Cc
Sarn	124	Cc
Sarnesfield	87	Ba
Saron	64	Da
Sarratt	74	Db
Sarre	46	Ca
Sarsden	91	Bc
Satley	206	Ba
Satterleigh	30	Dc
Satterthwaite	192	Db
Saughall, Gt.	159	Bc
Saul	69	Ba
Saundby	165	Ba
Saundersfoot	62	Db
Saunderton	73	Bb
Saunton	30	Cb
Sausthorpe	154	Ca
Sawbridge	112	Cc
Sawbridgeworth	76	Db
Sawley, Derby	149	Bc
Sawley, Yorks.	181	Bc
Sawley, Yorks.	184	Ca
Sawrey	192	Db
Sawston	96	Db
Sawtry	114	Da
Saxby, Leics.	131	Ba
Saxby, Lincs.	166	Db

Name	Page	Sq.
Saxby All Saints	176	Db
Saxelby	130	Da
Saxham, Gt.	97	Bb
Saxham, Lit.	97	Ba
Saxilby	166	Cb
Saxlingham	136	Da
Saxlingham Green	119	Bb
Saxlingham Nethergate	119	Bb
Saxlingham Thorpe	119	Bb
Saxmundham	100	Cb
Saxondale	150	Db
Saxtead	99	Bb
Saxthorpe	137	Ab
Saxton	184	Dc
Scaftworth	165	Aa
Scagglethorpe	187	Ab
Scalby, Yorks.	176	Ca
Scalby, Yorks.	200	Dc
Scaldwell	113	Ab
Scaleby	218	Cb
Scaleby Hill	218	Cb
Scalehouses	204	Ca
Scales	179	Ba
Scalford	131	Aa
Scamblesby	153	Ba
Scampston	187	Ab
Scampton	166	Cb
Scarborough	188	Ca
Scarcliffe	164	Cc
Scarcroft	184	Cc
Scarfskerry	324	Ca
Scarisbrick	169	Bb
Scarle, N.	165	Bc
Scarle, S.	165	Bc
Scarning	136	Cc
Scarrington	150	Db
Scarthingwell	184	Dc
Scartho	167	Ba
Scawby	176	Dc
Scawton	198	Ca
Scholes, Yorks.	164	Ca
Scholes, Yorks.	172	Da
Scholes, Yorks.	184	Dc
Scholey Hill	174	Ca
Scissett	173	Bc
Scole	99	Aa
Scone, New	270	Dc
Scopwick	152	Da
Scorborough	177	Aa
Scorrier	2	Da
Scorton	198	Da
Sco' Ruston	137	Bb
Scosthrop	182	Cb
Scothy	213	Cc
Scotch Corner	198	Da
Scotforth	180	Db
Scot Hay	146	Cb
Scothern	166	Db
Scotstown	265	Aa
Scotter	176	Cc
Scotterthorpe	176	Cc
Scotton, Lincs.	166	Ca
Scotton, Yorks.	196	Db
Scottow	137	Bb
Scoulton	118	Da
Scourie	319	Ac
Scrafton, W.	196	Cc
Scraptoft	130	Db
Scrattare	57	Ab
Scrayingham	186	Ca
Scredington, Lincs.	133	Aa
Scredington, Lincs.	152	Db
Scremby	154	Cb
Scremerston	243	Ba
Screveton	150	Db
Scrivelsby	153	Bb
Scriven	184	Cb
Scrooby	165	Aa
Scropton	148	Cc
Scrub Hill	153	Bc
Scruton	196	Db
Sculthorpe	136	Cb
Scunthorpe	176	Cb
Seaborough	16	Da
Seacombe	159	Ba
Seacroft	184	Cc
Seaford	25	Ac
Seaforth	159	Ba
Seagrave	130	Da
Seagry	70	Cc
Seaham	222	Dc
Seaham Harbour	222	Dc
Seaham, New	222	Dc
Seal	43	Aa
Sealand	159	Bc
Seale	40	Da
Seamer, Yorks.	187	Ba
Seamer, Yorks.	208	Ca
Searby	176	Dc
Seasalter	45	Ba
Seascale	191	Ba
Seathwaite	192	Cb
Seatoller	202	Cc
Seaton, Dev	15	Bc

Place	PAGE	SQ
Seaton, *Rut.*	131	Bc
Seaton, *Yorks.*	177	Ba
Seaton Burn	222	Ca
Seaton Carew	208	Cb
Seaton, Low	201	Bb
Seaton Ross	186	Cc
Seaton Sluice	222	Ca
Seatown	16	Bb
Seave Green	198	Ca
Seaville	216	Dc
Seavington St. Mary	16	Da
Seavington St. Michael	34	Cc
Sebastopol	67	Bc
Sebergham	203	Aa
Seckington	128	Db
Sedbergh	194	Cb
Sedbury	68	Db
Sedgeberrow	90	Da
Sedgebrook	151	Bc
Sedgefield	207	Bb
Sedgeford	135	Ba
Sedgehill	36	Cb
Sedgwick	193	Bb
Sedgley	127	Ac
Sedlescombe	26	Db
Seend	52	Cb
Seend Cleeve	52	Cb
Seend Row	52	Cb
Seer Green	74	Dc
Seething	119	Bb
Sefton	169	Bc
Seghill	222	Ca
Seighford	146	Dc
Seisdon	126	Dc
Selattyn	144	Cc
Selborne	40	Cb
Selby	174	Da
Selham	23	Aa
Selkirk	241	Ac
Sellack	88	Db
Sellafield	191	Ba
Selling	45	Ab
Sellinge	28	Ca
Selly Oak	110	Ca
Selmeston	25	Bb
Selsey	22	Db
Selston	149	Ba
Selworthy	48	Cb
Semer	98	Dc
Semington	52	Cb
Semington Lane	52	Cb
Semley	36	Db
Sempringham	133	Aa
Send	41	Aa
Senghenydd	66	Da
Sennen	1	Ac
Sennen Cove	1	Ac
Senny Bridge	86	Ca
Serlby	165	Aa
Sessay	197	Bc
Setchey	135	Ac
Settle	182	Ca
Settrington	186	Da
Seven Ash	33	Ab
Sevenhampton, *Glos.*	90	Dc
Sevenhampton, *Wilts.*	71	Bc
Sevenoaks	43	Aa
Sevenoaks Weald	43	Ab
Seven Sisters	85	Bb
Severn Stoke	90	Ca
Sevington, *Kent*	27	Ba
Sevington, *Wilts.*	70	Cc
Sewerby	188	Db
Sewstern	131	Ba
Shabbington	73	Aa
Shackerley	126	Db
Shackerstone	129	Ab
Shackleford	40	Ac
Shadforth	207	Ba
Shadingfield	120	Cc
Shadoxhurst	27	Ba
Shadwell	184	Cc
Shaftesbury	36	Cb
Shaftesbury Lane	36	Cb
Shafton	174	Cb
Shalbourne	53	Bb
Shalden	39	Ba
Shaldon	14	Dc
Shalfleet	20	Db
Shalford *Essex*	77	Ba
Shalford, *Sur.*	41	Ab
Shalford Green	77	Ba
Shalstone	93	Ab
Shandon	247	Ba
Shangton	180	Dc
Shanklin	21	Bc
Shap	204	Cc
Shapwick, *Dors.*	19	Aa
Shapwick, *Som.*	34	Da
Shardlow	149	Bc
Shareshill	127	Bb
Sharlston	174	Cb
Sharnbrook	114	Cc
Sharnford	129	Bc
Sharpenhoe	75	Aa
Sharperton	231	Ab
Sharpness	69	Aa
Sharpway Gat~	109	Bb
Sharrington	136	Da
Shatton	163	Ab
Shaugh Prior	8	Db
Shavington	146	Ca
Shaw, *Berks.*	54	Db
Shaw, *Lancs.*	172	Cc
Shaw, *Wilts.*	52	Cb
Shawbury	125	Ba
Shawclough	171	Bb
Shawell	112	Ca
Shawforth	171	Bb
Shearsby	112	Da
Shearston	33	Bb
Shebbear	12	Da
Shebster, E.	322	Da
Sheen	162	Dc
Sheepscombe	70	Ca
Sheepstor	8	Db
Sheepwash	12	Da
Sheepway	50	Da
Sheepy Magna	129	Ab
Sheepy Parva	129	Ac
Sheering	76	Da
Sheerness	45	Aa
Sheffield	163	Ba
Shefford	95	Ac
Shefford, E.	54	Ca
Shefford Hardwick	95	Ac
Shefford, W.	54	Ca
Sheinton	126	Cb
Sheldon, *Derby*	163	Ac
Sneldon, *Dev.*	15	Aa
Sheldon, *War*	110	Da
Sheldwich	45	Ab
Sheldwich Lees	45	Ab
Shelf	172	Da
Shelfanger	118	Dc
Shelfield	127	Bb
Shelford	150	Db
Shelford, Gt.	96	Cb
Shelford, Lit.	96	Cb
Shelland	98	Db
Shelley, *Essex*	76	Dc
Shelley, *Suff.*	78	Da
Shelley *Yorks.*	173	Ab
Shellingford	71	Bc
Shellow Bowells	77	Ac
Shelsley Beauchamp	108	Dc
Shelsley Walsh	108	Dc
Shelswell	93	Ab
Shelton, *Beds.*	114	Cb
Shelton, *Norf.*	119	Bb
Shelton, *Notts.*	151	Aa
Shelton, Lr.	94	Da
Shelve	124	Dc
Shenfield	59	Aa
Shenington	92	Cb
Shenley	57	Ba
Shenley Brook End	93	Bb
Shenley Church End	94	Cb
Shenston	109	Ab
Shenstone	128	Cb
Shenton	129	Bc
Sheperdine	68	Db
Shephall	75	Bb
Shepherds Well	46	Cc
Shepley	173	Ac
Shepperton	57	Ac
Shepreth	96	Cc
Shepshed	129	Ba
Shepton	35	Ba
Shepton Beauchamp	34	Cc
Shepton Mallet	51	Ac
Shepton Montague	35	Ba
Sheraton	208	Ca
Sherborne, *Dors.*	35	Bc
Sherborne *Glos.*	71	Aa
Sherborne *War.*	111	Ac
Sherborne Causeway	36	Cb
Sherborne St. John	55	Ac
Sherburn, *Dur.*	207	Ba
Sherburn, *Yorks.*	187	Ba
Sherburn Hill	207	Ba
Sherburn-in-Elmet	174	Ca
Shere	41	Ab
Shereford	136	Cb
Sherfield English	38	Cc
Sherfield-upon-Loddon	55	Ac
Sherford, *Dev*	10	Cb
Sherford, *Som.*	33	Bc
Sheriff Hales	126	Db
Sheriff Hutton	185	Ba
Sheringham	137	Aa
Sheringham, Upr.	137	Aa
Sharington	94	Ca
Shernborne	135	Bb
Sherrington	86	Da
Sherston, Gt.	70	Cc
Sherston Parva	70	Cc
Sherwood	150	Cb
Shettleston	249	Ac
Shevington	170	Cc
Sheviock	8	Cc
Shieldaig	297	Ba
Shieldhill	250	Cb
Shielfoot	273	Bc
Shifnal	126	Db
Shilbottle	232	Ca
Shildon	207	Ab
Shildon, New	207	Ab
Shillingford, *Dev.*	14	Da
Shillingford *Dev.*	32	Da
Shillingford, *Oxon*	73	Ac
Shillingstone	36	Cc
Shillington	75	Aa
Shilton, *Oxon.*	71	Ba
Shilton, *War.*	111	Ba
Shilvinghampton	17	Bb
Shimpling, *Norf.*	119	Ac
Shimpling, *Suff.*	98	Cb
Shincliffe	207	Aa
Shinfield	55	Bb
Shingay	95	Bc
Shingham	117	Ba
Shinglewell	59	Ac
Shipbourne	43	Bb
Shipdham	118	Ca
Shipham	50	Cb
Shiplake	55	Ba
Shiplett	49	Bb
Shipley, *Sus.*	23	Ba
Shipley, *Yorks.*	183	Bc
Shipley Bridge	42	Cc
Shipmeadow	120	Cb
Shippon	72	Db
Shipston-on-Stour	91	Bb
Shipton, *Bucks.*	93	Bc
Shipton, *Glos.*	90	Dc
Shipton, *Shrops.*	125	Bc
Shipton *Yorks.*	185	Ab
Shipton, *Yorks.*	186	Dc
Shipton Bellinger	37	Ba
Shipton Gorge	17	Ab
Shipton Moyne	70	Cb
Shipton-on-Cherwell	72	Da
Shipton-under-Wychwood	71	Ba
Shirburn	73	Bb
Shirebrook	164	Dc
Shire Green	163	Ba
Shirehampton	50	Da
Shire Newton	68	Cb
Shirs Oak	128	Cb
Shireoaks	164	Db
Shireshead	180	Db
Shirland	149	Ba
Shirley, *Derby*	148	Cb
Shirley, *Hants.*	38	Dc
Shirley, *Sur.*	58	Cc
Shirley, *War.*	110	Ca
Shirwell	30	Db
Shitterton	18	Da
Shobdon	107	Ac
Shobrooke	32	Cc
Shoby	130	Ca
Shocklach	144	Db
Shoeburyness	60	Db
Shoebury, Sth.	60	Cb
Sholden	46	Db
Shopford	218	Da
Shopland	60	Cb
Shoreditch	33	Bc
Shoreham, *Kent*	43	Aa
Shoreham, *Sus.*	24	Cc
Shoreham, Old	24	Cc
Shorncote	70	Db
Shorne	59	Bc
Shortgate	25	Ab
Short Green	118	Dc
Shorthampton	91	Bc
Short Heath	128	Cc
Shortwood	51	Aa
Shorwell	21	Ac
Shotesham All Saints	119	Bb
Shotesham St. Mary	119	Bb
Shotley	80	Ca
Shotley Bridge	221	Ac
Shotleyfield	220	Dc
Shottenden	45	Ab
Shottery	91	Aa
Shottesbrook	56	Ca
Shotteswell	92	Ca
Shottisham	80	Ca
Shottlegate	148	Db
Shotton, *Dur.*	207	Ab
Shotton, *Flint.*	159	Bc
Shotwick	159	Bc
Shouldham	117	Aa
Shouldham Thorpe	117	Aa
Shoulton	109	Ac
Shrawardine	125	Aa
Shrawley	109	Ab
Shrewley	110	Db
Shrewsbury	125	Ba
Shrewton	37	Aa
Shripney	23	Ac
Shrivenham	71	Bc
Shropham	118	Cb
Shuckburgh, Lr.	112	Cc
Shuckburgh Upr.	112	Cc
Shudy Camps	97	Ac
Shurdington	90	Cc
Shurlock Row	56	Ca
Shurton	33	Ba
Shustoke	111	Aa
Shustoke Green	128	Dc
Shuttleworth	171	Bb
Shute	16	Cb
Shut End	127	Ac
Shutford	92	Cb
Shutlanger	93	Ba
Shutta	7	Bc
Shuttington	128	Db
Sibbertoft	112	Da
Sibford Ferris	92	Cb
Sibford Gower	92	Cb
Sible Hedingham	77	Ba
Sibsey	153	Bc
Sibson	129	Ac
Sibthorpe	150	Db
Sibton	100	Ca
Sicklinghall	184	Cb
Sidbury, *Dev.*	15	Bc
Sidbury, *Shrops.*	108	Da
Sidcot	50	Cb
Sidcup	58	Dc
Siddal	172	Da
Siddington	70	Db
Sidemoor	109	Bb
Sidestrand	137	Ba
Sidford	15	Bb
Sidlesham	22	Db
Sidmouth	15	Ac
Sigglesthorne	177	Ba
Silchester	55	Ab
Sileby	130	Ca
Silecroft	191	Bc
Slifield	119	Aa
Silian	84	Da
Silkstone	173	Bc
Silkstone Common	173	Bc
Silkstone Row	174	Ca
Silksworth, New	222	Dc
Silk Willoughby	152	Bc
Silloth	216	Cc
Silpho	200	Cc
Silsden	182	Dc
Silsoe	75	Aa
Silton	36	Ca
Silverdale, *Lancs.*	193	Ac
Silverdale, *Staffs.*	146	Db
Silver Green	119	Bb
Silverstone	93	Aa
Silverton	32	Dc
Silvington	108	Ca
Simmondley	162	Da
Simonburn	220	Ca
Simonsbath	47	Bb
Simprin	242	Da
Simpson	94	Cb
Sinderby	197	Ac
Sindlesham	55	Bb
Singleton	40	Dc
Singleton Gt.	180	Cc
Sinnington	198	Db
Sinton	109	Ac
Sisland	120	Cb
Sissinghurst	44	Cc
Siston	51	Aa
Sithney	2	Cc
Sittingbourne	44	Da
Sixhills	167	Ac
Skail	321	Bc
Skaill	318	Da
Skateraw	282	Da
Skeabost	296	Cc
Skeeby	196	Ba
Skeffington	131	Ab
Skeffling	178	Dc
Skegby	149	Ba
Skegness	154	Db
Skelbrooke	174	Cb
Skelgill	202	Dc
Skellingthorpe	166	Cc
Skellow	174	Cc
Skelmanthorpe	173	Ac
Skelmersdale	169	Bc
Skelmorlie	247	Ac
Skelsmergh	193	Bb
Skelton, *Cumb.*	203	Ba
Skelton, *Yorks.*	199	Aa

Place	Page	Sq.
Skelton *Yorks.*	185	Ab
Skelton. *Yorks.*	175	Ba
Skelton. *Yorks.*	184	Ca
Skelton, *Yorks.*	196	Ca
Skelwith	192	Da
Skelwith Bridge	192	Da
Skendleby	154	Ca
Skene	293	Bc
Sken.rith	88	Cc
Skerne	188	Cc
Sketty	64	Dc
Skewen	65	Aa
Skeyton	137	Bb
Skidbrooke	168	Cb
Skidby	176	Da
Skilgate	32	Da
Skillington	131	Ba
Skinburness	216	Db
Skinidin	295	Ac
Skinningrove	199	Ba
Skipness	246	Cc
Skipsea	188	Cc
Skipton	182	Db
Skipton-on-Swale	197	Ac
Skipwith	185	Bc
Skirbeck	133	Ba
Skirbeck Quarter.	133	Ba
Skirlaugh	177	Bb
Skirling	239	Bb
Skirpenbeck	186	Cb
Skirsa	324	Da
Skirwith	204	Cb
Skitham	180	Cc
Slack	172	Ca
Slackhall	162	Db
Slade Hooton	164	Da
Slaggyford	218	Dc
Slaidburn	181	Bb
Slaithwaite	172	Db
Slaley	220	Dc
Slamannan	250	Cb
Slapton, *Bucks.*	94	Cc
Slapton. *Dev.*	10	Cb
Slapton, *N'hants.*	93	Aa
Slateford	251	Bb
Slattocks	171	Bc
Slaugham	24	Ca
Slaughden	100	Dc
Slaughterford	62	Ca
Slaughter, Lr.	91	Ac
Slaughter, Upr.	91	Ac
Slawston	131	Ac
Sleaford	152	Db
Sleagill	204	Cc
Sledmere	186	Da
Sleepshyde	75	Bc
Sleights	200	Cb
Sliddery	234	Cc
Slimbridge	69	Ba
Slindon *Staffs.*	146	Dc
Slindon, *Sus.*	23	Ab
Slinfold	23	Ab
Slingsby	198	Dc
Slipton	114	Ca
Sloothby	164	Da
Slough	56	Da
Slough Green	33	Bc
Slyne	180	Ca
Smallbridge	16	Cb
Smallbrook	68	Db
Smallburgh	138	Cb
Smalldale, *Derby*	163	Ab
Smalldale, *Derby*	162	Db
Smalley	149	Bb
Smallford	75	Bc
Small Heath	110	Ca
Smallholm	242	Cb
Small Hythe	27	Ab
Smannell	54	Cc
Smarden	27	Aa
Smeaton, Gt.	197	Aa
Smeaton, Lit. *Yorks.*	197	Aa
meaton, Lit. *Yorks.*	174	Db
Smeeth	28	Ca
Smeeton Westerby	130	Dc
Smethcott	125	Ac
Smethwick	127	Bc
Smisby	129	Aa
Smithfield	218	Cb
Smithtown	301	Ac
Snailbeach	124	Db
Snailwell	97	Aa
Snainton	187	Ba
Snaith	175	Ab
Snape, *Suff.*	100	Cb
Snape *Yorks.*	196	Db
Snaresbrook	58	Cb
Snarestone	129	Ab
Snarford	166	Db
Snargate	27	Bb
Snave	27	Bb
Snead	124	Dc
Sneaton	200	Cb
Snedshill	126	Cb
Snelland	150	Cb
Snelland	166	Db
Snelston	148	Cb
Snetterton	118	Db
Snettisham	135	Aa
Snibston	129	Ba
Snitter	231	Bb
Snitterby	166	Da
Snitterfield	110	Dc
Snittlegarth	202	Ca
Snodhill	87	Ba
Snodland	44	Ca
Snoring, Gt.	136	Db
Snoring, Lit.	136	Db
Snowshill	90	Db
Snydale	174	Cb
Soberton	39	Bc
Sodbury, Lit.	69	Bc
Sodbury, Old	69	Bc
Soham	97	Aa
Solihull	110	Da
Sollers Dilwyn	107	Bc
Sollers Hope	88	Db
Sollom	169	Bb
Solva	61	Aa
Somerby, *Leics.*	131	Ab
Somerby, *Lincs.*	152	Cc
Somerby, *Lincs.*	176	Dc
Somercotes.	149	Ba
Somercotes, N.	168	Cb
Somercotes, S.	168	Cb
Somerford, Gt.	70	Cc
Somerford Keynes	70	Db
Somerford, Lit.	70	Cc
Somerleyton	120	Db
Somersby	153	Ba
Somersha¹ Herbert	148	Cc
Somersham, *Hunts.*	115	Bc
Somersham, *Suff.*	99	Ac
Somerton, *Oxon.*	92	Dc
Somerton, *Som.*	34	Db
Somerton, *Suff.*	98	Cb
Somerton Door	34	Db
Sompting	24	Cc
Sonning	55	Ba
Sonning Common	55	Ba
Sookholme	164	Dc
Sopley	19	Bb
Sopworth	69	Bc
Sorn	210	Dh
Sortat	324	Fh
Sotby	153	Aa
Sotherton	100	Da
Sotterley	120	Cc
Sotwell	73	Ac
Soudley, Gt.	146	Cc
Soughton	159	Ac
Soulbury	94	Cc
Soulby *Cumb.*	203	Bb
Soulby *W'land.*	204	Dc
Souldern	92	Db
Souldrop	114	Cc
Sourton	13	Aa
Soutergate	192	Cc
South Acre	135	Bc
Southall	57	Ab
Southall Green	57	Ab
Southam, *Glos.*	90	Cc
Southam. *War.*	111	Bc
Southampton	21	Aa
Southay	34	Dc
South Bank	208	Cc
Southborough	43	Bb
Southburgh	118	Da
Southburn	187	Bc
Southchurch	60	Cb
Southcoates	177	Bb
Southcott	94	Cc
South Croxton	130	Db
Southdean	44	Da
Southease	25	Ac
South End	177	Bc
Southend	69	Bb
Southend-on-Sea	60	Cb
Southern down	65	Bc
Southery	116	Db
Southfleet	59	Ac
Southgate	57	Ba
South Hill	7	Ba
South Huish	9	Bc
Southill	95	Ac
South Lawn	71	Ba
Southleigh	15	Bb
South Lowestoft	120	Db
South Luffenham	132	Cc
Southmarsh	35	Ba
South Milton	9	Bb
Southminster	60	Da
South Molton	31	Ba
South Normanton	149	Ba
Southoe	95	Aa
Southolt	99	Da
Southorpe	132	Db
Southowram	172	Da
South Pool	10	Cc
Southport	169	Ab
South Raynham	136	Cb
Southrepps	137	Ba
Southrey	153	Ab
Southrop	71	Ab
Southrope	39	Ba
Southsea	22	Cb
South Shields	222	Db
South Street, *Kent*	43	Ba
South Street, *Kent*	45	Bb
Southtown *Norf.*	120	Da
Southtown, *Som*	35	Aa
Southwaite	203	Ba
South Walsham	138	Cc
Southwater	24	Ca
Southway	34	Da
Southwell, *Dors.*	17	Bc
Southwell, *Notts.*	150	Da
Southwick, *Dur.*	222	Db
Southwick, *Hants.*	21	Ba
Southwick. *N'hants.*	132	Cc
Southwick, *Som.*	34	Ca
Southwick, *Sus.*	24	Cc
Southwick, *Wilts.*	51	Bb
South Wigston	130	Cc
South Witham	131	Ba
Southwold	100	Da
Southwood, *Norf*	120	Ca
Southwood, *Som.*	35	Aa
South Wootton	135	Ab
Sowerby, *Yorks.*	197	Bc
Sowerby, *Yorks.*	172	Ca
Sowerby Bridge	172	Ca
Sowton	14	Da
Soyland	172	Db
Spalding	133	Bb
Spaldington	175	Ba
Spaldwick	95	Aa
Spalford	165	Bc
Spanby	133	Aa
Spargrove	35	Ba
Sparham	137	Ac
Spark Bridge	192	Cb
Sparkford	35	Ab
Sparkwell	8	Db
Sparsholt, *Berks.*	72	Cc
Sparsholt, *Hants.*	38	Db
Sparrownit	162	Db
Spaunton	198	Db
Spaxton	33	Bb
Spean Bridge	275	Bb
Speeton	188	Cb
Speldhurst	43	Ac
Spellbrook	76	Db
Spelsbury	91	Bc
Spen, High	221	Bb
Spennithorne	196	Cb
Spennymoor	207	Aa
Spernall	110	Cc
Spetchley	109	Bc
Spettisbury	18	Da
Spexhall	100	Ca
Speybridge	290	Da
Spilsby	154	Cb
Spinkhill	164	Cb
Spital	205	Bc
Spital-in-the-Street	166	Ca
Spittal, *N'land.*	243	Da
Spittal, *Pem.*	62	Ca
Spittal of Glenshee	279	Bc
Spittle	186	Cb
Spixworth	137	Bc
Spofforth	184	Cb
Spondon	149	Ba
Spooner Row	118	Db
Sporle	118	Ca
Spott	253	Bb
Spratton	112	Db
Spreyton	13	Ba
Spridlington	166	Db
Springburn	249	Ab
Springfield, *Dumf.*	217	Bb
Springfield *Essex*	77	Ba
Springfield, *Fife*	261	Bb
Springfield *Som.*	33	Ac
Springhead	172	Ca
Springthorpe	166	Ca
Sproatley	178	Cb
Sprotbrough	174	Dc
Sproughton	79	Ba
Sprouston	242	Cb
Sprowston	137	Bc
Sproxton, *Leics.*	131	Ba
Sproxton, *Yorks.*	198	Ca
Spurstow	145	Aa
Stableford	126	Dc
Stackpole	62	Cc
Stacksteads	171	Bb
Staddlethorpe	176	Ca
Stadhampton	73	Ab
Staffield	204	Ca
Stafford	127	Ba
Stafford, West	18	Cb
Stagsden	94	Da
Stainborough	173	Bc
Stainburn, *Cumb.*	201	Bb
Stainburn, *Yorks.*	184	Cb
Stainby	131	Ba
Staincross	173	Bb
Staindrop	206	Dc
Staines	56	Db
Stainfield, *Lincs.*	153	Aa
Stainfield, *Lincs.*	132	Da
Stainforth	175	Ab
Stainforth, Gt.	182	Ca
Staining	180	Cc
Stainland	172	Db
Stainley, N.	196	Dc
Stainley, S	184	Ca
Stainsacre	200	Cb
Stainsby	153	Ba
Stainton, *Cumb.*	203	Bb
Stainton, *Lancs.*	179	Ba
Stainton, *Yorks.*	196	Ca
Stainton, *Yorks.*	208	Cc
Stainton, *Yorks.*	164	Da
Stainton, *W'land.*	193	Bb
Stainton-by-Langworth	166	Db
Staintondale	200	Db
Stainton, Gt.	207	Bb
Stainton-le-Vale	167	Ab
Stair	236	Dc
Stairfoot	173	Bc
Staithes	199	Ba
Staken Bridge	109	Ba
Stalbridge	35	Bb
Stalbridge Weston	35	Bc
Stalham	138	Cb
Stali-field	45	Ab
Stallingborough	167	Ba
Stalling Busk	195	Ab
Stalmine	180	Cc
Stalybridge	162	Ca
Stambourne	77	Ba
Stambridge, Gt.	60	Ca
Stamford	132	Cb
Stamford Bridge	186	Cb
Stamfordham	220	Da
Stanborough	75	Bc
Stanbridge	94	Dc
Standeford	127	Ab
Standen	27	Aa
Standerwick	51	Bc
Standish, *Glos.*	69	Ba
Standish, *Lancs.*	170	Cc
Standlake	72	Cb
Standle	33	Ac
Standon, *Hants.*	38	Db
Standon, *Herts.*	76	Cb
Standon, *Staffs.*	146	Dc
Standwell Green	99	Aa
Stane	250	Cc
Stanfield	136	Ca
Stanford, *Beds.*	95	Ac
Stanford, *Hants.*	40	Ca
Stanford, *Kent*	28	Ca
Stanford, *Norf.*	118	Da
Stanford Bishop	108	Dc
Stanford Dingley	54	Cc
Stanford-in-the-Vale	72	Cc
Stanford-le-Hope.	59	Ab
Stanford-on-Avon	112	Da
Stanford-on-Teme	108	Db
Stanford Rivers	58	Ca
Stanford-upon-Soar	130	Ca
Stanghow	199	Aa
Stanground	115	Aa
Stanhoe	135	Ba
Stanhope	206	Ca
Stanion	113	Ba
Stanley, *Derby*	149	Bb
Stanley, *Dur.*	221	Bc
Stanley, *Perth*	270	Cc
Stanley, *Staffs.*	146	Ba
Stanley, *Yorks.*	173	Bb
Stanley Pontlarge	90	Db
Stanmer	24	Db
Stanmore	57	Aa
Stanney Lit.	160	Cb
Stanningfield	98	Cb
Stanningley	173	Aa
Stannington, *N'land.*	221	Ba
Stannington, *Yorks.*	163	Ba
Stansbatch	107	Ac
Stansfield	97	Bb
Stanstead	98	Cc
Stanstead Abbots	76	Cc
Stansted Mountfitchet	76	Db
Stanton, *Derby*	163	Ac

362

	PAGE	SQ.
Stanton. *Glos.*	90	Db
Stanton. *Staffs.*	148	Cb
Stanton. *Suff.*	98	Da
Stanton-by-Bridge	149	Aa
Stanton-by-Dale	149	Bb
Stanton Drew	50	Db
Stanton Fitzwarren	71	Ac
Stanton Harcourt	72	Cb
Stanton Lacy	107	Ba
Stanton Long	125	Bc
Stanton-on-the-Wolds	150	Cc
Stanton Prior	51	Ab
Stanton St. Bernard	52	Db
Stanton St. John	72	Da
Stanton St.Quintin	70	Cc
Stanton-under-Bardon	129	Bb
Stanton-upon-Hine Heath	125	Ba
Stanton Wick	50	Db
Stanwardine-in-the Fields	125	Aa
Stanway. *Essex*	78	Aa
Stanway *Glos.*	90	Db
Stanwell	56	Da
Stanwellmoor	56	Da
Stanwick	114	Cb
Stanwix	217	Bc
Stapenhill	128	Da
Staple	46	Cb
Staplefield	24	Da
Staple Fitzpaine	33	Bc
Stapleford. *Cambs.*	96	Db
Stapleford. *Herts.*	75	Bb
Stapleford. *Leics.*	131	Aa
Stapleford. *Lincs.*	151	Ba
Stapleford *Notts.*	149	Bb
Stapleford *Wilts.*	37	Aa
Stapleford Abbots	58	Ca
Stapleford Tawney	58	Da
Staplegrove	33	Cb
Staplehurst	44	Cb
Stapleton. *Glos.*	50	Da
Stapleton. *Heref's.*	107	Ab
Stapleton. *Leics.*	129	Bc
Stapleton. *Shrops.*	125	Ab
Stapleton. *Som.*	34	Dc
Stapleton. *Yorks.*	207	Ac
Star. *Pem.*	83	Ab
Star. *Som.*	50	Cb
Starbeck	184	Ba
Starbotton	195	Bc
Starcross	14	Db
Stareton	111	Ab
Starston	119	Bc
Startforth. High	206	Cc
Startforth. Low	206	Cc
Statham	161	Aa
Stathe	34	Cb
Stathern	150	Dc
Statfold	128	Db
Staughton. Gt.	95	Aa
Staughton. Lit.	95	Aa
Staunton. *Glos.*	68	Da
Staunton. *Worcs.*	89	Bb
Staunton-in-the-Vale	151	Bb
Staunton-on-Arrow	107	Ac
Staunton-on-Wye	87	Ba
Staveley. *Derby*	164	Cb
Staveley *Lancs.*	192	Db
Staveley. *W'land.*	193	Ba
Staveley. *Yorks.*	184	Ca
Staverton *Dev.*	10	Ca
Staverton. *Glos.*	90	Db
Staverton. *N'hants.*	112	Ca
Staverton. *Wilts.*	52	Cb
Stawell	34	Ca
Stawley	33	Ac
Staxigoe	324	Dc
Staxton	187	Ba
Staylittle	122	Db
Staynall	180	Cc
Staythorpe	150	Da
Steane	92	Db
Stebbing	77	Bb
Stechford	128	Cc
Stedham	40	Db
Steens Bridge	108	Cc
Steep Green	53	Bb
Steeping. Gt.	154	Cb
Steeping. Lit.	154	Cb
Steeple. *Dors.*	18	Db
Steeple. *Essex*	60	Da
Steeple Ashton	52	Cb
Steeple Aston	92	Dc
Steeple Barton	92	Cc
Steeple Bumpstead	97	Ac
Steeple Claydon	93	Ac
Steeple Gidding	114	Da
Steeple Langford	37	Aa
Steeple Morden	95	Bc
Steeton	182	Dc
Stemster	323	Bb
Stenton	253	Ab
Stepaside	62	Db
Stepney	58	Cb
Steppingley	94	Db
Stepps	249	Db
Sternfield	100	Cb
Stert	52	Db
Stetchworth	97	Ab
Stevenage	75	Ba
Stevenston	235	Bb
Steventon. *Berks.*	72	Dc
Steventon. *Hants.*	54	Dc
Stevington	94	Da
Stewarton	236	Da
Stewkley	94	Cc
Stewton	168	Cc
Steyning	24	Cb
Steynton	61	Bb
Stibbard	136	Db
Stibbington	132	Dc
Stichill	242	Cb
Sticker	6	Cc
Stickford	154	Cb
Stick'epath	13	Aa
Sticklinch	35	Aa
Stickney	153	Bb
Stidd	181	Ac
Stiffkey	136	Da
Stifford	59	Da
Stillingfleet	185	Bc
Stillington *Dur.*	207	Ba
Stillington *Yorks.*	185	Aa
Stilton	114	Da
Stinchcombe	69	Ab
Stinsford	18	Da
Stirchley	126	Cb
Stirling	259	Aa
Stisted	78	Cb
Stithians	5	Db
Stittenham	2	Db
Stixwould	153	Ab
Stoborough	18	Db
Stock. *Essex*	59	Ba
Stock. *Som.*	50	Cb
Stockbridge	38	Cb
Stockbury	44	Cb
Stockcross	54	Cb
Stockdalewath	203	Aa
Stockerston	131	Bc
Stockingford	129	Ac
Stocking Pelham	76	Da
Stockland Bristol	33	Ba
Stockleigh English	32	Cb
Stockleigh Pomeroy	32	Cc
Stocklinch	34	Cc
Stockport	162	Ca
Stocks	19	Db
Stocksbridge	163	Ba
Stockton *Heref's.*	107	Ba
Stockton. *Norf.*	120	Cb
Stockton. *Shrops.*	126	Dc
Stockton. *War*	111	Bc
Stockton. *Wilts.*	36	Da
Stockton-on-Tees	208	Cc
Stockton-on-Teme	108	Db
Stockton-on-the-Forest	185	Bb
Stockwith. E.	165	Ba
Stockwith. W.	165	Ba
Stodmarsh	46	Cb
Stoer	313	Db
Stoford. *Som.*	35	Ac
Stoford. *Wilts.*	37	Aa
Stogumber	33	Aa
Stogursey	33	Ba
Stoke. *Ches.*	160	Cc
Stoke. *Dev.*	29	Ac
Stoke. *Hants.*	54	Cc
Stoke. *Kent*	60	Cc
Stoke. *War.*	111	Ba
Stoke Abbott	16	Db
Stoke Albany	113	Ba
Stoke Ash	99	Aa
Stoke Bardolph	150	Db
Stoke Bliss	108	Cc
Stoke Bruern	93	Ba
Stoke-by-Clare	97	Bc
Stoke-by-Nayland	78	Da
Stoke Canon	32	Dc
Stoke Charity	39	Aa
Stoke Climsland	7	Ba
Stoke D'Abernon	41	Ba
Stoke Doyle	114	Ca
Stoke Dry	131	Bc
Stoke. East.	18	Db
Stoke Edith	88	Da
Stokeferry	117	Aa
Stoke Fleming	10	Db
Stokeford	18	Db
Stoke Gabriel	10	Ca
Stoke Gifford	68	Da
Stoke Golding	129	Bc
Stoke Goldington	94	Ca
Stokeham	165	Bb
Stoke Hammond	94	Cb
Stoke Heath	145	Bc
Stoke Ho y Cross	119	Ba
Stokeinteignhead.	14	Cc
Stoke Lacy.	88	Da
Stoke Lane	51	Ac
Stoke. Lr.	60	Cc
Stoke Lyne	92	Dc
Stoke Mandeville.	74	Ca
Stoke. N.. *Oxon.*	78	Ac
Stoke. N.. *Som.*	51	Aa
Stoke. N.. *Sus.*	23	Bb
Stokenchurch	73	Bb
Stokenham	10	Cb
Stoke Orchard	90	Cb
Stoke Pero	47	Bb
Stoke Poges	56	Da
Stoke Prior,*Heref's.*	107	Bc
Stoke Prior,*Worcs.*	109	Bb
Stoke Rivers	30	Db
Stoke Rochford	151	Bc
Stoke Row	55	Aa
Stoke. S.. *Oxon.*	55	Aa
Stoke. S.. *Som.*	51	Bb
Stoke. S.. *Sus.*	23	Bb
Stoke St.Gregory.	34	Dc
Stoke St. Mary	33	Dc
Stoke St. Milborough	108	Ca
Stokesay	107	Ba
Stokesby	120	Ca
Stokesley	197	Ba
Stoke Talmage	73	Ab
Stoke Trister	35	Bb
Stoke-upon-Tern	145	Bc
Stoke-upon-Trent	146	Db
Stoke. W.	22	Db
Stoke Wake	36	Cc
Stondon	75	Ba
Stondon Massey	59	Aa
Stone. *Bucks.*	73	Bb
Stone. *Glos.*	69	Ab
Stone. *Kent*	27	Ba
Stone. *Kent*	58	Dc
Stone. *Staffs.*	146	Dc
Stone. *Yorks.*	196	Cc
Stone. *Yorks.*	164	Ba
Stone Allerton	50	Cc
Stonebridge. *Som.*	50	Cb
Stonebridge. *Sus.*	25	Ba
Stonebroom	149	Ba
Stone Easton	51	Ab
Stoneferry	177	Bb
Stonefield	249	Ac
Stonegrave	198	Ca
Stonehall	90	Ca
Stoneham S.	38	Dc
Stonehaven	282	Db
Stonehenge	37	Aa
Stone Hill	28	Ca
Stonehouse. *Dev.*	8	Cc
Stonehouse. *Glos.*	69	Ba
Stonehouse. *Lan.*	238	Ca
Stoneleigh	111	Ab
Stone. Lr.	69	Ab
Stonely	95	Aa
Stonesby	131	Ba
Stonesdale. W.	195	Aa
Stonesfield	72	Ca
Stones Green	79	Bb
Stone Street	99	Ab
Stonethwaite	202	Dc
Stoneyford	15	Ac
Stoneykirk	209	Aa
Stoney Middleton	163	Ab
Stoney Royd	172	Ba
Stoney Stanton	129	Bc
Stoney Stoke	35	Ba
Stoney Stratton	35	Ba
Stoneywood	294	Cc
Stonham Aspall	99	Ab
Stonham. Lit.	99	Ab
Stonor	55	Bc
Stonton Wyville	130	Dc
Stony Houghton	164	Dc
Stony Stratford	93	Bb
Stoodleigh	32	Da
Stoop	216	Ca
Stopham	23	Bb
Stopsley	75	Ab
Storeton	159	Bb
Storkland	15	Ba
Storridge	89	Ba
Storrington	23	Bb
Storthwaite	186	Cc
Stotfield	303	Aa
Stotfold	75	Da
Stottesden	108	Da
Stoughton. *Leics.*	130	Dc
Stoughton. *Sur.*	41	Ab
Stoughton *Sus.*	22	Da
Stoughton. W.	34	Ca
Stoul	273	Ba
Stoulton	90	Cb
Stourbridge	109	Ba
Stour. E.	36	Cb
Stourhead	36	Cc
Stourmouth	46	Cb
Stourpaine	36	Cc
Stourport	109	Ab
Stour Provost	36	Cb
Stour Row	36	Cb
Stourton. *Norf.*	173	Bb
Stourton. *War.*	91	Bb
Stourton. *Wilts.*	36	Ca
Stourton Caundle	35	Bc
Stour. W.	36	Cb
Stoven	120	Cc
Stow *Lincs.*	166	Cb
Stow. *M. Loth.*	241	Aa
Stow. *Shrops.*	106	Db
Stow Bardolph	117	Aa
Stow Bedon	118	Cb
Stowbridge	116	Da
Stow-cum-Quy	96	Bb
Stowe. *Staffs.*	147	Ab
Stowe. *Staffs.*	128	Cb
Stowell. *Glos.*	70	Da
Stowell. *Som.*	35	Bb
Stowey	50	Db
Stowford	12	Bc
Stowlangtoft	98	Da
Stow. Long	95	Aa
Stow Marles	60	Ca
Stowmarket	98	Db
Stow-on-the-Wold	91	Ac
Stowting	28	Ca
Stowupland	99	Ab
Stow. W.	98	Ca
Strachan	281	Dc
Strachur	256	Dc
Stradbroke	99	Ba
Stradishall	97	Bb
Strasdett	117	Aa
Stragglethorpe	151	Ba
Straiton	224	Cb
Stramshall	147	Bc
Strang	190	Dc
Stranraer	209	Aa
Strata Florida	102	Aa
Stratfield Mortimer	55	Ab
Stratfield Saye	55	Ab
Stratfield Turgis	55	Ab
Stratford-on-Avon	91	Aa
Stratford St. Andrew	100	Cb
Stratford St. Mary	79	Ab
Stratford-sub-Castle	37	Bb
Stratford Tony	37	Bb
Stratford Tony	87	Bb
Strathaven	237	Ba
Strathblane	248	Ba
Strathcoul	323	Bb
Strathkinness	262	Ca
Strathmiglo	261	Ab
Strathpeffer	300	Cb
Strathy	322	Ca
Strathyre	258	Da
Stratton. *Corn.*	11	Ba
Stratton. *Dors.*	17	Ba
Stratton. *Glos.*	70	Da
Stratton Audley	93	Ac
Stratton. E.	39	Aa
Stratton-on-the-Fosse	51	Ac
Stratton St. Margaret	71	Ac
Stratton St. Michael	119	Ab
Stratton Strawless	137	Bb
Stratton. Upr.	71	Ac
Stratton. W.	89	Aa
Streat	24	Db
Streatham	57	Bc
Streatley. *Beds.*	75	Aa
Streatley. *Berks.*	55	Aa
Street	34	Da
Street Dinas	144	Cb
Streethay	128	Cb
Street. Lr.	34	Cc
Street-on-the-Fosse	35	Da
Strefford	107	Ba
Strelley	149	Bb
Strensall	185	Ba
Stretcholt	34	Ca
Strete	10	Cb
Stretford. *Heref's.*	107	Ba
Stretford. *Lancs.*	161	Ba
Strethall	96	Dc
Stretham	116	Dc
Stretton. *Ches.*	144	Da
Stretton. *Ches.*	160	Db
Stretton. *Derby*	149	Ba
Stretton. *Rut.*	132	Ca
Stretton. *Staffs.*	127	Ab
Stretton. *Staffs.*	148	Dc
Stretton-en-le-Field	129	Ab
Stretton Grandison	88	Da
Stretton. Gt.	130	Dc

Name	Page	Sq.
Stretton Heath	124	Db
Stretton, Lit.	130	Dc
Stretton, Lr.	160	Db
Stretton-on-Dunsmore	111	Bb
Stretton-on-Fosse	91	Ab
Stretton Sugwas	88	Ca
Stretton-under-Fosse	111	Ba
Strichen	306	Cb
Strickland, Gt.	204	Cb
Strickland, Lit.	204	Cc
Strines	162	Ca
Strixton	113	Bc
Stroat	68	Db
Stromeferry	286	Ca
Stronachlachar	257	Bb
Strone Argyll	247	Aa
Strone, Inver.	288	Da
Strontian	265	Aa
Strood	59	Bc
Stroud	70	Ca
Stroxton	151	Dc
Struan	278	Cc
Strubby	168	Dc
Strumpshaw	120	Ca
Struy	299	Bc
Stuartfield	306	Cb
Stubbin	164	Ca
Stubbington	21	Ba
Stubbins	171	Ab
Stubbs	174	Db
Stubhampton	36	Dc
Stubton	151	Bb
Studham	74	Da
Studland	19	Ac
Studley Oxon.	73	Aa
Studley War.	110	Cb
Studley, Wilts.	52	Ca
Studley, Upr.	52	Cb
Stukeley, Gt.	115	Ac
Stukeley, Lit.	115	Ac
Stuntney	116	Dc
Sturmer	97	Bc
Sturminster Marshall	19	Aa
Sturminster Newton	36	Ca
Sturton, Lincs.	166	Cb
Sturton, Lincs.	176	Du
Sturton Gt.	153	Aa
Sturton-le-Steeple	165	Bb
Sturry	46	Cb
Stuston	99	Aa
Stutton	79	Ba
Styrrup	164	Da
Suckley	108	Dc
Sudborough	114	Ca
Sudbourne	100	Dc
Sudbrook, Lincs.	152	Cb
Sudbrook, Mon.	68	Dc
Sudbrooke	166	Db
Sudbury, Derby	148	Cc
Sudbury, M'sex.	57	Ab
Sudbury Suff	98	Cc
Suffield, Norf.	137	Bb
Suffield, Yorks.	200	Dc
Sugnall	146	Cc
Sulby	189	Bb
Sulgrave	92	Da
Sulham	55	Aa
Sulhampstead Abbots	55	Ab
Sulhampstead Bannister	55	Ab
Sullington	23	Bb
Sully	49	Aa
Summer Bridge	183	Ba
Summercourt	5	Bc
Summerhill	294	Cb
Summerhouse	206	Dc
Summertown	72	Da
Summit	172	Cb
Sunbury	57	Ac
Sunderland Cumb.	202	Ca
Sunderland, Dur.	222	Db
Sunderland Bridge	207	Aa
Sunderland Nth.	244	Db
Sundon	94	Dc
Sundridge	43	Aa
Sunk Island	178	Cc
Sunninghill	56	Cb
Sunningwell	72	Db
Sunniside	206	Da
Sunny Brow	206	Ba
Sunton	53	Bc
Surbiton	57	Ac
Surfleet	133	Bb
Surfleet Seas End	133	Bb
Surlingham	119	Ba
Sustead	137	Ba
Susworth	176	Cc
Sutcombe	12	Ca
Sutterby	154	Ca
Sutterton	133	Ba
Sutton, Beds	95	Bc

Name	Page	Sq.
Sutton. Cambs.	116	Cc
Sutton. Ches.	160	Db
Sutton Essex	60	Cb
Sutton, Kent	46	Dc
Sutton, Lancs.	160	Ca
Sutton, M'sex.	57	Ab
Sutton, Norf.	138	Cb
Sutton, N'hants.	132	Dc
Sutton, Notts.	165	Ab
Sutton, Notts.	150	Dc
Sutton, Oxon.	72	Cb
Sutton, Shrops.	125	Bb
Sutton, Som.	35	Aa
Sutton, Staffs.	126	Da
Sutton, Suff.	80	Ca
Sutton, Sur.	42	Ca
Sutton, Sus.	23	Ab
Sutton, Yorks.	177	Bb
Sutton, Yorks.	174	Ca
Sutton, Yorks.	174	Db
Sutton-at-Hone	58	Dc
Sutton Bassett	113	Aa
Sutton Benger	70	Cc
Sutton Bingham	35	Ac
Sutton Bonington	130	Ca
Sutton Bridge	134	Db
Sutton Cheney	129	Bc
Sutton Coldfield	128	Cc
Sutton Courtenay	72	Dc
Sutton Crosses	134	Cb
Sutton Forest Side	149	Ba
Sutton Grange	196	Dc
Sutton-in-Ashfield	149	Ba
Sutton-in-the-Elms	130	Cc
Sutton-le-Marsh	154	Da
Sutton Lit.	126	Db
Sutton Maddock	126	Ab
Sutton Mallett	34	Cb
Sutton Mandeville	36	Dc
Sutton Marsh	88	Da
Sutton Mill	182	Dc
Sutton Montis	35	Bb
Sutton-on-Sea	168	Dc
Sutton-on-the-Forest	185	Ba
Sutton-on-the-Hill	148	Dc
Sutton Poyntz	18	Cb
Sutton St. Edmund	134	Ca
Sutton St James	134	Cc
Sutton St. Nicholas	88	Da
Sutton Scotney	38	Da
Sutton-under-Brailes	91	Bb
Sutton-upon-Derwent	186	Cc
Sutton-upon-Trent	165	Bc
Sutton Valence	44	Db
Sutton Veny	52	Cc
Sutton Waldron	36	Cc
Sutton, Wick, Berks.	72	Db
Sutton Wick Som.	50	Db
Swaby	154	Ca
Swadlincote	129	Aa
Swaffham	117	Ba
Swaffham Bulbeck	96	Ca
Swaffham Prior	96	Da
Swafield	137	Bb
Swainby	197	Ba
Swainsthorpe	119	Ba
Swainswick	51	Ba
Swalcliffe	92	Cb
Swalecliffe	45	Ba
Swallow	167	Aa
Swallowcliffe	36	Db
Swallowfield	55	Bb
Swallow Nest	164	Cb
Swalwell	221	Bb
Swampton	54	Cc
Swanage	19	Ac
Swanbourne	93	Bc
Swan Green	161	Ab
Swanington	137	Ac
Swanland	176	Ba
Swanley	58	Dc
Swannington	129	Ba
Swanscombe	59	Ac
Swansea	64	Dc
Swan Street	78	Ca
Swanton Abbot	137	Bb
Swanton Morley	136	Dc
Swanton Novers	136	Db
Swanton Street	44	Da
Swanwick, Derby	149	Ba
Swanwick Hants.	21	Aa
Swarby	152	Cb
Swardeston	119	Aa
Swarkestone	149	Ac
Swarland	232	Cb
Swarraton	39	Aa
Swaton	183	Aa
Swavesey	95	Ba
Sway	20	Cb
Swayfield	132	Ca

Name	Page	Sq.
Sweeney	124	Da
Swefling	100	Cb
Swell	34	Cc
Swell, Lr., Glos.	91	Ac
Swell, Lr., Som.	34	Cc
Swell, Upr.	91	Ac
Swepstone	129	Ab
Swerford	92	Cc
Swettenham	161	Bc
Swilland	99	Bc
Swillington	174	Ca
Swimbridge	30	Db
Swimbridge Newland	30	Db
Swinbrook	71	Ba
Swincliffe	184	Cb
Swinderby	151	Ba
Swindon, Glos.	90	Cc
Swindon, Staffs.	127	Ac
Swindon, Wilts.	71	Ac
Swine	177	Bb
Swinefleet	175	Bb
Swineshead, Beds.	114	Ca
Swineshead, Lincs.	133	Ba
Swineside	202	Db
Swinford, Berks.	72	Ca
Swinford, Leics.	112	Ca
Swinford, Old	109	Ba
Swingfield	28	Da
Swinhoe	244	Dc
Swinhope	167	Bb
Swinithwaite	195	Bb
Swinscoe	148	Cb
Swinstead	132	Ca
Swinthorpe	166	Db
Swinton, Berw.	242	Da
Swinton, Lancs.	171	Ac
Swinton, Yorks.	196	Dc
Swinton, Yorks.	198	Dc
Swinton, Yorks.	174	Cc
Swithland	130	Cb
Swordly	321	Ba
Swyncombe	73	Cc
Swynnerton	146	Dc
Swyre	17	Ab
Syde	70	Ca
Sydenham, Kent	58	Cc
Sydenham, Oxon.	73	Bb
Sydenham Dameral	8	Ca
Syderstone	130	Cb
Sydling St. Nicholas	17	Ba
Sydmonton	54	Dc
Syerston	150	Bc
Sykehouse	175	Ab
Syleham	99	Ba
Symington, Ayr	236	Cb
Symington, Lan.	239	Ad
Symondsbury	16	Db
Symond's Yat	88	Ca
Synod	83	Ba
Syreford	90	Cb
Syresham	93	Ab
Syston, Leics.	130	Ca
Syston, Lincs	152	Cb
Sytchampton	109	Ab
Sywell	113	Bb
TACKLEY	92	Dc
Tacolneston	119	Ab
Tadcaster	184	Dc
Taddington	163	Ac
Tadley	55	Ab
Tadlow	95	Bc
Tadmarton	92	Cb
Tadwick	51	Ba
Tadworth	42	Ca
Tafolwern	122	Db
Taibach	65	Ba
Tain	312	Cc
Tair Bull	86	Ca
Tai-yr-ysgol	65	Ab
Takeley	76	Db
Talachddu	104	Dc
Talaton	15	Ab
Talbenny	61	Bb
Talbot Road	66	Db
Talbot Village	19	Bc
Talerddig	122	Db
Talgarreg	83	Ba
Talgarth	87	Ab
Talisker	283	Dc
Talke	146	Ba
Talkin	218	Cc
Talland	7	Ac
Tallern Green	144	Ba
Talley	84	Db
Tallington	132	Db
Talog	83	Bc
Talsarnau	140	Db
Talwrn	156	Ab
Talybont, Brecon.	86	Da
Talybont, Card.	121	Bc
Tal-y-llyn	140	Cc
Ta-y-sarn	140	Ca
Tamerton Foliott	8	Cb

Name	Page	Sq.
Tamerton Nth.	12	Cb
Tamworth	128	Db
Tamworth-in-Arden	110	Cb
Tamworth Green	134	Ca
Tandridge	42	Db
Tanfield	221	Bc
Tanfield, W	196	Dc
Tangley	53	Bc
Tanmere	23	Ac
Tankersley	173	Bc
Tannadice	271	Ba
Tannington	99	Bb
Tansley	148	Da
Tansley Knoll	148	Da
Tansor	114	Da
Tantobie	221	Bc
Tanvats	153	Ab
Tanworth	110	Cb
Tan-y-grisiau	141	Ba
Taplow	56	Ca
Tarbert	245	Bc
Tarbet	257	Bb
Tarbolton	236	Dc
Tarbrax	250	Dc
Tarland	292	Dc
Tarleton	169	Ba
Tarlton	70	Cb
Tarnock	50	Cc
Tarporley	160	Dc
Tarrant Crawford	18	Da
Tarrant Gunville	36	Dc
Tarrant Hinton	19	Aa
Tarrant Keynston	18	Da
Tarrant Launceston	19	Aa
Tarrant Rawston	19	Aa
Tarrant Rushton	19	Aa
Tarring Neville	25	Ac
Tarrington	88	Da
Tarring, W.	23	Bc
Tarskavaig	284	Dc
Tarves	294	Ca
Tarvin	160	Cc
Tasburgh	119	Ab
Tasburgh, Upr.	119	Ab
Tasley	126	Cc
Taston	92	Cc
Tatenhill	128	Da
Tathall	181	Aa
Tathwell	167	Bc
Tatsfield	42	Da
Tattenhall	145	Aa
Tatterford	136	Cb
Tattersett	136	Cb
Tattershall	153	Ab
Tattershall Bridge	153	Ab
Tattershall Thorpe	153	Ab
Tattingstone	79	Ba
Taunton	33	Bc
Tavelty	293	Ba
Taverham	137	Ac
Tavistock	8	Ca
Tawstock	30	Cb
Tawton, North	31	Bc
Tawton, South	13	Ba
Taxal	162	Cb
Tayinloan	233	Aa
Taynton. Glos.	89	Bc
Taynton, Oxon.	71	Ba
Taynuilt	265	Ba
Tayport	271	Bc
Tayvallich	245	Ab
Tealby	167	Ab
Tebay	194	Ca
Tebworth	94	Ca
Teddington, M'sex.	57	Ac
Teddington, Worcs.	90	Cb
Tedstone Delamere	108	Dc
Tedstone Wafer	108	Dc
Teeton	112	Db
Teffont Evias	36	Da
Teffont Magna	36	Da
Teigh	131	Ba
Teigncombe	13	Ba
Teigngrace	14	Cb
Teignmouth	14	Db
Tellisford	51	Bb
Telscombe	25	Ac
Temple, Corn.	6	Da
Temple, M. Loth.	252	Cc
Temple Bar	84	Ca
Temple Cloud	51	Ab
Temple Combe	35	Ba
Temple Grafton	91	Aa
Temple Guiting	90	Db
Temple Hirst	174	Da
Temple Normanton	164	Cc
Temple Sowerby	204	Cb
Templeton, Dev.	32	Cb
Templeton, Pem.	62	Db
Tempsford	95	Ab
Tetbury	108	Cb
Tenby	62	Db

Name	PAGE	SQ.
Tendring	79	Bb
Tendring Green	79	Bb
Ten Mile Bank	116	Bb
Tenterden	27	Aa
Terling	77	Bb
Terregles	215	Ba
Terrington	185	Ba
Terrington St. Clement	134	Db
Terrington St. John	134	Dc
Terwick	40	Cb
Teston	44	Cb
Tetbury	70	Cb
Tetbury Upton	70	Cb
Tetchill	144	Dc
Tetcott	12	Cb
Tetford	153	Ba
Tetney	167	Bb
Tetsworth	73	Ab
Tettenhall	127	Ab
Tettenhall Wood	127	Ac
Tetworth	95	Bb
Teversall	149	Ba
Teversham	96	Db
Tevlothead	228	Da
Tew, Gt.	92	Cc
Tewin	75	Bb
Tewkesbury	90	Cb
Tew, Lit.	92	Cc
Tey, Gt.	78	Cb
Tey, Lit.	78	Cb
Teynham	45	Aa
Thakeham	23	Bb
Thame	73	Bb
Thames Ditton	57	Ac
Thanington	45	Bb
Thankerton	238	Db
Tharston	119	Ab
Thatcham	54	Db
Thaxted	77	Aa
Theakston	196	Db
Thealby	176	Db
Theale, Berks.	55	Ab
Theale, Som.	34	Da
Thearne	177	Bb
Theberton	100	Db
The Causeway	36	Ca
The Cleaver	88	Db
Theddingworth	112	Da
Theddlethorpe All Saints	168	D
Theddlethorpe St. Helen	168	Dc
The Hill	192	Dc
The Hollies	126	Da
The Hyde	57	Ba
The Knolls	124	Dc
Thelbridge	32	Cb
The Lee	74	Cb
The Lings	175	Ac
The Linleys	52	Ba
Thelnetham	118	Dc
Thelveton	119	Ac
Thelwall	160	Da
Themelthorpe	136	Db
Thenford	92	Db
Therfield	76	Ca
The Spa	52	Cb
Thetford	118	Cc
Thetford, Lit.	116	Dc
Theydon Bois	58	Da
Theydon Garnon	58	Da
Theydon Mount	58	Da
Thickwood	51	Ba
Thimbleby, Lincs.	153	Ba
Thimbleby, Yorks.	197	Bb
Thirkleby	197	Bc
Thirlby	197	Bb
Thirn	196	Db
Thirsk	197	Bc
Thirston	232	Cb
Thirtleby	177	Bb
Thistleton, Lancs.	180	Cc
Thistleton, Rut.	131	Ba
Thixendale	186	Da
Thockrington	220	Ca
Tholthorpe	184	Da
Thomas Chapel	62	Db
Thompson	118	Cb
Thongs Bridge	172	Dc
Thoralby	195	Bb
Thoresby, N.	167	Bb
Thoresby, S.	154	Ca
Thoresway	167	Ab
Thorganby, Lincs.	167	Bb
Thorganby, Yorks.	185	Bc
Thorington	100	Da
Thorlby	182	Db
Thorley, Hants.	20	Db
Thorley, Herts.	76	Db
Thormanby	197	Bc
Thormington	243	Ab
Thornaby	208	Cc
Thornaby-on-Tees	208	Ca
Thornage	136	Da

Name	PAGE	SQ.
Thornborough	93	Bb
Thornbrough	196	Dc
Thornbury, Dev.	12	Ca
Thornbury, Glos.	69	Ab
Thornbury, Heref s.	108	Cc
Thornby	112	Db
Thorncliff	147	Ba
Thorncombe	16	Ca
Thorndon, Dev.	12	Dc
Thorndon, Suff.	99	Aa
Thorne, Som.	34	Da
Thorne, Yorks.	175	Ab
Thorner	184	Dc
Thorney, Cambs.	115	Ba
Thorney, Notts.	165	Bc
Thorney, Som.	34	Da
Thorney, West	22	Ca
Thorn Falcon	33	Bc
Thornford	35	Ac
Thorngumbald	178	Dc
Thorngrove	34	Cb
Thornham, Kent	44	Ca
Thornham, Norf.	135	Ba
Thornham Magna	99	Aa
Thornham Parva	99	Aa
Thornhaugh	132	Dc
Thornhill, Derby	163	Ab
Thornhill, Dumf.	226	Db
Thornhill, Glam.	67	Ac
Thornhill, Perth	258	Dc
Thornhill, Yorks.	173	Bb
Thornhill Edge	173	Bb
Thornhill Lees	173	Bb
Thornholme	188	Cb
Thornley, Dur.	207	Ba
Thornley, Dur.	206	Da
Thornliebank	248	Dc
Thornsett	162	Ca
Thornthwaite, Cumb.	202	Cb
Thornthwaite, Yorks.	183	Bb
Thornton, Bucks.	93	Bb
Thornton, Lancs.	169	Ac
Thornton, Lancs.	179	Bc
Thornton, Leics.	129	Bb
Thornton, Lincs.	153	Ba
Thornton, Yorks.	186	Cc
Thornton, Yorks.	172	Da
Thornton Curtis	177	Bc
Thornton Dale	187	Aa
Thornton in Craven	182	Cb
Thornton-in-Lonsdale	194	Cc
Thornton-le-Beans	197	Ab
Thornton-le-Clay	185	Ba
Thornton-le-Fen	153	Bc
Thornton-le-Moor, Lincs.	166	Da
Thornton-le-Moor, Yorks.	197	Ab
Thornton-le-Moors	160	Cb
Thornton-le-Street	197	Ab
Thornton, Lit.	180	Cc
Thornton Rust	195	Bb
Thornton Steward	196	Cb
Thornton Watlass	196	Db
Thoroton	150	Db
Thorp Arch	184	Dc
Thorpe, Derby	148	Ca
Thorpe, Lincs.	168	Dc
Thorpe, Norf.	120	Cb
Thorpe, Sur.	56	Db
Thorpe, Yorks.	177	Aa
Thorpe, Yorks.	182	Ba
Thorpe Abbotts	99	Ba
Thorpe Acre	130	Ca
Thorpe Arnold	131	Aa
Thorpe Audlin	174	Cb
Thorpe Bassett	187	Ab
Thorpe-by-Water	131	Bc
Thorpe Constantine	128	Db
Thorpe Culvert	154	Cb
Thorpe Hesley	164	Ca
Thorpe-in-Balne	174	Dc
Thorpe-in-the-Fallows	166	Cb
Thorpe Langton	131	Ac
Thorpe-le-Soken	79	Bc
Thorpe-le-Street	186	Cc
Thorpe, Lit.	208	Ca
Thorpe Malsor	113	Ba
Thorpe Mandeville	92	Da
Thorpe Market	137	Ba
Thorpe Morieux	98	Cb
Thorpe-next-Norwich	119	Ba
Thorpe-on-the-Hill	166	Cc
Thorpe-on-the-Hill	173	Ba
Thorpe Roy	118	Ca
Thorpe St. Peter	154	Db

Name	PAGE	SQ.
Thorpe Salvin	164	Db
Thorpe Satchville	130	Ba
Thorpe Stapleton	173	Ba
Thorpe Thewles	207	Bb
Thorpe Tilney	152	Da
Thorpe Willoughby	174	Da
Thorrington	79	Ac
Thorverton	32	Ca
Thrandeston	99	Aa
Thrapston	114	Cb
Threapwood	144	Db
Threapland	182	Ba
Threckingham	152	Dc
Three Bridges	42	Cc
Threemile Cross	55	Bb
Threlkeld	202	Db
Threshfield	182	Da
Threxton	118	Ca
Thrigby	120	Da
Thringstone	129	Ba
Thrintoft	197	Ab
Thriplow	96	Cc
Throapham	164	Da
Throcking	76	Da
Throckmorton	90	Ca
Thropton	231	Bb
Througham	70	Ca
Throwleigh	13	Ba
Throwley	45	Ab
Thrumpton	149	Bc
Thruxton	231	Ba
Thrupp	70	Ca
Thruscross	183	Bb
Thrushelton	12	Da
Thrussington	130	Da
Thruxton, Hants.	38	Ca
Thruxton, Heref s.	88	Cb
Thrybergh	164	Ca
Thulston	149	Ba
Thundersley	59	Bb
Thundridge	76	Da
Thurcaston	130	Cb
Thurgarton, Norf.	137	Ba
Thurgarton, Notts.	150	Db
Thurgoland	173	Bc
Thurlaston, Leics.	130	Cc
Thurlaston, War.	111	Bb
Thurlbear	33	Bc
Thurlby, Lincs.	151	Ba
Thurlby, Lincs.	132	Da
Thurleigh	114	Cc
Thurlestone	9	Bb
Thurlow, Gt.	97	Ab
Thurlow, Lit.	97	Ab
Thurloxton	33	Bb
Thurlstone	173	Ac
Thurlton	120	Cb
Thurmaston	130	Cb
Thurnby	130	Db
Thurne	138	Cc
Thurning, Norf.	137	Ab
Thurning, N'hants.	114	Ba
Thurnscoe	174	Cc
Thurrock, Lit.	59	Ab
Thurrock, W.	59	Ab
Thursby	217	Bc
Thursford	136	Db
Thursley	40	Da
Thurso	323	Ba
Thurstaston	159	Ab
Thurston	98	Ca
Thurstonfield	217	Bc
Thurstonland	172	Dc
Thurton	119	Ba
Thurvaston	148	Db
Thuxton	118	Da
Thwaite, Norf.	119	Bb
Thwaite, Suff.	99	Aa
Thwaite, Yorks.	195	Aa
Thwaites	183	Ac
Thwing	188	Cb
Tibbermore	260	Ca
Tibberton, Glos.	89	Bc
Tibberton, Shrops.	126	Ca
Tibberton, Worcs.	109	Bc
Tibenham	119	Ab
Tibshelf	149	Ba
Tibthorpe	187	Bc
Ticehurst	26	Ca
Tickborne	39	Ab
Tickencote	132	Cb
Tickenham	50	Ca
Tickhill	164	Da
Ticklerton	125	Bc
Ticknall	129	Aa
Tickton	177	Ba
Tidcombe	53	Bc
Tiddington	91	Ba
Tideford	7	Bb
Tidenham	68	Db
Tideswell	163	Ab
Tidmarsh	55	Aa
Tidmington	91	Bb
Tidpit	37	Ac
Tidworth, N.	53	Bc

Name	PAGE	SQ.
Tidworth, S.	53	Bc
Tiffield	93	Aa
Tigerton	281	Ac
Tighnabruaich	246	Cb
Tilbrook	95	Aa
Tilbury	59	Ac
Tilbury-juxta-Clare	97	Bc
Tilbury, W.	59	Ab
Tilehurst	55	Aa
Tiford	40	Da
Tilley	145	Ac
Tillicoultry	259	Db
Tillingham	78	Dc
Tillington, Heref s.	88	Cb
Tillington, Sus.	23	Aa
Tillybirloch	293	Ab
Tillyloss	271	Ba
Tilmanstone	46	Cb
Tilney All Saints	134	Dc
Tilney-cum-Islington	134	Dc
Tilney St. Lawrence	134	Dc
Tilshead	52	Dc
Tilstock	145	Da
Tilston	144	Da
Tilsworth	94	Dc
Tilton	131	Ab
Tilty	77	Ab
Timberland	152	Da
Timberscombe	48	Db
Timble	183	Bb
Timsbury, Hants.	38	Cb
Timsbury, Som.	51	Ab
Timworth	98	Ca
Tincleton	18	Cb
Tingewick	93	Ab
Tingley	173	Ba
Tingrith	94	Db
Tinhay	12	Cc
Tinhead	52	Cb
Tinsley	164	Ca
Tintagel	11	Ac
Tintern Parva	68	Db
Tintinhull	34	Dc
Tintwistle	162	Da
Tinwald	227	Ac
Tinwell	132	Cb
Tipton	127	Bc
Tiptree	78	Ca
Tirley	89	Bb
Tirphil	86	Dc
Tisbury	36	Da
Tissington	148	Ca
Tisted, E.	39	Bb
Tisted, W.	39	Bb
Titchfield	21	Ba
Titchmarsh	114	Ca
Titchwell	135	Ba
Tithby	150	Dc
Titley	107	Ac
Titsey	42	Cc
Tittensor	146	Db
Tittleshall	136	Ca
Tiverton, Ches.	145	Aa
Tiverton, Dev.	32	Db
Tivetshall St. Margaret	119	Ab
Tivetshall St. Mary	119	Ac
Tixall	127	Ba
Tixover	132	Cc
Tobermory	263	Bb
Tocher	293	Aa
Tockwith	184	Db
Todber	36	Cb
Toddington, Beds.	94	Db
Toddington, Glos.	90	Db
Todenham	91	Bb
Todhills	217	Bb
Todlachie	293	Ab
Todmorden	172	Ca
Todwick	164	Db
Toft, Cambs.	96	Cb
Toft, Ches.	161	Bb
Toft, Lincs.	132	Da
Toft Monks	120	Cb
Toft-next-Newton	166	Da
Toftrees	136	Cb
Tofts, W.	117	Bb
Tokavaig	285	Ac
Tolland	33	Ab
Tollard Royal	36	Db
Tollcross	249	Ac
Toller Fratrum	17	Ba
Toller Porcorum	17	Ba
Tollerton, Notts.	150	Cc
Tollerton, Yorks.	185	Aa
Toller Whelme	17	Aa
Tollesbury	78	Da
Tolleshunt D'Arcy	78	Dc
Tolleshunt Knights	78	Cc
Tolleshunt Major	78	Cc
Tolpuddle	18	Ca
Tomich	300	Cb
Tomintoul	291	Ab
Tomnavoulin	291	Ba

365

Name	PAGE	SQ.
Ton	66	Ca
Tonbridge	43	Bb
Tondu	66	Cb
Tonedale	33	Ac
Tong, Shrops.	126	Db
Tong, Yorks.	173	Aa
Tonge	129	Ba
Tongham	56	Cc
Tongland	214	Cc
Tong Norton	126	Db
Tong Street	173	Aa
Tongue	320	Db
Tonypandy	66	Ca
Ton-yr-efail	66	Ca
Tookenham	70	Dc
Toot Baldon	72	Db
Tooting	57	Bc
Topcliffe	197	Ac
Topcroft	119	Bb
Topcroft Street	119	Bb
Toppesfield	77	Ba
Toprow	119	Ab
Topsham	14	Da
Torbryan	10	Ca
Torcross	10	Cc
Torksey	165	Bb
Tormarton	69	Bc
Tormore	273	Da
Torness	288	Da
Torpenhow	202	Ca
Torphichen	250	Db
Torphins	293	Ac
Torpoint	8	Cc
Torquay	10	Ca
Torran	284	Db
Torrance	249	Ca
Torrington	30	Cc
Torrington, E.	167	Aa
Torrington, W.	167	Ac
Torrisholme	180	Ca
Torry	294	Cc
Torryburn	250	Ca
Torry, Low	250	Da
Torthorwald	216	Ca
Tortington	23	Ac
Torton	109	Ab
Tortworth	69	Ab
Torver	192	Db
Torworth	165	Ab
Toseland	95	Ba
Tostock	98	Da
Totaig	295	Ac
Totford	39	Aa
Totham, Gt.	78	Ca
Totham, Lit.	78	Cc
Tot Hill, Sur.	41	Ba
Tothill, Lincs.	168	Cc
Totland	20	Dc
Totley	163	Ba
Totnes	10	Ca
Toton	149	Bc
Tottenham, Dur.	207	Ab
Tottenham, London	58	Ca
Tottenhill	135	Ac
Totteridge	57	Ba
Totternhoe	94	Dc
Tottington, Lancs.	171	Ab
Tottington, Norf.	118	Cb
Totton	38	Cc
Toulton	33	Bb
Tovil	44	Ca
Towcester	93	Aa
Towednack	1	Bb
Towersey	73	Ba
Towie	292	Cb
Tow Law	206	Da
Town Barningham	137	Aa
Town End	116	Cb
Towngate	132	Db
Townhead	293	Ac
Townhill	251	Ba
Town Kelloe	207	Ba
Townshend	2	Cb
Town Street	117	Bc
Towthorpe, Yorks.	185	Bb
Towthorpe, Yorks.	186	Ba
Towton	186	Da
Toxteth Park	159	Ba
Toynton All Saints	154	Cb
Toynton Fen Side	154	Cb
Toynton, High	153	Ba
Toynton, Low	153	Bb
Toynton St. Peter	154	Cb
Towyn, Den.	158	Ca
Towyn, Mer.	121	Bb
Trallong	67	Bb
Tranch	67	Bb
Tranent	252	Cb
Trapp	64	Ca
Traquair	240	Db
Travellers' Rest	30	Dc
Trawden	182	Cc
Trawsfynydd	141	Ba
Tre-Alaw	66	Ca
Treales	169	Ba
Trebartha	7	Ba
Trebarwith	11	Ac
Treborough	48	Cc
Trecastle	85	Ba
Trecynon	86	Cc
Tredegar	67	Aa
Tredegar, New	86	Dc
Tredington, Glos.	90	Cb
Tredington, War.	91	Bb
Tredunnoe	67	Bb
Treeton	164	Ca
Trefach	83	Bb
Trefasin	81	Bb
Trefdraeth	155	Bb
Trefeglwys	123	Ac
Treffynnon	155	Ba
Trefgarn	62	Ca
Tref-garn-Owen	61	Ba
Trefilan	101	Bc
Treflach Wood	124	Ca
Trefnant	158	Db
Trefriw	157	Bb
Tregagle	68	Da
Tregalan	156	Cb
Tregare	68	Ca
Tregaron	102	Cb
Tregavethan	2	Da
Tregeiriog	143	Bc
Tregibbon	86	Cc
Tregonetha	6	Cb
Tregony	4	Ca
Tregurrian	5	Bb
Tregynon	123	Bc
Trehafod	66	Da
Treharris	66	Da
Treherbert	86	Cc
Trelan	2	Dc
Trelawnyd	158	Da
Trelech	83	Ac
Trelech-ar-Bettws	83	Bc
Trelights	6	Ca
Trelleck	68	Ca
Trelleck Grange	68	Cb
Trelowia	7	Bc
Trelystan	124	Cb
Tremadoc	140	Db
Tremain	83	Aa
Tremaine	11	Bc
Tremeton	8	Cb
Tremeirchion	158	Db
Treneglos	11	Bc
Trent	35	Ab
Trentham	146	Db
Trentishoe	30	Da
Trent Vale	146	Db
Treorky	66	Ca
Trescoll	6	Cb
Trescowe	2	Cb
Tresham	69	Bb
Tresmeer	11	Bc
Treswell	165	Bb
Tre Taliesin	121	Bc
Treto	83	Ac
Trevalga	11	Ac
Trevanson	6	Ca
Trevarrick	4	Da
Treveighan	6	Ca
Treverbyn	6	Cc
Trevethin	67	Bb
Trevor	139	Bb
Trewen	11	Bc
Trewent	62	Ca
Trewidland	7	Bb
Treyford	40	Cc
Triangle	172	Cb
Trimdon	207	Ba
Trimingham	137	Ba
Trimley	80	Db
Trinnley	109	Aa
Trim-Saran	64	Cb
Trinant	67	Ab
Tring	74	Da
Trispen	5	Bc
Tritlington	232	Cc
Trochrie	269	Bb
Troedyraur	83	Ba
Troes	66	Cb
Troon	236	Cb
Troqueer	215	Ba
Trossachs, The	268	Cb
Troston	98	Ca
Trostrey	67	Ba
Trottiscliffe	43	Ba
Trotton, Sus.	40	Cb
Trotton, Sus.	40	Cc
Troutbeck	193	Aa
Troway	164	Ca
Trowbridge	52	Cb
Trowell	149	Bb
Trowse Newton	119	Ba
Troy	188	Ba
Truddoxhill	51	Bc
Trull	33	Bc
Trumpan	295	Ab
Trumpington	96	Db
Trunch	137	Ba
Truro	2	Da
Trusham	14	Cb
Trusley	148	Dc
Trusthorpe	168	Dc
Trysull	127	Ac
Tryddyn	144	Ca
Tubney	72	Cb
Tuckerton	33	Bb
Tuckhill	126	Dc
Tuckingmill	36	Da
Tuddenham, Suff.	97	Ba
Tuddenham, Suff.	99	Bc
Tuddenham, E.	118	Da
Tudeley	43	Bb
Tudhoe	207	Aa
Tuffley	89	Bc
Tufton	38	Da
Tugby	161	Ac
Tugford	108	Ca
Tullibody	259	Bc
Tullynessle	292	Db
Tumble	64	Ca
Tumby	153	Bb
Tumby Woodside	153	Bb
Tunbridge Wells	43	Bc
Tundergarth	216	Da
Tunley	51	Ab
Tunstall, Kent	44	Ca
Tunstall, Lancs.	194	Cc
Tunstall, Norf.	120	Ca
Tunstall, Staffs.	146	Da
Tunstall, Suff.	100	Ca
Tunstall, Yorks.	178	Cb
Tunstall, Yorks.	196	Db
Tunstead	162	Db
Tunworth	55	Aa
Tupsley	88	Da
Tupton	164	Ca
Turclossie	305	Ba
Turkdean	71	Aa
Tur Langton	130	Dc
Turleigh	51	Bb
Turnastone	87	Bb
Turnditch	148	Da
Turnershill	42	Cc
Turners Puddle	18	Da
Turnworth	36	Cc
Turriff	305	Ab
Turton Bottoms	170	Db
Turvey	94	Ca
Turville	73	Bc
Turweston	93	Ab
Tutbury	148	Cb
Tuttington	137	Bb
Tuxford	165	Ac
Tweedmouth	243	Ba
Tweedsmuir	239	Bc
Twenty	132	Da
Twerton	51	Bb
Twickenham	57	Ac
Twigworth	89	Bc
Twineham	24	Cb
Twinhoe	51	Bb
Twinstead	78	Ca
Twitchen, Dev.	47	Bc
Twitchen, Salop	107	Ca
Twycross	129	Ab
Twyford, Berks.	55	Ba
Twyford, Bucks.	93	Ac
Twyford, Derby	148	Dc
Twyford, Dors.	36	Cb
Twyford, Hants.	38	Db
Twyford, Leics.	130	Db
Twyford, Norf.	136	Db
Twyn-carno	86	Db
Twynholm	214	Cc
Twyning	90	Cb
Twyning Green	90	Cb
Twyn Llanan	85	Aa
Twywell	114	Cb
Tyberton	87	Ba
Tyburn	128	Cb
Tyby	137	Ab
Ty-cros	64	Cb
Tydd St. Giles	134	Cc
Tydd St. Mary	134	Cc
Tydweiliog	139	Ab
Ty-gwyn	64	Cb
Tyldesley	170	Dc
Tylerhill	45	Bb
Tyndrum	267	Ac
Tyneham	18	Db
Tynemouth	222	Db
Tynewydd	86	Cc
Tynron	226	Cb
Tyringham	94	Ca
Tysoe, Lr.	92	Ca
Tysoe, Mid.	91	Ba
Tysoe, Upr.	91	Bb
Tythecott	12	Ca
Tythegston	65	Bb
Tytherington, Ches.	162	Cb
Tytherington, Glos.	69	Ac
Tytherington, Som.	51	Bc
Tytherington, Wilts.	36	Da
Tytherleigh	16	Ca
Tytherley, E.	38	Cb
Tytherley, W.	38	Cb
Tytherton, E.	52	Ca
Tytherton Lucas	52	Ca
Tywardreath	6	Dc
Tywyn	157	Ba
Ubbeston	100	Ca
Ubley	50	Db
Uckfield	25	Aa
Uckinghall	90	Cb
Uckington	90	Cc
Uddingston	249	Ac
Udimore	27	Ab
Udny	294	Ca
Uffcott	53	Aa
Uffculme	15	Aa
Uffington, Berks.	71	Bc
Uffington, Lincs.	132	Db
Uffington, Shrops.	125	Ba
Ufford, N'hants.	132	Db
Ufford, Suff.	99	Bc
Ufton	111	Bc
Ufton Nervet	55	Ab
Ugborough	9	Ba
Uggeshall	100	Da
Ugley	76	Da
Ugthorpe	199	Bb
Uig, Inver.	295	Ac
Uig, Inver.	296	Cb
Uiginish	295	Ac
Ulbster	318	Da
Ulceby, Lincs.	167	Aa
Ulceby, Lincs.	154	Ca
Ulcombe	44	Db
Uldale	202	Da
Uley	69	Bb
Ulgham	232	Cc
Ullapool	309	Aa
Ullenhall	110	Cb
Ulleskeif	185	Ac
Ullesthorpe	112	Ca
Ulley	164	Ca
Ullingswick	88	Da
Ullock	201	Bb
Ulpha	192	Cb
Ulverston	192	Dc
Ulzone	188	Cc
Umberleigh	30	Ca
Uncleby	186	Cb
Underbarrow	193	Bb
Undercliffe	173	Aa
Underwood	149	Bb
Undy	68	Cc
Unstone	164	Cb
Unstone Green	163	Bb
Unsworth	171	Bc
Unthank	204	Ca
Uny Lelant	1	Bb
Upavon	53	Ac
Up Cerne	17	Ba
Upchurch	60	Cc
Up Exe	32	Dc
Upgate Street	118	Db
Uphall	250	Db
Upham	39	Ac
Uphampton	109	Ab
Up Hill, Kent	28	Da
Uphill, Som.	49	Bb
Upholland	170	Cc
Upleadon	89	Bb
Upleatham	199	Aa
Uploders	16	Db
Uplowman	32	Db
Uplyme	16	Cb
Upminster	58	Db
Up Nately	55	Ac
Uppottery	15	Ba
Upper Beeding	24	Cb
Upper Boat	66	Da
Upper Broughton	130	Da
Upperby	217	Bc
Upper Corris	122	Ca
Upper Gornal	127	Bc
Upper Green	173	Ba
Upper Hambledon	131	Bb
Upper Haugh	164	Ca
Upper Mill	172	Cc
Upper Penn	127	Ac
Upper Somborne	38	Cb
Upper Stoke	119	Ba
Upper Tean	147	Bc
Upperthong	172	Dc
Upperton	23	Aa
Uppertown	163	Bc
Uppingham	131	Bc
Uppington	126	Cb
Upsall	197	Bb

Place	Page	Sq.
Upstreet	46	Cb
Up Sydling	17	Ba
Upton, *Berks.*	72	Dc
Upton, *Bucks.*	73	Ba
Upton, *Ches.*	159	Aa
Upton, *Ches.*	160	Ab
Upton, *Corn.*	7	Ba
Upton, *Dors.*	18	Cb
Upton, *Hunts.*	114	Db
Upton, *Leics.*	129	Db
Upton, *Lincs.*	166	Cb
Upton, *N'hants.*	113	Ac
Upton, *N'hants.*	132	Dc
Upton, *Norf.*	120	Da
Upton, *Notts.*	165	Bb
Upton, *Notts.*	150	Db
Upton, *Pem.*	62	Cb
Upton, *Som.*	34	Db
Upton, *Wilts.*	36	Ca
Upton, *Wilts.*	54	Cc
Upton, *Yorks.*	174	Cb
Upton Bishop	89	Ab
Upton Cheyney	51	Aa
Upton Cressett	126	Ca
Upton Green	138	Cc
Upton Grey	55	Bc
Upton Hellions	32	Cc
Upton Lovell	36	Da
Upton Magna	125	Bb
Upton Noble	35	Bc
Upton-on-Severn	90	Ca
Upton Pyne	32	Dc
Upton St. Leonards	70	Ca
Upton Scudamore	52	Cc
Upton Snodsbury	109	Bc
Upton Warren	109	Ac
Upwaltham	23	Ab
Upway	17	Bb
Upwell	116	Da
Upwood	115	Bc
Urchfont	52	Db
Urmston	161	Ba
Urquhart	303	Aa
Urr	214	Db
Urswick, Gt.	192	Dc
Urswick, Lit.	192	Cc
Usk	67	Bb
Usselby	166	Ca
Usworth, Gt.	222	Cb
Utkinton	160	Dc
Utley	182	Dc
Uton	32	Cc
Utterby	167	Bb
Uttoxeter	147	Bc
Uxbridge	56	Da
Uzmaston	62	Ca
VALLEY	155	Ab
Vange	59	Bb
Vaynor	86	Db
Velindre, *Brecon..*	87	Ab
Velindre, *Carm.*	83	Bb
Venn Ottery	15	Ab
Ventnor	21	Bc
Vernhams Dean	54	Cc
Verwick	82	Da
Verwood	19	Ba
Veryan	4	Ca
Vexford, Lr.	33	Ab
Vickerstown	179	Ab
Victoria	67	Aa
Vinehall	26	Da
Virginstow	12	Cc
Virley	78	Dc
Vobster	51	Ac
Vowchurch	87	Ba
WACTON	119	Ab
Waddesdon	73	Ba
Waddingham	166	Ca
Waddington, *Lancs.*	166	Cc
Waddington, *Yorks.*	181	Bc
Waddingworth	153	Aa
Wadebridge	6	Ca
Wadenhoe	114	Ca
Wadhurst	26	Ca
Wadshelf	163	Bc
Wadsley	163	Ba
Wadsley Bridge	163	Ba
Wadworth	164	Da
Waen	158	Db
Waen-fawr	156	Cc
Wainfleet-all-Saints	154	Db
Wainfleet Bank	154	Cb
Waingroves	149	Bb
Wainscot	59	Bc
Wainstalls	172	Ca
Waitby	194	Da
Waithe	167	Bb
Wakefield	173	Bb
Wakeham	18	Cc
Wakering, Gt.	60	Db
Wakering, Lit.	60	Cb
Wakerley	132	Cc
Wakes Colne	78	Ca
Walberswick	100	Ba
Walberton	23	Ac
Walby	218	Ca
Walcot, *Lincs.*	176	Cb
Walcot, *Lincs.*	152	Ca
Walcot, *Lincs.*	152	Dc
Walcote	112	Ca
Walcott	138	Cb
Walderton	22	Da
Waldingfield, Gt.	98	Cc
Waldingfield, Lit.	98	Cc
Walditch	16	Db
Waldringfield	80	Ca
Waldron	25	Bb
Wales	164	Ca
Walesby, *Lincs.*	167	Ab
Walesby, *Notts.*	165	Ac
Walford, *Herefs.*	107	Ab
Walford, *Herefs.*	88	Dc
Walford, *Shrops.*	125	Aa
Walford Heath	125	Aa
Walgrave	113	Ab
Walkden	170	Dc
Walker	222	Cb
Walkerburn	240	Db
Walkeringham	165	Ba
Walkerith	165	Ba
Walker, Low	222	Cb
Walkern	75	Ba
Walkhampton	8	Da
Walkington	177	Ab
Walkers Green	88	Da
Wall, *N'land.*	220	Cb
Wall, *Staffs.*	128	Cb
Wallasey	159	Ba
Wallbrook	127	Bc
Wallend	60	Cc
Wallheath	127	Ac
Wallingford	73	Aa
Wallington, *Herts.*	75	Ba
Wallington, *Sur.*	42	Ca
Wallsend	222	Cb
Wallsworth	89	Bc
Walmer	46	Dc
Walmer Bridge	169	Ba
Walmersley	171	Ab
Walmley	128	Cc
Walmley Ash	128	Cc
Walpole	100	Ca
Walpole Highway	134	Dc
Walpole St. Andrew	134	Dc
Walpole St. Peter	134	Dc
Walsall	127	Bc
Walsall Wood	127	Bb
Walsden	172	Cb
Walsgrave-on-Sowe	111	Ba
Walsham-le-Willows	98	Da
Walshaw Lane	171	Aa
Walshford	184	Db
Walsoken	134	Cc
Walston	239	Aa
Walterston	66	Dc
Walterstone	87	Bc
Waltham, *Kent*	45	Bc
Waltham, *Lincs.*	167	Ba
Waltham Abbey	58	Ca
Waltham, Gt.	77	Bc
Waltham, Lit.	77	Bc
Waltham, N.	39	Aa
Waltham-on-the-Wolds	131	Ba
Waltham St. Lawrence	56	Ca
Walthamstow	58	Cb
Walton, *Bucks.*	74	Ca
Walton, *Bucks.*	94	Cb
Walton, *Cumb.*	218	Cb
Walton, *Leics.*	112	Da
Walton, *N'hants.*	115	Aa
Walton, *N'hants.*	132	Dc
Walton, *Rad.*	106	Dc
Walton, *Som.*	34	Db
Walton, *Staffs.*	127	Ba
Walton, *Staffs.*	146	Dc
Walton, *Suff.*	80	Ca
Walton, *Yorks.*	173	Bb
Walton, *Yorks.*	184	Db
Walton, East	62	Ca
Walton-in-Gordano	50	Ca
Walton-le-Dale	170	Ca
Walton-on-Thames	57	Ac
Walton-on-the-Hill	42	Ca
Walton-on-the-Naze	80	Cc
Walton-on-the-Wolds	130	Ca
Walton-upon-Trent	128	Da
Walton West	61	Bb
Walwick	220	Ca
Walworth	207	Ac
Walwyns Castle	61	Bb
Wambrook	16	Ca
Wamphray	227	Bb
Wanborough, *Sur.*	56	Cc
Wanborough, *Wilts.*	53	Ba
Wandsworth	57	Bc
Wangford, *Suff.*	117	Bc
Wangford, *Suff.*	100	Ba
Wanlip	130	Cb
Wanlockhead	226	Ca
Wannock	25	Bc
Wapsford, *N'hants.*	132	Dc
Wansford, *Yorks..*	188	Dc
Wanshurst Green	44	Cb
Wanstead	58	Cc
Wanswell Green	69	Ab
Wantage	72	Cc
Wantisden	100	Cc
Wapley	69	Ac
Waplington	186	Cc
Wappenbury	111	Bb
Wappenham	93	Aa
Wappenshall	126	Ca
Warbleton	25	Bb
Warblington	22	Ca
Warborough	73	Ac
Warboys	115	Bc
Warbreck	179	Bc
Warbstow	11	Bc
Warburton	161	Aa
Warcop	204	Dc
Warden, *Kent*	45	Aa
Warden, *N'land.*	220	Cb
Ward End	128	Cc
Warden, Old	95	Ac
Wardington	92	Da
Wardington, Upr.	92	Da
Wardle, *Ches.*	145	Ba
Wardle, *Lancs*	171	Bb
Wardley	131	Bc
Wardlow	163	Ab
Ware, *Herts.*	76	Cb
Ware, *Kent.*	44	Ca
Ware, *Kent.*	46	Cb
Wareham	18	Db
Warehorne	27	Ba
Warenford	244	Cc
Waresley	95	Bc
Warfield	56	Ca
Wargate	133	Bb
Wargrave	55	Ba
Warham All Saints	136	Da
Warham St. Mary	136	Da
Wark, *N'land.*	220	Ca
Wark, *N'land.*	242	Db
Warkleigh	30	Dc
Warkton	113	Ba
Warkworth, *N'hants.*	92	Db
Warkworth, *N'land*	232	Db
Warlaby	197	Ab
Warleggan	6	Db
Warley	172	Da
Warley, Lit.	59	Aa
Warlingham	42	Ca
Warmfield	174	Cb
Warmingham	146	Ca
Warminghurst	23	Bb
Warmington, *N'hants.*	114	Da
Warmington, *War.*	92	Ca
Warminster	52	Cc
Warmley	51	Aa
Warmsworth	174	Dc
Warmwell	18	Db
Warnborough	39	Ba
Warnborough, N..	55	Bc
Warndon	109	Bc
Warnford	39	Bb
Warnham	41	Bc
Warninglid	24	Ca
Warnsgrove	73	Ab
Warren, *Ches.*	162	Cc
Warren, *Pem.*	61	Bc
Warrington, *Bucks.*	94	Ca
Warrington, *Lancs.*	160	Da
Warsash	21	Aa
Warslow	147	Ba
Warsop	164	Dc
Warter	186	Db
Warthill	185	Bb
Wartling	26	Cb
Wartnaby	130	Da
Warton, *Lincs.*	169	Ba
Warton, *Lancs.*	180	Dc
Warton, *War.*	128	Db
Warwick, *Cumb.*	218	Cc
Warwick, *War.*	111	Aa
Washbourne, Gt.	90	Db
Washbourne, Lit.	90	Db
Washbrook	79	Ba
Washfield	32	Db
Washfold	195	Ba
Washford	33	Aa
Washford Pyne	32	Cb
Washingborough	166	Cc
Washington, *Dur.*	222	Cc
Washington, *Sus.*	23	Bb
Washwood Heath	128	Cc
Wasing	55	Ab
Waskerley	206	Ca
Wasperton	111	Ac
Wass	198	Cc
Watchet	33	Aa
Watchfield	71	Bc
Watendlath	202	Dc
Waterbeach	96	Da
Waterden	136	Ca
Water Eaton	94	Cb
Waterfall	147	Ba
Waterford	76	Cb
Water Fryston	174	Ca
Waterhouses	147	Ba
Wateringbury	43	Bb
Waterlane	70	Ca
Waterloo, *Lancs..*	159	Ba
Waterloo, *Lan.*	250	Cc
Waterloo, *Perth*	270	Cc
Waterlooville	22	Ca
Water Newton	132	Dc
Water Orton	128	Dc
Waterperry	73	Ab
Waterrow	33	Aa
Watersfield	23	Ab
Waterside, *Yorks.*	175	Ab
Waterside, *Yorks.*	172	Cc
Watersplace	76	Cb
Waterstock	73	Ab
Water Stratford	93	Ab
Water Street	65	Bb
Waters Upton	126	Ca
Waterton	293	Bc
Watford, *Herts.*	57	Ba
Watford, *N'hants.*	112	Db
Wath	197	Ac
Wath-upon-Dearne	174	Cc
Watlington, *Norf.*	135	Ac
Watlington, *Oxon.*	73	Bc
Watnall Chaworth	149	Bb
Watten	324	Cc
Watten, N.	324	Cb
Wattisfield	98	Da
Wattisham	98	Db
Wattlefield	119	Ab
Watton, *Norf.*	118	Ca
Watton, *Yorks.*	177	Aa
Watton-at-Stone	76	Cb
Wauldby	176	Da
Waun-arlwydd	64	Dc
Waun-y-clyn	64	Cb
Wavendon	94	Cb
Waverton, *Ches.*	160	Cc
Waverton, *Cumb..*	216	Dc
Wavertree	159	Ba
Wawne	177	Bb
Waxham	138	Db
Waxholme	178	Db
Wayford	16	Da
Weald	71	Bb
Weald Bassett, N.	76	Dc
Weald, South	59	Aa
Wealdstone	57	Aa
Weare	50	Cc
Weare Gifford	30	Cc
Weare, Lr.	50	Cb
Wear Head.	205	Ba
Wearne	34	Db
Weasenham All Saints	136	Cc
Weasenham St. Peter	136	Cb
Weaverham	160	Db
Weaverthorpe	187	Bb
Webbery	30	Cc
Webheath	109	Bb
Webscott	125	Ba
Weddington	129	Bc
Wedhampton	52	Da
Wedmore	34	Db
Wednesbury	127	Bc
Wednesfield	127	Bb
Weedon Beck	112	Dc
Weedon Lois	93	Aa
Weedon, Upr.	112	Dc
Weeford	128	Cb
Week.	33	Ba
Weeke	38	Db
Weekley	113	Ba
Week St. Mary	11	Bb

	PAGE	SQ.
Weeley	79	Bc
Weem	269	Ab
Weethley	110	Cc
Weeting	117	Bb
Weeton, Lancs.	169	Ba
Weeton, Yorks.	184	Cc
Weeton, Yorks.	178	Dc
Weighton, Lit.	176	Da
Weir	60	Cb
Weirbrook	124	Da
Welborne	118	Da
Welbourn	152	Ca
Welburn, Yorks.	186	Ca
Welburn, Yorks.	198	Db
Welbury	197	Aa
Welby, Leics.	130	Da
Welby, Lincs.	152	Cc
Welches Dam	116	Cb
Welcombe	11	Ba
Weldon, Gt.	113	Ba
Weldon, Lit.	113	Ba
Welford, Berks.	54	Ca
Welford, War.	91	Aa
Welford, N'hants	112	Da
Welham, Leics.	131	Ac
Welham, Notts.	165	Ab
Well, Lincs.	154	Ca
Well, Yorks.	196	Dc
Welland	89	Ba
Wellesbourne Hastings.	91	Ba
Wellesbourne Mountford	91	Ba
Well Hill	43	Aa
Wellhouse, Berks.	54	Ca
Wellhouse, Yorks.	172	Db
Welling	58	Dc
Wellingborough	113	Bh
Wellingham	136	Cb
Wellingore	152	Ca
Wellington, Herefs.	88	Ca
Wellington, Shrops.	126	Cb
Wellington, Som..	33	Ac
Wellington Heath	89	Aa
Wellow, Hants.	20	Db
Wellow, Notts.	165	Ac
Wellow, Som	51	Bb
Wellow, E.	38	Cc
Wellow, W.	38	Cc
Wells	34	Da
Wells-next-the-Sea	136	Ca
Wells-of-Ythan	304	Dc
Welney	116	Db
Welshampton	144	Bc
Welsh Bicknor	88	Dc
Welshend	145	Ac
Welsh Newton	88	Cc
Welshpool	124	Cb
Welsh St.Donats	66	Db
Welton Cumb.	202	Da
Welton, Lincs.	166	Db
Welton, N'land.	220	Db
Welton, Som.	51	Ab
Welton, War.	112	Cb
Welton, Yorks.	176	Da
Welton-le-Marsh	154	Ca
Welton-le-Wold	167	Bc
Welwick	178	Dc
Welwyn	75	Bb
Wem	145	Ac
Wembdon	33	Ba
Wembley	57	Ab
Wembury	8	Dc
Wembworthy	31	Bb
Wemyss Bay	247	Ab
Wemyss, E.	261	Bb
Wendens Ambo	76	Da
Wendlebury	92	Bc
Wendling	136	Cc
Wendover	74	Ca
Wendron	2	Cb
Wendy	96	Cc
Wenham, Gt.	79	Aa
Wenham, Lit.	79	Aa
Wenhaston	100	Ca
Wennington, Essex	58	Db
Wennington, Hunts.	115	Bc
Wensley	196	Cb
Wentbridge	174	Ca
Wentnor	124	Dc
Wentworth, Cambs.	116	Cc
Wentworth, Yorks.	164	Ca
Wenvoe	49	Aa
Weobley	87	Ba
Weobley Marsh	88	Ca
Wereham	117	Aa
Werrington, Dev.	12	Cc
Werrington, N'hants.	115	Aa

	PAGE	SQ.
Werrington,Staffs.	147	Ab
Wervin	160	Cc
Wesham	169	Ba
Wessington	149	Aa
West Acre	135	Bc
West Alvington	10	Cb
West Ashby	153	Ba
West Bay	16	Db
West Beckham	137	Aa
Westbere	46	Cb
West Bilney	135	Bc
Westborough	151	Bb
Westbourne	22	Ca
West Bromwich	127	Bc
Westbrook	52	Ca
West Buckland	33	Bc
Westbury, Bucks.	93	Ab
Westbury. Shrops.	124	Db
Westbury, Som..	34	Da
Westbury, Wilts.	52	Cc
Westbury Leigh	52	Cc
Westbury-on-Severn	69	Aa
Westbury-upon-Trym	50	Da
Westby	152	Cc
West Calder	250	Dc
Westcombe.	35	Ba
Westcot Barton	92	Cc
Westcote	91	Bc
West Cross	64	Dc
Westdean	25	Bc
West Deeping	132	Db
West Derby	159	Ba
West Drayton	56	Da
West End, Hants.	38	Dc
West End, Norf.	120	Da
West End, Sur.	56	Db
West End, Wilts..	36	Db
Westerdale, Caith.	323	Bc
Westerdale, Yorks.	198	Ba
Westerfield	99	Bc
Westerham	42	Da
Westerkirk	228	Cc
Westerleigh	69	Ac
Westerton, Aber..	293	Bb
Westerton, Sus.	22	Da
West Felton	124	Da
Westfield, Norf.	118	Da
Westfield, Sus.	26	Db
Westgate, Dur.	205	Ba
Westgate, Lincs.	175	Bc
Westgate, Norf.	137	Bb
Westgate, Norf.	136	Ca
Westgate Hill	173	Aa
Westgate-on-Sea	46	Da
West Gordon	242	Ca
West Grimstead	24	Cb
Westhall	100	Da
West Hallam	149	Bb
West Halton	176	Cb
West Ham, Essex.	58	Cb
Westham, Som..	34	Ca
Westham, Sus.	26	Cc
West Hampnett	22	Da
West Hartlepool	208	Db
Westhay	34	Da
Westhead	169	Bc
Westhide	88	Da
West Hill	50	Cb
West Hoathly	24	Da
Westhorp	92	Da
Westhorpe, Lincs.	133	Bb
Westhorpe, Notts.	150	Ba
Westhorpe, Suff..	98	Ca
Westhoughton	170	Dc
West Kilbride	235	Ba
West Kirby	159	Ab
Westleigh, Dev.	30	Cb
Westleigh, Lancs.	170	Dc
West Leigh, Som	33	Ab
Westleton	100	Db
Westley, Shrops.	124	Db
Westley, Suff.	98	Ca
Westley Waterless	97	Ab
Westlington	73	Ba
Westlinton, Cumb.	217	Bb
West Linton, Peeb.	239	Ba
Westmancote	90	Cb
Westmarsh, Kent.	46	Cb
West Marsh, Lincs.	167	Ba
Westmeston	24	Db
Westmill	76	Ca
West Monkton	33	Bb
West Moors	19	Ba
West Newton	135	Bb
Westoe	222	Db
Weston, Berks.	54	Ca
Weston, Ches.	146	Ca
Weston, Ches.	160	Cb
Weston Dors	17	Bc

	PAGE	SQ.
Weston, Herts.	75	Ba
Weston, Lincs.	133	Bb
Weston, N'hants	92	Da
Weston, Norf.	137	Ac
Weston, Notts.	165	Bc
Weston, Pem.	62	Cb
Weston, Shrops.	145	Bc
Weston, Shrops.	126	Ca
Weston, Som.	51	Aa
Weston, Suff.	120	Cc
Weston, Yorks.	183	Rb
Weston Bampfylde	35	Ab
Weston Beggard	88	Da
Weston-by-Welland	131	Ac
Weston Colley	39	Aa
Weston Colville	97	Ab
Weston Corbett	39	Ba
Weston Favell	113	Ac
Weston Hills	133	Bb
Westoning	94	Db
Weston-In-Gordano	50	Ca
Weston Jones	126	Da
Weston Lullingfields	125	Aa
Weston, Old	114	Db
Weston-on-Avon	91	Aa
Weston-on-the-Green	72	Da
Weston Patrick	39	Ba
Weston Rhyn	144	Cc
Weston, S.	73	Bb
Weston Subedge	91	Ab
Weston-super-Mare	49	Bb
Weston Turville	74	Ca
Weston-under-Lizard	126	Db
Weston-under-Penyard	88	Dc
Weston-under-Wetherley	111	Bb
Weston Underwood, Bucks.	94	Ca
Weston Underwood, Derby	148	Db
Weston-upon-Trent, Derby	149	Bc
Weston-upon-Trent, Staffs.	147	Bc
Weston Zoyland	34	Cb
Westow	186	Ca
Westowe	33	Ab
Westport	34	Cc
Westra	49	Aa
Westrop, Wilts.	71	Ac
Westrop, Wilts.	52	Ca
West Row	117	Ac
West Rudham	135	Bb
West Runton	137	Ba
Westruther	241	Ba
Westry	116	Ca
West Somerton	138	Dc
Westhorpe	164	Cb
West Walton	134	Cc
Westward Ho	29	Rb
Westwell, Kent	45	Ac
Westwell, Oxon.	71	Ba
West Wickham	42	Da
West Winch	135	Ac
Westwood, Kent..	59	Ac
Westwood, Notts.	149	Ba
Westwood, Wilts.	51	Bb
Westwoodside	165	Bb
West Wycombe	74	Cc
Wetheral, Cumb.	217	Bb
Wetheral, Cumb.	218	Cc
Wetherby	184	Db
Wetherden	98	Db
Wetheringsett	99	Ab
Wethersfield	77	Ba
Wetherup Street	99	Ab
Wettenhall	145	Ba
Wetton	147	Ba
Wetwang	186	Db
Wexcombe	53	Bb
Wexham	56	Da
Weybourne	137	Aa
Weybread	99	Ba
Weybridge	41	Aa
Weyhill	38	Ca
Weymouth	17	Bc
Whaddon, Bucks.	93	Bb
Whaddon,Cambs..	96	Cc
Whaddon, Glos.	69	Ba
Whaddon, Wilts..	37	Bb
Whaddon, Wilts..	52	Cb
Whale	203	Bb
Whaley	164	Dc
Whaley Bridge	162	Db
Whalley	181	Bc
Whalton	221	Ba
Whaplode	133	Bb
Whaplode Drove	133	Bc

	PAGE	SQ.
Wharfe	181	Ba
Wharles	180	Cc
Wharncliffe Side	163	Ba
Wharram-le-Street	186	Da
Wharton, Ches.	161	Ac
Wharton, Herefs.	107	Bc
Whashton	196	Ca
Whasset	193	Bc
Whatcote	91	Ba
Whatfield	79	Aa
Whatley	51	Bc
Whatlington	26	Db
Whatton	150	Db
Whaw	195	Ba
Wheatacre	120	Cb
Wheatcroft	148	Da
Wheatenhurst	69	Ba
Wheatfield	73	Ab
Wheathampstead	75	Bb
Wheathill, Shrops.	108	Ca
Wheathill, Som.	35	Aa
Wheatley, Hants.	40	Ca
Wheatley, Oxon.	73	Ab
Wheatley, Yorks.	172	Da
Wheatley, Yorks.	174	Dc
Wheatley Lane	182	Cc
Wheatley, N.	165	Bb
Wheatley, S.	165	Bb
Wheaton Aston	127	aa
Wheelock	146	Ca
Wheelton	170	Cb
Wheldrake	185	Bc
Whelford	71	Ab
Whelnetham	98	Cb
Whempstead	76	Cb
Whenby	185	Ba
Whepstead	98	Cb
Wherstead	79	Ba
Wherwell	38	Da
Wheston	162	Db
Whetstone, Leics.	130	Cc
Whetstone,M'sex.	57	Ba
Whicham	191	Bc
Whichford	91	Bb
Whickham	221	Bb
Whiddon Down	13	Ba
Whifllet	249	Bc
Whilton	112	Dc
Whimple	15	Ab
Whinburgh	118	Da
Whippingham	21	Ab
Whipsnade.	74	Da
Whipton	14	Da
Whirlow	163	Bb
Whisby	166	Cc
Whissendine	131	Bb
Whissonsett	136	Cb
Whistley Green	55	Ba
Whiston, Lancs.	160	Ca
Whiston, N'hants.	113	Bc
Whiston, Staffs.	127	Aa
Whiston, Yorks.	164	Ca
Whiston, Upr.	164	Ca
Whitbeck	191	Bc
Whitbourne	108	Dc
Whitburn, Dur.	222	Db
Whitburn, W Loth.	250	Db
Whitby, Ches.	159	Bb
Whitby, Yorks.	200	Cb
Whitchurch, Berks.	55	Aa
Whitchurch, Bucks.	93	Bc
Whitchurch, Dev.	8	Da
Whitchurch, Glam.	67	Ac
Whitchurch, Herefs.	88	Dc
Whitchurch, Hants.	38	Da
Whitchurch, Pem.	61	Aa
Whitchurch, Shrops.	145	Ab
Whitchurch, Som.	51	Aa
Whitchurch, War.	91	Ba
Whitchurch Canonicorum	16	Db
Whitcombe	18	Cb
Whitebrook	68	Da
Whitechurch	82	Db
White Colne	78	Ca
Whitefield, Lancs.	171	Bc
Whitefield, Som.	33	Ab
Whitegate	160	Dc
Whitehall	30	Cb
Whitehaven	201	Ac
Whitehill, Kent	45	Ab
Whitehill, Leics.	129	Bb
Whitehills	304	Da
Whitehouse	245	Bc
Whitekirk	253	Aa
White Lackington	34	Cc
White Ladies Aston	109	Bc

Name	Page	Sq.
Whitelye	68	Db
White Notley	77	Bb
Whiteparish	38	Cb
White Roding	77	Ac
Whitesmith	25	Bb
Whitestaunton	16	Ca
Whitestone	14	Ca
White Waltham	56	Ca
Whitfield, *Glos.*	69	Ab
Whitfield, *Kent*	46	Dc
Whitfield, *N'hants.*	93	Ab
Whitfield, *N'land*	219	Db
Whitford, *Dev.*	16	Cb
Whitford, *Flint*	158	Da
Whitgift	175	Bb
Whitgreave	146	Ca
Whithorn	210	Db
Whiting Bay	234	Dc
Whitkirk	173	Ba
Whitland	63	Aa
Whitley, *Wilts.*	52	Ca
Whitley, *Yorks.*	174	Db
Whitley Bay	222	Ca
Whitleybridge	174	Db
Whitley, Lr.	173	Ab
Whitley, Upr.	173	Ab
Whitmore, *Dors.*	19	Ba
Whitmore, *Staffs.*	146	Db
Whitnash	111	Ac
Whitney	87	Ba
Whitrigg, *Cumb.*	202	Ca
Whitrigg, *Cumb.*	216	Db
Whitsbury	37	Bb
Whitsome	242	Da
Whitson	67	Bc
Whitstable	45	Ba
Whitstone	11	Bb
Whittingham, *Lancs.*	180	Dc
Whittinghame, *N'land*	231	Ba
Whittinghame	253	Ab
Whittington, *Derby*	164	Cb
Whittington, *Glos.*	90	Cb
Whittington, *Lancs.*	194	Cc
Whittington, *Norf.*	117	Ba
Whittington, *Shrops.*	144	Cc
Whittington, *Staffs.*	128	Cb
Whittington, *Worcs.*	109	Bc
Whittington, Gt.	220	Da
Whittington Moor	164	Cb
Whittington, New	164	Cb
Whittinstow	125	Ac
Whittlebury	93	Aa
Whittle-le-Woods	170	Ca
Whittlesey	115	Ba
Whittlesford	96	Dc
Whitton, *Dur.*	207	Bb
Whitton, *Lincs.*	176	Ca
Whitton, *M'sex*	57	Ac
Whitton, *N'land*	231	Ba
Whitton, *Rad.*	106	Db
Whitton, *Rox.*	242	Ca
Whitton, *Suff.*	99	Ac
Whitton-cum-Thurlston	99	Ac
Whittonditch	53	Ba
Whittonstall	220	Dc
Whitway	54	Cb
Whitwell, *Derby*	164	Db
Whitwell, *Hants.*	21	Bb
Whitwell, *Norf.*	137	Ab
Whitwell, *Rut.*	131	Bb
Whitwell, *Yorks.*	196	Da
Whitwell-on-the-Hill	186	Da
Whitwick	129	Ba
Whitwood	174	Ca
Whitworth	171	Bb
Whixall	145	Ac
Whixley	184	Db
Whorlton, *Dur.*	206	Dc
Whorlton, *Yorks.*	197	Ba
Whyle	108	Cc
Wibdon	68	Db
Wibsey	172	Da
Wibtoft	112	Ca
Wichenford	108	Ca
Wichling	44	Da
Wichnor	128	Ca
Wick, *Caith.*	324	Dc
Wick, *Glam.*	66	Cc
Wick, *Glos.*	51	Aa
Wick, *Som..*	34	Cb
Wick, *Worcs.*	90	Ca
Wick, E.	60	Da
Wicken, *Cambs.*	96	Da
Wicken, *N'hants..*	93	Bb
Wicken Bonhunt.	76	Da
Wickenby	166	Db
Wickerslack	204	Cc
Wickersley	164	Ca
Wickford	59	Ba
Wickham, *Berks..*	54	Ca
Wickham, *Hants..*	21	Ba
Wickham Bishops	78	Cc
Wickhambreux	46	Cb
Wickhambrook	97	Bb
Wickham, E.	58	Dc
Wickhamford	90	Da
Wickham Market	100	Cb
Wickhampton	120	Ca
Wickham St. Pauls	78	Ca
Wickham Skeith	99	Aa
Wickham, W.	97	Ac
Wicklewood	118	Da
Wickmere	137	Ba
Wick St. Lawrence	49	Bb
Wickwar	69	Ac
Widcombe, N.	50	Db
Widcombe, S.	50	Db
Widdington	76	Da
Widdrington	232	Db
Widecombe-in-the-Moor	13	Bb
Wide Open	222	Ca
Widford, *Essex*	77	Bc
Widford, *Herts.*	76	Cb
Widford, *Oxon.*	71	Ba
Widmerpool	150	Cc
Widnes	160	Ca
Widworthy	15	Bb
Wield	39	Ba
Wield, Lr.	39	Ba
Wigan	170	Ca
Wigborough, Gt.	78	Dc
Wigborough, Lit.	78	Dc
Wiggaton	15	Ab
Wiggenhall St. Mary Magdalen	134	Dc
Wiggenhall St. German	134	Dc
Wiggenhall St. Peter	135	Ac
Wiggington, *Herts.*	74	Da
Wiggington, *Staffs.*	128	Db
Wiggington, *Yorks.*	185	Bb
Wigglesworth	182	Cb
Wiggonby	217	Ac
Wiggonholt	23	Bb
Wighton	136	Da
Wigmore	107	Bb
Wigsley	165	Bc
Wigsthorpe	114	Ca
Wigston Magna	130	Cc
Wigston Parva	112	Ca
Wigthorpe	164	Db
Wigtoft	133	Ba
Wigton	217	Ac
Wigtown	210	Da
Wike, *Yorks.*	184	Cc
Wilbarston	113	Ba
Wilberfoss	186	Cb
Wilberton	9	Eb
Wilbraham, Gt.	96	Db
Wilbraham, Lit.	96	Db
Wilburton	116	Cc
Wilby, *N'hants.*	113	Bc
Wilby, *Norf.*	118	Db
Wilby, *Suff.*	99	Ba
Wilcot	53	Ab
Wilcote	72	Ca
Wilcott	124	Da
Wilcrick	68	Ca
Wilden, *Beds.*	95	Ab
Wilden, *Worcs.*	109	Ab
Wildhern	54	Cc
Wildsworth	165	Ba
Wilford	150	Cc
Wilkesley	145	Bb
Wilksby	153	Bb
Willand	15	Aa
Willaston, *Ches.*	159	Bb
Willaston, *Ches.*	146	Bb
Willen	94	Cb
Willenhall, *Staffs.*	127	Bc
Willenhall, *War.*	111	Bb
Willerby, *Yorks.*	187	Ba
Willerby, *Yorks.*	176	Da
Willersey	90	Da
Willersley	87	Ba
Willesborough	27	Ba
Willesden	57	Bb
Willesley	70	Cc
Willett	33	Ab
Willey, *Shrops.*	126	Cc
Willey, *War.*	112	Ca
Williamscot	92	Da
Williamston, E.	62	Db
Williamston. W.	62	Cb
Willian	75	Ba
Willingdon	25	Bc
Willingdon, Lr.	25	Bc
Willingham, *Cambs.*	96	Ca
Willingham, *Lincs.*	166	Cb
Willingham, N.	167	Ac
Willingham, S.	167	Bc
Willington, *Beds.*	95	Ab
Willington, *Derby*	148	Dc
Willington, *Dur.*	206	Da
Willington, *N'land.*	222	Cb
Willington Quay	222	Cb
Willisham	99	Ac
Willitoft	175	Ba
Williton	33	Aa
Willoughbridge	146	Cb
Willoughby, *Lincs.*	154	Da
Willoughby, *War.*	112	Cb
Willoughby-on-the-Wolds	130	Da
Willoughby Waterless	130	Cc
Willoughton	166	Ca
Willsbridge	51	Aa
Wilmcote	110	Dc
Wilmington, *Kent*	58	Dc
Wilmington, *Som.*	51	Ab
Wilmington, *Sus..*	25	Bc
Wilmslow	161	Bb
Wilnecote	128	Db
Wilpshire	170	Ca
Wilsden	183	Ac
Wilsford, *Lincs.*	152	Cb
Wilsford, *Wilts.*	37	Ba
Wilsford, *Wilts.*	52	Db
Wilsham	47	Ab
Wilshamstead	94	Da
Wilshaw	172	Dc
Wilsill	183	Ba
Wilsontown	250	Dc
Wilsthorpe	132	Db
Wilstone	74	Ca
Wilton, *Herefs.*	88	Dc
Wilton, *Rox.*	229	Aa
Wilton, *Som.*	33	Bc
Wilton, *Wilts.*	37	Ab
Wilton, *Wilts.*	53	Bb
Wilton, *Yorks.*	187	Aa
Wilton, *Yorks.*	208	Dc
Wimbish	77	Aa
Wimbledon	57	Bc
Wimblington	116	Ca
Wimborne Minster	19	Aa
Wimborne St. Giles	37	Ac
Wimbotsham	117	Aa
Wincanton	35	Bb
Winceby	153	Bb
Winchburgh	251	Ab
Winchcombe	90	Db
Winchelsea	27	Ac
Winchendon, Lr.	73	Ba
Winchendon, Upr.	73	Ba
Winchester	38	Db
Winchfield	55	Bc
Wincobank	164	Ca
Windermere	193	Aa
Winderton	91	Bb
Windlesham	56	Cb
Windley	148	Db
Windrush	71	Aa
Windsor	56	Da
Winestead	178	Cc
Winewall	182	Cc
Winfarthing	118	Dc
Winford	50	Db
Winforton	87	Ba
Winfrith Newburgh	18	Cb
Wing, *Bucks.*	94	Cc
Wing, *Rut.*	131	Bb
Wingate, S.	207	Ba
Wingates, *Lancs..*	170	Dc
Wingates, *N'land.*	231	Bb
Wingerworth	164	Cc
Wingfield, *Suff.*	99	Ba
Wingfield, *Wilts.*	51	Bb
Wingfield, N.	164	Cc
Wingfield, S.	149	Aa
Wingham	46	Cb
Wingrave	74	Ca
Winkburn	150	Da
Winkfield	56	Ca
Winkhill	147	Ba
Winkleigh	81	Ab
Winksley	184	Ca
Winkton	19	Bb
Winlaton	221	Bb
Winless	324	Cn
Winnington	146	Cb
Winscombe	50	Cb
Winsford, *Ches.*	161	Ac
Winsford, *Som.*	48	Cc
Winsham	16	Ca
Winshill	128	Da
Winskill	204	Ca
Winslade	55	Ba
Winsley	51	Bb
Winslow	93	Bc
Winson	70	Da
Winster, *Derby*	148	Db
Winster, *W'land..*	193	Ab
Winston, *Dur.*	206	Dc
Winston, *Suff.*	99	Bb
Winstone	70	Ca
Winterborne Abbas	17	Bb
Winterborne Came	18	Cb
Winterborne Clenston	18	Da
Winterborne Herringstone	17	Bb
Winterborne Houghton	18	Ca
Winterborne Kingston	18	Da
Winterborne Monkton	17	Bb
Winterborne St. Martin	17	Bb
Winterborne Steepleton	17	Bb
Winterborne Stickland	18	Da
Winterborne Tomson	18	Da
Winterborne Whitchurch	18	Da
Winterborne Zelstone	18	Da
Winterbourne *Berks.*	54	Da
Winterbourne, *Glos.*	69	Ac
Winterbourne Bassett	53	Aa
Winterbourne Dauntsey	37	Bb
Winterbourne Earls	37	Bb
Winterbourne Gunner	37	Bb
Winterbourne Monkton	52	Da
Winterbourne Stoke	37	Aa
Winterburn	182	Db
Wintercott	107	Bc
Winteringham	176	Cb
Winterley	146	Ca
Wintersett	174	Cb
Winterslow	37	Bb
Winterton, *Lincs.*	176	Cb
Winterton, *Norf..*	138	Dc
Winthorpe, *Lincs.*	154	Db
Winthorpe, *Notts.*	151	Ba
Winton, *Hants.*	19	Bb
Winton, *Sus.*	25	Bc
Winton, *W'land.*	204	Dc
Winton, *Yorks.*	197	Aa
Wintringham	187	Ab
Winwick, *Hunts..*	114	Da
Winwick, *Lancs..*	160	Da
Winwick, *N'hants.*	112	Db
Wirksworth	148	Da
Wisbech	184	Cc
Wisbech St. Mary.	116	Ca
Wisborough Green	23	Ba
Wiseton	165	Aa
Wishaw, *Lan.*	249	Bc
Wishaw, *War.*	128	Dc
Wisley	41	Aa
Wispington	153	Aa
Wissett	100	Ca
Wissington	78	Da
Wistanstow	107	Ba
Wistanswick	145	Bc
Wistaston	145	Ba
Wiston, *Lan.*	238	Ca
Wiston, *Pem.*	62	Ca
Wistow, *Hunts.*	115	Bc
Wistow, *Leics.*	130	Dc
Wistow, *Yorks.*	185	Bc
Wiswell	181	Bc
Witcham	116	Cc
Witchampton	19	Aa
Witchford	116	Dc
Witchingham, Gt.	137	Ac
Witchingham, Lit.	137	Ab
Witcombe, *Glos.*	90	Cc
Witcombe, *Som.*	34	Dc
Witham	78	Cc
Witham Friary	36	Ca
Witham-on-the-Hill	132	Ca

	PAGE	SQ.
Withcall	167	Bc
Withcote	131	Ab
Witheridge	32	Cb
Witherley	129	Ac
Withern	168	Cc
Withernsea	178	Db
Withernwick	178	Ca
Withersdane	45	Bc
Withersfield	97	Ac
Withial	35	Aa
Withiel Florey	48	Cc
Withington, *Glos.*	90	Dc
Withington, *Herefs.*	88	Da
Withington, *Lancs.*	161	Ba
Withington, *Shrops.*	125	Ba
Withington, *Staffs.*	147	Bc
Withnell	170	Db
Withybrook, *Som.*	51	Ac
Withybrook, *War.*	111	Ba
Withycombe	48	Cb
Withycombe Raleigh	15	Ac
Withyham	43	Ac
Withypool	47	Bc
Witley	40	Da
Witley, Gt.	108	Db
Witley, Llt.	108	Db
Witnesham	99	Bc
Witney	72	Ca
Wittenham, Lit.	72	Dc
Wittenham, Long	72	Dc
Wittering	132	Cb
Wittering, E.	22	Db
Wittering, W.	22	Db
Wittersham	27	Ab
Witton, *Norf.*	119	Ba
Witton, *Norf.*	138	Cb
Witton, E.	196	Cb
Witton Gilbert	222	Cc
Witton-le-Wear	206	Db
Witton Park	206	Db
Witton, W.	196	Cb
Wiveliscombe	33	Ab
Wivelsfield	24	Db
Wivenhoe	78	Db
Wiveton	136	Da
Wix	79	Bb
Wixford	91	Aa
Wixhill	145	Bc
Wixoe	97	Bc
Woburn	94	Cb
Woburn Sands	94	Cb
Woking	41	Aa
Wokingham	55	Bb
Wolborough	14	Cc
Woldingham	42	Da
Wold Newton, *Lincs.*	167	Bb
Wold Newton, *Yorks.*	188	Cb
Woldridge	89	Bc
Wolferlow	108	Dc
Wolferton	135	Ab
Wolfhamcote	112	Cc
Wolford, Gt.	91	Bb
Wolford, Lit.	91	Bb
Wollage Green	46	Cc
Wollaston, *N'hants.*	113	Bc
Wollaston, *Shrops.*	124	Db
Wollaston, *Worcs.*	109	Ba
Wollaton	149	Bb
Wollerton	145	Bc
Wollescote	109	Ba
Wolsingham	206	Ca
Wolstanton	146	Db
Wolston	111	Bb
Wolterton	137	Ab
Wolvercot	72	Da
Wolverhampton	127	Ac
Wolverley	109	Aa
Wolverton, *Bucks.*	93	Bb
Wolverton, *Hants.*	54	Dc
Wolverton, *Wilts.*	36	Ca
Wolverton, *War.*	110	Dc
Wolves Newton	68	Cb
Wolvey	111	Ba
Wolviston	208	Cb
Wombleton	198	Cc
Wombourn	127	Ac
Wombridge	126	Cb
Wombwell	174	Cc
Womenswold	46	Cc
Womersley	174	Db
Wonersh	41	Aa
Wonston	38	Da
Wooburn	74	Cc
Wooburn Green	74	Cc
Woodale	195	Bc
Woodall	164	Cb
Woodbastwick	138	Cc
Woodborough, *Notts.*	150	Cb
Woodborough, *Som.*	50	Cb
Woodborough, *Wilts.*	53	Ab
Woodbridge	99	Bc
Woodbury	14	Da
Woodbury Salterton	14	Da
Woodchester	69	Ba
Woodchurch *Ches.*	159	Ba
Woodchurch, *Kent*	27	Aa
Woodcote	55	Aa
Woodcott	54	Cc
Woodcroft	68	Db
Woodcutts	36	Db
Wood Dalling	137	Ab
Wood Ditton	97	Ab
Wood Eaton	72	Da
Wood End, *Herts.*	76	Ca
Woodend, *N'hants.*	93	Aa
Wood Enderby	153	Bb
Woodford, *Ches.*	162	Cb
Woodford, *Essex.*	58	Ca
Woodford, *Glos.*	69	Ab
Woodford, *N'hants.*	114	Cb
Woodford, *Wilts.*	37	Ba
Woodford Green	58	Ca
Woodford Halse	92	Da
Woodford, Lr.	37	Bb
Woodford, Upr.	37	Ba
Woodgate, *Norf.*	136	Dc
Woodgate, *Staffs.*	147	Bc
Wood Green, *Staffs.*	127	Bc
Wood Green *M'sex.*	57	Ba
Woodgreen, *Oxon.*	72	Ca
Woodhall, *Lincs.*	153	Bb
Woodhall, *Yorks.*	195	Bb
Woodhall Spa	153	Ab
Woodham	207	Ab
Woodham Ferrers	60	Ca
Woodham Mortimer	78	Cc
Woodham Walter	78	Cc
Woodhay, E.	54	Db
Woodhay, W.	54	Cb
Woodhead	305	Bc
Woodhill, *Som.*	50	Ca
Woodhill, *Som.*	61	Cb
Woodhorn	232	Dc
Woodhouse, *Leics.*	130	Ca
Woodhouse, *Yorks.*	164	Cb
Woodhouse, *Yorks.*	174	Cb
Woodhouse Eaves	130	Ca
Woodhouses, *Staffs.*	128	Ca
Woodhouses, *Staffs.*	128	Cb
Woodhurst	115	Bc
Woodland	14	Cc
Woodlands, *Hants.*	38	Cc
Woodlands, *Som.*	51	Bc
Woodlane	128	Ca
Woodleigh	10	Cb
Woodlesford	173	Ba
Woodley	55	Ba
Woodmancote, *Glos.*	69	Bb
Woodmancote, *Glos.*	90	Cb
Woodmancote, *Glos.*	70	Da
Woodmancote, *Sus.*	24	Cb
Woodmancott	39	Aa
Woodmansey	177	Bb
Woodmansterne	42	Ca
Woodnesborough	46	Db
Woodnewton	132	Cc
Wood Norton	136	Db
Woodplumpton	170	Ca
Woodrising	118	Da
Woodsetts	164	Db
Woodsford	18	Cb
Woodside, *Aber.*	294	Cc
Woodside, *Dur.*	206	Db
Woodside, *Pem.*	62	Db
Woodside, *Perth*	270	Dc
Wood Stanway	90	Ca
Woodstock, *Oxon.*	72	Ca
Woodstock, *Pem.*	82	Cc
Woodston	115	Aa
Woodstreet	56	Dc
Woodthorpe, *Derby*	164	Cb
Woodthorpe, *Leics.*	130	Ca
Woodton	119	Bb
Wood Walton	115	Ac
Woodyates	37	Ac
Wookey	34	Da
Wookey Hole	34	Da
Wool	18	Db
Woolacombe	80	Ca
Woolaston	68	Db
Woolavington	34	Ca
Woolbeding	40	Dc
Wooldale	172	Dc
Wooler	243	Bc
Woolfardisworthy, *Den.*	29	Bc
Woolfardisworthy, *Dev.*	32	Cb
Woolfold	171	Ab
Woolhampton	54	Db
Woolhope	88	Db
Woolland	36	Cc
Woolley, *Hunts.*	114	Db
Woolley, *Som.*	51	Ba
Woolley, *Yorks.*	173	Bb
Woolley Green	51	Bb
Woolmer Green	75	Bb
Woolmersdon	33	Bb
Woolpit	98	Db
Woolstaston	125	Ac
Woolsthorpe, *Lincs.*	131	Ba
Woolsthorpe, *Lincs.*	151	Bc
Woolston, *Hants.*	21	Aa
Woolston, *Shrops.*	107	Ba
Woolston, *Shrops.*	124	Da
Woolston, *Som.*	35	Bb
Woolstone, *Berks.*	71	Bc
Woolstone, *Bucks.*	94	Cb
Woolstone, *Glos.*	90	Cb
Woolton	160	Ca
Woolverstone	79	Ba
Woolverton	51	Bb
Woolwich	58	Cb
Woore	146	Cb
Wootton, *Beds.*	94	Da
Wootton, *Hants.*	21	Bb
Wootton, *Herefs.*	107	Ac
Wootton, *Kent*	46	Cc
Wootton, *Lincs.*	177	Bc
Wootton, *N'hants.*	113	Ac
Wootton, *Oxon.*	92	Cc
Wootton, *Oxon.*	72	Db
Wootton, *Staffs.*	148	Cb
Wootton, *Staffs.*	146	Dc
Wootton Bassett	70	Dc
Wootton Courtney	48	Cb
Wootton Fitzpaine	16	Cb
Wootton Glanville	35	Bc
Wootton, N.	50	Dc
Wootton Rivers	53	Ab
Wootton St. Lawrence	55	Ac
Wootton Wawen	110	Db
Worcester	109	Ac
Worcester Park	57	Bc
Wordsley	109	Ba
Wordwell	98	Ca
Worfield	126	Dc
Workington	201	Bb
Worksop	164	Db
Worlaby, *Lincs.*	153	Ba
Worlaby, *Lincs.*	176	Db
Worldham, E.	40	Ca
Worldham, W.	40	Ca
World's End	54	Da
Worle	49	Bb
Worlingham	120	Cb
Worlington	97	Ba
Worlington, E.	31	Bb
Worlingworth	99	Ba
Wormbridge	88	Cb
Wormegay	135	Ac
Wormhill	162	Db
Wormingford	78	Da
Worminghall	73	Aa
Wormington	90	Db
Wormit	271	Bc
Wormleighton	92	Ca
Wormley	76	Cc
Wormley Hill	175	Ab
Wormshill	44	Db
Wormsley	88	Ca
Worplesdon	56	Dc
Worrall	163	Ba
Worsall	207	Bc
Worsbrough	173	Bc
Worsbrough Bridge	173	Bc
Worsbrough Dale	173	Bc
Worsley	171	Ac
Worstead	138	Cb
Worsthorne	171	Ba
Worston	181	Bc
Worth, *Kent*	46	Db
Worth, *Som.*	34	Ba
Worth, *Sus.*	42	Cc
Wortham	99	Aa
Worthen	124	Db
Worthenbury	144	Db
Worthing, *Norf.*	136	Dc
Worthing, *Sus.*	24	Cc
Worthington	129	Ba
Worth Matravers	19	Ac
Worthy	47	Bb
Worting	55	Ab
Wortley, *Glos.*	69	Bb
Wortley, *Yorks.*	173	Bb
Worton, *Oxon.*	72	Da
Worton, *Wilts.*	52	Cb
Worton, *Yorks.*	195	Bb
Worton, Nether	92	Cc
Worton, Over	92	Cc
Wortwell	119	Bc
Wothorpe	132	Cb
Wotton	41	Bb
Wotton-under-Edge	69	Bb
Wotton Underwood	73	Ba
Woughton-on-the-Green	94	Cb
Wouldham	44	Ca
Wrabness	79	Bb
Wrafton	30	Cb
Wragby, *Lincs.*	153	Aa
Wragby, *Yorks.*	174	Cb
Wragholme	168	Cb
Wramplingham	119	Aa
Wrangbrook	174	Cb
Wrangle	154	Cc
Wrangle Bank	154	Cc
Wrangle Tofts	154	Cc
Wrantage	34	Cc
Wratting, Gt.	97	Ac
Wratting, Lit.	97	Ac
Wratting, W.	97	Ab
Wrawby	176	Dc
Wraxall, *Dors.*	17	Ba
Wraxall, *Som.*	50	Ca
Wraxall, Lr.	51	Bb
Wraxall, N.	51	Bb
Wraxall, S.	51	Bb
Wraxall, Upr.	51	Bb
Wray	181	Aa
Wray, High	192	Da
Wraysbury	56	Da
Wrayton	181	Aa
Wreay	217	Bc
Wrecclesham	40	Ca
Wrekenton	222	Cb
Wrelton	198	Db
Wremingham	119	Ab
Wrenbury	145	Bb
Wrentham	120	Dc
Wrenthorpe Potovens	173	Bb
Wressell	175	Bb
Wrestlingworth	95	Bc
Wretham, E.	118	Cb
Wretton	117	Aa
Wrexham	144	Ca
Wrickton	108	Ca
Wrightington	170	Cb
Wrinehill	146	Cb
Wrington	50	Cb
Writhlington	51	Ab
Writtle	77	Bc
Wrockwardine	126	Cb
Wroot	175	Bc
Wrotham	43	Ba
Wroughton	53	Aa
Wroxall, *Hants.*	21	Bc
Wroxall, *War.*	110	Db
Wroxeter	125	Bc
Wroxham	138	Cc
Wroxton	92	Cb
Wyberton	133	Ba
Wyboston	95	Ab
Wybunbury	146	Ca
Wychbold	109	Bb
Wyche, Lr.	89	Cb
Wyche, Upr.	89	Ba
Wyck	40	Ca
Wyck Rissington	91	Bc
Wycliffe	206	Dc
Wycomb	131	Aa
Wycombe Marsh	74	Cc
Wyddial	76	Ca
Wye	45	Bc
Wyesham	68	Da
Wyfordby	131	Aa
Wyke	173	Aa
Wyke Champflower	35	Ba
Wyke Marsh	36	Cb
Wyken	111	Ba
Wyke Regis	17	Bb
Wykey	124	Da
Wylam	221	Bb
Wylde Green	128	Cc
Wylye	37	Aa
Wymering	22	Ca
Wymeswold	130	Ca
Wymington	114	Cc
Wymondham, *Leics.*	131	Ba
Wymondham, *Norf.*	119	Aa

	PAGE	SQ.		PAGE	SQ.		PAGE	SQ.		PAGE	SQ.
Wymondley, Gt.	75	Ba	Yarm	207	Bc	Yealmpton	8	Dc	Yockleton	125	Ab
Wymondley, Lit.	75	Ba	Yarmacott	30	Db	Yearsley	198	Cc	Yokefleet	175	Ba
Wynford Eagle	17	Ba	Yarmouth	20	Db	Yeaton	125	Aa	Yoker	248	Db
Wyre Piddle	90	Ca	Yarnbrook	52	Cb	Yeaveley	148	Cb	York	185	Bb
Wysall	150	Cc	Yarnfield	146	Dc	Yedingham	187	Aa	Yorkley	68	Da
Wytham	72	Da	Yarnscombe	30	Cc	Yelden	114	Cb	York Town	56	Cb
Wythburn	202	Dc	Yarnton	72	Da	Yeldham, Gt.	77	Ba	Yorton	125	Ba
Wyton, Hunts.	95	Ba	Yarpole	107	Bb	Yeldham, Lit.	97	Bc	Youlgrave	163	Ac
Wyton, Yorks	177	Bb	Yarrow	240	Cc	Yelford	72	Cb	Youlthorpe	186	Cb
Wyverstone	98	Da	Yarrow Feus	240	Cc	Yelland	30	Cb	Yoxford	100	Ca
Wyville	151	Bc	Yarwell	132	Dc	Yelling	95	Ba	Yoxhall	128	Ca
			Yate	69	Ac	Yelvertoft	112	Db	Ysbyty Ifan	142	Ca
Yaddlethorpe	176	Cc	Yately	55	Bb	Yelverton, Dev.	8	Db	Ysgubor-y-coed	121	Bb
Yafforth	197	Ab	Yatesbury	52	Da	Yelverton, Norf.	119	Ba	Yspytty Ystwyth	102	Db
Yalding	44	Cb	Yattendon	54	Da	Yenston	35	Bb	Ystalyfera	85	Ab
Yanworth	70	Da	Yatton, Herefs.	107	Bb	Yeovil	35	Ac	Ystradfellte	86	Cb
Yapham	186	Cb	Yatton, Som.	50	Ca	Yeovil Marsh	35	Ab	Ystradgynlais	85	Bb
Yapton	23	Ac	Yatton Keynell	52	Ca	Yeovilton	35	Ab	Ystrad Owen	85	Ab
Yarburgh	168	Cb	Yatton, W.	52	Ca	Yerbeston	62	Cb	Ystrad Meurig	102	Ab
Yarcombe	15	Ba	Yaverland	21	Da	Yetholm	242	Dc	Ystrdowen	66	Db
Yardley	110	Ca	Yaxham	118	Da	Yetlington	231	Ba			
Yardley Gobion	93	Ba	Yaxley, Hunts.	114	Da	Yetminster	35	Ac			
Yardley Hastings	113	Bc	Yaxley, Suff.	99	Aa	Yiewsley	56	Da			
Yarkhill	88	Da	Yazor	88	Ca	Ynys-bydafan	85	Bb	ZEAL, S.	13	Ba
Yarley	34	Da	Yeading	57	Ab	Ynys-ddu	67	Ab	Zeal Monachorum	31	Bc
Yarlington	35	Bb	Yeadon	183	Bc	Ynys-hir	66	Da	Zeals	36	Ca
			Yealand Conyers	193	Bc	Ynys-y-bwl	66	Da	Zennor	1	Bb
			Yealand Redmayne	193	Bc	Yockenthwait	195	Ac			

INDEX TO AIRPORTS

	PAGE	SQ.		PAGE	SQ.		PAGE	SQ.		PAGE	SQ.
Aberdeen (Dyce)	294	Cb	Edinburgh	251	Ab	London (Heathrow)	56	Da	Prestwick	236	Cc
Ashford (Lympne)	28	Ca	Exeter	14	Dc	Luton	75	Ab	Roborough	8	Db
Birmingham	110	Da	Glasgow	248	Db	Lydd	27	Bb	Southampton	38	Dc
Blackpool	169	Aa	Hawarden	159	Bc	Machrihanish	233	Ac	Southend	60	Cb
Bournemouth (Hurn)	19	Bb	Inverness	301	Ab	Manchester	161	Bb	Stansted	76	Db
Bristol	50	Da	Isle of Man			Manston	46	Da	Staverton	90	Cc
Cambridge	96	Db	(Ronaldsway)	190	Db	Newcastle	221	Ba	Swansea	64	Dc
Cardiff	66	Dc	Leeds-Bradford	183	Bc	Newquay	5	Bb	Teesside	207	Bc
Coventry	111	Bb	Liverpool	160	Cb	Nottingham	150	Cc	Valley	155	Ab
East Midlands	129	Ba	London (Gatwick)	42	Cc	Penzance	1	Bb	Wick	324	Dc

MADE IN GREAT BRITAIN

PRINTED BY MORRISON AND GIBB LTD., EDINBURGH AND LONDON

TABLE OF DISTANCES

The table shows the distance between any two towns at the intersection of the columns, which contain the names of selected towns thus:—

London to Brighton, 54 miles.

LONDON
498 **ABERDEEN**
211 440 **ABERYSTWYTH**
111 411 116 **BIRMINGHAM**
227 308 151 123 **BLACKPOOL**
103 561 198 143 266 **BOURNEMOUTH**
54 552 245 160 280 90 **BRIGHTON**
115 490 124 88 202 74 134 **BRISTOL**
159 358 133 63 72 206 212 146 **BUXTON**
56 451 217 101 202 156 110 147 130 **CAMBRIDGE**
58 548 270 169 285 156 75 174 217 99 **CANTERBURY**
154 493 110 102 206 118 178 44 158 173 213 **CARDIFF**
299 215 225 196 93 338 353 285 93 258 355 278 **CARLISLE**
245 258 307 109 197 255 299 255 105 143 197 294 74 **DARLINGTON**
74 563 285 184 300 172 82 189 232 114 15 228 310 268 **DOVER**
378 121 320 290 187 433 432 369 225 350 427 373 94 137 442 **EDINBURGH**
171 565 199 163 278 82 168 75 221 221 229 120 330 350 244 444 **EXETER**
248 497 57 168 208 223 283 149 190 262 306 112 282 283 321 377 224 **FISHGUARD**
395 145 321 292 189 434 449 371 239 354 451 374 96 168 466 44 446 378 **GLASGOW**
103 457 108 53 170 99 137 35 111 161 177 56 242 220 177 336 111 145 338 **GLOUCESTER**
258 430 106 147 141 279 306 209 134 244 316 203 215 217 332 309 284 163 305 111 **HOLYHEAD**
172 346 217 123 129 249 226 205 90 124 221 225 153 88 237 225 283 216 237 180 284 **HULL**
536 107 477 446 345 598 590 527 395 488 530 477 158 209 602 158 534 494 170 600 170 383 **INVERNESS**
254 260 180 151 46 294 308 230 98 216 313 233 45 64 328 139 305 237 64 600 170 128 297 **KENDAL**
193 314 171 110 73 247 246 196 50 145 242 208 115 60 257 193 271 228 139 305 115 56 351 70 **LEEDS**
57 404 151 41 135 160 150 116 63 69 155 137 206 151 171 284 192 209 30 177 179 161 441 135 73 **LEICESTER**
134 375 191 85 131 211 188 167 86 86 183 187 182 121 199 254 248 255 71 254 132 81 412 160 41 51 **LINCOLN**
197 335 105 90 46 228 250 161 53 178 255 165 120 182 276 216 214 237 162 243 95 56 201 135 86 109 118 **LIVERPOOL**
184 333 131 81 47 224 237 162 25 155 242 173 118 97 257 213 238 188 127 214 127 122 371 96 41 88 84 34 **MANCHESTER**
279 228 259 204 128 341 333 288 143 231 328 301 57 34 343 107 364 316 145 238 316 145 265 255 253 155 155 250 121 **NEWCASTLE/TYNE**
65 436 167 51 163 133 118 105 95 50 95 135 237 183 137 316 183 199 50 107 183 131 474 192 99 32 8 183 128 128 **NORTHAMPTON**
114 480 271 161 232 216 163 209 164 62 141 235 287 227 156 360 227 287 61 156 360 180 517 246 120 174 135 246 174 517 128 **NORWICH**
123 379 156 49 118 183 176 137 46 84 181 151 183 126 156 259 213 213 159 259 71 73 416 139 70 26 99 106 120 106 71 112 **NOTTINGHAM**
439 179 415 386 283 528 543 465 333 448 545 468 164 210 560 125 540 472 35 213 305 35 173 138 136 58 123 108 120 35 99 **OBAN**
56 473 157 63 186 91 97 70 124 80 104 258 220 129 353 141 193 353 48 209 164 120 405 225 115 42 42 144 69 415 26 260 372 95 **OXFORD**
213 608 242 206 320 124 118 124 285 263 271 162 393 373 287 487 43 267 573 153 287 43 326 348 313 141 234 279 233 646 141 234 372 528 448 **PLYMOUTH**
71 552 281 141 264 46 49 94 202 126 121 138 337 298 165 432 124 243 432 105 431 124 432 242 199 88 148 282 105 589 78 237 427 583 256 583 **PORTSMOUTH**
215 314 235 163 137 292 269 248 114 167 264 265 138 65 280 194 324 292 172 230 65 43 352 172 81 109 199 132 137 352 135 185 310 511 222 222 527 **SCARBOROUGH**
160 347 156 76 65 213 214 164 29 117 211 178 145 94 229 227 240 213 159 229 60 38 385 190 38 71 72 38 64 385 128 217 157 323 141 146 231 114 **SHEFFIELD**
154 388 141 264 46 49 76 85 131 107 163 227 265 179 227 384 131 267 267 129 418 91 267 278 107 46 117 159 53 385 57 134 207 575 132 38 173 201 38 93 **SHREWSBURY**
77 538 198 251 29 61 74 189 130 118 323 285 102 175 472 126 452 418 86 181 107 217 452 278 208 134 185 190 208 223 134 185 389 495 339 334 63 208 335 160 208 **SOUTHAMPTON**
401 232 327 298 195 440 455 377 245 360 457 380 102 175 472 126 452 384 86 452 126 255 255 253 147 217 308 220 222 575 208 389 157 389 285 247 183 219 177 187 266 **STRANRAER**
192 500 128 158 218 84 173 206 250 280 285 280 160 72 381 89 179 244 194 70 476 137 179 203 194 179 206 165 265 177 165 449 248 539 437 179 117 476 447 161 239 **SWANSEA**
258 650 384 248 363 169 255 160 306 308 316 205 415 415 332 530 87 310 521 196 369 310 369 366 390 277 328 323 369 687 208 625 325 625 211 247 158 398 398 179 409 **TRURO**
199 307 195 129 97 263 253 217 74 151 248 231 114 49 264 186 292 252 210 182 137 39 344 39 40 105 74 197 24 344 53 137 105 277 252 201 40 265 174 187 305 **YORK**

SIGNS WHICH MUST BE OBSERVED - *Continued*

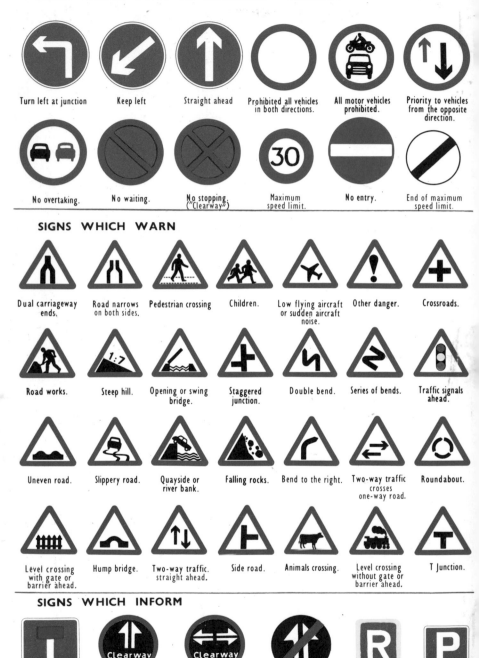

Turn left at junction	Keep left	Straight ahead	Prohibited all vehicles in both directions.	All motor vehicles prohibited.	Priority to vehicles from the opposite direction.
No overtaking.	No waiting.	No stopping. ("Clearway")	Maximum speed limit.	No entry.	End of maximum speed limit.

SIGNS WHICH WARN

Dual carriageway ends.	Road narrows on both sides.	Pedestrian crossing	Children.	Low flying aircraft or sudden aircraft noise.	Other danger.	Crossroads.
Road works.	Steep hill.	Opening or swing bridge.	Staggered junction.	Double bend.	Series of bends.	Traffic signals ahead.
Uneven road.	Slippery road.	Quayside or river bank.	Falling rocks.	Bend to the right.	Two-way traffic crosses one-way road.	Roundabout.
Level crossing with gate or barrier ahead.	Hump bridge.	Two-way traffic. straight ahead.	Side road.	Animals crossing.	Level crossing without gate or barrier ahead.	T Junction.

SIGNS WHICH INFORM

No through road.	Initial sign.	Side road sign.	Terminal sign.	Ring road	Parking place